809

D0670632

5/11

HAMILTON-WENHAM
PUBLIC LIBRARY
Hamilton, MA 01982

# Alfred Kazin's Journals

a Sketch-Book

# Alfred Jonathan Kazin

## I

May 14, 1933— . . And the true poetry of human life rarely appears in our souls, meagre, frost-begotten tissues of a warped life that they are!—is the true vestiges of a placid and beautiful externality. Life jags us beyond ourselves, distorts our powers of understanding into a passive, suffering receptivity to the great blindnesses that seep into us and flow out the light from noise of illusion. There is a type of poetry that is unity—the poetry of the intellectual mind having visaged the whole of the objects of his understanding, he fuses them into the white heat of his soul, illuminates the rote upon his passion and feels that the

# Alfred Kazin's Journals

Selected and Edited by Richard M. Cook

Yale
UNIVERSITY PRESS
New Haven & London

Frontispiece: May 14, 1933. All images of pages from Alfred Kazin's journals are reprinted courtesy of The Henry W. and Albert A. Berg Collection of English and American Literature, The New York Public Library, Astor, Lenox and Tilden Foundations.

Published with assistance from the foundation established in memory of Philip Hamilton McMillan of the Class of 1894, Yale College.

Copyright © 2011 by the Estate of Alfred Kazin, and Richard M. Cook.
All rights reserved.
This book may not be reproduced, in whole or in part, including illustrations, in any form (beyond that copying permitted by Sections 107 and 108 of the U.S. Copyright Law and except by reviewers for the public press), without written permission from the publishers.

Yale University Press books may be purchased in quantity for educational, business, or promotional use. For information, please e-mail sales.press@yale.edu (U.S. office) or sales@yaleup.co.uk (U.K. office).

Designed by Sonia Shannon.
Set in Bulmer type by IDS Infotech Ltd., Chandigarh, India.
Printed in the United States of America.
Library of Congress Cataloging-in-Publication Data
Kazin, Alfred, 1915–1998.
Alfred Kazin's journals / selected and edited by Richard M. Cook.
p. cm.
Includes bibliographical references and index.
ISBN 978-0-300-14203-7 (cloth : alk. paper) 1. Kazin, Alfred, 1915–1998—Diaries.
2. Critics—United States—Biography. I. Cook, Richard M., 1941–. II. Title.
PS29.K38A3 2011
809—dc22
[B]
2010045254
A catalogue record for this book is available from the British Library.
This paper meets the requirements of ANSI/NISO Z39.48–1992 (Permanence of Paper).
10 9 8 7 6 5 4 3 2 1

*To Jeremy, Charlotte, and Abigail*

# CONTENTS

## ACKNOWLEDGMENTS

I am grateful to a number of people for assistance with this book. Judith Dunford, Alfred Kazin's widow, encouraged me and provided moral and practical assistance. She has made everything possible. Curator Isaac Gewirtz, Steven Crook, and Ann Garner of the Berg Collection at the New York Public Library were helpful in providing access to material in the Collection. I am grateful to Alan Wald, Morris Dickstein, William Cain, and the late John Patrick Diggins for their encouragement and support. I thank the John Simon Guggenheim Foundation for a fellowship, which enabled me to undertake this book, and the University of Missouri–St. Louis Research Office, which provided me with a teaching leave to complete it. Jennifer Banks of Yale University Press was unfailingly enthusiastic and helpful throughout. Dan Heaton, also of Yale University Press, and Mark Schechner read the manuscript and did their best to correct my errors. I thank Hyun Jin Lim, Kimberly Misch, Matthew Kimbrell, and Ryan Smith, who helped me prepare, proofread, and occasionally decipher the entries. I am deeply indebted to my wife, Sylvia, for support and sound advice.

# CHRONOLOGY

| | |
|---|---|
| 1915 | June 5, Alfred Kazin is born, son of Gita Fagelman and Gedahlia ("Charles") Kazin |
| 1919–1927 | Attends Elementary Public School 66 in Brooklyn, New York |
| 1922 | Birth of Pearl Kazin, Alfred's sister |
| 1927–1931 | Attends Franklin K. Lane High, Brooklyn |
| 1931–1935 | Attends City College |
| 1933 | May 14, first entry in journal |
| 1934 | September 3, publishes first book review in the *New Republic* |
| 1935–1937 | Reviews books for the *New Republic, New York Times, New York Herald Tribune,* and *Modern Monthly* |
| 1937–1938 | Earns an M.A. in history at Columbia University |
| 1938 | Marries Natasha ("Asya") Dohn, begins work on *On Native Grounds* |
| 1942 | June, first visit to Yaddo, writers colony near Saratoga Springs, New York; July 10, hired as literary editor of the *New Republic;* October 30, publication of *On Native Grounds* |
| 1943 | May, resigns from *New Republic* to work at *Fortune;* November, begins affair with Mary Louise Patterson; November–December, travels around country researching *Fortune* article on "Education of Soldiers" |

| | |
|---|---|
| 1944 | June 6, arrives in Pasadena, California, on a Huntington Library Fellowship to study Blake's *Illuminations;* teaches fall semester at Black Mountain College |
| 1945 | February 11, sails for England, where, supported by a Rockefeller Grant, he researches material for *The Education of Soldiers* and gives talks on American literature and culture for the Office of War Information |
| 1946 | Reviews books for the *New York Times, New York Herald Tribune;* October 1, *Portable Blake* published; employed as editor-scout for Houghton Mifflin; marriage with Natasha annulled, begins relationship with Carol Bookman; teaches summer school at University of Minnesota; meets and befriends Hannah Arendt |
| 1947 | Begins *A Walker in the City;* May 23, marries Carol Bookman; July–August, lectures at the Salzburg Seminar in Salzburg, Austria |
| 1948–1954 | Reviews books for the *New Yorker* |
| 1948 | June 6, Michael Kazin born; fall, lectures at New School, where Jack Kerouac is one of his students |
| 1950 | Winter, separates from Carol; October 13, meets Ann Birstein |
| 1951 | January 19, divorces Carol; May 22, sails for France with Ann; July–August, lectures at Salzburg Seminar; October 31, publication of *A Walker in the City* |
| 1952 | May–June, visiting professor at University of Cologne; June 26, marries Ann Birstein; July, Fulbright Seminar on American Studies in Cambridge, England |
| 1953 | Fall semester, visiting lecturer at Harvard |
| 1954–1955 | William Allan Neilson Visiting Professor at Smith College; June 30, 1955, birth of Cathrael ("Kate") Kazin |
| 1955–1958 | Professor of American Studies at Amherst College |
| 1955 | November, publication of *The Inmost Leaf* |
| 1959–1966 | Columnist for the *Reporter* |

| | |
|---|---|
| 1959 | August, member of American Writers Delegation to the Soviet Union; fall semester, visiting professor at University of Puerto Rico; October 10, mother dies; named to editorial board of the *American Scholar* |
| 1960 | August, visit to Israel; reviews *Night* by Elie Wiesel, whom he befriends |
| 1961 | August 1, lunch with President Kennedy, on whom he writes a critical essay for *American Scholar;* fall, delivers Christian Gauss lectures at Princeton |
| 1962 | April, publication of *Contemporaries;* fall semester, Gallagher Visiting Professor at City College of New York |
| 1963 | Winter, Beckman Professor of English, University of California-Berkeley |
| 1963–1973 | Distinguished Professor of English, Stony Brook Campus, State University of New York |
| 1965 | October, publication of *Starting Out in the Thirties;* elected to the American Academy-Institute of Arts and Letters |
| 1966 | April 26, visits Washington with group of writers, where he confronts Vice President Hubert Humphrey on Vietnam War |
| 1970 | May 28, speaks against Vietnam War at Dag Hammarskjold Plaza in New York; September 23, father dies |
| 1971 | Fall, Ewing Lectures at UCLA |
| 1973 | May, publication of *Bright Book of Life* |
| 1973–1985 | Distinguished Professor, Hunter College and Graduate Center of City University of New York |
| 1977–1978 | Meets Judith Dunford; Senior Fellow at the Center for Advanced Studies in Behavioral Science, Stanford University |
| 1978 | May, publication of *New York Jew* |
| 1978–1979 | William White Visiting Professor of English, University of Notre Dame |
| 1980 | August 24, marriage of Michael Kazin and Beth Horowitz |

| | |
|---|---|
| 1981 | July, divorces Ann; August 18, purchases house in Roxbury, Connecticut |
| 1982 | February 11, heart attack followed by bypass surgery |
| 1983 | March 31, "Saving My Soul at the Plaza" published in *New York Review of Books;* May 21, marries Judith Dunford |
| 1984 | May 1, "Not One of Us," speech on George Orwell delivered at the Library of Congress; May, publication of *An American Procession* |
| 1987 | June 9, delivers Phi Beta Kappa Oration at Harvard |
| 1988 | Winter semester, Howard A. Newman Professor of American Civilization, Cornell; October, publication of *A Writer's America* |
| 1989 | November, inducted into the American Academy of Arts and Sciences; December publication of *Our New York* |
| 1990 | July, learns he has prostate cancer |
| 1994 | May 9–11, delivers William E. Massey Lectures in the History of American Civilization at Harvard, published the following year as *Writing Was Everything;* fall semester, teaches at Brown University as Annenberg Fellow |
| 1996 | January 8, receives Truman Capote Lifetime Achievement Award of $100,000; May, publication of *A Lifetime Burning in Every Moment* |
| 1997 | October, publication of *God and the American Writer* |
| 1998 | June 5, dies |

## BOOKS BY ALFRED KAZIN

*An American Procession* (New York: Alfred A. Knopf, 1984)
*Bright Book of Life: American Novelists and Storytellers* (Boston: Little, Brown, 1973)
*Contemporaries* (Boston: Little, Brown, 1962)
*The Inmost Leaf: A Selection of Essays* (New York: Harcourt Brace Jovanovich, 1955)
*A Lifetime Burning in Every Moment: From the Journals of Alfred Kazin, Selected and Edited by the Author* (New York: HarperCollins, 1996)
*New York Jew* (New York: Alfred A. Knopf, 1978)
*On Native Grounds: An Interpretation of Modern Prose Literature* (New York: Reynal and Hitchcock, 1942)
*Our New York: A Personal Vision in Words and Photographs,* text by Alfred Kazin, photographs by David Finn (New York: Harper and Row, Publishers, 1989).
*The Portable Blake*, selected and arranged with an Introduction by Alfred Kazin (NewYork: Viking, 1946)
*Starting Out in the Thirties* (Boston: Little, Brown, 1965)
*A Walker in the City* (New York: Harcourt, Brace, 1951)
*A Writer's America: Landscape in Literature* (New York: Alfred A. Knopf, 1988)
*Writing Was Everything* (Cambridge: Harvard University Press, 1995)

# INTRODUCTION

> Take this diary. Fundamentally, I write in it not to console myself, not to take notes, but to *write*, to write of all the things that I want to write of, and in just the spirit I damned want to write in. And I am not afraid to release it, to publish it all; of seeming "ridiculous." But is it not true that a diary like this, the record of a life-long commitment and meditation and quest, should be not merely a communion with oneself, but *also* an address to the outside world, precisely because this book holds what is truest and deepest in me?
>
> —Alfred Kazin, Journal, June 27, 1955

At the time of his death in June 1998, Alfred Kazin was remembered as one of the two or three most influential writer-intellectuals of postwar America, author of more than a thousand reviews and essays, several books of criticism and literary history, and three highly regarded autobiographies, including the canonical *A Walker in the City*. What was less well known is that in addition to his published writing, he had been contributing for more than half a century to a personal journal of seven thousand pages now held in the Berg Collection of the New York Public Library.

Writing in a journal had been an important part of Kazin's life since he was a child. Born on June 5, 1915, to immigrant Jews, a seamstress and a housepainter from the Minsk region of Polish Russia, he grew up in the predominantly Jewish Brownsville area of Brooklyn. Kazin remembers his childhood as mostly lonely and unhappy. Cursed (like his mother) with a bad stammer, he feared and hated school, had few friends, and turned for companionship and entertainment to books—on which he commented in a personal notebook. "As the years mounted, I was happiest when alone, reading and beginning to note in my school notebook what I thought of the books I was always reading" (*Lifetime*, 339). He would later look back on this youthful practice as a sign of things to come—his lifelong passion to read and write about books and his lonely "compulsion" to keep a journal, to write to himself what he could not easily say to others. Reading and writing in his notebook was a way to connect imaginatively and intellectually with the world outside Brownsville—"the open mind operating on the world." It was also "(alas) a way of communing with oneself, of trusting nothing and nobody so much as one's very own self. So it is a form of loneliness" (June 7, 1987). Though he worried that his daily bouts of journal writing could lead to more solitude and loneliness, he remained convinced that the journal was his best means for understanding the world and for discovering his rightful place in it. "It is not to favor the ideal self over the world or the world over this self," he wrote in a May 2, 1959, entry on the dangers of unchecked subjectivity, "but to bring the self back into the world as its natural home."

No journals survive from Kazin's high school years, the first available entries dating from May 14, 1933, when he was a sophomore at City College. There is a gap from late 1935 to 1938, when he was earning a master's degree in history at Columbia, and there are only a few entries between 1938 and 1942, when he was working on *On Native Grounds*. But from 1942 until four months before his death he very rarely skipped more than two or three days. The latest available entry is dated February 18, 1998—though Kazin's widow, Judith Dunford, says that he wrote in the journal virtually to the time of his death on June 5. Writing three or four times a week, he typically began the day with an entry—as the prospect of getting to his typewriter to record his thoughts and impressions prompted him to get out of bed. But he also wrote in the afternoon and evening, at home, on the subway, the train, and the plane—whenever the impulse or "compulsion" seized him. Writing in his journal was a necessary part of the rhythm of his life—"the need to get it down, to frame it, to record the passage from yesterday to today" (April 5, 1987). When a busy schedule occasionally kept him from his journal for more than a few days, he returned to it relieved and determined not to permit future lapses. "It is terrible the way I ignore this notebook, when I reflect how much I continually need it not only as an aid to composition but my spiritual well-being," he wrote in a May 13, 1948, entry. "I must make a practice of writing something in it every day."

Kazin liked to say that he had "lived directly and symbolically at the storm centers of the twentieth century," and he certainly felt the need to write as though he had—to take up "directly" and passionately what he considered the most pressing issues of the moment and to make them his own. This almost always meant turning first to his journals—"everything that is fundamental in me has first found its expression here" (August 20, 1950). Communism,

anti-Communism, Socialism, cultural nationalism, liberalism, existentialism, Israel, modernism, bohemianism, the American Jewish renaissance, New York City, the Kennedy administration, the Vietnam War, student radicalism, feminism, religious belief, the neoconservatives—Kazin takes up all of these topics in his journals, as well as more personal matters related to his identity as a writer, an American, and a Jew. While many of these subjects are discussed in his published writings, they typically got their first airing in the journals. It was there, working in "the lovely ease and freedom of the Journal form" (August 3, 1990), that he could try out new ideas and surprise himself with unexpected insights. "There is no joy like working out one's ideas for oneself, like coming to the root of the matter for oneself" (March 19, 1960). To read through a portion of Kazin's journal entries is to reexperience history as a series of daily discoveries by an alert, informed, adventurous, if often moody intelligence, developing an idea that had been troubling him, pursuing a sudden hunch or insight wherever it might lead—"the moment to moment life, the impulse and waywardness [. . .] This up and down so deep to my inner weather" (November 18, 1987).

It is also to encounter an interesting array of people and places (including the changing faces of New York City). As virtually all the reviewers of his autobiographies noted, Kazin had a genuine gift for literary portraiture. That gift is on display throughout the journals: in sketches of friends, enemies, wives, mistresses, and family members, as well as leading literary and intellectual figures with whom he socialized—Arthur Schlesinger Jr., Richard Hofstadter, Daniel Bell, Harold Rosenberg, Saul Bellow, Lionel Trilling, Hannah Arendt, Mary McCarthy, Edmund Wilson, Philip Rahv, Philip Roth, Elie Wiesel. Written on impulse after a meeting, a conversation, or moment of reflection, the sketch may entail little more than a quick, summary judgment—"Just as [Jacques] Barzun always makes me think of the fatal French vanity and public 'style,' so [Max] Ascoli reminds me of the fatal Italian smallness and corruption." But it can also open into an extended, thoughtful appreciation of a friend or acquaintance, such as the March 10, 1959, entry on Harold Rosenberg.

> Harold the old-fashioned man. Face out of the silent movies, tall in a way that fathers used to be, not young men; above all, the instinctive habit of independence and determination, which reminds me of Freud's saying that he used "sex" where he could have used "eros" in order not to give "any concession to faintheartedness." Talking to Harold, all my instinctive cultural loyalties come into play—my feeling for history, my admiration for radical personality, my belief in art as a comment on the

> world. With his hooked nose over his paternal moustache, his forthrightness, his delight in stating *his* case first, Harold gives me an acute case of nostalgia.

The sketches and portraits in the journals present an array of personalities and social/political types that vividly recall a milieu and an era that are now part of history.

While a number of topics and personalities appear and reappear in the journal, none occupied more of Kazin's attention and wonder than matters related to the meaning of Jewishness. "My autobiography," he wrote in a January 4, 1960, entry while working on *Starting Out in the Thirties*, "will always be most deeply the autobiography of a Jew," noting that his journal was his "true biography." (He once proposed *Jews* as the title for a book of his journals.) Much of his interest in the subject derives from his situation as a Jewish-American writer who at the age of twenty-seven established himself as an expert on "native" American writing with his groundbreaking literary history *On Native Grounds*, and who then proceeded in his autobiographies to depict his and his generation's rise from the Jewish ghetto to positions of power and influence. "The beggarly Jewish radicals of the 30s are now the ruling cultural pundits of American society," he wrote in a July 25, 1963, entry. "I who stood so long outside the door wondering if I would ever get through it, am now one of the standard bearers of American literary opinion—a *judge* of young men." The intensifying interest in the Holocaust in the 1960s and 1970s further deepened Kazin's interest in the Jews and Jewishness. "Because of the Holocaust, because the Holocaust would not go away, I became much more consciously Jewish," he noted in *New York Jew* (95). The journals reflect this growing consciousness as well as his fascination with the paradoxes of Jewish history—"So many incredible successes in the world of thought (to say nothing of finance) and so much ignominy, persecution, and murder," he wrote to an Israeli friend in 1997. In the months before his death, the majority of journal entries are devoted to reflections on Jews, Israel, and the contradiction between the Jew as victim and the Jew as "conquistador," "the High and the Low," " 'the prophet and the bounder' (Proust) the most creative and the most abject"—paradoxes he hoped to explore in a never-written book: *Jews: The Marriage of Heaven and Hell* (February 4 and 11, 1988).

Perhaps the most compelling interest of any journal is what it reveals about the personality of the writer—and Kazin's reveals a great deal. Though he saw a psychiatrist for much of his adult life and considered the sessions (sometimes three a week) essential to his emotional and creative life, he thought psychoanalysis went only so far. "There is everything to say, outside that strictly clinical room" that can only be discussed "here" (in the journal), he wrote following a 1948 session with his analyst. Only in the journal was he able "to come home" to himself, "because there is where the heart lives [. . .] the life that you do not share with anyone" (December 25, 1988). There he could talk about anything—the petty, "the stuff of life that one naturally feels superior to," and the profound, "such depths and secrets, such forgotten passageways as me soul contains" (June 27, 1965; October 25, 1986). One finds accounts of his (largely unhappy) Brownsville childhood, his early religious interests, his difficulties with his "dominant" mother and "reclusive" father, his lifelong bouts of loneliness, his dealings with magazines and publishers, and his sometimes uneasy relations with his children. There are numerous accounts of sexual liaisons and conflicted reports about his marriages, including "the hot depths and cold depths" of his life with Ann Birstein. One also encounters a surprising amount of self-criticism: a reassuring feature in a journal; he writes of his social awkwardness and resentments—the "proletarian youth in me"—his "mulish solitariness," his "irritability" and impatience with people, his need to be loved "that is infantile to the point of insanity," his self-assertiveness "on an absolutely unprecedented scale," and his "besetting" weakness as a writer flitting from assignment to assignment, leaving major projects unfinished (August 16, 1986; April 2, 1985; November 22, 1970; October 19, 1963; December 1955). A "critic-of-everything" forever in "the judgment seat," Kazin rarely spared himself his habits of uncompromising assessment.

While all journals are sui generis, taking their distinctive character from the personality and interests of the writer, Kazin's are exceptional for the variety and intensity of feelings on display. "I wonder if E[dmund] W[ilson] ever gets into his journals of the literary life anything as personal, harrowing, *mixed* as this," he wrote in a May 20, 1966, entry after reading entries from Wilson's journal published in the *New Yorker*. Was there anything in Wilson's crafted "set pieces" of disciplined "objectivity" comparable to "the open, suffering, deeply clamorous personal record that *I* write" (June 13, 1971)? Reading Kazin's journals, one is sometimes reminded of Wilson's as well as the recently published journals of Leo Lerman and Arthur Schlesinger Jr., writers from overlapping periods and milieus who like Kazin had a talent for literary portraiture. But Kazin was right to suggest that there is nothing in Wilson's journals (or for that matter in Lerman's and Schlesinger's) comparable to the "mix" of serious reflection, inspired portraiture, and the "open," "clamorous," sometimes brutally self-critical soul-searching to be found in his own. He was also correct to observe, as he frequently did, that the journals were essential to his life and thought. However entertaining and informative the journals of

Wilson and the others, each was in the end supplemental to its author's life and work. For Kazin the journals were primary; they came first; he liked to say that he "lived" in them. "I turn to this notebook as if it were my private lie detector, my confession, my way of ascertaining authenticity—and of recovering it—of making myself whole again," he wrote in a September 26, 1966, entry. And while we might wonder at times about his readiness to wrestle so exhaustively with his "suffering" soul, we can appreciate how high were the stakes, how urgent the need to think things through and set himself straight—"to lift myself by thought, by ideas, by words" (June 17, 1969).

Kazin hoped to publish an edition of his journals before his death. The closest he came was *A Lifetime Burning in Every Moment: From the Journals of Alfred Kazin* (1996). Though it contains a number of undated, edited, and rewritten journal entries, *Lifetime* cannot properly be called a book of Kazin's journals. Rather, it is a series of retrospective meditations on certain events and persons in his life written with varying fidelity to (and occasionally contradiction of) the original entries. In *Lifetime*, for example, he recalls his dismay on first reading Hannah Arendt's *Eichmann in Jerusalem* (1963), claiming that she "has made me suffer because of the tone she has taken to the doomed people" (179). But journal entries written when he read the book in manuscript indicate unqualified admiration for Arendt's views on the subject (December 22, 1962). "Hannah," he writes, is "one of the *just*. [. . .] She has the fundamental sense of *value*. She still believes in the right." It is not wholly clear why Kazin decided against publishing a selection of actual entries, or why he "refus[ed] to use the journals themselves" in *Lifetime*, perhaps because of the unhappy impression he felt too many of them would leave—"the fact is that the journals scare even me when I look them over—so much longing, so much resentment, so many names to worry about" (May 30, 1992; July 27, 1989). But the decisive reason seems to have been the prospect of reading though and making selections from seven thousand pages of entries—a daunting task for a man in his eighties struggling to finish a number of other projects. In the end, he acknowledged the hopelessness of the assignment—"the pile up of words there seems impossible to break through" (May 30, 1992). It was a major disappointment that the journals, "my precious life blood," would not be published in his lifetime (August 3, 1990).

The entries included in this volume represent approximately one sixth of the journal housed in the Berg Collection. In selecting and assembling them I have tried to faithfully represent the range of Kazin's interests and the tenor and depth of his thought. As he readily acknowledged, he was not a systematic thinker; he was, however, capable of sustained and passionate reflection, moving from image to insight, from feeling to idea, from association to discovery, surprising himself, Emerson-like, by what he never knew he knew. I have also tried to preserve some of the catch-as-catch-can flavor he valued in a journal—the randomness, the abrupt transitions, the "very fragments and sputtering and interruptedness that are so hard to read [and] are the real connecting stones, the primary elements" in any journal (May 26, 1985). A journal lives in its unpredictable responsiveness, its freedom to react erratically, even at times to stammer. Kazin occasionally stammers in his journal as he did in his speech—hesitant, unable to find the right word or complete the thought. Yet it is the opposite quality that comes through most predictably and powerfully—the rush of words, the cascade of ideas and impressions, "uncalculated and headlong and indiscriminate" (June 27, 1965). Fluency has special meaning for the stammerer; and Kazin clearly rejoiced in the upsurge and flow of words and ideas—"the pouring river of all my associations"—that could sweep him forward when he was writing in his journal (December 9, 1961). The daily entry was a relief and a release stirring the depths of consciousness, registering the "impact of language on the amazed and grateful brain" (October 5, 1951).

In 1980 Kazin attempted (unsuccessfully) to dissuade a Ph.D. candidate from writing a dissertation on him. It is too early, he explained. His career was not over, and he had more books to write. "Nor," he added, "will it ever make sense to write about me without some knowledge of my lifelong Journal, which has been the most exciting and influential form of my life." Though Kazin had misgivings about the self-preoccupation, "the me, me, me," of journal writing and occasionally feared losing himself in the "labyrinth of my own soliloquy" (December 10, 1962), he had no doubts about the excitement and pleasure and value the journal brought to his life. Described variously as his "true autobiography," his "precious life blood," his "private lie detector," his "confession," his "way of ascertaining authenticity," the journal was both a personal necessity and a reason for living. "What joy and relief this lonely Sunday to be able to set down things here as they are," he wrote in a March 7, 1997, entry, not long before his eighty-third birthday. "I must never be too tired to write in this book—*it is the one place where I can deal with the unexpected* that every day is made of" and the one place where life never becomes routine, where "life is ever new, and the day is its constellation right in my head."

I first encountered Alfred Kazin's journal in the summer of 1985 when I was researching a book on American public criticism. Hearing that he had recently deposited sections of the journal in the New York Public Library, I thought they might suggest some interesting connections between the private Alfred Kazin and his role as one of the country's most influential public critics. Soon after I had begun reading in the journal, I saw that it told a more interesting story than what I planned to say about American public criticism—a story I wanted to tell. When I met Kazin later that summer, I told him I found the journals fascinating, that he obviously "lived in" them, and that I would like to use them in a biography. He was pleased by my interest in the journals. But he was not at all sure about a biography and even less sure about me. "But you're not Jewish!" he exclaimed with emphasis. How could I possibly understand where he was coming from? I acknowledged the steep learning curve faced by a native of northern Maine (the son of two Baptist ministers) attempting to write the biography of a self-proclaimed "New York Jew" from "darkest Brownsville." But I had read enough of the journals to believe that the story was worth the effort, and eventually I convinced him. We disagreed for a time on the nature of the biography—he wanted an "intellectual biography"; I wanted the whole story. In time he agreed, on the condition that I be fair to his four wives.

Like all biographers, I searched out material wherever I could find it—published writing, news items, personal correspondence, reviews, interviews, publishers' contracts, strands of gossip. But the journal was my most valued resource. Without it *Alfred Kazin: A Biography* would not have been written. The journal not only told the inside story of Alfred Kazin; it demonstrated why it was worth telling—because there was so much inside—ambition, excitement, enthusiasm, fear, pride, hurt, resentment, euphoria, depression, passion, guilt, shame, humor, and wit. Reading in the journal I was privy to the thought and impressions of an acute mind and restless sensibility responding daily to a world of opportunity and threat. It was "my sensitivity to the world, my lightning-quick reactions to everything around me, that has always prepared me for this capacity for pain," Kazin wrote in the April 17, 1959, entry. "If you want maximum exposure, you must pay for it. This 'violence in the soul' that somebody described as the artist's quality, this fear of going mad, because of the writer's fundamental extravagance and saturability of experience." There is much more to the journals than "violence in the soul," but there is a good deal of turbulence and pain—as Kazin acknowledged. "What will not be forgiven me by the reader of these diaries is my obstinate unhappiness" (February 3, 1968). I have not edited out the unhappiness, loneliness, and pain in the selections that follow; they are as essential to the journal as the excitement Kazin felt in discovering a new writer or friend, the sardonic pleasure he took in portraying a colleague or acquaintance, the hope and determination with which he anticipated and planned his next book. Many things attracted me to the journal when I first encountered it in 1980s; it granted me access to a life, a milieu, a period in history that I felt privileged to share. It impressed me with the unsparing honesty with which Kazin confronted and assessed his conflicted, troubled nature—"the violence in the soul."

But the quality I found then (and still find) most engaging and reassuring is the obvious pleasure with which he exercised his gift of self-expression—"the bliss of writing. How lucky I am to be able to write, to be able to write this quickly. To be able to tune in whenever and wherever" (November 16, 1961). Kazin's journals are the work of someone who lived to think and to write. One reads and returns to them with a heady sense of creative contagion while sharing (at least for the moment) in his often expressed hope that salvation would, indeed, come by the word.

## Editor's Note

I have divided the book into chapters corresponding to distinct periods in Kazin's life and provided brief introductory accounts of the signal events of those periods, including especially those discussed in journal entries. While accuracy was my primary concern in presenting the entries, I have made the following very slight alterations in the texts for purposes of consistency and clarity. I have corrected obvious typos and misspellings, regularized the punctuation and Kazin's often erratic use of ellipses. I have expanded most of his contractions, substituted "and" for "&." I have rendered in italics his frequent underlinings except where different penstrokes indicate the underlinings were added at a later date; and I have italicized titles of literary works that he did not underline. I have not reproduced Kazin's random indentations, nor his use of characters (++, //, ##) at the beginning and conclusion of entries and paragraphs. When it is clear that Kazin misdated an entry, I indicate the correct date followed by his date. Because of space restrictions, it was not always possible to include entire entries. I indicate my elisions with bracketed ellipsis [. . .]. Unbracketed suspension dots are Kazin's.

# 1
# Starting Out
## 1933–1942

THE EARLIEST SURVIVING JOURNAL ENTRIES were written in May 1933, when Kazin was a sophomore at City College. His years at City were not happy ones. Irving Howe, Daniel Bell, Irving Kristol, and other notable alumni would look back fondly on City College in the thirties as a "wonderful place" (Howe), where one made friends through political association while sharpening one's polemical skills through vigorous political debate in the college's famous alcoves. Kazin did not participate. He detested the "fanatical" political atmosphere, stayed away from the "odorously male" alcoves, and chose to study by himself in the Great Hall, where he could listen to the organist playing Bach. It was a lonely time, and for companionship he often turned to his journal much as he had in his high school years.

The entries of this period are what one might expect from a bright, bookish sophomore excited, overexcited, by his reading, by music, by large (not always coherent) ideas about religion, art, and politics. Kazin says little in these early entries about the daily events and people in his life. The journal entry was primarily an opportunity to reflect on books, politics, and such expansive topics as "the true poetry of human life" and the artist "as the happiest and most accursed of men." It was also a chance to test and extend his fluency—and to experiment with grammar. Kazin often seems as interested in riding a flood of words as in making a coherent argument or clarifying a point of view. "I write words not within the planes of cognition or even common fancy, but of a terrible and pulsating musical sense" (November 18, 1933). He understood the risks of fluency. "I want to express everything and am therefore fated neither to express or understand anything" (September 20, 1933). But they were risks he was willing to take, hoping to tap into expressive (musical) reserves—"the fragmentary mutterings of a myriad of harmonies" (November 18, 1933)—that he believed were essential to his growth as a writer.

He was less willing to sacrifice clarity when politics was the subject. A young Socialist from Jewish Brownsville, Kazin was familiar with recent European history and the course of European Socialism. Reviewing the events leading up to the naming of Hitler as the German chancellor on January 30, 1933, he saw the collapse of the Second International at the beginning of World War I as a sign of things to come. An organization of socialist and labor parties founded in 1889, the Second International had disintegrated when the members abandoned their antiwar pledges and sided with the war aims of their respective countries. That failure and the subsequent failure of the German Social Democratic Party to consolidate and extend its power in the 1920s led Kazin to question Socialism's relevance to twentieth-century realities and to look to the "gusto and force" of the Communists (August 5, 1934). However, unlike other young radicals (including his friend Richard Hofstadter) he never joined the Communist Party nor made public statements in support of Communism—a decision, or nondecision, for which he would have no reason to apologize. "The only reason I escape[d] some of the absolutes" in the thirties, he wrote in a November 25, 1967, letter to Matthew Josephson "was that I couldn't get over the discovery of myself as a writer. It was grace."

No journal entries exist between June 5, 1935, and December 3, 1938—busy years when Kazin wrote book reviews for the *New Republic*, the *New York Times*, and the *New York Herald Tribune*; earned an M.A. in history at Columbia (1937–1938); taught courses at the New School and City College; and began work on *On Native Grounds*. In October 1938 he married Natasha Dohn, a research biologist working for her doctorate. Shortly thereafter, he and Natasha ("Asya") decided that each should keep a "daily record" of their lives. He did not write often in his journal while working on *On Native Grounds* (1938–1942), but he did find time for the occasional entry—on the war, on the state of modern criticism, on music, on Henry Adams (a subject of ongoing debate with his new friend Hofstadter), and, most memorably, on what writing his history of American literature and culture meant to him.

## May 14, 1933

A Sketch Book Alfred Jonathan Kazin

And the true poetry of human life rarely appears in our souls, meager, frost-begotten tissues of a warped life that they are! is the true vestiges of a placid and beautiful externality. Life jags us beyond ourselves, distorts our powers of understanding into a passive, suffering receptivity to the great blindnesses that seep into us and flow out, the light [illegible] noise of illusion. There is a type of poetry that is unity—the poetry of the intellectual mind—having visaged the whole of the objects of his understanding, he fuses them into the white heat of his soul, illuminates the note with this passion and feels in that the simple wholeness of passion that was Walt Whitman's simple anti-intellectualism when "he heard the learned astronomers," that is hysteria, the hysteria of the untutored, bare soul, in conflict with the flashy, hard crabbedness of pure conceptualization as in mathematics that is the world, piteous, exalted cry of the Lawrences of the world. [. . .] I have a horror of simple anti-intellectuals as I have of the eunuch scholastics. Life calls us to nothing more than passionate and rigorously logical (truthful) introspection. There is no externality but the outpourings of the self—no life spirit but the natural poetry of the human soul. The continuity of man's spirit is a grandiloquence and literal apotheosis possible of consummation solely under the light of man's own self. The self is a unity, an integrated body of apperceptive responses to a reality that is really but an individual creation. [. . .]

## May 29, 1933

[. . .] The world of today is at the crossroads—The whole scheme of aimless capitalism and the last dregs of traditionalist nationalism are being seen more clearly in their death-struggle. [. . .] The war gave our times a finality, but it was a finality left incomplete, for the vital dynamic that produced the bloodbath was left with hard, protruding edges and the very forces of idealism and strength of intellectual purpose that had seemed bulwarks against the patriot-murderers (read the Second International). But the artists suffered—and suffered so complete and so humiliating a disillusion that the objects of their artistic processes became blurred and indistinct—The forces of human life lost any sequence or coherence believed possible for them and, left as they were with only their receptive artistic senses, they turned it upon themselves and lost the beautiful, the enduring woods for the trees. [. . .]

It is idle to wish ourselves different from what we are—idle and tragic. We must fit the bone into the designated socket, and live with a naturalness, a freedom, an all-enduring, all composing veracity that will remain the last and most satisfying expressions of our life upon earth. That is why I love the moderns so much—Joyce and Lawrence, Maugham and Robinson,[1] the political and social thought of Einstein, the revolutionary work of Freud. "Honesty, Honesty," as Carlyle[2] said on his death-bed—the honesty to face life completely and frankly, and to accept it all as a totality of wonder, knowing the *responses* we give to each to be the best in the end. [. . .]

## July 24, 1933

[Alfred loves Nancy; Alfred loves Sex: Nancy!][3]

The essence of fascism is not so much the capitalist as it is the nationalist ideal. It is of course a platitude that the use of nationalism since the 13th and 14th centuries, particularly in Western Europe, has been marked by adherence to the laissez-faire theory of economics *and* the bourgeoisie side of the class-struggle, but what I want to bring out principally is that fascism, being a mass-spontaneous

1. William Summerset Maugham (1874–1965), English novelist and playwright; Edwin Arlington Robinson (1869–1935) American poet, three-time winner of the Pulitzer Prize.
2. Thomas Carlyle (1795–1881), influential Scottish essayist, historian, and biographer.
3. Added at the top of the page; editor's brackets.

movement, has fundamental roots in that blind, implacable chauvinism so dear to the heart of every moron. Fascism's essences are militarism, chauvinism, the arrogant Narcissism of Germany and Italy. Fascism is natural and real for the average individual. Even American Communism, most demagogic and fascist-like of all contemporaneous social (and particularly Marxist) creeds is often a stimulus for the average of the hoi-polloi. When a Social-Democrat aids the capitalists he does not become a "Social-Fascist," but a bourgeois. A Social Fascist is a Trotskyite Communist, with his asinine and pernicious doctrines of permanent revolution and exaggerated leftism. The Fascist influences in the modern Communist parties are the stress upon the violent features of the class-struggle with the incredible demagoguery of boring from within, the "bonus riots," the teacher's mess, etc., and the actual militarization of the proletariat. Did I not see young Pioneers[4] wearing uniforms? Communism believes that the social-pacificsts of the world are dangerous and obstructing influences in the class-struggle, that pacifism, if sincere, deluded and intellectually effeminate—and, if "hypocritical," obviously and manifestly the instrument of the bourgeoisie.

Marxism, in its theory of dialectical materialism offered to the contemporary thinking world a secularism so audacious and so cosmic that even we of today fail to appreciate the purely intellectual revolution it excited. The 19th century was the consummation, the climax of the Italian Renaissance, the vortex of an aimless secularism and a vast, desperate individualism. Marxism, of its own essence, propounds the most amazing denouement of the Copernican revolution and its subsequent non-metaphysical ramifications—it makes man historically and continuously an animal, an animal not so much of Darwin's purely physical aspects with its major allusions of brutality and infinite, omnipotent struggle, but an animal devoting its speculative, clarifying, cognitive and social powers to the promulgation of evil social cultures. Intellectually Marxism represents the climax of intellectual honesty. It marks the determination on the part of the intellectual individual to see the history of man's social and mental cultivation and refinement from the perspective of the organic and scientific method—viz—to envisage man's intellectual odyssey, not in terms of an idealistic ethic as did Goethe, Herder, and Spengler, but in terms of a dispassionate reality.[5] Marxism marks the *overthrow* of man's omnipotence and egotism. Organized religion of the 19th century and particularly contemporary fascism have their fundamental roots in this specious

4. A Communist youth group.

5. Johann Gottfried von Herder (1744–1803), German philosopher, poet, philologist and critic. Oswald Arnold Gottfried Spengler (1880–1936), German historian and philosopher, whose *Decline of the West* (1917) became a influential best-seller in the 1920s.

and hypocritical ethic—an ethic of delusion and criminal projection—since it is a theology of materialism, an idle and irrational ramification of the silly idealism of the Era of Enlightenment. It is here apropos to deal at length with the added features of Marxism: that it is a fundamental or *final* idealism of the scientific method—the attempt to reorganize an idealist society, a noble utopia with the instruments and clarifying powers of a rigorous and brilliant logic. But it is a logic of extraordinary scope and dimensions because it gives the final blow to the anthropocentric myth.
[Written in the top margin:]
(Sex and mental Pathology)
H. Ellis—Sexual Inversion
Freud—Three Contributions to the Sexual Theory
Kraft-Ebbing—Pyschopathia Sexualis
McDougal—Abnormal Psychology
Corot—Problems of Sex

## August 3, 1933

*Thomas Mann and Buddenbrooks. Buddenbrooks* is in itself a perfect piece of art because it is so completely accurate and satisfying an expression of a mode of life that is ordinary and stable, inherent in human life. Outwardly, it is but the rapid recital of the births, development, marriages and deaths in a prosaic and prosperous family. But what does not go on within this dull exterior! What a wealth of exaltation, tenderness, and super-humanized mystery. Reading it one seems to be living sheerly immersed in the very [illegible] and proportions and a lasting well-built monument to a class and creed approaching the spiritual in its fanatical devotion to a material essence and a material Deity. It is interesting to compare this novel with the *Forsythe Saga*! Galsworthy's work has certain elements of the melodramatic in it—that is to say, the feud between Irene as the implacable, victorious sense of beauty and Soames as the devotee of the sense of property and righteous morality is doubtlessly not a common idea, nor is the feud extending to young Jon with Fleur Mont valid as a transcription of actual experience. What is most extraordinary in the work, however, amounting to an idea of genius is that the accredited force of evil, Soames, is made into so comprehensible and even likeable a human being. The feud is a fissure, an adjunct. What is at the heart of the novel is the extraordinary feeling and tenderness approaching the cosmic moments of the Russian novel, that we are made to feel for one who is so obviously and completely a pernicious influence and whose power and ability are sufficient to ruin the lives of the most able and the most enduring of the book's characters. But *Buddenbrooks* is placid and normal. It is normality exalted to literature. The only character who approaches anything like individuality of a marked sort is Hanno, and Hanno is the consummating and most complete irony of the novel, for it is precisely Hanno who by his dreamy effeminacy, his love of music, his common dullness throws into grotesque relief at once the pitiful decline of the house and the fundamental, terrible, and disheartening dichotomy born in temperament and experience between the fourth and the fifth generations. The novel is superb in its titanic serenity, its reticence, its artistic form. [. . .]

## August 5, 1933

[. . .] The "Epilogue" to *Crime and Punishment* is not only one of the most beautiful and impressive scenes in the whole of fiction, it represents with an extraordinary clarity the whole spirit of the Russian novel of the 19th century and more important, of the Russian people. This has its chief interest in me because the Christ-spirit, conceived by me to be the greatest idea and passion ever given to the Human race, is so completely consummated in art by the Russians. Think of these intellectual and spiritual titans, Tolstoy and Dostoevsky, each of whom turned, the one in the flower of his creative period, the other at the close, to a repercussion of the Christ idea in terms that verged on the abnormal!—

For it is Christ and Christ alone who sums up the human race in its greatest significance!—its contradistinction from animalism. It is Christ who by his theory of love for one's fellow man expresses finally and *irredeemably* that divine understanding of man and his stature and significance in a universe of hostile and unrelenting inhospitality—it is Christ who more than the oriental prophets rings clear forever and forever to the soul-piercing declaration of man's solidarity with man and the hatred of injustice, inequity, and, above all, violence. For the essence of Christ's teachings is love and the divine rationalism that is pregnant with so complete and cosmic a fatalism. It is Christ who is the secular pacifist and anarchist—the great spirit of love and pity. Christ's pity is not condescension or even aid. It is love, a love of such divine proportions that it realizes inequality among men, the inequality of talent, strength, and innate organic temperament to be nothing but a pitiful joke, and realizing the wisdom of Lucretius' atomism, it seems to say: "My brother, I pity you not as one stoops to lift a less able brother from the dust, but as a fellow-creature. I realize with you such a comradeship, that I recognize in you my desires, my defects, my exaltations, and my despairs. [. . .]"

## August 7, 1933

The music of Mozart presents some of the most curious implications for the philosophical critic. In its purity of form, its ease, its jollity, it seems at first glance the unaffected happiness of eternal childhood. But it requires no deep-set penetration to realize the classic imprint of the more tragic emotions—particularly in the violin concertos and the chaste and reticent suffering of the 4th Symphony. Mozart is the greatest representative of Classicism because he, more than any other, includes with a subtle and major influence, the spiritual strivings of the Romanticists, its passionate and intense individualism and emotion. [. . .]

## September 5, 1933

*Form is Substance.* One of the most ludicrous and pathetic features of "critical thinking" is the incredible short-sightedness and pedantry of its views. Our critics seem too often unable to see into a problem of thought or expression save when bulwarked by a comfortable traditionalism and a body of established ideas and axioms which are conveniently made to influence all problems, whether or not the thinker becomes conscious of a differentiating necessity. It is the lack of intellectual courage that is most repellent and even pernicious, for fanaticism and falsehood thrive only on half-truths and [in] that dark and sequestered region of intellectual impotence and repressiveness. If thought has any value as a part of one's individual experience, it has precisely that dynamic influence upon a man's common experience that seems so alien to the majority of our folk and so precisely with form. Now, it seems to me that logic is too often seen (when it is seen at all in a conscious, brilliantly alive philosophical sense) as a convenient instrument for coherent dissertation. Form is viewed as a categorical vehicle, of a static and permeable influence alone which one may work upon at will and make one's own but possessing no active, dynamic-relevancy to the matter at hand, forming, of course, the main issue at hand. Wrong. What is obviously lacking here is a perception of the vital unity of an artist's consciousness, of the sharp immediacy of impressions, comprehensions, exultancies, perceptions that go to make up the thriving nameless, a natural expression of his being as he works. For substance does not *follow* or enter into form—it *makes* form. [. . .]

## September 12, 1933

[. . .] And all philosophies of history suffer for their grandiosity and the pathetic pompousness of individual positiveness of assertion and complete belief.

But deep, deep in the soul of man, reinforced by that superb intuition that is great with the profound sense of the abiding tragedy in all human life is the knowledge of the complete flux and transitoriness of all things and that solely that miraculous poetry that floods the dull and dismal crevices of life rises forward to a new and more complete conception of man, and his instrumentality of existence, the soul.

## September 20, 1933

I want to express everything and am therefore fated neither to express or understand anything.

## November 18, 1933

I can say with Schiller that the bases of my artistic consciousness are in music. I write words not within the planes of cognition or even common fancy, but of a terrible and pulsating musical sense. I feel the whole brunt of what I say held fast within music—and music fills my being with a sense of completeness that literally compresses me out, and then further into words. I write them out of a compulsion that is musical—I can hear the fragmentary mutterings of a myriad of harmonies pulsate and fly upwards dealing out sparks of fiery and brilliant life and come to even sense, sometimes, a new Being growing within me, large and rich with life, crying out in its wonder and beauty and holding me fast. O, music, it is nameless and terrible. [. . .]

## December 3, 1933

We respond most easily and really feel the greatest ultimate pleasure in that which helps us to live. I feel a necessity for solitude, even loneliness. I need to be alone. I desire it and take it upon myself and feel a yearning peace and glorious self-sufficiency in it. And how curious and logical that my artistic and intellectual masters are themselves men who saw this necessity for loneliness—Heraclitus, Plato, Plotinus, Coleridge, Keats, Beethoven, Brahms, Caesar Frank and Lawrence and Joyce![6]

6. Heraclitus (c. 535–c. 475 BCE), pre-Socratic Greek philosopher, best known for his theory of change: "everything flows"; Plotinus (c. 204/5–270 CE), influential philosopher of late antiquity who argued for a "neoplatonism" that subordinated the material world to ideal forms; César Franck (1822–1890), Dutch-Belgian-French pianist, organist, and composer.

## December 7, 1933

[. . .] I was walking at dusk in Highland Park[7] today, carried away by lovely memories, and in the incredible beauty of the waters, the silhouetted trees, and the fanciful nebulous shadows. I have loved there, been happy and miserable. It is the scene of my most intense moments. I was carried away, and would have plunged further had not a sudden burst of white struck my eye in the declining brightness. I walked on further, and what I saw pierced me cruelly; more so that my mood was so removed from all somberness or reflection. The graves of the soldier-dead lie there, in the jetties beyond the reservoir, sunk deep in the cut grass and the wet earth, and I thought to myself: what did these men die for? They must have been nearly as young as I was when they died, some of them may have been here as I was there then, exulting in freedom and a beauty that was formed part out of the God's and part out of mine own elements. They died, killed in legalized murder-scenes, and they died so that Wilhelm of Hohenzollern might be replaced by Adolf Hitler! O, my God—when I think of such things, when I witness the sickening and terrible degeneration of the 2nd International, the growing intensification of nationalism, hate and prejudice, I all but give up the struggle. Idealism is less than useful today, it is blind and pitiful. The war is coming, I know it, the war will come; and the patriots and the jingoes, the pompous Pilates will throw more blood on the fire. They will make another Versailles, and then, perhaps, even the Comintern[8] will follow its unlamented step-brother, "noble, idealistic" Social-Democracy. If the party of a Bebel could have produced a Noske,[9] what in the name of sanity will the party of Djershinski[10] do? I sometimes think that Christ was fortunate to die when and how he did—such a darkness as will now infect me and my generation would have led him to deny his own Heavenly Father.

It is not so much the imminence of war that frightens me; it is the complete paralysis of all proper agencies to defeat it, and the dynamic power of Reaction. Before the last war, the International Trade-Unions drew up definite plans for general-strikes, sabotage, and the like. Many workers realized the imminence of

7. Straddling Brooklyn and Queens, Highland Park figures prominently in *A Walker in the City*.
8. Comintern, a contraction of Communist International, also known as the Third International, was formed in Moscow in 1919 after the collapse of the Second International.
9. August Bebel (1840–1913) was one of the founders of the German Social Democratic Party of Germany. Gustav Noske (1868–1946), a leader of Germany's Social Democrats, crushed the Sparticist Communist movement in 1919.
10. Felix Dzerzhinsky (1877–1926) was head of the Soviet secret police under Lenin.

the peril and were drawn up determinedly to counteract it. But we of today have no such agencies. The only power of any consequence against war and fascism, the Comintern, is too weak and too rutted in theoretical plans of action to seem to me of any use. It is Fascism, the mouth of Capital that is the force, Fascism, the hideous evil that is to be combated. But how? Look what happened to the Reichskammer and the boasted "vanguard of the Proletarian Revolution," the Red Front Troops in Germany! Was Italian Communism or Italian syndicalism less cowardly than Italian Social Democracy in 1922?

The alternative is too easy, pitifully easy. Cynicism, debauchery, and a complete world-suicide will inevitably result if there is no solidification of righteousness in action. Otis remarked at the students' hearing today that we ought to get out (we homo sapiens) and give the fruit flies a chance! *I* cannot help but feel that they could not make a more miserable botch of living than we have. What a miserable, stinking animal man is when he runs in packs! Perhaps Judas was the wisest of the Apostles!

## March 31, 1934

[. . .] I know that I am often shocked by the destructive quality of my sexual affinities. I love coarse women—the women that are frank, volatile, daring, and pre-eminently physical. May it be that the cynical remark that Huxley[11] makes somewhere (in *Brief Candles*) that prostitutes have a definite service in that they make the advances that so many shy men are unable to make for themselves can apply also to men who see a definite and intoxicating beauty in such women? I feel that I am quite forthright enough in my advances to women, and I am anything but shy—and yet I love the atmosphere of brothels, the tangible, earthy, rollicking obscenity of it. I love women who can encompass me and make me feel a partner to a great physical energy and robust charm. What has always revolted me in the position of women in conventional morality is the possessive attitude of men—the attitude that women have no sex promptings of their own. Only prostitutes (quelle ironie!) seem to be forthright and thoroughly honest. And I dream the dream of the shimmering and pear-dripping breasts—to be held with my face pressed deep downwards in great, white, hanging breasts—my lips on black nipples and my whole body pressed down in the sudden tingling of desire.

11. Aldous Leonard Huxley (1894–1963), English writer, author of the collection of short stories *Brief Candles* (1930) and, most famously, the novel *Brave New World* (1932).

## May 5, 1934

The artist must endure the presence of thoughts and ideals, which, in any other form would be anti-social and positively immoral. The artist can understand that a mystical attitude toward government becomes the servant of reaction, of fascist deceit and economic evil. And yet he will deliberately seek such an attitude in his personal life, or visualize the contours and forms of it otherwise. Why? Because being an artist he is essentially amoral. Political/social idealism are studies and operations in the particular. They are ethical studies because they are embedded in a naturalistic way of looking at things. The artist is not a naturalist or even a supernaturalist. He is a totalitarian eclectic, and because he can probe into the linear and the obvious he escapes the logic of ethical naturalism and can visualize things irrationally and irresponsibly.

## August 2, 1934

In the novel, effects can be gained, appearances making for impressive solidity gained, and ideas distilled that would, in any other art-form, fail completely. The novel breathes the air of life—if it is a novel with conventional literalness one partakes of the consciousness of life in one's reading moment of consciousness, when the concentrated straining of the reader becomes a self absolutely divorced from and yet psychologically aligned to the normal, ordinary self. [. . .]

## August 5, 1934

The great difference between Social-Democracy and Communism is that Social-Democracy rests upon ethical, general bases—ideas that are essentially drawn from the tradition of 19th century liberal humanitarianism and that Communism deals with particulars, with the living, seething contemporaneity of contemporary capitalism rather than of a vague and general reformism. Communism came out of the maelstrom of the war's politics—it was created not so much, it seems to me, as a development of Lenin's 1903-London theses[12] as of a general impatience with and revolt against the ineffable debacle of Democratic Socialism during and after the war.

Social-Democracy is *not* a consciously motivated aid to capitalism, as the Communists would have us believe, but an essentially noble idea distorted by the cold and brutal logic of antagonistic events. Social-Democracy belongs to

12. In a 1903 meeting in London, the Russian Social Democratic Labor Party split into two factions: the Mensheviks and the more radical Bolsheviks led by Lenin.

the era of the liberalistic status-quo. Its mainstay was the concept of a free and steadfast democracy in which to employ the mechanics of a social rationalism. The best index to the "mind" of Social-Democracy is the thought and form of Shaw's work. Shaw's great essence is his rationalistic insistence that by discussing problems in the whimsy-fancy of the play-world, people will actually and conjointly, too (under, I suppose, the flush, of a fully realized impressiveness) aid in the process of a radical social amelioration. Social-Democracy too believed in persuasion, but it was successful until reality became insistent and articulate. The reason the Socialist parties successively succumbed to the force of war, etc. was not that they were enemies of proletarian revolution—it was rather that having no real consciousness of proletarian ideals, they could not, when the time came, adjust themselves to a perniciously forceful situation. The Socialist parties before the war, as now, did not want Socialism because they had no realization of what Socialism was. They could speak yearningly of a "worker's world" and such a "worker's world" uses an alloy of Billy Sunday's Heaven and Bailey's Beach,[13] but their very comical naiveté betrayed the source and true nature of their Socialism. They had no real consciousness of social-mechanics, of the forces going to influence social ideas—they came to their philosophy out of an earnest desire to ameliorate themselves; and they allowed, successively the emotional fervor of their earnest idealism to take the place of pragmatic ideas, social psychology, and the realistic awareness of life which were super-necessary for the realization of the social-idea. Consequently, when capitalism really became incisive and obdurate, Socialism collapsed—not out of the capitulatory case of treachery, but of the debacle of psychical and organic collapse. The Socialist parties had not trained themselves to fight a truly *realistic* situation. Capitalism to them was either an idea of a social state or the impressionism of local conditions. They did not understand, because it never occurred to them to understand, that the state and the status of proletarian strength were of commensurate importance for the winning of Socialism. They did not realize that Socialism was a matter of complete debacle for one class and complete victory for another—They had no fundamental realization of the essential brutality of all social struggles because they had not envisioned the scope and range of the social state.

Social-Democracy existed as an "ideal" alone. This is perfectly borne out by a study of their press. How, for example, does the *New Leader*[14] handle the

13. A private beach club for wealthy families in Newport, Rhode Island. William "Billy" Sunday (1862–1935), professional baseball player turned popular evangelist.
14. A fiercely anti-Communist journal founded in 1924 to support Socialist and liberal causes.

great majority of present-day news? By ignoring it. It writes principally about the vagueness of social idealism—running flamboyant cartoons of strangely heroic-looking steel-workers marching on to the dawn etc.—all this with perorations on the side about the beauty of a co-operative strength, and the images of workers (who never work) envisioning (!!!) the social apotheosis.

Social Democracy failed then because of its major and essential fault: unintelligence. It was that rather than social-fascism that created the specter of fascism and fascist victory. It was unintelligence that made Arthur Henderson[15] spend years in Geneva instead of Downing Street; unintelligence that made the Wells talk nonsense before the Hitler Reichstag about honor when a dignified silence would have been infinitely more impressive and less dangerous, personally. It was the same driveling, childish self-encroachment that made for the policy of the "lesser evil," and allowed a Hindenburg[16] when any Reichsbanner[17] war-veteran could have told the flunkey in the *Vorwärts*[18] that Hindenburg couldn't be trusted. The tragedies of English labor, of American laborism, of French division, of French debacles and Austrian procrastination—how can one see the horrible, engulfing tragedies save under the unusual symbol of naive dunder-headedness?

The point is that once confronted with forceful and brutal capitalism, Socialism lost its props and betrayed the fact that it had no consciousness of the meaning of Socialism and therefore no desire for Socialism. Socialism was a pipe-dream; when Lenin showed that it meant war and courageous struggle, they [the Socialists] collapsed. Think of the irony of the Weimar Socialists! For almost fifty years they had preached the gospel of socialization to the masses. When, in 1919–20 they finally achieved power, had Scheideman as Chancellor and Ebert as President, they appointed a committee (under Karl Kautsky's chairmanship!) to investigate the possibilities of socialization![19] This has always seemed to me the culminating irony of Social-Democracy. To steadfastly preach Socialism for half-a-century and then, when able to embody their preachings in resolute and decisive actions, they set out to investigate!

15. A leader of the British Labour Party.
16. Paul von Hindenburg (1847–1934), Germany's president, appointed Adolf Hitler (1889–1945) chancellor of Germany in January 1933.
17. An organization of war veterans formed to defend the German Republic against militant groups on the left (Communists) and the right (National Socialists).
18. A liberal-left newspaper published in Berlin.
19. Philipp Scheidemann (1865–1939) and Friedrich Ebert (1871–1925) were leaders of Germany's Social Democratic Party. Karl Kautsky (1854–1938) was a Marxist theoretician who denounced the Bolshevik Revolution.

This is not insincerity but palpable, almost grotesque obtuseness. Socialists did not go to jail and suffer all the penalties of a true social martyr fate out of a cunning demagogism—no, they really believe in what they were suffering, but they believe alone. They did not accompany their otherwise admirable beliefs with planning and a forceful, deep-rooted ideology.

Social-Democracy was born out of an unrealistic vein of life, and it collapsed; as soon as it came face to face with reality, it betrayed its integrated ill-logic. Communism, however, it seems to me, derives straight from the attack on Social-Democracy. Communism as we know it today owes its essential psychology to the atmosphere and events of the October Revolution and the seething activity of post-war class-struggle. What is most evident in Communism is not so much the mind of Lenin diffused into conglomerate social-action, as the fusion of Russian Socialism with the definitive and lasting form of crisis. Communism thrives on the offensive—it began with the struggle against debacle reformism, and it gains its strength hourly (I am thinking particularly now of the United States) through the continual struggle against immediate, particular things. Communism has nothing of the airy generalizations, the pompous, platitudiness vacuities of the Vandevelde-Wells-Abramovich[20] school. It lives within and almost *because* of action. Communism has method, substance, and form. It lacks the sentimentalism of Social-Democracy, that particularly opprobrious impediment which disguises the ineffectuality of endless reformism by poetry of the dish-water variety. Communism, in short, is a 20th century movement—of the gusto and force of the contemporary weltanschauung. Social-Democracy rather is the expression of the out-moded world of gentle aspirations and gentle lives. It is a relic of a time when life could be divorced from politics and when the forces of reaction were vulnerable only (it was felt) through the force of argument and rationalistic impetus.

## August 19, 1934

In "Faith and Transfiguration" I am writing a satire upon human life—I give the history of one who arduously and painfully attempts to piece out the nebulous qualities in himself which will make for calm and transcendence of his experience. Jonathan finds out that the only faith that can lead to transfiguration is the faith that man is capable of understanding his world—he learns that life has no meaning in itself but acquires a meaning, or rather a set of

20. Henry van de Velde (1863–1957), an architect, and H. G. Wells (1866–1946), a novelist, wrote about the relationships between socialism and art. Raphael Abramovitch (1880–?) was a Russian Social Democrat, a Menshevik.

colored values that stem directly from the heart of every living being. He learns, then, that life is nothing but that perception and consciousness are all. [. . .] Jonathan conceives of himself as an artist, and the problem that interests him almost above all others is the psychology of [the] artistic personality.

Jonathan is drenched with the loneliness of the far-seeker, the painstaking visionary. For him, art holds the highest promise of human life. [. . .]

## June 5, 1935

While re-reading P. M. Jones's *English Critical Essays*, I was thinking constantly of a remark Nathan made (*Passing Judgments*) about the effeminacy of most contemporary English drama.[21] Well, I don't know much about the drama; but certainly much of the criticism, while acute and really good is sissified. I miss a robust and realistic sense. The humor is the hypothetical, wheezy, old humor of the professor who wants to show what a good fellow he is. It strikes me as rather funny when I think of how I longed for England years ago. Now I wouldn't want to live in it any more than I would in Tibet. Culture (literary) in England when it's not accompanied by a real strength and some definite talent like V. Woolf or Eliot is flat and dull competence. Emotion becomes the sentimental repetitiousness of a man like Murry.[22] Well, what's wrong? Of course the caste system and the resulting unreality about most of what happens to them. When a man like Lawrence comes out of the lower class he's an *eccentric*—in the good sense of the word. Or [Arnold] Bennett, in his personal *life*.

## December 3, 1938

Before Asya[23] and I were married, we decided to keep a daily record of our lives, but of course we won't. I do need a notebook-journal-diary, however, as I've always needed one; and this may be it. . . . Incidentally, I'm happier that I ever thought I could be. I've always believed in my bad fortune, feared marriage and the worst in it as my special dispensation, my special dispensation always being bad. But Asya is like nothing I ever anticipated or even dared to hope for. She's priceless.

21. Phyllis Maud Jones, ed., *English Critical Essays* (Oxford, 1933); George Jean Nathan (1882–1958), drama critic, co-edited the magazine *The Smart Set* with H. L. Mencken (1880–1956).
22. John Middleton Murry (1889–1957), English writer, critic, and editor.
23. Natasha Kazin, née Dohn.

## December 4, 1938

Reading, reading, reading. Who was it (Leslie Stephen?[24]) who said Gibbon had composed his life in reading? I'm reading Emerson because I want some light in the background, and because he gives me always a sensation of purity. Also, I'm very ignorant.

## April 29, 1939

[. . .] A bright thought, and I ought to know: People who do not tell the truth are afraid. I used to be a terrible liar. I could say, as most writers so often do say (and beneficent psychologists, gushy folk, literary people and fond mamas and papas), that such a disposition merely suggests a literary talent. In part, yes. But it is part of the complex in me, the perpetual radiating complex dating from Brownsville, which allows me to stammer.

## June 24, 1939

"Truth can never be told so as to be understood, and not be believed."[25] I understand that, I believe that, I stake my life on that. It is perfectly meaningless to most of the talented, ambitious, generally preeminent of my contemporaries and especially of my own generation. [. . .]

What a baboon I am. I am still, for all my efforts at self-discipline, perpetually surprised by deceit, by envy, by shallowness, by that gangster hardness, that mechanical cynicism, which my generation abounds in. Apparently I have not grown too far since those hot, exultant, feverish days in Highland Park when I was so, so strong in my knowledge of self, and so close to exaltation. I grow cold when I think of those days—the moon on the ice-pond, the hills above Highland Boulevard where Nancy I used to walk every evening, the trees out of El Greco's Toledo-Spain, and the happiness, the poignance, of knowing that I had that living, breathing awareness, that power to compose the scenes of life in the frame of a restless imagination, without which life is impossible.

Every man bears a secret: the private legend of his ambition, which is a salient and ambiguous and perpetual marshaling of his resources.

24. Leslie Stephen (1832–1904), English writer, critic, and editor, father of Virginia Woolf.
25. A favorite quotation from *The Marriage of Heaven and Hell* by the poet William Blake (1757–1827).

Me and my contradictions: I love mystics and rebels; I love independence, the tigers of belief: Donne, Blake, Baudelaire; but I prefer Tolstoy to Dostoevsky.

Spinoza, as Goethe said, proved not that existence demonstrates God, but that existence is God. Does not that signify a comfortable, delightful, challenging truth? Does it not mean that man has responsibility and that truth, properly conceived, is open to us? It signifies liberation; most ideas on and of God curtail, repress, bind, hurt, mortify.

## September 23, 1939

Henry James on criticism.[26] Save, Kazin, save: it's wonderful. And listen: "To lend himself, to project himself and steep himself, to feel and feel till he understands, and to understand so well that he can say, and to have perception at the pitch of passion, and expression as embracing as the air, to be infinitely curious and incorrigibly patient, and yet plastic and inflammable and determinable, patient, stooping to conquer and yet serving to direct; these are fine chances for an active mind, chances that add the idea of independent beauty to the conception of success. Just in proportion as he is sentient and restless, just in proportion as he reacts and reciprocates and penetrates, is the critic a valuable instrument."

## November 1, 1939

The tragedy of today is simply this: never before has capitalism appeared so barbaric, so repulsively hypocritical, so formless, so irrational; never before has Socialism in theory appeared so remote, or in practice—and I mean the Soviet Union, I mean the thinking and morals of most Communists in this world, their complete inhumanity and sterility, their lack of culture, their muzhik[27] sense of life—appeared so unattractive. On this day Russia attacked Finland; on this day workers in Helsinki were bombed by the army organized by Lenin, Trotsky, Tukachevsky, Frunze,[28] and the aspiration of the world's toilers.

26. Henry James (1843–1916), "Criticism" (1891).
27. A Russian peasant.
28. Mikhail Nikolayevich Tukhachevsky (1893–1937), Soviet military commander, victim of Stalin's 1930s purges; Mikhail Vasilyevich Frunze (1885–1925), Bolshevik leader of the Russian Revolution of 1917.

## January 7, 1940

Is it not curious how the most intense and voluble modernism of our day (but of course all modernism is voluble; if it could not talk of itself and perpetually proclaim its intentions, it would not exist), so somber or even tragic in theory, so angular a view of the world, is always so *prankish?* . . . Perhaps the answer lies in the essence of so successful a modern book as *The Enormous Room*.[29] Begin with horror too horrible to seem horrifying and you must end up by playing the clown.

## January 25, 1940

On Henry James: nothing is so typical of his ambivalence of spirit, lost between his *image* of Europe and his *conception* of America than his half-playful, half-apologetic, use of what English gentlemen in the eighties would certainly have thought of as improper colloquialism. Or even worse. James was never English, never too perceptive a student of the English; he was too *genteel* and too American at once. How many times in his letters, essays, novels, does one hear that recurring note of distress, of the many ejaculations of loss, of irritability?

## April 8, 1940

I received a Guggenheim Foundation Fellowship this morning. Mama said: Zwei toisand toller: Far vus [Two thousand dollars: for us]?

## April 27, 1940

The place of literature, of art and scholarship, in this war-riddled world just now is symbolic, and that is its value and, I might add, the *method* of its evaluation. When the Nazis talk their drivel about Shakespeare being a "German" dramatist, and a Daladier[30] talks about la belle France, le France de Voltaire, Rousseau, et Foch, it's the same.[31]

29. A 1922 autobiographical work by E. E. Cummings (1894–1962) recounting his life inside a French prison during World War I.
30. Édouard Daladier (1884–1970) was prime minister of France at the beginning of World War II.
31. Ferdinand Foch (1851–1929), French soldier and military theorist, supreme commander of the Allied armies during World War I.

## August 11, 1940

Provincetown: Properly understood, Romanticism is not a literary or artistic form, but the symbol of an epoch. What in literary terms, does a Goethe have in common with a Renan,[32] a Whitman, an Oscar Wilde that they all do not have in common with the qualities of say, of Marx's early prose, European nationalism, and Napoleon?

## December 26, 1940

Reading Henry Adams's late letters, with their macabre and really frightening sense of doom, one enjoys the luxury of self-mockery and the historical irony. If Adams thought what he did of the nineties, what would he have thought of us? . . . Yet Adams didn't really approximate his emotions in thought—least of all the historical formulaic thoughts, the facile Hamlet-Spengler doom! doom! of his letters. He dramatized himself *in* his social position. Also, he had—what most men today can never appreciate for almost physiological reasons, such a wealth and vivacity of mind, such a need to come alive, to observe, that it is little wonder that he often said more than he meant to. Character is fate. And it is also conversation.[33]

## December 27, 1940

Middle-class philistinism is bad enough, but radicals—especially a certain type of Jewish, city Marxist, possess and impose a Philistinism that is far more frightening than anything else. It is their knowingness, their complacent and puerile materialism, that total refusal to entertain even in hypostasis (not to say dialectically!) any possible alternative or controversion or to understand anything different. . . . Tell a certain type of lumpen intelligentsia that religious significance—if only as an idea—and a more scrupulous, conscious sense of ethics are indispensible, and his face will grow blank. He will not disagree with you; he will merely not understand you.

## January 7, 1941

I play with an image—the point at which all types of greatness in the arts will converge—H. James pressing harder, deeper; Michelangelo flat on his back

32. Ernest Renan (1823–1892), French philosopher, scholar, historian.

33. Kazin and Richard Hofstadter (1916–1970), who at the time often worked at the same table in the New York Public Library, frequently quarreled over Adams. Hofstadter said that Kazin was too willing to overlook's Adams's anti-Semitism because he was good writer.

painting the Sistine Chapel ceilings; Bach at his Leipzig organ. . . . Then, a point at which a career becomes a corpus—as again in H. James—the writer, artist is physically futile, personally even a little ridiculous—"he has found his happiness in his work"—and his life's evidence is . . . a row of books on a shelf.

Sainte-Beuve: "Soyons les derniers des delicats." [Let us be the last of the refined.][34]
Renan—"The essence of criticism is to enter into modes of life different from our own."

The naturalist, Flaubert to George Sand—"We must treat men as if they were mastodons or crocodiles."

How does a writer become great today? In the Victorian era it was often enough for him to assert a moral criticism of the age, of being a lay protestant, a realist in the sense of being a 19th century reformer-prophet. From 1890 to 1920, say, literary distinction of the highest and most obvious kind—historically—meant the creation of new methods, radical insights that would devastate the old and point the way—society, Shaw; craft and language, Joyce. The balance of the times, the balance between epochs, were so delicate that to tip it ever so slightly, like Shaw and the general Fabian-Socialist-Wellsian mind in art, c. 1910, was to "achieve" originality.[35] Anti-bourgeois-c'etait assez [To be antibourgeois was enough]. Today? The bourgeois has lost all prestige—lost even faith [in] himself, which is one way of saying that he has often become a Fascist—but épater le bourgeois [to shock the middle-class] has become silly. A writer today with Shaw's élan would not be a pamphleteer; a writer with Carlyle's intensity would not be a moralist. Who are our great writers of the future and how do they propose to dominate their age and inspire and excite and unify? Where is their instigation? Where shall they attach themselves to the main line, the preponderant theme, the central focus? Literature has not been truly progressive since 1919. The great writers of the post-war period have been rhetorical morticians. Indeed, our contemporary literature is rhetorical in the same way that Pope's and Gay's was.[36] I almost said Congreve,

34. Charles Augustin Sainte-Beuve (1804–1869), leading French literary critic of his era.
35. The Fabian Society, a British socialist society hoping to advance socialism through reform rather than revolution.
36. Alexander Pope (1688–1744), eighteenth-century English poet and satirist; John Gay (1685–1732), English poet and dramatist, author of *The Beggar's Opera* (1728).

perhaps even Donne—we are metaphysicals, that is, superior to romanticism and too disorderly for classicism.[37] Yet Donne's arabesques and devotions—yes, even his devotions, are truly alive and catholic—a man excited by his own gifts and appetites, potentiality. Our vivacity is neurotic, impressionable, gluttonous. [. . .]

## January 8, 1941

Beware of a writer quoting too much; he may be quoting all he knows.

## January 13, 1941

Heard the *Eroica*[38] this morning, first time in ages—and I've been weeping in a sad, aroused excitement in my heart ever since. Oh, the challenge of it, the overflowing, irrepressible joy in life of the last movement—like seven-league boots conquering the world! What I hear in that last movement, always, is an army terrible with banners—the fields of the dead are suddenly alive with spears. . . . That look on Thomas Hardy Louise Bogan[39] wrote of: the thrust head, the living heroic, exuberant self-assessment and triumph in achievement, that ineffable dignity of aroused spirit—the exuberance of victory.

Criticism today is not an art, perhaps never may, even never should be one; but it has a become a *branch* of art. That's the important consideration.

## March 16, 1941

Yeats's *Autobiography* is one of the very few books I have ever read that suggest a great spiritual personality, achievement, imaginative life, capacity—yet remain full of good, hard common sense—and the c.s. steals in and out of the honeyed prose. It's like an undertone—a monumental and profoundly impressive sobriety of the mind. His amazing gift—to convey limpidly and perfectly his dissatisfaction with Oscar Wilde—life as rhetoric—"I shall write beautiful words, with beautiful characters," etc.—yet, hating "vague impressiveness," succeed[s] with devastating, disdainful superiority to it in conveying the music of language

37. William Congreve (1670–1729), English playwright of the Restoration period; John Donne (1572–1631), leading English "metaphysical" poet, Dean of St. Paul's Cathedral.
38. Beethoven's Symphony No. 3.
39. Louise Bogan (1897–1970), American poet and poetry reviewer for the *New Yorker*.

inherent in Irish literary speech. . . . It is a book which is simultaneously—yet easily, quietly; quality of great repose in the prose—both witty and *noble*.

## March 17, 1941

The character in Yeats's autobiography—BELIEF MAKES THE MIND ABUNDANT.

## March 21, 1941

When one has a temperament like mine, one can either drive it or be driven by it. There is no other course—unless one can endure the sacrifice every day.

## April 17, 1941

The critic as undertaker: secretly he wishes for the death of his subject, so that he may see the arc close, the analysis final.

## June 13, 1941

Think about the peculiar and philistine irresponsibility of so much academic scholarship in America—the fundamentally *mindless* exhibitionism of accumulation of data, the lack of any personal and dynamic consciousness of need, value, purpose, sense. What is so depressing is the irony inherent in any activity concerned with the history of forms, culture, but vitally unconcerned with and even stupid about culture. Think of the ransacking of facts, the pillage of libraries, the tireless scrutiny and dissection of detail—and of the utter vacuity, the sinister complacency and spiritual laziness, which direct it! In a "degenerate" age—which, of course, ours is not—this would be Byzantian.

## August 2, 1941
### (dated October 2)

In every way ours is not "the end of an era," the end of everything we like to think; the world, the best part of it, seems to be waiting, waiting, in a spirit not unlike the climacteric in eighteenth century Europe upon which followed the Romantic movement. The world is waiting for assurance of its own worth, of human worth and activity; it is waiting for a new romanticism, a new prophecy. It is waiting for those calm new men, prophets and realists of our own time, who will offer confidence in its own need to survive. The new romanticism will be religious without religion; oracular, but sophisticated; and *simple*.

## August 18, 1941
### (dated October 18)

My mind reverts to the vault-like appearance of City College in the old days—the Great Hall, the darkness stealing through every pore of Townsend Harris Hall—ah, bitter chill it was! The biological museum on the third floor of the Main Building. And remembering how I used to sit alone in the evenings, loath to go home to Brownsville, under the memorial windows of the Great Hall, looking up at the flags of the European universities—Salamanca, Dublin, Oxford, Paris, Munich—with the old text-book of mathematical analysis in my hand.

## September 17, 1941

Reading *Partisan Review*[40] this morning (a magazine I admire and am indebted to). I cannot help but feel how strikingly a certain kind of Marxist disputation has become pure scholasticism—

## October 1, 1941

Reading through George Dangerfield's[41] piece on pamphleteering in the current *Virginia Quarterly*, I saw immediately why British style—the tone and weight of its prose—is so much superior to ours—why Brogan's[42] book on France seemed to me so remarkable in its poise and personal mastery of the material. It is because they have real *assurance*, belief, and confidence in (1) their allusions, their taste, their education—(2) greater sense of history—almost a sense of the historical comedy. They do not see things as collections of torments—they have the long view. Hence, when they care to do so, they are so much more moving, detached, even in their intensity.

## October 19, 1941

Difference between the morality of teaching and the morality of writing. In teaching "impressing" one's audience too often seems to be all.

40. *Partisan Review*, American journal of literature and politics, published quarterly from 1934 to 2003, closely associated with the rise of "New York (mostly Jewish) intellectuals" in the postwar years. Though Kazin read and published in it, he distrusted its editors and was never a member of its inner circle.
41. George Dangerfield (1904–1986), journalist and historian, author of *The Strange Death of Liberal England* (1935).
42. Sir Denis William Brogan (1900–1974), Scottish historian, professor of political science at Cambridge.

Why does the modern Jewish artist fail so often today in real creativeness—always suggesting instability, lacking of staying power, some dark background of restlessness and self-doubt.

## December 8, 1941

Yesterday, Sunday, Japan declared war on us, attacking Hawaii and the Philippines. Sunday: we had just returned from a week-end in New Jersey and had no knowledge of the event until after seven. It sounded incredible, as it still does; in Times Square, about ten, Asya and I bought the newspapers, watched the crowds and looked at the news bulletins on the Times Building. It was frozen cold; a few drunken sailors crowding around; otherwise absolute calm, even seeming indifference or disinterestedness. Roosevelt will speak, asking for a declaration of war, at 12:30 today.

I feel absolutely numb, excited as it were, from some distance. In a week nothing will be as it has been; very soon everything may be changed. My first thought—selfish as it may see—was about the book. It's going to be a struggle to finish it.

Just talked to Gene Mudge;[43] he is in the reserves, which may be called up immediately.

## December 9, 1941

I want to *do* something, if only to serve as a warden at the college. Like William Morris,[44] I feel "the true secret of happiness lies in the taking of a genuine interest in all the details of daily life."

Planes flying overhead constantly, a few minutes ago, eating my lunch in a beanery on Queens Boulevard, an ambulance sounded its siren; and for a moment I felt like the beginning of an air raid.

"The country"—us—how moving and [breaks off]

## December 23, 1941

A bad day on the book. I suddenly realized that I've been trying to do too much, aiming too hard and too narrowly, in the chapter on Marxist criticism. But I don't mind that, and shall start again tomorrow.

43. Eugene TenBroeck Mudge (1912–), American historian who received his M.A. at Columbia in 1937 while Kazin was working toward his.
44. William Morris (1834–1896), English writer, artist, and socialist, associated with the Pre-Raphaelite Brotherhood.

But I feel depressed and particularly unhappy. I've never had more confidence in the book, never felt so passionately how right it is, how imperative its insights, how much it can and must mean to us at a time when general ideas seem to have grown shabby. And yet I feel so overpoweringly lonely doing the book; I feel as if I were writing it in a hermetically-sealed chamber, as if its passion and exactitude and purpose were locked up inside of me, with nothing but a few friendly hands—so very few—outside, waiting to reach and be reached. I believe in it as I believe in my individual spirit; I believe in it as I believe that something must come out of all the agony and hopelessness and stifled energies of contemporary humanity. But it's hard, hard to go on at a time when criticism—particularly the kind of criticism I wish to write—seems so remote almost so futile. I say again, with all my boyhood religion, God keep me, God spur me on. But knowing that it is "God inside of me that worships God," I know that my purpose is closed within me.

## December 26, 1941

A jolly little woman in my New School class, Dorcas Campbell, took us out to dinner last night. I met at her house an extremely interesting Gerald Sykes[45] whom I want to see often. He looks, as Asya commented, like a young Charles Laughton;[46] grave, round, parliamentarian English face, soft voice, and an ambiguous look of portentous solemnity. Yet he is wonderfully clever, a good human being, and a fine person to talk to. Clever: we were talking about Phil Rahv,[47] and he laughed: "Rahv looks like the chairman of a grievance committee."

What I like best about him is a firm, central, artistic intelligence. He's finishing up a novel for Simon and Schuster; lives on Bank Street, apparently a little hard-up at this moment. Worked for *PM*[48] for a while, didn't like it too much. We talked about criticism and *novelists*; I wanted to go on talking forever. He's one of those rare critical minds who think in creative terms—his creative terms. Begins with technique and sensibility, and yet keeps central issues clear. A rounded mind, subtle and careful and human; full of salt. His reticence is half-sadness; there's been a lot of disappointment for him in the past. But there's a

45. Gerald Sykes (1904–1984), novelist, critic, philosopher, taught classes at Columbia University and the New School.
46. Charles Laughton (1899–1962), an English-American stage and film actor, perhaps best known for his roles as Quasimodo in *The Hunchback of Notre Dame* (1939) and Captain Bligh in *Mutiny on the Bounty* (1935).
47. Philip Rahv (1908–1973), editor of *Partisan Review*.
48. *PM*, New York newspaper, published 1940–1948.

curious heartening feeling of critical litheness about him which cheered and touched me: it's so rare.

## December 27, 1941

Homosexuality as a fact in contemporary art and literature. We were talking last night about the flood of homos in high places. Names: I've already, as I seem to every day, added a dozen to my list. For me it is a fact of social interest—horrifying, yet curiously illustrative of my perpetual growl about the quality of contemporary degeneration—worse, *passivity*. I remember how I was reading a book of criticism by John Crowe Ransom, and suddenly, with a knowledge based almost entirely upon the movement of the prose, the coziness of his thinking, the curious elliptical direction of his thinking—homos think in mirror-words—I suddenly realized that he was one! And then my talk with H. and learning that he was one, too![49] ... Curious to note, what one sees in H's writing and N's personality, and M's big, famous book, how muffled their writing is.[50] They have every gift except the gift of primary motive; their minds are cushioned. And this is something tragic, where the fairies on the beach in Provincetown, or knitting with elaborate self-consciousness on the porches on Commercial Street, were merely funny.

## January 10, 1942

I never learn—never, never, never. I was raised in a school of toughness; and I've always lived militantly, thinking hard, working my life out hard. Yet I've never learned to accept and dismiss people at my own interior valuation of them—I seem always to need them so desperately. And so I fling myself—no, not at them, but out upon them—and am always disappointed that the return is not what I had expected. Adolph, that gangster, was perfectly right when he laughed at me last year, telling me that I was forever opening my heart to people and then dropping them when I realized my illusion. I've never learned to be tough, to husband my resources and be content with them; to take myself openly at my own proud evaluation. When I was a kid in Brownsville,

49. There is no evidence that the poet and critic John Crowe Ransom (1888–1974) was homosexual. He did once turn down a poem, "An African Elegy," for the *Kenyon Review* when he learned that its author, Robert Duncan (1919–1988), was a self-professed homosexual. Ransom was one of the Agrarian New Critics, a group Kazin attacks in *On Native Grounds* for "extreme neoclassicism" and "professional snobbery" (431).

50. H was Howard Doughty, a friend of Kazin's (see note 74); M was F. O. Matthiessen (1902–1950), author of *American Renaissance* (New York: Oxford University Press, 1941). N was the critic Newton Arvin.

I remember asking idiot kids who bored me whom I despised: you're not *sore* at me? And I haven't grown up one bit since then, for all *practical* purposes. I can't sit back and be what I know I am; I must be forever beseeching, trying to find the necessary ecstasy from people who are tired or dull or perfectly respectable and nothing more. And then there are the long nights of terror and self-recrimination. What a child I am! What a stupid, stupid child! To have lived [so much in] my mind, to have taken the range of so much, known the roundness of experience, yet never to accept my knowledge as a principle of conduct!

## January 16, 1942

I see by the papers that the *Southern Review* is about to close up shop.[51] So it goes. The *New Republic* views with alarm, and notes that a resolution has been sent to Huey Longites to keep the thing going.[52] Yet, even if it does, what will it mean? Writers—will find it harder and harder to keep going. Curiously enough, I don't feel panicky about myself. I've never believed that the book would be a great success, yet I've never believed it would be a thankless offering. But what worries me profoundly is the atmosphere that is growing everywhere—an atmosphere of unintelligent determination that is as bad as panic and in one sense its companion. What we are seeing now is a failure of writers to justify themselves—a failure of the literary mind in our time that is the outgrowth of the long alienation between writers and the people; between writers and any coherent dynamic purpose of their own. The *Southern Review* will not be missed, save by people like myself—and God knows my own critical ideals never found expression there!—but the important thing is that people will find it easier and easier to do away with literature.

I should like to do my last chapter now—a rousing paper on "The Failure of Modern Criticism," the failure of modern literature.[53] In this war that is at bottom a war of ideas, how significant it is that ideas will find no place in America!

51. The *Southern Review* ceased publication in 1942 and resumed in 1965.
52. Huey Pierce Long, Jr. (1893–1935), charismatic populist Louisiana governor and senator of 1920s and 1930s.
53. "Criticism at the Poles," the third-to-last chapter in *On Native Grounds*, attacks the criticism of the New Critics and the Marxists, but it praises the work of Edmund Wilson (see Chapter 2, note 6), Lionel Trilling (see Chapter 3, note 6), Mark Van Doren (1894–1972), and Louise Bogan.

## January 17, 1942

A Sunday afternoon walk to the river with Asya. In this industrial kitchen of Long Island City, where the factories lie scrubbed and waiting in the sun like so many pots and pans hung up on the wall to dry, there is a weariness in the air, and the river is not the sluice of the harbor it usually is, but a pallid, turgid stream breaking languorously against the lonely docks and piers and river dumps. Sunday: the fog over the river and the long line of yellow lamps all along the subway line near the project houses, where the Italians live in moderne-arte slums, cut and parceled like cheap dresses in a factory. The Italians play an odd game with a few balls and a hole in the ground; it always needs a little ground, a wall, a gutter in which to play a game!

Sunday: I always remember the sadness of Sunday, the waiting, the fear that grips the heart before the soul returns to its treadmill. I remember how I used to sit on the sand at Coney Island as a child, alone in the emptying crowds, looking out to sea, and so sad at heart that I could cry. Sunday: a walk in Highland Park with Nancy, and the long line of yellow lamps again across the embankment near the park—the hills of dumped earth across which we used to walk over to the playing grounds, where the boys played a last game of association football in the twilight, and we would sit on the benches near the reservoir, and look out at the YMCA lights. Sunday: playing Bach duets with Anne Mattus,[54] and the Polish cups of tea, the lemon and the French lessons to be remembered. Sunday: always Highland Park and the water around which Zisowitz[55] and I walked, talking about my first essays when I was in high school. Sunday: always Highland Park and the trees in the darkness, the flower garden above which we walked; the darkness, the darkness, the darkness! The walk through the Italian neighborhood to home; the butcher shops busy of a Jewish Sunday; the pushcarts on Belmont Avenue, and the little room with the bed and the desk, Sophie's[56] old closet. And sitting there, looking out on the street, the history of civilization looking out on Sutter Avenue and crying Israel! Israel! Why Have you Forsaken Me?[57]

54. Anne Mattus was a childhood sweetheart with whom Kazin played violin duets. He recalled that his mother was anxious about his relations with "the shining gleaming Poilesha."
55. Samuel Zisowitz, Kazin's English teacher at Franklin Lane High School. Many of the images in this entry appear in *A Walker in the City*.
56. A distant cousin, Sophie Kaminkowitz lived with the Kazins until persuaded to go off with a mysterious lover in 1943, who abandoned her in the Midwest. She lived the rest of her life in an asylum in Clarinda, Iowa, recognizing no one.
57. Kazin paraphrases Psalm 22: "My God, my God, why hast thou forsaken me? why art thou so far from helping me, and from the words of my roaring?"

Sunday: the long-remembered pain, and Nancy's rhinestone dress, and huddling together against the wall of the toilet, hoping that they would not come home too soon. Sunday: and the waiting, the waiting, the benches in Highland Park, the cold, the kitchen sink, the water in the reservoir. Sunday.

## January 27, 1942

The book is to be finished by April or so, and published in the early Fall. As ever, it goes slowly—the multiplex process of reading hundreds upon hundreds of books, the dovetailing, the insights, the pattern to be made. Yet hard as it gets, unbearable as it gets sometimes, something drives me on. Whenever I catch myself panting for breath, hoping to be released from it even for a minute, a day, I realize—almost with as sharp a sense of sin as one of my rabbinical forefathers must have looked at a pretty breast—that I shall have no release until I am finished with the book and put it from me. Then I may begin to live again, to travel, to get back into the stream. But until it is done, I am a prisoner of my conscience, prisoner to a project that I began almost four years ago without any clear idea, and which has steadily taken such shape in my mind and heart that it has become more than the crux of my young manhood, the pinnacle of my first aspiration; it has become the living design of existence for me, the cross I must bear until I can see it through the press.

## February 8, 1942

[. . .] Where are we all of us going? The Nazis stand in the night with their spears; waiting, waiting, waiting; and we don't know. We don't yet know how much this war is our war, the only real war fought in hundreds of years. We say we know, or we think we know. But each man wants to finish his book, enjoy his snooze, go on in his own way. And so much to be done! When I read of these lectures the Army boys are getting from soldier-brain instructors, and I think of how great an opportunity for education lies there—the fields so fallow—my depression generation, "lost between two wars with all the street lights out"—when I think of what could be done, and how it will not be, I get sick.[58]

58. Kazin would not become a "soldier-brain instructor," but he would report on the education of soldiers in the United States for *Fortune* and in England for the Rockefeller Foundation.

## February 17, 1942

More and more the avantgardiste of our time takes on the apocalyptic character and fury of the primitive Christian in the wilderness. The type is now Henry Miller, now James Agee,[59] now one or another of the illegitimate descendants of Baudelaire on the one hand (the technical-art side), and Lawrence-Whitman (the prophetic-comrades—love me all comrades) side on the other, so dear to the aboriginal John Humphrey Noyes[60] Communist in certain artist Americans. I insist upon the analogy of the primitive Christian; I never felt it so vividly as when squirming through the tortured, hot pages of Miller, or lately, James Agee's improvisation on a sharecropper theme—*Let Us Now Praise Famous Men*. And what is this character, more precisely? It is the sectarian—the Christian heart dreaming of the furious world beyond, the world of peace and freedom and *knowledge*. Living in the wilderness on locusts, he dreams of his hatred of the *gentilum*.

Pound's poetry and Whitman's in the American line—catalogue of impressions—going by symbols—ransacking a continent.[61]

## February 19, 1942

The most significant political phenomenon on the Allied side right now, which is the side of progressive, middle-class culture, is the reluctant, dazzled admiration of Stalin. It came out in Churchill's lachrymose speech on the fall of Singapore; one hears it everywhere. More and more He is becoming the symbol of the dash, the organization, the Allies long for and need—is he Jeb Stuart or Bedford Forrest[62]—the enemy respected? Or is he the dim vision of the future and the prestige that can make that future? Yes, I admire the old bastard as never before. But this morning, on one of my daily walks from the library, I stopped

59. Henry Miller (1891–1980), American author, known best for his quasi-autobiographical fiction, *Tropic of Cancer, Tropic of Capricorn*, and *Black Spring*; James Agee (1909–1955), American journalist, screenwriter, and film critic, best known for his account of southern poor whites in the Depression, *Let Us Now Praise Famous Men*.

60. Utopian Socialist, founded the Oneida Colony in New York State.

61. Ezra Pound (1885–1972), American poet and critic, experimented with verse forms as did his earlier compatriot, Walt Whitman (1819–1892). In a 1913 poem titled "A Pact" Pound reluctantly acknowledges Whitman's influence: "It was you that broke the new wood/Now is the time for carving."

62. James Ewell Brown "Jeb" Stuart (1833–1864), a Confederate Army general famous for his raids and reconnaissance missions against the North; Nathan Bedford Forrest (1821–1877), a daring cavalry officer in the Confederate Army, who became a Grand Wizard of the Ku Klux Klan that terrorized blacks during Reconstruction.

to look at some Soviet war posters in the windows of Bookniga—and there was a cartoon of a heroic Red Army man preparing to stamp out, with the butt of his musket, three grisly figures—Hirohito, Hitler, and Mussolini—three figures walking along in blood and hatred—and beside them is a gallows, and on the gallows is a dreadful caricature of a bird, a carrion-crow, a viper—Trotsky.

## February 24, 1942

I love to walk, to take long, running leaps and lunges on the leisure-class streets of New York—Fifth and Madison and Park. Every day that I work at the Library[63] I walk at least a mile up from 42nd Street and Fifth Avenue to the station at 59th and Lexington. The women of this new bourgeoisie, with their fantastic sensuality and their fantastic coats and dogs and manners. The shops, the people, the start and rush of the human traffic at three in the afternoon up Fifth Avenue. And as I walk, two thoughts recur to me over and again—thoughts that make me happy, yet have a poignant taste to the mind. I remember how for three years now I have sat in the Library, reading, reading, reading; how I have traced the pattern of my book, up from the ghosts of those early documents and novels of the nineties and 1900's, who are like the very architectural stuff this library is built of. [. . .]

## February 28, 1942

Every once in a while some token, a sentence in a book, a voice heard, will recall for me the fresh instant delight in the sense of being a student of the American landscape and culture that I felt first two years ago, only after I had begun serious work on the book. The sentence this morning, fresh as a spring wind, comes from Constance Rourke's book on Audubon,[64] on the sudden realization that his ornithology has the token of a national sense of scale, that like Whitman and the others he was a great voice of the American nationality. Yet what it does for me is to recall the excitement under which I lived for weeks on weeks early in 1939, when I suddenly realized, and for the first time consciously, that I had a passionate and even professional interest in American culture and literature. I remember now how in those weeks of almost

63. New York Public Library on Fifth Avenue and 42nd Street.

64. Constance Mayfield Rourke (1885–1941), pioneering scholar of American culture, published books on the ornithologist John James Audubon (1785–1851), Davy Crockett (1786–1836), and other American cultural figures. Her most influential work is *American Humor: A Study of the National Character* (1931).

incommunicable delight and energy and faith in the future I used to walk up and down the halls of the Metropolitan American rooms, looking at the portraits of solemn Colonial and Revolutionary figures—or pictures by Eakins,[65] always a hero for my spirit—or dull, glazed transcriptions of a Sunday morning in deare olde Flatbush in 1836. Pictures that suddenly brought back to my mind the delight I had always taken as a child in pictures of Colonials, in American history texts; delights in biographies of the American, at all times and in all conditions (when I was a senior at college, one of my jobs as a worker for NYA was to read and comb the DAB[66] for biographies and lists of American college graduates; I never got tired of reading the stories). . . . I have never been able to express the pleasure I derive from the conscious study of "Americana." As a writer and student of writing I get fulfillment out of only a very few American writers, actually; when I think of writing, I think always of Blake and Tolstoy. Yet the very words—"poet of the American nationality"—or the mere lists of Americans—Cope, James, Ryder, Peirce, Dickinson, Franklin—as in Lewis Mumford's little books, or the Forward to a book like Beer's *The Mauve Decade*—or notebooks out of the nineteenth century—or the letters of William James, the curious sensation of talking of Albert Ryder and Henry James, of Whitman and Dickinson and Emerson, etc., in the same breath, gives me an extraordinary satisfaction.[67] Why I'm not too sure; yet when I think of a career like Constance Rourke's or William James's[68] or Audubon's or so many others in the American vein—makers and movers and thinkers—great takers of notes—observers in the profoundest sense—I feel happy. I love to think about America, to look at

65. Thomas Cowperthwait Eakins (1844–1916), American realist painter.

66. National Youth Administration, a New Deal agency under the Works Progress Administration, employing high school and college youth; *Dictionary of American Biography*.

67. Edward Drinker Cope (1840–1897), American paleontologist, who discovered a thousand species of extinct vertebrates in the United States; Albert Pinkham Ryder (1847–1917), American painter known for his allegorical style and the dreamlike qualities of his land and seascapes; Charles Sanders Peirce (1839–1914), American philosopher, logician, mathematician, and scientist, considered by many to be the most original and multitalented of American philosophers; Emily Dickinson (1830–1886), a favorite American poet of Kazin's; Benjamin Franklin (1706–1790), American printer, writer, inventor, diplomat, and signatory of the Declaration of Independence; Lewis Mumford (1895–1990), American philosopher, historian, literary critic, best known for his writing on cities and urban architecture. Kazin identified Mumford's *The Brown Decades* (1931) as a source of inspiration for *On Native Grounds*. Thomas Beer (1889–1940), American author, historian, biographer; Kazin in *On Native Grounds* writes that Beer was "the perfect example of what a rich, traveled, superior, and comfortable leisure class had come to in art" (240).

68. William James (1842–1910), American philosopher of "pragmatism," who wrote on psychology (he invented the term) and religion, brother of Henry James.

portraits, to remember the kind of adventurousness and purity, heroism, and *salt*, that the best Americans have always had for me.

Or is it—most obvious supposition—that I am an outsider; and that only for the first American-born son of so many thousands of mud-flat Jewish-Polish-Russian generations is this need great, this inquiry so urgent?

Yet the most extraordinary element in all this is something it is difficult, perhaps hazardous, to express; that is, the terrible and graphic *loneliness* of the great Americans. Thinking about them composes itself, sooner or later, into a gallery of extraordinary individuals; yet at bottom they have nothing in common but the almost shattering unassailability, the life-stricken I, in each. Each fought his way through life—and through his genius—as if no one had ever fought before. Each one, that is, began afresh—began on his own terms—began in a universe that remained, for all practical purposes, his own. [. . .]

## March 30, 1942

I was thinking of John Dewey[69] this morning. Some weeks ago as I [was] walking to the subway from my day's work at the Library, I saw Dewey on Lexington Avenue with a lady I presume to have been his daughter. I looked at him with a certain pleasure and affection in my recognition. He stared at me. When I looked back, after half a block, to see what had become of him, he was still staring at me in the street and talking to his (daughter), as if to say—"Now, when did I have *him* in my classes?"

I was thinking of Dewey because my own impression of his career and significance is so curiously different from that of most people. For me Dewey always represents not the pragmatic adaptable 20th-century intelligence which was going to fit philosophy into a new age; rather, he seems to speak with the security and quiet serenity of a vanished world. And when I think of him, it is not of his lack of "art" or the clumsy handiwork of his style; it is always of his nobility, his steadiness, the work of immense and quiet usefulness, of a moral art, that he has made of his life. In my book I have already written at some length of Dewey's influence upon, and embodiment of, the "H. G. Wellsian" period of uplift in Progressive Wilsonian America. All that has turned to ashes long since; but Dewey represents its vital force still. The tang of the Vermont woods;

69. John Dewey (1859–1952), American philosopher and educational reformer.

the philosopher of the frontier; the good American teacher and scholar, doing his work, teaching with a real integrity and quiet—if not inaudible—originality. Why do I think of Dewey in this light? Because more than any American scholar of his kind—it goes without saying that he is not the peer of William James—he has made and given to others a great happiness out of his career. He has proved that a man can give his whole devotion to the academic career and its responsibilities, and make of it a great moral and intellectual example. James, of course, was a genius, and his personality was his greatest contribution to philosophy. But if one understands Dewey aright, it is not absurd to say that his career—his example—is as great a contribution to modern American thought as his social psychology and the galvanizing influence of his attacks upon the old education. . . . For I do not think that Dewey has given us a new—or truly serviceable—education; he merely helped to destroy the old.

## May 5, 1942

[. . .] The situation at school [City College] has become impossible—financially and professionally.[70] I am determined not to go back in September and will try my hand at journalism on the Donovan committee or *Fortune*.[71] A period in my life is coming to an end. How long it will be until I'm called up into the army, I don't know. My great hope is that I shall have some interim between the completion of the book and my induction. . . . The war is coming closer, as God knows it should. But how little yet it means—waiting in line for sugar—rationing and test blackouts of 20 minutes!—But the blackout last night was rather beautiful. I have always hated in my heart this raw, makeshift suburb.[72] But last night, looking at the dark and quiet streets, it seemed extraordinarily clear, almost—and the brilliantly-lighted trains crossing the curve at the Boulevard, like the mazda-lit bowels of ships at night, startling.

## May 13, 1942

More and more these last few months, I've come to hate criticism—the strain, the false knowingness, the attempt to find what men in books so often do not have, and what, for me, is only inside of me—crying, welling up for release. Like

70. Kazin was teaching classes at City College as well as the New School.
71. A committee of journalists was recruited to help in the war effort under the overall leadership of William Donovan (1883–1959), head of the Office of Strategic Services (OSS). Henry Luce (1898–1967), publisher of *Fortune*, had invited Kazin to write for the magazine.
72. Long Island City, Queens, Kazin and Natasha's residence while he completed *On Native Grounds*.

so many in America, I may have come to make too much of criticism—but the truth is that it no longer even begins to satisfy me. When I write criticism, I feel as if only a quarter of my mind—and too much of my strength—were going into it. I often think that if I had not been so afraid of being lost when I got out of college a few years ago and began to write criticism; if I had had the necessary courage—or desperation—to break away entirely and go away somewhere, travel, learn to live the hard way—I might have begun to do my stories right off. But in a way I'm glad it's happened this way. I didn't know *anything* then! Now at least I know how little I know. I know what to look for in writing—I know something, *something*, of the meaning of America—I know enough to avoid the kind of desperate personal romanticism I might have been thrown into. [. . .]

## June 12–30, 1942

Yaddo.[73] North studio. The lovely Negro whores on Congress Street. The sunshine through my north window. I learned something at Yaddo—I learned a new sympathy for writers. I felt a new solidarity with all the lonely men in the lonely rooms. I came back to correct the last few chapters of the book. It is almost entirely finished. Curious feeling of holiday in the air; warm, moist July nights. The dark streets. Last night the blackout was beautiful, like a cool hand placed on the fevered brow of hot, rattlingly tense New York. All the streets of the city suddenly seemed gone for a moment. The red [illegible] in Astoria hung suspended in the night. Then the mail plane came over, winking in the darkness with red and green lights. The beacons flashed over the sky, probing, probing, and for a moment the plane was caught in their triangle. . . . Curious feeling of detachment I feel. The book has exhausted me so much, yet though I seem incapable of fresh thought on any subject, I feel a poetic lightness, an airiness. I'm so afraid for the book, so terribly afraid it's not good enough. And yet I've done all I can—I've established in it, *for its subject* (and I've hated, hated the subject) all I have to give at the moment. Newton Arvin[74] read the last four chapters up at Yaddo and apparently disliked them. I'm not sure I know why. Inflated? Over-done? I was able to guess something of this from Howard, who talked to him about it at Grafton two weekends ago. I begged H. to tell me what Newton *thought*. I wanted reasons; I wanted candor. But I could learn nothing. Of course my rather bitter attack on the Left debauch in the thirties may have

73. A writer-and-artist colony located outside Saratoga Springs, N.Y. Kazin would be a frequent visitor.

74. Newton Arvin (1900–1963), a critic of American literature whom Kazin admired, whose lover was Howard Doughty, Kazin's neighbor in Long Island City.

irritated him.[75] But why couldn't he *talk* about it? Only a weak amiable smile and nothing. I was terribly hurt at first, but I feel detached now. To hell with it! To hell with it!

## July 7, 1942

John Chamberlain[76] wrote in the *Times* this morning that I was the only new voice in criticism to come out of the thirties. Who, me? Corrected and revised about one-third of Chapter 14—on criticism. Hate the stuff now—and yet I wrote it once with so much joy, so much certitude and passion! All that Marxist wrangle . . . wrangle, wrangle. Went over to the Carnegie Corporation in the afternoon to explain that I was approaching the end sooner than I had anticipated and wanted to give part of the July–August check back. Then went over to the *Tribune*. Talked with Gertrude and Sophie and Lewis Gannett.[77] Asya and I then went over to Lewis's for supper. [. . .]

## July 11, 1942

I completed the final draft of my book at 5:30 this afternoon. Yesterday I was appointed to the staff of the *New Republic*.

75. Kazin singled out for special abuse Granville Hicks (1901–1982), editor of the Communist *New Masses*, Arvin's friend and colleague at Smith College.

76. In *Starting Out in the Thirties*, Kazin credits Chamberlain (1903–1995) for helping him get his start as a book reviewer.

77. Lewis Gannett (1891–1966), journalist and editor.

# 2
# The Break
## 1942–1945

LOOKING BACK YEARS LATER, KAZIN would describe the period between the completion of *On Native Grounds* and the end of the war as "the break"—a break in history, a break in belief, and a break in his personal life. After four years of disciplined routine on a project that had become his "living design of existence," he found himself released into "the whirl of New York" and a brilliant new life (January 27, 1942; October 27, 1942). He was just twenty-seven and exhilarated by his prospects—"open, disrupted, ready for anything," as he later put it in *New York Jew*. On August 3, 1942, he became literary editor of the *New Republic*, a post formerly held by Malcolm Cowley and Edmund Wilson. On October 30, his book appeared to rave reviews—"Not only a literary but a moral event," according to the *New York Herald Tribune*. Lionel Trilling in the *Nation* called it "quite the best and most complete treatment we have of an arduous and difficult subject." In May, enticed by a higher salary and hoping for an overseas assignment, he left the *New Republic* for *Fortune*. The overseas assignment failed to materialize; he was asked instead to report on the education of soldiers in various training camps across the county. Kazin, who had been turned down twice for military service because of an undescended testicle, welcomed the opportunity to contribute to the war effort. He also calculated (correctly) that it might lead to a Rockefeller grant to report on the education of soldiers in England.

When he boarded the train in November 1943 to army outposts in Michigan, Wisconsin, Colorado, and points west, Kazin had more on his mind than the trip ahead. He had recently begun an affair with Mary Louise Petersen, the wife of a UCLA philosopher, Hans Meyerhoff, now in the service. An affair of a few months, it would lead to Kazin's separation from Natasha and a long period of self-recrimination and loneliness. Forty-seven years later he would write in his journal that the affair had cut his life in half—before Mary Lou, after Mary Lou—"the fall of Rome was nothing compared with the 'fall' in the heart of Alfred Kazin." He did not regret what he had done—he had been passionately attracted to Mary Lou and he had wanted to make a break from his past—but he was not prepared for the loneliness, fear, and paralyzing feelings of guilt that had followed. "To this day (and today I am seventy-five years of age) he cannot think without a gasp of pain of all that it cost him then to be unfaithful to Asya. And what it costs him still" (June 5, 1990).

Hoping to alleviate the suffering, he began seeing a psychoanalyst, Janet Rioch, with whom he would continue to have sessions (sometimes three a week) until the early sixties. He also turned to his journal to think things through. There was a lot to consider—the war, the "post-Stalinist interregnum" following the eclipse of the "revolutionary" thirties, the mounting evidence of destruction of European Jewry, recurrent feelings of loneliness and guilt. In one of very few essays published in the mainstream press on the destruction of Europe's Jews (*New Republic,* January 10, 1944), Kazin discussed the recent suicide of the Polish Bund leader Shmuel Zygelboym, who wrote that he was killing himself to bring the world's attention to the plight of Poland's Jews. Reflecting on Zygelboym's suicide and the three million already dead, Kazin wrote that "something subtle and suspended and destructive" had broken out in Europe. Though unprepared to say what that "something" was, he knew there had been a "break," that there was no returning to the radical dreams and hopeful assumptions of the thirties. New thinking was necessary—about the nature of man, about the direction of history, about God, about "what is permitted."

Kazin's trip for *Fortune* was the first of many wartime journeys. In the summer of 1944 he traveled to Pasadena, California, where he worked at the Huntington Library on an edition of William Blake for Viking Press and visited with members of the Group Theatre now making films in Hollywood. He taught the fall semester at Black Mountain College in Ashville, North Carolina. In January he sailed for England, where he worked for the Office of War Information (OWI) while gathering material for a Rockefeller report on the education of soldiers. In July he flew to liberated Paris to speak to a gathering of professors about American literature. Kazin loved to travel, to give public lectures, to meet new people (most of the time), to gather impressions. Traveling sharpened his perceptions; recording them in his journal sharpened them further, providing images and memories to be revisited and realized in later work. "I write in order to embody the actual, to capture in its approximate sense of place what I have lived through; to realize, to recapture, to renew" (March 11, 1952).

## September 3, 1942

I began work at the *New Republic* a month ago today. After four years of loneliness and doubt, trudging to the library and school, I feel exhilarated by being at the center of things, meeting people constantly, and as exhilarated by the money, for after three weeks Bliven[1] gave me a raise when *Fortune* offered me $100 to come to work there. I couldn't see *Fortune*—yet: not that super-plush superficiality. I like the job here, though I'm a little frightened by the time one spends reading bad poetry—and other people's book reviews. I haven't much

1. Bruce Bliven (1889–1977) was managing editor of the *New Republic*.

responsibility, and my job is hardly an important one. But I am learning much about the technical side of journalism, and the prejudices of journalism. I am learning much, too, about liberalism—the liberalism into which I had slid after losing my brief admiration for totalitarian Socialism. One curious effect of the job on me has [been] to make me lose my fear of people, my fear of writers. How much bad writing there is in the world! How different these glossy or assertive people are who come in and—shocking me by the total absence of anything like the self-consciousness I used to feel when I would come to see Cowley[2]—prove to me how silly I was, how jejune, to quake so before the little powers of the earth! When I read some of the stuff here I am reminded of Emerson's wry pleasure in Andrews Norton's[3] attack on him, anonymously printed. "How rare is good writing in the world!" . . . Meanwhile, my evenings are taken up with proofs on the book. I want so much to write in this journal and think through it about the hundred different things I study every day here. But there's so little time. . . . Yet a writer should have time for nothing so much as for a note book like this: Emerson's Savings Bank, Beethoven's Letters, Katherine Mansfield's Journals.[4] Not Amiel,[5] not the excuse, the compensation. But the working material.

## September 4, 1942

The revolt against Joyce. Interesting to note how sharp and even violent is the feeling against Joyce and all he represented.

I, who dislike much modern poetry—I, please God, am now the defender of the right here on the *New Republic*. Bliven won't print any verse that any reader of the *NR* might possibly object or, or feel that he doesn't understand. And I have to argue with him about it.

The *New Republic* is a liberal magazine whose deficit is paid by the wealthy Elmhirsts (Dorothy Elmhirst is the daughter of that old, sleek crook and crony of [President Grover] Cleveland in the Gilded Age, W. C. Whitney). But it wants, oh aches so, to be a popular, a paying magazine. Well, why not? But it doesn't and won't—so it's in limbo.

2. Malcolm Cowley (1898–1989) was literary editor of the *New Republic* from 1929 to 1944.
3. Andrews Norton (1786–1853), Unitarian minister and theologian who denounced Emerson for his 1838 "Divinity School Address."
4. Kathleen Mansfield (1888–1923), English writer of short fiction, married to the critic John Middleton Murry (see Chapter 1, note 22), friend of the novelists Virginia Woolf (1882–1941) and D. H. Lawrence (1885–1930).
5. Henri Frédéric Amiel (1821–1881), Swiss author and philosopher, best known for his Journal.

Edmund Wilson's[6] name must not be mentioned here at the *NR*. Of course, *I* mentioned him the very first day.

Ralph Bates[7] came in yesterday. Soft, pompous, intellectual, cockney son-of-a-bitch. I admired his early novels very much; dislike him personally, and intensely. He came in swaggering, Dr. Johnson[8] hard-breathing wise obesity—the English are an ancient people. Patronizing, careless, proud of his special skill, his writer's talent. But crafty and dull. A dull man, a politico-journalist of our era.

## September 6, 1942

This morning on Second Avenue near the bridge I stood near a fruit-stand while waiting for the bus. The fruits and vegetables out under the awning, still dripping with the water from the can, suddenly aroused in me by their look of careless richness, a whole world of memories about the summers in Brownsville when I was a kid. The early summers, when I was either too young or we too poor for me to go to camp. The hot afternoons and the tenement women coming back from the market. And then that moment (this it was always that *made* summer: the moment of pause, the enervating season) when mama would say (after hours at the machine): "Oh, it's too hot, too hot!" And I would walk down to [Public School] *66*, where the other children would gather to play in the cool basketball-sweat of the halls downstairs. The fruits on the stand, the jacks on the cool brown floor in the dust, mama in her house dress. Why does this memory seem at once so dim, trivial and yet so inexpressibly dear to me? Looking back now it is like opening my mind to everything out of that childhood I've wanted so desperately to lose and can never lose.

## September 9, 1942

They are killing us off in Europe; they are killing us off by the thousands from the Rhine to the Volga. The blood of the Jews is like the vapor in air that Faustus saw when the Devil claimed his due; but no one claims us but death; our due is, apparently, the "sympathy" of a few men of good will. From this morning's *Times*, however, I learn that French Catholic priests have been fighting Vichy's

6. Edmund Wilson (1895–1972), literary critic, historian, and essayist, former literary editor of the *New Republic*, later writer for the *New Yorker*, whom Kazin greatly admired.
7. Ralph Bates (1899–2000), English novelist who organized support for the Spanish Republic during the Spanish Civil War.
8. Samuel Johnson (1709–1784), English poet, critic, biographer. and lexicographer.

submission to the Nazi Jewish policy. Saliège,[9] the Archbishop of Toulouse, has written this pastoral letter: "There is a Christian morality, there is a human morality, that impose duties and confer rights. These duties and these rights derive from the very nature of man.[. . .]

"Why does the right of asylum no longer exist in our churches?

"Why are we a vanquished people?

"Lord have pity upon us!

"Our Lady, pray for France!

"These Jews are men; these Jewesses are women; these aliens are men and women. All is not permissible against them, against these men and women, against these fathers and mothers. They belong to mankind. They are our brethren as are so many others. No Christian can forget that.

"France, beloved motherland; France, who preserves in the conscience of all children traditional respect for the human individual; chivalrous and generous France, I do not doubt that thou art not responsible for these errors." [. . .]

## October 13, 1942

Tom Sancton.[10] When you try to argue with Tom about anything, he says with his petulant sweetness—"Oh, I can't meet you in dialectic—I only know what I feel!" Me, dialectic! Shades of Morris Raphael Cohen![11]

Tom wants more emotion. Oh, solar plexus Tom—Tom is what the *New Republic* is today—half *Readers Digest*, half nothing.

This is unfair—an intellectual fragment, superficial. Tom has wonderful qualities.

## October 27, 1942

[. . .] I'm excited by the book's coming out. But also the reviews, the whirl of New York the high, lean, proud tower of Radio City, the most beautiful American building for me except New England frame houses—both types make up our American civilization. Excited by the women in the morning light, the proud, the beautiful women of New York, the breasts and hot purple mouths of the

9. Archbishop Jules-Géraud Saliège (1870–1956) was an outspoken critic of the Nazi's deportation of the Jews.
10. Thomas Sancton (1915–) became managing editor of the *New Republic* in 1943 at the age of twenty-eight, the youngest editor of the magazine.
11. Morris Raphael Cohen (1880–1947), famous professor of philosophy at City College, whom Kazin disliked.

Bergdorf Goodman women, the fantastic sensuality of New York—hot and cold at once, an interior, unreal, cruel sensuality, but dreadful for me to see, dreadful to dream about. For I do dream, continually, and am so ashamed—but not so ashamed that I do not wish to go on dreaming and wanting.

## November 5, 1942

Stark Young—a Regency buck.[12] I can see him in tight trousers perched on top of a cabriolet—horse and four rather, crying—What ho! What ho! Clever, malicious, *sadly* feminine—a [illegible] like a machine caricature of the New York sybarite. Of social sense he has none, though he is probably one of the most perceptive minds in the whole history of American criticism. Very conscious of his "aristocracy"—and of his isolation and relative failure. Praised my book a little hysterically, but hated me [beseechingly, with the actor's rattle and the Southerner's rattle, making believe he was not beseeching at all, but only mocking][13] for not writing him up in it. I was a little drunk on three martinis he gave me and was sleepy and bored.

## November 10, 1942

I never knew what music was for, though I thought I had spent my whole life in it, until I came to understand Beethoven's last quartets. The fist out of the darkness, the pith and range, the wildness of the truly dramatic imagination—until, like in the last plays of Shakespeare, one sees the human imagination at the peak—beyond this no further; and *that* enters into its knowledge.

## November 14, 1942

Gorky on Chekhov—"All his life Tchekhov lived on his own soul; he was always himself, inwardly free."—[C.—"Everyone should speak his own language."][14]

There is something so frightening about success for a real writer—the world's success. They tell me my book is good. They praise me and write me letters; they even buy it. But essentially this has nothing to do with me—nothing. I am in the book, as the book is in me—but that is *my* affair. And I realize that all the more keenly when, reading what they say of me, I find that they can praise more

12. Stark Young (1881–1963), *New Republic* drama critic, also a novelist and popular lecturer.
13. Kazin's brackets.
14. Kazin's brackets.

easily than they can read, and that when they do read, they either dishonestly present my thoughts as theirs or else quote inaccurately.

The new barbarians. One of John Crowe Ransom's[15] emissaries comes to see me. We talk of our disagreements. He says that Beethoven's *Eroica* is nasty. He uses the word "stomach" when he means courage, militancy, personality: Viz: "Van Wyck Brooks has no stomach." But when I use the word "shit," he is shocked. I say it again—shit!

*Russia. We have not come* to grips with Russia: We don't think truly of Russia; we only repeat ourselves, and flatter our prejudices, and make conversation. The Left—particularly in England and America—has failed us most. *The Russians have taken the skin off their old world.* They have been tyrannical, inhuman, brutish . . . Russian. But we do not try to understand them, least of all do we every try to help them. Of course, it is quite possible that we can't help—the American Communists always get in the way, as in a way the Russians do themselves. But the problem remains, and now—25 years after the great event, we are farther away from real comradeship than ever. But there are superficial and even dishonest ways of solving this problem—*to confuse our admiration of R's military success with the Stalinist rationale*—to join in the shocking and contagious acceptance of the Stalinist version of the Moscow trials. We must attain that kind of knowledge and fraternity vis-à-vis Russia that will allow us to keep our minds on the essential truth of this greatest single social fact of our epoch, and yet *see* it—yet keep our minds upon it, and know that it is not our truth completely. . . . Of course, these reflections come from reading Chekhov, from seeing and hearing him talk about the old Russia. So that one must say—God damn it, *they have pulled the diseased skin off that old Russia*—and it's enough, enough! It almost justifies everything!

Yes, to a Russian. But Chekhov never read Thomas Jefferson and Altgeld,[16] and the Communists are not even alive in America at all.

The elder Henry James—"the inestimable satisfactions of obeying one's highest convictions."

15. See Chapter 1, note 49. Van Wyck Brooks (1886–1963), critic, biographer, historian, received the 1937 Pulitzer Prize for *The Flowering of New England.*

16. John Peter Altgeld (1847–1902), a progressive Democratic governor of Illinois, 1893–1897, on whom Kazin wrote a short piece for *Fortune.*

## December 5, 1942

*Too much literature*, too much criticism—too much thinking about literature, and not enough literature. Maybe what's wrong is that so many of the young writers are in 4F. There's something wrong when so many young writers are being closed to the greatest single experience of their generation. Worse still, being contented about it.

## December 21, 1942

In Durham, N.C., a week ago, I saw a young white boy throw a lighted cigarette at a Negro soldier, hoping it would burn his hair. Bob Wunsch[17] of Black Mountain College told me that when he was a boy he was once studying at the family table and an uncle of his came in and threw something across that left a red splotch on the white paper. It was the finger of a Negro the uncle had just lynched. The Education of a Southerner: Wunsch now wants to admit Negroes to the College, and spends much of his own time in Negro education.

## December 25, 1942

What has the Socialism of intellectuals ever to do with the people? Think of Edmund Wilson's socialism so humanist, meditative, and the rest—but it is as self-consciously personal as Flaubert's hatred of socialism; both artists merely talk about their particular vision of the world and their horror of it.

## April 3, 1943

Nothing in the jargon of American "educationists" makes me so mad as the phrase "personality-problem." I picture the iron file-card mind—social problem, a, b, c, part three—a world gone to hell, ridden with greed, "perishing for want of kindness"; and "personality-problem," type c, psychoneurotic, likes to write symphonies. When you reduce the differences of men to problems of "personality," and personality to a "problem," you have at last seceded from that abstract glory—the human race.

## April 12, 1943

A critic, a student of literature, ought to carry a little talisman around with him, a sacred medal—and on it should be printed, in high, defiant letters, the

17. Robert Wunsch, English and drama instructor at Black Mountain College.

word IMAGINATION. The ark would always be before him, and he would be less likely to make mistakes.

## May 1, 1943

Rejected: but there's another chance.[18]

## May 27, 1943

Paine[19] took me to lunch with Henry Luce this afternoon. My memos on American writing may have interested him, and there had been some talk of the philosophy series. Luce seemed to me a very negligible man, but rather different from what I had imagined him to be. He's shy, vaguely charming, wonderful eyes and beetle-brows, getting bald, but hair in back very long, so that he looked rather like Jerome Mellquist, if Mellquist ate regularly. The luncheon was on the 64th floor of the RCA building in the private dining room of the *Time* executives. Much gloss, tablecloth gentility, etc. I could not always understand everything Luce said—he has what I call the Yale mumble, the mumble that I've heard on Paine, John Chamberlain, Charlie Poore, and others.[20] It's the speech of Fitzgerald's sad young men generation—now in their middle or late thirties; and what it means to me is not so much bad upbringing or stammering, but a symbolic colloquialism and friendliness. The mumble, you see, symbolizes their divorce from the formality, dignity, remoteness, etc., of power-life in their fathers' day. It shows their youth and happy carelessness.

Luce wanted to talk about AMERICA AND WHAT'S WRONG WITH IT. He confirmed, involuntarily, what I had suspected about the philosophy series in *Fortune*—that it's a *naive* attempt to bring meaning, purpose into the lives of the business class by buying pronouncements on the good life by Hocking, Whitehead, Hutchins, et al.[21] It's not vicious or misleading; on the contrary, it's

18. The undescended testicle that led to Kazin's rejection by the army was later corrected, but he was never called up for service.

19. Kazin had recently resigned from the *New Republic* to work for *Fortune*. Ralph Delahaye Paine Jr. (1906–1991) was a special assistant to Henry Luce; Jerome Mellquist (1905–1963) was an art critic for the *Nation*.

20. John Chamberlain, journalist and book reviewer for the *New York Times*, editor at *Fortune* (see Chapter 1, note 76); Charles Poore, editor and daily book critic for the *New York Times*.

21. William Ernest Hocking (1873–1966) and Alfred North Whitehead (1861–1947) were prominent Harvard philosophers. Robert Hutchins (1899–1977) was president of the University of Chicago.

an attempt to find intellectual order and security on the part of people who have everything but that.

But the hitch is that, Mortimer Adler-like,[22] they're trying to add this to *Time*, Inc. culture. And that's why all this nauseates me a little. *Time* is neutral in everything, or worse. It lives by cunning, promptness, smartness. It's dead-cold so far as a single ideal is concerned; and its chief purpose, so far as I can see, is to make capsules out of the news—and to titillate the great middle class. The old Satevepost[23] formula won't work anymore; this is a world-conscious generation, etc. So *Time*, and the March of Time, and the glossy pages of *Fortune*.

I was talking of John Quincy Adams and of Emerson—and spoke of the disillusionment after the Civil War of Henry's generation. Said we had to know now that the Emperor has no clothes on. Luce looked puzzled, then angry—said What Emperor? I said, with my fingers crossed, the Materialist Emperor. But America is not materialist! cried Luce. *Fortune* was not organized to celebrate business, but to explore it! Yes, I think that's true. Only *Fortune* is now part of what it had already set out to explore—and there's the catch. Part of the Luce mind deeply, genuinely, really wants to know about things today. But just as the Luce-*Time* always insists on good manners, etc., at the very moment that it writes up the most awful vulgarities of word and spirit, so here it wants the Hutchins idea; it wants purpose, etc., without losing anything.

I love John Dewey especially at this moment—because Henry Luce—Henry Luce!—said that "Dewey had sold philosophy out." That kind of amateur snobbery irritates me to death. The most pragmatic salesman in America complaining that the pragmatist is—not an Aristotelian. And good old Hutchins is.

The most vivid impression Luce left with me is that he is a puzzled man rather than a stupid one, and a better man in every sense than his life and his present eminence allow him to be. It was charming going back with him, from the RCA building to the *Fortune* office—he had got on to his pet idea about political knowledge and freedom being the key to everything,

22. Mortimer Adler (1902–2001) was an educator who with Hutchins founded the Great Books of the Western World program.

23. *Saturday Evening Post*, a popular bimonthly magazine that published articles and short stories until its demise in 1969. It was revived in 1971 as a quarterly that published articles on health matters and topics of general interest.

etc., stuff that I didn't fully understand but which seemed to me to be leading up to the American Century—and it was as if he was begging Paine and me to believe in the thing. He's terribly in earnest, but full of blocks, strains, and little swaggers. A young face, and a young mind—preserved in aspic, as it were, with all the childhood feelings and young-college-senior benevolent disputatiousness left, and thus lifted (not a fold in the silken covers) to his present level. Here is this journalistic machine he has—all those researchers, elevators, luncheons, and bowing editors. He doesn't kid himself; but he has been hypnotized, as it were, while keeping his memory. So that, feeling the power he has—or the simple responsibility of all those words spurting like lava out of the mountain, oozing over the heads of the thirsty American public, he wants terribly to make the thing click. For the first time he's been forced to think about the whole human-American equation. It's a question of mind, not integrity—and, naturally, his conception of mind drives him to the Hutchinses, and now the John Chamberlains, who "prove" that labor has always wanted to swallow the state, and must be discouraged.

The death of the heart—The Polish Jewish leader's suicide—Zygelboym—Blake—if it is true, comprehensible, it must be believed.[24]

## May 29, 1943

Every writer has his own rhetoric, which is both the primal beat and essential trick he gives his work (what his mind reads back to himself). Sidney Hook is logic-chopping.[25] An ordinary writer, when he is tired or lazy, falls into expansiveness, diffuseness, etc. Hook says—"Now let us examine A and A1."

## May 31, 1943

This, especially from the radical point of view, should be called the era of *the disappointed. Aldanov, Burnham, Nomad, et al.—Marx cheated us!*[26] It ain't

24. On May 12, 1943, Szmuel Zygelboym (b. 1895) committed suicide in London to draw attention to the Nazis' murder of three million Polish Jews. Kazin would publish the suicide note and his response in the *New Republic* (January 10, 1944): 44–46.
25. Sidney Hook (1902–1989), professor of philosophy at NYU and an authority on Marxism, was famous for a combative style in ideological debate that Kazin found offensive.
26. Mark Aldanov (1889?–1957) was a historian of the Russian Revolution. James Burnham (1905–1987), a one-time Trotsky supporter, argued in *The Managerial Revolution* (New York: John Day, 1941) that capitalism would evolve into a non-Marxist form of bureaucratic collectivism. Max Nomad (born Max Nacht, 1881–1973), a philosophical anarchist, author, and educator, taught at NYU and the New School.

true! And therefore the new conservativism, and the deification of spiritual laissez-faire.

Poor Burnham, who has lived so long and read so much Greek philosophy, only to learn that the history of society (considered as society) is a history of force. The very fact that he can write about it in his horrid book [*The Managerial Revolution*] only proves that the history of man as man is the attempt to off-set the history of force.

[Force and Love. Hate and Justice.][27]

## June 7, 1943

Yaddo—Sometimes it seems as if one gets the purest intimation of tragedy from naturalism rather than from myth or symbolism.[28] The heaped-up record, the massed detail, end by giving the musical effect of a *single quality*—the multiplicity, or the mindlessness, makes for an essential and penetrating unity of understanding. Conversely, the art of explicit suggestibility, intimation, etc. flickers and makes for dimness. You have to pick up too many pieces—the energy is not spiritual, *something properly received*, but willed, sly, artistic in the modern sense.

In the same way the supernaturalist, the naive man, and the participant in superstition (for superstition is only the *willed*, or naive attempt to set up in reality what the spirit only knows, and can only know, in itself) who create spiritual entities and thereby, by the act of forced creation, sacrifices himself, his own deepest knowledge, to the enshrined myth, the symbolic half-knowledge. To look at life pitilessly, from the point of view of a deep naturalistic acceptance, is really to see the mystery. Reality is horrible, joyful, fleeting—reality. The *sense* of reality is wonderful, if it is completely honest. Then you really see the shadows; then you know that you have no control over the shadows, but that they are what they are, and that, properly considered, they represent the legitimate unknowability of man's existence. There is no substitute for understanding, and the counterfeits the mind offers to itself for them never satisfies.

27. Kazin's brackets.
28. Despite his attack on the "realistic savagery" of naturalist fiction in *On Native Grounds* (371), Kazin would be one of the few defenders of literary realism and naturalism in the postwar years.

[And so much here depends on the reader—naturalism is curiously modern in this sense—it assumes a power of reaction and sophistication (the material itself is like a palimpsest) on the reader's part that is like a creative suggestion in itself.][29]

The greatnesses of art, like the phases of the moon. And the great artists, Lawrence's "great souls, the only riches." High over head, as we come between them and eternity—the flecks of darkness. Only—sometimes we do have to turn our faces away from them.

The writers-artists-great spirits a man really *knows* are like nests of flame, and far apart—especially from him. He warms himself at their fires, and he can feed his own from them; but life is not a hearth-side; it is the pilgrimage from fire to fire. And there are so many spaces between.

## June 17, 1943

I now carry a poem or two of Blake's with me in my wallet—a talisman, and a medal of light. Oh, holy! holy! holy!—The highest praise I have for Jesus is that he must have been something like William Blake.[30]

The modern doctors have discovered that the mind can disorganize the body—and that it does rule it. But do you know what mind is? Mind is a hand clutched in space—a seeking-mind is the signature of all your human resources—mind is the imprint of all your desire. Therefore I say spirit, not mind: and I know that the spirit does rule the body—that is its victory.

This morning I am at peace again—for I have told the truth—I have been honest with myself for once—my life is anchored again—

But we shall never have peace so long as we believe that fascism is an aberration only, or the organization of power only—made by the tyrants and controverted by the Red Army only—we shall never have peace until we see that each of us carries fascism within him or helps to build it every day—like the dark Satanic mills in our own minds—fascism is the organization of all the negations—it is the hardening of all those invisible spheres "that were formed in fright."[31]

29. Kazin's brackets.

30. Kazin had a contract with Viking Press for the *Portable William Blake* (1946).

31. "Dark Satanic mills" is from Blake's Preface to *Milton*. "Though in many of its aspects this visible world seems formed in love, the invisible spheres were formed in fright" is from *Moby-Dick*, chapter 42.

## June 23, 1943

Realism and naturalism are a perfect picture of 19th century society, of the theory of progress, and especially of the liberal and radical philistinism of the new revolutionary movements. That is why symbolism begins with the decline of the old materialist faith—and why the truly representative art of our time is preoccupied with evil, with religious questioning, and above all, with the primal question—"*What is a man?*"

This is the atomic age—man is back to himself again—[down to himself again.][32] The trouble is that in losing our faith in progress—a good thing to lose per se—we have in a way lost our sense of historical continuity; or are too much bothered by our special disillusion; our special difference.

[Sin is disorder—man attained virtue that he might not go mad—][33]

Just as the whole story of Melville is the attempt to find an ontology, equal in capacity and individual heroism to the faith of his fathers, so today we are recovering almost gnostically that conception of responsibility, individual integrity, etc., which the church once imposed on men almost against their wills. Our mistake is that of superstition—we know that supernaturalism is a lie, and therefore miss its truth as myth—as the theory of human correspondences. We want religion without revelation—that is, factitious order. Whereas the only meaning of religion is revelation—that is, the meaning and worth of religion come to self-knowledge.

## July 1, 1943

Often I ask myself, as if I were directing the question to another person, how do you attempt to reconcile your belief in the sacral with even your rudimentary socialism? But I see no need to apologize for believing, with the same will, that man has a moral nature which he must obey, but that beyond it is a truly human community in which he must believe. It was not I who made the division between them.

## November 2, 1943

Neither original sin nor original virtue.

A journal is an exercise in reason—a tool in the effort to make oneself *reasonable*.

32. Kazin's brackets.
33. Kazin's brackets.

## November 28, 1943

On way to Chicago—First week Washington—second week—Washington, Camp Lee, Virginia.—Bainbridge, Maryland.

A white plume of smoke over the brown crusted earth in Ohio. [. . .]

All night long, bouncing in the upper berth of car 73. Where? Where?

Yet it is a happy train—a good Sunday morning. Overcast: but I am full with love, expectant of love, no one for a while, please; no more company, thinking, friends for a while. I have committed my sin and want to think about it. I feel that I want to be alone with my sin. Strange, I feel no *easy* pain—the sin was committed in my mind long before. When you have done, you have not done—for I have more.[34]

## December 14, 1943

[. . .] Paolo[35] is right—I am stubborn, not steely. Yes, but I am going through with Lou. And I am going through—I do want to see the other edge of the woods. Steely alone—where is the meaning that will flow out of the love?

Asya is going away. There is a crack in me that I do *not* want to heal.

Why did I say it was wrong to sit quietly and not be in the melee? What is it? What meaning has it? This endless flow of news? This continuity of steps in the dark? If I could read *Lear* every morning in the bus, not the *Times*, I would feel clean. [. . .]

Lou riding me in the bed. Riding, riding—the shifting sands once the sword has broken the dyke. That is why women are so grateful, so rhapsodic when the break comes? In man the orgasm is vertical, a slow mounting up the ladder. The unfolding is of a lop-sided accordion. In woman it is the onrush of the sea. Henry James's lake and the steeple. But they hadn't expected: they hadn't dared to believe. Because so much more is engaged of them than in the man? Because it is so complete a submission? (Mary McCarthy's unforgettable sentence on the Brooks Brothers shirt man:[36] "She waited for the man to exhaust himself.")

34. Kazin's "sin" was his affair with Mary Louise Peterson.

35. Paolo Milano (1904–1988), a professor of Romance Languages at Queens College and future literary critic for *L'Espresso*, was a friend of Kazin's.

36. "The Man in the Brooks Brothers Suit," in *The Company She Keeps* (New York: Harcourt, Brace, 1942).

But think, how *poetic* an end it is for a woman: fundamentally, the terrible joy of the ecstasy. That is why the pain, the groans, the *gratitude* (which presumably keeps her from being completely carnal). The man has established her identity, her blissful *truth*, to herself. And now she cannot be coy, or expectant, passionate or afraid.

The man has experienced a pleasure in this or that degree. It has or has not been an experience.

This is what I must know now. This is what terrifies me—to be reconciled to the final egotism of man. The ultimate in the pleasure-principle, the ultimate in the lie. Is there no more than this—that love is not love *for*, but the improvisation and fulfillment of the occasion? That the deepest love may spring only out of insecurity?

[. . .]

## December 16, 1943

The really extraordinary thing about Whitehead is his *feeling* for eternity. He is in the celestial halls. A quality of spaciousness and patience.

Asya left last night. I have been ill and alone all day. Whatever it means, whatever comes, it has been wonderful to be whole again for a while—and to be so quiet in my loneness.

## January 24, 1944

How foolish to call oneself, to wish to be, a supernaturalist. How can anything supernatural be credible or good? Even at their highest pitch of belief, men are only inverted pantheists. The wise man says that existence is God; the merely religious one hopes to show (even when he does not know what he hopes to show) that God *spells out* existence.

But to call oneself a transcendentalist (I am here thinking not of literary history, but of the inner logic of names) is beautiful—for the highest truth lies in the wish for and expectancy of *transcending*, of moving through, not of super-anything, to incorporate within yourself the idea of the transcendentalist passage; to prove the wish a fact, and to live it; to have a sense of the intertwining, the planes, the channels of human movement and liberation; finally, to *transcend*, to be greater than the seeming necessity, by knowing what the necessity is, and by completing it—that is a provisional and decent human hope. [. . .]

Sometimes she [Mary Lou] frightens me by her scatteredness—I think of her on this morning, when we are so far away from each other, as someone so young and beautiful, dream-lost and confused, floating—endlessly—being pulled by so many tides.

She needs patience, love, tenderness. She is not hard only meditative without a center, without the experience of a *center*. Without the experience of great ambitions and joys.

Is thoughtfulness, ultimately, only an act of safety?

## January 26, 1944

[. . .] Two days ago, when I first began to be troubled by Mary, I stood in the middle of the street, enclosed within the greyish afternoon, the scattering cars, the people so lonely, so unexpressed—all the loose atoms, normally contained within boxes called images, books, society now flung out absently as blocks may be cast down by a child's hand—and thought, in my pain, my sudden bewildering sense of loss—how *funny* Life is—how funny and strange.

*For Blake*—The marked, post-Stalinist, interregnum materialist. Which sees a kind of inductive pointillism (Bergson?)—the rethinking into expressive insight of man's involvement *in* nature. The sense of the mysterious continuity.

A true book on religion would be a book *on the nature of human peace.*

## January 29, 1944

To be the historian of genius? Yes—and not enough.

The most curious thing I have had to learn is that people learn the great lessons—some people do—without ecstasy. I never dared to believe it—I wondered how they could—categories are names, but not substances.

Happy tonight. Very happy.

## February 10, 1944

The soul is like a moon over round waters. Once it fell into the lake of its own being, and lay at the depths, sending up a thin shaft of light that whimpered at the face of the sky.

## February 14, 1944

L[ou] left tonight: Record of a week. I now live utterly alone, which is apparently where I've been headed for ever so long. The caster-off. For what? Now we shall know.

## March 3, 1944

Between the depths and so great a promise. But why always this painful alternation, so that one can never ever live *between* them, but only at the poles?

Met Denis de Rougemont two days ago. Like Silone, Schweitzer—*a man of the third camp: my camp.*[37]

De Rougemont's Swiss spare idealism—"super rational, super-racial, super-linguistic."

Vinet[38] quoted the Swiss maxim—"I want man to be master of himself that he may be the servant of all."

## March 11, 1944

God is only a name for our wonder.

## March 15, 1944

Living in a miserable hotel bedroom on University Place, the Hotel Albert. I heard once that the hotel was owned or managed by Ryder's brother, who named it after him.[39] This thought has always pleased me and has made me think of it. But Ryder's spirit is not here now.

Yet I pray for a little rest here, and want so much to be quietly alone. So glad to be out of Barrow Street[40]—how much darkness is associated for me with

37. Denis de DeRougement (1906–1985) is the author of *Love in the Western World* (1940). "Third camp" refers to those who reject both Russian Communism and the inequities of American capitalism. Ignazio Silone (1900–1978), Italian novelist and politician, much admired by Kazin; Albert Schweitzer (1875–1965), Franco-German theologian, organist, physician, and recipient of the Nobel Prize for his philanthropic work in Africa.
38. Alexandre Rodolphe Vinet (1798–1847), Swiss critic and theologian.
39. William Ryder owned the Albert Hotel in Greenwich Village, named after his brother Albert Pinkham Ryder (1847–1917), who lived and painted there. See Chapter 1, note 67.
40. The apartment of Kazin's friend the literary critic and novelist Isaac Rosenfeld (1918–1956).

those rooms—endless processions of dirt that disappeared only to found new shapes. Gloom and Isaac's special gift of humiliating himself and the world he lives in.

It is cruel to live in the house of your friends, and to have to discuss money with them. What is most cruel is to learn so much about them from the objects they have handled with such intimate comfort, lust, or distaste—not knowing that the friend will come and live, even though he may not want it, may not help it, and learn too much about you.

Went with Esther[41] to buy an overcoat for England. It was pleasant talking with her; I felt full of affection and peace.

## April 3, 1944

I see them in the gateways of the city, in cheap cafeterias, in subways. And always I know them by their own peculiar combination of hopelessness and bravado—the sallow flesh, the empty flash of the eyes, the general flavorlessness of human personality which has risen as they have fallen. I never knew so much about them until, in these last few terrible months—the most important single period of my life, and the part that has tested, and made my humanity as nothing ever has—I became, for all practical purposes, one of them. I mean those who are essentially, by their present constitution of life, homeless, intellectual, and desperate. Homosexuals or [those] on the verge of homosexuality sometimes; certainly always "bright," full of brisk judgments; intimates of that nameless despair in the heart which is like a great sweeping fog. Their life, or their destruction of life, is to be read in their eyes. This morning, entering an uptown express at Times Square, I passed one of them who was standing in the corner of the train as I entered. He gave me the eye—and I thought, half in humiliation, half in a cheerful despair—hah, he knows me; he knows his own kind. And I thought of that terrible scene in Charles Jackson's *The Lost Weekend*, not a very piercing novel but proficient in gloom to the point of giving solid evidence, in which the drunk watches the homosexual orderly trying to dissolve his (imaginary) defenses against homosexuality. I know you, bud.

The wretches—in which homosexuality plays only a small part—know you all, bud. When I first realized that my own bitterness and hopelessness at times gave me away, I was frightened. Now I am no longer afraid: everything could have driven me to go their way, except my quaint need to survive, to go home to my own spirit. "Was das Leben mir versprach werde ich ihn halten

41. Kazin's aunt.

[I will hold onto what life has promised me]." And I shall redeem, I already have in that perilous corner where the real battle is waged, where the soul is torn, and where—if the promise of life is great enough—one wins. Always the bargain is made with oneself; the battle is waged with oneself; peace comes only from that thorny but imperative reintegration of self. . . . I say this in calmness, in joy, and with expectancy, but since I am physically still in the circle of danger, I can write it with a certain ruefulness, and an appreciation of the distress that has accompanied my life in these last few months.

## April 5, 1944

[. . .] Reading Freud (as in reading ourselves!) we naturally supposed that the vast system of repression, of guilt, of the strivings for "instinctual gratification," that are so checked and displaced everywhere by the established forms of conscience and culture, are like a veil under which the "natural man" still lives, and despite which he must find expression in terms which will liberate him from the darkness of our original being. But what if man, acting in accordance with some ancient terror-principle whose authority has penetrated so far into his collective history, has a natural teleology which is something different from instinctual gratification per se? Values become substances, ends become means; there is a saving caution in man as well as a strained spirituality, a desire for a symmetry that is all the more real for its being so deeply embedded in the imagination. The purposiveness of human existence can be shown to rest on a fiction i.e., it can be shown to have deeper origins than it knows, and a more "animal" life than it can confess. But why do we suppose (and surely this is one of the great prepossessions of romanticism, and one of its great dangers) that the uncovering is merely to a new release of the pleasure principle? Why do we suppose, in short, that for all its foundations in myth, that the "humanity" of man is anything less than a *natural* need to *make* purposes equal to his discovered powers? So it may not be merely the natural man who is uncovered, but the natural priest, prophet, etc. This is not to say that all these things too do not have their psychoanalytical-biological foundation. But it does mean that the inheritance, on the part of man, of an involved transparent and even tender sense of purpose is more complex than we know—yet even more inveterate.

Another way of saying this—why is Pascal wiser than Freud?[42] Why is the following Penseé more true than the truth of what is most unimpeachable in

42. Blaise Pascal (1623–1662), French mathematician and philosopher; Pascal's *Pensées* were favorite reading of Kazin's.

Freud's diagnosis? "*Men are so necessarily mad, that not to be mad would be only a special kind of madness.*"

Because P's perception of "madness" is a summing up of the whole being and *tone* of man, seen in relation of man to himself, man to infinity. His madness is our whole being; Freud's health is a state of suspension—a legend, buried deep under civilization, and yet considered as the farthest projection of it.

P's madness is our health; Freud's health is a symptom, or a wish.

Yet there is something unclean and pitiful in Pascal's Christian morbidity, in his talk of the necessary hatred between men in the world. Is the opposition, then, between the philosopher and the doctor—between the *penetration* in "mysticism" and the summary values of man's life? Without P's morbidity, we would not have his cosmology. With Freud's sanity, we have, at bottom, the ethics of the pleasure-principle. Where is the union of insight and health? Of essence and normality?

P's *schema* is true—for men who can bear it. We do bear it and yet it is not right that we should. A need, but a thinking need? A God, but a yearning God.

## May 18, 1944
### (dated April 18)

This book is not a journal; it is an exercise-book, a disorderly pile of shavings.

## May 19, 1944

Last night, at Esther's, Harvey Swados[43] talked about his experiences as a seaman and mostly about New Orleans and London. Dressed in whimsically outrageous shirt and silk tie, [illegible] beard that curiously accented all his native sensibility and youthfulness, he talked about whores and the House of Parliament, of New Orleans nightlife, and English labor. Harvey is the only war-intellectual I know—the only war-man, and listening to him rolling off his experiences so quickly, I realized that it would take him ten years to recover from the wars.

The Jews are the great watchers—from eternity on. [. . .]

43. Harvey Swados (1920–1972), American novelist, brother of Felice Swados (d. 1945), Richard Hofstadter's first wife.

## July 11, 1944

The one real thing I have learned from the terrible experiences of the last months is a knowledge of how far we human beings are from each other.

## August 1, 1944

I always feel, in reading Stevens,[44] as if I were running my hands over great cool marble slabs. The marble is the color of flesh and has the texture of flesh, but there is a coldness in it that suggests to me too expert a withdrawal on Stevens' own part.

## July 24, 1944

Proust as the great modern Elizabethan—not only in the obvious sense of so manifold an exploration, but in the ostentation, the fullness, the laughing fine-spun richness of observation.[45] The key: that the instrument should be equal to the scene, and a scene in itself. Not rhetoric but proud sensuality.

## August 30, 1944

Provincetown; another bedroom/Left Monhegan Island [Maine] on Monday afternoon and arrived in Boston late that evening; Went to Dixon's[46] in Berkeley Street and to bed. Just before waking that morning early I dreamt of Paul Goodman.[47] He was walking with me somewhere, and suddenly he stopped and with a "cruel" smile said, "Well, shall I start asking you questions about Blake now?" . . . I awoke with a shiver, and suddenly felt the old familiar panic of depression again—a fog sweeping in to me from an unknown sea. I lay in bed shivering and almost weeping, powerless to get up, when suddenly I thought to myself, no, no, it can't go on like this; no, no, I must fight it! Fight it not with will, but with understanding; enter the conspiracy and break it up by standing between the parts, and examining them.

44. Wallace Stevens (1879–1955), American poet whose difficulty, mandarin manner, and philosophical musings were not always to Kazin's taste.

45. Marcel Proust (1871–1922), French novelist, essayist, and critic, best known for his modernist masterpiece *À la recherche du temps perdu* (*In Search of Lost Time*, or, as in its first English translation, *Remembrance of Things Past*), published between 1913 and 1927.

46. Dixon Wecter (1906–1950), American historian.

47. Paul Goodman (1911–1972), writer, sociologist, activist of the left, best known for *Growing Up Absurd* (1960).

At my first interview with her, Dr. Rioch[48] said she found a pattern in my relations with women: that I was always in love with those who rejected me. The fear of loss always drives me into panic; but the symptom is not sorrow but fear. Paul in the dream was *threatening* me: why? Because he had become the person who would show me up. So always I have felt, in school, in the crises of the book, in quarrels and in that which led to quarrels, in the twisted strands of my relations with Asya, that the loss of something I had in my own mind discounted, or the loss of something that had simply become habitual and necessary, *threatened me with extinction*. Somewhere in my early psychic history, not as a result of the testicular business merely, I was threatened, shown up; and ever after my real psychic disease has been panic. [. . .]

My neurosis is a toxin that has infected my whole being, slowed up my movements, made me horribly aware of all the possible slights, cruelties, indifference, a man may suffer. But my disease is shallow and no less serious for that. Somewhere in my early childhood, under the stress of Mama's profound anxieties over herself and over me and my early illnesses, I was made consciously and excessively aware of life's hazardousness; and from that point I must trace and date all my life-long terror of insecurity. The stammering was a symptom of my insecurity: literally, the brokenness of my link with the world. I did not suffer because I stammered; I stammered because I suffered. The wound was inner. Rioch is right, too, about the testicles: it was a condition that joined psychic experiences; it was not itself the cardinal cause of trauma. When I remember the gashes, I think of that day in the Lane annex at high school when I stammered so helplessly in class, and felt everyone looking at me in a pitying but remote circle. I went down to the toilet and standing near the slate-gray walls, wept my heart out. I remember asking the children when I played with them: but you're not *sore* at me? Why was I afraid that they would be sore at me? I wasn't; I was greedy for solace and friendship; thought I could bridge the gap between me and them *anyway*: with words, with assertions of companionship. So with Asya and Lou: I have never had real relations with them; I was only using them. And that is what horrifies me now; the realization that Asya had become a symbol for the safety of home, and Lou a symbol for my sexual release.

I did not really love Lou until I went to Maine and saw how she was suffering, how I had contributed to her suffering, till I saw her in her own sinewy unhappiness. My aggressiveness has been terrible; my lack of love and understanding has been terrible. All my life I have lived like a bullet going

48. Janet Rioch (1905–1974), psychoanalyst whom Kazin saw (sometimes three times a week) into the early 1960s.

through walls: I have thought only of my own progress, and in the end there has been no progress, for in my life-long terror, in my never-ending anxieties, I have lived only for myself, so that now I am left only with myself.

Left here; so I shall start here.

## September 1, 1944

Chiaromonte[49] said yesterday on the beach in Truro: socialism means an essential change in human relations; human relations cannot be changed by . . . fiat (law and order). But cannot we defend the destruction of the old intolerance between races and peoples (the one argument I know of for the revolutionary state; where it succeeds)? As Leonard Ehrlich[50] said long ago at Yaddo—the tearing the skin off? Chiaromonte smiled and said: yes, a situation has been changed, but what of its inner quality?

The quality is what, however? Not perfect? But a change has been made. Refusing everything but the summum bonum (it comes to that, in the actual order of our thinking), we are still what we are; and in actual experience, under capitalism, that means a constant retrogression of the fundamental moral and creative sense.

The Stalinist converts his ends into means; the moralist supposes that his means can become ends. But the dichotomy is always too crude, and innerly false. The great moral content of the revolutionary drive—the will to remake history, is moral; the conception of education, persuasion, vital individual change in politique de la personne [personal politics], is a kind of purposive action. It is really the naked defense of terror, the articulation of the contempt for the individual, that stuns us into devising a new category for the revolutionary. Hitherto the argument has always been too simple between both parties, for it is supposed that the planes of action are parallel in both. That is manifestly untrue; the moralist finds his modus operandi in the individual; the "Stalinist" his in the mass, the class, the patterns of social revolt, administration, etc. The Stalinist's argument is based on time: in the long run individuals will be different; the moralist's on experience and habit: if you make your mistake in one individual, you are set on the wrong path ever after.

49. Nicola Chiaromonte (1905–1972) was an Italian anti-Fascist and journalist of the anti-Communist left who wrote for the *Partisan Review* and other liberal/progressive journals during and after the war.

50. Leonard Ehrlich (b. 1905), proletarian novelist of the 1930s.

No individual life is actually sacred; it is the idea of such that has ennobled and filled man's spiritual history. . . . And even in the times of the Swastika, men are units, individual souls, in everyone's mind.

## September 3, 1944

[. . .] I am a Jew, a socialist, a comrade to those who are dying tonight in Hitler Europe, and will die tomorrow, and the next day, and the next. Why am I so alone: why? Because my awareness of where I have failed has been greater than real failure and has made it; and my awareness will not let me rest till I have become one with it. [. . .]

## September 22, 1944

Black Mountain.

The tyranny of love in Proust; fills all the spaces occupied formerly by custom, law, religion. It is the private man's last expression of his finiteness and longing for the infinite. The irony implicit in his own suffering; his own awareness of his suffering, of its intrinsic greatness and triviality; of its being a substitute value for so much else.

American barrenness, resulting from reliance on a merely individual life. What is exterior is really only outside forms of pleasure. The code of sensation: *that* will bring us home! The *wolf*: we must be wolves, or else *what is* there? I shall never be able to put out of my mind the scenes I saw last night in Asheville—the broken saloon types, the soldiers looking around aimlessly, the terrible American search for home.

How profound—Proust describing Paris bombed, the background for Charlus chained to his bed in the male house of prostitution: *the last of the aristocracy—until the day when this willing Prometheus had had himself chained* by force to the rock of pure "matter."

## September 24, 1944

Went last night with some girls from the college and soldiers from the neighboring Moore Hospital to a "folk festival" in Asheville, a three-days running vaudeville show. The emcee was a fat, friendly, little man in a white suit; the audience was cordial, baffled, in quest of excitement—answered at the high moments with the Rebel yell. The "folk" was jived square dances; stringed strumming; a seven-year-old boy propped up in a chair next to a microphone, whining "God Bless America." The performance was true to contemporary folk, certainly; but it was meaningless and pathetic otherwise. The only performance that seemed to have a real purity and dignity was an almost spontaneous little dance launched by a middle-aged man with the seamed look of a carpenter and old black moustache, who stepped out into the wooden extension of the stage under the high, blank lamp and tentatively, affectionately performed a few steps of his own. Then another man came out, and at the other end reproduced and varied the steps of the first; and the fact that he was wearing a dark, city suit, collar, and tie made his self-assertion all the more beautiful; then another man, and still another; till finally there was a ring of men, most of them looking like city lawyers, doctors, business men, each dancing quietly and absorbedly in his own corner. I realized then the great beauty of separateness in dancing and most of all, of *men* dancing—beautiful in itself and not least because of the surprise embodied in the act of such men, at such a dance. . . . For the rest, the evening was dull hooplah, and later, on thinking it over, gave me an insight into the now negative cast of "folk" in this region, famous so long because of the pockets of resistance to urban federalized culture it is supposed to have kept.

I walked the Asheville streets with Betty Schmitt,[51] while waiting for the bus to take us back. The Saturday night in Asheville—the leaky neon colors; the look of banned liquor between soda-pop bottles; the soldiers propped up in front of cigar stores and ice cream parlors, waiting for that which is beyond them to give them pleasure, but the vital connection with which, since it must always be in the self, or the self entire, is missing.

## September 25, 1944

Went to bed early last night, and for the first time since California, had a dream—a violent dream about Mama in which all the data I've collected with Rioch were embodied in my wish to see her dead. It hurts to write this even here, yet I want to set down the dream for what it is. I dreamt that Mama had fallen ill, somewhere in this region, and was being taken to the hospital, on the top of an enormously high car or wagon. She lay on top there, the car jolting through the streets as if on parade; the streets seemed to be full of spectators. Suddenly she fell off into the street, and was dead. I was painfully, almost intolerably stirred; but stirred not out of grief so much as out of surprise at the event, and surprise at my realization (in the dream) that I could accept this without violent protest. My first impulse

51. Elizabeth Schmitt, dance student at Black Mountain College.

was to tell everyone within reach, or rather to let it be known, that Mama was dead. Entering through the doors of a restaurant I encountered Fadiman[52] and a stranger accompanying him; he was in Asheville on a lecture tour or something; he was indifferent rather than hostile in his general attitude, and when I told him about Mama, he and his friend smiled coldly, as if amused by my surprise and loneliness, and went off.

The meaning of the dream is clear enough—since, through my talks with Rioch, I have come to realize the great hostility I bear Mama, I wanted to demote her from her high repute; to say to the world, *she* did this to me, and though you condemn me and have so little patience or love for me, yet you believe in her unswervingly! . . . I woke up suddenly; it was only two; and felt a kind of bitter-sweet calmness at the divulgence of a secret emotion; happy that "reality had caught up with me." My state was one of cold, bitter acceptance; but the acceptance was good; the surprise was gone.

The loneliness here is very great; solid and thick, and yet tolerable, entirely normal-seeming, in a way it never did in California. My mind is full of projects and ideas, full of the desire to write; this morning, lying in bed, I formed the conception of a book about childhood and modern literature, a conception stemming not only from my own increased awareness of how dominant the patterns of hostility and worthlessness Mama showed me became, in my later psychic life, but from the obsession with childhood in contemporary American writing, particularly among writers of my own generation. The possibilities of inclusive truth in such a book are enormous: dovetailing of studies of fantasy and symbolism with real social-political history; analysis of particular works of art; history of personal history and of the idea of personal history.[53]

## October 5, 1944

The real joy of writing comes from surprising oneself.

[. . .]

## October 29, 1944

[. . .] Nakedness and grace. Rhetoric is an enclosure, a sheath—writing should be proportionate to what one has to say; that is its nakedness. Proportion, flexibility,

52. Clifton Fadiman (1904–1999) was a friend and book review editor of the *New Yorker* (1933–1943).
53. The conception and techniques of *A Walker in the City* (1951), which Kazin called a "personal history," are indebted to the "obsession with childhood" found in Joyce and Proust as well as in the American writer Sherwood Anderson.

tone. We write with our whole being, if we wish to write honestly, as well as from the point of view of "objective truth." (We, too, are the objects.)

The rhetorical and redundant qualities of my writing so far come from the over-emphasis necessitated by uncertainty, and tentativeness. I am never content to say, A is B; I must add—it is really B; or, it is that B which follows second in this order. A is B: which B? That should be indicated once and finally. . . . But "simplicity" as such has no meaning. Writing is tentative in its grasp, final in its innerness, but it is not a series of statements. It is an imposture, too; an interweaving of every costume has its artificial, its imposed and external qualities. Language is artificial precisely because it may express so much that needs merely to be *expressed.*

## November 7, 1944

The Fall lingered on for days; but now the cold has set in. The grass near the dining hall frozen-white, bathed in early morning light and mist from river. [. . .]

Melville, Whitman, Crane.[54] Three examples of the democratic, impassioned, literary imagination in America cut off from the love of women. "Homosexual" is a word that applies here only to Crane; but Whitman and Melville reflect a condition of American revolt that needs badly to be understood, with dispassionate and even tender understanding for their inner ambiguity, struggles, and fate. . . . The world to them is a woman who has betrayed, or has proved too remote. Melville's mother-wife, Whitman's mother.

How fragile are these leaves, O Lord,
Yet symbols endure, and in them we dream of our renewals.

## November 8, 1944

Received news from the Rockefeller Foundation that they can probably get me over to England at last, by the first of the year or so. The news left me unexpectedly passive, and a little sad. Black Mountain has been the first real home I've had in a year, and for all the loneliness and searching in my heart to cross over this period of uncertainty, I've been happy here and a workman

54. Hart Crane (1899–1932), poet, whose poem *The Bridge* (1930), inspired by the Brooklyn Bridge, held special significance for Kazin.

again. Last night I thought over and over the convulsive migrations of this past year, and suddenly felt a need to put down the external addresses, at least, in this notebook, as a jagged line of my wanderings since Asya and I broke up. . . . Hotel New Weston; Lou's room at 36 Morton Street; our 85 Barrow St.; Hotel Albert; with the Hertzbergs at 21 W. 11th;[55] W. 94th; University Residence Club; California; Hotel St. George; Maine; Provincetown and Truro; Sutter Avenue; Black Mountain College.

Emerson—"Art . . . teaches to convey a larger sense by simpler symbols."

## November 10, 1944

I devoted my Blake class this morning to a general talk on Blake's life and personality, on the artisan status and independence shown in his career, and on the slow and crippling restrictions placed on his means of earning a livelihood. It all began with my attempt to ascertain what in English life at the end of the eighteenth century, brought to so concentrated a focus the interest in the child, and thinking about the new interest in the child and its sensibility led me to a discussion of Blake's extraordinary place in the economic history of English culture. I never realized so keenly before, I think, the paramount importance of the artisan's role in Blake's career—with its retreating independence, its concentration in the illustrated and hand-made book, the byplay of his own independent and often conflicting picture-illustrations to other texts, and of course his fierce yet entirely natural integrity and simplicity of life. Blake, I saw it here again, but somehow more clearly and movingly than before, represents in his career, as well as in his thought and vision, the last margin of independent sight open to the artisan in his time. Neither a middle-class man nor a proletarian, but the son of a hosier early apprenticed to the engraver's craft, Blake led a life of independence that fed on the inner fires of his own resentment against the brutalization of spirit as it fed on his physical limitations as an independent worker. The artisans holding on to the last margin of selfhood, still making their piece-goods in their own cottages. But Blake is also a city man. Had he been a peasant his career would have been as broken, as "naif" and purely folklorish, as Burns'; but he was in the center of the new life, and still worked at the last margin of the old pre-factory independence. . . . I must

55. Sidney (1910–1984) and Hazel Hertzberg (1918–1988). Sidney was journalist and political activist, Hazel a professor of history at Columbia Teachers College. They are parents of the journalist Hendrik Hertzberg (1943–).

make an independent study of the history and traits of the artisan class in English and European life.[56]

## December 18, 1944

[. . .] The darkness of these hills in Winter; the effect of this landscape on the bleak, potential violence of the mountain people. Everywhere the mountain wall fencing one in; only yesterday, walking through their orchard with the Stokeleys, and looking north to Kentucky did I get a feeling of uninterrupted space; a feeling that one could here look beyond. In the first fall days when I came, the light of the sun expanded one's sight; made the mountains like tiers of one's own perception. Now, in the early winter darkness, amid the rain and slush, the effect is sad, no longer liberating. Yet I like it. The loneliness I have had all year has now become a physical fact in the mountains around me; and with a bare dozen of us left here at the college, and so many houses dark, I sit and mediate my isolation in a kind of attentive peace and confidence I did not have last night, or before, or so many nights before. . . . Now at last I am like the man in my own story, "Going Home";[57] I can no longer clearly see *her* face before me. I dread going "home"; this isolation is a harmony; the mingled companionship I shall know soon enough in N.Y. will be disharmonious, for I am no longer part of that life.

I would speak here of Asya, but I cannot; the wound has gone so deep that I no longer can go over the old, old calculations of self-blame, of her blame, of longing and idle wish. If only she knew—if I knew—but we both know, and there is nothing, apparently, that I can do about it at this stage. It is hard to be alone this way; but it was hard to be incompletely together before, even harder. And now that she will not even speak to me; now that there is not only the old familiar barrier and raw hurt between us, but absolute moral hurt and a deeper, more speechless estrangement than before, I am speechless in the full depth of my agony, and cannot resolve it in words. How long it has gone on, this death-in-life, with neither

56. In *Black Mountain: An Exploration in Community* (New York: Dutton, 1972): 222–223, Martin Duberman (1930–) describes Kazin's "impassioned manner" in the classroom. "He was a kind of evangelist for Melville and Blake—a Jewish evangelist, something akin, as one student put it, to 'the Holy Schlemiel,' rhapsodizing eloquently one minute, playing the inept joker the next, mixing gossip, profundity, calculated impetuosity and exhortations into such a staccato, stammering, testy brew, that his students, or at least those with literary aspirations and a taste for the histrionic, left class intoxicated, drunken, and reeling."

57. In "Going Home," *Harper's* (April 1945): 476–478, Kazin's only published work of fiction, the protagonist, following a stay in a sanatorium, decides against returning to his lover.

death nor life to come between the dilemma; how long; how sickeningly long, when a little more intelligence, a little more radical and human impatience, even, would have turned one horn away. And now I go on; to New York; to Europe: one kind of end, for the present, being Europe.

The body moving through space and in time. "Matter is motion loathing itself"—matter in motion seeking through its own highest yearning for identification to understand itself—even as it lives the impulses it seeks to comprehend. This mysticism is a biology—a suspension of the habitual human divorce between existence and *being* (in comprehension).

## February 14, 1945
### [On board the *Hart Crane* in a convoy to England]

Choppy sea. Slight sea-sickness and depression. High wind. Direction turning more northerly after going SE, then due east. Radio stations heard in saloon New England. Boston Stations. Father Godfrey Wolf, Dawson, Bell, Kazin[58]—Four civilian passengers in hospital room tightly wedged together. Convoy yesterday—53 vessels, plus escort vessels of Canadian Navy. More vessels expected to join us in convoy from Halifax in a day or two. Men on board all in *my age-group; extremely likable Jewish second radio operator from Bronx.* Captain Robert Fairbairn. Long lines of vessels in convoy look like dames in quadrille—mother ahead, with chicks plodding obediently and uncertainly after. *Endless rumors*, though everyone seems very confident. The third mate played the accordion to a violin I borrowed from a gunner's mate. Then taught the 3rd assistant engineer German. Began Prescott's *Conquest of Mexico* this afternoon. The enormous eating that goes on here—Muzerall, the 3rd mate, accompanies every bite of bread, meat, or potatoes, with a thick slab of butter. Wind increasing all through the day.

## February 16, 1945

[. . .] Anxiety and thoughts of home. The steward of French Canadian descent (Rioux?) on the subject this morning of the *fucking* British Empire. That is their favorite word here—the cuss word of greatest mechanical power used like spread over every word, did convey the greatest possible impotence. Intense loneliness

58. Father Godfrey Wolf, Franciscan cleric sent to replace an ailing Franciscan cleric in Liverpool; Reverend Dawson, a Baptist missionary on the way to France; Bell, a "radio engineer who sleeps all the time" (*Lifetime*, 33).

and boredom of this life for most of them—boredom and the unrelenting threat of danger. Submarines, storms, collisions, bombings. *No joke standing watch 4 hours at a time in this intense cold.* The three mates: Clark, Heal (apple-cheeked boy from Maine), Muzerall. No superficial patriotism from any of them and much cynicism and weariness about the war; but great individual pride in power of country's material and military resources, etc.

## February 27, 1945

In St. George's Channel. At daybreak saw lights around dark water; pilot at breakfast. Cleared by 5 and went walking around streets [of Liverpool] with Bell. *Redburn: His First Voyage* described the poverty in the docks of L; saw same small Launcelot's Hey.[59] Drab paint signs along the docks: Hands Off Greece. Priest eating in cafeteria, shoveling with genteel voraciousness beans on knife. The courtesy and delicacy of the tired girls in the shops; first view of bombed areas. Slept on board ship.

## March 2, 1945
### [London]

Lunched with David Glass; saw *Henry V;* talks with Yeaxlee[60] in morning; O'Brien in afternoon. Henry cream-colored Shakespeare; excellent taste; pleasant political re-editing; young Prince Hal played by Laurence Olivier. Article defending D. H. Lawrence in *Tribune*; poor article but important for itself. The blanket darkness of the streets at night part of atmosphere of my alienation. England adds institutions on institutions; paleogenesis all the way through, in terms of form, if not function. Yeaxlee outlined general scheme; a reader in educational psychology at Oxford. The bare line of food—sugar not only scarce, but battered when it comes; dirt on dishes. General subdued feeling that big push soon coming. The old gentlemen with wing collars; general appearance of people better than I had anticipated; so many stores boarded up; stone walls like great blank shields against the street in front of many tube stations and stores. Rosy children playing in the dull dead twilight at night along the alleys. Low-massive palaces. Royal society rooms at Burlington House; chipped statues. General feeling of grime, fatigue, but inner confidence and cheerfulness.

59. Launcelot's Hey is a street where Redburn sees a starving mother and child in an 1849 novel by Herman Melville.
60. David Glass (1911–1978), English sociologist, friend of Kazin's from the United States; Basil Yeaxlee (1883–1967), a leader in the British adult education movement.

Great question in my mind always how they keep from hating the home folk—saw GI's lined up by the dozens in P[iccadilly] Circus; always in front of American movies! Glass says that on their tour five American senators most anxious to be photographed with Bob Hope,[61] and one or two of them actually invited him to accompany them to 10 Downing Street; it had to be whispered in their ears by Winant that the thing wasn't cricket.[62] Uniforms everywhere; all the English and Scottish colors: our drab private's khaki and sleek officers' uniform. Sailors sitting in Chicken Coop restaurant chuckling over bare English diet; idea of material possessions, easy power and comfort, so great to us that anything else seems deserving not of fellowship or imaginative pity but of condescension. Homesick officers in tube chewing Wrigley's. Reverse Lowell's essay: now On a Certain Condescension in Americans.[63] Yet afraid of English; conscious of superior tone—part of it the higher, graver, more lilting and more musical tone of English speech. If their graver note heard, impossible for us to deliberately go one lower: France ugly after Frawnce. Tight restriction on all news of V-2;[64] great search lights combing the sky from or around Hyde Park. Need more time to prowl around for myself; time to read and reflect, and to be alone more. European soldier/male along Oxford Street, reminds me of picture of Sophie's brother, grand in Czarist uniform and enormous moustache. Knight-type; the noble and handsome figure of chivalry? Our dominant type not striking but aggressive or proud looking; successful lawyer—now successful major. . . . Too much talk all around me about America-Britain, sterile and futile comparison of civilizations; superficial and based on surface differences in top-level history, nomenclature, etc. Broadway and Piccadilly (and there isn't much difference, except that P. is more compact, less blatant, and as shivery in the spasmodic hunt for pleasure) (the peristaltic American belt moving at night) as the hard, green-red neons along Broadway are. More and more convinced that the only basic category in which people think, politically, spiritually, emotionally, is the purely received notion of the nation, made aggressive by war. What is the history of the nation in these times? Contemporary life soaked in all the unconscious attributes of nationalism; yet we know little or nothing of its emergent history. Greater superiority and depth of local place-names in England. Every American knows English names—stations, streets, etc. from their novels: our landscape is

61. Bob Hope (1903–2003) was an English-born American entertainer and comedian who regularly entertained the troops.

62. John Gilbert Winant (1889–1947) was the U.S. ambassador to Britain, 1941–1946.

63. Kazin is referring to a 1869 essay by James Russell Lowell, "On a Certain Condescension in Foreigners."

64. V-2 rockets fired by Germans into London in the last months of the war.

unconsciously the landscape of the wilderness, in its unknowability, its forward remove, the rhythms of our migrations. The "Churchillian renaissance" problem to study. Silence of streets at night eerie; hard to tell if people have left many blitzed-looking houses, or still live in them. Old private dwellings in which all of us move or live; little grate fires; superior neatness; quality of desk-order. Slower, gentler, more *inner;* restrictions are or flow into institutions: a great moving jelly; yet innerly more people's intelligence, interest in government, etc., everywhere. Hazard from the air: any moment; where; who. The sharp-cutting defensiveness of Americans in streets. The subway-sleepers: old lady with glasses down her nose reading *Church Times*.—How hard, with their deep sense of privacy, to have to double up everywhere!

## March 4, 1945

Went on a tour with some OWI people and touched briefly on the East End.[65] The chauffeur, hired with his car for the occasion, was ignorant and snobbish, and when I pressed him several times to go to Whitechapel, he demurred and explained that there wasn't much to see there—only lower-class dwellings. The bombings in the E. End savage and terrible: whole blocks of houses destroyed; and what I saw was a dirtier, grimier East Side. Walked around Bloomsbury and the British Museum area. Lunch in a casual "Greek" restaurant nearby very bad.

## March 5, 1945

Saw Madge briefly at Pilot Press and went over to Jonathan Cape. Lunch with G. Wren Howard, who I presume is chief editor.[66] Gentle and fatherly-looking man, not very exciting; rather indifferent and absent-minded about my book. Had long talk with W. E. Williams.[67] The handsome scholarly Englishman: very breezy and casual, terribly bored, racked by a slight but persistent stammer. Talking with him moved me very much, not for anything he said but for the community of feeling I had with him, of which he was probably totally unconscious, because of my own history. Lost my way on the subway and then on the bus trying to get back; mostly because I was suddenly overtaken by terrible depression and went into a fog. Dinner at the billets and stayed for the

65. In addition to gathering material on the education of soldiers in England, Kazin worked with the Office of War Information (OWI) to inform English citizens about America.

66. Charles Madge (1912–1996), poet, journalist, sociologist, was a director of Pilot Press. Jonathan Cape was the English firm that published the British edition of *On Native Grounds*.

67. William Emrys Williams (1896–1977), British publisher and educator.

movie. Lana Turner. How they all loved it; and though I was seeing it for the second time, and it was trash to begin with, I got a kick out of seeing our natural resources so lavishly displayed.[68] The homesickness in the OWI room could have been cut with a knife. . . . Blackout and rain after dinner last night made a traditional London vignette. Over and again, walking about in the evenings, I have had the curious sensation, looking at the completely blanked-out houses and stores, that no one is living in them at all. In the daylight many of the houses look so battered and decayed that one supposes them vacated; in the evenings they are so dark that they still look empty. But the town is crowded.

## March 6, 1945

The shortages of many common things easy to get back home are very acute here, but my impression is that many items are distributed more equably than they are in A. [. . .] In the evening went to one of Laski's[69] open-house nights Addison Bridge Place. A clever man, a scholarly man—not profound, not secure enough to be humble; when you listen to him, you listen to *him*, not to his ideas. What interested me, far beyond the nerve-racking habit of referring to all the world's great by their first name, was the shocking, conventional "realism" of his position on Poland, etc. I recognize the difficulty of choosing in this situation, or rather the inability to choose at all, between losing Russia as an ally and trying to support the dubiously "democratic" government of Poland. But since the choice has to be made this way, within present limits, it should at least provide a lever for candid thinking about the depths of our situation. Instead the dangers inherent in big-power control are passed over, and we thank our lucky stars that S. is not against us; that we are still alive, etc. [. . .]

## March 7, 1945

House of Commons in the morning. The backbiting from the conservative benches about Poland. Long Navy speech by Alexander.[70] Talk with Mrs. Anderson at the *Tribune*. Stressed the exhaustion of those people who could pursue a higher education; actual difficulty of studying in lower-class dwellings.

68. Lana Turner (1921–1995), American actress known as "the sweater girl" for her extraordinary physique.

69. A leading intellectual in the British Labour Party, Harold Laski (1893–1950) wrote Kazin's publisher that the author of *On Native Grounds* was "among the best six critical minds America has had since Emerson."

70. Harold Alexander (1891–1969) was a British general and statesman.

At random: how do these rosy, often strikingly beautiful children, turn into the stiff-backed white-faced adults with their bad teeth, their horrible black spectacles, and that special look of always peering stiffly ahead—?

## March 12, 1945

Cambridge as Brogan's[71] guest at Peterhouse. Brogan's mind is entirely journalistic, tirelessly, full of great knotted cords of historical association. I teased him with being "disinterested" in his historical thinking; I meant cynical. His quickness of mind absolutely amazing: a photo-electric cell with violent, accurate, and perhaps shallow illumination. Felt his impact on me as the impact of an endlessly revolving sky-rocket, and admired the genuineness and force of his culture, but did not feel any human contact with him. A compulsive type; but what is his compulsion? Took me on a flashing tour of the colleges. When I went into King's College Chapel the delicate groined beauty moved me beyond expression. Cambridge is a greyhound, I said once; but the word was nonsense even in the deepest meditation on the English race (I mean the competition, not the people). The lawns, the first crocuses, and the narrow winding river; everyone on bicycles, with their winding college scarves in the wind and babies on papoose perches on the backs of the bicycles. Dinner with the fellows in great state. The master looked like a wizened andiron and to every bright remark from B. flashed a mechanically appreciative smile.

## March 18, 1945

Phantasmagorie de Nuit. Chambermaid told me this morning that she fainted while lying in bed, when she heard rockets close to her. . . . Twice I have been awakened, before daybreak, by most hollow boom in the center of town. . . . Long line in front of shop that had all its windows knocked out—Sunday crowd, or tribute?

## March [nd] 1945

I lifted the receiver this morning to give a number to the operator. Suddenly I heard a deep smashing note. "Oh," the operator said, "My windows have just gone." I asked her if she didn't want to hold off for a minute; said she was used to it.

71. The Cambridge historian Denis Brogan (1900–1974) had written a favorable review of *On Native Grounds* in the *Times Literary Supplement.*

Brig. Sewall—Negroes' minds stop developing after 15. Sheep grazing by the sea. The enclosed fields, like little Chinese walls, meandering up and down the hills and the mountains. The little village of North Harlech.

## April 4, 1945

Listened in at Central Hall, opening session of the National Union of Teachers, and then walked over to the National Gallery for the lunch-time concert. The "Budapest Trio" was uneven, the first violinist very nervous and scratchy, but the occasion itself was more important than the performance. As always I felt surprise and admiration at the rightness of such moments as these Myra Hess has provided—the tight little chairs wedged up against each other; people a half to three-quarters of an hour waiting and ready for the concert, nibbling meanwhile at their sandwiches and out of the ubiquitous little containers (milk, sugar) that they all carry.[72] The "interior court" itself where the concert was held as grimy and empty as all the great houses and museums in London now, but always with that look of a high regal look which the great squares keep. . . . In the evening after dinner the new double-summer time[73] gave us light, and Ruth Hooper and I walked to Waterloo from Park Lane—through Green Park and St. James to Westminster, across the bridge and so onto the border of the East End. Somehow I had become dulled, these last few weeks, to the city; but on this twilight walk I felt as if I were seeing it all for the first time, and by a light that gave what I was seeing a subtle last clarity. Walking through the quiet and leafy park, I felt as if the light had suddenly renewed itself at the end of the day.

## April 6, 1945

Went down this Friday afternoon to the East End. In one section, itself not blitzed, the street is lined on both sides with alley houses so dark, small, and leveled together in a brown anonymous mass that I almost wept on seeing the street itself half-filled, every ten yards, with shelters that took up whatever air and space there may have been before. Tyne Place, Aldgate East—a dirtier, grimier East Side, but all shuttled together by the bombings. . . . The scooped out squares now used as storage tanks; the faint lines of structural supports left.

72. The pianist Myra Hess (1890–1965) persuaded the government to allow her to organize concerts, Monday through Friday, in the National Gallery (stripped of its paintings) for the duration of the war.

73. British Double Summer Time. During the war the British advanced the clock two hours beyond Greenwich Mean Time.

All the bombed buildings are now an arch through which you can see, if not pass; Liverpool Station so murkily beautiful late this afternoon; the roof half away, as in so many London railway and underground stations, and the light fiercely reflecting the hurrying crowds, the tea wagons, and the dirt.

## April 8, 1945

The circle of hymn singers in Hyde Park this Sunday evening. The chapel spirit and release—the ugly, mealy, downtrodden faces and the fresh clear voices—the enthusiasm. O dear Lord, take them up tenderly.

I was deeply impressed by the hymn singers, for never had I seen so clearly the unifying and the liberating effect of a religious act on people who were suddenly made to look human because of it. Hyde Park on a Sunday evening: end of a war. The lean-boned, middle-aged man in the center; the rather pretty little woman in the smart suit and shoes, with a fur jacket over her shoulders for warmth; and all around us the blotched faces of prematurely old, lower-middle-class Englishwomen, singing with such clarity and sweetness, such practiced contrapuntal sense, that it suddenly seemed to me the greatest human proof one could ask for of the rightness of such devotion.

## April 17, 1945

Discussion meeting of Civil Defense group in first-aid station, Walthamstow, London. The best and most humanly impressive discussion group I have yet seen and heard. The evening and morning (I stayed over when the discussion went so late that I could not obtain transportation home) constitute the most satisfying personal experience I have had in England. Chairman, middle-aged volunteer nurse, Mrs. Poultney, who sat at the head in the shed, surrounded by medical equipment, cots, blankets, outlined salient information and possible approaches to problem—Is Gambling Necessary, etc.—and then invited discussion. Middle-class people, shopkeepers, lower specialists-telegraphists, etc.; very intelligent, morally conscious. Station going full blast despite end of danger; formerly twice a day hot water bottles were made ready under blankets for shock cases; now, Mrs. P. said a little apologetically, only once. 24 hours a day duty on, 24 off. *They miss the feeling of danger and being together*. About 200 patients have passed through. One of the doctors a Persian Moslem. Absolute straightness and devotion to duty of these people beyond description and praise. Discussion of America, which I led, centered around education and our "opportunities."—Woman's point of view: it was the dirt brought into the shed by the casualties that they remember most. Night the telephones went and all the lights; they were too busy to be frightened. Hut with inner consecutive rooms, like pictures I remember of shelters for communications at Bataan. The community spirit—stress that gambling might impair the morals "of our nation." Absolutely easy, natural patriotism; real feeling for country. Charming ignorance about A[merica]: *had never heard, when I pronounced it, the word Wisconsin;* but were so eager to learn more that I felt ashamed to tell them so little that was basic and meaningful.

## April 23, 1945

One of the leaders of the national fireman's service said to me tonight in Islington that adult education in England now plays the role that religion once did for the people—an inquiry into the meaning of life. I went down with Mary Zimmern of the Home Office to the station, a regular fire station. The men had been called out four or five times during the day, mostly on false alarms—"malicious" alarms in England—and were still eating when we arrived. I served on the brains-trust with a man called Hewitt, a Cambridge graduate who is preparing to take a doctor's degree soon at London, his chief interest being 17th century tragedy—Webster and Tourneur;[74] and another man—both very good types. The meeting was exceptional, not only brains-trust but a combination of open discussion with remarks from the table. Questions like: should religious education be compelled in the schools? At what age should sex education begin? The firemen, all fairly simple people, but very left. The discussion of Fascism was on a very intelligent level, and everyone agreed that it was shallow and perhaps suicidal to confine our thinking to revenge against the leaders. In the middle of the discussion the alarm rang and in three seconds flat, as it seemed to me, the men were on their wagons rushing out. It was another malicious call, and when they returned we continued the discussion. I felt completely at home with their thinking on international affairs, and admired them very much. Waiting for the bus in the darkness, Hewitt and I talked about Blake.

## May 1, 1945

For more than two months now I have been living at the Billets, and for more than two months now I have met every day a young man of about my age whose name is really Johnnie Smith. He is a kind of assistant porter, and a general

74. John Webster (c. 1580–c. 1634), English playwright, author of *The White Devil* and *The Duchess of Malfi*; Cyril Tourneur, English playwright (1575–1626), author of *The Atheist's Tragedie.*

utility man, and he speaks in very broad cockney. Johnnie has never known that I am a brother to him; that I am as scared as he is; and he always calls me sir. Not sir at the beginning or the end of sentences, but Sir, as a part of speech that serves intermittently for preposition, verb, adjective. Well, sir, yes sir, how do you sir do yes, sir. Sir. He stammers, he is crestfallen, and in his recessive speech is all the plaintiveness of the poor and the frightened. Once, when I was shaving, he called me twice to the phone, and in an irritable mood I spoke crossly to him. His face flushed and he actually fell back before me. How ashamed I felt—not merely because I had been the cause of frightening him, but because of the false relations of man and master that persisted between us. This morning (having since established better relations with him) I at last requested him not to call me sir any longer; explained that it grated on my nerves, was a ridiculous servility, etc. He smiled sheepishly, but with some suspicion, and when I emphasized the point said, stammering a little, But that is how we are trained in England (I transcribe the words; he did not of course actually say it this way). Johnnie Smith is a lesson to me, to *me*, and not about England.

## May 3, 1945

Interview with T. S. Eliot, at his offices (Faber and Faber). Eliot, now, if I calculate correctly, must be 57; face has aged and relaxed greatly, so that one's first impression of him physically is of a rather tired kindness as opposed to the otherworldliness and hauteur of his early pictures. He was extremely kind, gentle, spoke very slowly and hesitatingly, livened up a bit when I pushed the conversation on to literary topics (at first, because of my official business, he spoke a little about popular education and his own experiences teaching for the WEA and LCC). He looks like a very sensitive question mark—long, winding, and bent; gives the impression that his sensibility is in his long, curling nose and astonishing hands. I was so afraid that he would be standoffish or just reluctant that I spoke more than I wanted to, just to keep the conversation going. He said things which just verged on "you Americans," but I grinned when he spoke of Truman and Missouri and he grinned back. When I gave him Spencer's regards, he brightened up considerably and asked me if I was a Harvard man.[75]

75. Benjamin Spencer (1904–1996) was a professor in the Harvard English Department.

## June 27, 1945

The American in Europe. S, a press-agent and newspaper man from the West, went to see the family of his English girlfriend. They know about the romance, and I presume about S's family back home. Talking to me about it this morning, he said: Golly, they're funny people, they're so different from us; they don't care a hang. He was shocked.

On the other hand, Shirley and Larry washing the windows. She's literally young enough to be his daughter.

British "messing through" may have its philosophic roots, but in the ordinary run of affairs it comes from the reluctance of the upper classes to do what the others want, and it comes from a deep conservative unity, shared by all classes. *England is a raging class struggle, but it is also an island*—and it has to a remarkable degree profound class tensions set within the fabric of its unity—a unity deepened in every way by the British *feeling of remoteness* from other countries and superiority to them. The remarkable change-over from coalition unity to the present election atmosphere.

Re-reading *Crime and Punishment* for the first time since I was a boy. How presumptuous it was of me to rely so long on merely a juvenile experience of it. It is Dostoevsky's *Hamlet*, and like *Hamlet* itself, records the crisis of an intellectual who suffers in his own person the war of orders within the state. Razumikhin=Horatio. Dostoevsky loves Raskolnikov. The difference between the two heroes is the difference between a prince who suffers because he is tied to a vision of life that has been destroyed by his father's murder and his mother's marriage and an intellectual who tries to rise *above* life by being a *schismatic*. R's error is intellectual pride—his disease, a willed aggressiveness that rises entirely in deep frustration, the injury he inflicts on others by his need to rise [above] his weakness. Objectively, D reports all this as the sin of heretical and perverse individualism—man has lost his deep inner relationship of faith, and by stepping out of the body of Christ inflicts mortal injury on some member of it. But D. loves Raskolnikov; he uses him to report the full measure of his self-punishment, but for all this, R. in his eyes is still a prince among men=still the noble heart, in Horatio's phrase for Hamlet.

Dramatically, both works deal with *the duplicity of the intelligence in crisis*. Neither Hamlet nor Raskolnikov is mad. They unconsciously impersonate madness to save them from the confrontation of their fears and actions. It is a form of moral escape, a collapse as much *fabricated* as recorded in the mind.

Both men turn away from women! Raskolnikov, in a frenzy of injured pride because he is ashamed of his condition and resentful that Dounia has betrothed herself to a man she dislikes, breaks with her and, in an ecstasy of self-abnegation, joins himself (the murderer to the harlot) to Sonia. [. . .]

## July 10–13, 1945

I was supposed to leave for Paris on the three o'clock plane, but the day was foggy and rainy, and after getting into the plane and circling about a little we went back, and I had to spend the night at Bevingdon Field. At ten the next morning, after some uncertainty, we went off at last: it was my first flight. There was so much mist on the field and beyond that I had no sensation of leaving the ground; suddenly I looked down, and saw that we had ascended, and that was all. The wings purred with power before we went up. My seat just looked over the left wing, and it seemed to me as if all the power of the plane had suddenly and tensely been locked up in the quivering wings.

For a half an hour we flew through a white mist above the clouds; it was all utterly unreal—all I could see was the wing, floating slowly like a bird feather against the white walls of mist. I had no sensation of height, distance, or flight; we were floating. Then I looked down and saw the breakers in the channel. Toy boats were plowing a furrow; there was no land, and for the most part not even the sensation of moving at all.

Then the channel wall, and France. A mosaic of farms: brilliant, red, purple, brown, and gray: squares, crescents, and triangles. Clusters joined by arteries of roads; a wood, a few houses, then a small town, and everywhere, the long winding narrow roads joining men together. At ten o'clock we saw the Seine, then the Eiffel Tower like a watchtower over the city. Orly field is to the NE of the city; as we flew steadily lower, I saw hundreds of orange-red roofs.

Then the bus into Paris, through long suburban avenues of drab shops, warehouses, and fields. We stopped at the ATC office in the Place de Vendome; I went over to George Stevens' office, arranged my affairs and a room at the Astor, and went to look at the city.[76]

76. George Stevens (1904–1975), American film director, a member of the U.S. Army Signal Corps, head of a film unit that documented D-Day and the liberation of Paris.

Paris at the moment reminds me a little of the atmosphere of the World's Fair: there is a nervous holiday mood, the look everywhere of a bazaar. The booths along the avenues, selling trinkets, tickets to the national lottery; amusement games. Everywhere American soldiers; girls in white blouses and gaily colored peasant skirts riding bicycles. The only transportation is by private car and the Metro. The great palaces sporting flags; the enormous show of Crimes Hitleriens at le Grand Palais. The whole show of Nazi atrocities arranged with terrific passion and skill. In one of the main rooms is a large expanded photograph of a corpse found on the ground of a concentration camp, his skeletal arm outstretched like Christ on the Cross. At the door, as you leave, a placard reading:

Tous ces morts
Tous ces martyrs
Vous Disent
Souvenez Vous[77]

Everywhere the signs of the resistance groups; everywhere fresh evidence of the pleasure the French get in pronouncing their own name. Overwhelmingly: la France, les Francais et les Francaises, la résistance, la republique, la patrie. [. . .]

## July 14, 1945

Last night (the 13th) had dinner with Sylvia Wright, Jo Felts, and Armel Guerne and his wife.[78] Guerne is a young leftist who escaped to England during the occupation, was arrested by the English while his wife was in a labor camp run by the Germans near Pilsen. He was extremely bitter at De Gaulle and the present Government, and for all his courtesy, not less bitter at the Americans. He reported that an official of the American military police said that the Americans would intervene in any French revolution and destroy it with flying fortresses. [. . .]

On the surface all the political activity and all the newspapers seem to come from the Resistance, but their function at the moment is still to resist: this time De Gaulle.[79]

77. All these dead/All these martyrs/Say to you/Remember.

78. Sylvia Wright (1917–). Daughter of the utopian novelist Austen Tappan Wright (1883–1931), Sylvia made a powerful impression on Kazin, who would remember her as the "girl I left behind me." Armel Guerne (1911–1980), French poet of the Resistance.

79. The French Resistance refers to those groups of citizens who fought a clandestine war inside the country against the German occupiers and their French collaborators. Charles de Gaulle organized the Free French Forces, consisting of French generals exiled in England during World War II. He later became prime minister and president of France.

Went after 11 to a "veillée des morts pour la liberté [vigil for those who died for freedom]" held at the Arc de Triomphe. Walking in the Champs-Élysées, we met some officers in a jeep and hopped aboard. Behind us was a small group of Resistance and army veterans who were using the jeep to steer their own path to the Arc. It was fun until we got into the great crowd near the Arc itself; and then we realized what a shameful picture we made, riding gaily in an American jeep to a ceremony and got off. Nothing illustrated so perfectly the present position of the Americans in Paris.

The ceremony itself was overwhelming as a rite and as a meeting. The Champs was massed with people along both sides. The largest flag I have ever seen, a tricolor draped on one side in black, hung in the center of the Arc; before it, like the fires at a pagan sacrifice, were red, smoky lights. All down the avenue loud speakers hung along trees bellowed, with terrifying intimacy, the words: patrie, resistance, à c'est a vous reconstruire la France [homeland, resistance, it is for you to rebuild France]. Soldiers and their girls move along munching ice-cream or petting in the privacy of the crowd. The topmost height of the Arc was lit up in a pearly white, reflecting the names of Napoleon's great victories. The flag was the center of all, however; it seemed to me that we were all worshiping the flag, that it had become a kind of idol at that moment, and that all the lights that bathed it, the speeches that attended it, the watchful and noncommittal crowds who stood uneasily before its fascination, were the accompaniments of an old ceremony. [. . .]

Politically, we are all a little mad these days, for no matter how clearly and knowledgeably we may think, our thoughts and our possibility of action have no relation to each other. But there is the trivial madness, among thoughtful people, that is the stagnancy of powerlessness. Among those whose participation in events is roughly equal to their ignorance of their meaning, politics is an exploitation of personal incoherence and weakness. Viz. the spectacled army bookkeeper I met yesterday: his only approach to Germany was that he wanted to get up in a plane over it and piss on it. Or Elliott Hagle, the young infantryman, who is boxed up, living drunkenly on commercial and sexual orgies (le marchand noir in goods and sex), and who says that he just *hates* the Germans.

It is not that I have a solution; my own belief in humanist-socialism is only a private ideal; it has no actual political meaning at the moment. But ideals are psychological goals, necessary to the health of the mind; they symbolize a belief in the broad life process and testify to our links with our inheritance and our interest in the future. These hard-boiled petty cynics have no life in them at all, no awareness of the relations between men, and between men and society. They are sleepwalkers telling time by physical sensations.

## July 20, 1945

At eleven at night the air in the streets seems to have turned blue, and the bronze horses on the bridges are golden.

It is now almost a law: the intellectuals instinctively resent the public expressions of their innermost thoughts. And they are most sure to dislike most of those works, like Silone's *Seed Beneath the Snow* and Koestler's *The Yogi and the Commissar*,[80] that are palpable realizations of their innermost thoughts, for in them they realize that these works are not founded on anything except a wish similar to theirs.

The greater freedom of discussion of Russia in France than in England.

80. *The Seed Beneath the* Snow, a 1942 novel by Ignazio Silone (pseudonym of Secondino Tranquilli, 1900–1978) depicting the efforts of Pietro, a Christian and Socialist, to aid the peasantry in the Abruzzi region of Italy; *The Yogi and the Commissar*, the 1945 lead essay in a collection by Arthur Koestler (1905–1983) indicating the choice open to modern man between the radical transformation of society and the mystical acceptance of the world as is.

# 3
# A New Time
## 1945–1950

"IS IT GOING TO BE A NEW TIME—IS IT really going to be a new time?" Kazin asked himself some months after returning from England after war. "How wonderful it would be not to look back anymore, not to have the familiar, stabbing regrets about Asya" (March 22, 1946). It would be a new time. In his last weeks in England, he had met Caroline Bookman, a New Yorker working in London who had returned with him on the Queen Mary. When he learned that Natasha was unwilling to patch up relations, he began seeing Carol regularly. The daughter of Judith Wertheim Bookman and Dr. Arthur Bookman, Carol came from a line of wealthy, assimilated German Jews, very different from Alfred's family in "darkest Brownsville." Despite their different backgrounds, the relationship flourished; and in May of 1947 they married, each for the second time. They spent an extended honeymoon (May–December) in Italy, where Kazin luxuriated in the beauty of the Italian setting. "I felt as if my whole being were re-dedicating itself" (June 28, 1947). In July, Kazin left Italy for Austria and a six-week stint at the Salzburg Seminar. Organized to familiarize young Europeans with American culture and institutions, the seminar brought together students from seventeen countries for lectures and discussions with notable American academics and thinkers. Kazin and Harvard Professor F. O. Matthiessen taught American literature in a series of lectures that the anthropologist Margaret Mead remembered as the greatest moments of the seminar.

When the Kazins returned to New York in January 1948, Carol was three months pregnant and Alfred uncertain about how he was to support his young family. He signed up to teach courses in the fall and winter at the New School (where he would have Jack Kerouac as a student); took a position as an editorial scout for Harcourt Brace, and wrote reviews—for the *New York Times,* the *Herald Tribune,* and the *New Yorker.* He appeared on the radio program *Invitation to Learning* to discuss writers and literary works with other critics and scholars. Initially worried about a return of his stammer, he discovered that he could hold his own with the experts on radio and later on television. "God, how I can bathe in cultural perceptions, in sheer play of critical point and critical wit" (June 17, 1963). But his primary concern at the time was a book he had begun while working on a 1946 piece about the Brooklyn Bridge with the photographer Henri Cartier-Bresson. Writing about the neighborhoods touched by the bridge, he envisioned a longer meditation prompted by walks in various districts of the city. It would be a "personal journal," he wrote in a January 3, 1949, letter to Van Wyck Brooks, "based on the inner world of a man walking in the streets," a "spiritual autobiography" describing "one man's relations to certain problems, memories, institutions that pressed on his consciousness walking about New York." He hoped to draw on resources very different from those that went into his first book that he believed engaged "only a quarter of my mind." But uncovering new resources proved frustrating—"I have gone through all the possible hells of confusion and conflict," he complained after a discouraging day at his desk "—on the one hand recognizing how deeply necessary the book is to me; on the other hand trying to escape it" (August 14, 1948). In the end he found his way—partly by shifting its focus from different New York neighborhoods to his experiences growing up in Jewish Brownsville. When *A Walker in the City* appeared in 1952, it was hailed by reviewers as an achievement as impressive in its way as *On Native Grounds,* though it was purchased (the journal entries make painfully clear) at considerable cost to its author—and to his second marriage.

While Kazin's personal life and creative efforts are the dominant concerns in the journal of the immediate postwar years, evolving political conditions are never far out of mind. Like most Americans, Kazin had hoped the end of the war would usher in "a new time" politically. But following Russia's refusal to leave Poland and the Baltics, Churchill's "iron curtain" speech, and the 1947 announcement of the Truman Doctrine, it was clear the country was headed into a new kind of geopolitical struggle. Alarmed by Soviet behavior, Kazin was also unhappy with the response of Americans, particularly American intellectuals intent on turning anti-Stalinism into an all consuming moral-political philosophy. "Opposed both to Communism and 'anti-Communism,'" he wrote in a November 9, 1948, letter to Matthiessen, and unwilling to abandon his socialist hopes, he looked for "a third-camp" that rejected the injustices of capitalism and the belligerence of both the East and the West. He also looked to his new friend Hannah Arendt—"I'm a sucker for this kind of advanced European mind" (*Lifetime,* 109)—who grasped the seriousness of present conditions without yielding to the fashionable pessimism and "'guilty' apocalyptic morality" (December 10, 1945) that he saw seeping into the thinking of onetime radicals since the war. And he looked to his journal. There, "against all policies of the lesser evil, in one's life as in one's politics; against pessimism glossed as social interpretation," he could remind himself daily of the need to keep faith with his literary goals and his increasingly threatened political ideals (April 2, 1947).

## December 10, 1945

Themes of the real history of our time.
Struggle for integration of the self.
The psychologism of sex. Infusion of journalism.
The petty release of verbal aggressiveness.
The "guilty" apocalyptic morality. Falsification-theatricalization of style. [. . .]

## March 22, 1946
### [Pineapple Street, Brooklyn Heights]

Finished the final draft of the Blake introduction this afternoon. No longer know whether it is good or not, have worked too long at it and Blake *had* become too important. But it is finished, and I can now turn to fresh and less morbid work. Walked across the bridge, bought a musette bag for walking trip and hiked back. Very tired all this afternoon but happy, surprised, and peaceful. Sitting in my rocker and looking at the roofs and chimney pots, I suddenly realized how long I have been living by my will—an earnest apprentice to a new life, so dogged upon his lesson that I have forgotten how to laugh.

Is it going to be a new time—is it really going to be a new time? How wonderful it would be not to look back anymore, not to have the familiar, stabbing regrets about Asya—I have worked so hard these last few months and have been so grimly conscious of the need simply *to break in a new way of life* that it was only this afternoon, as I say, that I felt how long it has been since I laughed simply—how long since I felt a certain mild and accustomed state of well-being, *of being simply in tune* with my *surroundings.*

The straw-hat on the man in the Stieglitz[1] picture before me nods his head gravely in meditation before a new world.

Early spring dusk—a hush in the Saturday street. Reading Elizabeth Bowen's Ivy Stories[2] this afternoon made me think of the hush of the London streets. What a waste I made of those months. But I know I shall have them again—at flood-tide, no longer in retreat.

A star blew out in the sky.

## August 3, 1946

Down with pathos! It is not sincere unless it is tragedy, and if it is tragedy it is not pathos.

1. Alfred Stieglitz (1864–1946), American photographer, used his art galleries in New York to promote the art of photography and the modernist art movement. Kazin chose one of his photographs, *The Steerage*, for the frontispiece of *A Walker in the City*.
2. *Ivy Gripped the Steps and Other Stories* (New York: Knopf, 1946).

## August [nd] 1946

I went back to Highland Park in the rain, looking for the Chinese cemetery.[3] In the old days, when you could get into the park only by climbing the three soft mounds that led into the park from the boulevard like a back yard, and long before they put down gravel walks and a dozen tennis courts and emptied the old reservoir of its green, unused waters, there were half a dozen stones there: odd little blocks, resting on the earth like three-cornered paper hats, marked in hieroglyphs. I remember Sam Z[isowitz][4] and I looking at them once, after hours walking around the reservoir, reading my essays aloud. It then began to rain. It must have been the memory of the rain that brought me back in another rain.

In the old days the Chinese cemetery—so far as I can remember it now at all—was somewhere off in a corner of the main cemetery, full of great cold stones commemorating the burghers of Bushwick. And the road to the cemetery led in from the outside track of the park. In those days it was not really a park: more like a reservation or a half-tamed swamp. I remember always the wildness of its desertion; as if the city had built itself around it, and had forgotten—just forgotten, not in contempt—to include it.

You came into the park through strange huddled little streets, full of garages and little frame houses in which there was never any light. Whenever Nancy and I went to and from the park we stopped in the corner of the street, so indistinguishable in its human emptiness from the park itself, and embraced there. There was one lamppost at the end of the street, now really part of the park itself. Sometimes it was illuminated; most often it was dark itself. We would walk down that street, past the lamppost and into the park.

The entrance through the hills. We would walk along the boulevard, on our way from the library, and climb the hills and walk along the mounds, creaking on old boardwalks as we went. Once, I remember, we went on an evening just after I had had a tooth pulled. My mouth kept flushing a little blood—when I kissed her on the hill, I said in embarrassment: can you taste my mouth full of blood?

3. In this entry Kazin recalls images and experiences that would appear in *A Walker in the City*.
4. See Chapter 1, note 55.

## August 12, 1946

[. . .] When I look back at these notes from time to time, it seems to me that their main burden is passive suffering, complaint, and yearning. I feel ashamed—not because I have suffered or revealed my suffering, but because I have not sufficiently defined my suffering, or been sufficiently generous, loving, and therefore challenging toward it. The task is to *use* our suffering and to use it so well that we can use it up.

In reading [Edmund] Wilson one is conscious of his disproportionate effort at lucidity—as if it were the painful resolution of ideas into some harmonious-appearing sentence structure, rather than the functional balance between form and content, *passion*, that is wanted. So great is his inward struggle for lucidity, and his necessary struggle for form, that he reminds me of a man in a rut who jolts against a fence every time he attempts a fresh step.

Yet it is in this struggle for lucidity that W's value is gained. He gives us as readers too the sense that we have been reading the summary account and plausible conclusions of a long and complex train of thought.

## October 2, 1946

The uses of simplicity. Gide's *Journal*[5] a great example of a writer gathering together all his resources and achieving heresy by his simplicity.

## October 3, 1946

Strange to lie in bed this morning, meditating on a discussion I had had in a dream with Trilling,[6] and to realize how real is the relationship I have with writers I have rarely or never met. There are writers in the past with whom I have love affairs, estrangements, quarrels, that in intensity of pleasure and sorrow exceed anything I have had with people. My affair with Blake was really becoming a scandal. Milton is an old uncle, stern and reproachful, whom I am always slightly afraid to meet. In the present I have intricate entanglements with writers whom it always shocks me slightly to meet—so real have their thoughts been to me, and so pressing the amount of agreement, instruction and

5. Andre Gide (1869–1951), French novelist and autobiographer, winner of the 1947 Nobel Prize in literature. Kazin would review his *Journal* in the *New Yorker*.
6. Lionel Trilling (1905–1975), prominent postwar literary critic and Columbia professor, who Kazin believed prevented his obtaining a position in the Columbia English Department.

divergence, that their personalities always come in the moment of meeting, like a banal anti-climax. "J'ai vecu en lisant" [I have lived in reading], said Gibbon.[7]

## October 7, 1946

From today on I shall try to write something in this notebook every day as a discipline in reasonableness. I have devoted so much time and thought to the analysis that I see now that I have come to assume that talking to Rioch three times a week would take care of my confessional needs. But Rioch's business is to take care of my irrationality; I can only lead up to the point with her of saying what it is I want to affirm and how I wish to live. The definitions and the constructions belong here.

Went down to Columbia early this morning to ask Campbell for a part-time job.[8] He seemed to think it very likely. My first thought was a kind of surprise at his welcoming me so cordially as he did. He's a bright-faced twinkling little man whose whole kindness is in his eyes, rather than in his face or manner. He was a little abrupt; I was glad, business being sketched out, to get away. My second thought was again surprise at myself to realize how much having one foot on a campus, being nearer people, could warm me all through suddenly and penetrate the dryness and paltriness into which my loneliness thrusts me. Yet why should I be ashamed to declare openly to myself that I cannot live entirely alone as I do? That for me it is always unnatural and debilitating? I can never write by force, and when I get unbearably conscious of my solitude, writing becomes either mawkish or impossible—the same thing for me. As it is now, I am writing 1/10th of what I could; and the writing is always accompanied by a wasting and over-deliberate quality. When I feel in with people, my mind suddenly takes wings—the dry twigs of insight suddenly become tender and growing, and new seeds drop into my thought all the time. [. . .]

## October 11, 1946

Style from one point of view is the socket in which the bones of a man's thought move. From another it is always a secret thought, the surface that is

7. Edward Gibbon (1737–1794), English historian, author of *The History of the Decline and Fall of the Roman Empire.* Kazin wrote his Columbia M.A. thesis in history on Gibbon's literary criticism.

8. Oscar J. Campbell (1879–1970), professor in Columbia's English Department. Columbia did not hire Kazin then or in the future.

the silent content. Reading one of Genet's[9] coldly brilliant articles from Paris in the *New Yorker* today, I was struck by the intention of her style—which is plainly to show a curtain of indifference. The words, as words, sentences and ideas, convey her inner motivation not less than the outward quality of the style—its chic, its cold and formal symmetry of movement. I would suspect that the greater part of her effort as a writer goes into the lacquering of her surface—producing the suggestive simplicity of an expensive dress. The clue is indifference: the writer is describing the agony of the "peace," the slow erosion of so many hopes, the deadlock between East and West. Yet she must assemble these things in such a way that a distance, at once cool and familiar, will appear between her and her material. One sees this especially in the lines of her prose—adroit, of a coldly regular movement, and with a certain clickety-clack.

Indifference in writing is poisonous; "emotionality" is self-destructive. True style is that which raises one's most serious and most dramatic thoughts to a new level. Style is the face of the speaker, when he speaks well; the face blends with the words to give us a human image. False style—*Time* and the *New Yorker* are together on this—is fundamentally the division in personality, and therefore in intention. It is half-writing.

## November 20, 1946

[. . .] Process and value: realism and the moralists. After I came home last night from Yaddo and had unpacked my things, I read the current number of *Politics* and felt again how attractive and yet sterile this pure approach by "values," absolute values, is. For the inner thread of Macdonald's position is its relevance on abstention and perpetual alienation. It assumes that its criticism is useless, that there are two objects in the world—that which is outside and institutional and is bad and that which is subjective, moral, and hopeless.[10]

What I object to in Macdonald's position is not that it is "impractical," but that it is self-righteous to the point where it identifies *all* power with evil and its own powerlessness with good. Someone else would say—he doesn't compromise sufficiently; he's not "realistic." Thank God! We are dying of "realism," and can live only by vision. No—What is wrong with Macdonald is that he does not distinguish between opposition to the established culture,

9. Genet, pen name for Janet Flanner (1892–1978), Paris correspondent for the *New Yorker*.
10. Dwight Macdonald (1906–1982) founded, published, and edited *Politics* (1944–1949).

which is good, and the *ceremony* of alienation, which is a self-protective neurotic device.

The immediate consequences of political and moral avant-gardism in the present moment of world agony is exaggerated sensibility, recklessness, lack of that particular application of the truth in which real vision, or continuous creative attitude, consists.

There is a meaning which we must not *defy;* lyricism is not the whole of poetry, and truth does not lie merely in defiance of the bad, but in continuous disclosure of its roots in the nature of society and of man.

## November 22, 1946

O city girl, stripped for action at 5 in the winter dusk—colored glasses, skirt hoisted to the maximum possible point at the garter line, black bag dragging from the shoulder like a doctor's or a soldier's baggage, mouth a thick ocean of wet lipstick—

O city girl, wandering so determinedly down the street, where are you going so fast, so fast? O, where are you going? Breasts rippling in your blouse like silent cries. Your handkerchief in the wind like a flag; your face framed in glasses and lipstick and mascara that are not your own, only bars between which your true soul appears, legs it does not matter how ugly, for they glisten in the winter with nylon sex, o where are you going, or where? [. . .]

To Charles Olson, to Dahlberg[11] and all other such Melvillians, who, taking fire from their master, know not what to do with it and burn themselves with it—: Apocalyptic is a *means,* not an end. It is a tunnel, not an altar!

## November 24, 1946

In every artist there is a magician and a scientist—a man who attempts to charm nature and a man who seeks patiently and by knowledge to control it; one who seeks to defy and one to transform.

## November 26, 1946

The weather has been sickeningly warm these last few days. Coming out of Isaac [Rosenfeld]'s house tonight, where we had been talking with a young merchant

11. Charles Olson (1910–1970), American poet, allegedly coined the term "postmodern" in a 1949 letter to the poet Robert Creeley (1925–2005). Olson's first book, *Call Me Ishmael* (1947), was a study of *Moby-Dick.* Edward Dahlberg (1900–1977), novelist and essayist, was an early Melville enthusiast who later regretted his enthusiasm.

seaman named Harry Hershkowitz, a curious and almost mystical person, we stood on Barrow Street talking of the weather. Suddenly the talk took on a note of fantasy—obviously, Isaac said, atom bombs were being shot off somewhere, and there was a vast decomposition taking place in the solar structure. We were drawing nearer the sun, and were going to dry up, etc., etc. . . . What interests me in this is the renewed awareness of how large a part the bomb plays in all our thinking these days. It is a particularly warm day—somewhere, in the fear of our days, it becomes the natural thing to say that the bomb is working on us—that bomb which like a leukemia, a cancer of the blood, a blight slowly eating away in the unconscious, swims so obscurely and menacingly in our thoughts. I take this as another sign of the reign of fear under which we live nowadays: fear whose content is the feeling of absolute loss of control. We live, study, eat, love, write; life goes on; how else can we believe but that it does, that it must? Yet here is the phantom that pursues us now and day, not because it is so terrible a bomb, but because it is so peculiarly uncontrolled a force, and has so many links with that nature which we can manipulate so cruelly, till living we erode ourselves into its first victim.

What this evening brought to my mind above all was the atmosphere of soothsayers, portents and signs; as in that scene in Shakespeare's *Julius Caesar,* before the assassination of the tyrant, when a dream is described of trees being torn up from their roots and of great storms in the streets, of blood running through them.

Robert Lowell: the triumph of talent over confusion.[12]
Hannah Arendt, Henri Cartier-Bresson, Carrado Cagli, Paolo Milano[13]

## December 5, 1946

Went out with Henri[14] to take pictures of Brownsville, and walked about most of the morning and early afternoon in the cold. I hadn't been in the Negro section

12. The poet Robert ["Cal"] Lowell (1917–1977) was a friend of Kazin's.
13. Hannah Arendt (1906–1975), prominent writer and political philosopher, refugee from Hitler's Germany, best known for *The Origins of Totalitarianism* (1951) and the controversial *Eichmann in Jerusalem: A Report on the Banality of Evil* (1963); Henri Cartier-Bresson (1908–2004), French photographer; Carrado Cagli (1910–1976), Italian painter, who moved to the United States during World War II; Paolo Milano (see Chapter 2, note 35), Italian literary critic and professor, lived in New York during World War II. Kazin felt privileged to know and befriend European writers and artists who moved to or visited the United States. "I'm a sucker for this kind of advanced European mind" (*Lifetime*, 109).
14. Kazin and Cartier-Bresson collaborated on a *Harper's* article on the Brooklyn Bridge (September 1946), prompting Kazin to make plans for *A Walker in the City*. He was unable to persuade the photographer to collaborate on the book.

for years, and was horrified by the emptiness of the faces, the drunkenness, the kids playing in the dirt, the rubble yards. Henri stopped to snap some cute little Negro kids, and a woman came rushing out from the yard—a demented face, eyes rolling in her head like a violently beating heart, screaming at us that she knew what we were doing, all right, couldn't fool her, etc. Are these your kids, I asked? Yes, she said. Is your husband around? I'm married to everybody, she said, and grinned. . . . What tableaux in the empty afternoon air, with the winter sun proving the cruel emptiness of the street—a Negro man, about fifty, who sat in front of his house, just staring ahead; a pregnant woman, drunk with an Empress Eugenie hat, feathers and all, perched on her head; a man with a wooden leg, a leg like Long John Silver's.

When I walk with Cartier-Bresson, I take his kind of picture in my mind.

## December 10, 1946

Every time I go home to Brownsville, or even to Ben's[15] on Crown Street, it is as if I were entering a foreign country where the people *look* like the inhabitants of the country where I am living but have stubbornly, slyly kept some rich difference in their speech. Under the plastic aprons, the chromium features, the Yankee dresses and suits, an unchanging, deeply resistant Jewish life goes on—but a life not really "Jewish," but half and half in everything. It is this mixture, coarse, opportunistic, exuberant, that makes the real quality of the immigrant life and gives it its funny as well as vulgar qualities—the humor being sometimes a kind of vulgarity, a kind of surprise and overreaching through the surprise, as who should say—"Look! We made it!" and sometimes being honest self-commentary. . . . In fact, Jews know themselves better than one might sometimes think they do. They parody their lives secretly. They know the effect they have on others, and persist not only because they can't help it, but because they also enjoy it.

## December 11, 1946

A human being like a bell, telling its health by the fullness and depth of the tones.

## February 17, 1947

[. . .] I feel the reaction in America creeping around me like the blast of a cold wind.

15. A friend of Kazin's, Benjamin Seligman would become a noted labor historian.

## February 27, 1947

Worked most of the early day on the Blake lecture. In the afternoon went to a party given by Houghton Mifflin for Henry Wallace, which was the strangest collection of big shots and literary cocktailers. John Winant,[16] one of the most extraordinary faces I have ever seen. It is the face of one of the dark British Celts. His shyness and nobility fantastic in a politician. Characteristic useless talk with Bliven, who would at least be a man if he weren't so fearful and fatuous. Struck again by the characteristic pessimistic flightiness of him, which contrasts so amusingly with his public, progressive, pragmatic optimism. Full of airy, cynical talk about American[s] being children, etc. He spoke to me about his childhood in Iowa, and with eyes suddenly grown soft and near to tears told me that hunger was always a living threat, though his people were farmers. . . . The Rococco of the Ritz-Carlton, American plush hotel, stripped with gaudiness. . . . Blake lecture went off pretty well; there were moments when I almost enjoyed it.[17] My father in the audience, awkward and pleased. We had coffee together afterwards, and then, two amiable acquaintances, went to the subway. Always it is I [who] feel like the father, and he is my oldest boy. Always deeply touched by his faith and pride in me, the *naches.*[18]

Extremely stupid article by [Harold] Laski in the *Nation,*[19] explaining the mystery of Russia by pointing on the one hand and yet on the other. Interesting trend: the attempt to portray Stalin as someone different from the Stalinist politbureau and bureaucracy. Poor Joe, who does not know what is happening around him!

## March 6, 1947

Wrote until 4 to finish the "Mrs. Solovey" section.[20] After years of trying to write her story, it startled me to realize that I had done it at last. Feel an increasing confidence in the book, though am troubled by the sparseness of the entries in Part I. The whole book needs baking in after I have finished the first draft. Walked across the Bridge. Every day the harbor looks different, yet every day it is the same. Picked Carol up at the office and had a drink with her, then went home and read and wrote letters till after midnight. A gleeful holiday feeling this morning now as

16. See Chapter 2, note 62.
17. Kazin delivered a series of lectures at the John L. Elliot Institute for Adult Education.
18. Yiddish: the joy Jewish parents derive from their children's success.
19. "Why Does Russia Act That Way?" *Nation* (March 1, 1947): 239–242.
20. A section in *A Walker in the City*.

I write. My mind is full of memories, like ballet music, of that happy last year in high school, 1931. Memories aroused by my exploration backward and inward for the book, taking off a lot of dead skin. Well, even if the book does not come off as it should, I have been enjoying a wonderful creative experience again. [. . .]

## March 7, 1947

[. . .] I have a dream of an infinite walk—of going on and on, forever unimpeded by weariness or duties somewhere else, until the movement of my body as I walk becomes the shadow of the world as it turns on its axis, until I in my body and the world in its skin of earth are somehow blended in a single motion. [. . .]

## March 16, 1947

Discussing the case of Richard Wright,[21] Paolo countered my complaint that his mind had little penetration by saying—a writer's intelligence consists in fidelity to his own experience. This seems to me an immense truth, and one susceptible of subtle interpretations. Viz.—fidelity to one's own experience is the most difficult, not the easiest, thing for a writer to practice—for it necessitates a real understanding and acceptance of one's own singularity, one's special fate—an ability to separate what we learn from others from the temptation to hide ourselves under the mask of others.

Lovely afternoon at the Bronx Zoo; absolutely entranced by the beauty of the lion, so full of gravity and intelligence and a kind of weary forbearance of his own captivity.

The moving story of Paolo's cousin, Enzo Sereni, who as an Italian Jew went to Palestine in the middle twenties and became a leader in the Labor federation, Histadruth. When the Nazi massacres began he deliberately went back to Europe to be with his people and was parachuted by the British, caught and imprisoned as an Italian partisan. A Polish Jew in the cell was complaining about his lot, his inability to fulfill his religious duties, etc.; and E.S. in comforting him divulged his real identity and was killed like the rest. The most remarkable item in the story somehow seemed to me this: that the night before he was sent down behind the Nazi lines, he explained to a Zionist comrade why he believed in the immortality of the soul.

21. Richard Wright (1908–1960), American writer of African-American descent, author of the 1940 canonical novel *Native Son*.

## April 2, 1947

Why one keeps a journal. Essentially, because I am a writer and want to develop my thoughts for future use. Even the most casual and banal observations about one's daily life have some purpose in developing one's sense of observation. But perhaps I keep a journal, irregularly as I keep it, because one wants a record of the days that die so forgotten. Deep in this is the old struggle with death—something far more real and continuous than the fear of death, which like all fear is occasional, whereas the struggle is unremitting and is lost only when the other antagonist wins. Nothing seems so important to us as our own life. It is pitiful to think of the waste of so many days. At least, then, let us try to make a record of what has gone by. Not to save what is unsavable, but to define what is peculiarly mine.

The never-ending problem of faithfulness, which can never be really solved, but which every day presents afresh. How to live and speak and write and feel in accordance with one's own sense of the truth. How to recognize one's own errors and exaggerations and deficiencies without yielding to the temptation to be "like the others." To see in oneself so great a portion of existence, simply because one is A. K. and not three thousand million other people, that one plants a standard thereby. To recognize that there is more richness and joy in the faithfulness to one's own idiosyncratic universe than in losing oneself for a fictitious superiority. To see that "absolute frankness is the only originality." And the absoluteness of the frankness is the absoluteness of self-acceptance, which accepts not the self that I am in the world, but the whole interior world which is me.

Not to be afraid because the world seems more and more divided between Moscow and New York, and because in the world they bray that you must believe this and not the other. Not to be taken in by the "realists," who are only people with a deadline psychosis and very little to say. Not to surrender to life construed only as politics. Life does not end because there are bad and hopeless days; life will survive even this totalitarian ice age. Always and always to hold out for cardinal values, and to live by them, whatever "they" say, whoever "they" are at the moment. Against all policies of the lesser evil, in one's life as in one's politics; against all pessimism glossed as social interpretation; against all theories which begin by fitting our human universe to their iron measure.

## April 8, 1947

The hot, stale, always faintly not-clean atmosphere of Isaac's house. The babies were crying; the windows so tightly closed I could barely breathe. Yet he sat there, telling me the plot of a new story, with such enthusiasm and wisdom in the planning, that I realized over again how remarkable he is, though the effect is often curiously barren. Without any great knowledge of life, provincial as a mouse, he has yet managed, while having to retreat entirely into himself, a whole imaginative life based on general principles. His mind speculative, abstract, not at all the mind of an artist, but rather rabbinical, playing fiction as the Israelite sages played cosmology. [. . .]

## April 13, 1947

[. . .] Interesting to compare the journals of Thoreau and Gide. One is a record of solitude seeking an environment, both in nature and in literature, that will allow him the freedom to make his life exactly as he likes without his having to change his moral opinions. The other is the record of solitude seeking legitimacy for its own feeling of strangeness. Thoreau finds his "objective correlative" in morality and independence; Gide in the manners of human thought, conceived as an expression of man's own nature. To both the real work of their lives is keeping a journal, for both suffer from that radical solitariness and tentative vanity that compels certain writers to keep journals.

Their differences in style so great as to be amusing. Thoreau naturally likes to exalt everything—he is not plain at all, except to himself, and *that* is why he likes to appear grand. Gide's style a masterpiece of economy, nuance, truth in rendering his sense of reality.

## May 23, 1947

Married Caroline Bookman this day.

## June 5, 1947
### [On board the Polish ship *Sobieski*, bound for Genoa]

My 32nd birthday. Utter feeling of unreality. Hard to believe that I am already *32*—hard to believe that I am married, going to Europe—and that I am not alone anymore. The contrast with other birthdays these last years very sharp. [. . .]

## June 15, 1947
### [Florence]

Meeting in the Piazza della Signoria in the morning under auspices of pro-Communist Socialists to hear Nenni—who said very little. Afternoon going around Berenson's villa near Florence under guidance of Leo Stein—who turned out to be a charmingly irreducible American of some seventy summers, less interested in art than one would assume, and chiefly preoccupied with the problem of lying and psychoanalyzing himself.[22] I liked him very much, but found it hard to establish contact with him because of his deafness. The Berenson villa itself very beautiful, very stagey—some excellent pictures and a magnificent library, but the whole house so carefully imagined and decored in every particular as to be deadly static: the last word in connoisseurship as a personal principle, but not enough to raise connoisseurship to a creative level.

Wonderful story, somewhere in Berenson, the Lithuanian Jew settled in Florence—and in Leo Stein, the Pittsburgh Jew. L.S.'s one remark about his famous sister Gertrude, and said with a certain resentment—"she always took herself for granted, I never could."

## June 16, 1947

Wonderful drive with Raimy Alexander[23] from Florence to Rome—a whole day full of sun, of olive trees with their silvery glint in the sun, and of the Italian countryside, eating cherries and singing as we rode past. Lunch in Siena opposite the *Palazzo*. Rome rather depressing in the evening—

Very important for me to yield myself at this point—not to be so prudent and so everlastingly careful. This is, in its smallest and most trivial ugliness and defects, a very great portion of human experience new to me. I must give myself to it more—not worry about the unfinished book, the unplanned life, the unplanned days. Like all neurotics, I am an incurable bourgeois—amazingly modern feeling of Rome. [. . .]

## June 28, 1947

Early morning bus to Assisi. I was ill with cramps all the way, and wedged into a tight seat where I could barely move my knees. It is harder to be ill in Italy than

22. Pietro Nenni (1891–1980), Italian socialist and senator; Bernard Berenson (1865–1959), American art historian, made his fortune authenticating paintings from the Italian Renaissance for collectors and museums; Leo Stein (1872–1947), American art collector and critic, brother of the writer Gertrude Stein (1874–1946). Kazin had been asked by the editors of *Partisan Review* to report on the political situation in Italy, where it was feared the Communists would come to power in the first postwar European election. See "From an Italian Journal," *Partisan Review* (November–December, 1948): 550–557.

23. Ramy Alexander, a mutual friend of Kazin and Paolo Milano.

anywhere I have ever been—on every side the world is so incomparably beautiful and green, and the sun shines with such evenness on everything in sight that you feel ashamed to be locked up in a complaining body. I am so enchanted by Italy and feel so *inferior* to it, so lacking in the grace I see all around me. We got off in the valley and went up the hill to Assisi into a beautiful little hotel, up into a room full of sun which looks out on the valley. I stared; I could not believe it; I kept staring. Cecchi[24] said to me the other day that he had the same feeling in Assisi that he had had in Olympus, that something great had happened here. And, he added, he did not particularly admire St. Francis. Walking the two long streets that lead upwards to the main square, past the houses in which flower pots are hung in rings on the walls, where at every interval the valley reappears, I felt so awed by the beauty, the silence, the earth-colored stone, the incomparable peace which seems to lie in the curve of the hills and the passive, majestic spires of the churches, that I felt as if my whole being were re-dedicating itself. There are many crucial experiences I have had in my life that I expected, in some way or other. But nothing prepared me for Assisi, and as I walk here I cannot suppress a sense that this is not real. As it is not, in terms of the civilization I have known and the kind of person I have always been. I mean here specifically not so much a lack of understanding in myself as a lack of harmony. In Assisi all is harmony: there is nothing but the silent fulfillment of a spiritual ideal. The secret of its beauty, I am convinced, is that it is itself a church—a twelfth century Italian church in which the flowing, rocky upwardness of the streets directs the ascent of the eye and the heart, and from which the world is seen *below*—it is beautiful, the valley is an elaborate abstraction in all the Mediterranean shades of green, but it is *below*. I feel in Assisi, as in a church, the controlling and expansive power of a great conception; something past but not dead. There is a design here that is more than the form filled out by a city built on a hill; the design molded the city, not the other way around. The details of stone, streets, and houses are not *capricious*. [. . .]

## July 30, 1947

Now here [in Salzburg] a little more than two weeks—a very busy period for me, full of study and lecturing, and new people, that made it difficult to write in this journal. [. . .] Vividly see before me the cabbage plot surrounded by barbed wire; the erosion of the rock on Mount Untersberg. Perfect unreality of much of Austrian life at this moment, cooped up with a "seminar in American

24. Emilio Cecchi (1884–1966) was a well known critic of English, American, and Italian literature.

civilization." Subtle strains of life with F.O.M. [Francis Otto Matthiessen], a lovely, little, gentle scholar-man with more rivalry to me than I would have expected, full of odd little strokes of malice. A man I like, or *could* like very much, if he would let me, let himself. Not original, intellectually a good deal of a pious prissy, but careful and orderly in many of his processes—essentially a teacher, and a very good one.

## August 13, 1947

[. . .] Went to the DP [displaced persons] camp with V and Carl Kaysen[25]—oh misery, oh Jewish brothers. We climbed over the fence of the DP camp; I climbed back into East Europe, and we Americanos gave out our chocolate bars and bobby pins and razor blades and listened sympathetically to a 28-year-old woman, looking anywhere older than that, telling again the old incredible story of the war. Odd touch about the camp, which must at one time have been run by the British Army, or some colonial derivation thereof—one hut named after Jan Christian Smuts,[26] of all pompous, racist bastards; another after his moronic majesty the sixth George of England. It was not my old friend Herskowitz, the camp policeman, or his wife (his brother's widow) that drew us most; but a woman of perhaps 45, not at all "Jewish" looking, stiff and proud in a black dress—faintly mottled skin, thin mouth—very strong type. Nu, she said to me, smiling at my own *Yiddisher ponim* [Jewish face]—how do you like the way we live here? Twenty four of them in a room the size of my bedroom here, just a little larger. A concentration camp of a room, wooden slats—dirty, unkempt food in pails or sizzling on little burners. Copies of Yiddish newspapers from N.Y. (packages from the relatives?) all around; sick people; ten children or so. With the black-dressed woman (she also wore, a characteristic touch, little curled gold earrings) was a woman who might have stepped out of Sutter Avenue—so much so that looking at her and the *Day*[27] on the table, I almost forgot that I was in a DP camp. The black dress was bitter, humorous, proud: I loved her spunk; her face cracked with inexpressible, useless defiance. Everybody has gone home now, she said, only we are left; only we have no home to go to. You American Jews, she said, you American Jews—do something! Etc., etc. But for herself she wanted only to go to Palestine. The tailoring shop, the shoe repair shop, the

25. "V" was Vida Ginsburg, a professor at Bard College; Carl Kaysen (1920–2010) was an economist who would later serve in the Kennedy administration.

26. South African prime minister and military leader, Jan Christian Smuts (1870–1950) was defeated in the 1948 general election for refusing to support apartheid.

27. The *Day*, a New York Yiddish newspaper.

garage. The crowd around the American sergeant, the little man with the snow-white hair saying in perfect British English why do we never get white bread anymore? And the American sergeant saying with great clumsy ease and good-feeling (this surprised me and made me very grateful) that it was difficult [to] get white bread now, that it was expensive—imagine, 12 cents a loaf in America.

There are about 1400 in the camp; 500 children—I think, though not entirely sure, about half of them or more are orphans. In the children's play room pictures of Eretz Israel with the Zionist blue and white flag around it; pictures of Herzl and Chaim Bialik.[28] Incredible broken-down look of everything—the little Polish Jew, with the traditional cap and little beard, selling tiny green pears at a shilling each, which he had bought in town. [. . .]

Struck the other day, listening comfortably to FOM's lecture on Dreiser, by how fascinatingly concentrated so much American material becomes when one is away from home—how much more tolerant and humanly curious and wise one becomes when not immediately caught up in the singing lava of America. Feel something of the self-tender homesickness I used to have in London in '45—always remember that silly picture *Meet Me in St. Louis,* awful, fake thing, but sitting in the movie house weeping for the past that never was, that I never had, for the goldenness of all American nostalgia, the greatest, the most child-like, the most pathetic in the world, weeping for the part of my own childhood that how insistently against all reason, except personal, centers around the kitchen—oh, dear Mama, where is it, where is it all gone—that never was on land or sea but is yet true, is, is. [. . .]

## August 15, 1947

Reflecting upon the mingled impressions of these days, I come back again and again to the Leopoldskron Strasse as a central symbol. The long white road lined at one point by the Jewish DP camp, at the turning by the camp for Nazis, the workmen and migrants walking up and down in the August heat, the dust stirred up by the wheels of American military cars blowing into their faces. Europe full of wandering herds of men, endless lines of the homeless, the displaced, walking up and down. The winter was the coldest ever, they say; this is the worst summer in many years. The details fit coldly and nastily together as in a poem by

28. Theodore Herzl (1860–1904), journalist from Austro-Hungary, was father of modern Zionism and spiritual founder of the State of Israel; the Russian-born Jewish poet Chaim Bialik (1873–1934) moved to Tel Aviv in 1923, wrote and published poems in Yiddish and Hebrew, and is now recognized as Israel's national poet.

Eliot—the dead season, alas. Think of the Nazi and American Negro Army deserters living up in the north woods of Italy; the Jews huddling miserably together in the stinking barracks formerly a prison camp; the Latvian "displaced girl" and the Jugoslav white Russians—all of them living crouched, in a state of absolute human insecurity, where everything is provisory, where nothing is settled. And in the heat, the dust, the face of the past—Baroque fortresses, all looking blankly on.

Long talk with Adam Wandruska, late of the Afrika Korps, doctor of philosophy U of Vienna in history, the man with the typical Austrian double-facedness, but yet more honest and more interesting than the others here. Agreed with me that the hypocrisy of the Austrians—what? We were Nazis? We were an occupied people, etc.—really revolting. A view of the Nazi mind—looked around carefully to see if anyone was listening, told it to me with great air of pain and hesitation, but confessed that he could not prove the racial purity of his immediate ancestors up to 1800. He had a Jewish great-grand-mother! Curious face in two levels—one buttery, confiding, intellectual; the other, especially when he is in repose, the perfect face of the Nazi officer. Tried to appeal to me, without his fully realizing it, on the basis of the Nazi inefficiency—we were not supermen, etc. As well I know it; and so what? But fundamentally not a bad type at all, and one I almost like at times. [. . .]

## September 3, 1947
### Piazzale del Museo Borghese

Dinner with Carlo Levi[29] last night. [. . .] Levi wonderful to be with: looks like either a benign old Roman or a sturdy Jewish grandmother. Marvelous confluence of the Italian and the Jew. Walking with him through the Corso on the way to the restaurant was to get a new intimacy with the city. At the restaurant there were letters for him, people always sitting down at his side. [. . .]

## October 28, 1947

Meeting last night with Bernard Berenson at the Hassler Hotel right off Trinita dei Monti. Wonderful lucidity and delicacy of perception in everything he said. I even enjoyed the little snobberies, so much was he of a piece.

29. Kazin reviewed the novelist Carlo Levi's (1902–1975) *Christ Stopped at Eboli* in the *New York Times Book Review* (April 20, 1947): 1–2.

We wrangled a little about Santayana,[30] which is in itself a curious story, for B.B. never sees Santayana, though they have both lived in Italy so long. Said his wife told him not to read Santayana's autobiographies, he would be too distressed. They went to Boston Latin School and Harvard virtually together (S. always a year ahead, as he is a year older)—Berenson unique example in my experience of the old Russian-Jewish gentry which kept its place perfectly in the gentry of the world—seems [a] pure international product, as much Boston as old Europe, as much England as Boston itself. I told him frankly that he was different from his house—I meant more interesting. Yet it is striking how much, now that I have seen him, he resembles that house—its cultured neatness, "taste," and his own fundamental *unregional* quality in every sense. B.B. born June, 1865—50 years to the month before I was. Berenson as an example of the man of culture, the analogue of the Henry James era, the man who crossed borders without difficulty and combines a little bit of every country in himself. Yet how different from Henry James!—something one sees immediately. The "man of culture," the critic, the connoisseur who reflects the liberties of the world before War I, an intellectual *fineness* in every aspect of him, yet not an expatriate in the basic creative sense in which James combined personal revolt with unforgotten and unforgettable saturation in a specific region. Berenson corresponds in his situation to Santayana; and without S's genius for absolute dependence on himself, suggests the same quality of being in his own person, his only locality. I can see now, writing these lines, why with all his feelings of inferiority etc. vis-à-vis Santayana, B.B. should feel a relationship with him that even enmity could not destroy. Easy enough to imagine the two little foreigners in Boston in the 1880s. But here I am on the verge again of exaggerating the importance of locality and "roots" and the pains of foreigners. I am a foreigner in America. I have been a foreigner in the world: a fact to accept and to *use* as an instrument of explanation but not to dwell on too long and sentimentally, as I tend so often to do. [. . .]

## December 17, 1947

[. . .] Walked about in the late morning, silently saying good-bye to everything around me and aching for Italy as if I had already left it. I want to go home—God knows why!—but I hate to leave Italy—I haven't the words to express my love for it. Bought Volume I of the Pléiade edition of Flaubert and read in it the rest of

30. George Santayana (1863–1952), Spanish-American philosopher and essayist. Santayana and Berenson, both American immigrants who returned to live in Europe (Italy), were friends in their years at the Boston Latin School and at Harvard. Santayana later ended the friendship.

the afternoon. Dinner with Carlo Levi and Silone at the [Hotel] degli Amici—in the midst of the noise and the quickly sputtering Italian, of which I caught, as usual, very little. [. . .] Silone a great disappointment—mulish, ungiving sort of man, cluttered with stale politics and journalism. Very southern, occasional flashes of the humorist.

## December 20, 1947

[. . .] A critic must reveal *why* we read him [a writer]. Everything else—the historical associations, the comparison with other writers, the placing in a school, the social, moral, and political significance thereof—all that comes later. The first question a critic should ask himself is: in what does this man's interest to us as a writer primarily consist? Why do we read him and *what* do we read first? The value of a critic can be defined by the extent to which he remembers that he is a reader and by his cleverness and passion in applying that remembrance to the service of his readers. [. . .] The better the critic as a reader, the more he will want to establish in some orderly fashion the *ground* of that experience of reading which is synonymous with communication. I go further: reading should be a sensual experience, and the critic is useful only in so far as he opens our senses to the work before us. Perhaps, if I remember these things well I will not make the mistakes I so often have made—faults, not I think of my sensibility, but of my anxiety and impatience, in my approach to literature. Art is valuable only as far as it helps us to the health of life—Criticism is meaningful only in so far as it aids us to deepen the quality of our experience. [. . .]

## December 21, 1947

[. . .] Intense cold. A very quiet Sunday, mostly hovering around the fire. Deeply touched by talk of the coming child. Greater ease and love in my feeling for Carol: She is so different from me that I am sometimes repelled. And as if I were calling to her across a great gulf. And at other times that very difference—her deep solidity, her naturalness, her humor and irony, simply delicious. [. . .]

## January 9, 1948
### [New York]

Arrived early in the morning after an all-night wait in quarantine. New York in the harsh early morning light, slush under foot. *The violent quality of people's* energy. The brutal cop pushing the Italian woman back on the curb.

## January 24, 1948

Struck more and more by the extent to which the technical ease and power of American life support *without their seeming fully to realize it as a living fact in their own lives* a good many intellectuals, amateur savants precieux, in their own *uninterest* in American society. In proportion, as these people are *made free by* their environment *they become unable and unwilling to study it fully. But then, only a society which is struggling against some pressures from below is capable of basic revolutionary and social thought, and this pressure does not exist in America* today. Protest is turned inward: the individual is all the more conscious of himself, of his frailty, his "happiness" and fate: as he is given the opportunity to be so self-absorbed.

## February 15, 1948

Reading the Russian accusation against Western Powers, one has the sense that behind all the formal denunciations and counter-charges is a deep emotional bitterness, a kind of unforgivingness toward all of us, *outside of Russia, who have not shared in what its people have gone through.* This is not new in Russia: it can be found in the tone of moral superiority taken by Dostoevsky and many other 19th century figures. "How can *you* hope to understand us?"

*Gide in 1930 journals:* "The only drama that really interests me, and that I should always be willing to depict anew, is the debate of the individual with whatever keeps him from being authentic, with whatever is opposed to his integrity, to his integration. Most often the obstacle is within him. And all the rest is merely accidental."

## February 29, 1948

Impressed more and more by the duplication of language between Soviet apologists, all quotations from Soviet press, and the Nazis. The key to a mind is always in its use of language, and the degeneration of the Communists is to be seized exactly here. It would [be] interesting, if I had time now, to make a double column of Nazi and Stalinist expressions in all their similarity.

## March 10, 1948

The primary type of originator, like Marx and Freud, who isolates a cause or phenomenon from the context of custom and analyzes it to the point where it gives us a new illumination of life. It does not matter how they may exaggerate this, how ungenerously they will denounce their opponents, or refuse to concede any qualification of their thought from the outside. They have created a key image of ourselves which we can never lose. Their own enemies know it, too, for they continually pay tribute by draping their criticisms on the structure already provided here for them.

## March 14, 1948

*Invitation to Learning* program this morning on Ellen Glasgow's *Barren Ground,* with [Lyman] Bryson and Jonathan Daniels.[31] Foolish book and oratorical bluster of the Southern liberal; but it seemed to go very well. So exhausted after the accumulated tension had worked off that I was almost alarmed. The "intellectual" performers. Vida [Ginsburg] said the right thing afterward—why didn't I say: "Mr. Daniels, you and I are not discussing the same thing."

First meeting at Dwight Macdonald's of Europe-America Groups. God knows what will come of it: but I want to make some effort for it. Weldon Kees's house later—Jean Malaquais and Michael Frankel. Not very interesting.[32]

## March 24, 1948

Leon Bloy[33] and Kafka: plus religieux que les religieux. Amazing identity of religious inspiration. The fate of the religious outside any church.

Those large cocktail parties, like this one last night for Koestler, are always such particular agony for me. The literary charge, or: what value does that

31. Radio talk show on WCBS in which three scholars and critics discuss a book or an author. Kazin would be a frequent guest. Ellen Glasgow (1873–1945), American novelist, awarded the 1942 Pulitzer Prize for *In This Our Life*. In *On Native Grounds* Kazin calls her "the most biting critic of Southern Romanticism" (258). Lyman Bryson (1888–1959), American educator and media consultant for CBS; Jonathan Daniels (1902–1981), American author, educator, editor, former White House press secretary.
32. Europe-America Groups was founded in 1948 by American anti-Stalinist intellectuals to give moral and financial support to European writers. It folded before the end of the year. Weldon Kees (1914–1955), American poet, critic, and short story writer; Jean Malaquais (1908–1998), French writer of Polish-Jewish descent.
33. Léon Bloy (1846—1917), French novelist, poet, essayist, passionately devoted to the Roman Catholic Church; Franz Kafka (1883–1924), Czech short story writer and novelist, regarded by many as one of the giants of modern literature, best known for *The Trial*, *The Castle*, and his short stories "The Metamorphosis" and "In the Penal Colony."

smile place on *me?* I am always amazed, awed, disgusted by my own silent, upwelling pleading in these things. My craving for fame, prestige, "love," seems uncontrolled at such times. I have this picture of myself like a prisoner on the bench, waiting for judgment to be passed on him.

## March 25, 1948

On my way home about 5:30 stopped into Emanu-El on a sudden whim, and on even more of a whim found myself enduring an evening service in the chapel. If there is anything more depressing, unctuous, and insincere than this kind of high-church Reform Jewish service, I have never seen it. The "reader," a fat and oily looking business man or Ethical Culture type, read out the words with such deliberation that whenever he would come to GOD, he would stop, prepare himself for the ordeal, and pronounce the word as if he [had] taken on new dignity merely by being in its neighborhood. About five or six depressed looking middle-aged people reading the familiar old litany of praise and homage. Oh Lord, you who knowest best, you who are the mightiest. Praise and praise to the mighty Jewish Lord who can somehow not be flattered enough. I was so bored and distracted that when I rose at one point I neglected to note that only mourners were expected to be up at that point, and so foolishly stood up there listening to the opening words of the Kaddish recited for my benefit. Terrible image of the mighty Lord, the master of all. An absolute and (it is to be hoped) possibly benevolent monarch.

The trance-like amiability of weak-chinned people. The shallow kindness and expectancy imposed on certain faces by the lack of harmony in the bony structure.

## May 13, 1948

It is terrible the way I ignore this notebook, when I reflect how much I continually need it not only as an aid to composition but for my spiritual well-being. I must make a practice of writing something in it every day—especially a time like this, when I am so much immersed in the *Walker* that I hate to take time "off." It is always at such moments of the greatest pressure on me that my writing here is most unconscious and therefore most useless. And it is no longer true that my weekly sessions with Rioch relieve me of the need of "examining myself" here—there is everything to say, outside that strictly clinical room. [. . .]

I notice that Matthiessen [in *From the Heart of Europe*] has me leading the singing of the "Internationale" at Schloss Leopoldskron last year. The dog, did he have to put that in and so little else? Carol jokes that I may not be able to get a passport. It would be horrible if some reactionary jackasses could get me that way.

The reason for this journal: I get about 1/5,000,000 of my daily thoughts, fantasies, miseries, ambitions—oh, the sheer tidal flow of my consciousness—into what I write and say. I must use this book from now on as a knife to cut off the dead skin of custom. It should be a real daybook, filled to the brim with everything possible, no matter how foolish. It is only by following my follies to their end, to their very end, that I shall know wisdom.

Reading Gide's Journals for the *New Yorker*,[34] and hence, of course, my sudden freedom in writing these notes. I still have as my most real personality only the character of the man I am reading: i.e., if I like him. A completely literary creature, that's me: born by the book, sleeping by the book, and will die aching to be like the end of another man's sentence.

What it is that pleases me about Gide: a whetstone, a way of observing, literary tone. What it is that annoys me: *a man for whom everything is fundamentally literature.* Life like a mirror of books. *The man walking with a book in his hand.* The fear of time, of death, of being serviceable in the Protestant sense: this is the key to the link with the radical Protestant tradition and Thoreau: I must account for every minute of my time to my maker. The Jew says: I must please Him. The Protestant: I must not be found in idleness. [. . .]

## May 15, 1948

Eretz Israel is the "State of Israel." I have always been against the idea of a Jewish state, and now that it is here, I find myself as moved by it and as eager to defend it as if I had been a Zionist. Unable to read any of the newspaper articles without bursting into tears. Yet I keep thinking a) that history is made by acts, and the consequences follow often from the facts of particular people; b) that nothing shows up so clearly the nature of our time, for this new nationalism is the greatest possible proof that for millions of Jews throughout the world the promise of "modern history" in the Dispersion is over. What it will do to Jews outside of Palestine is a muddled and possibly tragic business. [. . .]

34. "The Journal Keeper," *New Yorker* (June, 12, 1948): 91–94. Kazin reviewed books regularly for the *New Yorker* from March 1948 to October 1954.

Saw [William] Shawn[35] at the *New Yorker* office late yesterday afternoon. Very charming and sensitive little man—how much of his charm lies in this being so unlike the expected picture of the *New Yorker* managing editor hard to say. Had a red jacket sweater under his coat, and bustled around timidly in that high comedian's whiny voice, full of anxiety. Yet very firm under all this, and beautifully sincere. The old business about "fitting" the style of the magazine, about heavy critics and light critics, and Wolcott Gibbs,[36] whom they all so much admire because he writes "by not saying things." Certainly. How can I ever get down on paper the really fantastic business of magazine writing in N.Y.—the wearing need to fit the writer into shape, to take him into just the required space and tone? Fundamentally all this is obscene, for it rests on real hatred of the writer as individual spirit. Nothing so far from their minds as wanting the best of the writer, of serving, releasing, providing opportunity, for *him.* [. . .]

## May 16, 1948

Hannah Arendt's remarks on the Palestine situation refreshed me morally and gave me more to understand than anything I have read or am likely to read on that subject for a long time. I count her as one of the few really valuable people I know.[37] [. . .]

## May 19, 1948

For me thinking about style is not a trivial concern, as it is for many writers who naturally write better—that is, with more ease and confidence. I notice in going over The Neighborhood section in the *Walker* that the writing becomes bad the minute I try for external connections that the sentences themselves actually do not support. I must get into my writing the spontaneity of this Journal. Above all, I must get away from that bane of my life, the "well-organized" paragraph, which leads me into mechanical compound sentences again and again. I must have the courage to let my paragraphs fall off by the wayside as it were, and not lay them together like bricks of the same size. If I depend less on the artificial unity of the paragraph, I may be able to get away from these camels with humps in them that my rigid sentences resemble now.

35. William Shawn (1907–1992), editor of the *New Yorker* from 1951 to 1987.

36. Oliver Wolcott Gibbs (1902–1958), writer, humorist, and drama critic for the *New Yorker*.

37. Hannah Arendt, in "To Save the Jewish Homeland: There Is Still Time," *Commentary* (May, 1948): 398–406, warned that the creation of a Jewish state that ignored the rights of Palestinian Arabs would be a political and moral tragedy leading to a militarized state permanently at war with its neighbors.

This is directly related to the candidly impressionistic note—the entrance into the text of real dreams—that I have not gotten yet. There must be an infusion in the *Walker* of real dream-life states. Now many pages have a look of editorialized fantasies. The firmness I seek in my writing will come only from definite commitment to the inspiration I have had from the beginning—images of solitude that embrace the world by defining the distance between it and the walking man. The separation in time (longing for the past). The separation in space (the difference between the street and the city). The separation in comradeship (the moral gap between our hearts and our lives). [. . .]

So long as I keep thinking of this journal as a form of personal prayer or training in devotion, so long will I keep it from hindering my vital communication with others.

## June 1, 1948

Reading Henry James's *Notebooks.* Fascinating in its shop-talk, and, as always, in the spontaneity and freshness of the writing. James's style itself is one of the great achievements of the literary mind in English—all thought and feeling and *hovering,* like a rustle of the mind's wings. But it is a little dismaying to realize how little he was interested in general ideas. So far, not a word, not a note, that was not for the particular purposes of plot. And the picture of him: returning every night from his society dinners, nursing some piece of gossip into a plot. Will it go? How can I turn it right? etc. In one sense the notebook is like the account book of a broker, noting his little deals. Had neglected to realize how much J. is, here, right in the tradition of the plotters and melodramatic spinners of 19th century drama. His feeling for plot extraordinary—all full of subtlety and immediate instinct. And to be fair, not perhaps so much in the line of the "well-made" play or novel as in terms of the psychological complication between characters that he got from his own upbringing and saturation in Hawthorne. The meeting of nations in the "international" novel. It would be interesting to study. [. . .]

## June 7, 1948

Michael Kazin [born]. After Carol and I had decided on the name I raised my pen above the blank to write it in, and felt a strange sense of presumption at deciding in advance so important a part of his life as his name. But it is a sound, strong name, and I am glad we chose it. [. . .]

In the rainy silence tonight, alone at home, heard again that voice of perfect peace and love—that voice I once heard when I was alone like this years ago, and again when I sat in the library one morning reading Blake, and the morning more than a year ago when I sat by the Delaware, thinking of my approaching marriage, and heard the voice say so clearly: Do it; do it; aim for the whole of life again.

## July 4, 1948

Moved, baby, baggage, book and all, to Hill Farm[38] today. Day of glorious sun. When I see Michael in his out-of-doors screen crib under the willow tree, I feel so ashamed to be fretting over my work, when the wonder and the intrinsic beauty of him fill me up every time I look at him. Curiously benign associations I always have with any kind of screening or mosquito-netting over a crib; must go back to some half-remembered early pleasure in my own childhood.

Michael. He floats amid sensations of heat, light, thirst, hunger, rage, joy. I keep thinking of him floating on the materials of life, in an elemental sea.

## July 22, 1948

Went off to New York Tuesday after finishing the Huxley review for the *Herald-Tribune.*[39] Looked forward so much to being on my own in New York for a day or two after seeing the ear doctor and taking care of the necessary chores. But the city so unbearably hot and lonely for me that I found myself wandering about in a deep state of confusion, the "wasted" weeks here, the unfinished book, throbbing in my mind. The heat and deadly dampness of the city affected me more deeply than I can remember it. I was looking for something—a girl? A chance for a quick, easy lay? The blousy half-nakedness of the girls in the streets, with that peculiar languor of summer, the faint drops of sweat on their lips, drove me crazy with desire. But deeper than my desire was a fear of the guilt I would feel if I did sleep with someone: a panicky return to that knowledge of my whole world gone bust I still carry with me from that unforgettable week in Washington during the war when Lou came down. This part was childish, but I think I am sincere when I say that another reason was my desire to be patient with myself and Carol, to ride this period out in the hope that things would change soon for me. What part of this was "honor," what part my love for C., what part mere cowardice, and worse than cowardice, superstition? I wish I knew. Sentimentally, I kept looking at my wedding ring.

38. Vacation home of the Bookmans in Bucks County, Pennsylvania.
39. "Fantastic Forecast of the Post-Atomic Age," review of *Ape and Essence*, *New York Herald Tribune Weekly Book Review* (August 22, 1948): 3.

All confusion these last few days, a deep sadness. Last night I even went back to Balilla in Bleecker Street for dinner, as if to recapture something of that past which, when I think about it honestly and coherently, was far more sterile and unhappy in every way than my life now. Sitting there alone, in the almost empty restaurant, while at the bar the locals were looking at the baseball game, with nothing to read but a twice-read copy of the awful *Star,* an English Penguin introduction to the Bible (!!!). The manicotti was too hot, the place dismal; truly, under new management. Then when I got home, I was so weary and depressed that I could not even take in the music on the radio to which I had looked forward so much to re-fill me; kept peeking nervously at books (what have I lost? who has taken this away from me?), reading Harvey [Swados]'s ms. Never have I realized so deeply my compulsive need of books, the silent question I ask of myself when I turn to a new one: is it with this that I will be complete at last, lose my long fear of being found out? When I went to take a shower, I put my head against the bathroom wall, even with the water falling on me, and cried. "I won't give up!" I said. "I won't." So low, then, have I gone because my progress on the book has been temporarily slowed up. So low, after everything I have learned, after all the patience I (in my mind) have taught myself to acquire. It seemed to me in this pitiful day and a half in New York, after all the silent weeks of misery here, that I had learned nothing after all, acquired nothing that would help me back to the needed serenity; that I was as full of anguish about myself, and, oh, let me dare to say it even here, hatred of others [. . .] who are "better," more efficient, who do not flatter and love me unceasingly. I am poisoned by it; it takes me violent efforts and ruthless self-urgings to lift myself out of that pit. And being so conscious of this in myself now, after Rioch's excellent and unsparing course of instruction, I cannot fool myself a minute, cannot lose it ever. It exists. The price of such profound self-doubt as I have known all my life is infliction upon others, distortion of ideas, guilt beyond words. The chaos in my nature fills me with despair.

Yet coming back here to the farm this noon, the quietness in the grass, the understanding in C.'s face, and that unreal, beautiful Michael refreshed me instantly. So quickly do I change, to change again, perhaps; yet when I came into my study here to write these words and go back to work again, a tremor of renewal seized me, that happiness which, by contrast, can be so violent in me that I never know which book or paper to take to first. I feel then that I could lie in the fields, humbly kissing each leaf, out of gratitude at having found myself back from death again, at being human, active, and loving again. [. . .]

## July 24, 1948
### [dated June 24]

[. . .] Read the USSR issue of *Politics:* remarkable article on the dictatorial tradition in Russia by the anonymous author of *The Dark Side of the Moon.*[40] Impressed despite Macdonald's arid and rather smart-alecky writing, by the essential dignity of the fight for freedom, *per se,* for fundamental independence and truth. After Matthiessen's *From the Heart of Europe,* which sickened me by its compromises and bad faith, all the more impressive. What creative-critical activity in our age really stands for—support of human curiosity, *the deepest sympathy for human suffering—against all claims of* necessity and "*historical*" logic.

But by contrast, and as a reminder of the sterility of purely avant-garde effort, note Irving Howe's essay on Popular Culture.[41] All these definitions, made, surely from the outside, fundamentally useless; for they do not show the involvement of the writer. The assumption of independence in the body of the writing, the claim to the critic's superiority and "independence," is false. In writing about Popular Culture, it is not *what* you say, but how you say it—i.e., your awareness of your own relationship to the material that is the real guarantee of your approach to the truth. For "popular culture" is belief debased, belief institutionalized, and not the "commonplace" as seen from a social angle.

## July 26, 1948

[. . .] What shall I do? What can I do but face bravely up to the need to write out the book as my heart dictates without constantly looking over my shoulder to the imaginary reader and scoffer? I cannot go back on my original inspiration; I can only deepen and subtilize it, remain true to it by giving all my *present* resources to it.

My theme more than ever: the alienation of man from present institutions; the moral estate of man in the city; the solitude that must follow upon man's effort to examine his deeper and more sincere relations to, and rejections of,

40. Anonymous, "The Background," *Politics* (Spring 1948): 78–81.

41. Irving Howe, "Notes on Mass Culture," *Politics* (Spring 1948): 120–123. Irving Howe (1920–1993), literary critic, biographer, historian, editor of *Dissent*, best known for *World of Our Fathers: The Journey of the East European Jews to America and the Life They Found and Made* (1976). Though both Howe and Kazin came from similar Jewish immigrant backgrounds, went to City College in the 1930s, shared liberal left political views, and taught at Hunter College and the Graduate Center of the City University, they never became friends. Kazin considered Howe an unreconstructed "ideologue" and sensed latent distrust, called *Dissent* (now edited by his son Michael), the "dullest magazine in the world."

present-day society and culture; the call to *integration,* i.e. the involvement of his total self in his living activity; the mode of walking, or meditation.

## August 14, 1948
**[dated July 14]**

[. . .] I have never been able to take society for granted, and least of all my own place in it. That is one of my values: I am always concerned with the central situation, precisely because I have always felt myself on the periphery. I write these words now because they help me better to understand the difficulties I have been having so long with the *Walker.* From the outset—and the book is a very old thing with me; in the deepest sense I cannot remember when its central theme came into my mind—I have been moved to write this book in order to create a portrait of moral solitude within the social disorder. For a long time, then, I have been struggling with just that which has always been dearest to me. But at the same time I have been trying to get away from it—to diminish its force, its essential acerbity, its necessary lyricism. And so, being unable to leave my topic, or to *say* it, I have gone through all the possible hells of confusion and conflict—on the one hand recognizing how deeply necessary the book is to me; on the other hand trying to escape it.

## August 28, 1948

[. . .] When I read through the stories in Schwartz's[42] book [*The World Is a Wedding*], I asked myself if I had not been guilty of my usual hostility in advance to hide my secret fear, in not writing some words of praise to New Directions to help it on—a book which certainly needs help from all those who understand its curious merit. When the stories appeared in the *Partisan,* I was *put off by their over-conscious simplicity, to which I attributed a certain nasty irony.* I could not even read them through. Yet now I have gone through the book, and I am conscious in myself of the fact that I avoided reading it attentively before out of resentment against Schwartz. A difficult matter for me to decide on here—on the one hand the stories do not attract me; there *is* something repellent about them—an excess of manner, an abysmal lack of certainty! Yet they move me. I think of them as psychological fables, and though the *narrative* quality of the stories is either dull or just missing, I get the point of them. Why, then, did I fail to encounter them honestly and directly before? What was it made me shirk a fair judgment of them?

42. Delmore Schwartz (1913–1966), American poet and critic, poetry editor of the *Partisan Review.*

Whatever guilt I feel toward S in the matter, the greater thing to seize here is the lesson of how much my resentment of the *PR* group, my unending fear of their scorn, has led me astray. There is no, there cannot be, any real sympathy between Rahv and myself. But that is a fact by itself: it must not lead me to such arrant cowardice and such unfairness before any of them, particularly Schwartz, who is a real poet, and a writer to whom I am attached by many ties in our common situation and critical understanding. Behaving this way, I do not even give myself a chance to fix determinedly on what it is I disagree with: I distort the matter in advance.

All this still in the psychological realm: the behavior of someone who at 33 is still haunted by the terror-images of his childhood. I could weep when I realize how much time I waste, how many creative opportunities I have thrown away, how much *fiction* I am occupied with day in and day out, hour by hour, by my anxiety, my useless shadow-boxing with the imaginary censure and rejection by others. *Trance*: my automatic drive to improve on my activities and judgments, the opinion of others; an empty quarrel with authorities who rationally do not exist.

How much more life giving it would be, if I really *used* this notebook to study carefully the meaning of my experiences—and not as I have so often done, to touch them on the margin, as if I could exorcize them from my mind by naming them. The heart of the terror is not in what is actually there, but in my refusal to search it. For when I have fully confronted any one of the innumerable things which, in their abstract, burden my life by all the imagined destructiveness they seem to merit, I find that I am no longer *struggling* but have already come over on the other side, into nothing more terrible to bear than loneliness, yet with a gentler, graver kind of understanding for it. [. . .]

## September 27, 1948

Although I have not seen Faulkner's *Intruder in the Dust,*[43] I was impressed by the warmth of Gregory's and Bert's[44] reviews in the Sunday papers because of the *contagious passion* that even reading [about] Faulkner makes possible. That air of deep human truth, that nervous American style hurling itself onto tragedy, that *sounding* of all our immense possibilities for good and evil—the

43. One of Kazin's regrets as a critic was his dismissive treatment in *On Native Grounds* of the American novelist William Faulkner (1897–1962), who won the 1949 Nobel Prize for literature.

44. Horace Gregory (1898–1982), poet and critic, reviewed Faulkner's *Intruder in the Dust* for the *New York Herald Tribune*; Harvey Breit (see Chapter 8, n. 27) reviewed it in the *New York Times*.

haunted awareness by the American of his peculiar domain in the world. But Faulkner actually evokes something far more immediate: the relationship of the oppressor and the oppressed, seen from the point of view of the oppressor himself—the former master, the white man in the white-Negro relationship. Thus reminding us with full force what it is the Southern writer has that other American writers lack, what makes the others so thin, so morally coarse, so *unfounded* on anything but this discovery of himself, if that. It is the awareness, the Southern writer's, of the *relationship* between master and servant, between guilt and history, and the fact that this relationship is seen from above [that] is all the more significant to his own possession of the complexity of his experience.

Compare the situation of the archetypal Southern writer with that of the Jewish writer. In both the perception of the relationship is upper most, but the role each sees for himself in it is different. The Jewish writer usually thinks of himself as the oppressed, the alienated, the man things are done to, despite his genius. Kafka is still the paradigm of the Jewish writer who always feels that the world is pressing on his back, that it is simply enemy or Gentile enigma: in a word, not for him. Yet still the idea of a relationship is paramount: the fact that he is a Jew means that he is always conscious of the other; the Jew of the Diaspora at least, could not exist if there were not a non-Jew always before him: Jew and Gentile are plighted to the same misunderstanding.—The important thing here, however, is the class of writer for whom this idea of a relationship is uppermost, whether he knows it or not; who lives—how can I put it more directly?—in consciousness of another: whether as oppressor of the oppressed, or as oppressed of the oppressor. That would be the title of my fable or essay: and its moral, that the oppressor-class writer is often the greater, because he has not lost his dignity by abjection, and has even added to it by understanding of his guilt. The oppressed has the consciousness of his ethical superiority; the oppressor of his central place in the human domain.

## September 30, 1948

*Stammerer:* from the Anglo-Saxon *stamerian:* "to speak with involuntary stops in uttering syllables and words." Involuntary? But let us go on to a more imperative question: Why, having been engaged all my remembered life with stammering, or the fear of stammering—why, having attained a tyrannical fluency so that I might never be found gaping and gapping—why should I not turn this into a psychological fable or essay: on the stammerer-writer: the man haunted by difficulties of speech—Billy Budd on one side of the picture—Billy, whose stammer cost his enemy and himself their lives. On the other, Demosthenes, Charles Lamb, Maugham, etc.[45] The man who could not stop talking. [. . .]

## November 2, 1948

Election Day. Like a damn sentimental fool voted for [Norman] Thomas,[46] but with deep misgivings, and glad I could vote with the Liberal Party for the other offices—Not that there was much of a choice, since the Socialists, characteristically, didn't even bother to nominate candidates for the legislature and local offices. [. . .] Wonderful feeling of Dewey's evident defeat: how his face freezes even his own supporters! The total Democratic, especially the labor-liberal, strength in the country, is amazing. Though Truman is not in as I write—10 A.M.—it is clear that he will squeeze through somehow, if not now, then in the run-off in the House. I loved the whole evening and its excitement; above all, I had a sudden feeling of pride in being an American and in realizing that the liberal core of the country is still so solid. [. . .] The fact is that the country wanted a Republican administration but simply could not stomach in Dewey the obvious coldness and success-mongering. Truman is mediocrity incarnate, which is why I could not vote for him; but Dewey represented something essentially repellant even to many conservatives. I rejoice in his defeat.

## November 6, 1948

[. . .] Whenever I had a chance, I kept at Merton's[47] autobiography, *The Seven-Story Mountain;* moved me so deeply that I got a little scared at one point that I was falling back into my old abject jealousy of les religieux again. But it seemed to me as I stood there on the porch, thinking hard and close on it, that the real reward of such a book is not in the discovery or rediscovery of Catholicism, which is fundamentally not important to the book, but in Merton's own quality. In sum: and a good thing to get clear in my head for once: not the creed, but the believer. What moves me so much about the book, of course, is

45. Billy Budd, character in Melville's novella of the same name, frustrated by his stammer, strikes and kills a senior officer who has falsely accused him of mutiny; Demosthenes (384–322 BCE), orator and politician in ancient Greece who stammered as a child; Charles Lamb (1775–1834), English essayist afflicted with a lifetime stammer. A stammerer himself, Kazin was interested in other stammerers, including his student at Harvard (1954), the writer Edward Hoagland (1932–), "the worst I ever encountered."

46. Norman Thomas (1884–1968), perennial Socialist candidate for the presidency.

47. Thomas Merton (1915–1968), American Trappist monk and prolific author, best known for his autobiography, *Seven Story Mountain* (1948).

my identification with Merton based on the fact that we are almost the same age, that we have both gone through so many of the same experiences (we were both taking our MA's at Columbia in '38, though I did not know him) and that he, unlike so many of my generation, has really won his way to clarity. But what it says about his own abysmal upbringing and early orphanage, and our culture, that he should have found this by becoming a Trappist monk! [. . .]

As for Catholicism; I can best state my feelings about it as a creed this way: if I knew a Jew, of my own age, who wrote with the love, the passion, and the cardinal simplicity of Merton, it would not change my mind in the least about *Judaism.* Gandhi did not make me a believer in Hinduism; Blake did not convert me to "mysticism"; I love the Quakers but am bored with Quakerism; the more I recognize my debt to Christ, the less I can follow "his" church. But let me put the general fact plainly: I am a *religious*, my eyes are always half-closed, looking within.

## November 17, 1948

This is the age of extreme manifestations and therefore of extreme explanations. But would the manifestations always be so extreme (since we only see what we are prepared to see) if we had not gotten into such a pattern of extreme explanations? More and more, it seems to me, we automatically look for clues that are *abysmal.* In politics, take the idea that everything rests on the lust for power; in psychology, on anxiety; in literature, on the absolutely naked self.

[This is one clue to the attraction of Melville for our age: the sense of the extreme has replaced the *human* matter (i.e., "society" in Jane Austen's sense); men facing the world alone is all—"My splintered heart and maddened hand."][48]

We discount our own experience in its *fineness;* we have replaced the complex and contingent truths of our daily life with crushing absolutes of guilt, lust, solitude, hostility.

Last night at the E-A meeting, found myself regretting, as I always do when I see Macdonald, that I have so often pooh-poohed him superficially; in his strivings and daily attitudes, more creative than anyone else in his group. Yet though I admire him, fundamentally I find him boring, and I think now that I know why—it is because everything he is and says is on a level of radical journalism

48. The quotation is from *Moby-Dick:* Ishmael on the state of his soul before meeting Queequeg. Kazin's brackets.

and avant gardism rather than on the level of *art.* He is a utopian journalist rather than a creator; when his mind stops shaping explanations, he relapses into trivialities.

## November 18, 1948

We moved today to 415 Central Park West. Enormous business of packing and unpacking my books, which I have been carrying on my back for so many years. Lord, how I would like to get free of all these *things* sometime. I date my maturity from the day I realized there were books I could get along without. Yet obviously I am crammed full of obligations left over—since I have as yet only a small portion of my library here. "Simplify, simplify,"[49] but every week there are more possessions, and in this great barracks of an apartment house every real or imaginary requirement of our living calls for still more. [. . .]

## December 19, 1948

[. . .] I like what Heinrich Blücher[50] said the other night at Hannah's, his reminder that socialism is only an instrument towards internationalism. Which is why the Germans, having seen the socialists drop internationalism, were able to convert "socialism" into fascism. This is a reminder we need more and more these days, to get us free completely of the fetishism of socialism as an end in itself, and thus at the same blow, to restore socialism as an idea to its rightful place in the great tradition. Once we free ourselves of the purely Marxist and working-class trappings of socialism, we can recapture, as in terms of our personal activity and everyday culture, those very values that have become purely formal end-terms in the Socialist and Communist movements. All of which is only a roundabout way of saying that for us, in an industrial culture, the values of socialism can still be separated from the statist theory and practice. But in peasant countries like Czarist Russia and present-day China? As I write, China seems fated to go completely Stalinist, and there is probably nothing we can do about it, for there, as in the Russia of 1917, the dominant class is completely bankrupt. In China, it is a question of elementary rights withheld from the masses.

49. "Economy" chapter in *Walden.*
50. Heinrich Blücher (1889–1970), philosopher and educator, husband of Hannah Arendt, friend of Kazin's.

## December 24, 1948

At the farm. Long wretched day getting myself back in order. Michael's look of serene curiosity as he takes every new object in the world into his ken. The lighthouse of the child's incipient mind turning now to this, now to the other. When I watch Carol playing with him, I think with amazement and gratitude of how different his childhood is from my own—and should I not add, from hers? Since her wonderful intuitiveness comes, too, from her feelings of exclusion and unattractiveness as a child, and the strategic advantage she took *over* her own unhappiness—*in* her silence—her daily air of reading life absolutely straight? [. . .]

## January 4, 1949

Yesterday afternoon, after fussing unsuccessfully all day with the Dreiser review, took my first walk after my being in bed most of the week—across the park and down to the Society Library. Felt weak, dispirited, horribly sorry for myself, etc., but noted with interest as I went down Madison—about 86th or so—that old sensation of late afternoon, goes back with me to sometime in the late '20s, when I used to go to that "speech clinic"—a kind of key or connective with the smell of biscuits coming out of a chain bakery, the light falling away from the streets, myself in a strange "American" neighborhood—about to go home to Brownsville—and the depth of the sensation all, curiously, made up of the brilliance of the winter frost on the windows, the shoppers in the streets, the people sheathed in their thick winter coats. What is it here, what *was* it, that keeps returning at such odd moments—that makes the smell of the biscuits so unforgettable, and the look of the windows, of the people in their coats, so *new?* It seems to me now, as I write these hurried notes, that what I felt most then was a feeling of initiation, of departure from the old ways. The background of this afternoon reverie is completed by the going home at last, of sitting in my old place at the head of the kitchen table, and trying to account to myself for what had taken place that afternoon. [. . .]

## January 31, 1949

[. . .] At Claire Nukind's party afterwards, had a talk with Clem Greenberg,[51] whom I have come to like more than I have, for a certain direct and "separatist"

51. Clement Greenberg (1909–1994), art critic, author of influential 1939 essay in *Partisan Review* "Avant-Garde and Kitsch," defending modern art.

intelligence—a way of always being himself though he is certainly lacking in grace. Yet the value of such a man is outside all those considerations: and what interested me in his ideas, general appearance, etc., was the forthrightness of what he had to say about the homosexual syndicate and then his own face as he talked. The ripe young man about 40 or so; the sharp edges of teeth protruding from his mouth, and a way of going back and back to the topic—that homosexuals have collective politics, like Jews, but more unconscious; that they really band together, etc. I like most what he said on this—that he would like to know what the homos' idea of safety is; if he knew that, he would have the secret. And meanwhile, as he talked, I felt his own clumsiness, ruggedness, harshness—sometimes a little manic and exaggerated, full of black and white propositions, yet again and again coming back to things with incontrovertible truths. [. . .]

## February 10, 1949

In the Tourneau watch shop on Madison Avenue. The Jews with magnifying lenses screwed into their eyes on rugs behind the glass showcases—they walk with cat-like steps, careful to avoid breaking anything in this house of glass. The lenses, thicknesses through which they look at themselves in the convex, modernistic mirror, emblems of the trade. (An infinity of mirrors, each penetrated by its special chromium-plated lamp.) The rugs, the velvet pads on which the gleaming, jeweled watches are placed: the bijou must barely rest on the creamy mat, for it may be tarnished; the store itself so expensive, everything about of such immense and innate cost, that the men yearn to obtain to the condition of the things they guard. The woman refugee comes in: matching of her accent for *theirs.* And vat can I show you? This is trooly a splendid piece. This is among our most *outstanding* creations. Could I perhaps ask you, Madame, where you have derived that excellent neckpiece?

Etc., etc. snobbery of the jeweller-watchkeeper, who is at once technician and salesman. The money is kept out of sight, in some invisible tier on *his* side [of] one showcase. The adoration of *luxe,* by the men who confer upon themselves the dignity which eunuchs do in the service of kings.

## February 12, 1949

Let me put the content of my romanticism this way: Although my whole effort as a writer is to convert images into thoughts, experiences into concrete details, symbols into universals, something, still, is always left over from my writing that is pure emotion. And to this I cling, whenever I find it emerging absolutely from the end of my thought; in this alone, for me, is the germ of other thoughts.

## February 16, 1949

There are no words to describe this daily struggle I fight with my book—as if I were trying to write it and unwrite it at the same time. Whenever I can get away from it enough to look back at my work, all its possibilities flame up in me again; I feel as if I were dancing on air, and there *could* be no joy so great as working out an idea so grand and flexible as this. Yet here I sit mechanically day after day, accomplishing at most a page or two, often making my way ahead only by a few sentences, and making everything else gray and torpid. Truly, it is like a weight I drag around on my legs. Yet the first thought that comes to my mind as I write this is, *I* am still missing from it. It was for a certain abundant *O altitudo!* arising entirely from my nature that I began the book at all: it was for this, to put into an intelligible frame, the indefeasibility of my own soul. And what is it? For what did I waste and torture myself all last summer when I could have *sung* out the Bridge part and in fact had been waiting this long only to sing?

Oh God, I am so tired of defrauding myself like this day after day. I seem to see the truth always at an angle. In my mind's picture I am walking toward it into open arms, but when I come up to it, it has changed its shape. I cannot recognize it.

## February 20, 1949

[. . .] Story of a marriage here between a frustrated writer and his wife: the writer acting out on his wife all that he has not found in his life and work and therefore condemning the marriage as well.

## February 24, 1949

[. . .] Last night the sky of New York was "brilliant," metropolitan—a sky lit up from the underlying electric torches of the skyline around the park. When I got out of the subway at Columbus Circle I was astonished by the drama of all those separate glowing monuments under the sky—illuminated clocks, Christopher on his pedestal, the long, even blaze of the marquees down Broadway, the swinging pendulum, lighted glass and electric red roses of the whiskey sign. A three-ring circus, in the open air, and the sky overhead bearing down, lit up from below but still bearing down, overreaching it all, qualified but untouched.

And if we look up at the sky with such surprise and pleasure, is it not because we are wearied by the absolute unrelatedness of these buildings?

Walking along Amsterdam yesterday from the post office, I felt my mind crushed by the inexpressible anarchic rot. I do not ask for an eternity of Rockefeller Fifth Avenue smoothness, on the contrary. But the totally *accidental* landscape of New York is what makes these streets so ugly. There is no reason why *this* should be *here* rather than *there.* The pile, the rubbishy pile: the refuse of commercialism strewn along the streets. Jutting out from each store like an arrested arm: the store sign, writing the man's name above the pavements.

## April 5, 1949

[. . .] Consoled myself when I got back [from a walk] by reading through the rest of Chaim Weizmann's[52] autobiography. I'd never before felt much interest in him and certainly did not expect to feel admiration and even affection. But I am so *particularly* raw these days on Palestine and the whole Jewish question that I found myself moved to tears again and again; I realized to the quick how very right he has been and that his conception of the Jewish *people* is incontrovertible—from the point of view of the Russian Jews, of whom I am certainly, by everything except the accident of birth, one. The book roused my interest in Palestine to fever-pitch. I realize, of course, that I see all this now in the special context of my book, my "return" to Brownsville, and my irrational, my cowardly, fear that I've "betrayed" my own by criticizing the Jews so much—!!! I can see that Weizmann's lifelong fight was just, and I feel *intimate* to him, to it, by every deep-felt association of my own life in the ghetto. It strikes me, I add *seriatim,* that Zionism was, up to '33, peculiarly the aspiration of Russian Jews, for whom it was the inevitable step from the Pale. The Russian Jews did feel their relations with the Russians were as with neighboring and hostile states. What I got, further, from W's book, is the fact that the religious practices of the Jews were the *folklore* of this people, not merely, not formally, its theology. Hence the logic, which once I failed to see, in Weizmann's reprisal of the *nation,* the homeland, the incarnation of our long history in *Eretz Israel,* despite his own evident lack of sympathy with the synagogical. The real clue to Zionism is the aspiration toward the "normal," Weizmann's insistence on agricultural colonies and his bitter opposition to the commercial and urban, the manipulative and petty bourgeois character of Jewish life in the *Galut.* His mind was evidently racked by the furtiveness and abstractness of Jewish city life.

52. Chaim Azriel Weizmann (1874–1952), president of the Zionist Organization and first president of the State of Israel. He was also a prominent chemist who developed a process for producing acetone used by the British in the manufacture of explosives during World War I.

## April 18, 1949

Last night spoke with Irving Howe on Melville and Hawthorne at the "Labor Action Group." It went off all right, and in fact cheered me up considerably. But I find myself thinking this morning not of Howe or what we said, but of the battered Trotskyite hall on W. 14th above the factories, and of the girls and men we had coffee with later—dry, tired faces, all skepticism and "experience," faces that brought home to me, against the banners in the hall and the creak of the chairs—splinter group, all splinters in your hand—the unutterable dreariness of New York, for all the human joy one ever sees in its people. [. . .]

## May 8, 1949

Along the River Road. Picking up the old life as I go, walking parallel to the river, I feel that I march alongside my hidden genius, who sleeps in the river at my side. How slowly and gently he paces me, leading me on.

At night the towers are hooded, and in the faint light up from the boats in the river and the lights from the other side, they *hulk* over the bridge. When you start from the Brooklyn side in the misty rain, you see—first and last, the towers over the bay. Their gray is luminescent despite the mist, concentrated by the mist—They gleam over the bay, pyramids and watchtowers, the first and the last things here. It is toward them that you go, always toward them, yet central, omnipresent, with thin veins of light shining over them in the mist, they proclaim something here that is older than man. Their granite force is rooted in the bottom of the river and their ogive eyes stare you straight through, leading you on, implacable tho' trancessible [*sic*], saying—we are taking you through, but we shall close ourselves up as soon as you have passed.

As soon as I look up to the coil and swing of the cables, I am threaded through, caught up and threaded through, by millions of lines. Going through the arches of the towers I slowly and unbelievingly make my way through the eye of the needle; then, with the lines streaming back and forth, and up and down on every side of me, I am threaded through, I am led on. Into the thousand thicknesses and coiled strength of the lines, I am led on.

*This* is my only understanding of the divine . . . in the continuing, in the apprehension of an interminating [*sic*] energy, and infinity of suggestiveness. How the lines course and return and course back again on every side of me! *Plenitude over the river,* in the full light of day. I open my arms to the plenitude.

In the day it is the threads that I see, for it is in me that they do their work. At night, in the rain and the mist, it is the towers—the implacable surface of the divine.

*The bridge on different days and in different weathers.* Early in the morning on weekdays it is a sheer currency, a busyness; as soon as you start, you must go over immediately. There is the smell of coffee roasting, the impatience of the cars: the trolley rings and rings its bell as if afraid that it might be stopped *en route;* the ships in the harbor strain at their piers, impatient to get on. But on Sundays you linger, you wait, there under the coolness of the Brooklyn tower, in sight of the connecting piers—straight down the curved fastnesses of the tower arch.

But especially I think of the Bridge as I have walked across it on a hot day . . . a day when the metal plates that reinforce the worn, wooden floor are glowing in the heat, when the boards of the promenade seem to come up to meet you, and *melting,* expanding, warm, the worn gray and sooty, sooted blocks of the promenade clumped back by your feet. You feel that the whole bridge is fluid, *familiar to every sense,* its lines, its odors, its deeply engrained familiarity swimming in your blood.

Then the bridge in winter, the black roofs on the other side in that miniature of winter I saw that late afternoon through the window of the New School. A late winter afternoon scene, each line in it as rigid and still as in a mezzotint engraving, while beating along its track, on the topmost level of the buildings, the train, like a serpent, maneuvers its way in and out of the house-clumped streets.

## May 12, 1949

In the train to Washington.

"All those who do not aid in my perfection—Zero."—Henri Michaux[53]

What is it I associate so keenly with the summer smell and sensual keenness of Prospect Park?[54] I started thinking of this a few weeks ago—the first image that came back to me was of the curving road leading away from the lake there, the old boathouse and the "restaurant." Then, some days ago, walking past the rocks in the park on my way to the subway, and suddenly aware of the intense greenness of the leaves, that same happy, yet mostly vague and *excited* feeling came back to me. In some way the path there to and from the old boathouse is crucial to my mind. And as I write, I think of something more and finer—the old gas lamps in the park, row on row, there where the path itself was so wonderfully

53. Henri Michaux (1899–1984), Belgian-born French poet and painter.
54. A Brooklyn park, the largest in New York City and, like Central Park in Manhattan, designed by Frederick Law Olmstead and Calvert Vaux.

*wide,* and their paper filaments, budding like flowers, row on row of them all along the path, waited for the lamplighter to come along with his torch. This is what I remember with the greatest pleasure of that scene: the lamplighter—making his rounds, *raising his [torch] high to each pole* till the gas blazed under his hands, and then going on again making the whole flame as he went. [. . .]

## May 23, 1949

Schubert. Sonata in G major, Op. 78. A musical work I go back to every time I am at Yaddo, and one that is *nearer* to me than any other piano work I know. It moves me and changes me so profoundly that for once I can understand Lenin's fear of music as a diversion from "real" life. That is, for me Schubert's sonata acts as an absolute escape from life. When it is over I literally come back to earth and am dazed and really frightened by the shock of the contrast. [. . .]

It is this freedom, swift ranginess, alternation of mood, yet steadfast line all through and around the caprices of the mind, that I seek for my book. My book, also, is a sonata—i.e., a game of wits between the journeyings of the self and the ineluctability of the theme.

## June 4, 1949

[. . .] Read *PR* and *Commentary;* read Hindus's fantastic record of his meetings with Céline in Denmark.[55] The story in itself is hilarious and tragic—the young Jewish intellectual fallen in love with the virulently anti-Semitic genius, and trying to vindicate to himself his—"strange taste" that [brings] only honor to his own taste and probity as an intellectual. I've always been something less than warm toward Hindus and have usually been even a little afraid of a certain manic instability in him. Yet putting all my personal feelings aside here, so far as I can, I note above all my respect for his own "queerness" in approaching Céline and a certain grim honesty in recounting his own feelings—even to the risk of seeming ridiculous by all "smart" standards. The truth is, as I see it now, that Hindus has always sought, above most of the young intellectual Jews I have known, to be himself. As a portrait of Céline himself, for example, his record is

55. Milton Hindus, *The Crippled Giant: A Literary Relationship with Louis-Ferdinand Céline* (New York: Boar's Head, 1950). Anti-Semitism in certain English and "modern" writers, including Céline (see note 57), T. S. Eliot (see note 57), and Ezra Pound (see Chapter 1, note 61), was the subject of a *Commentary* symposium in which Kazin participated: "The Jewish Writer and the English Literary Tradition: A Symposium: Part II," *Commentary* (October 1949): 367–368. See also October 22, 1949 entry.

negligible, badly written, gauche in every sense. But as a journal of his encounter with Céline, it has a certain pathos and candor that make it interesting.

The dilemma involved in such a literary infatuation as Hindus is a terrible one—all the more terrible in that the burden of anti-Semitism upon *us* has so long made impossible *real* criticism of Jews and an accounting of their equivocal relation to those whom they respect for their intellectual and artistic gifts, but who are hostile to the Jews. Hindus's pamphlet is a harrowing illustration of this. With bowed head and clenched lips, trying both to do justice to the artist and to *neutralize* the oppressor, the Jewish intellectual has to perform so many functions at once. His own respect and proffered love are turned against him; *he,* in his full racial and historic personality, is despised by the man to whom he offers his love, and his *opinion* is negligently and ironically accepted. Yet worse than all this is what must be obscured and slurred over in the heart and mind of the young Jew himself. For after all, he does not, himself, wish to "defend" the "Jews" in toto—The particular burden of the Jewish question is that it forces the Jew to defend more than he wishes to, more than any human being living among his fellows actually can. What he should like to do, at most, is to show up in his idol that vulgar prejudice which, after all, is conventional, unconscious, auxiliary to the writer's own genius. But the idol-writer being non-Jewish, cannot himself so discriminate. Hence the curious burden of the Jew, and at the same time, a certain advantage in having to *distinguish*—it is the importance of both his physical survival, of his self-respect, of his moral growth at the same time—he does more than is called for by any other individual and wedges open the ambiguities of history at the same time.

But if, like Hindus and so many others, he leaves the question there, saying in effect: "I will not permit you to attack *my people*"; or, "everything you say against the Jews is false and vicious about us as a whole. It would be so about any people." Then he also retreats from the crucial point, that from which all modern Jewish self-consciousness might start into a truly creative understanding of the Jews, what is a Jew, how far we should accept and how far deny our tradition.

Most important, but always so obvious, tragic that we fear to say it and leave the most emphatic definitions of this role to others; by being continually forced into this contradiction, the Jew wears the great burden of history—it is for this reason that only out of such a people could the Christ-story have risen and in that "no man's land" of which Veblen spoke, he sees more: i.e., he sees both sides at the same time.[56]

56. Thorstein Veblen, "The Intellectual Pre-eminence of Jews in Modern Europe" (1919).

The burden is one we must accept. The burden is of life itself in all its deepest contradictions. And it is a *prophetic* burden: we honor the creative function in him who, still, would slay us. We exemplify in our own lives the division that must continually be made between the creative and the conventional. We bear witness to something greater than the genius-attacker himself: we point to the essential principle he in part denies.

And this, too, this cleaving function on the part of the Jewish intellectual, is what men like Eliot and Greene and Celine[57] hate in us. That *we* are without "orthodoxy" frightens them. The figure of the "usurer" in the medieval legend has been transposed, in the Judeo-phobia of modern intellectuals, into the figures of the *stranger,* the wanderer, the man who "belongs nowhere"—this is the real animus in Dostoevsky, in Stalinist patriotism, with its horror of the "pitiful and unpleasant," figures—the "quiet skeptics," the "passportless wanderers," the "rootless cosmopolitans." If we accept this condition with dignity, with the needed prophetic awareness, we uphold the very principle of freedom; we point to the condition of the intellectual, the *free thinker* as a whole.

## July 30, 1949

[. . .] Music the God. In these last days of intense nervousness and distress I have been conscious as never before on how much I depend on music for my life-strength. Last night, visiting with my parents and Pearlie[58] after dinner, the unspoken strain of these meetings afflicted me so hard that I thought I would break down completely—when suddenly, out of memory, I began to sing arias from Mozart's operas, and sang and sang. I could not bear to leave off singing, until I was quieter in myself. [. . .]

## August 5, 1949

On the nature of the ideologue. He is the man brought up for an age of revolution who finds himself summarizing its failures. He is the man who accounts for everything in terms of the *new* philosophy. He is a Bolshevik who has lost

57. T. S. Eliot (1888–1965), American-born poet and critic, whose 1922 poem *The Waste Land* was the most influential literary work of its era. Graham Greene (1904–1991), English novelist and critic. Kazin met him at a London party in 1945 and resented what he believed to be Greene's evident distaste for his Jewish looks. Céline was the pseudonym of the French novelist and doctor Louis-Ferdinand Destouches (1894–1961), an influential and controversial French writer who wrote anti-Semitic satires and supported Vichy France during World War II.

58. Pearl Kazin, younger sister of Kazin, critic and essayist, wife of the Harvard sociologist Daniel Bell.

everything of Bolshevism except its habits of mind. He is the critic who patronizes the artist. He is the man who invariably thinks that mystics are stupid. He is the man for whom *systems of thought* are more precious than insights.

The ideologue, created for an age of revolution—Diderot. The ideologue, washed up by the despair of a class—Alfred Rosenberg.[59] The ideologue, descendant of a Talmudic tradition, but without the belief—Isaac [Rosenfeld], Harold Rosenberg, etc.

The ideologue as conventional man: fundamentally, he is unable to step out of the patterns laid down in the past. Wishes to impress his audience, not to liberate it.

The ideologue—"thinking his way through the crisis," on his way from one philosophy to another.

## August 19, 1949

[. . .] I have never felt so close to Carol, so conscious of how much I admire and love her. As I watched her face under the lamp last night, so tired and worn and dismayingly thin, I felt a pang at the unrelieved hard work of her life with Michael. And at my own fundamental unshar[ing] in the parental life. I do *something,* I help out when I can—but I can't kid myself that I do anywhere enough. When I'm with Michael in the afternoon, watching him steer his cart around the lawn, I love him with all my heart, but my mind isn't always on him—too much on my work. In some way, too, I exploit the strength he so obviously has, and which I am learning to have only so long after my youth. All those simple boyish things I have never freely, easily done he's beginning to do with radiance. When I see him going to the dog, giggling his head off as the dog licks him, I am amused by my own lifelong fear of dogs, my total unnaturalness to so many things which kids take for their own as a matter of course. But I try to keep up with my son; and I do, honest God, do my best to pay attention. If only I didn't exploit his

59. Alfred Rosenberg (1893–1946), leading racial theorist of National Socialism, executed following Nuremberg trials. Denis Diderot (1713–1784) was a French philosopher, critic, and writer. An important figure in the Enlightenment, he is best known as cofounder, editor, and contributor to the *Encyclopédie*. Harold Rosenberg (1906–1978), writer, philosopher, art critic who coined the term "Action Painting," later called abstract expressionism, which he once explained to Kazin, meant essentially "fucking up the canvas." Among Rosenberg's varied accomplishments was the idea of "Smokey the Bear" as a mascot for the U.S. Forest Service.

young beauty so, and tell myself that he doesn't need a father as much as *I* do. I am perfectly aware that I invented my father. Michael must wake up his.

## September 20, 1949

After a week's fussing on it, finally brought the Mrs. Solovey story to Shawn at the *New Yorker*.[60] When I handed it to him, I was sweating so profusely that I could not stand his looking at me, and fled as soon as I could. The whole day weakened and unreal, but happy, for having delivered myself of this at last.

Shawn's eyes are extraordinarily blue and piercing and "Irish." It is only when he looks straight at me that I get some insight into the curious severity under his fumbling shyness.

## October 10, 1949

When I hear European Jews, "refugees," like Hannah and Paolo, discussing European and American civilization, I feel that they alone—whom "Europe" rejected, really still love it, and understand it, and are now patiently trying to explain it to others.

Last week played the Beethoven Concerto for the first time in years. It is made up of scales and of the *echoing* tones of the scales. [. . .]

## October 11, 1949

I have been catching in myself all these last few days a more sympathetic, unconsciously loving, attitude toward the city, which has nothing to do with *liking* it better. It is merely that the great insight of my recent life has been *acceptance,* an inexpressibly delicious feeling of being *me,* no one else, of not wanting to be anyone else, of being grounded in this life, this city, this body, and in no other. Walking in the street as usual, between boredom and fatalism, I nevertheless realize to the depths of my being something I have so rarely admitted to myself—that I am grounded in this city, these streets, among these people, as a matter of course, without even the possibility of hypothetical denial. Essere: to be: to be of this existence of which I am threaded through and through. [. . .]

60. The story, a section of *Walker*, was not published in the *New Yorker*. It appeared as "The Woman Downstairs" in the February 1950 issue of *Commentary*.

Imagine a group of Jews, crazed by being years in the concentration camp, who decide that they alone are the true Christian-*founders* of the religion of Jesus and go about attacking the established churches.

## October 22, 1949

[. . .] How awful, how shameful, more and more in retrospect, is the self-pity and theatrical isolation of that contribution of mine to the *Commentary* symposium.[61] Far from being a "stranger" in this Anglo-American literary tradition, I am morally at the very center of it. I [may] not belong to the "official party," and thank God that I do not: I am rather a sentinel of the truly universal experiences, and far, far closer to the central moral problems in Modern literature, by reason of my being a Jew, than I can possible say. This morning, as I was walking along the Cutalossa Road, I realized more deeply than ever before that so many of the cultural fixtures I mechanically equate with pain are, in truth, sources of very deep pleasure and enrichment to me—America itself, in the largest sense, and myself as a Jew. What has always kept me from affirming my positive affirmation for them more clearly, as I see now, is my fear that if I did, I would be false to my inner estrangements, to my untiring awareness of the rift at the heart of our culture. Yet as I grow older, more deeply planted in the earth of my being, with all its attendant loyalties and attachments, I find that far from diminishing or softening my *radical* view, I at last give it focus—to see things in something like their *necessary* proportion. [. . .]

## November 8, 1949

[. . .] Out of my erotic ache, sharper these last few weeks than ever because I have been so impotent on the book. There was a young woman in the train—not at all attractive, glasses, tidily coupled with her equally uninteresting companion. But as I watched her (plainly unsensual) as she sat on the seat, or walked up to the aisle, clothed in her white blouse, I thought again of the imponderable sensual value a blouse always has for me. A woman's tactile values are never so real for me as when she is in a blouse. Transparency, filminess: I have the woman's skin in her clothes; and there is a progression of delight from seeing her breasts ripple, from the shoulder straps outlined against the skin (magnified by the blouse itself, as if it were a second skin)—to something even more delightful, both in my mind as I watch them and in the sticking and

61. See Note 55.

unpeeling of the blouse to the skin. For in a blouse a woman's sensual *being,* her secret, the thing a man always tries to reach and which evades him even when he penetrates her below, somehow remains, is *invested* in the transparency in which she is all clothed of herself and her second skin. As I watch her in a blouse, I feel her deepest femininity is all *there,* and—most delightful—that she is conscious of it. Not coyly, not necessarily even provocatively—but held by deep inner satisfaction of her own abundance—a kind of warm, inner strength moving from [the] openness of her breasts and shoulders to her limbs below. They walk more slowly, happily, when they are clothed like that. They have put on a question to which we are expected to answer. And sometimes when I see a woman walking like that, secretly looking up and down herself, wherever her gaze may seem to be directed, I wonder if she is not as enraptured with her own abundance as I am, and if, should I be making love to her, we would not be joined, the two of us, in adoration of something that is still as mysterious to her as it is to me. This secrecy in a woman, as I call it, or better still, her unalloyed sense of being, as compared with an over-conscious and, by nature, aggressive man—she who *receives* us—is to me at once the most vexing and yet the most delicious aspect of the feminine principle. It is to this that I make love, and will never be tired of making love—for I can *never* solve the secret, I can only shape its enchantment for me in different ways, and the nearer I get to it, the more I realize that *she* shapes it with me, for she is as far from knowing there is a secret as I am from solving it. Yes, it is always out of the woman that life comes, and to the woman we return for the *presence* of life at its deepest.

## December 9, 1949

The more I go over my sexual situation, my longings for C., and for how many other women I rarely confess to myself, the more I realize how much this distress in myself, my continual *wanting* and strain and anxiety and guilt, are exacerbated by my refusal to face the facts of my own character and simply what is. I keep on wanting two things—the family, and freedom of sexual exploration; "security" and the elementary rights of my complicated, sensual, and propulsive nature. Which is all right, which is a very human craving, which is a deep and serious human conflict without easy resolution—but which is something very different from the absolute strain and self-deception and continual oscillation in which I always put these things. I can bear the pain of living so long as I know where I am, because I know what I am; what I cannot bear, and what robs me of growth and soundness, is this elusiveness, this reference of all these real problems to some arbitrary idea or romance of "happiness" as virtue, as anything, for me, but the acceptance of my double need: or a more truthful word than acceptance, realization.

The fool of virtue, or the soul of Kazin crying and lost to be saved from the fierce hungry sharks of his own nature. I already see a story in this, have I not lived this over and over, so that I have done everything but realize it? Not a satire, but a loving, tender, affectionate, uncompromising study of such a man as I have always vainly tried to be, a slave to the fantastic absolute of "security" and "normality"— this on the surface, while remorselessly, and oh how mercilessly, he seeks to find in one woman both the ideal mistress and that ideal, that Russian woman ideal, and Mrs. Solovey and that Palestinian woman in the park last Sunday, and Leuba,[62] who is Sophie the better mother, the mother that never was. In the story, my Myshkin[63] does what all men do, and more; he is susceptible all the time, and his unconscious air of entreaty—the way, shall I say, in which he puts himself at the disposal of women, his revelatory air of regarding them as his fate—makes him more attractive to women than he dares admit to himself. Yet they never have him, and he never has them—for his mind is always on something else, on that ideal. And rather than take his place *in* the world, and eat his fill of the abundance given to him, and satisfy himself and her in the same movement of completion, he destroys himself, inch by inch, by undoing himself in mind what he does in fact, by devaluating it in reference to his lost paradise, his idea. He wants two contradictory things at the same time—to have the world (simply because he is a man), and to arrest it in moral terms. Trying to become more than a man, he becomes less. And shall I add that his "recompense" in this, his legend—the very thing that makes him singular—is his "goodness," his "virtue"?

It is only on this new understanding that I can go ahead with the *Walker:* no more posturing, no more forcing; this book is already inside of me and demands to be *adapted,* not manipulated, from the immediate wealth of my consciousness— what it is I do think and feel.

## January 17, 1950

Pearlie and I think that we are soft because we suffer so much. But because we suffer so much, we have been turned hard—and it is from this hardness, now, that we continue to suffer. [. . .]

62. Kazin's dentist.
63. Prince Myshkin, the Christ-like hero in *The Idiot*, by the Russian novelist Dostoevsky (1821–1881).

## February 25, 1950

After listening to the *St. John Passion*[64] at Carnegie last night: the epic of Christianity is the connection of millions with the story of Jesus, how he lived and died—how one man suffered the complete gamut "for us." So it does not matter, I say as a Jew, that the story is perhaps dubious, and that the language directed against Jesus's fellow Jews all through time! is so bitterly offensive to us. For human experience dominates all, in the end. That millions have wept over this man and been charged all over again with the story, each time they have heard it—that is the meaning of the lesson, not its abstract claims for Him as a God. He has entered, as no one man entered before, into the heart of the human race.

Thought again of the connection between Bach's passion music and the old morality plays. The touching naiveté with which they act out the parts, with which the lesson is transfused into music, each of those "simple" Christians at the altar in the old church playing the various parts—that is the best proof of what I said before. It is the experience of Christianity that the Jews overlook in their bitterness against "Christianity."

I am so tired of being told my writing is "moving." I want to be told it is convincing.

## March 19, 1950

[. . .] As I walked up the road early this morning before breakfast, I realized again how much I have been trying to fit myself to Carol,[65] to "adjust" to her—at the cost of myself, and how wrong and wasteful it is from every point of view, how impossible it makes even love for someone else, for her. Well, then, has it all been wrong from the beginning because I *have* always tried to adjust to her, because I have constantly compromised? Yes and no—for under this strain, I have not had even a chance to find out what my real feelings toward her are. [. . .]

## March 21, 1950

[. . .] Horrible *Commentary* dinner last night. Insufferable to be in that gaseous, anxious, self-congratulatory Jewish atmosphere too long. I never realized so

64. *St. John Passion*, oratorio by Johann Sebastian Bach (1685–1750), based on the Gospel of John.
65. On March 6, Kazin and Carol separated; he moved into a sublet at 339 East 58th Street.

firmly how little I have in common with those people. Imagine meeting with people and trying to induce some deeper affection between us than we possess—from the fact, simply, that we are Jews! A pox on all such incestuousness.

Among non-Jews I wish to be myself and so only too often stress to them what I am on the most rudimentary level—i.e., a Jew. Among Jews I wish to be myself, and so, only too often stress to them what I am *not,* on the most rudimentary level—i.e., not simply and exclusively a Jew. I need to stop this, and easily can, for the conflict is not as great as I had thought: I can simply be what I am—with Jews or non-Jews. "Our desire," said Spinoza,[66] "is not that nature may obey us, but on the contrary, that we may obey nature." [. . .]

## Easter Sunday, 1950

John [10:16] "And other sheep I have, which are not of this fold: them also I must bring, and they shall hear my voice; and there shall be one fold, and one shepherd." [. . .]

I, who am not a Christian, who may become one by the time this journey of reflection is finished, but strongly doubt it. I cannot approach Yeshua without thinking first of the stupendous wealth of love and faith which Christians and non-Christians have poured out on his name and image and story. It is meaningless to look for "real" Yeshua, the Jew—as so many Jews have done—as if Christian devotion to him were simply an extravagance or a mistake. No matter how well Jewish scholars may prove that he was a good and faithful Jew, that the greater part of his personal teaching is in the Jewish tradition, that the image of the Christ, as Christendom has created it, is based upon superstitions and mysteries unworthy of his own joy in the God of Israel—the real story of Yeshua is still in the inspiration that he, in the shape of Jesus as God, has given to the human race. How many millions have wept over him, how many centuries have they tenderly recounted his sufferings and his death, have believed in Him, have found their way to God because he lived and died. And how truly he did live and die for them, whatever the "real" Yeshua may have been, since, after all, the inner history of Christianity is a human experience, of the most sacred delicacy and transcendent intensity, and not of a doctrine which may or may not (and I think it was) have been at variance with his original teaching. [. . .]

66. Baruch Spinoza (1632–1677), Dutch philosopher of Portuguese Jewish origin, one of Kazin's intellectual heroes.

And so this book [*Walker*] is an attempt, not to find the "real," the Jewish Yeshua, prior to what Christianity has made of him,—what possible satisfaction can it be to discover the "true" Yeshua in order, as many Jewish scholars unconsciously wish, only to lose him—but the Yeshua who is *in* Jesus. If I, a Jew, find joy in the fact that millions adore one who was himself a Jew, it is not *because he* was a Jew (that would be shallow national pride), but because I can still find my way to Yeshua through those teachings of his common to both Jews and Christians. [. . .]

## June 28, 1950

A dream of fair women. All afternoon—on my way from Rioch's, and then to and from Leuba's—I found myself walking with my eyes absolutely glued on the women. I had never before in my life found them so thick on my sight. I was mad with hunger, wandered in an orchard of breasts like fruit, of bodies like great trunks, in a jungle of great growths, and clinging vines, and wild underbrush below.

## August 20, 1950

[. . .] I really must write in this old notebook more often than I do; everything that is fundamental in me has first found its expression here.

## August 30, 1950

New York again, dregs of summer. The air is thick and moist, the sun behind its overcast gleams pale and liverish. Pale under the Coney Island sunburn, the young girls stand on the corners, sucking defiantly at their cigarettes, their print skirts flaring around their knees, the design in the print pressed against their sallow flesh like a cockamamies. Tornadoes of dust in the air, thunderstorms of noise, screeching of whistles, groans of busses, burglar alarms, peanut whistles, wheeze of emergency breaks. The air hangs heavy; we all walked slow; the last of summer; dregs of summer.

When I think of the block, I think first of the cavern it made between the houses—the long black asphalt ground of Chester Street between the rotting farmhouses.[67] This was the ground, the bottom ground of all my first discoveries in space. How I played one-o'-cat there by myself in the twilight, fishing that ground up and down. Beyond the Wassermanns' house lay the new country—

67. The third chapter of *A Walker in the City* is titled "The Block and Beyond."

the way to Betsy Head[68] and the vegetable gardens and the pavilion, with its smell of emptiness and cool dusty air, and its steps where the little girls played jacks, and the ailanthus trees around the wading pool.

The block at evening I identify most deeply with "countries." The magic circle with its spokes, in each the name of a different country. Then, at the signal, we all ran—I remember that best, the running into the darkness where the monument works were, hiding there. Exploding into space; the centrifugal burst.

Lights and blackness. When you fought a boy in the evening, you fought within the narrow dark circle made by the lights over the candy stores. Then, when your head hit the sidewalk, the soul-shivering thump, the fright was in the ground at last, which usually you had fought, had tried to bend to your wishes. The ground, the wall of our house against which we played handball, trying to reach higher and higher as you went. Simulation of mastery. The little swagger in the boys as they played.

The narrow ground—and then, to the fields.

## September 8, 1950

Worked steadily until about 9 last night, and then ate at my 60th St. trattoria, walked about in a state of high excitement and exhaustion—there is a whole new dimension of strength in me every time I work at night; the hell with all my inner aches and pains! I can work anytime I please! Slept badly of course, from the continued strain; it seemed to me that I was thinking, thinking all night. But the morning is good, though weary. Was so pent-up that as I read that banal article of Rabbi Bernstein's[69] in this morning's *Life* on "What the Jews Believe," I burst into tears. But just a moment ago, thinking about the Rabbi's description of the place the Pentateuch has in the Jewish religion, I suddenly realized something about the Jewish orthodoxy about time, the past, the foundation stones of their own earliest religious history—something that has been deep in me for years. I mean that the Jewish commitment to the world's oneness, their sense of themselves as the "first" people, has, in me, and certainly in many other Jews, led to a peculiar belief that beyond their standard, their tradition, all other experiences are only

68. Betsy Head Memorial Playground in Brooklyn.
69. Rabbi Philip Bernstein (1901–1985), president of the Central Conference of American Rabbis. "What the Jews Believe" appeared in the September 11, 1950, issue of *Life*.

modifications and extensions, not equally "real." That despite the centuries of persecution and exile, etc. there has always been a feeling among the Jews that everything after themselves, or slightly off the line of their own tradition, is an accident, superficial. For myself, this is one clue, at last, to that persistent orthodoxy and even sacramentalism conferred upon the past I have suffered from so long—the unwillingness to accept, as equally real, anything that has happened late, or to other peoples; the feeling, particularly, that the period in itself, with whatever it may bring, is interesting only as a reflection of a tradition or a breaking away from it.

This has been a great intellectual and even moral weakness, a refusal to accept the flexibility and even the chaotic spontaneity of life in all its inward manifestations, to see the period, different peoples, etc., etc. as they are, simply in existence.

## September 23, 1950

[. . .] Lunch with Jim Farrell[70]—who dismayed me as much as usual, but whom I like, as usual, with a fellow-feeling that is never between our minds. Jim has discovered that Lincoln and Whitman were the greatest Americans, utters banalities by the bushelful. A deeply tormented man, as insecure as a drunken chick, with a fundamentally uninteresting mind, but full of good will. I understood for the first time today how much of the lack of direct contact with him is due to his eyes—those bad, heavy eyes that never fix on anything, always look as if they were trying to focus on something. The deeply awkward boyish slouch of his body. Plod, plod, plod. Told me he writes 5–10 pages everyday as a matter of course; that is his system. Never worries about it. Then rushed to my appointment with Marian K—an apartment full of diddley-diddley things, so girlish I did not know whether it made me laugh or suffocate. She came back here, and I made love to her for twenty minutes. She attracts me violently, I want her so badly, yet she is a not over-intelligent, rather childish girl, with a great power of provocative, ladylike reserve. I listen to her talk about her father, a doctor, and the Jews among whom she doesn't belong—why paint your arm green, she said, if the dominant culture doesn't believe in it? I do not respect this girl; being with her is full of that unverbal sultriness I am so used to; and I am worried, worried stiff, that I want her so badly.—why?

70. James T. Farrell (1904–1979), Irish American novelist, best known for the *Studs Lonigan* trilogy, friend of Kazin since the thirties.

A day of confusion, of mental dishonesty, of silent weeping. Let me try to put myself in order; it has not been so bad for a long time. I must not lose the thread so soon again, after working so hard to regain it.

## September 25, 1950

In the train on the way back to NY from Josie's[71] where I spent yesterday. [. . .] Josie is sick, worried, more withdrawn than usual. She is to go to NY hospital in three weeks or so (whenever they have a free bed) for an operation. A growth on her back. The day with her was a little boring, a little moving—as always, a little strange. Ever since I have known her (but can admit to myself only now) I've felt in her a kind of inner panic, almost a queer, hypnotic disintegration. Her genius is entirely as a person, from the heart. She is inexpressibly precious and rare, for one can depend on her, as on so few, for absolute spontaneity, goodness, considerateness. But years in that house alone, a long and tormented stewing over John Herrmann[72] *have sapped her body.* With me she is painfully submissive intellectually, too humble; and as always this makes her pallid within. Josie's is a tragedy of the writer *qua* writer, perhaps especially of the woman writer who is almost too nice without, too *decent, too* womanly, without a sufficiently combative, asserting intelligence to find her complete balance either as a woman or as a writer. As a human being, pure and simple, she is of the most homogeneous goodness. Echoes of the old Sioux City, of the Valley of Democracy in the early sweet 1900's. And now she is frightened, almost penniless, very much alone in that house. The stillness around her twists my heart—uselessly. Yesterday at twilight as I sat across the living room from her (each of us looking steadily and mutely out to the green outside the other's window), it twisted me, it twisted me in a heavy, silent grieving to see her face so yellow and sick—pale in the light—the person contracted within her own fear. But then I saw her *young face,* the chin leveling out to a square, wisps of blond-gray hair (her absolute naturalness). It always repels me to see the way she sucks on cigarettes half-way down. Every ash tray in the house is full of those gray pulps. Yet this, like the way she talks in that

71. Josephine Herbst (1892–1969) was a prominent novelist and journalist in the 1930s whom Kazin met and befriended in 1950. She lived in a farmhouse in Erwinna, Pennsylvania. They would remain close friends until her death in January 1969.

72. John Herrmann (1900–1959), divorced husband of Josepine Herbst. Herrmann was living in Mexico. He had worked in the New Deal administration and was a member of a group that allegedly funneled messages to the Soviet Union through the CPUSA. Herrmann introduced Whittaker Chambers (1901–1965) to Alger Hiss (1904–1996), a former State Department official whom Chambers accused in an August 3, 1948, congressional hearing of having been a Communist and Soviet Spy—a charge Hiss vehemently denied.

growling tobacco-sputtering voice, or the way she drives, is [illegible] tenderly and wisely considered, of her wonderful directness, naturalness, lovingness—something of the quality I observed the other day in Jim Farrell despite all his heaviness and ploddingness. I mean the way the writer's constant indwellingness upon his own thought (we are all heavy inside with our own thought) throws him upon every object in his path: how more slowly, cumbersomely, he makes his way (as differentiated from others). [. . .]

## September 29, 1950

Better this morning, but still weak. Unable to fix very long on anything. Was thinking, however, that if I can remember anything at any moment, if, as it so often seems, there is a core of simultaneous memory in us, that we might imaginatively see ourselves as living differently in time than we do. I.e.—it is possible to say now that I am "remembering" (back now to this incident, now to that one), that I at this fixed point am remembering back to another, but that my whole inner life of memory and sensation and idea is simultaneous in its inspiration of ordering: that this movement in me is primary, not my stationary self in space looking back to the movement.[73]

*The Girl.*[74]
It was that late spring, just before the end of war in Europe.

## October 8, 1950

[. . .] Went up to Heinrich and Hannah's for dinner with them and the Koyrés.[75] Heinrich as usual started by lecturing, saying the same (very brilliant and independent) things he's said over and over. But the lack of contact with him last night was my own fault. So drawn to Hannah these days that I resent him? I'm not in love with her, just adore her as a human being, with all my heart. Heinrich's heaviness, Cherman, Cherman, got me down, nevertheless. The dinner excellent but I too tired and depressed to do very much. Liked Koyré a lot, obviously a man of parts. At first reminded me of Irwin Edman[76]—which is

73. Kazin's "Proustian" theory of memory as described here informs the structure of *Walker*.
74. A story, set in war-time London, that Kazin hoped to write but never did.
75. Alexandre Koyrés (1892–1964), an influential philosopher of science.
76. Irwin Edman (1896–1954), professor of philosophy at Columbia, gave *On Native Grounds* a rave front-page review in the *New York Herald Tribune: Books*, calling its publication "not only a literary but a moral event."

absurd. Sandy, thin hair, a lot of bad teeth in gray metal fillings; his mouth looks like the remains of an arsenal. The talk was not very good, mostly general—was surprised and a little nettled (downfall of the idol?) by Hannah's surprising eagerness to please, her complyingness, and Heinrich's rather obvious "good manners." [. . .]

## October 18, 1950

And now let us get to work. Janet [Rioch] is perfectly right; I must finish the *Walker* before I go to Europe. I must bend every effort. Now that the divorce is in hand and there are no more illusions about Carol of any kind, I must stop looking back and frittering away my time. Yesterday was a beginning—really dug into the summer part in which the Commie street meetings figure. In the afternoon saw the lawyer at the Pecora Campaign H.Q., Sidney Davis, who seemed nice enough, then went on to [Clifton] Fadiman's house, then Janet for what I hope and believe is a windup, then met Saul [Bellow] outside the Museum of Modern Art. Saul very gray, jaded, worried—the evening was in some way disappointing, but we came together by the end, I felt it.

Thinking of Nehru's beautiful face brooding over the current situation.

## October 23, 1950
### [Yaddo]

Elizabeth Bishop's[77] hair is thick and rises electrically up her head—that crisply warm voice of hers goes on, shyly picking out the syllables, and alights on something she cares about (Dylan Thomas a moment ago) the hair seems to shoot up straight, connected node to node by sparks. . . . That upsweeping electric hair is the poet's helmet, his rooster comb. Used to notice it in Robert F,[78] and in Lowell, and many others—it is the shield on which they take the blows, but it is also the flag breaking out in excitement. The electricalness of it is what I love—straight up and down, politely burning.

77. Elizabeth Bishop (1911–1979), American poet, winner of a Pulitzer Prize, poet laureate of the United States, 1949–1950; Dylan Thomas (1914–1953), Welsh poet, carried on a torrid affair with Kazin's sister, Pearl.

78. Robert Fitzgerald (1910–1985), American poet, critic, and celebrated translator of many Greek classics.

## November 2, 1950

The only way I ever get anything written is by getting up the material so thoroughly beforehand that writing consists in lopping off what doesn't belong.

## November 4, 1950

[. . .] Thinking last night about the Negro artist Beauford Delaney, whom I like so much but bores me so with his spiritual clichés. He goes around being *grateful* for everything, loving everything by design. Add this to what they do to "minorities" [in] America (Jim Farrell as well). They make the Negro so grateful, so simple. Just as they make the Jew too canny, too full of "angles." The usual Jewish intellectual and Beauford the Negro artist meet on the periphery of the circle, running from each other as they try to avoid the gimlet eye of the white Aryan Protestant in the middle. Both types are distortions. How hard for the Jewish intellectual to be *simple;* how hard for his Negro fellow to be militantly wise, or openly skeptical, without sourness (that awful Negro big-shot intellectual, the little knowing smile, I met at Frank Taylor's[79] house that evening in 1944).

Read the second [issue] of *Freeman.* The tone of this is impossible: ex-liberal and Commie intellectuals rolling all the great issues of our times down the hill at a single word of command: Down with Stalin! It occurs to me that the real pressure toward conservativism now is being applied almost exclusively by intellectuals of this stamp—Chamberlain, Schlamm,[80] etc.; the "captains of industry" are simply not much interested. This is an *examen de conscience* purely, and so narrow-minded and cheaply aggressive and *lateral* to the masses of our time that the thing becomes comical.

## November 9, 1950

The whole idea of the *Walker* to be based entirely upon Brownsville, the only way. The book to come only from the heart, entirely from mood—no more

79. Frank E. Taylor (1916–1999), editor at Reynal and Hitchcock, which published *On Native Grounds*; later editor in chief at McGraw Hill.

80. A liberal-left columnist for the *New York Times* in the 1930s, John Chamberlain (see Chapter 1, note 76) later became a leading conservative journalist, writing the Introduction to William F. Buckley Jr.'s (1925–2008) *God and Man at Yale* and served as contributing editor to Buckley's *National Review*. Former Austrian Communist and adviser to Henry Luce, William Schlamm (1904–1978) edited the *Freeman* and helped Buckley found the *National Review*.

qvetching, no more note-book outlines and straining. I have it now; I have it all—just 4 years to the week I began that primitive first draft up in the farmhouse at Yaddo!

## November 28, 1950

The coldest day of the year. The crucifixion day. On such a day one either dies or is reborn. Saying goodbye to Michael—yes and to Carol, too, on a rainy morning in a lawyer's office on Fifth Avenue. So that for a moment, remembering the warm, yellow sand that day Hannah and I walked at Manomet, I shivered exactly as if a spear had split me.

No, I say, it doesn't matter about the money and how often she has blocked and starved me: one must love, to us has been given this gift—we must love.

Why I do not like Saul Bellow, no—*au fond,* I don't: a *kalte mensch,* too full of his being a novelist to be a human being writing. [. . .]

# 4
# The Fifties
## 1951–1957

ON JANUARY 18, 1951, ALFRED AND CAROL divorced. By then, he had persuaded himself that the marriage was a mistake. For three years he had stifled "the doubts and protests in my heart," he wrote in a July 15, 1950, note to his new friend Josephine Herbst. "I was living a lie." He was less successful adjusting to the separation from his son. Thinking about a future without "normal" relations with Michael, he felt "a tight band of ice" forming around his heart and "a kind of fatality" (June 20, 1951). There were compensations, however. Except for minor revisions he was finished with *A Walker in the City*, a book that had turned out better than he had hoped. In addition, he had met Ann Birstein, a "wise-cracking" twenty-three-year-old rabbi's daughter and author of a prize-winning first novel, *Star of Glass*. Kazin was strongly attracted to Ann, not least because he sensed a sympathetic literary intelligence very different from that of the "statuesque philistine" who was divorcing him (November 7, 1951). Ann had been awarded a Fulbright Fellowship to study in Paris; Alfred, who was scheduled to attend the Salzburg Seminar in July, joined her on the trip over, continuing a courtship that would conclude in their marrying (in Basel, Switzerland) when he returned to Europe a year later.

Kazin had returned in the spring of 1952 to take a visiting professorship in American studies at the University of Cologne, to be followed by a Fulbright Conference in American Studies in the summer at Cambridge. The Cold War fifties were a good time for cultural ambassadors and students of American studies, and Kazin was nicely situated to benefit—"nothing like working your way through Europe on the strength of *On Native Grounds*" (*Lifetime*, 141). Nor were opportunities confined to European fellowships. Kazin was invited to teach American literature at Harvard during the fall of 1953. The following year he was named the William Allan Neilson Visiting Professor at Smith College. The next year he accepted a permanent appointment in the American Studies program at Amherst College.

But if the Cold War created opportunities, it also created difficulties—particularly for a former radical recalling the hope and collective excitement of the revolutionary past. "Whatever the thirties came to, there *was* a feeling of having one's beliefs shared," Kazin wrote in a June 27, 1955, entry. "Nowadays, I not only feel alone in my belief; I hardly find it possible to feel that most people around me believe in *anything*." Struggling to make sense of the moral-political changes that had occurred since the war, he envisioned a book that would track the revisionary journeys of certain New York intellectuals who had started out in the thirties. "The American orthodoxy book," as he called it, would be "about the intellectuals, about New York, about the ex-left, about Fiedlerism and Hookism and Trillingism, about everything I know and have been a part of.

[. . .] I have it, all of it, inside me" (October 15, 1955). The book would eventually become two books, *Starting Out in the Thirties* (1965) and *New York Jew* (1978).

Kazin was planning another book during much of the fifties. Titled "The Western Island," it was to focus on the American writer's search for meaning in lonely confrontation with the American landscape. Or, as he put it in a (successful) application for a renewal of his Guggenheim fellowship, it would consider America as "something apart," a "*terra incognita*" that was always being rediscovered and reimagined in the consciousness of its writers. Kazin did not finish the book, though two versions of it would later appear as *An American Procession* in 1984 and *A Writer's America* in 1988. He did, however, complete a number of essays (some of his very best) on writers—Melville, Thoreau, Emerson, Dreiser, Faulkner—whom he had intended to include. He also wrote frequently and extensively about the "Island book" in his journal as he searched for underlying connections that could become the basis for a coherent plan.

Though he complained about "the nervous gentilities" of college life, the "brainlessness" of the Amherst English faculty, and the "dry, belchy" look of Amherst students—"the way [they] lie back in their seats as if they were 106 and just recovering from coronary thrombosis"—Kazin was not unhappy living and teaching in Northampton and Amherst (September 17, 1954; December 4, 1956). He was passionately interested in the material on which he was lecturing; he had a few friends among the faculty; and he luxuriated in the natural setting. "I feel terribly wealthy and lucky just to be in this part of the country," he wrote in a June 7, 1955, entry when considering the Amherst position. "Is not the secret of this 19th century American writing I love really its grasp of rhyme and colors from nature? The sea, the leaves, the ponds, the forest?" (June 22, 1955). Ann did not feel so lucky. Trapped in the role of faculty wife and mother—their daughter, Cathrael, was born June 30, 1955—unable to move ahead in her own writing, she missed the excitements and social connections of the city. The love affair and marriage that had promised so much in New York, Paris, and Cambridge closed in on her in rural New England. In the fall of 1956, she informed her husband she would not stay another year in Amherst. Though worried that rural New England was not the underlying source of their marriage difficulties, Alfred agreed that Amherst had become impossible for them. He submitted his resignation in January.

He would be returning to New York with a family and without a steady job—but with few regrets. Stymied by his lack of progress on "The American Island," he hoped that a change of venue might shake things loose or point him in a more promising direction. Perhaps it was time to look beyond New England, "that old landscape of dreams and wonders" (October 1, 1956), to come to terms with "the *realness* of America" (August 11, 1957). If New York lacked the ponds and the forests of rural Massachusetts, the hushed quietness of a New England snowstorm, it remained a place where a writer could observe life at its broadest and keenest in "the full concentrated force of the living moment" (August 11, 1957).

## January 25, 1951

Living here.[1] [. . .] I came back among my own. It was hard these first days returning here, the worst was my own snobbish shame and my endless grieving over Asya and Carol. But now I am back among my own, have pierced through the shell of old habits and disorders, to begin my real, my new acquaintance with the people here. Tom Nelson my super, the man on the city. Mrs. Ackerman's bakery. The other day when I was there I was cloven through and through by a special vision—all those lonely men sitting there over their cake and coffee. There was one especially, who sat holding long rumpled sheets of newspaper in his hand and staring at the headlines disgustedly. Over and over he recited the names of old New York newspapers, now gone, and of the magnates—the *Globe*, the *World*, the *Sun*, Munsey, Pulitzer. It was like a roll-call, not only of the past, but of the New York of any to forty or fifty years ago. Our New York wobblies, our solitary working men, our city tramps. This is what I caught in that man calling the roll in the bakery, and from the men along the piers this morning, and the super Tom Nelson—here along the middle streets, the wall of the harbor.

## February 3, 1951

How I recognize my love. That when I look at her face it should seem to me so amazingly beautiful that I should wonder that all others looking upon her do not feel the same thing. This is what I used to feel about Asya; yes, and about Carol; this is what I felt the other afternoon at Lindley's[2] looking at Ann. [. . .]

## February 16, 1951

The whole Harvard experience glorious, even though I read my paper much too quickly.[3] A day of real satisfaction. In the evening at Murdock's read parts of

1. After giving up his sublet on East 58th Street, Kazin moved back to Pineapple Street in Brooklyn Heights, where he had lived before his marriage to Carol Bookman.
2. Denver Lindley (1905–1982), Kazin's editor at Harcourt.
3. Kazin had just returned from Harvard, where he had read a paper on William Faulkner and a chapter from *A Walker in the City*. The visit led to an offer to teach there in the fall of 1953 but not to the permanent position he hoped for.

the WALKER to a group that included Thornton Wilder and MacLeish[4]—Wilder understood everything instantly.

## February 24, 1951

[Albert Pinkham] Ryder: "Have you ever seen an inchworm crawl up a leaf or a twig and then, clinging, to the very end, revolve in the air, feeling for something to reach? That's like me. I am trying to find something out there beyond the place on which I have a footing."

As a boy, it was always Ryder's *biography*, and the biography of so many people like him, that interested me most. And now I see why—it was that remark of Ann's apropos of my wavering interest in Thoreau's Journals that led me to understand. For I was seeking *sanctions* for my own kind of search. Unless I could find that a Ryder, a Thoreau, a Whitman, a Melville had lived—unless it became real to me from reading Mumford's *Brown Decades* that Ryder had actually walked New York streets, I could not believe that what I sought so doggedly and furtively was real. So they gave me sanction, and so, in a very real sense, it was this that led me to criticism—not entirely for this reason, of course, but at least I fully understand now why I could not give my most scrupulous objective understanding to writers—of which I was certainly capable, as I see now!—I was too busy seeking sanctions of my own kind of search. [. . .]

All the smooth oily dark surfaces of those paintings in the Metropolitan entranced me in themselves—literally, entranced; looking at them I found myself coasting along the varnish into sleep, and thought that after I had left, had walked down the great steps, I would still be looking at them with my eyes wide open in sleep. The smoothness, the duskiness of them closed the doors around me of another world. It was like that small corridor-looking room on the second floor (?) of the Metropolitan where they hung the still lifes up and down the walls with a certain negligent disdainful profusion, hid them in an alcove near the elevator, so that in the gloom I had to crouch, get up as close to the wall as a I could, to see them. But blinking there in that alcove I stood face to face with those pictures of the Civil War, those old street scenes of people walking in the snow around Union Square, of skaters in Central Park—breathing in the gloom and the dark at twilight as if that corridor room hung on the main walls with worthies of the

4. Thornton Wilder (1897–197–85), novelist and playwright, awarded the Pulitzer Prize three times, best known for his play *Our Town*; Archibald MacLeish (1892–1982), poet, essayist, librarian of Congress. Kazin would later write that "there was nothing A. MacLeish turned to that he did not turn into still another success."

Revolutionary period was lit with gaslight. The whole room turned into its narrow gas-lit shape; I was uprooted, now in truth, only to be transplanted again. [. . .]

## May 11, 1951

What lovely mornings. What lovely days, with my *Walker* finished at last and Europe ahead—with Ann. Now spring up, my love: go straight ahead without looking back. Only there is steadiness, not in carefulness or second thoughts, but in following my bent to the end. And I will. Now my real life begins: my apprenticeship is over.

## May 26, 1951

On board the Ile de France. The fog horn blasts and blasts, and the sea outside and the air and the planks underfoot are all very wet. Long peaceful days on board with Ann, on my way to Paris. Have never known such uninterruptedly happy days, and even with shipboard languor and boredom such vigor and simple electric joy. So I abandoned my old big notebook for this summer and will write of this summer here, in my little notebook and *en route*. [. . .]

## June 6, 1951

[. . .] I have discovered what my journal is—not a diary or sketchbook, not anything that can be named by its contents, but simply a book that takes its measure from the spontaneity in which I write here. Anything goes in here that I wish to say to myself, *and in advance.*

I cried a little when I saw the boys and girls in Chartres cathedral—those girls of 11 and 12 all in white with their prayer books, those boys with the white sashes around their left arms, for I was thinking of Michael and perhaps of all childhood itself, with its infinite dumb expectation.

## June 20, 1951

[. . .] Michael. All day long and for how many days now I have gone about plodding about thinking of him, missing him. Whenever I catch sight of his picture in my wallet the tears rush to my eyes. I miss him. I miss him so dreadfully, there are no words to say it, and when I think how little I am with him and all the absences that have been and will be, I feel a tight band of ice form about me, a kind of fatality. [. . .]

## July 24, 1951

[. . .] Every original Jew turns against the Jews—they are the earth from which his spirit tries to free itself. Every original Jew recaptures Jewish history by passing through it. The vice of Jewish solidarity—it is an unexpressed compassion without love. The glory of being in the truth, Jewish or not Jewish, is to find a love higher than solidarity. [. . .]

## October 5, 1951

[. . .] What I got most from Hannah last weekend in the country was a more intimate view of her essential *simplicity*—i.e., by which I mean her naturalness, her healthiness in the highest degree. She is so slow, often, on the "pick-up" simply because she cannot really imagine what [it] is *for anyone else to be unnatural.* On the whole, she seems to me the most conclusively *human* creature I have ever known. Not so original as Heinrich, of course, but incomparably more interesting because she is so *compacted* of the human quality. [. . .]

## October 5, 1951

What will give me rest from all this (added three or four days later) but to write myself out; to have it out? I come to bring not peace but a pen.[5]

*Saying the words over to myself as I write.* It is the rhythm of the words and phrases still, that I do not take naturally enough. Constantly awed by our own power of language! Amazed by the simplest phrases, etc. But surely, there is a deeper signification to this *re-saying* in my mind as I write, a stirring of the deepest embers of language, a harkening back to the initial impact of language upon the amazed and grateful brain. This re-saying, re-speaking, points to the inherent doubleness of language: the cleft between existing silence and the dawning speech: to our amazement at language.

## October 12, 1951, 10 PM

Went back to Brownsville for Friday night supper and to give my father and mother a copy of the *Walker*. Walked down from the Brooklyn Museum, where I had gone to look at an exhibition of old photographs. Wonderful one, "Stieglitz and Kitty," (1905) taken by Steichen.[6] So I went home again, fully five years from

5. See Matthew 10: 34: "I come not to bring peace but a sword."
6. Edward J. Steichen (1879–1973), American photographer, painter, and museum and gallery curator.

the day I conceived the book. It *still* looks like a foreign country, more than ever. And shall I tell you a secret? I don't feel like a Jew. Never did—no, not in my soul. It is all a foreign country to me, which is what I said here in this notebook 5 years ago—not my country, the country of my soul at all.[7] No never did; and have spent all my life running away from that fact, trying to be nice and agreeable about being a Jew. How often I have punished myself for a totally fictitious "disloyalty."

Now peace, oh my Lord, some peace. I have begun my work with the *Walker* and now must go on. I don't feel lonely at all any more, though the house is so alone, and there is not a soul on the staircase of this house to even speak my language.

The peculiar unbearable frying smell they have downstairs; how I have to shut my door against it. The little Puerto Rican boys in cowboy uniforms.

Nothing but Yeshivas and temples and *suchul* halls all the way down E-Parkway.

Pussy, I love you with all my heart.[8] What is this world, this strangeness, this world?

## October, 22, 1951

It is Marxism itself that belies historical materialism. Was there ever in the world (as of course there was! It is the presence of this in Marxism that is so striking and bizarre)—ever in the world such a fanaticism entirely of ideology—such a contempt for the real facts of any situation, such a cult of the abstract? What are these bastards making war for? What are they so eternally *mad* about, but ideology, a claim, an abstract? Man's tyranny is always in and from the head. *The mind-forged manacles*[9] is one of the profoundest *descriptions* of the human state ever made.

I think I am learning some objectivity as a critic.

7. See December 10, 1946 entry.
8. "Puss" or "Pussy" was Kazin's affectionate name for Ann, from Edward Lear's (1812–1888) "The Owl and the Pussycat."
9. "Mind-forged manacles," a favorite phrase from William Blake's "London."

## October 29, 1951

Publication date: *A Walker in the City* [. . .]

## October 31, 1951

We construct models or analogies by which to afford a world we cannot, after all, carry around with us all the time. Then we forget that the model is not the world, that analogy is never the truth, but only a provisional way of confronting it. Then we exact authority to the model itself. Viz—obedience to a leader, a hierarchy, a Pope. Obedience *to* the truth, fitting ourselves to the inner disposition of the world, is replaced by the rigid subservience to a model or construct of *the* "truth": the church, the Pope!

Without the model, no construction or operation at all, not to see through the model, dogmatism and superstition; to love the model and yet to see behind and all around it, the heartbreak of trying every day to wed the symbol back to the world from which we extracted it, and yet to keep them: free.

## November 7, 1951

Always when I leave Michael the sadness of it grips me, the total lack of any real communication with Carol. Tuesday, after a futile day before, it was worse—I was mad with loneliness, and at Chambers St. suddenly got into the rain, walked about in a stupor—whom to call up, what movie to go to, etc., etc. But really, the die *is* cast, there is so utterly solitary a road reserved for me; there is not room in it for mere loneliness anymore, or resentment against that statuesque philistine I was married to. [. . .]

## November 8, 1951

[. . .] Remarkable piece by Trilling in the *Reporter* on Dreiser, Anderson, and the problem of the anti-social, the utterly isolate American writer.[10] Remarkable because it sums up his own position, or rather his *findings*, vis-à-vis the British situation—*and* illustrates his need to legislate the situation away (in America) by reason. And confirms in me his deep seated fear of the genuine artist (Dreiser,

10. "Dreiser, Anderson, Lewis, and the Riddle of Society," reprinted as "An American View of English Literature" in *Speaking of Literature and Society*, ed. Diana Trilling (New York: Harcourt Brace Jovanovich, 1980): 260–269. Sherwood Anderson (1876–1941), American novelist, best known for his short story sequence *Winesburg, Ohio;* Sinclair Lewis (1885–1951), American novelist and playwright, first American winner of Nobel Prize in Literature (1930).

Anderson) and his long repugnance to me, thoroughly based, I see now, on a *fear* of the "extremism" or what not he finds in me. On the lowest, the purely personal and vexed problem of his relations with me, the article helped to heal something of the continuous ache about Lionel and his nervousness with me, for it told me as clearly as can be that it is *myself*, inherently and initially and potentially, that troubles him, exactly as Dreiser and Anderson do, and that nothing whatever can be done about this. I seize this opportunity, I who have so often been needlessly bitter about him and how many others who seemed to reject me out of hand—I seize this irremediable opposition between us, to (from my own part, as far as I can tell) be more just to him, less petty and therefore less anguished. What is in these matters *is*, as it was with Carol: there can be no bridge made here without falseness.

But on a higher and more objective level I am glad of this article, too, because it gives me a chance to review my own thinking as a critic—to see *all around*, for once, this continuous problem of isolation in American literature. No, I was not wrong when, starting from my own situation 14 years ago—but doing surely something more than *starting* from it—I saw isolation as a concrete and historic fact in American literature. Nor, in the bitter yet glowing winter of my discontent 6 years ago here, I [saw] *The Western Island* growing out of Melville's own isolation. *I did not invent these facts;* my literary reason did not play me false. The mistake was in founding my work, my necessary personal work, on outside documents; and on narrowing my range to that. Now that I am *in* my own work, I can really see around the subject, can really address myself in all reason and with light and shadows in the picture. God damn it all, I *am* a critic. And have somehow lost all desire to be one.

## November 29, 1951

My New York, I thought yesterday, having a coffee in that cafeteria at Lex and 59th where Pussy and I used to sit going over the finished pages of the *Walker*—My New York remains the New York of the cafeterias, the salesmen, the evening session students, the countermen, the kibitzers—the New York of the tired men who eat in their overcoats and with their hats on, of the dressmaker old maids on their way from the Amalgamated, of the Jews and the Greeks.

Only cafeterias in NY are places for me to sit down in.

## December 6, 1951

In the drugstore yesterday, I watched one of the Fulton Street drunks buying nitre. While I walk between the skylight room and my desk, drinking water and passing water, the drunks spend their time drinking whiskey and passing water. Why do I never *notice* more of these men in this life? There they stand in front of the warehouse and flophouse, every day I pass to and from the subway. *Think of the whole day being spent like this.* This is what afflicts the heart. That they should do nothing else but this—this watching and waiting.

*The Girl*[11]

The color of the war for me was a sooty gray. The season was always dead winter. Hanging over the bombed and bruised streets were the prongs of barbed wire. Yet at the flat earth's unimagined corners the pools of water were my oases, my heart healed each time I passed one. And every day in those English streets there was some small gentleness, some kindness, some civility, that made me stop and gasp with surprise. On those quiet and cold streets it was the English who brought me back to love. Each time a stranger spoke to me with simple English kindness I awoke from my dream of Asya, I could for once see my own lacerations.

Oh ladies of Walthamstow, oh kind ladies, oh sweet and good ladies, who would not let me go that night—oh my cockney angels, who fed me and talked to me and saved me—you with the old-fashioned specs, and the dry gravity of tone, oh sweet comrades, oh my good nurses of war, how we watched all that night long over the men and the women in their separate rooms—all of us together, the Arab doctor, and the German refugee, and the English ladies with their bad skins and yellow teeth and their goodness, their goodness—they brought out the bacon and the marmalade for me, the American, and all night long we watched and talked over the men and women sleeping in their separate rooms.

At intervals, all through the winter, the little lisping words, Fuck, fuck you, it fucks. Fuck, fuck, the lapping of the waters fuck, fuck. But the little fireman leading the hymn singers in Hyde Park, with even the lipsticked fairies joining in. Hymnal of my days on the two-penny chairs in Hyde Park—past the broken hospital where Keats studied, the Irish volunteer in the dark who said Bless, bless you—not *God* bless you, but invoking and conferring the world's blessing, and so we talked in the dark. It was always in the blackout that my greatest moments came, the prostitute who took me back to that room behind the Haymarket where I saw the Jewish owner's picture on the bureau; the German refugee whom I met on my way to Swiss Cottage station; the long lines

11. See Chapter 3, note 74.

of prostitutes going round and round in the dark; Graham Greene that night at Kathleen Raine's[12] talking about authors; the prim lady with the fur collars I met on my way from the scientist's meeting full of commie intellectuals like J. D. Bernal and Solly Zuckerman[13] (?)—then hearing *The Messiah* echoing and re-echoing through Westminster Abbey, how sweet it was, and how distant trailing between the tombs. Oh that worn English decency. [. . .]

## December 7, 1951

Ten years since Pearl Harbor. Asya's life and mine. This morning awoke to read in the *Times* of J. Edward Bromberg's death in London.[14] Oh, that time I sat in the 2nd balcony of the Belasco and wept over *Awake and Sing*. I am beginning to feel that I belong, truly, to a *passing* generation—not that we are passing, but those closest to us, from the day before yesterday. [. . .]

## December 12, 1951

First snow. Rivers of snow pour down on the black streets, course between separate funnels; and when they meet, they meet on the low roof just outside my bedroom window.

Old Brooklyn, Old London City, the city. Those fall noons, working in Remsen Street on *On Native Grounds*, I used to walk down to Borough Hall, the Exchange Buffet (honor system) for my lunch; between the stationers (crackle of parchment, high ceiling sheen on the oily waxed filing cabinets) and the banks and the insurance companies. Small islands of business, of officialdom, of impersonal, clean banknotes—small island in which I had my lunch on the honor system. Always when I lived in Remsen Street with Asya, I felt myself surrounded by a vast hum. The clean paper noise of Brooklyn city and the Borough Hall, the Town Hall, all around me.

12. Kathleen Jessie Raine (1908–2003), English poet, critic, and scholar, who wrote on William Blake and W. B. Yeats.

13. J. D. Bernal (1901–1971), an English scientist who made important discoveries in crystallography, was a onetime member of the Communist Party who remained sympathetic to the Soviet Union. Solly Zuckerman (1904–1993), English biologist, was scientific adviser to the Allies in their bombing campaign against the Germans. He was a strong advocate of nuclear nonproliferation after the war, but it is unclear why Kazin refers to him as a "commie."

14. J. Edward Bromberg (b. 1903), actor and founding member of the Group Theater that first produced Clifford Odets's *Awake and Sing* in 1935.

*Old* Brooklyn, so near London City: churches and graveyards, monuments and toppling stones. Black roofs, soot of age on the roofs. Walking in the city, I thought of old Brooklyn city; among the black coats of London, the clerks, the stiff collars. I longed for lunch hour in Court Street, between the lawyers, the rotting pillars of the courthouses, the clean crackle of the lunchrooms, the newsstands, and the old library on Montague Street; for Trinity church and the Battery and yea, even for the banks.

## January 1, 1952

Ann, Hannah, Heinrich—more than any other people I have ever known, these live by principle. So that loving them you love the good *they* love, by which they live and (vis-à-vis) which they regard themselves as smaller, as servants.

Celia Koron. Each time a new human being, who is really a rounded *being*, swims into our lives, it is a miracle. At first we look around wildly for landmarks, whom she reminds us of, traits we can place. And then bit by bit she emerges as completely herself, this individual of whose existence we were not even conscious a week ago.[15] [. . .]

## January 3, 1952

[. . .]Bit by bit, one learns, even so stupid a one as I, to follow certain rules.

a) *Don't try to overcome anything.*

b) *Never call Carol when you are ill, or lonely, or disturbed*: you always try to take it out on her.

c) Don't force yourself to write more than you feel like writing, or to persist in writing when something is obviously wrong—i.e., when the intelligence does not function *lightly* or joyously.

d) Don't expect people to give *you* more than they give themselves.

e) Don't, not even at a party, and after too many drinks, exaggerate to make a point or tell a story for "artistic" reasons—i.e., to create an effect, to jolly up a party. On the other hand never reproach yourself for being abandoned, natural, happy.

15. Kazin would continue an affair with Celia Koron until the late 1950s.

f) Take your temperature, establish your daily latitude and longitude, i.e., recognize your physical and mental state of the day, *and respect it*. If you're ill, as today, tense, uncertain! ready to pick a fight—lay off, comfort yourself with every possible comfort; *stop mauling yourself*.

So this notebook is a deep necessity for me, then: by *it*, chiefly have I learned to recognize my heart and to learn how I might yet obey it.

## January 26, 1952

Rain, rain, rain. The other day at the Whitney for the John Sloan show,[16] was overjoyed to find a reproduction of Edward Hopper's *Sunday Morning*, which now hangs on the wall before me as I write, one of my new talismans. How that picture has spoken to me from the day I first stumbled on it when I was tormenting myself over the old version of the *Walker*. That street, that Sunday morning, that charged silence—that is my country, that is where my soul still lives, and to which it returns. When I saw the reproduction behind a desk at the Whitney, it was if someone had stretched out a hand to me and was saying—Take heart, Alfred, all that is good is still here; take heart, we have not gone away—That rose, that rosy pink, deep in the forehead of those dear commonplace, little Brooklyn or Chicago houses, flushed there with Sunday early morning. That is my country, that is my native country.

The hidden God. My God is no God shining on an altar in a nimbus of gold-painted spikes, but the hidden God, the God that waits to be disclosed, as we wait—to find him. Between Him and me what silence, what long preparations and rehearsals, what a deep shyness.

In all these early city scenes of John Sloan I love so much, the men sit still and anchor the pictures in time, but the women dance and drift like smoke—They weave, they are constantly in the same joy of motion, their bodies uncurl, they dance. It is always in those women of the period, those lyrical women that Sloan catches the joyful innocence of the [word crossed out]. A discovery is made entirely through women.

16. John Sloan (1871–1951), American painter, prominent figure in the Ashcan School specializing in realist paintings of New York neighborhoods; Edward Hopper (1882–1967), American painter, noted for his rendering of empty city and landscapes and solitary figures.

## January 28, 1952

Last night, after I had *finally* got home, after that long weary day, I suddenly took it straight through and through that I am going to marry Ann, that I'm striking out for life at last. It was the deepest, the clearest, the happiest hour I've had in months. I'm going to accept my wife through and through. I'm not going to shirk my happiness. Oh, the tenderness of it, the joy, the wealth, the radiant rightness of it all through and through me every inch of the way. Oh Pussy, pussy, my darling—we're going to live.

## March 11, 1952

[. . .] Do you know what writing my *Walker* scenes and poems mean to me? What that full afternoon light means: that the commonest, nearest objects suddenly come within my reach, are saved from death. I write in order to *embody* the actual, to capture in its approximate sense of place what I have lived through; to realize, to recapture, to renew. That is why I cannot, fundamentally, write these books except by the most excruciating faithfulness to the actual experience, for it is for all the joy of recapturing them—that is, of claiming my life as *mine* that I write. . . . Otherwise, the abstractness of death that I have been thinking of all my life takes over. [. . .]

## May 15, 1952

After conference at Boppard am Rhein.[17] The deep ancestral power over me of the German language, of German names (literally with fire in them) as Bremer, the thin-lipped official at the conference today and yesterday. *Tief*, *arbeit:* root words for me. Root feelings that go so far back. . . . Meanwhile, the Germans maimed (the glove over the left hand), hobbling along with a stick, always frowning stiffly. *Only the children laugh*. But oh, that child screaming as she ran after her dog on the University grounds.

## May 17, 1952

How unused these people are to strangers; how *caked* and long hardened they are in their automatic fear of anyone different from themselves. When I went into the little café a few minutes ago, the girl stared and grinned at my khaki pants and blue, American shirt as if I were a zebra. . . . Notice, too, what great

17. Kazin was a visiting professor (May and June) at the University of Cologne.

starers they are, generally. In the tram, for example, you will see them staring and staring ahead, endlessly lost in their own thoughts. And really square heads—the frightful haircuts they give themselves on top, while everything below looks as if it had been hastily gone over with a rusty lawnmower.

## June 26, 1952

Basel—My glorious wedding day. My great unbelievable new gift. Tonight my spear is tipped with fire. Tonight, tonight, a whole new world has opened for me.[18]

## July 4, 1952

[. . .] The lame, the halt, and the blind of Germany. Everywhere I go in this wounded and accursed land, I see the tell-tale glove hiding the stumps of amputated hands, the yellow, three dotted armbands proclaiming the blind, and the men hobbling along on crutches. How many like Helmut Fribourg (?) with the new-grafted skin around the nose and mouth. Accursed land, wounded people, somber, stark people. The long hairs of their taffy-blond hair drawn straight back: the whole life of their thought drawn back in their faces as if to strike. [. . .]

## July 10, 1952

*In the train going back to Cambridge* [for Fulbright Conference on American Studies]

London, my London, with its white pillars transparent against the milky-blue sky. The brass plates have been considerably polished since I was here last, and against the gleaming fresh paint, the city looks like a set of andirons in an antique shop. The flowers in their little receptacles will never smell and seem papier maché, the people walk with sedate merriment. It is another city from the one I trudged up and down in, froze in and half-died in, seven years ago—and God knows I am another man, here now with Puss, and so deep in my happiness, so warm and afloat in my own life for once.

Just beginning to get over my awe of them [the English]. They are so contagious—I feel the authority of their style: the last two days have been a dream from which I have awakened into self-consciousness. But now I am beginning to sit back and can just *enjoy* them. Notice again the fantastic, half-comic *show:* the tense assertiveness of place and background in every syllable.

18. Ann and Alfred traveled to Basel, Switzerland, to be married.

How much we Americans look at our own country from the point of view of *all* history. Even Henry Commager[19] this morning, rattling off the names of the continents and the proportionate weights of the other ages: all avenues leading up to this spotlighted center: *us*.

The great bad style of the heaped-up monuments in Westminster Abbey—like the English sideboard crammed with family pewter and silver, and lined with heavily framed photographs.

## August 5, 1952

Another article sent to me from some Jewish magazine in NY attacking Jewish writers of my "ilk" for not accepting the true faith. What irks me in all this is that these little worms, frightened by the slightest suggestion of intellectual freedom, should always speak *for* the "Jews." Why is Ludwig Lewisohn[20] *the* Jew, and not Kafka? Why do these nauseating little *shameses*,[21] anxiously patrolling a non-existent synagogue, always assume their mediocrity, their provincialism, and their cowardice as *the* nature of "*The Jews*"? [. . .]

## August 23, 1952

Through love of "country," a natural place to begin with, do you ascend the ladder of affections to love of man and even love of God. Look at Simone, at Melville, at Bloy[22]—all these deeply universal spirits, all passionately pledged to something material through whose interstices they catch a boundary of the divine. I distrust people who do not love enough even to love a country. [. . .]

## September 10, 1952

Motto of this journal: "Life consists in what a man is thinking of all day." Emerson

[. . .] American-Europe: always the same bifurcation, always one as the hammer and the other as the anvil. We praise America vis-à-vis Europe; we

19. Henry Steele Commager (1902–1998), American historian, taught at Columbia and Amherst, probably best known for *The American Mind: An Interpretation of American Character Thought since the 1880s* (1950), longtime friend of Kazin's.
20. An American Jewish writer, critic, and educator, Ludwig Lewisohn (1882–1955) was a passionate Zionist who argued strenuously against assimilation.
21. The light that lights the candles on the Menorah.
22. Like a number of other intellectuals in the 1950s, Kazin was attracted to the French philosopher and writer Simone Weil (1909–1943), whose *The Need for Roots* (New York: Putnam, 1952) argued for maintaining connections with one's origins. Leon Bloy: see Chapter 3, note 33.

select the heights of Europe against the depths of America. But always the same difficulty in all these searchers for America, in us: that we are not truly at home yet here, that it simply exists.

I remember now that odd, odd sense of wonder I had so often during the war—that perhaps, if America lost, America would die out entirely; my curious surprise at America's *permanence*.

## September 15, 1952

Was thinking as I read Hemingway's *The Old Man and the Sea* yesterday—Hemingway is a country boy and he writes well, Faulkner another country boy and he writes well. The city boys—Dos Passos, for example, always aimed at an abstraction, "capitalism," the big city. The country boys wrote out of memory, and they had something to remember. How long ago, it seems to them now, they had put down a solid rock of primitive impressions. They anchored themselves in the present only out of a kind of rage; they always know where "home" was, the real, the old. All the best American writing even of this epoch is always commemorative; it celebrates in its writing the rituals of excellence life itself no longer possesses for them.

In the beginning, said John Locke, all the world was America. In the beginning, said Melville, was the whiteness into which man interjected his spot of color, and so knew one color from another, and that in the beginning the world was not for him. The spheres were formed in fright.

In the beginning. That is the great theme of so many American books. They always start with the void, the emptiness, and *then* see man as "new" in it, for man is really the unaccustomed fact. So man is not *in* nature, but always in front of it, as an emblem (kept illustratively apart from it). Brown with dirt and leaves, physically blended with this environment, he is still not homo factor, but a *scout*, an explorer. Projecting his shadow before him, his double, he ceases to be part of all he sees the moment he begins to think: the moment he becomes *man*. (He projects his own image before him as a form of protective coloration, carries it before him like the leaves of the forest in *Macbeth*).

To see that straight backwards into time, to declare that there was a beginning, and that America *was* it, requires a wish to be made new, starting from some extreme degree of historical sophistication. Hence the looking back you get in all the key American books with their wonder-land of the American boyhood along the river, hunting in Northern Michigan. Man declares a stop, makes himself into a signpost, and then, looking back, says—In the beginning was America, and every man who went into it was made new. All here is new because we—who see it so—have declared that the world must have a new dispensation, and from here on, *in this region*, all things are as they never were before. Yet (Jefferson's dream) we (having stilled the spokes of time) have builded perfection, we have an apprehension of the fully illuminated truth: and now we, in order to build a more perfect union, build for all time.

In the beginning. What an awesome phrase. *That man can think himself back to the beginning, that so late in the play* he can dismiss all thoughts of its authorship, of the scene, and (dwelling on the creation itself rather than on the creator) simply unroll time, can think of himself as first entering the play again. [. . .]

America—an earthly paradise projected out of the heart of man, and not within it, and so doomed always to magnetize, to be compared, and to disappoint.

## October 6, 1952

The literary *profession*—What a misnomer, what a horror. This very profession (of faith!) to which I entrust my life (for by that I mean my thinking) is also a mad scramble for social prestige *and* a job. So that at every point (but obviously most on Sunday night, before the treadmill gets me back) I oscillate between the native purity, the *relative* selflessness of my inner thought—and this splintery, *tormented, boring, boring* attempt to *get* things by my *profession*—my name on this list, my bank account full. *The profession which by its incarnated incarnation* the nullity of egotism serves (how often!) *only* our egotism.

What a monster it is, then, this being not a writer, a thought-bearer, but a *WRITER*, quoted on the jackets of the latest books, much sought-after by summer workshops, an object of mystery, a perpetual mode of unbelief to the vulgar—"and do you write under your *own* name?" as if most us wrote for any purpose other than publicizing our own name!

No name, no writer.

"The literary profession"—an essay in journal form on the conflict in the writer's heart. This is the passage from Maurice de Guerin[23] that Melville

23. Georges Maurice de Guérin (1810–1839), French poet and diarist, who wrote evocatively about nature.

marked and annotated. "There is more power and beauty in the well-kept secret of one's self and one's thoughts, than in the display of a whole heaven that one may have inside one. . . . The literary career seems to me unreal, both in its essence and in the rewards which one seeks from it, and therefore fatally marred by a secret absurdity."—on which Melville wrote: "This is the finest statement of a truth which everyone who thinks in these days must have felt." [. . .]

## November 6, 1952

[. . .] America in a conservative mood [following election of Eisenhower]: the generation brought up under Roosevelt wants to keep what it has—and, I suppose, deny it to others.

## December 13, 1952

[. . .] Improbably as it may seem to the others at this morning's further conference for Nevins's magazine of popular history, for I spoke more sharply against it than they did—I enjoy such bunk, I like moving in the company of these distinguished salesmen of letters and the arts.[24] No longer do I arise in righteous wrath and denounce iniquity precisely at the moment I learn of it. No sir, for I have learned manners, I practice detachment; I breathe in with pleasure the aroma of civilized good manners. Because I want to see how things work, I want to know what is going on, I shall conspiratorially go along. Once I would have felt *guilty:* my Hebraic compulsion to make the world perfect again, to remind man of God's own image, would have caused me to cry out, to walk out. And I would have been left—not even with my protest, for protest must retain that which it complains against, and by driving my pen through the paper, I would have been left with neither pen nor paper. But not now: I enjoy in sweetness my own secret (all this is a parody).

## December 30, 1952

[. . .] George S. Kaufman[25] dropped from a television program for having made a quip about the commercialism of "Silent Night." God almighty, I ask myself every day when I look at the papers—am I a coward for not fighting all the

24. Despite Kazin's opposition, Allan Nevins (1890–1971) succeeded in turning *American Heritage* into a successful magazine of popular history, one to which Kazin contributed a number of pieces including his 1987 Phi Beta Kappa address, "Where Would Emerson Find His Scholar Now?" (December 1987): 93–96.

25. George S. Kaufman (1881–1961), drama critic, playwright, humorist, and director.

time and in every way against this stinking fog of orthodoxy creeping over the country.[26] Yet when I look at the *Nation*, as I did last night, and for a moment feel the fine flush of revolt—in sympathy—I note at the same time the utter lack of conscience in these people. "From Prague to Washington all governments seek scapegoats." This in criticism of the indictment of Lattimore, as if the [Meyer] Lansky trial and the indictment of Lattimore could be put on the same plane.[27]

## January 3, 1953

[. . .] Was it providential, this discovery of America—or merely an accident? Of course it had to be considered providential, for the white man, European man, by the very "range of reason," had access to the secret of creation—knew why the continents had been arrayed as they had been, and could guess at what lay beyond the seas; could invent the wheel and round out even the last European cape to Thule. Europe lay in the center, the white man was the appointed of God; he inhabited the temperate zones; he knew reason, i.e. could manipulate nature, could bend it to his purpose, *and recreate himself to it.*

Was it providential or an accident? The latter theory obviously absurd in a world that accepted Godly order as a matter of course.

## January 24, 1953

The old doubt that women are really *people.* Reading a student paper by a woman student in which she refers slightlingly, but on the basis of considered judgment, to another woman—the *strangeness* interjects itself, that an objective "normal" criticism (as by a man of another man) can be made. *Sophie*[28] *and Mama:* Mama did not consider herself simply a person (oh, no, I sacrifice myself continually for others) and therefore all her criticism of Sophie seemed both fundamental and irrational, *especially in that it was made of a woman at all?*

Mama did not eat like others (in fact she did not eat at all *publically*). She did not dress like others. She just worked and worked. Sophie, on the contrary, tried

26. Kazin did write to Irving Mansfield (1908–1988) at CBS (December 31, 1952) calling the removal of Kaufman "disgraceful and cowardly" (Kazin correspondence, Berg Collection, New York Public Library).
27. Owen Lattimore (1900–1989), a China expert accused by Senator Joseph McCarthy (1908–1957) of being a Russian spy, was indicted for perjury, charges that were later dismissed. Meyer Lansky (1902–1983) was a prominent gangster.
28. See Chapter 1, note 56.

openly to find happiness, thought of nothing but marriage and satisfaction. Her nose was always pressed to the windowpane. She looked out and out wistfully to life. So there was condemnation of her; *she thought of herself as a person.* That condemnation seemed to me basic and necessary! Women existed only as mothers—to "serve"! Any sensuous self assertion was horrible and unnatural—*as was any friendship between women*, any pleasant natural enjoying of each other.

## March 6, 1953

Death of Stalin, and I have absolutely nothing to say about it. Except that I am sure as I can be about anything that the triple-chinned and gimlet-eyed Malenkovs who come now will be far worse. What has been *immediately* horrible this week: the way a whole world has waited on this man's death as if to ascertain its fate. Perhaps that is why I have found it difficult to feel *anything* very sharp about Stalin's death, when politics is reduced to one man's biography and that biography itself = the unpredictable. Then there *is* nothing to feel, except disgust for someone who has so disgraced the human essence and pity for us who have to bear it.

But what a revolution Pussy brought me to last night with her clarification of *The Western Island.* What I have gained from this new positiveness, to see all my work as the successive, organic unfoldings of a single craft: the essay. How it all comes back to me now, my particular concern with the sonata, the free exercise within a loose but resolute form, the reordering of the world as contemplation.

## May 1, 1953

Back last night from Cambridge and Cape Cod, and as I sit here now preparing to go to work again after three dry, empty days of apartment-hunting and seeing people, I feel I want to spew out all the so irrational resentment and sudden depression I felt at Harvard.[29] Still trying to determine my place, my career, still driven by occasional idiotic resentment at not having a full academic post—O Lord, I'm almost ashamed to admit this even in the privacy of my notebook, were it not that I learn more from admitting things, from looking at things as they are than from walking around choked up with all that silliness—and then, always, scared to death at losing myself, my writing, my innermost self, whenever I do come too close to the academics. I found myself Wednesday

29. Kazin had been invited to teach at Harvard in the fall of 1953.

night in Cambridge just miserable after the long business of making talk with Jones and Miller.[30] Instead of accepting them, from just accepting myself, of recognizing the differences between us and of enjoying the contact we could make, I found myself afterwards breathing strange, desperate death-breaths of loneliness as Pussy and I wandered around Boston. [. . .]

Jones was talking about Judge Wyzanski of Boston, and spoke about his "photographic mind." I thought of some other Gentile speaking of Laski's[31] "photographic mind," and got a little sore—how I hate to see mental faculties reduced to mechanical gifts. There is no photographic memory outside of one's special vision of life that entails one. The Jew often does have this kind of memory, the over-eager scholar, as Dr. Johnson did; and all this does imply a whole view of a civilization, a particular kind of learning need, and not just a mechanical trick of memory.

## May 15, 1953

McCarthy and McCarthy, and McCarthy again. Every day now, in every way, he gets louder and fiercer and more uncontrolled than ever. Sink British ships if they bring goods to China, we are strong and can go it alone, etc. But the appalling record of yesterday's Senate debate attacking Britain, when only one senator, John Sherman Cooper, had the decency even to speak up, is completed really with Senator Dirksen's[32] threat to cut aid to Britain. Notice the hysteria of these people, the absolutely uncontrolled and uncontrollable way they sound off—this is what is so ominous in the present situation.

## June 10, 1953

Monday night it was McCarthy and Rahv; last night Kermit Lansner.[33] A long procession of intellectuals, *intellectuelles purés* wind through my evenings and my days; and Lord, O Lord, how sick I am of them—I mean bored, excruciatingly bored, bored all over. The minute you enter the house, see the

30. Howard Mumford Jones (1892–1980), writer, literary critic, professor at Harvard, friend of Kazin's; Perry Miller (1905–1963), literary critic, intellectual historian, expert on American Puritans, professor at Harvard.
31. See Chapter 2, note 69.
32. Everett McKinley Dirksen (1896–1969), U.S. senator from Illinois, 1951–1969.
33. Mary McCarthy (1912–1989), prominent critic, novelist, whom Kazin intensely disliked; Kermit Lansner (1921–2000), editor of *Art News*, later editor at *Newsweek*.

drinks laid out, the first conversational gambit given, you know it all in advance. The point is that the intellectual without originality, without real heart or vision or grace, an intellectual by habit, a competitive soused-up intellectual is a mockery of the artist's and the religious man's vision—he comes in always walking in shoes that are too large for him, he talks by habit, he lives in a routine. You never know with these people whether you are talking criticism or gossip. I'm sick to death of all this talk, self-perpetuating, competitive talk. [. . .]

## June 11, 1953

In times like these the "country" seems more than usually attractive because we cling to something known and familiar and unexpectedly dear. Trilling's observations in *Perspectives* show how one comes on one's country after light years of instinctive estrangement.[34] "But there also comes a moment when the faces, the gait, the tone, the manner and manners of our own people become just what one needs, and the whole look and style of one' s culture seems appropriate, seems perhaps not good, but intensely *possible*. What your compatriots are silently saying about the future, about life and death, may seem suddenly very accessible to you, and not wrong. . . ." This can be a very real experience, and just because it can be so real—because, that is, the category of culture is so deeply implanted in the modern mind—it can be easily falsified and must therefore be subjected to critical analysis of the strictest kind.

## September 25, 1953
### [Beacon Hill, Boston]

Friday morning, warm and good—the brown paving stones of Chestnut Street glow in the sun just as "my old village" did in my dreams long ago—New Haven as a child, Brooklyn Heights; all those old villages, lost villages, reclaimed villages, particles of memory, of purely imaginative memory, I had stored away so long and returned to and returned to so long in my dreams of getting away. And now I have gotten away—last night walking up and down the cobbled streets of Beacon Hill under the crepuscular lamps, my other land! my other land! at last. . . . [. . .]

34. In "The Situation of the American Intellectual at the Present Time," *Perspectives* (Spring 1953), Lionel Trilling restates his positive revaluation of American society and culture made in his contribution to "Our Country and Our Culture: A Symposium," *Partisan Review* (May-June 1952), reprinted in *A Gathering of Fugitives* (Boston: Beacon, 1956): 60–78.

## October 7, 1953

Walked from Harvard to Boston this afternoon, mostly along the riverfront. A wild, stormy day, constantly breaking into sunshine and shouting back again into storm. Trees gnashing their teeth in rage, the sky so low that the large, pulpy, blue-white clouds seem to make another sky. Walked along the riverfront: factories and experimental stations and technology, hardly another person on the path, and felt brimmed-up to choking as I walked, so full of projects and plans and ideas and the people walking through my life and my utter joy and confidence in being here, and when to do this and whether not to do that—suddenly decided not to pick and choose, to make the day heavy with false decisions, but to do *everything*.

Erich Heller last night at the Leontiefs:[35] a man I like so much and am so much attracted to, but who always leaves me panting, as if he were saying something slow and incommunicable, hiding a deep secret of his own, a culture secret, behind the mask, the English front, the *grappling* efforts of his speech. A lonely man, as Puss says, reduced to shining in company.

## October 14, 1953

Last night at Zelman Cowen's, Isaiah Berlin,[36] whom I'd heard so much of for years and now finally met—to my immense satisfaction. They were all "English" there last night, with a handful of Australians to mark the edge of their Englishness, and when we went home Zelman said God bless, just as they used to in England . . . during the war. A society, I thought, friends—all that pining and envy of the English for being a *society* came home to me suddenly, the hardness and graspingness and assertiveness of my American world suddenly eased up and warmed and blotted out. Yes, I went home enchanted, as always, with the goodness and manners of these people, with their *kindness*, their fine social intelligence. But going to class this morning, to talk on Thoreau, my Western Island came home to me in a rush, said not to pine and to envy, but to take *this*, this created, evermore-being created American world, this adventure into space, this idea forever being made flesh, this where we are, this reality, with all its jaggedness and rawness. Was it not simply *my* loneliness I wanted to write

35. Erich Heller (1911–1990), a literary critic and Germanist, whose seminal work on truth and art, *The Disinherited Mind*, was published by Farrar, Straus and Cudahy in 1952; Wassily Leontief (1905–1999), a noted Harvard economist and Nobel laureate (1973).

36. Zelman Cowen (1919–), Australian lawyer and educator, served as Australia's governor-general (1977–1982) and as provost of Oriel College Oxford (1982–1990); Isaiah Berlin (1909–1997), social historian and philosopher, major voice for philosophic liberalism in the postwar years.

about in the English story, and could not, because it was only my loneliness—and not England itself, not the thing in itself? All my days now are filled with an unceasing, an almost uncontainable adventure of thought—the greatest I have ever known in my life—and the cup brims over, brims over, the waters flood me beyond speech—with this knowledge above any I have ever known, that we are *privileged* to be here on this earth, nothing less—privileged and to be grateful every day of the living year for that which is—for this mind we have been given amid all this infinitude in which we think we drown. [. . . .]

## October 25, 1953

Israel today is no longer a religion, but a state. By every sign, the state will become increasingly nationalistic, military, cynical, and, in the fashion of states, hypocritical—that is, it will live in that middle distance between high professions and actual practice which it is the nature of states to live in. And what was once a religion has become an ideology—which is worse than no religion, for it is false religion and exploits the memory of a great religious experience.

The Jews are historically a chosen people; they were chosen, in history, to teach all around them the inexpungable memory of the divine source from which our lives come. As a state they can only misuse, exploit, and even kill this mission. The Jews have been Jews only in the diaspora, for among the nations they served to *remind* the world of the transcendent source and meaning of this experience. In a sense, Christianity took up this mission, but the Jews resisted it because they were afraid of being swallowed up in it; nevertheless, it becomes increasingly clear, as "Israel" ceases to be a faith and becomes an ideology, that Christianity alone does justice to the historic mission of the Jews—that it is only *as* Christians that Jews can remain Jews. Still, when the Jew becomes a Christian he ceases to be a *reminder*, he has been swallowed up in the general community of faith. So the Jew must remain in the diaspora, must accept gladly and proudly the condition of independence both from the "Jewish homeland," which never was and never can be, for Jerusalem is no longer a holy city, and from the impersonal normality of "Christianity," which itself tends to lapse into worship of itself. [. . .]

## November 10, 1953

Dylan[37]—How much light goes out with the passing of our wizard, our beautiful, careless singer? With everything you can say against the automatism, even the

37. Dylan Thomas, who died on November 9, 1953, had had an affair with Kazin's sister Pearl.

lovely self-infatuation of this man, he embodied the deepest cry of poetry, he *was* our young singer. What lovely pride I say. What unforgettable bounty of the word. It is this bounty, this true, rich, singing fluency, the *manner* entire, the big stance, the word flowing, flowing, for which I remember him with so much love this gray morning. [. . .]

Dylan the speaker, and Huck [Finn] the speaker. *Always* in our romantic writing the single self-heard voice that is the entering wedge into the world and binds the world together. The speaker is a magician—he casts a spell, we are held together by this veil. As I write, I sometimes hear myself saying the words over to myself. Between the echo of some greater voice I hear in my head and the look of the words on the page, I am always a speaker selecting words. But sometimes the voice, having found itself, gathers strength and swells beyond what it *knows*. We are then bewitched prisoners of our own spell, and if we go on, can sing praises only to this spell itself. This what Dylan often did, I think—the voice, once heard, becomes our refuge from the eternal abyss of the silence. [. . .]

## January 23, 1954

So I come back to my old notebook again—after weeks in which I thought I had done with it. Always and always one needs a place, perhaps it is the place, where one can turn an idea over for its own sake alone, where one can talk to oneself in perfect privacy of heart. [. . .]

## January 24, 1954

That fatal particle of vulgarity in Irving H[owe], which gets between everything he says like sand.

## February 15, 1954
### [New York]

Ruth Draper[38] last night. A monologist, a woman alone on a stage, acting out *all* parts. A very *feeling*, loving woman, her *feeling* itself (like Chaplin's) already a little old-fashioned today, like her "immigrants" and shy, young lovers and her giving of a number to the *operator* instead of dialing it herself. I am fascinated by the *monological* strain in our American tradition anyway, this single voice

38. Ruth Draper (1884–1956), monologist admired by George Bernard Shaw, John Gielgud, Katharine Hepburn, Laurence Olivier, Henry James, Henry Adams, and Edith Wharton.

that *mimics* voices of a society, this personal *dream* that living within the privacy of a single heart, impersonates and *embraces* from *afar* so many other *shadows* impinging on the single heart.

## February 16, 1954

Evening—Went down to the Village to see Josie and seemed to see nothing but these damned, mannish young women in slacks and belts, great, thick, leather belts, patrolling the streets. They all look like *soldiers*—apache soldiers. How military they all are now, these young women with their bags slung over one shoulder and their chins stuck out as they walk their Bohemian round in the Village.

Josie—after all that illness, that loneliness, that cold inside and outside the heart, has finished her book on the Bartrams, has another coming out, is working on another. What courage to that woman, what whole loveliness—you can touch her anywhere, and it rings true. In our time of spies and patriots how many people do you know whom you can really depend on as you can depend on that woman, who gave herself so utterly to a young stranger in his terrible year of need and gave, gave, never thinking of herself at all?[39] [. . .]

## February 18, 1954

Morning—last night, from the viaduct over 125th Street, saw the sky angry and remarkable behind the Riverside Church, and thought of describing it here, starting with the homely anchor of 125th Street. Now why was the very thought of giving the number of the street, of this grimy workmanlike street, this most ordinary of passageways—why did it give me such pleasure? Because I had seen something *from* the ordinary, because the rest of this vision was, in my own city experience, bound up with something one mentions so casually everyday as "125th Street." This is the key to what is so beautiful in the aspiration of Emerson and the practice of Thoreau: this is what lies behind much of the fragile, shivery beauty of so much American writing. For what we seek to capture in the end *is* the actual, to make it tangible: to wrest out of abstractness, the generality, the anonymity of the daily, unthinking experience, the miracle of the real. It is not the vision I saw *from* 125th Street that made the experience so noteworthy; it was rather, that the vision made me realize the full and unexpected depth of 125th Street itself.

39. Nineteen fifty, following Kazin's and Carol's separation.

## April 24, 1954

Sat in a bar most of yesterday afternoon looking at the swinish McCarthy hearings. That one should even *accept* this pompous lying, these horse-faced theatricals, as anything real, is enough to make a man vomit with disgust. . . . I notice, by the way, how on every side people come to accept the pressure, how instinctively they respond to the charged situation with a little shrug of the shoulders. At a time like this only the man who will *remember*, who will hold out, is really good for us.

## July 8, 1954
## [Wellfleet, Cape Cod]

I take up this notebook now almost a week later (Thursday morning, the 8th of July), after days of inward storm and stress, of strange bitter-sweet anxieties and convulsive hopes, to record on what looks now like my first full day of peace, something of my being here.[40] Perhaps that is what one takes up such a record as this for—to record *en soi* one's being here. For nothing else, I see, does one keep a notebook of this kind, of so coherently private a nature. It is not, I see now, to enlist one's thoughts in for future use, but so entirely for present use, for this moment alone, July 8, 1954, when the gold sand outside my window yields up its green pine growth; and this morning, after a day of wind and unexpected storm (a day when the wind seemed to blow all the wrong way), promises under thick, white clouds to clear and to be hot. This moment of our presentness, then, is what one seeks to get down in a private notebook—this median point so intangible, almost so invisible—a point toward which we yearn from so far away which is equated with distance, with the ungraspable and the unnamable, and which, though it so often seems to dissolve in the very flush of its own being, is nevertheless the one experience which contains the gist of life itself. [. . .]

## August 16, 1954

So this, I see now, is what is happening. All though the weekend with the Hofstadters in L.I., I was so resentful with Pussy, [. . .] because I felt "guilty," wanted her approval about what I am thinking and writing in *The Love of*

40. The Kazins (and many other writers and New York intellectuals) would vacation in Wellfleet during the 1950s and 1960s.

41. Kazin would not write "The Love of Women," although he would include a number of the planned portraits of the women in his life in *Starting Out in the Thirties* and *New York Jew*.

*Women.*[41] So I see this now, and see how it relates to the story, to all these stories in which I wish to praise God's plenty of women, to praise human freedom and love and desire—and of the hard, hard pilgrimage of the soul to this point, of the world constantly pointing to us, making us feel sneaky and ashamed. This, surely, is the real theme of what I have been trying to say in this book—that we have the gift of love, of desire, that we want, that we want overwhelmingly, and that then the world gets in our way, makes us "ashamed." [. . .]

New York the capital of this—between the girls in the Village,[42] Lou, Katey, the sorrowing ex-mistress of all the krims[43] and krums, Connie Smith, who said to me, "But I always have my journal," *and* the Trillings, the literary couple always talking about Freud and blaming themselves for aggressive or homosexual impulses, and being so damned psychological-biological about everything, and who watch and watch—this damned naming, I say; while in the Village these single heretics from small towns, these girls who think themselves "ugly," who are the most loving and the most generous, who are the only women who ever treat men as true brothers and friends, as partners, who want to give to men, who can talk to them only in bed, it is these girls who run up the failures, everlastingly, who are passed on from man to man, who are treated this way. (This must be the background of the girl from the Village story, this background of "lost" girls, from small towns in the Midwest, *Gentile* girls, the mistresses of Jewish intellectuals, the girls who give themselves without the Jewish tremor and veil-cloud over sex)—and who themselves yearn for the distinction and intellectuality of these Jewish intellectuals, who give of their bodies, who yearn for the kind of "home" life and stability which these intellectuals have, and who in turn give the intellectuals the challenge, the for-once unprotected woman-experiences they want, but who expose them *so* much to the cold, cold world that these women become the martyrs, the mothers-in-turn.

## August 20, 1954

[. . .] New York earth colors: damp brown of the soil behind the black fences in Riverside Park. As I walked along, I suddenly saw a long, wormy tail, nothing else, just the tail, winding out from an animal hole below the sidewalk. Motto: keep your eyes posted even in the city: this brown soil which looks as if it had

42. Kazin describes "the girls in the Village" in "Midtown and the Village," *Harper's* (January 1971): 82–89, a version of which appears in the "Midtown and the Village" and "You Must Change Your Life" chapters of *New York Jew*, 35–98.

43. See July 20, 1963, entry and note.

been pushed under the pavement, this is not as emptily uniform as it looks. Look a while longer, and you will see it literally crawling with life. How I love to see that expected pattern of sameness (and emptiness) suddenly change.

## September 22, 1954
**[Smith College, Northampton]**

First day of school[44]—first day of real fall, red leaves on every bush, wind pouring down the street—lovely young pullets in shorts and red socks riding on their bicycles, leaves turning, bicycles turning, vague sense of unrest and beginning everywhere you look.

## October 6, 1954

Raining. Morning. It flashed in on me somewhere in my long, thinking night, that absurd review by Schorer in the *Times* of this gimcrack, weak book by Wright Morris.[45] Schorer is always consistent: give him a book with a trick gimmick to it, something voulu, showing all its seams, and he responds: Aiken's made-up *Ushant*, this Wright job;[46] Schorer's own novel, *The Wars of Love*; always this man goes to the *scheme*, to the "intellectual" rather than to the felt—and so misses everything. Fundamentally, it seems to me, one does better, on the whole, considering all the risks; one does better responding to the felt amount of emotion or authentic individual experience. There is a kind of explosion, true: but one can sort out the pieces. To respond directly in this way is to have that true creative gift and knowledge which is "naiveté," the gift of exposing oneself, of taking at one blow more than one fully understands—which is the pattern of true perception anyway. The boat rocks, one shivers trying to adjust oneself to the force of the blow, but one is in the direct path of life. These damned schemers and finaglers are always looking for subjects, for things to write about—they start with the way things look rather than the way they are: or to put it another way, it is only their fund of ideas they are sure about, and which they carry around from place to place, trying to press this onto available "subjects" or occasions. The "naive," the feeling man exposes himself directly to the subject. [. . .]

44. Kazin was William Allan Neilson Professor at Smith College for the 1954–1955 school year.
45. Mark Schorer (1908–1977), a professor of English at Berkeley and friend of Kazin's, reviewed Wright Morris's novel *The Huge Season* (New York: Viking, 1954) in the *New York Times Book Review* (October 3, 1954): 4. Wright Morris (1910–1998), American novelist, photographer, and essayist.
46. Conrad Potter Aiken (1889–1973), American novelist, poet, and autobiographer.

## November 8, 1954

Sugar grains of frost curled within the leaf, tightening it shut with cold. Cold coming down.

By their renegades, I say, shall you know them. By its renegades, I say, Marxism reveals itself as *not* a doctrine of hope and love and progress, but as a blueprint to be seized and used by intellectuals who fancy themselves in "the vanguard of humanity." There is no emotional residue in these people who have left it that points to anything much greater than themselves which they may have believed. Bitterness that a reasonable doctrine is not enough/scorn for those who do not know it/cold contempt for those who may be the victims of "history," still. The renegades from Christianity still feel respect for the power of love, and the renegades from Judaism will never cease to long for the promised land. But the renegades from Marxism all act like commissars out of a job: and even worse, are dumbfounded and outraged that they can be *disappointed* at all.

## November 9, 1954

Just finished washing the dishes and before I tackle my papers and other such gloomy tasks of a schoolteacher, I sit down to this. A day, a whole solid day spent fighting with Pussy, making up with Pussy, then going to movies with Pussy, then fucking with Pussy. Such is my life and has been for so long, this intense doubleness I bear throughout everything and can barely acknowledge to myself after all the years of pining and loneliness. I thought I was angry with her, and perhaps I am, and know damned well how unreasonable she was this morning, etc., etc. But quite apart from the fact that we are going to have a child, praise God, and that this *will* make a woman petulant and strange, especially an artist-woman like my wife, I note for the record [the] overwhelming fact that this whole day has been spent—and I note it with a kind of awe—in the most passionate screaming inner closeness with Pussy; even the terrible fight of half the day ended only with my shivering like mad when I went out for myself in the afternoon, and as I sit here now, typing this. I can still feel in my loins the long delicious withdrawal of sensation, the ebbing of the beautiful fire I knew, we knew, between fixing up the sauce and setting the hot water on for spaghetti. Praise God, praise God, praise God for this doubleness, and if I ask for anything now, this night, after this long crazy day that has ended so deliciously, I ask never, never, never to forget that I am never alone.

## November 10, 1954

Wednesday morning: Frosty and clear. What it *did* mean to me to be able to write about what really happened yesterday. This morning, lying in bed, I suddenly realized all at once how much I have used even this book to protect myself, to guard my feelings, to walk alone. I suddenly wanted to break through—to write truthfully and actually, *here*, of the actual tangle and conflict of every day's experience, instead of using it only for personal reveries and passive notes on the weather. [. . .]

## November 18, 1954

[. . .] *Mama, Mama yesterday at the hospital, Mama under an oxygen tent* her head wrapped in towels and looking older and weaker than I could ever have seen her.[47] Two days in NY going back and forth from 111th to the hospital and then standing on the roof walk yesterday with Pussy, a light rain, gulls flying, wet brick and the yellow rose I had bought Pussy for her picture. This rose in her belt, *this rose already too far swelled and gone*, but the only color at all on that wet, dark, dark brick roof. Mama. It was a catharsis—not tragic so much as *awful*, penetrating you like a sword-stroke to see Mama there gasping for breath. [. . .]

## November 20, 1954

It is raining, and it has been raining for some days now. In the few minutes I have before my class, I want to get down here something that has been teasing my mind for several days. The entries themselves in this journal are always curiously short—short, that is, in proportion to the life of the day. I have never tried to put the day itself down, only to capture in brief, telegraph strokes something of the basic thought that has held that day down. And from time to time, looking these pages over, I feel sick at how much I have not put down—how much, with my love of this form and my attachment to it and my secret knowledge of it, I *don't* put down of the day. This is partly because I am not a realist, and because external events as such never seem as real to me as my own thought or real except through the impression I have of them, *which* I try to capture. But the telegraph strokes themselves which correspond to heart-beats, and like my heart beats, are always the intensity of my thought—these strokes, dots and dashes, this shorthand of thought, *is* what one wants to write. The figure molds itself as it is molded, and when it is done

47. Kazin's mother, diagnosed with cancer, would die on October 10, 1955.

it is done, and the shape it takes *is* what we wanted, even when we knew it not. [. . .]

## November 29, 1954

Monday morning. Rain. . . . That afternoon weeks ago in the television studio, I was talking on Melville and looking straight at that picture of him which I have been looking at so long and listening to the reading of the Pacific chapter, and though I was on television and chattering away in a composed and business-like way about H.M., I did have the distinct feeling that I was dreaming, as so often I *have* dreamed of Melville and the Pacific. What had been locked up in me so long, I thought in wonder, *this* picture and *these* words, is now broadcast alive to millions; the smallest link and detail of my inner life is now an open secret, publicized and manipulated to "millions," and I am not only dreaming on television, but am looking on with these others at my dream. [. . .][48]

## December 28, 1954

When one finishes a book, one's first sensation, I think, is of how detestably easily it fits into the codes and formulas and genres of culture—this book that has been the life to us, our life. When one begins a book, as I am at last beginning my "Western Island," one's first thought is of how much of life is in it—all life. My greatest problem, like that of all craftsmen, is in realizing the limits of my subject, which will release the hidden scope of my craft. I am constantly trying to put everything I am and everything I think into a book, and it takes me years to realize just what I can make a book of. Undeniably, one root of this in me is my anxiety, my constant fear of not making the most of my experience and my knowledge and my thought, for I am constantly writing down the tracer of everything I think, and when Puss and I, at our best, sit together really discoursing and thinking, I always feel shocked by the thought of how many of these ideas may slip away from me, how I can best realize them in my writing, etc., etc. [. . .]

48. Jack Kerouac (1922–1969), who heard the broadcast, wrote Kazin: "You were as great as you ever were at the New School" and commended his "unselfconsciousness before the camera millions" (Jack Kerouac to Kazin, October 27, 1954), *Jack Kerouac: Selected Letters, 1940–1956*, ed. Ann Charters, (New York: Viking, 1995), 449. Kerouac might have been even more impressed had he known that his former teacher had once been a stammerer.

## January 3, 1955

The holidays, behind me at last, Pearlie and Michael and all that visiting, I can get down to work at last. . . . Thinking the other day that what *really* characterizes the hardened journal-keeper, like me, is not so much the hugging to oneself of thoughts, or the confessional habit, or the contemplative one, but *the inborn disposition to put things in brief*, to get quickly on the pith of the day's experiences or lesson, and then move away. All true diarists are known by *the short breaths they take in* their writing—and it is *this fundamental shortness* of one's thought rather than the end of it that distinguishes someone like Thoreau (or Emerson) from the heavier, slower-moving, and also more patient type of mind.[49] But another profound (and limiting) characteristic of the diarist is the desire to keep control of one's experience, or, to put it as sharply as possible, that *the quick short flight of one's thought is a way of limiting*—of assuming control over one's very expression of things, and thus of course over those things themselves.

And it is this self-conscious control that is so bad in the journal as an artistic form, which, of course, it is. The journal is too plastic to our hand, does not force us to go farther than we intend to go, does not lead us to some inherent quality of its own, to vital discovery, and does not *fight us*, insist on its own needs.

Perhaps it is in these terms that we can understand why contemplative and "religious" natures like Thoreau's take to the journal. For one prime quality of such minds is precisely the fierce, tense moralism, the subjection of all experience to principle, the tendency (so painfully clear in Thoreau's appallingly literary journals) to see everything in the light of a mastering idea, and of some confining principle. Then the brevity of the journal becomes an expression of the *superfluousness* of pure thought, and confirms the moralistic-religious tendency by never letting one's thoughts get into some *foreign shape*.

But the method of art, whatever the stringency of its final form, *is* to let experience have its lead, to let life tell its own story, *to be led* by, rather than to lead, the events of one's experience. For Thoreau the art is all in the *shaping* of one's sentences—in the molding or rearrangement of one's materials, rather than in the choice of them. *But the greater artist is he who looked* the deepest and in the unconscious devotion with which he looked—*in his silence rather than in his speech.*

49. See "Dry Light and Hard Expressions," *Atlantic* (July 1957): 202; and Kazin's Introduction to *Emerson: A Modern Anthology*, ed. Alfred Kazin and Daniel Aaron (Boston: Houghton Mifflin, 1958): 7–13.

## January 30, 1955

This beautiful text from Whitehead's *Science and the Modern World* that has always moved me so deeply by its recognition—"Religion is a vision of something which stands beyond, behind, and within the passing flux of immediate things; something which is real, and yet wanting to be realized, something which is a remote possibility yet the greatest of present facts, something that gives meaning to all that passes, and yet eludes apprehension, something whose possession is the final good and yet is beyond all reach, something which is the ultimate ideal and the hopeless quest."

## February 7, 1955

[. . .] We write in order to become that which we write of. We write in order to lay claim to that which we would like to become, and which, in the act of writing, we feel ourselves becoming. The hand with which we write is flexed to take possession. [. . .]

## February [nd] 1955

By the inmost leaf, then, I mean that individual core of genius which each true artist represents, and which, though we do not know where it comes from or where it exists (any more than we know where the soul exists) and what even its true name should be (for the inmost leaf is the magical site we apportion to it), represents the creative element, the continuous revision and recreation of "reality."[50] It is as much of a site, of an actual background, as we can locate in man's creative struggle. But the horizon toward which that creativity yearns, that is the nameless, the to-be-created, and it is precisely this that causes anxiety. "But I feel that I am now come to the inmost leaf of the bulb, and that shortly the flower must fall to the mould." We identify this genius with a place even in ourselves and think that once we have come to that place (perhaps once we can even *name* it), we have come to the barrier, and that is no more. But that is the continuing, perhaps the purely inward story of talent; what we are concerned with is that inner gift itself.

A critic is a writer, and can perhaps be best defined as someone who lives in literature. But one does one's work without always knowing why one does it, or what is the ostensible and nameable theme. As I look over these essays, written

50. "The inmost leaf," a phrase from an 1851 letter by Melville to Hawthorne, is the title of Kazin's collection of essays published in 1955.

over the last twenty years, I can see that I have always been driven by the same need to define this individual core of talent, "the gift," and it is this individual creative element, this continual discovery of alternatives and revisions of "reality," that interests me, the joyful surprise constantly presented to the world by each newborn talent. [. . .]

## June 7, 1955

With the [Smith] girls all gone, and in our reasons for this mood, I suddenly feel utterly negligent, calm, easy, well disposed to laze and ruminate and float. The delicious quietness and solitude of Northampton just now fill me with delight, and I feel terribly wealthy and lucky just to be in this part of the country, as when we came last September. [. . .]

## June 20, 1955

It is impossible to talk to people like Newton and Elizabeth Drew[51]—in fact, I do all the talking, and they listen to me with a snotty little smirk on their faces. For they are critics and have good taste; I am a writer and interested in everything I can see and read and feel and touch. Yesterday on our terrace I suddenly realized, running around getting drinks for these people, that I had just had enough of trying to talk to them, to enlist their attention, their sympathy, their friendship. Bah! Here I am, still trying to persuade them to talk, to *interest* them—but Miss Drew is not interested in England, only in lit'ry criticism, and Mr. Arvin, dear little lord fauntleroy arvin, is not interested, period. [. . .]

## June 22, 1955

[. . .] Melville's "linked analogies," his sense of the sea's eternally recurrent beating as the tidal-beating of the earth, this conveys to me in his obvious identification of his style with the sea, his deep understanding of prose in its immediate life-relation. Whitman's rhythms, both in the poems, where his prose-sense actually gets him to write a new kind of poetry, and in his diaries and essays, also seem to be founded on a living closeness to nature—in his case to the "compost," the dry paths, strewn with leaves: the scattered path, all brown and natural and informal, all carelessly abundantly heaped up. Is not the secret of this 19th century American writing I love really its grasp of rhyme and colors from nature? The sea, the leaves, the ponds, the forest? [. . .]

51. Newton Arvin and Drew taught in Smith's English Department.

## June 27, 1955

Fundamentally the "idea men," be they historians or critics or philosophers, find themselves absolutely without effect in this country—except on each other—which is why they find it so hard to think of themselves as *writers*, as having an artistic function or in aspiring to one. Van Wyck [Brooks] has always thought of himself as a writer because he stems straight from the English-Continental tradition of the critics as law givers and national sages, and because he was in the beginning part of a movement of writers. [Edmund] Wilson, in his way, has had the same equal relation to writers and has been influenced even more by French examples. But today, part of my constant feeling of being isolated and of not being a recognizable part of any literary tendency comes from the fact that I, who am a writer to my finger tips and never had a thought in any literary direction that is not instinctively a writer's, find that I have to tell myself that in the very act of doing criticism. This comes not only from self-doubt, acute enough in my own case, but from the lack of permissiveness, encouragement, understanding of the kind of literary talent that is excited by ideas. Fiedler,[52] though I rather despise him, seems to me a particular case of an intelligent critic who is constantly making statements of wide, even national reference, which in the actual run of things, do not include him. He is addressing the smallest possible number of confederates in experience—i.e., the Committee for Cultural Freedom.[53] And this keeps him from being as much of an artist as he could be, in the only field, probably, where he *is* an artist. [. . .]

And when I ask myself, what it is that keeps me from writing this preface to *ONG* for Anchor, what makes every and any essay in contemporary literature such an ordeal for me, it lies, I see this now, not in my lack of courage to say "no" to pissers like Fiedler and Rahv and how many others; but in the simple courage to say "yes" to what, so often feels like the craziest, most unbelievable, most unbearably *private*, self-centered Alfred Kazinish kind of thought. It is not lack of "courage" that keeps us from saying our piece, from going through with our vision. It is the sickly feeling of being ridiculous, in being *only* this, ourselves alone and *only* ourselves. And there is no use in being heroic about isolation,

52. Leslie Fiedler (1917–2003), American literary critic and essayist, best known for *Love and Death in the American Novel* (1960), a study of the homoerotic strain he found in American writing.

53. The Committee for Cultural Freedom was a group of cultural commentators (secretly funded by the CIA) that promoted the values of Western democracy against the cultural influence of the Soviet Union. Kazin did not belong to the CCF, nor did he write for its primary organ, *Encounter*.

though of course we stick to it, and will die by it, if necessary. (For we will die without integrity; this is a matter of course.) No, what kills us *is* the isolation, the lack of dialogue, of growth in ourselves that comes from talking to each other.

Take this diary. Fundamentally, I write in it not to console myself, not to take notes, but to *write*, to write of all the things that I want to write of, and in just the spirit I damned want to write in. And I am not afraid to release it, to publish it all; of seeming "ridiculous." But is it not true that a diary like this, the record of a life-long commitment and meditation and quest, should be not merely a communion with oneself, but *also* an address to the outside world, precisely because this book holds what is truest and deepest in me?

In any event, I see today, working over the Fiedler book for my review,[54] how much I do keep myself from contemporary materials like this, not because I am afraid of defying contemporary taste, but because—see how I began this very note some pages back!—I feel that I do not belong to any of it, that I am not classified or classifiable, that I do not belong as a "writer," or as an abstract "critic" either, and so tend to hug my ideas, fancies, my very love, until they feel like grievances; when, in fact, they *are* only love, and it is ultimately of what I love, in the sight of this overreaching great sky, that I want to write of. If someone could come to me and say what Ann says by spirit, by word, by her love, all the time, I believe what you believe—what this would not mean! what this would not mean! For it is not encouragement we want, not "understanding," or psychology, but *belief*. Ann believes what I believe, and this has given me everything, everything that I have had. But nevertheless, I do feel alone, for there are few others who believe what I do, and this, this, this, is the damned coldness and inhumanness and frightfulness of everything I hate about this period. Helena C. was saying it the other day, and it awoke a deep thankfulness in me—it is this period that sets the tone by the utter selfishness, or at least, self-contentedness, self-reference, self-seeking of everything. Whatever the thirties came to, there *was* a feeling then of having one's beliefs shared, of being with others because of this. Nowadays, I not only feel alone in my belief; I hardly find it possible to feel that most people around me believe in *anything*. Newton, even Dan[55] in a way, certainly most of the literary crowd in NY—and perhaps especially the younger academic crowd; to say nothing of this as the thing one felt especially in Dylan: always this

54. "The Uses of Innocence," review of *An End to Innocence* (Boston: Beacon, 1956) by Leslie Fiedler, *New Republic* (August 29, 1955): 20–21.
55. Daniel Aaron (1912–), professor at Smith and friend of Kazin's.

nihilism, this actual specter that is menacing us, of nada, nothing to believe in. PSYCHOLOGY IS THE BELIEF OF THOSE WHO HAVE NO BELIEF AS IDEOLOGY IS THE METHOD OF THOSE WHO HAVE NOTHING TO THINK ABOUT. Silone said it in that *Encounter* piece, "A Choice of Comrades," and surely it is this quality in S. that always makes him so lovable; as it is this, again, that I went to in Simone Weil (and I noticed that Silone does, too); that I cannot find in someone like Niebuhr,[56] that I find so utterly missing in so many of my friends and colleagues. For me everything sooner or later comes down to this warm, glowing coal of belief that I do feel burning away inside me; and which warms me, inside, when I am least conscious of it, apparently, wandering in my sleep through the forests of the night. But by day, in the fight of the day, how often it goes from me, this good angel of mine, my love, my love, only because I shudder, I truly shudder, with the loneliness of it, the utter queerness of it, and so *am* a coward for not standing my place, where sometimes, it may be enough to say, all by oneself! Lord, Lord, I come, I come.

Fiedler finds his answer in the sophistication of post-Stalinism, and I mention this only because he is a bellwether, and recalls to me what was beautiful, as a belief, in our Socialism, and the cost of its perishing. Probably Judaism, which was passed on to us, and in the most formalistic fashion possible, never in its losing meant so much to us as our Socialism, for we were never so *conscious* of losing Judaism, and, so far as I am concerned, I did not lose it, but retained the best of it in deliberately passing beyond it. But Socialism did have the true quality of a belief, in the number of unconscious attachments it included—to the "oppressed," to Europe itself as the umbilical continent of our Socialism, and to "solidarity." When you think about it, one real effect of the loss of the Socialist belief was to exaggerate the value of solitude (this construed as the mark of integrity) precisely because this was the only way in which so many people could revenge themselves on the false "solidarity" of the Communist period. But they went too far, we all did, and ended up by denying the value of solidarity at all; which meant, in actuality, an arrogant contempt for the values of the "people." In one way or another, the *unreal*, false, all-too-conscious quality of our lonely integrity comes out in the need to give our position on everything, to define our relation to everything lest we be fools again or just be *thought* fools. The real beauty and meaning of a belief is the amount of unconscious

56. Reinhold Niebuhr (1892–1971), influential American theologian and political essayist during the postwar years, turned the Christian doctrine of "original sin" into a useful concept for interpreting recent history.

creative life that it releases. The worst of our period, of the "disillusioned," has been the need to make a position out of everything *personal*, out of one's tastes in cooking, houses, people; the need always to show oneself anti-"progressive," on-the-alert. In short, since this is (at its lowest) fashion and at its most ambitious (ideology), we have, along with their brothers, "methodology" and "taste," the perfect opposition between belief (which is creative and in the best sense involuntary; it captures us) and ideology, which does just the opposite of what religion does in releasing us; ideology *establishes* us as its owner; it is, finally, the method of egotism.

## July 12, 1955

The flight from "history" itself is what is recorded in the contemporary reaction against the historical. Eliot the high priest of this movement in criticism, reviews the "contemporary situation" as something frozen in its own despair, shut-in from the past, and destroyed in the supernatural disgust with it that is expressed in Thunder.[57] Then the present, that time of "confusion and anarchy," is given up altogether, and man looks only for *redemption*, deliverance. At this point, too, man begins to find his reality in works of art, and as Wittgenstein[58] said, "the limits of language become the limits of the world"—in all this man sees himself as creating reality by his perceptions, is endlessly *subjective*, posed entirely on his own effort and, as Schorer remarks this morning in his review of René Wellek's *History of Criticism*, Wellek's skill is shown inter alia, "in the ease with which causality is eschewed."[59] Wellek's own statement on this is—"All causal explanation leads to an infinite regress, back to the origins of the world." [. . .]

The Eliot vogue really arises from the attitude toward history revealed in *The Waste Land*, "Tradition and the Individual Talent," that is, of the present, first as *totally condemnable and unworthy* as compared with the past, hurrying to empty itself out at the maw [of] the dirty city river . . . utterly blasphemous and unworthy—and then of the past as living only in the mind's right perception and reordering of it. The famous influence of the present upon the past and

57. Refers to "What the Thunder Said," the final section of T. S. Eliot's *The Waste Land*.
58. Ludwig Wittgenstein (1889–1951), Austrian philosopher of logic, mind, and language, taught at Cambridge from 1939 to 1951.
59. René Wellek (1903–1995), Czech-American comparative literary critic, founded the Comparative Literature Department at Yale. His eight-volume *History of Modern Criticism, 1750–1950* remains an authoritative account of the subject.

the resettling and rearranging of this past in our mind—does this not somehow suggest above all, that the past has come loose, has broken from its moorings so that the subjective intellect does not merely "work" on it but actually recreates it in such fashion that it is felt to be alive only in his mind? *The past*, the *tradition* ceases to have any authority in its own right.

These are, *considered in themselves*, the broken tablets of forgotten gods. Yet above all, the unhistorical mind becomes a supplement to the spirit of the past itself, *begging it to exist*, and full of apprehension that it may not.

The seemingly "timeless" quality of the past in these anti-historic minds really means that the past is not really felt to exist, that *it* is only our "idea" of it and *so* it does not move and grow within us and upon us as organic beings, but is *moved*, like a dead weight, or is *worked* on, like a chemical substance (precisely the image on which Eliot ends his essay ["Tradition and the Individual Talent"]). [. . .]

## July 27, 1955

The subjectivity of the transcendentalists was their way of holding on to the chief Jewish-Christian feeling: man as the child of God, man as image of truth, as a vessel appointed to receive him. *This* personal, endlessly subjective element is what Emerson saved from the tradition and made into a new tradition, unfortunately, one dependent on his genius. For unlike the old tradition, he had to keep saying, "*I* see it! *I* see it!" and his audience had to believe in the sight of his rapture. Otherwise, the whole system, so delicately made up of personal insights, of rapturous flights, of balances held together only in this man, and by him, fell apart.

Nevertheless, Emerson held firm to the tradition—in the vital sense that life makes sense, that there is a design. It is Melville who, adopting the Romantic-transcendentalism symbolism, nevertheless sees man, the "agonist," the contestant, as someone who seeks meaning, and finally despairs of it, but in the end—gives forth this profound image of the deep, the waters outside of man's ken, as in themselves they may really seem. It is this image of the sea as the great natural force, of the shroud rolling on as it rolled five thousand years ago, of the natural force and sinews of this natural element that surrounds us, in which we barely swim for our lives—it is this vision of the deep that gives us the measure of Melville's greatness, for it is a vision not of the world still holding itself together in the small, secondary light of the Romantic ego, but of man seeing as far as he can—the waste of waters that does not include *him*, except as an eye to see it with.

## July 29, 1955

A little angel with a book in her hand jutting out from the cornice of the Episcopal church on Elm Street. When I saw it, I felt washed by memories of Paris, by a beauty which for me is always *Europe*. By contrast with the thoughts that have kept me boiling these last days on "The Western Island," the sweet European angel, *the* American is oh so leathery, sweating-hard, troubled and troubling, a sliver in the brain, a pick in your eye. Beauty is of the gray stone gathered in its sweetness over the centuries, well-tended like an English lawn, the memory well-tended even in Northampton. The American is oh so sweating *new*, every man alone in history, no sweet past to comfort him, no angels, no Gothic, except the synthetic Yales and Princetons. And yet it is not the existentialist acuteness, the final horror, man alone, but the light this newness throws, and out of the very nakedness, the immensity of the world-metaphor which the American grasps as one. No beauty, no; precious little sweetness, combing of the past down. But here everything asks to be defined again, everything to be discovered, life sinks like a stone to the very bottom of our minds. The very abstractness which DeTocqueville was so afraid of, the lack of concrete social examples to go by, to keep one's thought "sane," all this, granted its harsh angularity and self-gnawing, also widens its hold on the world as one, on a single image of life's being.

Fundamentally, the American as new man has always excited the European as old man, because the new man is always a laboratory, an experiment, where old conceptions can be tested and new ones discovered. The new man, this American, is a chance to *set up conditions*, to test and to try. And how much has the American done this himself, in his images of the West, of the great untried, of the newness of which he himself has been so conscious?

## July 30, 1955

[. . .] These forms—epic, lyric, "pastoral," and historical, the drama, the lyric poem, the essay, the dithyramb—each speaks for a different faculty or appetite of the mind, like Kant's categories.

## August 16, 1955

[. . .] The real torture and doubt of modern man—the fear that the world has no purpose—this is the real background of the book; and Ahab's determination to *find* Moby-Dick and to follow him to his death expresses the modern hero's desperate attempt to defeat the nihilism that seems to be setting in.[60] But Ahab *loses*, is conquered—as every hero is, by the superior strength of nature; and it is exactly the extent to which the *scribe*, Ishmael, can harmonize this struggle *and* its human pain by finding the power to absorb it all comprehensively in his consciousness: by showing man as equal to some vital music of the creation, *if not its chosen child*, that the book ends on the picture of man bobbing up and down on a coffin buoyed up on the waste of waters that is their field—not defiant of the universe but speechlessly humble before it.

## August 18, 1955

I suppose that what it is I dislike most in Trilling's writing is this specious air of reasonableness which he gives to his prudences and fears and prejudices; this air of connecting logic which makes so many of his points seem external. Compare it with the way Wilson or Malraux[61] writes, and you see the difference between someone (the latter), who writes straight from within, who is feeling his thoughts, rather than someone who is trying to think out what he is supposed to feel, or would like to show that he feels, rather than what he actually does. Trilling's writing is so completely audience-minded, in this sense; it is the style of a lecturer, whose very turns and pauses and connecting phrases show that he is thinking of the audience.

But in any event, this contrived and external reasonableness seems to me the mark of an imitative and timid and second-rate mind: a mind that does not have a particular vision to bring out from its own depths, but is trying to fit its convictions to the existing usages and standards and prejudices. But everything that is really good—in Wilson, in Malraux—has the quality of coming undiluted and fundamentally even unmediated—from a personal insight that he neither contrived nor could edit. I dislike Trilling's specious "reasonableness"—I fear it; for behind this air of prudent good sense and modest tentativeness, I always feel the presence of someone who is trying to arrange a "structure," rather than trying to get a fundamental point made and said; so that his deepest notes, his most tragic confessions, always sound as if he could not control them, and for a moment, had given way to his heart. [. . .]

60. Kazin was working on the Introduction to *Moby-Dick* (Boston: Houghton Mifflin, 1956).
61. André Malraux (1901–1976), French author, youthful adventurer in the Far East, best known for *Man's Fate* (1933), fought on the side of the Republicans during the Spanish Civil War. He became minister of cultural affairs during de Gaulle's presidency.

## September 3, 1955

*Amherst* Moved in Monday, 29 August[. . . .] *Amherst is a long, long* street: you just get out and start walking and trust to luck. There is no visible place to turn or to turn off, no little sidestreets and mysterious alleys, no secret passageways. Just one long street up and down, for miles it goes, and always named Pleasant. On this Pleasant Street, then, life is lived, up and down, past the college and the golf course and the Ayshire farm. The sidewalk is narrow, the main street soon empties out into a highway; there is no mystery about it, and yet an immense long-suspended quietness trembles behind the blinking face of the night-lamp on our corner. That washed-down, immensely regular, almost convent-regular quality I have always detected in Amherst people. *The quality of people who have lived in the same* house and have worked at the same college and have looked at the same street and trees for a very long time. [. . .]

## September 10, 1955

[. . .] When you read *Moby-Dick*, you remember that the idea of God was born in the desert, in the great open places, in the lonely places, in the sands that like water itself, becomes the mirror of itself, cancels out all distinctions, and across the great empty bulk of which, man reaches to God. There is one simple point that no one can get away from: God is born of loneliness. Where man has no one else to talk to; when the desert or the sea gives back the meaningless reflection of his own face or effort, then these immense spaces recall to him, as from some forgotten art of his own being, an idea of the creator commensurate with the non-human vastness of the world around him. This is what Melville meant when he wrote about the pyramids that the idea of Jehovah was born there, and what Abraham had felt in the desert. But where, as today in America, all reality is conceived as social or psychological and the whole of the universe equated with the human; when loneliness is conceived of as weakness rather than a state of being, the incipience of the search; then the very ground of faith, the private apprehension and wonder and terror, vanishes, simply because man cannot trust his loneliness, flees from it, tries to "know" himself—in the sense of trying to operate better. [. . .]

## September 11, 1955

THE AMERICAN ORTHODOXY Sunday noon/I notice in this morning's *Times* that a special committee of the American Legion has absolved UNESCO of the charge that it is communistic. [. . .]

What with one thing and another, the American orthodoxy seems to reduce itself to the "code," as in *Babbitt*[62]—Yet my feeling about the *new* orthodoxy is that it supplies a whole creed (or the appearance of one), as opposed to the class or philistine or prosperous code of the 20s. And this time the creed or code is actively mustered in defense of "America," which is seen combatively and ideologically, vis-à-vis Russia. Fundamentally, I believe that the icon is shaped in this image in order to have an "American" face because it is the secular creed par excellence, the faith of those who have no transcendental faith. Everything leans to this as a matter of course—the legend of America as a world-spirit and world hope, the enormous hypothetical and unrealized possibilities of a country like America, the equation that still exists for us between democracy as the fullest development and encouragement of the individual and religion as the culture of the individual; the peculiar enlisting of the pagans (immigrants, unwashed) into America. And above all, the fact that America is always felt to have a meaning, of utterly transcendent and spiritual character, which can never be truly defined. (Scott Fitzgerald's feeling that we are neither a country nor a people.) Primarily it is this enormous emphasis on the future, which as in religion emphasizes the possible enrichment of the individual, that makes a religion out of America. And the first thing about a religion like this is that it must be organized, that it cannot be flying apart at the seams all the time. When, I ask, was this religion codified? Reminder to study more closely the emergent history of American nationalism here.

Today, too, it is the intellectuals (in retreat from Marxism or whatever) who hold on to America as orthodoxy. And they are, even when more honest or thoughtful than the Partisan Reviewniks, honestly caught here in a quandary, because, on the one hand they are genuinely attached today (the era of good feeling and prosperity) *and* repentant of former attachments (with particular reaction against theories of alienation) that involved them in so much more, dangerous and false to their actual feeling of happiness about the country, which *is* a classless society. But above all, they bring the news to their own kind, who may not yet know of it; and here the constant danger of propaganda comes in precisely because, in strictly honest terms that the European knows nothing of, the American honestly celebrates what he has and wants to tell the world of it; and at the same time, in the method and spirit of his culture, he cannot help *selling* it. Every creed in America becomes something that you sell, precisely because you so often like

62. George F. Babbitt, the protagonist in the 1922 novel *Babbitt* by Sinclair Lewis that satirizes American middle-class culture, society, and values.

the "originator" of it (and the value of an idea in America *is*, too often, in terms of its origin; this confers prestige); and because it is *needed*.

Nevertheless, the intellectuals as orthodox Americans are always in a tough and essentially impossible position. For their America is a concept rather than a reality—i.e., what thrills them is the idea and even the unexpected, the scandalously "bourgeois" idea of it. And just as "Russia" pleased them because it connoted so much more than the actuality of the Revolution—i.e., the past, or the future—so "America" for them is not the suburban paradise so fundamentally far from the intellectual's heart (how else could it be?) but the token by which they reject so many past mistakes.

If ever there was [a] society which disproves Marx's thesis that the material problems solved, human life truly begins, it is this.

## September 23, 1955

The sun shines, the trees positively glow in this superbly clear New England fall light; I like teaching, I like my house, I like my marriage and my daughter and I even like the way I think these days. Contented, occasionally rapturous, and so even happy, much of the time, I nevertheless chafe against the pricks, I look for trouble, I long for discord. Is it true, then, is it true, as Puss said last night, and as I could feel in myself when I made the date with Celia in New York, that I was looking for trouble, for tension? It is true enough, I feel; and what strikes me in it is the rhetoric of time, for there is a sense in which we hold on to ideas that we no longer really believe in, to hatreds that we do not feel, to opposition of which we have lost the rationale. It is true that Amherst is, vitally speaking, boring—charming and boring; but it is also true that I have my work to do, that I need not look for conversation where there isn't any. [. . .]

## October 11, 1955

I will do what I think is right, I will act on what I believe, and nothing, *nothing* will keep me from it. In case after case, whenever I have tormented myself with the possible loneliness or exclusion or disdain, in punishment of a certain act (as in the Fiedler review), I have been unable to remember anything I wrote there that I would take back. And that, surely, is the decisive point, the only one.

Oh, it is difficult, difficult, difficult for two writers who have always taken their freedom for granted, bitterly difficult for them to live together like this with a child and manifold duties, responsibilities, quarreling constantly as we do about who does what or not. The *only* way I can see in all this is to give, to give, to give unceasingly and unreproachfully. And yet, and too, not to suffer from every blow and reproach, not to be constantly on edge with one's self-righteousness. This above and this, go hand in hand—only as I know that I cannot even imagine apologizing for what I know is right and for what I believe will I lose that everlasting fear of *not* realizing my heart's wish that is behind my anxiety. And surely this is exactly the same for Pussy, who, God knows, has not felt free, herself, for more than a year now. I cannot relieve her of being a mother, and my irritation with her is based on my outrage that she should not accept all this gladly. Oh miserable man, that I am to be so blind and selfish—and stupid, too, in my very lack of patience, of gentleness, of clear firmness for her to rely on. For if she is a lousy "wife" (but a supreme lover), I am a lousy husband and father in the same way. I am in despair when I think how hard it will continue thus for us—and yet as it is love and love alone that explains why I broke my deepest obligation to stay loving, so it is love and love alone that will make *our* living together at all tenable. I have not been able to confess to myself *how* profoundly irritated and disillusioned I have been ever since she became pregnant and began, as I felt, to complain and complain. I have been pissed off, disgusted—but this woman is *me*, turned inside out, *me*, in bondage of a kind that I would not tolerate for an hour. When I think how I roar and balk at the slightest check and grievance, I can hardly—in justice—complain of Ann. And I do hardly confess to myself *how* hard it is, and how far away from her I had come to feel. But bad as it all seems to me, now, *I* must stand firm and not be afraid of every possible storm and break-up as threatening my "security." Great God, what security have I got living with a temperament just like mine—What security have I ever had, *will* I ever have, with a mind like mine and a *wife* like mine? I give it up, all up—all these images I *may* ever have had, *if* I have ever had them, and want only to be *true*, whatever the case, to be true to what I *love*. Which means that I must stop thinking of Ann as in any sense a "wife," and to go back to the only kind of wife she has ever been for me, as a comrade and lover, and fellow-writer. In the same way that I *spit* on any and every possible threat to my *inward* power to speak the truth—as I dare more and more to face death itself with open eyes, this fear of death that has been the lifelong enemy and poisoner of my spirit. So I face *everything*, *everything* that can possibly happen to me; I face it—everything, up to the final homelessness, and *want only to have my say*, to be free and firm and clear in my heart. [. . .]

## October 14, 1955

Tremendous winds all morning—everything shakes: the year is beginning to show its teeth.

Reading these reviews of the "ultra-frank" new Mailer novel, *The Deer Park*, which has shocked silly Orville Prescott[63] out of his pants; and thinking of me, longing and lusting after Celia in my dreams; of my dear wife, who has her private dreams; of everybody I know, walking around with this deep sexual privacy and longing locked up inside him, I see that this private longing, this sexual "dissatisfaction," is practically the only way of protest against everything. The real meaning of this everlasting sexual burn and itch, I see now (and *this* is why it is so often accompanied by hatred and "power" rather than by love)—the real meaning of it is that it *is* private, that it is our way of saying that we are unappeased and perhaps unappeasable, that we cannot be brought into line, at least not within! Only this can explain why we hold on to our "dissatisfactions" like grim death, would hate the very idea of "fulfillment" even if the possibility were conceivable. The clue, I repeat, is the feeling of angry self-satisfaction we feel in proclaiming our dissatisfaction; the sense of self-indulgent independence we achieve at last. Several times in the recent unhappy times with Ann, when I have found myself reproaching her and storming about my dissatisfactions, I have had a horrible memory of myself sitting in the same air of complacent anger, lecturing Asya and then Carol. And the fact that Carol was as efficient as Asya was numb did not make any difference! No, it never does. This is the real meaning of the Freudian revolution—the up-raised fist, the silent grimness, the desperate search, as who was it—Andree Vilas?[64] years ago confessed to me—"for sexual satisfaction." This is the way we proclaim our selfhood—and the despair we instantly feel about its necessary frustration by society, by the great machine. This is the way we insist upon our liberty, the only real definition of liberty being a state of mind, a conception of life, rather than a function towards something specific. O poor modern rebel, raising your fist against your loved one and looking elsewhere for what you do not even wish to find. O blind stirrings of the human gut, which speak for more than you can ever know.

## October 15, 1955

[. . .] All this morning, even before I got up to feed the baby, I have been in a lather of excitement about the American orthodoxy book—which, how deeply it came to me this morning, is about the intellectuals, about New York, about the ex-left, about Fiedlerism and Hookism and Trillingism, about everything

63. Orville Prescott (1906–1996), daily book reviewer for the *New York Times*.
64. Unknown reference.

I know and have been a part of. I don't want to look anymore for what I want to write; I have it, all of it, inside me.

## October 18, 1955

[. . .] Dick [Hofstadter]'s book [*The Age of Reform*] came and I looked though it; and I've already [read] reviews which tell me what I can see, that it is brilliant and realistic and true. But my objection to all this "status-politics" stuff, this new realism, this post-liberal move in our generation is simply the level on which all this is written, on which it is thought. This is the damned trouble with all these people—from Trilling up and down; it is not that the particular point they are making that is ever wrong, for Dreiser does write badly and "realism" did let us down, etc., etc. What is wrong is the whole careful, saving, prudential, political point of view—they are always within the circle of what they are criticizing. And in a sense, this is the battle I have with all these ignorant kids, that one has all the time in this culture. Which is simply the level of discourse, the unbelievable smallness and materialism and group-mindedness and psychologization of everything. Who can quarrel with Dick about the silly populists? And who can feel that *this* is the level on which to wage criticism of the "age of reform"—which in itself deserves everything, and more, that it is coming in for, and which in itself is no worse than half a hundred things these guys go in for? No values, no real values, no conscious values, no definitions, no respect for humility, no intactness of the soul, no sense of anything but this damned materialistic culture in itself. This is the case, the only possible case, on which the damned thing can ever be fought out against the left (and now the new right). Everything else is just a waste of time and of words.

## October 25, 1955

[. . .] When I stopped for coffee at the College Drug Shop, corner of S. Pleasant and Main, old working-on-third-novel, David Jackson, Merrill's boy friend and house mate greeted me.[65] Squashy soft. All these little butterflies are so boringly *young*. To be young is to be arch. Asked much after my friend, my best friend, Annie. I kidded her about it—a little maliciously, after so many nights of no f. And it is true, and it is true, that she does inspire a fearless affection in fairies. But not only in them. God knows. I am sore and hurt and bruised and starved all over, for lack

65. James Merrill (1926–1995), Pulitzer Prize–winning poet, graduated from Amherst in 1947. David Noyes Jackson (1922–2001), poet, life partner of Merrill's, collaborated with Merrill in the latter's most productive years.

of f. But I love her, I love her, and I pray for the power that makes warm, that relaxes and expands and makes warm. All that nonsense last week and how many other weeks, on my part about f., when it is love that opens and attaches and secures. For me at least. The only road to my body, to any body, is through the spirit. [. . .]

## November 18, 1955

[. . .] As I read Panofsky's[66] charming autobiographical epilogue to his Anchor collection of essays, I find myself nettled, as usual, by this "humanistic" fetish of our Jewish intellectuals—no extremes, please, let us be sensible, etc. . . . And thinking it out on my walk just now, I came up with a theory: the Jewish intellectual sees the world through a model, usually in the native culture, which he accepts as the norm. Thus, the German-Jewish intellectuals of Panofsky's generation, *obviously* chose the humanist, the old German fuddy-duddy scholar (as see P's loving notes on the type in his youth, who taught him Greek and history); Hannah's generation, more "radical," brought up on existentialism, took Nietzsche and Jaspers, Kafka and . . . Chesterton.[67] . . . The Russian Jews I have known took the type of the Russian liberal-revolutionary-intellectual, say Chernischevsky[68] or even Tolstoy. Thus, point 2—the model is a national type of *liberator* or constructive force: the model must be slightly old-fashioned, as in the English liberals or even the English aristocrats who are so much admired (here see [Harold] Laski on Churchill, even, but certainly . . . [Oliver Wendell] Holmes, etc., etc.) All this reverses [Edmund] Wilson's essays on Holmes seeking Jewish sons:[69] brings us back to Jewish sons seeking fathers, the "goyish" culture. Trilling the respectable professor—TRent [*sic*] one like that? I had my model in people like Mark Van Doren, but more especially in the American religious radicals and spiritualists, like Emerson and Thoreau and Whitman. The model must be a relaxing, a "vague" kind of director (in terms of limitation) but firm as a character to be followed. In any event, Trilling, Levin, Panofsky, even Edgar Wind[70]

66. Erwin Panofsky (1892–1968), German art historian, who emigrated to America, best known for *Studies in Iconology: Humanist Themes in the Art of the Renaissance* (1939).
67. Gilbert Keith Chesterton (1874–1936), prolific English writer, wrote on philosophy, art, and poetry; staunch defender of orthodox Christianity.
68. Nikolay Gavrilovich Chernyshevsky (1828–1889), Russian revolutionary democrat, led the revolutionary democratic movement of the 1860s, influenced Lenin and Emma Goldman (see Chapter 5, note 54). It has been argued that his novel *What Is to Be Done* was a greater influence on the Russian Revolution than Karl Marx's *Capital*.
69. Edmund Wilson, "The Holmes-Laski Correspondence," in *The Bit Between My Teeth* (New York: Farrar, Straus and Giroux, 1965).
70. Edgar Wind (1900–1971), a German-born British art historian, student of Erwin Panofsky, taught in various American colleges and universities, including Smith, before becoming the first professor of art history at Oxford University.

(particularly homeless and deracinated as an un-German Jew brought up in Germany)—all, as I have known the type, have always had the academic humanist as model; where Harold Rosenberg has gone after, say, Rimbaud, or Saul [Bellow] after Lawrence. . . . Obviously a *purely* Jewish model makes for too much restriction, too much nostalgia. . . . NOW: I advance the theory that the really original and brilliant and brave Jewish intellectual has no model that is particularly national, local, in time (Einstein) . . . or seeks it very far in the past . . . I question, given the kind of cultural ambiguity from which so many Jews start, whether it would be possible to sail into this "foreign" culture completely, without a model. . . . It follows too that for most Jews in America, the example is bad, cultureless, practical—hence the revolting muckerism of American Jewish alrightniks as opposed to the complacent humanism of the German Jewish intellectuals. . . .

Item: the model, I suspect, is identified with the type which liberated the Jewish intellectual but is not too close to the Jew himself to be tarred with his own inferiority. He represents the model, perhaps, of an *age* of liberation—i.e., the rationalists of the French Revolution who freed the German Jews; the social critics and Marxists who freed the Russian Jews. No one freed the American Jews, but correspondingly, there has been less inspiration.

If my theory is right, as applied to the intellectuals, it would follow that with, say, Kafka or Simone Weil, one has an amazing amount of self-definition, and that here, precisely, is one explanation of their immense burden and suffering, which would consist in the lack of immediate (national) background. Simone Weil always sought this national background, proclaimed her roots as French and classical, but in the absence of an immediate national cultural model to fall back on, in her revolutionary and creative attitude of resistance to the whole French present, she unconsciously found her true Jewish identity and became a figure for our time.

It follows from what I have said that the endemic and typical vices of the Jewish intellectual are: a) cultural piety and humility; b) rhetoric (i.e., lack of directness and personal *point*, as in [Harry] Levin); c) reliance on personality and psychology for explanation of all motivation (since the immediate inspiration is *personal*). And, of course, "respectability"—i.e., reliance on status, the German professor at his worst, etc.

Now this "positivism," sensibleness from Sidney Hook up, or down, all this also indicates, independently, the enormous disillusion with the faith, the patient endurance of this world, the Jew's well-known shrug—of fatigue and sheer, continuous, cumulative discontent, through the ages, of search and aspiration.

Conversely, it must be said, the "strong" model-less Jew, Yeshua or Marx, Simone Weil or . . . becomes a model for the whole culture, starts from well outside it.

## December 1955

The Gift of Conviction:

THE INDIVIDUAL STRENGTH. All my life I have been seeking—in the last few years, more and more positively—what may be called the individual strength, the core of maturity, the power to be strong and free inside oneself. This maturity is actually the great ideal of the individual in our society, who always defines himself in terms of his society and of his relative freedom from it. This power begins as the search for "self-knowledge," and then becomes a search for strength—i.e., what the Freudians call ego, the crystallization of one's knowledge of oneself in such a way as to enable one to draw upon the sources of strength in one's unconscious life. This "ego-strength," which Freud himself made the principle of his life and represents for our generation, is defined in terms of one's power to resist—to resist bodily ills and fears, to resist conventional opinion, to enable one to go one's own way. This is strength, individual strength—and involves an unflagging power of resistance, a scrupulous attention to all one's innermost needs and thoughts. This is "maturity"—i.e., one is not deceived by secondary goals or deflected by conventional power or discouraged by the mediocre trials of life. It is measured by serenity, a conscious awareness of one's independence and vigilance. It may be expressed as defiance (Ahab) of the powers of life and death, the wish to carry out to the uttermost one's exploration of the unknown; Freud himself felt this power as that of the "teacher," or the father—the great Moses figure, he who transmits the law, who shapes into a social, modern experience what he himself has grasped in the lonely and awesome confrontation of God (Nature), and who now orders life, whole generations, to the vision which he has transmitted. [. . .]

What these reflections come down to, I see, is that the basis of modern search for integrity lies in the lack of any philosophy, of what to think. Or rather, in the fact that each individual has been summoned up to the ark to read of the book of life for himself and to discover the truth for himself—so that, given the extreme perilousness and loneliness of this, the individual clings, almost as a point d'appui [base of support], to the psychological struggle. More and more, it is clear to me that what I suffer from is the lack of a working philosophy, of a strong central belief, of something outside to which my "self" can hold and, for once, forget its "self." And the more I see of life around me, the more I am convinced of the utter lack of any true opinion in most places, of there being no solid core of thought anywhere. The real joke of our modern egomania may not be that we are struggling with an unconquerable passion for ourselves, but that for the moment, we may have nothing else very sure to talk about. [. . .]

My besetting weakness: an inability to stay with the subject, to devour it through and through. I am always flitting—and the weakness, I see, comes from this same anxiety that I will not have it all, meaning all my interests. I am devoured by so many interests, I cannot help responding to so many calls on my imagination, that instead of taking it all full in the face, or staring each one through and through, like a hunter his quarry, like a jeweler his stone, I tend to get as much of anything I need in order to establish a meaningful relation to it, and then disappear. . . . But it is exactly in proportion to this direct "crushing," full concentration of all our power on an object—a subject—that the real work is done. [. . .]

## December 23, 1955

[. . .] How I have been bemused and puzzled and discouraged by the academics [at Amherst], whether it be Marx's hurtful review of the leaf or by the [Cesar Lombardi] Barbers[71] and other such horrors here, the unthinking no-brains—constantly thinking of the kind of "objectivity," of "objectivity," Oh Lord, whatever that can be, for a scientist of letters, for whomever, it is not and has never been for me, and only my persistent forgetfulness of my own soul, my cruel and shameful lack of faith, my lack of heart, of trueness to myself and my deepest need and conviction, surrounded by these braying voices, these noises, these nothings "objectively" addressing themselves to their new-critical shit and straw. [. . .]

This is the trouble of a writer's notebook: a writer uses it constantly to gain clarity, to seek clarity, to define his terms, but unless he catches his torment, his obsession, on the wing, as it were, in terms of the subject itself, he tends, as I so often do here, to define the problem rather than to face it, to make words, psychology, instead of the thing, which is writing. . . . On the other hand, the notebook has to be used like good liquor, to stimulate, but should not be confused with food, the work itself, which alone can nourish. . . . The notebook is a training-ground, to remind him of the kind of intimacy, the utter withinness *in* which the writer lives; it is not and cannot be the fearful facing of the presence, the standing-up to the ghost, the unbelievable exertion of removing the stone from the tomb. [. . .]

The trouble with so many writers, who are real writers, and to be known by this quality of personal necessity, is that they cannot face up to the often

71. Leo Marx, "Kazin and the Religion of Art," *New Republic* (November 8, 1955): 18–19. Leo Marx (1919–), American literary critic and historian, became professor of American studies at Amherst following Kazin's departure; Cesar Lombardi Barber (1913–) taught Shakespeare at Amherst.

unexpected width and reference *of* their need (which has been true of AK and today explains for me the constant gap and seeming division between the autobiography and my essays). Or, as is true of Trilling, they also *want* to be successful, in the worldly sense: they are tormented, exigent, demanding writers all right, real writers—but the profession, in LT's case, comes stealing in, and says "scarcely," and wears a black homburg, and in general, alas, although his critical work is exciting precisely because it comes out of need—the opposing self, the liberal imagination, the middle of his journey—wants also to be a judicious man, a father to many students, an influence, a success. . . . So he keeps sneaking and stealing to Freud the way a man might try to sneak a feel from a girl—and sees the individual torment at the bottom of himself? Oh, no, the crisis of *our* culture.

## January 22, 1956

[. . .] I have never been more convinced than I am just now of how well fitted for criticism I am and how much I love it. But I can only signify this by taking my job as a critic very responsibly indeed—by *seeing* what it is I do and by *presenting*, teaching, solidifying, making *clear*. I have not merely spent too much time "defending" myself—I have, alas, even rejoiced in the false feeling of isolation that it gave me—which released me from having to do some *genuine work*.

## March 8, 1956

Went in this morning to see Cole[72] to talk about leave, and to leave a big hint of my irritation and dissatisfaction, and went out as usual feeling not only that he had charmed me into conceding what I had not planned to concede and said what definitely I had not planned on saying, but that I had in some subtle way lied myself into more conventional postures than I can sincerely stand up in. It is a mark of Charley's charm, and efficiency, and presidential effect on me, that I do constantly, when I am in his office, sound to myself like a conventionally eager, soundly patriotic teacher. And this under the influence of a boy of the twenties who still parts his hair in the middle, has the complexion of a junior who has been feasting on ice-cream sodas, and talks to me, man to man, as one sophisticated intellectual to another! . . . This, my son, is ability on his part as much as it represents some infernal conventionalism on mine. And I sit down to note this as much out of a feeling of puzzled admiration for him and irritation

72. Charles Cole (1906–1978), Amherst president, 1946–1960.

with my own goody-goodiness. Cole has charm, and he works on you in the formula of the Greek god—i.e., he *shines*, and you bask in his light. [. . .]

## March 12, 1956

The American Dream and the European Nightmare. I have just finished reading papers on immigration in my American Problems courses, and I am sick at heart at the utter piddling, puerile "realism" of these little stinkers. For them the whole problem resolves itself into a) "realism"—the cold war will be aided or not by immigration or b) sentimental pluralism, it's good for *us* to have a little eytalian blood or c) "humanitarian." What has not occurred to them, except Tracy Wiggin, is that America as an idea, as a civilization, is founded on the very idea of immigration, on the idea of a world-civilization and a world-frontier. . . . But beyond this, the utter piddlingness of these young shits is what takes my breath away, the American "good sense" and American "moderation" and "decency." It seems not to occur to most of them that America has any transcendent principle whatever—or that anybody else has, for that matter. America the great adding machine, American dream and European nightmare, in truth.

## April 18, 1956

[. . .] The growth of "American" studies today has brought with it a new insistence on showing that America has a mission, or at least so exceptional a character, that all other facts have to be fitted to it. . . . Just as America would never have been discovered or colonized if someone had not *though*t of it first (say what you like about Columbus, he was searching for something more than India), so America in its history seems never to be described for "its own sake," but appears as the adjunct to someone's thought. And the reason, of course, is that America, unlike all other countries, is a conscious *creation*, and there must always be a reason for creating something—if only we can remember it. [. . .]

## April 20, 1956

The trouble with most critics is that they think like men in a corner; they can deal with a work only at close quarters, by commenting on what is put directly before them. If the art of criticism means anything, it means the gift of *primary* thinking, of originality, which puts a principle where we did not know one before; which establishes laws, which overhauls custom. [. . .] The greatest critics are either the primary philosophers of art, like Aristotle, or the wisest of craftsmen in dealing with their fellows, like Eliot, or the sages of life in general and of the artistic faculty in particular, like Johnson, or the innovators like Coleridge. The most useful of critics are the real *kenners* of fellows' work, like Matthew Arnold, those who hold a whole art in their hands and make you see all its possibilities in their pages. There are also entertaining critics (destroyers of a festering tradition) like Shaw; true spiritual critics or upholders, like Emerson or Lawrence. . . . But the greatest of critics are those who restore to us a conscious reason for liking what we like, for disliking what we [dis]like, who practice the art of judgment and analysis, the empirical arts of criticism and all the time lift this empirical work into universal significance, who connect it with systematic human knowledge.

## April 29, 1956

I spoke yesterday at the College English Association at Storrs and was fascinated, if that is the word, by the extraordinary two-dimensional world in which teachers live. Everything consists of a flat, hopelessly mediocre amiability, good manners, pleasantness and pleasingness. And I suppose it is this inner reference these people always seem to be making, to some authority or code of good manners or "scholarship," that explains the fearful *dryness*. I always have the impression with such people that they do not speak for themselves and in themselves, but like the good little boys and girls they were once in school, look up with eager submission to the right thing to feel and say. The *cautiousness* of such people is only a manifestation of the larger habit of constantly checking themselves in accordance with somebody's say-so or footnote.

Now if you put such people against an utterly new-made campus like the U. of Connecticut, which tires you out by its bigness and utter superficiality, then the boredom becomes absolute. How many lunches, how many academic meetings, how many octagonal glasses I have looked on since I became a visiting fireman at these things.

Yes, these people are the leavings of the once great ministerial class. But without any intensity. They are to the old ministers what the genteel liberal tradition is to Emerson.

The real significance and justification of the historical approach to literature is [that] the good writer always speaks to forces (and out of forces) larger than himself, and that these constitute, often as unexpressed assumptions, the ground on which he works—In order to understand his distinction, it is important to understand the precise change he has made in the tradition he may (unconsciously) be trying to express.

## April 30, 1956

AT THE ALTAR OF HENRY JAMES

Whatever James may have suffered at the hands of his critics during his lifetime, and just after it, the new dispensation has made up to such a point that I see literary pilgrim after literary pilgrim delicately genuflecting before his altar and putting upon it one paper flower of praise. That one of the most profoundly idiosyncratic writers who ever lived, a writer whose greatest merit lies precisely in his idiosyncrasy, and who is admirable largely because he converted his glaring deficiencies into such formidable assets of a highly exaggerated kind—that such a writer should now be thought of as "classical" in style, as "traditional" for the novel, seems to me one of the real jokes of our time. [. . .]

## May 21, 1956

[Edmund] Wilson was here last night; we drove into Northampton for dinner and later stopped in at the Aarons's.[73] He seems milder and mellower in many ways than I have ever known him, yet for the first time in my life I feel utterly detached from him, am often bored and impatient with him, and can see him with the shallower exactitude of a lack of affection than I ever could before. From the time I was a boy, his writing thrilled me—I use the word advisedly—because of its virtuosity, its consummate proof of the art that could be brought to criticism. And I suppose it was this that so long made the example of E.W. so important to me, since my own hunger was always to be a writer, an artist, not a "critic;" and it dumbfounded and baffled me to find that so many usual genres for a literary artist—the novel and poetry—were not for me. And since I have always approached all literary and critical questions with the instinctive quick sympathy of the writer, not with the objectivity or heaviness of the critic, I suppose I found in E.W. the one solid proof that my own kindred literary personality was real. . . . But year by year, as I have learned to depend on myself and not to seek an example in others, I have found myself growingly impatient with E.W.'s lacks, as well [as] painfully self-conscious that I could never meet him as a scholar, as the relentless student of all literature and languages that he so wonderfully is. I love him for his seriousness, for his abstractness, for having the courage, in so difficult a field as literary journalism, to take himself au grand serieux and to take the field. And as I watched him last night I was fascinated,

73. Daniel Aaron (1912–), American literary historian and long-time friend of Kazin's, taught at Smith and Harvard, best known for *Writers on the Left: Episodes in American Literary Communism* (1961).

too, by the seriousness with which as always he takes all his likes and dislikes—so that in that interminable card-catalog of his memory, he refers back always to what he has thought, to what he might have thought, with the same matter-of-fact egotism with which, having explained to us that he has high blood pressure and is forbidden salt and (much) alcohol, he downed about seven martinis before dinner. . . . This "egotism," as shallow people would call it, is the *sine qua non* of a mind which functions by referring everything back to his own reactions. These reactions are not necessarily "subjective," but they are *personal* to a quite remarkable degree, and it is in this steadfast reference to the writer's reactions that the fundamental artistic quality of such a mind as Wilson is found. That long cherishing of one's own reactions, this involves a remarkable degree of instinctive *training* and of the memory that will store away those reactions and assort them in their proper places. Wilson told me he had not looked at *The Scarlet Letter* since 1915, but that he remembers *disliking* it. . . .

To such a mind, other "critics" are of not the slightest importance and may, indeed, be a literal obstruction. It is always his personal attitude that counts. But what lies behind this huge dependence on his personal reactions is, of course, nothing psychological at all—but the hoarding and cherishing and daily sharpening of a *gift*. The gift that led him by the eyes from the time he was at all conscious of himself. All "egotism," as the shallow call it, consists in the protection and furtherance of this gift, which to the writer is the only life that means anything. Where the question of "egotism" *does* come in, for E.W., is in respect not to his personality but to the gift itself, to the length and breadth of its field of vision.[74]

## May 30, 1956

All this talk about only "imagination" as real—or how we need *myth* in order to *support* our existence. I believe that the world is real, that this reality is boundless, that it supports our imagination, not the other way round, that we are children of the world, of *this* world, of the everlasting reality, not that this world is a function of *us*, of our imagination.

74. In a journal entry recalling the evening in Northampton, Wilson wrote that it was his "first real talk with Alfred, who though self-important, is shy and needs drinks to loosen up. . . . I hope the time will come when he gets over his lack of confidence and comes out with something really important." *The Fifties: From the Notebooks and Diaries of the Period*, ed. Leon Edel (New York: Farrar, Straus, and Giroux, 1986), 417.

## June 8, 1956

The danger to America—that it will become not like Russia, but like Switzerland. It is not the fear of ideas we are suffering from but the lack of ideas—not the police state but the bourgeois habit of mind—not terror but inhuman self-contentment. It is from a lack of *vision* that we are suffering—not from a lack of "dissent."

## July 27, 1956

[. . .] The young Jew, the Augie March hero of Saul's book, this thoughtful stranger in America, this eternal traveler, this philosopher of eros, ex-Socialist and lover of many women—from the soapbox to the orgone box, from bed to bed, from the mother to the wife, from city to city—this type, as Saul described him, took on the masquerade of the half bum, half-philosopher. The man who would not be taken in, innocent and tough, skeptical and lyrical at once. The man whose greatest dream was fullness of experience, for he saw himself sailing from orthodox bonds and the chicken coop of the ghetto into the imagined fullness of the modern world. Infinitely self-resourceful, yet imaginatively, indescribably dependent; empirically, thoroughly learned, yet always feeling himself sharply in need of a new dispensation, a great new idea. His great value is that he possesses a past and has no plans for the future; that he is in touch with history but contemptuous of ideology; that he believes in *history*, respects the accumulated stream of things, society, the masses—but above all wants to be himself free [as] a person. This hero, AK, Augie, Isaac [Rosenfeld], even someone like [Leslie] Fiedler, corrodes like acid any society he finds himself in; *he sees through it* all at a glance; he is forever in a hurry to keep an appointment with his freedom. He thinks himself soft, blames himself continually for not settling things more satisfactorily so that he can be "happy." But his softness = *his thudding sensitivity to things plus his terrific ability to identify himself* with the condition of all those in the world who cannot think of their lives as "successful"—who unconscious of how much they suffer, still obscurely sense that *this* world is not the promised land. This young Jew, this traveler, is happiest when he is in touch with the earth—when he is *combatively* free, blazing away shackles and rotted negations. He is a *force;* he is a stir in the world and a force, a critic who criticizes from love, a poet who lives in ideas. The only fault of this man is that he can mistake his sensitivity for *personal fault*, and so blame himself, that the accumulated coldness and impenetrability and hate of the outside world will tempt him into thinking of himself as a spectator, a stranger, instead of a critic, a living bond between the intelligence and the world—a living and fiery particle of spirit. His real problem is always how to think of his origins not as exotic but as *necessary* and even, in terms of each human being's aspiration toward freedom, *symbolic*. It is to think of his road as an essential and fundamental journey from freedom (realized in the personal sense) to a free love *of the world as our earth*.

## August 19, 1956
### [Nice, France]

Sitting here on the balcony overlooking the sea. Puss is asleep in the living room. My heart is so full of what we said to each other yesterday, and in particular of what she said to me—of its truth, of its piercing hard and painful truth. The truth is that I have lost my writer's way in the last few months and almost years, that I *have* come to accept, to make do, to think of my comfort, I could say, with equal truth, that my own feelings of pettiness, of unworthiness, of boredom, all that comes from the fact that I am no longer *fighting*, comes because, like everyone else of my generation and background, I have "graduated" from suffering. I have joined the great middle-class world of daily self satisfaction. . . . What has happened *is* the story of America. The "success-story" for America *does* blunt and dampen all one's fires by its belief in "happiness" and fulfillment. All those fat Jews—Jason Epstein[75] and my own Richard H[ofstadter], all the Beichmans[76] and Cultural Freedom overseers—all this represents the death not merely of "alienation," but of the vital and fiercely hungry intelligence. . . . We wanted to get *out* of Brownsville, the steerage—and we got into the "American" business. *This* is the real story to follow the *Walker*, I see it now—the end of protest, or rather, the inability to remain *outside*, to be a free and single agent. [. . .]

## September 16, 1956

[. . .] What it means to be able to write from the heart in a journal like this. What it means to be able to *listen* to oneself and to transcribe the tones with utter ease and quickness. What it means, symbolically and in the fact, *to listen to oneself*, to speak the truth as one knows it. The limitations of the journal are the limitations of solitude—there are truths we never arrive at by ourselves, *truths that can only be realized in dialogue*. But within these limitations and

75. Jason Epstein (1928–), American editor, publisher, writer, and editorial director at Random House for forty years; cofounder in 1963 of the *New York Review of Books*, one of the cofounders of Library of America.

76. Arnold Beichman (1913–2010), prominent anticommunist columnist, later a research fellow at the Hoover Institute.

outside of the crippling suppressions and nonsenses that society (which too often lacks all true dialogue whatever) forces upon us, solitude has the virtue, not so much, I should say of wisdom, as of *authenticity*. Carrying your value proudly through a crowd of foes. And my first sentiment and inclination to the contrary, there is nothing to regret in the urgent necessity of private testimony and self-communion. For if there are truths we arrive at only in dialogue, there are forays into life that we can experience only in solitude. At least that is my poet's way of working, my writer's way of responding with infinite wonder and respect to the inner voice. For after all, writing to oneself, in the deep, deep intimacy of a personal journal, *is* not the same as casual introspection. There is, in the very act of writing, definition, crystallization, and in the very choice of the right word rather than the wrong one, obedience to the great and beautiful force of intellectual honor. So I am really excited by the privilege of keeping my journal. After so many years in which I have done just this without recognizing the inviolable necessity of a private place at all, I feel as if I have at last recognized in full light the sacredness of the private personality as against the innumerable temptations to facility, convention and untruth. It seized me that delicious afternoon in Oslo, lying in bed reading the Colin Wilson *Outsider* book,[77] that, after so many years in which I have tried so hard to find a use for my journal, I have at last been able to recognize that I keep it for the urgent pleasure of saying in it just what I think. And if this carries just now a special overtone because of my constant effort to *appease* Ann, then I must acknowledge that it is because of my situation that this notebook has become such a driving necessity. The truth is that I neither do what I want nor let Ann acknowledge fully what she wants. I have been sleepwalking, going along and trying to make do, for so long now! Because I couldn't acknowledge how much our life had changed, Pussy's and mine. I couldn't recognize that there was such a constantly and bitterly dissatisfied woman living with me and that all these scenes have been fundamentally her own way of expressing her bitterness. I thought it would blow over—I thought she would find some maternal pleasure in the baby or some new faith for herself. But quite apart from the fact that she can't, that she *is* terribly young, if not as young as she is in her rooted picture of herself, all our scenes result from my naive and stupid amazement, over and over again, at her bitterness. So that when her explosion comes, as sooner or later everyday it comes, I fall into the same trap by expostulating by suffering, by tears. I've lacked perspective and good sense utterly, utterly—I've constantly

77. In *The Outsider* (Boston: Houghton Mifflin, 1956), Wilson examines the perspective of writers and artists as "outsiders."

shut my eyes to this profound and deep bitterness she feels at being "caught," at having a baby. I've constantly been *amazed.* And oh God, much as I love her and always will, there *is* this fire there all the time, this resentment, this suffering at her lack of liberty and the truth is that the beautiful, beautiful world of our love comes back to us at moments now only when we are free of the baby. And as she feels bitterness, I feel disappointment—above all, I recognize with grim and calm sight this morning that I've constantly shut my eyes and held my ears against this seething volcano, *this bitterness*, this bitterness. I've constantly erupted into anger or collapsed into tears—neither of which was the slightest avail or meaning in this tense situation. I suppose in some sentimental way I had even deprecated perspective as unloving, as a betrayal of all our passionately identical ecstasies. But *perspective*, detachment, is an absolute necessity—I must at all times remember the real truth, offensive as it may be to my damned romantic memory, or I shall never get off my feet—or awaken from this strange inner torpor. So it all comes down to the closest possible attention to the truth, to the purpose, the profound and deep and painful *necessity* of truth which calls this journal into being, and so it all comes down to the same task.

## October 1, 1956

The trouble with Henry Commager, I decided this morning, is that he (like Van Wyck Brooks and how many people I know and admire, or rather love) is in the fairy tale of American history, which is a fairy tale that sometimes has no possible relation to anything else and where, by constantly appealing to your own past, you fall into the error of assuming that everybody else is off the track. The 19th century America, the old landscape of dreams and wonders, to say nothing of the endless love letters exchanged between oneself and oneself in this adoration of the American past, until, like Brooks or Henry, you get angry at the challenge to this fairytale world presented by the outside. And the appeal, I see more and more, is that it is a romance, this American history tale, a romance being a story that obeys no conditions but those inherent to it; it is not checked or challenged or tormented by anything outside.[78]

78. In a letter to Commager's biographer, Kazin is less dismissive. Commager is "a remarkable savant and one of the few historians left who is a true man of letters," quoted in Neil Jumonville, *Henry Steele Commager* (Chapel Hill: University of Carolina Press, 1999), 268–269.

## October 12, 1956

All this failure to grip the object solidly, to *see it*, comes from internal conflict, doubt, hesitation *in accepting the new commitment already inwardly made.* Reading Trilling's new book of essays [*The Opposing Self*] yesterday, I realized to what extent I agree with him, with his attitude toward America and to what extent I have not been able to *admit* what I know and feel. I used so long to think that I had to find "courage"—I see now that all I have to *be* is plain. . . . This has been an immense and painful transition for me, for so many of my generation, from alienation to acceptance—and I can see that it is indeed my struggling *against* acceptance, against the plain commitment to one's happy actuality—above all, the commitment to *partial* and fragmentary answers, that marks the new man I am. For in the past one had so many universal and comprehensive answers—either God or Socialism taken alone or together, were always systematic and abstract. More and more I feel, honestly, that *I do not know*, that I am sure of some things and all too unsure of others—and it has been my resistance *to* this commitment, my hiding of my real unsureness that has worked against me so long.

And this *unsureness*—how much it explains, this painful *transition*, our general haltingness, our lack of sweep, our sense that things are desperately tied to events—the generation [sentence breaks off]

## November 6, 1956

[. . .] Look at us now, this week of murder and bloodshed unspeakable in the world—in Hungary and Egypt.[79] We all go on planning things, planning so comfortably and idyllically, thinking about our souls and the progress of our culture and our lives, and all the while these tremendous human forces working in and around us, working *us*, if not as the Marxists say, completely, still so smashingly that it's both a comedy and a horror to realize for one single moment, when we pick ourselves up dazedly from the floor, that all our thoughts about and from ourselves consistently miss the dynamic, historical element that has put us where we are. [. . .]

This week of Egypt and Hungary has brought me back to my historical sense, to my sense of life as a process, as action; to the tragedy that we begin to recognize as soon as we see that the will is certainly not absolute.

79. Kazin is referring to the Hungarian revolution that led to the Soviet invasion of Budapest the first week of November and to the Suez Crisis, the attack on Egypt by France, England, and Israel after Egypt nationalized the Suez Canal.

## November 23, 1956

A light powdery snow on the ground this morning, a pleasant gray edge to the sky. Came back yesterday from Boston and Cambridge, where we had stopped with the [Howard Mumford] Joneses, and where I [had] gone to attend my first editorial lunch at the *NEQ* [*New England Quarterly*]. The genteel tradition: the fire, the martinis before lunch, the drapes, the cigars, the pleasant, o pleasant comfort. And above all somebody called Walter Muir Whitehall (???), the Athenaeum librarian. A moustache that looked as if it had been pasted on, a sort of mock-military mustache, flying out into ambiguous wisps. Every phrase, like putting still another smear of butter on a piece of toast. Phrases, ready-made phrases by the millions, and above all, this air of saying everything around the dinner table, the constant acknowledging of someone else, of a group, of the right way to think and the right way to say it. . . .

The genteel tradition—what is it but money, habit, tradition in an old and settled place: plus a certain Englishy lack of sensuousness and an Englishy love of solid comfort and the conscious polishing of still another corner of the dining table? What is it but high-living and the *tradition* of some high thinking as well? The clubiness of it is so striking; has anyone pointed out that the genteel tradition is founded on the clubman's idea of solid comfort, on the clubman's clubiness—on a world that is without sex, and without risks? The genteel tradition is the Century [Association] in NY and the Colonial Society in Boston, it is the academic, the pleasant and the womanless. . . . Is this why there are so many honorific references to women—why the woman is the absent god, the judge, of the genteel world?

Above all, a world of *money*. No money, especially no solid money, no gentility. [. . .]

Reading Lawrence's *Chatterley* till my knees begin to buckle. O life, O life, the life-giver—O to be this warm-hearted fucker—

To fuck with all one's heart—to believe that you love; to know what you are, and so to fuck with all one's being, straight into the core.

The "invisible flame of another's consciousness"

## December 4, 1956

One of the tests of any place, or time, or relationship, is its ability to charge us, to tempt us to exceed ourselves—in any event, to live more passionately! And by this test, Amherst is certainly a bust. How easy it is, how fatally and dreadfully easy, to fall languid, to find excuses for not doing things, to "husband" one's energy [. . .] the way the students lie back in their seats as if they were 106 and just recovering from coronary thrombosis. How much of this dry, belchy look I have seen so often on the faces, and in the figure, of the students—and the fat upholstered look of someone like Tuffy MacGowan, or the idiocy of the Art director Morgan.[80] . . . [. . .]

## December 7, 1956

We were talking in class this morning about Ahab the superman, and that good Smith kid remarked on the 19th century cult of the superman, the romantic genius, the Satanic intellectual. I was suddenly seized with a sense of shame at how little of our own period has gone into these last few years of meditating Emerson and his kindred, and thought again of the easy assumptions of progress or of damnation, for that matter, which dominate 19th century thought as opposed to our own. . . . My shame comes from my forgetfulness that one's own period is like a living person, that it *is* life, life to which one always owes the supreme allegiance, life that needs to be understood and met on its own terms, not those of the past. All history at least the kind that *I* know enough to write, *is* contemporary history: or, rather, since a history of the living world is in some sense impossible, is an attempt to meet this contemporary world, to discover something of its nature, to understand something of its structure. [. . .]

## January 18, 1957

The end of Auden's Oxford lecture on poetry seemed to me beautiful in its feeling for "sacred objects."—without worship, without respect, without *wonder* without the great work with which our wonder and awe plunge us, *what* is there—*what?*

But the "modern" epoch is precisely that in which each of us must discover our gods for ourselves. This is why so much in our language reverts to the idea of a *fall*, a descent. As Satan fell, to rise again as a prince of life, so we fall into this maelstrom, this madness—this world in which nothing any longer is *given* to us—to discover, in pain and awe, our own sacred objects.

80. Tuffy MacGowan, technical assistant for the Amherst College theatrical productions; Charles Morgan (1902–1984), first director of the Mead Art Gallery at Amherst College.

This is the true meaning of "romanticism"—of the private and personal effort found in it.

The long, long lost day. A day like a labyrinth, out of which one hopes to come free at last.

## January 29, 1957

Big snow again today, and I love it. Ann hates these solitudes, and I love it. I love it suddenly with ease, not furtively, for, as the picture of "American solitudes" unrolls before me for the book, I am beginning to realize how much, in these regions, but a century ago, incomparably more solitary than they are now, solitary as they are still, these American writers tended to find in such landscapes the materials of thought, the keys to fantasy, the brooding worlds of Ishmael, of "Monsieur du Miroir," of Whitman's Adam and Hawthorne's new Adam and Eve. . . . The writer in such a situation, starting from his long religious training and his solitary bent in a new and pretty uninhabited world, the writer does not think of reality outside, or of reality as something to "copy." He sees the natural world as a language to be understood, not as a picture to be copied. He feels a kinship with it whose actual terms of expression, fitting both him and it, are found in the middle, as it were: in the language of symbolism which he shares with the subject that supplies it.

The long loneliness of these writers, with their historical fantasies in a too-too new world, their sense of themselves as queers and different ones in a violently expansive society that nevertheless does share with them a kinetic individuality—and admires it. . . . Above all, such loneliness is an act of criticism, and like all real criticism suffers from an essential formlessness; tends to express itself in fits and starts, in marginal glosses. Hence the lumber of Hawthorne's stories and Emerson's journals and Poe's tales: the profound inner formlessness of Whitman, the long, lazy lines, each seeking the great mother to take it home. These sensitive, solitary brooders and fantasts, working with a language too *outside* the bustling big world, these men inevitably wrote the criticisms of a society whose *fundamental* postulates they shared—and wrote—but from which they felt personally alienated,—because of the kind of interests which they had—and society hadn't.

The literary imagination and the big, big world.

American writers before the flood: the unhappy few. The heroes and teachers, the prophets, the "sky-men."[81]

## January 30, 1957

[. . .] The "Jewish character" as such in a book by non-Jews. We Jews do not realize how odd, how fantastic, how mysterious and historically evocative Jews appear. They do not *have* to *do* anything, these Jewish characters, to be distinguished; they *are*. Shylock's malevolent plot is itself portrayed as the logic of his character, not as a spontaneous *deed*.

## June 2, 1957

Trust to the contradictions and see them *out*. Never annul one force to give supremacy to another. The contradiction itself *is* the reality in all its manifoldness. Man from *his* vantage point can see reality only in contradictions. And the more faithful he is to his perception of the contradiction, the more he is open to what there is for him to know. "Harmony" as an absolute good is for the gods, not for man. A thinker (like RWE) misleads us as soon as he promotes harmony as the exclusive goal, and especially misleads us when he preaches harmony as a *method*. Man's life is full of contradiction and *must* be; we see through a glass darkly—we want more than we can have; we see more than we can understand. But a contradiction that is *faced* leads to true knowledge. Today, thinking over the contradiction between my *Walker* poem and my critical work, I suddenly realized how false it is to try to "think it out" to a solution. All these contradictions are on the surface, the symbols of deeper and more fertile forces that can unleash the most marvelous energy when they are embraced. Never try to achieve "order," sacrifice symmetry—seek to relate all these antagonistic forces, not to the elimination of one to the other. The idea of "God" as perfect order is perilous to man as an ideal, for *us* to follow. [. . .]

## June 6, 1957

The delusion of Mary McCarthy that "frankness," "honesty" is *all*.[82] What is wrong here is that the approach is based on defiance and on a certain contempt

81. Kazin saw these American "sky men" or "Luftmenschen" inhabiting "the 'spiritual' or Hebraic period in American literature"; see July 24, 1960, entry.
82. Kazin may have been referring to McCarthy's recently published *Memories of a Catholic Girlhood* (New York: Harcourt, Brace, 1957). Kazin made McCarthy the subject of an extraordinarily harsh portrait in *Starting Out in the Thirties*.

for herself. The *will* dominates. Horrible as I am, here is the whole truth about *myself*, which is more than you can say about yourself, and this makes *me* outstanding—But what I require of *you* is something superior and lovable, anything better than myself and better than your ordinary self. Only if the frankness makes a connection to something better than yourself *is* it useful.—Who cares about the theatrical confessions of bad or weak people?

## June 14, 1957

To Concord yesterday. The Genteel tradition is full. If an institution is the lengthened shadow of a man, Concord is certainly, as an institution, only the shadow of a shadow, itself nothing. Yet how vividly it seized me yesterday, listening to Mrs. Margaret Lothrop tell me around the Alcott-Emerson house, that all the lovely autumnal glints of New England waysides and authors and authoresses that used to be passed out to us in school and the children's museum of American lit.—That all this was in truth the genteel tradition, formed as of the end of the century. By the time of the 80s, the old Transcendentalist-passion had simply got itself left by the wayside—was a museum. *This* is the period of Whitman's gazing at the dummy butterfly,[83] of "nature walks" *as* the recreation and rest from industrialism that was all Lowell had been able to see in Thoreau's doctrine, the period when Burroughs, Edison, TR and assorted railway kings went camping in the woods, the period of William James's Norfolk Jacket, knickers and Concord address. By the '80s, indeed, we get Henry ,James's satire in *The Bostonians* against Elizabeth Peabody,[84] and the leftovers of the Transcendentalist circle. America had become its tradition, and the schoolroom walls featured "our poets."

The dear, dear days beyond recall. The beautiful cemetery, and the man brushing away at Alcott's white tombstone. The Concord school of Philosophy, the white busts and the wooden stage.

*Yaddo:* more and more yesterday in Concord I realized how much all that represents the Genteel Tradition. The key is the aspirant for "*culture*" (where Emerson had aspired to religion); the Italian masters on the wall, the religion of Dante, the growing Anglomania, the pride of family and caste.

Thoreau's works all in the local Antiquarian Society Museum.

83. A famous photograph of Whitman gazing at a cardboard butterfly on his arm.
84. Elizabeth Peabody (1804–1894), American educator, opened the first kindergarten in the United States. A pioneer in progressive education, she is the apparent original for the satirical portrait of Miss Birdseye in Henry James's *The Bostonians*.

## June 15, 1957

[. . .] I see now that these early American books, these Ishmael journeyings and *Leaves of Grass*, these *Walden* and *Forest Essays* are all efforts at the individual religious experience through a re-consecration of the homely materials. *This* explains the overwhelming sense of place, the *site* of experience. Each of these books is a spiritual autobiography that attempts not merely to consecrate individual experiences but to show that such consecration can come *only* from the matter-of-fact elements of personal experiences.

Consecration—the real realism, the only matter-of-fact, is to give *hope*. Man cannot regard himself from the outside and be pitiless toward himself: he is the essence of his own destiny and must feel alive in order to live.

## July 1, 1957

[. . .] Now I know what romanticism means: it means Emma Bovary's answer to St. Flaubert: it means the supremacy of life, life's mystery, life-the-miracle, life the great, good gift over "meaning" and words. . . . and, alas, and so tragically, like all religion, it means the effort to capture this life-spirit, this flood and twist, this . . . incommensurable in the blood. This is what Dylan and all true "romantic" poets sought: not to lift language above life, but to get "all" of life, all of the experience, into words: i.e. to eat your cake and have it at the same time.[85] . . . And this and this always is the tragedy, and the unconquerable wish, of the romantic heart: i.e. of the religious imagination thrown out into the world, the whole world, for material; of the imagination eating *upon* the world. [. . .]

The truth is that in America Dylan was constantly put to it to out-rival himself in "intoxication" by a hundred thousand stimulants—called admirers. The poor boy from Swansea now found himself living at a pace which is not only unthinkable in quiet down-at-heels, moldy Wales and almost-as-quiet London, but found that he, the romantic rhetorician and auto-stimulant par excellence, was in the land of romanticism, of "possibility,"—the land where every love affair promises happiness, and a poet, if he is famous enough, stands out from the crowd enough to be admired by everyone. . . . America itself worked on him like whiskey—as New York did on Hart Crane.

85. Kazin was writing an essay on Dylan Thomas, "The Posthumous Life of Dylan Thomas," that would be published in the *Atlantic Monthly* (October, 1957): 164–168.

## July 22, 1957

Herb Gold's[86] explosive little piece on "the mystery of personality" in the novel, current *PR*, made me think of the explosive feeling for absolute freedom, indirection, the exultant insecurity, that young Jews are capable of.[87] The explosion is from, against, the tremendous hold and anchor of—not security but "purpose," God as meaning, God as law. [. . .] The real mark of so many young Jewish writers, I started to say, is in this opposition to *certainty*, to the false-complacent knowledge rather than to the mystical ecstasy of surrender to Him as the unknown. . . .

Obviously, too, the kind of explosiveness you get in this piece of Gold's, as in Saul's later work, stems not from revolt against our own background but against genteel-protestant-philistine America. "Breaking out" in favor of the mystically mysterious and free human soul is a way of asserting one's identity beyond the pale of synonymity we have to live with.

## July 23, 1957

The more I go over the events of the last few years, of the whole postwar time and starting back a little before, the more I feel how much my experience is that of a *baffled* generation—a generation brought up to ideas of radicalism, of freedom and independence and revolutionary militancy, brought down to a period more or less statist, "big," bureaucratic, reactionary. I feel that my preoccupation these last few years with Emerson and the romantics has been a way of feeling my way back to the beginnings, the spiritual fires, of the "modern" movement. And equally, that one's whole tendency for so long to "make do," to come to terms with that whole set of miserable, reactionary literary philosophers, Eliot and the Southerners, goes back to the immense and terrible defeat suffered by so many free men as a result of the 1st world war. It was then that, in answer to the threat of "chaos," there came in the new authoritarianism, in one way or another, whose final horror of the modern and the free was Hitler. . . . And this, deepening in the thirties (when the free writer and the "times" diverged to the point where the free writer could be used entirely by the reactionary ultra-Slavic philosophy of communism and be deluded that he was joining it) ended in the decade of war and the next decade of state socialism everywhere. . . . The new generation, born in the '30s, is not baffled but "inside the whale" born to the

86. Herbert Gold (1924–), Jewish-American novelist, whose work Kazin did not admire.
87. "The Mystery of Personality in the Novel," *Partisan Review* (Summer, 1957): 453–462.

comfortable slavery of the suburban culture and the permanent war state. . . . But my generation, born in the war that brought an end to democracy as a living real movement, to the generous hopes of the "century of hope," has been [a] living contradiction of its own basic elan. . . . I feel this all the more these days in that I seem to be arming myself for the next *Walker* book, for *something*, it is clear to me, in which I can assert my sense of the awful division in which so many of us have had to live these last few years, brought up to generous ideals of freedom and human expanse, and confronted as we have been by the snivelly philosophers of slavery, the Eliots and Tates[88] and the rest. . . . In one way or another, I see it all so clearly now, the job has been to stand up and to shout as loudly as one could for these old generous ideas and ideals, for all these things so easily condemned these days as "sentimentality," for feeling that is a moral judgment on the world, no matter how directionless it seems. . . . Can it be that the *Walker was* written out of nostalgia for my poor, old, revolutionary home—can it be that my obsession more and more with the heroic isolation and eternal fightingness of the real Jews, the true Jews, the few Jews, deals also with this longing for the old militancy, the old expanse? I feel more and more that what happened to me during the war years was not simply the loss of Asya but the loss of the old hope so intimately identified with her—and that the tendency to blame oneself, to analyze oneself ad infinitum, torturedly, that went on so long then, came from the loneliness of having lost one's instinctive, true, spiritual home. Odd that it should be Lou's husband, Hans Meyerhoff, who in that review of *The Inmost Leaf*,[89] pounced on my tendency to blame the writer, not the world. But oh, oh, how faithful I have been, how obstinately and stupidly and unswervedly faithful to my old ideal, my old love, my old pre-war rousing flag, when all the time, forgetting what I was fighting for, I fell into the trap, so easy! of fighting myself. . . . The other day, thinking [of] my "egotism" and my this and my that, I suddenly realized, with a shudder almost, of how easy it is to fall into this other-imposed trap of trying endlessly to correct and reform oneself, in accordance with this and that, one's idea of the right person to be, when all the time, one is not merely "stuck" with oneself, as one is rightly enough, but one suffers from constrictedness, from reaction, from the million-and-one reasons, so boringly personified around one in one's contemporaries

88. Allen Tate (1899–1979), American poet, literary critic, and poetry consultant to the Library of Congress, member of the "Southern Agrarian" group of writers and critics who competed for influence in the postwar years with the New York intellectuals associated with *Partisan Review*.

89. "A Critic's Point of View," *Partisan Review* (Spring, 1956): 278–283.

and half-friends and stupid, genteel colleagues, who are always telling us over again that man is bad and sinful!—interesting to remember, in a flash of light like this, that the insistence on man's guilt and sin comes from the Southerners who have been brought up on the guilt of slavery, and not only feel guilty themselves but want everyone else to feel so too. A pox on these everlasting nay-sayers and reactionary little tates, dead ones indeed! We are baffled all right, I am and Saul is, and most of us old fiery ones are—but let us not forget *why* we are so! [. . .]

## August 11, 1957
### [New York]

Still looking for an apartment—have been all alone in 54th Street [Rabbi Birstein's apartment] for two days, pounding the pavements and getting increasingly fed up with NY. The whole Latin-American, dark Cuban-night side of NY does disgust me; and the reason, whether here or in Cuba, is the *naked*, shabby, serf-like quality of these people. I've always felt instinctively that Latin America is the ass-hole of the universe; and the more I see of Latin-America-in-NY, with its vomit-making *bodegas* and that supine speech, the more I realize what *lowness*, what cravenness, are in these people. It is the idea of America as the slag-heap of the nations, of all America as a junk-pile and refuse station, the "last" place and the awful place, the forbidding place, the detention camp of the nations—all this that so revolts me in those dark slave faces. For me the "Western Island" was always the *naked place*, the stony land, the uninhabited island, the face of the rock, the country made inhuman by its strangeness and unavailability to man—the country in the West always too harsh for man to get an easy foothold on it. It meant the reverse of the over-domesticated green lawns and palaces of Europe. The Western Island: Man's fabled new home in the West and the fabled home of the *new* man!—But when I walk around all these those rotting garbage cans off Columbus Avenue and watch the Puerto Ricans sitting on the steps of those flaking brownstones—color of caked shit—then I realize all over again how little I have come to grips with the *realness* of America, the absolute driven into us by the full concentrated force of the living moment, the present hour. Last night, when I sat in the Fifth Avenue movie house looking at a film celebrating modern photography, *The Naked Eye*, mostly about Edward Weston, I suddenly had a sense of the profound solemnity attached to the living, no matter how ugly—of the *holiness* of the place where so many human beings gather. Much as I fear and dread NY, I have to admit that I am much more in *touch* here, than I ever could be in NE.—It is so important to keep the eye glued to the reality of the *actual* holiness! When I saw those Times Square faces in Weegee's[90] pictures yesterday, the women with that horrible fat and those indriven eyeglasses, I suddenly saw the beauty of the actual living hour in the human struggle of those faces—and of those faces alone. Somehow only the human being *tells* the story, only the human breath counts. The honor only the human heart ever *knows*. "As scenery consists of trees, so people make up the world." And even when one lonely transcendental heart stands poised upon an empty rock looking out to sea, it is *this* man, this mind, that *makes* the scene—not the rock and the sea, but the human eye that alone has united them. The human mind alone makes the radius to every point on the circumference, the great wheel on which we ride. The human eye alone unites the world—by perception. . . .

## September 6, 1957

From 110 Riverside Drive, Friday morning. New York. I am percolating inside with excitement, can't stop bubbling. It's New York again, New York. Is all this trouble worth it—for a *place?* Are places this important? It certainly feels it, just now—New York! with the old soft ooze of Klassical moosic on WQXR, and the sun in the windows, and an inch of blue sky above the television aerials. That single framed inch of blue sky concentrates everything wonderfully: *is* nature, for me, is life; while across the way a Negro maid in a white slip and loop earrings and a bandana goes about her work. . . . So much recent happening has gone unwritten in this book, weeks and weeks of packing, now unpacking. My dreams have been full of that last bitter visit to Englewood, and of Carol's "situation" with Mrs. Miles; the days have gone by running after dear Katie,[91] whose eyes are still, as it were, unfocussed on any single *thing*, are like dark slates that catch the light.

## September 7, 1957

Only the passionate encounter between the writer and the book makes for real criticism—for the constant sense of new *discovery*. It is this *voyage of discovery* that counts, this passionate journey of perception that counts; the freedom and speculative richness of [the] discovering mind that counts. I must have the same attitude of passionate discovery toward books that I do toward any other element in my experience.

90. Weegee, pseudonym of Arthur Fellig (1899–1968), Austrian-born American photographer and photojournalist who specialized in pictures of urban crime, fires, and other dramatic events. He had an uncanny ability to be first on the scene and a notable talent for capturing New York faces and personalities.

91. Cathrael "Katie" Kazin, daughter of Kazin and Ann Birstein, born June 30, 1955.

## September 19, 1957

In the subway on my way to meet my first class at NYU. My dear little wife has done it again—this time a whole story about herself and Sidney and me—and the portrait of "Max" was so brutal—it made me wince. But why should I go to pieces because of this? The truth is that as a *writer* Ann is often another of those literary females who sucks one's blood. If I allow myself to take this seriously, I shall go mad. But I won't, I can't, take this seriously. I must regard it simply as something which is not my business.[92]

Awful day, awful. So bitterly unhappy again.

## September 28, 1957

The critical imagination is distinguished by its voracious curiosity. I was so touched, as by an old ambition, to read in a *New Statesman* account of French literary journalism that a young critic, Roland Barthes,[93] has for some time written (in *Lettres Nouvelles*) "a regular monthly feature, *Petite Mythologie du Mois*, an astonishing series in which he commented on contemporary phenomena (anything from the Music Hall to Minou Drouet) with an approach and a style which mark a fine critical imagination."

How I've longed to do this!—to make of this private notebook a public journal, to have a chance for regular articles in single magazine![94]—And how I've longed, above all, to see an awareness of this in American critical opinion, instead of the everlasting "textual" study!—But this retreat from curiosity, from interest in the outside world as continuously interesting, comes from our lack of politics, our lack of faith in the possibility of change, above all from the change of *problems*, so that the easy socialist-meliorist philosophy of the past no longer has any meaning for us. [. . .]

But this "mythologie du mois" was just what I saw the *Walker* creating—a world of perceptions, of true commentary, of living intelligence. Only, I had to start

92. Ann's story, later published as "Love in the Dunes," in *Summer Situations* (New York: Coward, McCann and Geohagan, 1972), 11–69, describes a brief affair (modeled on a real affair) between a woman very much like herself and a young man modeled on Kazin's friend Sidney Monas. Max (Kazin), "a lump on the beach," is the cuckolded husband.

93. Sonia Orwell, "French Monthlies," *New Statesman* (September 7, 1957): 283–284. Roland Barthes (1915–1980), French philosopher, literary critic and theorist.

94. Kazin wrote a regular column in the *Reporter* from 1959 to 1966. The *Reporter*, published biweekly from 1949 to 1968, catered to an intellectual elite, including literate politicians and statesmen. See introduction to Chapter 5.

from the observer, I could not pretend that I was a disembodied intelligence coolly reading the times!—The problem, of course, is not to go too far the other way into introversion. And probably the safest path is always to think of the observer as a developing, living, *growing* agent, so that the self that is engaged in thinking out the world will feel itself growing only as the thoughts grow.

But meanwhile, the day, the living day, the actual moment, the pang of real life,—to be faithful to this, one must always pay attention, one must never dismiss anything a priori as too trivial. Nothing is too trivial, for what the writer may make of it.

I am excited this morning with the possibility of a "public journal," of realizing in my work the already visioned unity of my life *and* thought.

## October [nd] 1957

Grieg's *Lyric Suite* in my ears and the memory of three people walking down a street in Brooklyn—twenty-six years ago! Mary Salerno, Trudy Weitz, Felix Nigro, Eddy Peshkin, Sadie Tolmach. Twenty-six years ago. Another twenty-six and it will all be finished for us. My heart breaks for us, for all of us, tonight—for all those hopes, all of Trudy's pathetic actress vanities and Eddy Peshkin's father, and Eddy and Felix's sister. What breaks my heart about them, as about Sophie, is how little they mean to anyone. Their lives are utterly wrapped in silence. If *I* were not here, writing, as I always do, to that honest Grieg schmaltz, what *would* it all come to? Nothing, and less than nothing. When I see walking along that lamp-lit street on the way back from Highland Park, when I see again Mary Salerno's sweet face, it all hits me again. . . . How *little* human beings, all those hopes, count for—after all! The group of us walking along the dark street—and suddenly it's nothing. The dying fall, the voice unheard, the deadness of the dead. [. . .]

## November 28, 1957

How alive the city is, how alive, how alive, how alive. Each of those windows has someone behind it, each of these streets is a current under my feet. A network of people, a living field—each grass a soul, each grass alive. So let us give thanks after all, and be glad, and rejoice. To be in life with so many people!

# 5
# Return to the City
## 1958–1963

"OCTOBER 13, 1956–OCTOBER 13, 1961, GREATEST period of my life," Kazin wrote in a moment of exultation four years after his return to New York City from Amherst. He had reason to be happy. Leaving the security of an academic income he had plunged into the New York cultural milieu and succeeded in making a living as a freelance literary critic and essayist—assisted by the occasional visiting professorship. By the early sixties Kazin was arguably the most sought-after and widely published critic in the country, with essays and reviews appearing in the *Atlantic*, *Harper's*, *American Scholar*, the *New York Times Book Review*, *Commentary*, *Partisan Review*, *Reporter*—and *Playboy*. Ted Solotaroff remembers him as the "go-to guy" on the most recent work by Saul Bellow or Norman Mailer and for the latest assessment of current literary/cultural trends. His most influential work appeared in a biweekly column in the *Reporter*, a highbrow journal on culture, politics, and world affairs read by opinion-makers and statesmen, including U.N. Secretary General Dag Hammarskjöld, who invited Kazin to lunch to discuss a recent article. Other indications of his growing prominence included an invitation from the State Department to join the first "cultural exchange" with the Soviet Union (1959) and an invitation from the state of Israel (1960) for a visit in which officials tried (unsuccessfully) to enlist Kazin's support for emigration. In August 1961 he was invited to a private luncheon with President Kennedy for an *American Scholar* article he was writing on the presidency.

Kazin enjoyed his role as literary arbiter and cultural spokesman—"I love my worldliness, my snobbery, my ease" (January 2, 1959). But he was not pleased with cultural trends. He had returned from rural New England intending to reengage with the present by writing about contemporary fiction—a project he hoped would lead to a book. But he soon became convinced that contemporary fiction, reflecting current attitudes, was more about disengagement than engagement—the lonely self disengaged from ideas, from society, from tradition, from history. "It is as if the pure flame of consciousness had nothing to burn on but itself" (May 2, 1959). One consequence, as Kazin saw it, was a reduction of individual will to mere willfulness and pointless acts of defiance flagrantly apparent in the self-indulgent antics of the Beats. Not all the trends were bad. Kazin saw hopeful signs in the growing influence of Jewish writers and novelists. "Who can doubt the immense cultural authority of all us Jewish writers and critics?" he wrote in a January 21, 1958, entry. But even the most promising talents—Saul Bellow, Norman Mailer, Bernard Malamud—were, he felt, prone to a self-absorption that diverted them from the novelist's primary responsibility, "to elicit and prove the world we share" (*Contemporaries*, 217).

By the summer of 1961 Kazin's interest in writing a book on contemporary fiction had been overtaken by his desire to add a second volume to his autobiography. He had originally intended to call it *The Love of Women* and to focus the narrative on the women in his life. That focus now shifted to his experiences in the thirties and the war years—"the years of my apprenticeship, of my basic formation" (May 20, 1964). Looking back to those formative years, Kazin would be drawing on many of the same feelings that had inspired *A Walker in the City*—"to be an initiate again, to write the story of youth, to look forward to everything [. . .]—starting out" (May 13, 1960). Recalling his radical past, he would be reconnecting with history, reminding "the alone generation" of a time when writers had been concerned with something more interesting than their solitary selves. He could also raise questions similar to those raised in *Walker* about what it meant to be a Jew—questions that were taking on new resonance as the Holocaust became increasingly a subject of reflection and discussion.

The journal entries of this period can turn dark and bitter—about Jewish suffering, about the complacency of a generation that "never had it so good," about a "self"-centered culture looking to literature as "therapy" rather than a point of connection with the larger world of politics and ideas. But Kazin's temperament is nothing if not volatile. A walk with Kate, a conversation with one of his heroes (Hannah Arendt, Alex Mieklejohn, Eric Heller), a stroll through Riverside Park, a reading or rereading of a particular writer can suddenly lift the mood—"Marx on Feuerbach—wow! Blake's gates of the imagination opening up again!" (April 20, 1961). Following a terrible fight with Ann, he suddenly and gratefully recalls the sources of his affection. "What brought me out of my old hole of loneliness and despond was Ann, from '50 on. This was 'public' life, true life, lived not by the solitary will seeking to pierce through by intellectual effort alone, but by companionship and understanding, by love and dialogue"—the journal as barometer of the daily mood—"this up and down so deep to my inner weather" (July 23, 1963; November 18, 1987).

## January 1, 1958

New Year's Day. Weary and heavy of soul about the oncoming move to Amherst.[1] To hell with Amherst. Why am I bothering with this at all so much—making so much of an issue of it between Ann and myself. I suppose that last night at our party it was Germaine Bree[2] talking to me about Cargill's duplicity that set me

1. Kazin would be returning alone to teach his last semester at Amherst. He had just taught a semester at NYU and had learned that Oscar Cargill, the English Department chairman, had decided not to offer him a permanent position.
2. Germaine Bree, French-born American authority on modern French literature, taught at a number of American colleges and universities.

off—as if her refusal of me as a man made me identify her with rejection and bad news. Anyway it is and must be NY for me after the spring, and a long, hard pull it will be all around. The book on the "Twenties and After" *must* be done at the same time. I've been tossing around much too much with "The Western Island," which will *never* get off the ground.[3]

Tonight I pray with all my heart for patience and understanding and lovingness. Let me be good to Ann and not afflict her with all my stormy preys and doubts. Whatever will happen this year *must* happen, and there's an end of it.

## January 21, 1958

All this stuff on the young men and the period, etc., etc., is so boringly *sociological.* The literary interests are always few and far between. The only really interesting insight in Fiedler's usual auto-intoxicated remarks,[4] is on the *influence* of the Jewish intellectual pattern of struggle and accommodation. It is this excessive need of respectability that is so irritating about Trilling. But for the rest, who can doubt the immense cultural authority of all us Jewish writers and critics, the *particular* role that we play as internationalists, global culture-vultures, teachers of the tribe? As a teacher, a *critic*, I am always a father, a prophet, a layer-down of laws and a pointer out of parallels. But as an autobiographer, I am still a son—still looking for enlightenment and the future I *already* live! It is this over-insistent search for personal enlightenment that, as I see now, keeps me from losing myself altogether in the fatherly critic-teacher life. Or to put it another way, *my* way of seizing things dramatically is and must be by way of enlightenment, the discovery of meaning. And it is as a struggle for light, to see the whole pattern, that I cling to my ambition of personal history. [. . .]

## February 7, 1958

It suddenly came over me this morning, thinking of Salo Baron's[5] lecture last night on "Liberalism and the Jew" that *everything* I hold dear, *every*thing that moves my work at its best and that at its best becomes the content of my work, is embraced by the word "liberalism"—or freedom by the full power of criticism. No wonder that I have always been so nostalgic for certain periods, that I have

3. It would rise again in different form as *An American Procession* (1984).
4. Leslie Fiedler (1917–2003), "The Un-Angry Young Men," *Encounter* (January 1958): 3–12.
5. Salo Baron (1895–1989), prominent American historian of the Jews, taught at Columbia from 1930 to 1963.

always shied away instinctively from all forms of authority, accommodation, adjustment, coercion. But above all, no wonder that I instinctively watch my own period always as if I were on guard, and regard it as my enemy. It is so clear now and has been so clear for the longest time how much I feel *outside* this period.

But one must have perspective on what is really happening. It is beautifully clear to me this morning that the purpose of the autobiography is to show the struggle of the free man with the age. And perhaps above all to show that the real struggle now is against the "torpor." The growing institutionalization of life.

## May 28, 1958

Closing up shop in Northampton. Marking papers all day and walking at intervals through Paradise Woods and the lovely quiet streets. In a few days it will be over, all over—and I am glad. It will be good to have done with the Aarons, straight-nosed, stiff and spare un-Yankee Aarons, and the bad breath of Amherst library and my own recent revival of Miss Lonelyhearts. [. . .] Sad news from France [the election of de Gaulle and defeat of the Socialists] another nail in the coffin of the old free world that is my world forever. Hurrah for self-communion again, and for the subversive, the indefeasible truth of the human heart. [. . .]

When I moved in with Lou in Barrow Street, my head was still full of socialism, though I did not realize that by paying so much attention to utopianism, I was marking the end of my belief in socialism—I had already turned to the personal principle. This was the hunger that possessed me in that love affair made up not only of my honest and long-defeated lust, but of Macdonald's *Politics* (the magazine which among the intellectuals signalized the end of politics). The real story of—'43 and after, I see now, is the attempt to work out the personal principle—to *work* it out, as it were, on the thin and talcum-flavored body of Lou, vanilla-flavored like the flesh of a Negro, and then, in the midst of the world's war, the terrible and all-punishing war, the war that felt to everyone like a cataclysm, a God-sent punishment for some terrible human guilt, and which I accepted in those terms, so that my already strong sense of guilt and "sin," of having transgressed the moral authority that backed up my world became hopelessly exacerbated and inflamed—and I ran shrieking for home and mother and country; only there wasn't any more of any. Sophie was "dead,"[6] and for all practical purposes my mother was "dead" too; and there

6. See Chapter 1, note 56.

I was, choked with guilt and loneliness. No wonder that I identified myself so eagerly with the Nazi hangmen when *they* were hanged.

The guilt, *my* guilt, was everywhere, for if there weren't, *what* was all the suffering about, the mass rootlessness, the loss of all the accustomed landmarks, safeguards?

Yet the real struggle of those years was the achievement of *the personal principle*. It lay in the realization that the old "moral" order of the world, a fiction at best, really *was* dead in that the lonely, lonely self had to convert its loneliness into heroism, its desire into fact, its pain into understanding.

End of—'43. For the first time I had the courage to confront the intensity of my desire. For the first time I had the courage to *dare* the hunger that had always itched at my belly, my balls, a hunger which I had put away because I had feared to face the imagined cost of my self-assertion. It was not only the operation [on his undescended testicle] that gave me courage. It was the sudden, lonely prominence given to my "self-hood" by the destruction of so many barriers. Everything—Sophie's removal, her "death," my larger and larger experience of the world after the publication of the book—everything said: *now* is the time, chance it, *be*.

## July 6, 1958

[. . .] Oh god, for five minutes before dinner, watching the damned hamburgers, I looked with belly full of longing at a woman in a black slip across the way, and wondered just what *this* is all about. Thought: maybe Ann has been right all this time in saying that I don't really want her. Maybe I do want somebody else, a woman I can put my hands on and squeeze and fuck hard and take, a woman I can take, I can take, I can take—not my eternally elusive, complaining, solitary wife. I want a *woman* and I want her soon.

## October 20, 1958

Right after seven, when the hoarse alarm croaks madly, great streaks of redness can be seen jutting off the bare patch of sky. The extravagance of sky against the regular blocks of cells. But it is this panorama of windows that increasingly excites me in NY—the different look of light on each window. [. . .]

## October 22, 1958

Mark Van Doren's autobiography is out, and I read in the *Herald-Trib* that he was "a model of grace and gratitude." He loves everything and everyone, he has been a supremely happy man, and that Mr. Van Doren "is no man to let the world's corners go unpraised."

Twenty years ago, when I took my M.A. at Columbia and wrote reviews each week for Irita,[7] Mark Van Doren was my beau ideal. What a model of grace and deportment he was, what charm, what ease. . . . It is a token of my growth 20 years later, that Mark Van Doren now inspires me with contempt and disgust. No poet, a safeguarding, pursy[8] little man forever congratulating himself in rhetorical little phrases on the right way to live and the right way to think. . . . Mark Van Doren's way has not been my way. Mark Van Doren's pursy little prudence and little bucolic poems and empty phrases about the noble voice have not been my way. Once I thought this would be my way: that marriage, teaching, even the place in the country, would give me the warm, tight, little secure existence in which Mark Van Doren writes his golden, little, hollow sentences. . . . Now I know that every break, every "loss," every danger, every fright, every lonely room, every stab of loneliness, has been necessary for *me*—that my life can never be Mark Van Doren's, never tidy, never "secure," never pursy. Only, it hurts, it hurts always when one lacks the courage and insight to be the tiger one naturally is; it hurts when one has an idea of life as a certain shape, a certain design, and life breaks it up. When I think now of Remsen Street and Mark Van Doren, and all that neat little world I wanted so to hold on to; when I think of Van Doren as my beau ideal at all, I have to laugh. God give me the courage to be myself, to bear my life with truth and courage. God give me the honesty never to ask for "security," for grace and ease, but to follow out my love wherever it may lead me. God give me the courage to live without whimpering, to bear the truth spoken to me by my own mind and my own courage. God, who is God, God the only God, give me the dignity to bear my life with courage. [. . .]

## October 26, 1958

[. . .] There are women (as there are men) who possess sexual authority as a matter of course; they are competent, confident, easy. I have known several such women and had unforgettable satisfaction from them: Lou, Sylvia Marlowe,

7. Irita Van Doren (1891–1966), wife of Mark Van Doren's brother Carl, was the book review editor of the *New York Herald Tribune: Books* in the 1930s. Carl Van Doren (1885–1950), Columbia professor and literary editor of the *Nation*, persuaded Kazin to write *On Native Grounds*.
8. Kazin seems to be suggesting by "pursy" not shortness of breath, the usual meaning, but careful and controlled as one who purses one's lips to control breathing.

Celia, Vivienne, Jean Garrigue, Rose.[9] They are women who make everything easy, who have this side of their nature as a gift. Sometimes they are lovable like Celia; sometimes awful, like Carol; but this side of their nature gives warmth and life to a man whether he loves them or not, and this in itself is quite separate from love. With Ann, who looks for this sexual confidence in me and does not find it; with me who looks for it in her and does not, love exists, will always exist. The question is whether this sexual authority, this inner confidence, will also come. Without it, God knows, we are always on the prowl for each other and never find it. [. . .]

## November 1, 1958

In paying tribute to Pasternak yesterday over Radio Liberation,[10] I said that P. gives the writer a lesson on how to deal with the everlasting violence of our era. More and more, it becomes clear to me that the writer can respond to our time only by being, as the Soviet yahoos said yesterday, "a self-enamored effete and aesthete." Which translated into decent language, means to be a person, to stand up for certain principles, for the truth of the spirit, and above all, not to try to meet the violence and hysteria on its own terms, but to stand up for art, which is its own demonstration, and for spiritual truth. . . . We are already entering into the ice age. The helplessness of governments, the fatalism of political opinion, the increasing drift, in fear of total war, toward a total peace that will be simply the inevitable compromise between the great powers—everything points up the alternate role in political life of violence and inertia, and the necessity of the writer's position as a free spiritual conscience. Quietism, contemplativeness, personalism, above all, the free religious spirit, bringing us back to the self we have for so long not dared to be, the awareness of the immense responsibility placed upon the individual in our totalitarian and hysterical age: this is what we need more than ever to have confidence in and to live by.

## November 2, 1958

The keynote of intellectuals in our age: nothing is certain, everything is to be discovered, we are all *en route*. Nobody has a philosophy; we philosophize;

9. It is unclear whether Sylvia Marlowe was the famous harpsichordist (1908–1981); Jean Garrigue (1912–1972) was a poet.

10. Boris Pasternak (1890–1960) had recently been awarded the Nobel Prize for Literature. Radio Liberation broadcast to the Soviet Union, just as Radio Free Europe broadcast to Eastern Europe.

nobody has any faith; we are in search. The occasion, the moment, the issue, our immediate *Existenz*, these alone decide or can. . . . So in the same way, only persons count, not history; and in persons, the moment, not the life; the event, not the thought. . . . A picture is an occasion for picture-making; a poem, a chance to poeticize. We are all *en route*. [. . .]

## November 5, 1958

Election Night, ooze of television commercials, Jason Epstein, the child of this generation saying petulantly, I just don't *like* Harriman.[11] If ever there was a generation that intellectually lived from hand to mouth it is his—this. The lack of all general ideas, the fear of having any conceptions that might be serviceable beyond the moment's experience, the sullen inarticulateness—these are the marks of people who simply cannot make sense of contemporary reality, who fear ideas like the devil. [. . .] The increasing lack of any connection with philosophy itself is what is so pitiful and dangerous now. Instead of a radical movement in favor of experience, which is sustained by connections with some older and healthier tradition now become subterranean, we have a fear and rejection of ideas per se. And in a society in which it increasingly takes effort to have any ideas at all, in which the natural thing is to swing and drift with the well-established patterns of affluence and comfort, the slob in us exploits the coward and rejoices the drifter. [. . .]

## November 8, 1958

[. . .] The "Love of Women" book, to be true, must start from my passion, not my fear, from the acceptance I feel and know every day *now*. I should like to write about Carol, about Italy, about 55th Street and the mornings after love—about Celia and the feel of her tits in my hands as I stood behind her and the beads broke in my hand—about that incredible Vivienne, with the breasts that flogged me like a lion's mane, and her screams when I pounded in that delicious ripe cunt of hers, and the feeling of holding her over me as I danced her. I should like to write the true story of intercourse, of the socket and the holding, the solid and the fluid, and above all that sense of the running, the dance, the flight, when the two are one and the one is one because it is one of two. O happy love, o happy love, this is the bliss of life, the threshold of all joy.

11. William Averell Harriman (1891–1986), elected governor of New York in 1954, defeated for second term by Nelson Rockefeller, served as ambassador to the Soviet Union and to Britain.

## November 15, 1958

When I read Wilson's beautiful essay on Pasternak[12] the other day, my feeling was gratitude, but also the profoundest envy. Why, I thought irritably, can't *I* have the patience, the learning, above all the meticulous curiosity, to do an essay like this? The answer is deep down inside me. I always know so well what I think, the gift of conviction is so firmly and inescapably in me, that like Emerson I build a house without thinking of the stairs; I am so concerned with the essence of things that I seem to go straight to it, and as a result my things are usually short, fragmentary, and repetitive. I don't think I need to find out this much about anything. Scholem says in his book on medieval Jewish mysticism[13] that the distinctively Jewish literary forms are usually short, and in my own case, too, the need to wrest the essence out of things, to get at the heart of experience, to see the spiritual identity beneath the material form of any problem, always results in this lightening trip straight to the center. Yet it is precisely this that makes for Jewish conceit, or Jewish incuriosity, for we feel that we already know the answer—and I agree that we do. Except that in the great revolutionary era which opened before men with science and democracy and a general emancipation, the Jewish intellectuals thought it more necessary to discover the facts than to correlate the ideas; and it is a mark of Wilson's freedom from the confining narrowness of experience that a Jewish background is likely to instill that he still has to work everything out for himself, that nobody's prior opinion impresses him, that he regards everything as a discovery—and not, as it is for me, a "confirmation." The great Jewish success, intellectually in modern times, has lain in the ability to carve out new fields, to seize utterly unexpected possibilities for human consciousness; and it is this *radical* penetration of learning that has been so overwhelming in the examples of Marx and Freud and Einstein, as it is the naked and radical confrontation of life by the Jewish artist that has been so important to us. . . . The "revelation of unity" that Lipschitz[14] once spoke of is so native to the Jew that he must learn, as it were, to suspend it—to look at the radical disharmonies of life for their own sake, to learn to describe life as it exists in time instead of seeking the figures that are so easily reconciled under the aspect of eternity. [. . .]

12. Edmund Wilson, "Doctor Life and His Guardian Angel," *New Yorker* (November 15, 1958): 213–238.
13. Gershom Scholem, *Major Trends in Jewish Mysticism* (1941).
14. It is unclear which Lipschitz Kazin was referring to, possibly Rabbi Israel Lipschitz (1782–1860), who wrote an influential commentary on the Torah. Another possibility is Jacques Lipchitz (1891–1973), a sculptor and contemporary of Kazin's.

## December 15, 1958

History—the unleashed force of a billion human wills. For every human being is "reality." The hungry gorge of reality. Every human being, who is unique because he can interpret human destiny, multiplied in force and lust and anger a billion times. No wonder that society is always a cockpit and "mankind" always at war.

Jim Farrell may not always write well, but he is right to think that his own story gives him literary sanction. In America it does—or in a society that is based on the future that discredits all links to the past, the "minority" individual (who is such because of that national tradition which is not identifiable with the abstract American identity) has, in his mere person, immense symbolic value—this is why I recognize the possibility in my own autobiographical impulse. Only in writing about "myself' " do I, in this country, *connect* myself with the country.

*Time*—always says, even adjectively, U.S., not *American*. Quite right, *Time*. U.S. is a tradename for the national corporation, *America* a mythical and true symbol.

## December 18, 1958

Faculty meeting yesterday at the New School. The German Jews sitting around the table with the meek American Dr. Jones of the Middle States Accreditation committee. The German Jews—each one slightly more grotesque, more Cruikshank-looking than the other. What a race, what a group. Like hawks, waiting to pounce down on a subject, what a clever boy am I. And what tenseness in them because of the control, the politesse, the civilizing and hold-in-leash of so much passion. . . . Meanwhile, the harsh suspicious face of Doctor Simons,[15] the autocrat looking out and down on his charges.

## December 29, 1958

Yesterday, Sunday, walking back from Columbus Circle, I came to the great intersection at Lincoln Square, and the sky suddenly rose, widened, colored, with the wash colors, the end-of-day dispersion of colors that I remembered from great walks over the bridge in sight of the whole harbor and lower Manhattan. Moments of unforgettable depth, poignancy and charm. [. . .]

15. Hans Simons was president of the New School for Social Research, 1950–1960.

## January 2, 1959

Hannah and the Greeks. Classical limitations and classical knowledge. The path to deeper understanding of her lies in that over-pious sense of cultural loyalty, which I discerned in the art-historian Panofsky and in the "domination of Greece over Germany."—We must not get out of bounds. The last word on the subject has been said by so-and-so.

I love my worldliness, my snobbery, my ease.

Hugo—concision in style, precision in thought, decision in life.

## January 6, 1959

The act of remembering, like the act of thinking. From inside the castle of the mind, messengers go out every minute, and every minute, come back.

For the first time, I have security in my profession. I feel that I have only to sit down every day and to *think* in order to get my work done. The world becomes increasingly fuller, richer, denser, more beautifully complex every day. [. . .]

## January 16, 1959

[. . .] Every Monday night at the New School, the Russian Jew in advanced middle age, who couldn't wait for me to finish my lecture before he said, clearing his throat: Now I should like to say some reflections, and turned to the piece of yellow paper. The class in dismay, shame, annoyance, on every hand. And yet, although he's taken lately to patronizing me, I admit there is something marvelously old-fashioned and upright in this gent.

Whenever I write close to the bone of personal experience, the prose becomes neat, direct—and *nimble.*

Mensch—mensch—who always picked inferior and weak girls, so that they would not upset him.

## February 23, 1959
### [dated January 23, 1959]

The other day, reading Nabokov's *Gogol*, I found myself getting jittery, just as I did when reading the complete *Lolita.* I was not surprised to hear from

Herb Gold yesterday, in from Cornell, how much Nabokov himself disliked my piece apropos of Dick Lewis'[16] book [*The Picaresque Saint*]. My sense of claustrophobia, of being immersed in pure screaming eccentricity, was not off—this is a mind as different from mine, as utterly unhistorical, as can be imagined. God knows this eternal business of "placing" oneself in the stream of time, of making out the historical weather, can be overdone; but my own commitment to this kind of thinking, in and out of literature, my sense of politics in the Greek sense, is such that I cannot read an utterly idiosyncratic and farcical-eccentric mind like N without some slight sense of hysteria. Amazing realization that such a mind can take me so far below the anchors of the bridge. N's hatred of Nabokov [*sic*, meaning Boris Pasternak]—Gold says that he regards even Pasternak's poetry as "feminine," like Emily Dickinson—obviously springs from impatience with just that quality in *Zhivago* which moved me most.

## March 5, 1959

I know what I think, I know what I believe, and I know that much of the contemporary literature I read nowadays is bad. *Henderson*[17] was bad, the books I reviewed in recent months have been tepid-to-bad, even Behan[18] seems to me the triumph of a temperament over mind. . . . I certainly thought Ann's story yesterday was thin, and what to say to my wife, to my friends, to my would-be and very hostile friends, like Herbert Gold or Harvey Swados, or Monroe Engel, or Ralph Ellison, that I think their works are poor-to-bad? I am surrounded by lovely and fascinating people, most of whose works seem to me insignificant, c'est tout. As a critic, all I have is my diagnostic power, my honesty and my gift for judgment as one. If I am wrong, then I am utterly mistaken in my judgments; but the fact is that much of what I read now does seem to me bad, and that the more isolated and acute this critical power of mine becomes, the more obstinately alone I must remain. [. . .]

16. Richard Warrington Baldwin Lewis (1917–2002), American literary scholar, won a 1976 Pulitzer Prize for his biography of Edith Wharton. A friend of Kazin's, he was Niel Gray Professor of English and American Studies at Yale University from 1959 to 1988.

17. *Henderson the Rain King* by Saul Bellow (New York: Viking, 1959).

18. Brendan Behan, "The Causes Go, the Rebels Remain," *Atlantic* (January 1959): 65–67. Behan was an Irish playwright, novelist, and short story writer. He was also a member of the Irish Republican Army.

## March 8, 1959

[. . .] I never liked Bernie[19] so much as yesterday, never respected the artist self, in all his humility and unspoken sureness, so much as yesterday. There are times when he has not only the style of a master (as in the first part of the current *P*[*artisan*] *R*[*eview*] story, "The Maid's Shoes," though the story itself doesn't altogether succeed), but when, as yesterday, he has the true wisdom of the writer in the face of life and its manifold complexities. Yet his hold on life, the true Brooklyn experience, is still so delicate that he sometimes seems to tremble in the wind. He said extraordinary things: talking about his mother's early death and his brother's "condition," he remarked that anguish had set in so early in his life that it left room for growth. What I like most about Bernie's stories, I suppose, is that the actual *conditions* of life are realized imaginatively, that the actual color and tone of the seemingly colorless, inbred-with-eternity quality is actually rendered. [. . .]

## March 10, 1959

[. . .] The art of representation: when details are put into a scene or touch up a character for purely formal reasons to make something come alive. . . . Natasha's pigeon toes and blouses—Mary's patent leather shoes and dull bun of hair—Arthur Berger's short neck, so that his head seems to swivel dangerously on his shoulders—Nechama's[20] Chinese, twinkling face, Aunt Ida's *springy* quality, like a chicken— [. . .]

The art of representation. Harold [Rosenberg] the old-fashioned man. Face out of the silent movies, tall in a way that fathers used to be, not young men; above all, the instinctive habit of independence and determination, which reminds me of Freud's saying that he used "sex" where he could have used "eros" in order not to give "any concession to faintheartedness." Talking to Harold, all my instinctive cultural loyalties come into play—my feeling for history, my admiration for radical personality, my belief in art as a comment on the world. With his hooked nose over his paternal moustache, his forthrightness, his delight in stating *his* case first, Harold gives me an acute case of nostalgia.

The art of representation. Food is the trail that leads back to the mother.

19. Bernard Malamud (1914–1986), American novelist and short story writer. Kazin helped him secure a publisher (Harcourt Brace) for his first novel, *The Natural* (1952).
20. See Chapter 6, note 123, on Aunt Nechama and Uncle Berl.

Historie morale. Historie contemporaine. The feeling for history is the sense that the intelligence of man, a foreseer, really works to carry man into an imaginable—not always imagined—future. Time is not only in man's head, but on man's side; he works toward it, and for himself. He is not a stranger to his own creative resources.

The rebel—vide Freud—keeps the mother tight in an Oedipal situation, so as to revolt against her. The rebel needs the mother so as to sustain the rebellion; the stranger knows there is no mother any more, knows that he is alone. [. . .]

Real freedom is the freedom to do something about one's destiny, and in this sense very few people today have any sense of historical freedom. The sense of personal powerlessness has replaced active politics—replaced active politics—dread about "annihilation" has replaced political thinking. The world gets more and more fixed in the pattern of *absolute* politics of the totalitarian pattern. No wonder that the twenties now seem the last *real* period in which men still felt that they were free to do something about their destiny. The world gets more and more *grim*. [. . .]

## April 15, 1959

[. . .] All the popular philosophies of our time—Freudianism, existentialism—are based on distrust of external convention, society, rhetoric, even language. The inner man, the chaotic unconscious, these are the truth; philosophies of history, religions, the transcendent as more than the individual's wayward intuition, these are considered false and wrong. Our morality is entirely negative, to avoid phoniness; our thinking is entirely critical, to detect inflation and illogic and pretense. To escape disillusionment, we avoid hope; to escape scorn from others, we play it tough. But in this we go item by item, step by step only; and the worst of this negative morality, this avoidance at all costs of illusion and error, is that we are always so self-conscious, so careful, so methodical; we carry our own lives in our hands all the time, as it were; we do not *live*, we avoid folly.

But in this negativism, this choice of the moment over the whole, of the individual's *feelings* over the hypothetical falseness of language, religion, society, we play a false role, too; it is not natural for human beings to be so careful, so hopeless, so negative. It is not natural for human beings so *completely* to pretend non-attachment. In point of fact, we are fools of love, God-sick believers, we believe where there is no reason to believe, we love where love alone holds us up "like a candle in the midst of the almighty forlornness."[21] It is not natural for human beings to be so conscious of themselves thinking (rather than of their *thoughts*). . . . Worst of all, this negativism finally becomes a tiresome sophistication; the same habit of mind that is rooted in the *trust* of one's innermost conscience forbids us to distrust everything but other people's opinions! Too much of contemporary disbelief is rooted in the fear of being scorn[ed] by the majority of hard and tough unbelievers.

One must trust. It is impossible to live by the will, by the will to distrust, the will to be careful, the will to be anything but what one is prepared to be. One must trust, one must believe that this delicate membrane that through thought ties us to life, holds us firm, no matter what we may will.

## April 17, 1959

Went out an hour ago to deliver book to Dessauer's[22] house; then wandered disconsolately down Broadway to barbershop. On way, it did not surprise me to see a man carrying a shopping bag and leading a monkey by the hand (the monkey was wearing a leather sports jacket). The day so hot, my heart so heavy, everything zany all over again as in the worst of times years ago. [. . .] It is just that I am so damned sensitive, so quick to be hurt, so raw, so empty-hearted at the least blow! With this absurd sensitivity, it is bad enough to live life on the raw, to feel so much pain. But it is really worse, it approaches madness, to think that if maybe one thinks differently, just a little differently, it will all work out! When I look at those undated thoughts I wrote above, it seems to me that I am still looking for a position, a philosophy, which will help me to escape pain. Whereas, all the time, it has never been my position, my thinking, even "mental condition," even at the worst pain, that has ever been wrong: it is only my vulnerability, my horror whenever some deep attachment is broken, my fear of pain. [. . .] As for this rawness, this sensitivity, this eternal cry for love and warmth and security—Mama did not do all this either. True, she cooked us good and plenty, Pearlie and me; and it is unforgivable in one sense, that we should have been given such a lifelong sense of insecurity and even terror about everything. But it is also my sensitivity to the world, my lightning-quick reactions to everything around me,

21. A favorite allusion to *Moby-Dick*, where Queequeg is described holding up a candle in a sinking boat waiting for rescue.
22. Reference not clear, possibly John P. Dessauer, author of *Book Publishing: What It Is, What It Does* (1974).

that has always prepared me for this capacity for pain. The specific bending and twisting that came from my mother was in my readiness—mentally—to revise my thinking, to find a thought that would get me off the hook. Somehow the place I stood in became an abyss if I seemed to be standing there *too* alone. But all these excessive gentlenesses and submissions, as I can see from Michael,[23] are fundamentally rooted in nature, are a trick of character, and if they are sensitive enough, are the writer's fundamental sympathy with life, his openness to experience. And if you want maximum exposure, you must pay for it. This "violence in the soul" that somebody described as the artist's quality, this fear of going mad, because of the writer's fundamental extravagance and saturability of experience, that restricts the writer and causes him to feel blocked—it is this fundamental painfulness *because* openness of spirit that one must not only respect but cherish. THERE IS NO THOUGHT THAT CAN SAVE ONE, THERE IS NO REPRIEVE GRANTED TO CONFESSIONS AND SUBMISSIONS. We all know what we think and we know what we are like: the problem is to sustain oneself, not to yield to the delusion that one can be let off by pretending to be someone else. In point of fact, there is no tribunal that can grant one reprieve—there is no official, no judicial philosophy that can grant one surcease, or tell one what to think. The problem is to bear oneself up, to go through to the end, to *be* and to grow and to deepen with everything one *has*. [. . .]

## April 18, 1959

[. . .] The secular culture of the Russian Jews (and their American children) reaches back only as far as the 19th century. Zionism, socialism, nationalism, liberalism—all these familiar programs are the programs of the 19th century. No wonder, as Hannah says in reference to Sidney Hook (*Dissent*, Spring 1959)[24]—"How little he understands human dignity, however much he may be concerned with social opportunity." The *only* cause, the only conscious cause, of the Hooks and everyone else I know brought up in this background, has been "social opportunity." Human dignity simply does not reach back very far for them. Philosophy, religion, metaphysical concerns of the nature of man—these do not go back very far; and anyone who does go back, as Hannah does to the Greek and Christian and classical traditions, is resented.

23. Kazin's son Michael, who was about to turn eleven.

24. Kazin is referring to Arendt's "Preliminary Remarks" to "Reflections on Little Rock," *Dissent* (Winter, 1959), in which she defends her article against an attack by Sidney Hook.

In a sense this lack of background, of religious and philosophic background, has always been the besetting ill of America in modern times. It is one thing, as the greatest Americans have always known, to live amid the destruction of traditions; it is something else not to know that there *are* any.

## April 23, 1959

Wilson at lunch today—"I get so excited talking to people in the city that I get sick"—then he goes right back to the Civil War, 19th Century Russia, etc.

## April 29, 1959

Dr. Carl Stover of the Brookings Institution on the phone—"I just want to double-check with you re your appearance here on the 19th. . . . Allrightee . . . Bye, bye." (*Passim*—"Don't have any fear of being critical.")

I read this article of Mrs. Cooking Spoon (Diana Trilling) in the new *PR* with absolute fascination, like a snake preparing to strike.[25] I must desist from this foolish fascination from someone so vulnerable, from someone it is so easy to humiliate and to destroy. My real anger is with Trilling, not with her, and I get into a rage at her only to strike at him. Desist!

## May 2, 1959

"I am a conservative," says Irving Kristol[26] at lunch. And so are we all these days, we sons of the radical tradition. We have made good; we have made it; and like the hungry bourgeois that we have always wanted to be, we make all the right noises about our servants, our country places, our creativity and the rest. But damn it, the world is not conservative; it leaps ahead every day into new social forms that are obviously in the irresistible rhythm of our time; and all our cultural loyalties, whether to 19th century American individualism or to English romantic poetry or to the novel in its palmy days—all reflect a past world, not the world struggling to new birth before our eyes. More and more it comes to me that without a strong radical orientation these days, without fundamental sympathy for socialism and an understanding of the social patterns working

25. Diana Trilling, "The Other Night at Columbia," *Partisan Review* (Spring, 1959): 214–230. In *New York Jew* Kazin would quote from Diana Trilling's piece as illustrative of a "certain intellectual contentment" among the postwar New York intellectuals (194).
26. Irving Kristol (1920–2009), American journalist, later called "the godfather of neoconservativism." Kazin deplored his onetime friend's turn to the right.

themselves out into the shape of the present, it is impossible to understand what is happening in literature or anywhere else.

After the Straus party the other day, really a *PR* party, of course, it seemed to me, trying to define my disgust, that everything I saw and heard was a caricature of what a priggish Communist would call "bourgeois decadence." Mrs. Trilling and Miss McCarthy and the feeble little Gregorys, and the Hollanders, and, etc., etc.[27] But, more important, I have this sense in myself, about to speak of "the promise of America," about to explain "what happened to the novel," always mentally affirming "the end of modern literature," living in a country whose leadership seems paralyzed, not only because the leaders are old and sick, but because their minds are so incapable of grasping what is happening in the world today—I have this sense, I say, of the utter triviality and materialism of most of the culture around me, of living for the values of a vanished period. Anyone over forty now lives for a vanished period, while the younger writers no longer know what to live for, except themselves, find themselves treading water, are alone and lost in the great big void.

For more than 15 years, more or less, and more or less in intention and execution, I have tried to show what in the individual escapes the mesh of history, to give full marks to the pure flame of consciousness, which is the real spell of individuality. But it is exactly the lessening and darkening of consciousness just now, its trivialization, its cheapening, its self-concern only, that troubles me more and more about my cultural loyalty to individualism. It is as if the pure flame of consciousness had nothing to burn on but itself, as if the individual, with nothing to affirm but his own freedom, found himself affirming only his own personality traits, his middle-class greeds, his animal appetites. It is the increasing trivialization and self-concern of contemporary culture that are diminishing individual consciousness, until it has nothing to hold on to—that is, the secular forms, and I suspect most of the "religious" ones as well—except themselves. But these *selves* are not sacred to themselves, even; they exist as particles of consciousness, now closed-off, closed-in. [. . .]

The literary radical, the pure Protestant spirit—the individual as consciousness: from the beginning it feared science as its enemy. But is scienza, gay or not,

27. Roger W. Straus Jr. (1917–2004), publisher at Farrar, Straus and Giroux; Diana Trilling (1905–1996), literary critic and essayist, whom Kazin disliked almost as much as he disliked her husband, Lionel; Horace Gregory (1898–1982), American poet and critic; John Hollander (1929–), Jewish American poet and critic, professor at Yale University.

is knowledge ever the enemy of consciousness? In Blake's fear and hatred of science is the key to almost two centuries of fated opposition between literary intelligence and the broad developing forms of modern society. The key lies in the fear that consciousness will be hindered in its ideal freedom, that essence will have to submit to mere existence. But it is exactly this submission that ever gives us freedom from that insistence on our own essence which cuts off the world in its rough and disorderly actuality, that separates the soul from history. Just as we must show that the development of society is not the paradigm of the individual soul, is not "rational" as a model of the human being's own rationality, so we must insist that the individual soul must not reject history because it is uncapturable by the free religious consciousness. Is not this sense of the uncapturability of history, this abstract fear of science, what lies behind Blake and Lawrence in their rejection of society?

Or to put another way—if the great Communist heresy is to identify society with history, the romantic-religious heresy is to reject society and history as together the record of the individual soul. One should never identify society, any society, with "history." This is as bad as identifying the R.C. Church with the vision of Christ, or anything temporal with what is essentially a religious conception of history. But to overlook society in favor of "ideal" history—Pasternak's romantic-literary version of Christianity—is equally bad. If the first is idolatry, the second is self-communion. And it looks more and more as if the alternatives of Commissar and Yogi[28] are the only ones the people see just now.

To be a true radical is to be in favor of knowledge, of an openness toward society, experience, history, the world. It is not to favor the ideal self over the world, or the world over this self, but to bring the self back into the world as its natural home. And history is the world, temporally considered: is the present plus our aspiration, the present made by our aspiration. History is the world in the inclusive sense of time. . . . The value of the religious radical over the social one, I see, is that it makes harder the idolatrous confusion of society with history. But society also exists, not as ideal, but actuality, *as* the world; and it is the increasing rejection of the way the world is going, in favor of our own personality alone, that seems to me the really decadent and self-referring thing about contemporary American society.

28. In his 1945 essay "The Yogi and Commissar," Arthur Koestler describes the radically different choices facing modern mankind as either cultivating one's inward, spiritual self (the yogi) or radically changing the external world through forceful political action (the commissar).

## May 4, 1959

The critic, too, has his negative capabilities. Yesterday, all through the re-reading of *Man's Fate*, I was the revolutionary; today, preparing to write on *Chatterley*, I am the religious radical. . . . Again, one knows what one is really thinking of, au fond, by *how* one feels.

It is not their fucking revolution I loved, it was the revolutionaries. It was not a system, any system; it was man at his bravest, at his most loving, at his most far-reaching, O brave, O more brave, O mighty hearts! The new *system* after all was only to have better men, a new truth between men. [. . .]

## May 15, 1959

Just back from lunch with Bob Silvers and Walter Kauffmann,[29] the latter as deadly a German prof. as I had thought he might be. Anyway, when I like somebody as much as Bob Silvers, I notice that a) I expect and virtually demand complete agreement b) that I tend to try imaginatively to get into his mind, to anticipate his responses and thoughts. Apparently *liking* someone for me means complete identification with; it occurs to me more and more, in view of the exceedingly important last session with Rioch, that I try to get so much into someone's mind, to see someone so completely from his point of view, his purposes, as if to assure holding on to him. My, my, the lesson is one of identity, for I notice that every subtle increase, every *minute* increase in my sense of differentiation, of my own particular thought or responsiveness to things, always gives me the most immense, immediate joy, as if I were entering into a gift I had not expected to enjoy. [. . .] I can see now that always, as with the Europeans whom at first I panted to acquire as permanent friends—Paolo [Milano], Hannah, etc., etc.—always the anticipation of their point of view, the eagerness to enter into their minds. The eagerness and the *ability* to do so!

## May 26, 1959

The real courage I long for, the real daring, is not in furtive and half-assed flirtations, but in *living fully*, to the root, with one woman. To live with one and to sneak off with another is not courage but *cowardice*, not the intense truth I

29. Robert Silvers (1929–), editor of the *New York Review of Books;* Walter Kaufmann (1921–1980), Princeton professor and Nietzsche scholar.

dream of but bourgeois hypocrisy and complacency. Better to break with Ann than to *sneak.*

Yeats?—The great poet finds truth imbued in "the mystery of words."

HISTORY OF A LITERARY RADICAL.[30] End of the hope that the unsupported, "free," individual could sustain in himself through his free and undirected insights, the vision once imposed on him by the church. From orthodoxy to freedom to sluttishness. From the individual as vessel of the truth to the individual searching for his identity. From the rebel to the hipster. From the vessel of God to the addict. . . . The smaller the individual feels today, the more he phonily enlarges himself, becomes "power," as in the Corso poem in *Big Table.*[31] . . . Kerouac, associating himself with the mediumistic vision of the truth.

Mailer: sex itself has gone wrong, so we have to camp on this ice-floe. Lawrence: sex is the medium of the spirit.

Part II. From the rebel to the hipster. From the lover to . . . Mary Lou Petersen and Paul Goodman . . . .

## June 11, 1959

Lunch with Mailer—"You are a 19th century man, still close to your own emotions. I am mid-twentieth century, all assaulted and besieged and assailed."

## June 14, 1959

[. . .] Torpor is terrible. It hurts. All these evenings, though long finished with Celia, I am tempted to call her up again, to make quick and easy use of her, as always I knew I could. Took the children to see Chaplin's *Modern Times* again, and the touchingly archaic Chaplin, the touchingly archaic shots of tramps and strikers and unemployed, the seeking, wistful tenderness of C's typical music, made me break down again and again in the darkness. But there is no going back to that—or to any nostalgic and psychological "radicalism." What finished it in America, where it never had any real roots except in a few classes, was simply

30. Early title for *Starting Out in the Thirties.*
31. Title of magazine publishing "Beat" writers, first issue appeared in spring of 1959 and included pieces by Jack Kerouac, Gregory Corso, and William S. Burroughs.

the "success," the embourgeoisement of the immigrants and their immediate descendants. I come back to that—hardly see how you can avoid it. [. . .]

What gentle, good children I have. What an idiot I am ever, when meeting Mike, to mistake his own excitement and worry for coolness. And Katie! The pinnacle of delight, the plus adorable du monde, the daughter of my heart.

## June 17, 1959

Rabbi B[irstein] was operated on Monday afternoon, and it was so serious that I called Ann to come back. She traveled all night and came back early yesterday. . . . Monday lunch with [Dag] Hammarskjöld at the UN. I thought, going up in the elevator, that I had never experienced such a pure sensation of delight, such a forgetting of everything else immediately around me; reminded me of the bliss of Europe at first experience, the sense of having been carried utterly into another world. The lunch was exquisite, the view from the 38th floor reminded me of Jesus being shown the mountains of the earth and tempted. I half-regretted some of my jokes about Ben-Gurion with Hammarskjöld, feeling I had fallen too much into his "sophisticated" mood, but later, thinking it over, I remembered that the subject had begun with Hammarskjöld quoting B-G on Pasternak—"the most disgraceful book ever written by a man of Jewish origin"—and I thought again of how one's instinctive judgments are always correct, because they flow from the center of one's thought as an *individual*, the exceptional fact that one is—and only then does one begin to check one's thoughts with one's superegos as citizen, Jew, and the rest. . . . [. . .]

## June 20, 1959

[. . .] Lunch yesterday with Sidney Hertzberg, still so meek and mild, sensitive and good that I felt positively 12 feet tall standing over him, arrogant and powerful. In the evening, Nat Glazer[32] came over, then his Japanese Amy. . . . Part of my trouble with Nat is that he reminds me of the Jewish butcher relatives of my youth, the Lazars and such, with their kinky hair, the voices that rumble as if from the belly. Belly-types, big eaters and rumblers. And Nat talks in jumbled sentences, in gesticulated gestures. Yet it is interesting and moving to see someone essentially so strong so visibly affected by the breakup of his

32. Nathan Glazer (1924–), American sociologist, best known for *Beyond the Melting Pot* (1963), a study of ethnic groups in New York City.

marriage. Fundamentally, so non-literary that he has the skeptical look of the City College chemistry major in the face of the English department intellectuals. But his own comparative intellectual success is not accidental. I was kidding him about sociology and "masses," and all the rest of that mass culture crap; and he said that sociology for him is a way of writing contemporary history. Exactly the phrase that always haunts me. And I know why. For to write contemporary history is, by covering the present to the best of one's ability, to seek the future, to press the future for a solution. It is to restore the "present" as the total scene of man, in our time. Historie contemporaine, historie morale.

## June 23, 1959

[. . .] The obsession with Melville in those years [1940s]. Drift, sea-drift \ a waste of waters is their field. Above all, the fight in Melville's own heart, between the Promethean hero, would-be magician, the listless observer Ishmael, spinning with the hurricane but quiet-dead at the heart of it; and Pip, who cast overboard, saw God face to face and never saw anything else. . . . The Melville years, the years of Existentialist *Geworfenheit*, the outcast, the abandoned.

Such a lovely feeling tonight, restless, full of the built-up excitement of those years. Ach, how short life seems when one has a memory like mine and sixteen years ago seems yesterday.

The great warm Broadway crowd, the lighted shops. It might all be the East Side of sixty years ago—certainly very little about the Jews ever changes. But walking along the Drive, the sudden smell of honeysuckle from some unseen bush and the nostalgic, round lamps at the entrance to the houses, makes the past seem beautiful again.

## June 29, 1959

Rabbi B[irstein] still very ill; yesterday, transfusion. We never know from day to day whether he will last, and Ann seems utterly numbed with the anxiety of it. In the midst of this all, the Russian trip in August seems almost real. Weise of the State Department told me this morning on the phone that if the Russians give their formal permission (expected), it will go off. . . . It will do me good to go to Russia. I will hate it, but it will do me good to get away from the West for a while. In this madly spinning world, I still occupy a mental universe whose center is Paris, the French Revolution, and tiled bathrooms. I am less disposed to discomfort than any other writer who has ever lived, and my thinking has fallen into such regularities and traditionalities and correspondences that it will do me good to get jolted out of the comfort and refinements and sterilities of my usual existence.[33]

Torrid heat today.

## July 27, 1959

Hot again. Rains gone for a while. Last night, went out suddenly to Mama's after that idiot Lazar Kaminkowitz[34] pressured her into saying what was wrong with her. Poor mama, poor last days of fear and agony, poor father, my father. When he walked me to the bus, I asked him to kiss me and there was a big grin on his face. I would miss *him* more than anybody, though I am amazed to find how much I love *him*. Mama lying in bed, sheepish and grateful. . . . Then the low, long blocks of Brooklyn suburbia. Everything around there looks so new, so brown-brick, so New York my city. Oh God oh God, they are squeezing the life out of my mother, and with every new squeeze, I find myself gasping in rhythm with her. It is all so ordinary, so terrible, so human. The brown-bricked little family houses, Irving Weiss my taxi-driver from Flatbush Avenue, the housing project. I thought of those sulphurous and electric summer nights of my boyhood in Brownsville—it seems so strange to have my mother dying anywhere else!—and seeing a group of young girls standing outside the project, on Batchelder St., I thought back to my own boyhood and felt a pang, of how little these kids know of my boyhood, of my mother, of that whole life that already seems historic. . . . My mother asked for the picture of her parents that she gave me when I was writing the *Walker* and my father for the picture of *his* parents. Time, time, time—all we have left is this delicate membrance in the mind!

Yesterday, wrote the piece on Pound and the Freshmen, then read proof on the *Holiday* piece on NY, the *Harper's* piece on contemporary fiction. When I see from how many different memories, learning periods, the assembled sentences in an essay come, I am staggered and awed by the amount of training that goes into the actual race I run in a particular piece, by the amount of training that must still go on, day after day and moment after moment, before the race will be run again.

33. Kazin was a member of a small delegation of writers, including the historian Arthur Schlesinger Jr., the playwright Paddy Chayefsky (see Chapter 8, note 82), and *Atlantic* editor Ted Weeks, invited to Russia in the summer of 1959.

34. Lazar Kaminkowitz, an uncle of Kazin's.

These vulgar explosions of temper, regression, not strength. *Weakness*, just vulgar weakness. Disgusting on my part. I am ashamed.

## September 6, 1959

Puerto Rico. Today is Sunday. Arrived here Wed. afternoon. Life has been stupefying and dull and utterly depressed. I'm *not* sorry I went to Russia, and unloving and cold as I feel, I'm not going to pass it by. Puerto Rico itself utterly flavorless and meaningless.[35]

## September 24, 1959

[. . .] I see now that what I liked in Russia was not fortune or happiness, neither of which in my sense it possesses, but its old solemn sense of purpose, its stubborn faithfulness and religiosity. It was the absence of this stinking frivolity and mindlessness and skepticism, this poisonous careerism, that I liked. Holy Russia worked for me; which does not mean that I equate its holiness with the holiness of Communism, on the contrary. I do not believe in the new God of Communism or the old God of the synagogue—I believe in God. I cannot live without the belief that there is a purposeful connection that I may yet understand which I can serve. I cannot be faithless to my own conviction of value.

Man comes and goes between the idea and the "phenomenon," but he always comes back.

## October 25, 1959

[. . .] Every thought of my mother is of an inexpressible poignancy[36]—not sorrow so much as a clear note of amazed loss. When I look at her picture on my desk, I feel as if each time I had to acknowledge an emotion, a break for which I do not have the words. I seem to hear an unprecedented *tone* in my mind—infiniteness without return. When the mind has to carry the burden of recalling what in actual fact will be never be seen again. [. . .]

35. Kazin taught at the University of Puerto Rico the fall semester of 1959. There are no journal entries written while Kazin was in Russia.
36. Kazin's mother died on October 10, 1959.

## December 14, 1959
### [New York]

Conversation with D. Bell on N. Mailer—I admire him emotionally if not intellectually (sub-voci. Just as I admire *myself* intellectually but not emotionally.)

In the paper, pert, cute model's face. A face whose look and pose are *framed* entirely to solicit a response. A woman's face, look, pose, are like a question or a suggestion designed to elicit an answer—approval. Women are still a minority, looking to the majority for answer, status, *confirmation*.

## January 4, 1960

I am a serious man, and if I am to portray twenty-five years of my life in seriousness and truth, I must portray myself as a serious man, as a seeking mind—not just as a "sensitif." "Girl Who Loved Jews"[37] seems possible to me, for the first time in years, because there will be a real spiritual clash or problem involved, and the question of belief, throughout, must be foremost. My autobiography will always be most deeply the autobiography of a Jew. [. . .]

## January 12, 1960

[. . .] As a Jew and American investigator [in England during the war], the outsider among all those fluted voices. . . . Smug little society, even in the midst of war. The Laborites fundamentally inferiority-complex, as when the Labor ed. man confessed that he could not imagine winning.

Great thing about the [Labour] election of 1945—social action in view. Acceleration of social action. Masses in the streets—like immense emotion of returning on Queen Mary to the lights and bands in the harbor. Transfigured night. Society, a mass, acting in concert with you, *expressing the deepest part of you*, the unconscious part of you, in fact (just the opposite of being submerged in the crowd). This is the positive sacramental side of society as an institution: working for you, with the energy and unconscious but positive wisdom that you do not immediately find in yourself.

37. "The Girl Who Loved Jews," a portrait of Kazin's lover Mary Louise Petersen, would appear in *New York Jew*.

Here the London crowd in Whitehall—literary memories of great crowd in Wordsworth's *Prelude* and in Coleridge. The true meaning of the collective as the deeper part of you. [. . .]

What was wonderful in Britain was the sheer direct humanness and goodness of so many. And the English rough irony, absence of crap—gallows humor of Blitz people—*of people in trouble.* As Harold [Rosenberg] said about U.S. being at its best in time of trouble (thirties) so the British were truly up against it. By contrast, the Americans never had it so good, and felt up against it.

The new fatalism—expressed in laughter at Piccadilly theatre about Belsen prisoners. Too much for us. No real end to the war—[38]

The American Jew not fitting in so neatly as the English Jews: the unassimilable quality. . . .

## January 16, 1960

[. . .] At the *American Scholar* dinner in the evening—Barzun,[39] terribly stiff and carefully well-mannered. Brown double-breasted suit like a Frenchman's. Very efficient mind, I guess, but carefulness of manner threw me off. Another handsome and white-haired actor like Lionel Trilling. Never realized how much of an outsider Barzun must feel—from his manner, like a diplomat's. O, so careful.

Randall Jarrell,[40] already past his peak. Childishness of mind, concealed for so long by his bright adolescent sauciness, now comes out in his puzzled but heavily bearded face. [. . .]

## January 18, 1960

Cocktail party. The juice of New York. The accumulated *personal* energy of these people (sex-power-position), standing together, an energy machine.

38. In *A Walker in the City* and *Starting Out in the Thirties* Kazin describes the shocked, embarrassed response of the audience in a Piccadilly theater in 1945 to a film of the liberation of the Belsen concentration camp.
39. The French-born American critic and cultural historian Jacques Barzun (1907–) was a professor, dean of faculties, and provost at Columbia.
40. Randall Jarrell (1914–1965), American poet, literary critic, essayist, poet, who it seems was not past his peak. Jarrell's collection of poetry *The Woman at the Washington Zoo* won the National Book Award in 1960; in 1965 he published the poetry collection *The Lost World*, which many consider his best work.

## January 23, 1960

After the party is over, is over, and the tug of nausea is in your stomach, then is the time to think of upper-class bohemia, for it is right here. Maids, liquor, wine, children at good schools—but the intelligentsia are ready to come to blows, at a moment's notice, over a tear as an intellectual thing.

Upper class bohemia—Dwight MacDonald. Upper-class bohemia, Adele Mailer,[41] whose attitudes are all "beat" as a matter of course and *unconsciously*. Upper-class, bohemia or not, still seeks sensation, *pleasure*.

## March 8, 1960

The Fiedler book [*Love and Death in the American Novel*] shocks me by its unrelieved tone of ministering to American writing as if it were a patient. I am wearied and stupefied by the busy, busy tone, the stridency, above all, by the lack of modesty and aesthetic concern. What in hell is it that makes Jewish intellectuals so unbearably ideological and didactic in everything they—we—do? I turned to *The Boys in the Back Room*, and discovered Wilson, as usual, writing as a *literary* critic: judging *novels*. Aesthetic criticism. The only thing a critic can do. Fiedler also has a bit of the nut in him: the book takes the theme and develops examples. You go from cultural personification to cultural personification. This way Fiedler can never honestly feel that he is *learning* anything; he is just developing a thesis.

As with [Paul] Goodman, something false in his tone when he calls himself compassionate. A *macher*. *Too much concern with critical roles* (i.e., society) *and not enough with culture* (i.e., values).

## March 16, 1960

[. . .] The thirties—the bombardment of time. Yuri Yaroschevsky said in Russia, if you are brought up in our society. . . . And it is true, to this extent, that a society is the larger skin of oneself, the second body in which one lives. Sitting in that subway car on the way home from City, 1934, was like sitting in a gondola immersed below the water, or in a plane being shot at by ack-ack guns. The

41. Adele Mailer, second wife of author Norman Mailer, stabbed by him on September 21, 1960, when he returned drunk from a party.

pressures, ye gods, the pressures! No wonder I used to feel, rocking back and forth on my seat, as if I were traveling in no-man's land. . . .

Be plain, be plain, and let the cringing heart feed on the mind's self-respect. . . .

The *drama* of time. The goddamned Thirties and the organizational mind. Toujours the attack!

## March 19, 1960

"I must create my own system, or be enslaved by another man's."[42] All day long we are presented with other people's "pictures" of the world, which hold us captive so long as we treat them with unexamined respect and deference. Guilt is always deference to other people's dogmas. We are instantly punished with the loss of "togetherness." We have only to say no, I am not sure, maybe.

There is no joy like working out one's ideas for oneself, like coming to the root of the matter for oneself. But to do this one has to take for granted the supremacy of truth over "human relationships," of truth over the appearance of truth. That line of Wittgenstein's seems to me extraordinary in its freedom-giving power, "A picture held us captive. And we could not get outside it, for it lay in our language and language seemed to repeat it to us inexorably."[43]

Always get outside the picture, see the picture as outside yourself.

## March 20, 1960

[. . .] In the Pittsburgh airport yesterday morning, waiting for my plane to Marietta, I finished re-reading Miller's *Tropic of Cancer*, and by God was impressed. A *poet*'s book. Miller has real innocence of eye; he enters with genuine gusto into that dead Paris world of piss and brothels and rotten cheese. He has true good will, and this is why it is impossible in reading him not to like him, to feel exuberant, to enter into the experience of the senses.

42. From William Blake's *Jerusalem*: "I must Create a System or be enslav'd by another Man's./I will not Reason & Compare: my business is to Create."

43. *Philosophical Investigations*, No. 115.

As Proust says, we "reason" too much to avoid letting the object penetrate into our souls. Miller knows how to register this effect of objects on his soul. He makes me remember that fine saying of Ransom's, that the emotion that we associate with ourselves really belongs to the object. There is a kind of strickenness, a nakedness of soul, a baring unafraid of consciousness to the rain of objects on his head, that I love in Miller. [. . .]

## March 22, 1960

Snow this morning. The day after the first day of Spring: knees and chest tired from Desiree[44] yesterday, head tired from too much lecturing and not enough writing. Somebody anonymous left on my desk in class last night a record of Ralph Richardson[45] reading Blake; and when I played the opening of the first side this morning, I was struck again by the immense good will in Blake, this openness to the world that had surprised and delighted me in Henry Miller. A teacher in America these days teaches these men of good will, of open mind and heart, to students who always look . . . skeptical. Always the Jewish good look of disbelief, of having been squeezed so damned tight over the years that only a little eye, one little eye is left, looking suspiciously out of a yellow face.

Without *some* kind of innocence, no writing is possible. One must give oneself to the world, uncomplainingly, no matter what. . . .

And do you know what I think? I think it is possible only if one lets go, if one kisses goodbye to all the stale attachments. It is not that we distrust the world, it's that we don't recognize it! We have enveloped it in so many stale systems of thought that understandably the gap between things-as-they-really-look and things-as-they-are-supposed-to-look has wearied us, we fell into it. Only by forgetting one's old subjective attachment to this and this and this and this, by standing back for a moment and breathing hard in a state of blissful non-attachment to wife and mother and child and country and what-not; only by breathing deep into one's lungs one's own blissful unimportance in the scale of things, can things look fresh and sharp again. We are so preoccupied with the cost of everything that we have narrowed the world down to our own human scale, and like the old Jews I grew up with, have lost all, but *all* power of enjoyment. [. . .]

44. Kazin's physical therapist.
45. Sir Ralph Richardson (1902–1983), English actor for stage and screen.

## April 3, 1960

[. . .] The *Dissent* piece on the Jews gives me the wonderful opportunity to do a piece on the illusion of normalization, the attempt to be just like everybody else—which fails because in regard to others, the Jews have too much to explain, and in regard to themselves too much experience for the bourgeois will itself to dissolve.[46] Last night at Sandy Pearlman's[47] birthday party, the doctors, the lawyer, the Long Island suburbanites. Cezanne sketches on the wall, a Soutine; yet life is for these people what it always was. Ann think[s] they are becoming like the first generation. But was the first generation's awkwardness entirely a social matter? I think of Hilda Rotenberg and the religiosity of the "third" generation at Smith and Amherst. Isn't this return to Jewishness just the opposite of Judaism—an attempt to fit into the expected pattern, to show that they have a creed and a church and a people, like everybody else. Whether it is Trilling and the "lost cause" of English literature or Kristol, the conservative, or Bell, the end of ideologist, or Fiedler, the Lenin of the sex organs, or, apart from the intellectuals, my sweet little boy with his McCann Erickson[48] of a mother, no Jewish training whatever, nevertheless, discovering that he is a Jew in an Englewood full of Jews, and the Jewish Community Center, the fact remains that everything conspires to give the Jew the illusion of "normalization" of his status only because he lives in a country full of abnormal types like himself, and that whenever he tries to find an end to his search in Zionism or Socialism or country-clubbing, he is simply looking for his terrestrial home in ideology.

What has given the illusion of normality to the Jewish experience in America is the lack of any real concrete religious convictions, of any solid tradition, left to the Gentile-Americans. Anti-Semitism, I insist, has its roots in the rivalry of orthodox Christianity (Catholicism) with Judaism. In America the very looseness of all religious thinking, the substitution of sociological categories for religion ones, the end, among many Protestant clergymen (Niebuhr) of even the traditional proselytizing of the Christian church, has given the Jew the illusion

46. Kazin did not publish a piece on the "illusion of normalization" among Jews in *Dissent*. His only article to appear in *Dissent*, "They Made It" (Fall 1987): 612–617, is an attack on the "super-patriots" among successful Jewish writers and a warning that all was not as good for American Jews as they might wish.
47. Sandy Pearlman (1943–), son of a successful drug store magnate, Stony Brook student, future poet, songwriter, and record producer.
48. Carol worked for the advertising agency McCann Erickson.

of friendship when what he more often has are duplicates of his condition, or confederates against Christianity. [. . .]

## April 21, 1960

[. . .] So many thoughts I have been pent-up with, especially my insight that so far as the *New York Jew*[49] is concerned, and perhaps especially this New York Jew, life has been all too much a history of humiliation, of taking-it, of the supposedly inferior position. Isn't this what all the thick incestuousness and cousinship of New York Jewish life comes down to, the insularity, the hanging-together, always with an eye back to the Russian horror, and then to the German one? Oh God, how we Jews have lived—what incredible meanness of spirit, lowness, humiliation, we have been forced down to over the centuries, and how it all comes back to me that just behind the easiness and the prosperity of our life just now, there hangs this constant memory *and* threat of the past.

## April 22, 1960

The Jews—between the "anus mundi" and the heights. Between mass extermination as the victim and the Einstein brain that split the atom. Always extremes of wretchedness and power, of ignominy and spiritual exaltation. No wonder that the Jew is always so *conscious of himself*, and no wonder too, that Dwight MacDonald is always so conscious of *him* as the local intellectual opposition in New York. [. . .]

## May 13, 1960

Faster goes the train—faster, faster. And all our sorrows and regrets are that life is changing, that society is not and *cannot* be what it was.

Sadness of the Thirties

William and Edna Phillips[50]
Gertrude Hayes[51]

49. At the time Kazin envisioned writing a single autobiographical volume to follow *A Walker in the City*. He would later divide that volume into two autobiographical works, *Starting Out in the Thirties* (1965) and *New York Jew* (1978).
50. William Phillips (1907–2002), critic and essayist, cofounder of the *Partisan Review*.
51. Gertrude Hayes, wife of the poet, novelist, and screenwriter Alfred Hayes (1911–1985).

Ed Saveth[52]
Malamud (and M's characters)

Brooklyn is the country of dreams, of wishes, of youth longings. Night after night my skin clutches when I think of walking up Saratoga Avenue to the library. O what lonely excitement, What wistful hope! But Manhattan is the country of actuality of middle age. It is all here now, and more—everything I longed for, and these last few days and nights, especially now that the vexing chapter for AMS, Jr. is in the works,[53] I've had such a sense of looking forward to nothing, of having made it. I want in my heart, obviously, to be an initiate again, to write the story of youth, to look forward to everything. Surely that's the excitement, again, of the new book—*starting out.* [. . .]

## June 10, 1960

The Sacco-Vanzetti play on Channel 2 was very good indeed, but am struck by the fact that it was directed by Sidney Lumet, and that the emotional passion behind it was so strongly directed from the "foreign" group in American life. Czolgosz murder of McKinley, the Haymarket affair, the Sacco-Vanzetti case—all represent directly or indirectly the hated "foreigner" group in American life. And last night the children of the immigrants got their innings in.[54]

## July 10, 1960

[. . .] Everything *works* for me these days, but life has no volume anymore, no more surprises. Being 45 is above all, boring; there is little new in oneself to

52. Edward N. Saveth (1915–2010), American historian.
53. "The Realistic Novel," in *Paths of American Thought*, ed. Arthur Meyer Schlesinger Jr. and Morton White (New York: Houghton Mifflin, 1963), 238–253.
54. Directed by Sidney Lumet, the play dramatized the 1920 trial of two Italian immigrants and anarchists, Nicola Sacco and Bartolomeo Vanzetti, for allegedly robbing and murdering the paymaster and guard of a factory in South Braintree, Massachusetts. Seven years later, following sustained political controversy, the two men were executed. The trial recalls for Kazin the assassination of President McKinley by Leon Czolgosz, a fanatic of Polish descent, who was influenced by the anarchist writings of Emma Goldman (1869–1940), as well as the trial and conviction of eight anarchists (and the execution of four) following a bomb-throwing incident and riot that took place in 1886 in Chicago's Haymarket Square. As in the Sacco-Vanzetti affair, the lack of evidence tying the accused Haymarket anarchists to the crime proved less important to the jury than the fact that the defendants were anarchists of foreign descent.

discover. It is the boredom that kills me just now—I can't truly bear all these straight lines, these schedules, these rituals. I want to put my whole head into the advancing wave and feel the shock of the cold water and for a minute get out of myself. [. . .] If there is a God, let him surprise me these days—I need a surprise, I want to get off the regular track.

And yet what shall I do but dig deeper in my work? I don't do footsie with those types who are types of Dan's cretinous girl friend, and I don't want to take dope, fuck a man in the ass. I want a girl; I want lots of girls. I want to follow that line down to all those warm and giving tits I miss so much these days, the thin thread of cleft leading down the summer dresses to all the places I don't get these days. But there is no going back to anything. [. . .]

## July 24, 1960

[. . .] Emerson, Thoreau, Melville, Hawthorne, Whitman, Dickinson. The "spiritual" or Hebraic period in American literature. The fires burned out a century ago in New England, but in an occasional Jew, they burn still. The same fires, the same closeness to God, the same turning back and forth of the loving, doubting man.

## July 31, 1960

End of the month, Sunday morning. Ann ill for two days from shots for our trip. Reading Dickinson for my piece. A mind like a sunburst in the splendor of its subtlety and suppleness. A mind working in *shafts*. Illustrates how fundamental is the gift for separation. Detecting the minute differences that make up our sense of the actuality of *one* object. We see things as themselves only by separating them from other things. Do we then see *them?* No—but we have extricated [them] from the dizz[y]ing sameness; we have liberated them from the blur.

This is the beauty of writing, of thinking. Every day my cup runs over. I have so many perceptions. They bombard me. I have only to wait for them. How with this gift, *my* gift, can one be unhappy? What fortune for me. What daily bliss! It suddenly came over me, lifting the fog of the usual self-pity. Great God, *Good* God, how can one be unhappy when I can think so well every day? What else is there in life one can so much look forward to? Where else this constant breadth of possibility—One has only to get up in the morning to face in the direction of hope.

Dear God, sweet Lord, never let me forget the *depth* in my daily experiences—the gratitude I owe you for this gift, *my* gift. WELCOME to the Hero as Thinker.

## August 26, 1960

Wrote away at the criticism lecture for Minnesota. Two phone calls, but no one on the wire when I went to answer. Egon Hostovský[55] called about his book [*The Plot*]. O mighty Kazin, the critic, whom all authors supplicate for a good word (while mighty Kazin shivers all day long in his boots). I mean, I don't want to bother you, have you received? On phone with Bob Bingham about future books. On phone with Tom Lowry about Dickinson and Freud proofs. Afternoon went to Israeli consul for scheduled meeting with Shimson Arad.[56] Whatever for? Niente. The[n] back, bought wine and soda for dinner with Dick Fisher. Uri [Ranaan, Israeli consul] and wife over for dinner. Good talk about Jews.[57] Fussed around in Garnett ['s] *Golden Echoes* for additional selection to prose anthology.[58] Read in Crossman's *A Nation Reborn*.

## August 28, 1960

Woman across the way is washing dishes wearing rubber gloves, but nothing above the waist. How intimately she gives herself to the sight of the scouring powder and brillo, but would run screaming if she knew I was watching. Blessed tits. Imagine walking about with this front on your body. [. . .]

## August 30, 1960

Tuesday morning. Continued smolder, pinch and burn. Late summer heat. Katie unwell from diphtheria shot. Michael is here.

Feel very "Jewish" these days. Eretz-Israel. One might indeed. For what is it I draw my basic values from if not from the Jews! And it is as a *Jew* that I *judge* societies. A forgotten passion. A burning necessity. [. . .]

55. Egon Hostovský (1908–1973), Czech writer and novelist, living in New York.
56. Tom Lowry, editorial assistant at the *Griffin*, an organ of the Readers Subscription, a highbrow book club founded by Lionel Trilling, Jacques Barzun, and W. H. Auden. Shimshon Arad and Uri Ranaan, representatives from the Israeli Consulate.
57. Kazin visited Israel in September at the invitation of the Israelis.
58. *The Open Form: Essays for Our Time*, ed. Alfred Kazin (New York: Harcourt Brace, 1961).

## September 9, 1960
### [Israel]

Israel is all sunlight and happy progress during the day, and at night for this Jew, bad dreams. Israel breaks up the barely-concealed synthesis with which one lives every day, and the violent new concentration [and] realignment of forces and ideas that Israel represents smashes on the existing arrangement; and the ghosts of father and mother begin to drift and to transform themselves. The mental home on the Citadel in Acre—the dark, young woman walking the grounds. The old prison and the new hospital. Male nurse in *yarmulke*. Judith [illegible]'s *private* life and her public (Israeli diplomat) world.

## October 30, 1960
### [New York]

[. . .] I *must* write something long and right about the new Bohemians, the fake Bohemians, the Village Voices and the self-pitiers. The separate peace boys, the new fashionable pessimists—these hedonists who fake philosophy. Yet my irritation with these "islands of separateness" (William Barrett) comes from my dislike of the increasing abstractness and hypotheticalness of so many attitudes toward life and death, the selfish and passive glorying in the absence of control.

Society is now so rich that it permits us to pretend that we are moralists—when we are merely its spoiled children. The very richness and complexity of the great organization permit the fiction of "the separate peace." [. . .]

## November 25, 1960

After the party is over. Parties and more parties—we gather only in parties, as it were, and the other day at Kristols, I had such a sense of all the ex-radicals in New York being able to talk to each other only in and as a party that the depression of it lasted with me all night. To see all these people at a party, so full of their present positions and their ex-grief at being in possession of so special a form of disillusionment, this is indeed a remarkable situation. . . . The peculiar self-pity of these people, the look of being victims of history, above all, the extraordinary spiritual unemployment of people who are born radicals and who find themselves constantly having to make excuses for the inexcusable—this is indeed a comic situation, comic only in the sense that it is so *unnatural*.

The literature of knowledge and the literature of power. Knowledge to De Quincey[59] meant "prose," scientific or intellectual knowledge as opposed to poetry as power. . . . Yet the use of power over nature by means of the knowledge acquired as literature, stands out as the great theme of literature since the Enlightenment.

## March 30, 1961

Ever since I wrote the little Eichmann piece on Saturday, I have been seized, I have been pregnant with the Jews.[60] The fascination of this subject, when I find myself in it again, is such that I feel as if I were big with the Jews, as if they occupied a space in me. For in some way the Jews, not consciously, have the secret of life and death attached to them. And the key to this, surely, is that they are older, the "eternal people," as we say. They share in a sense of the eternity that earth alone has. Not only their own continuity is unbroken, back to the beginnings, but their life as a people communicates the unspeakable age of the earth. And as believers—why, their belief is only in the age of the earth, in the remote deeps from which their God comes. It is not in a fairytale God who came down to earth as man, in the fairy tale [word crossed out]: it is in eternity itself, in the depth of that time we touch on but cannot know. Eternity is finally out of time. [. . .]

## April 8, 1961

[. . .] Saintly Elie—what a contrast with my torn and angry nature. Walks with God—a good man.[61] [. . .]

## April 17, 1961

Back from Washington after hectic jaunts with Ann and the two kids. I must say that whatever my own tensions and guilts and resentments about Michael, the boy is so good and so sweet that I feel more than ever ashamed to be anything but gratuitously loving and good to him.

59. Thomas de Quincey (1785–1859), English author, best known for *Confessions of an English Opium-Eater* (1821).
60. "Eichmann and the New Israelis," *Reporter* (April 23, 1961).
61. Kazin's glowing review of Elie Wiesel's autobiography *Night* in the *Reporter* (October, 1960) was one of the first to appear in a major publication. Over time he would grow disenchanted with Wiesel's public persona and "platform" manner. Eliezer Wiesel (1928–) is a Romanian-born Jewish American writer and Nobel Laureate best known for *Night*, in which he describes his childhood experiences in the Buchenwald and Auschwitz concentration camps.

We went to Arthur [Schlesinger]'s office after taking the tour of the White House.[62] Arthur as a type of the "positive personality" whose interests are always so *definite*. [. . .] Arthur in the seats of power is no[t] really different from Arthur in the seats at Harvard. What does all his intellectualizing apart from Washington—the writing of history, the lecturing about history—really come to but the question of how to get into power and what you do with it when you are there?

How easy it is to be taken in by these "positive" personalities. The worst of them for me, is emphatically not Arthur M. Schlesinger, Jr., but that sinister actor, Barzun. The actor, the con-man, the accent, the cuff links, the manner—the actor! the actor! everything about him just sickens me. I imagine him going out of the room and collapsing into something unrecognizable—behind the scenes. Ugh, how that man revolts me with his frigid smoothness, his showy phrases, his transparent cynicism. [. . .]

## April 20, 1961

[. . .] [After] reading in a collection of Catholic essays that I had borrowed from Ed,[63] I got more excited reading an account of Marx's theses on Feuerbach,[64] with their typical affirmation of man's radical discovery of his powers. It was Blake, it was Nietzsche, it was the whole dynamic side of the Enlightenment again, which, after Ed's typical namby-pamby recitation of his catachistical lessons, was a breeze of fresh air.

Marx on Feuerbach—wow! Blake's gates of the imagination opening up again!

## April 21, 1961

It takes nerve to be president, and once you are in, it takes more nerve to keep from being pushed into extreme positions. Kennedy, the intellectual in his speeches, showed all the signs of being a liberal like us. Now that the "revolt" in Cuba[65] has ended in a disgraceful loss for us as well as for the rebels, he is

62. Schlesinger was a special assistant to President Kennedy.
63. Edwin O'Connor (1918–1968), Pulitzer Prize–winning novelist and friend of Kazin's.
64. In his "Thesis on Feuerbach," which contains the famous statement that "the philosophers have only interpreted the world, the point is to change it," Marx argues that a valid materialist philosophy would have to recognize human activity as a force always in the process of shaping history. Therefore, why not shape it deliberately?
65. The failed Bay of Pigs invasion (April 15–16).

no longer the man in the middle (us) but the defender of the West in extremis, taking a "tough" line. Goldwater is pleased, David Lawrence is pleased, The [New York Daily] *News* and New York Daily *Mirror* are pleased.[66] I am full of doubt and wonder. As an intellectual *pur*, nothing but an intellectual, as it often seems to me, I find myself wondering more and more how long it is possible to remain in the middle. The pull of political gravity these days seems physical in its force. All of us liberals and intellectuals, so firmly in the middle, committed to "principle," like Kennedy, find ourselves being pushed and pulled.

## April 26, 1961

*Russia As Alibi.* After this Cuban fiasco, I am more sure than ever that there is nothing for *us* to accomplish by fighting the cold war anywhere. Only in America will we accomplish *anything* and only by creating our society in a positive and radical sense. *We* have no ideas just now to export, and Kennedy's major ideas which he calls "liberty" cannot even be exported by the C.I.A. to countries that have never known "liberty." It is our own society that we must *humanize*. Russia must no longer serve as an alibi for those who take refuge in Russian villainy from the tasks here. [. . .]

## April 30, 1961

The look of those abandoned children at the NY infirmary the other day when Katey was having her operation. How dare *we* be so superior to "health" when these kids and so many like them live this way every day. They too were made to be happy, to say *yes* to life.

## May 1, 1961

It's May Day, it's May Day, it's May Day—and last night we were at a soirée, a real soirée, honest, at the Frankfurters on Park Avenue.[67] O Lawd, all it needed was the Prof with his nose in the air, and he was there too, the Trilling. Mr. Frankfurter made conversation about Russia, and Mrs. Shaw, the press agent of the Museum of Modern Art, whom I would have liked to grab but not make

66. Senator Barry Goldwater (1909–1998) advocated an aggressive military posture against the Soviet Union and its allies. David Lawrence (1888–1973), newspaper publisher, editor, and conservative columnist.
67. Alfred (1906–1965) and Eleanor Frankfurter. Alfred was editor of *Art News*.

conversation with, talked about what Allen Dulles[68] told her in Paris; and there was a cute number, a Mrs. Luytens or something, and there was all these painters, even great ones like Hans Hofmann and Bill de Kooning, and Tom Hess with his fish-like look of deprecating the group before it deprecated him. So it got so dull they put on music, and everyone stood around as if waiting to hear where he was expected to go. Ah, nuts, ah soirée, ah poo-poo-nuts. Such cultural lah-de-dah and self-consciousness all over the place.

## May 2, 1961

Letter from Sidney Hook in this morning's *Times* explaining that the peace movement assists Communism. Mr. Hook is one of those people who long ago learned the art of sounding positive, about anything he thinks at the moment. The crusades change, the crusader never. Anyway, I am jealous at the moment, for I sure don't know what I think. I feel squeezed to nothingness by the number of alternatives I see to every question. Certainly only people who have been thoroughly formed in other, earlier systems of thought—Walter Lippmann[69] in American "liberalism," Hook in Marxism—ever seem to be positive these days about anything. [. . .] It is a mark of my submission to political "realism" that whenever there is evidence of the influence of intellectuals on government, of theories on government, I feel *surprise:* as if intellectuals are *supposed* to be powerless and unavailing. [. . .]

## May 8, 1961

Reading a little yesterday in Hannah's new book of essays, *Between Past and Future*, and struck above everything else by the feeling of spiritual liberation that she gives in these days when the real uniformity is not that everybody thinks alike but that we are more and more deprived of the means by which to think differently. It came over me the other day how much Marxism is the heir of 19th century capitalism and scientism; and by contrast, reading Hannah, one can see that if she marches to a different drummer from the rest of us, it is because she has not been, like everyone else, limited to the same cultural resources, the same formulae, the usual liberal or radical "consensus" of our time. Hannah's chief longing, I would guess from the passionate invocation of classical literature and philosophy, is to get unstuck from the modern age; it is for once to *see*

68. Allen Welsh Dulles (1893–1969), director of the Central Intelligence Agency from 1953 to 1961.
69. Walter Lippmann (1889–1974), American writer, reporter, and political commentator.

with different eyes from the rest of us. And this is why she is always tonic and bracing; she gives us relief from the weight of banality. This is what every true writer does.

The fact that she does this in the style of *Kulturgeschichte*, using names as tokens to play with for the highest stakes—this is something else. She is actually an essayist, not a philosopher; a defender of the prophets, in her spirit, not in her language, a prophet herself. She replenishes my imagination by listening to a voice from afar. When I read her, I remember, for a brief instance, a world, another world, to which we owe all our concepts of human grandeur. Since we are all mortal, only immortality can measure us. Without God, we do not know who *we* are. This is what she recalls to me, and for this I am grateful.

## May 30, 1961, Decoration Day

This old-fashioned house. Studios. Man downstairs playing Bach. Only on the bottom, on greasy, broken down 14th Street are people at home on Memorial Day playing Bach.[70] Like something out of Willa Cather's *Stories of Washington Square*.

Reading Fuchs for *Griffin*.[71] The sour, hysterical, clownish, screeching thirties. What a *period* to identify with—if to identify with any period were not idiocy enough!—I see myself walking out of that period, fighting that period with my God-given words, my God-given eyes, *my* sense and vision of things.

## June 17, 1961

Benda's old word, *clerc*—the intellectual is the carrier of value.[72] This was the whole point of the career of someone like Emerson, for whom the old Protestant priestly function remained the same when he became a man of letters. But the point of modern intellectuals is that their vocations *are* different. Emerson may have thought that all curiosity is a form of religion or poetry, but the specialized curiosity of the sociologist working with a set of given propositions entirely in a mechanized technique, makes the idea of him as "*clerc*" a bit ridiculous. Specialization has become a routine that replaces the old free curiosity. In this

70. Kazin rented a "studio" on 14th Street, where he could work and meet girlfriends.
71. Daniel Fuchs (1909–1993) was a novelist and screenwriter. The *Griffin* was a magazine for the high-brow Reader's Subscription Service for which Kazin wrote occasional reviews.
72. Julien Benda, *La Trahison des Clercs* (1925).

sense the romantic was right to resist modern science for what it *does* rather than for what it believes, for he had the intuition that what it does would become all important and replace what it believed. Emerson as free seeker had been right to hold on to the sermon-essay, the general reflection, as a carrier of free, seeking. By contrast, probably nobody in administration today can even begin to see the "long view," much less the philosophic view. Hence, with someone like Kennedy, the special value given by journalists to his adaptability to the infinite number of details connected with the job.

## July 8, 1961

As a critic I am certainly not partisan. Anything with the touch of real transcendence in it wins my heart; any kind of authentic intellectual nobility and disinterestedness immediately makes me cheer—I cheer for Emerson the Christian, and Adolph Joffe, the idealistic Russian Jewish communist, for Gandhi and for Hannah Arendt, for Elie [Wiesel] and for Mauriac.[73] Maybe it is the Jew in me, finally, who wants only the good and the God-like and the true, no matter whether it is my *position* or not. As a critic I don't even have *positions*—that is for philosophers.[. . .]

## July 14, 1961
## [Wellfleet]

After drinks with the Hofstadters after a day of conciliating and loving, and immediately I am in a tizzy. Feeling lost and jealous of the Hofs and their money. The Kennedy piece obviously makes me feel that I may have incurred troubles![74] But my only peace is in being as independent as possible, in not letting myself feel odd in the company of prosperous professors.—I must pursue my own intuitions to the end, be calm and dignified about what I *myself believe*.

## July 16, 1961

Dear Marian [Schlesinger].[75] It was good talking to you at dinner last night. I was touched by your friendliness and by wearing my glasses (this sort of made us kinfolk

73. François Mauriac (1885–1970), Nobel Prize–winning French writer and ardent Roman Catholic, who persuaded Wiesel to publish *Night*, for which he wrote a Foreword.

74. "The President and Other Intellectuals," *American Scholar* (Autumn 1961): 498–516. Published after Kazin's private lunch with Kennedy on August 1, the piece argues that Kennedy was a "would-be intellectual" who used intellectuals to give his administration the "latest style."

75. Kazin is following Bellow's epistolary mode in published portions of *Herzog*, writing unsent letters to acquaintances and others.

in the generations, very different from the old papa bear that my whiz-kid wife always gives me). But most of all I was touched by your worldliness. You remembered that evening at our Boston house, when I was so full of Albert Schweitzer and nobility and all that (really as a way of getting back at too successful Arthur), and said I was a "dope" that evening. Yup—I was a dope that evening, just as I was a dope this morning when I awoke very early, full of sick, nauseous despair, and said to myself, in my usual style, where's the rock bottom self to hold on to? Where is the firm foundation in myself, etc.? In myself, as my dear friend Hannah Arendt says in her *Between Past and Future*, there really isn't anything *real* in that so private self. And as my dear friend Saul Bellow says in his brilliant *Herzog*, "Intelligent people without influence have a certain contempt for themselves."

I've always looked for the firm foundation, and now look at me, absolutely sick every time my wife disappears from my loving gaze in her well-known now you see it, now you don't.

Ah me, that firm foundation, when it takes two to make one! So thanks for your company last night. Thanks for reminding me. I was thinking of committing suicide this morning. I often think of committing suicide. But that too, alas, might be a way of saying to my wife, fuck you dearie for letting me down.

Oh Marian, Marian, there is a world, a great big world, a world? There is?
[. . .]

## July 17, 1961

[. . .] Dear Dr. Freud—You once wrote (seemingly in passing and in a tone of curiosity) about man's tendency toward a certain "overvaluation" of women. Now, maybe I'm wrong, and maybe this sense of depression, which sometimes feels like death in the heart, is due to other things than my temporary misery just now with Ann. But shall I confess that most of my life I have looked for my happiness to some woman or other? that when I feel this low, I attribute it to my relationship with Ann? that women have in fact always seemed to hold me in thrall; that in women I look for my happiness and to women I attribute my unhappiness? Talk about over-evaluation of women! I honestly feel on days like this that I can't *see* anyone but Ann. Yet so mad must I be at her in my stifled and anxious and grudging heart that I wait for her smile; I look to her to say that everything is all right. Everything is all right, Alfred. The world's o.k. I'm not angry with you anymore. Everything's all right, Alfred, all right.

Yes, Mama, I'm 46 yrs old, and you've been unbelievably in the grave for almost two years, but I certainly over-valued you in life, and the shadow of your power is still on me. Look at me, I'm so unhappy I could die, I'm so unhappy with all my bottled-up rage, with my need to get power still against you, o easy-to-over-value Mama.

At least when I write like this, and not in some pompously analytic style like the rest of this fucking notebook, I can say that I feel pain. I feel pain! I'm in pain! Half of the time I want to throw myself in the water and end it all because of your power over me, your fucking power, your unhappy power. That's the worst of it for me, I guess you found your power in and through your unhappiness. That metal javelin of your unhappiness is still in my side. And with everything to look for—for I *know* that I can trust my thought, that my thought is sound—I suffer agonizingly still when my wife's light is removed from me. Just as I asked you to make peace when I saw how good I was—appease you, bury the hatchet.

No, too late for that now. Unhappy mother who left your unhappiness like a curse on your gifted son. Look at me, now, afraid to assert myself, bending and breaking each way for a smile from Ann. Too late now to change. All I can do is to know and to be patient and not to let today's agony be—"overvalued." This too will pass, this too will pass. The other days smile at me. Today my unhappiness grips me in the throat like nausea. I'm sick with it. But I must see all around and see ahead. I forgive you, wretched old mama, mean with unhappiness, goodbye.

## August 1, 1961

Kennedy—In America success is in personal terms, and ultimately becomes unsatisfying; in totalitarian countries, the individual success is swallowed up in the group—[76] [. . .]

Malraux and two sons. Jackie. "He ignored me," and now "of course" Malraux is Jackie's favorite writer—

John Birch society—come out whenever we are in power— [. . .]

Allan Nevins[77]—Arthur, maybe we'll help your reputation while you are here—"wish I could take a course with him"

76. Earlier in the day Kazin had lunch with President Kennedy and Arthur Schlesinger Jr. at the White House. This and the following are notes Kazin made after the lunch.
77. Allan Nevins, prolific American historian, professor of history at Columbia. See Chapter 4, note 24.

Khrushchev—Polish election laws freer than in your own country—

Veiled hints on Cuba—generals give you information only 20% correct—

Tired green eyes—monograph on shirt—

Scott Fitzgerald and Sheila Graham[78]—I read it, bet you guys didn't—

Gives things that extra-little nudge: Garrison[79] good at those phrases—

Byron's mirror—and the outlets for the Eisenhower t.v.!

## September 12, 1961

[. . .] *Contemporaries:*[80] an argument against the alone generation, against lostness as a cause, for a transcendent sense of the public realism. A look backward to the days when lit. had a more *directly* prophetic function. A cry out of another consciousness than that which prevails. [. . .]

## September 19, 1961

[. . .] Read Introduction to [Edmund Wilson's] *Patriotic Gore* and was properly shocked. The small town American atheist and crank, it's all animalism etc. I don't agree, but honestly it does one good to see E.W. going at things exactly in his own way. *This* is why he can rewrite all his pieces, and polish his lenses. It has to be put down just the way he sees it. What a pleasure in hitting the bull's eye. Even in this little letter to Bob Giroux[81] yesterday on Bernie [Malamud]'s new book, I had this pleasure of seeing my own language quiver to the mark. Getting it down just to the shape you see it in. Elsewhere, language comes these days [in] readymade packages, already frozen, just heat and serve up. I love Wilson for saying it wholly in his way. What bliss!

78. Sheila Graham (1904–1988), syndicated Hollywood gossip columnist, companion of the writer F. Scott Fitzgerald (1896–1940) when his wife, Zelda, was in a mental institution.
79. Garrison reference unclear, may refer to William Lloyd Garrison (1805–1879), who published the *Liberator*, an antislavery newspaper, from 1831 to 1865.
80. Kazin's selection of essays, *Contemporaries*, would be published in April 1962.
81. Robert Giroux (1914–2008), influential editor at Harcourt Brace, later publisher at firm of Farrar, Straus and Giroux.

And even greater bliss for me in answering him.[82] The word right zing to the mark. Getting it down right. [. . .]

## October 2, 1961

Jack Ludwig[83] over to speak of possibility of joining the new State University of NY. Talk of 20, even 25 thousand. Today, an advance against royalty on a new collection of essays on Salinger,[84] with my piece to be the star. Every day, it seems to me, something new, something richer, not just in money but in quality of the opportunity it opens up. The booming society, with even a critic booming along with it. The big welcome now—and a depression generation, formerly the depressed generation.

## October 3, 1961

Whenever I sit down to my desk at the New School class, I feel like a lion in the zoo tempted to act up for the curious open-mouthed class outside. Whether it was fatigue on my part or the bad air in the room (as usual), I have the sense of not being in touch with the class—i.e., of their merely *watching* me, of their being a kind of dead weight. And so I am tempted to amuse them. I feel that I am too much a "personality" in their eyes and don't function enough as a thinking teacher.

Just as Barzun always makes me think of the fatal French vanity and public "style," so Ascoli[85] reminds me of the fatal Italian smallness and corruption. Sat with him in his elegant office yesterday to arrange a new contract: he tried to go get me to attack Kristol and *Commentary*—he lied about this and about that. What pettiness. . . . And this is the man whose "position" I so often agree with! I think I agree with.

Reading Hook in this new October *Commentary*. Always proving his point at the expense of others—always winning the little victory—always the provincial little Jewish boy putting his foot on the conquered antagonist. I'd like to write suggesting that he give up, for the good of his "party."

82. Kazin reviewed *Patriotic Gore* in "Our American Plutarch," *Reporter* (May 24, 1962): 43–46, criticizing Wilson for equating human with animal motives.
83. Jack Ludwig, chairman of the SUNY–Stony Brook English Department.
84. *J. D. Salinger: "Everybody's Favorite"* (New York: Atlantic Monthly Press, 1961). J. D. Salinger (1919–2010), reclusive novelist and short story writer.
85. Max Ascoli (1898–1978), publisher of the *Reporter*.

Hook talks constantly of Western values, but doesn't discuss them, doesn't understand or illuminate them, doesn't help them grow—as does Hannah. Acts as a realpolitiker, not as a philosopher—

So I feel about myself last night, as I feel always about Hook, the special Jewish strain of competitiveness, the excessive consciousness of *someone* to beat or to impress, rather than the deep inner solitude of truth. The enormous competitiveness of us all! Making our way so hard!—No wonder that Hook's *manner* is so ugly to me.

Yet our very eagerness and force and strength are what give us special vividness on the American scene. To say nothing of the deep intellectual Puritanism that made it possible for Hook (exactly as I do) to sound like a prophet reproving the backsliders and pagans.

My whole day ruined by this disgusting, outrageous letter of Hyman Levy[86] in the *New Statesman* defending the Soviet Test! Ridiculous, this swift access on my part to political outrage. They *all* outrage me; the sanctimonious Hook and the idiotically smug Stalinists, and the crooked Nixon. It's as if there were just a few voices who ever speak for me and for my values. And all the rest are so quick to defend murder and murderers. Even pure value, as in the case of poor Camus,[87] seems to count for so little! But value perhaps *can't* be looked for anymore in this racket among these racketeers! I can't allow myself every day to be so nauseated and frightened. I must do *my* work, not just react in outrage to *theirs*.

## October 9, 1961

The class-obsessed English take out their resentment of America by being "socialized"—the lower class Americans take out their envy of English *style* by pretending to be moral.

Obituaries by Lionel Trilling: The last time I saw Mallarmé[88] I was very, very angry with Mallarmé.

86. Hyman Levy (1889–1975), Scottish mathematician, member of the Communist Party until expelled for his criticism of the Soviet Union's treatment of Jews.
87. Albert Camus (1913–1960), Algerian French novelist, philosopher, and journalist, winner of the Nobel Prize for literature in 1957, best known for his novel *The Stranger*.
88. Stéphane Mallarmé (1842–1898), French symbolist poet and critic.

## October 23, 1961

New week, brisk winds. Long, almost winter sleep last night, full of delicious thoughts of fucking married women, women with the sheen of marriage on them, "respectable" women, women already made. Glowing in the darkness, earrings softly pulsing from their ears, their asses professionally comfortable on the pillow and their legs straight back, they get it deep down. All those "failures" with married women, Arabelle, Joan, even Rosalind, suddenly fall away from me now as I remember Lou, who was still married, the most married woman of all. The deliciousness of the married woman, taking literally what belongs, or had belonged to someone else! A dream of *taking* the mother—so keenly wanted, so long, that it shocked? But in the case of R, there was that old too much wanting on her side? Anyway, the memory of Lou, and the sweet, deep dreams, last night, when I felt for once that I was getting into the hidden places, makes it all seem strong and unafraid today.

Trilling, the prime example that "more writers fail from lack of character than from lack of intelligence." The bourgeois rut of the incisive mind. One could write such a *Death in Venice* about *his* fall—the fall of the Freudian intellectual kept the revolt all in his mind. Trilling in the *New Republic* part, Book II? The older man in the village.[89] [. . .]

## October 27, 1961

In the kingdom of the Communist intellectuals, once you have made it, you are naked or "innocent," as Bertrand Russell says—you are sheltered from life by "positions." You may have the "wrong" position or the "right" position, but you always have a position. You are never in doubt as to the "meaning structure" of things. Nature has been replaced by ideology, and where other men see death, you see the physical destruction of the representative of a position.

## October 28, 1961

Saul's [Bellow] beautiful, or at least his *ringing* voices. The voice of the writer is also *his style*—voices—of poets, of course, but also of novelists.

89. Kazin included a very critical portrait of Trilling in *New York Jew*.

## October 30, 1961

Just as I have always been secretly fascinated by the sadist (and the masochist) in me represented by the Nazis, so I can see now that all this irritable hatred of the Communists on my part represents now the Marxist swashbuckler and magisterial mind in me represented by the Communist.

For obviously, this close attention, this constant fascination, this irritable hatred, represents attachment to some secret faculty, some ambition that has had to be foregone. And it is exactly this secret attachment, so to speak, this inner resemblance, that has to be uncovered and made clear in the autobiography of intellectuals. The starting point generally is those who always see life in the character of intellectuals, from the safe-cover of a "position." In Marx's thesis on Feuerbach, it is self-consciousness with which the intellectual begins; and it can be said, I think, that this "self-consciousness" has always been a destiny-consciousness. In some way to discover what one possesses in one's brain is to discover the hidden power to others.

But more than this, the "intellectuals" theme explains the supremacy of ideology of experience and the possibility of the Establishment. Someone like Isaiah Berlin, who has never faced a worker in his life.

## November 16, 1961

[. . .] Evening—writing—the bliss of writing. How lucky I am to be able to write, to be able to write this quickly. To be able to tune in whenever and wherever.

## December 9, 1961

Cambridge. My style consists in the *flow*, the pouring river of all my associations—the utter *giving out*—the flow, the flow, finding in the rhythm the connection of all the buried associations. So that *everything* is a kind of working out of the buried material. Everything for me is a kind of outpouring of this *material.*

## December 17, 1961

Elie—on "open mind"—I had a thirst—I waited for a general sense of outrage.

He forgot why Freud succeeded Marx as the Jewish saint.

[Harry] Levin and Trilling. The simple secret of it all—social ambition and shame of the "lower-class" or too intense Jew.

## January 13, 1962

Saturday morning—they interrupt the television programs to announce the death of the comedian Ernie Kovacs.[90]

How badly we are brought up, we children of Old World parents—how little dignity, how little ease, how few manners. Everything is an excuse for outrage and bitterness. . . . I can see it in myself all day long . . . everything slightly out of the way upsets me. . . . I'm forever trying to make things conform to the expected pattern of success. . . . I must say that here, with Ann in such misery half the time, I *do* get horribly intolerant of her sufferings and failures. I want life to slide in with perfect efficiency and happiness *all* the time,—and if anything goes wrong, if Ann is plagued and despondent, as God knows, she often has reason to be, my instinctive feeling is one of irritation with her for upsetting the apple cart. [. . .]

The English magazine, a purely *social* intelligence. Guessing what the other fellow is likely to think, and surprising him.

Social intelligence: society has *such* standards! All over the place—like telling time from Greenwich.

Social intelligence: just the opposite of our aggressive, self-pitying existentialist intelligence, which really says, *what* is there but me? And what is to be believed in?

The American way of surprising—to emit a false universal. The English way, to startle by a display of social impudence. [. . .]

## January 31, 1962

[. . .] This notebook, my spiritual exercises. Trying to get to the root of everything . . . so that I can be right, even as my father in heaven is right. [. . .]

## February 16, 1962

Walked down to 72nd St. subway this morning. On the little curve of sidewalk just in front of the subway entrance, a miserable looking young Negro woman

90. Ernie Kovacs (1919–1962), popular television comedian noted for his on-air experimental manner and style.

with that look of stupefaction that you so often see on Negroes, who are probably looking for a job. A man pushed her aside to get into the subway, and she looked more miserable. The city is full of these miserable faces, miserable people. [. . .]

There's no getting away from just how proscribed, painful, unmentionable, the subject [of the Spanish Civil War] is just now. And that's why, maybe, I feel fear and trembling about entering on it again. The road is laid out for me, and I *cannot* shirk it. I must go through the 30s as I went through Brownsville. But it is exactly because the truth is *not* simple that I must work it out in its own terms.[91]

## February 19, 1962

Real wintry weather, freezing rain, sleet, slush. Like the feeling of politics in our age, when everything has been politicalized. The storm of events.

Yesterday, program on WBAI commemorating Isaac [Rosenfeld].

The thing to catch about [Paul] Goodman in II is the radical as *nag*.[92] The old radical conscience turned into doctrinaire nag—everything less than utopian or extremist is a compromise with the status quo.

Someone said on the program about Isaac that he was pure intelligence trying to turn himself into pure instinct. And the hint that he died of this attempt is certainly justified. Isaac, quite apart from his wonderful unworldliness, was certainly a man who died of the intellectual passion to become unintellectual. He turned himself inside out, looking for his "spectre." "I was amused," says pundit, Goodman, about the milk-and-meat story.[93] But Isaac was not doing this for old megalomaniac Goodman—he was trying to find his shadow, his spectre, the sensuous old man . . . and it was a hopeless quest.

The main thing that came to me yesterday, listening to Saul and the others on Isaac, is how rarely this typical intellectual-Jewish experience ever gets into print. I found myself straining to get the door open, to let it all in.

91. In *Starting Out in the Thirties*, Kazin describes the historical conditions that turned the Spanish Civil War into a "sacred" cause among thirties radicals. He would later describe the war as "the wound that will not heal." See October 25, 1986, entry.

92. "II" refers to a section of Kazin's autobiography covering the 1940s originally intended for *Starting Out in the Thirties* but later included in *New York Jew*.

93. A reference to Isaac Rosenfeld's 1949 *Commentary* essay, "Adam and Eve on Delancey Street," in which he made an off-color joke about a penis that did not sit well with the magazine's sponsors on the American Jewish Committee.

*Starting out*—driving ambition—the desire to see everything, to know everything, to gain access to everything! But in the beginning we seek to rise on other people's terms, to fit the categories that *they* hold out to you. With growth we seek to win on our own terms. But always the victory is in sight, the true flag to win.

Saul and Isaac—the writer and his creature. The success and the failure. Isaac at the abyss, never so honored in his life as in Saul's golden obituaries.[94]

## February 26, 1962

That note on the English woman reading in the teashop while eating. I was faintly shocked at myself at that detail being so disposable and movable. But what it pointed to, of course, was *perspective*, the self different from the subject. So the details are movable and disposable. . . . That is the sense I must have on the thirties book—that the process of growth it describes, the chapters of the journey, are disposable and movable and changeable—fiction under the form of autobiography— [. . .]

## February 27, 1962

This business of the autobiography haunting me night and day. Thinking of Josie in her coop, struggling to show that she was part of a great movement once. Whereas so much of mine seems to be concerned with the descent into hell, with the indemnification of old sins. . . . Mrs. Flint[95] up at the *Atlantic* was right when she said that they were not the *bitter* thirties, not in my mss anyway. Josie's example is, whatever the reason, the right one.

My reason for being positive and golden about it all is that one takes up the struggle for value in one's *own* way—no political myth can ever be *my* carrier of value all the way. The reason I get so much [out] of criticism is that it does get to work every idiosyncratic, odd corner and lobe of my brain. And the autobiography must be a journey into wholly individual thinking, into all the old corners and lobes of *my* mind. A spiritual autobiography, a spiritual journey, in the truest sense. [. . .]

94. See Saul Bellow's "Zetland" in *Him with His Foot in His Mouth and Other Stories* (New York: Harper and Row, 1984).
95. Emily Flint, managing editor of the *Atlantic Monthly*.

## March 20, 1962

Elie over last night. We had dinner, and then he accompanied me to my lecture at the New School. Finally, he *is* "Hungarian"—i.e., on an ice-floe in the middle of Europe . . . or a great, deep forest. I somehow sense that he lies because he does not believe that anybody or anything has to be reported to.[96] On an island in the midst of Europe, the island of Jewishness, where one consults only one's own fancies and hopes and ideas. A mixture of dread and contempt. [. . .]

## April 5, 1962

FOR GOUCHER[97] A plea for scholarship. If we connect all the past to ourselves and work with "the past in our bones," if we can forever show that everything is tied in with everything else, then we will never even notice what lies outside our scheme. . . . I am more and more desirous of the unassimilated and unassimilable past, of the past that lies not in our hearts but just below the threshold of our consciousness. The tendency to world culture on one hand, and the increasing assimilation of the past into the total self-exposure of the present, makes for a smooth and dangerously unopposed "image" of the past rather than fresh interest in it.

The French disease of pride—to possess the truth in logic, a woman in sex—always to be in fine control.

My book certainly asks a question about the possible end of the "modern" period that I cannot give a happy answer to. But what have we Jews got for our tradition, and our emancipation, *but* this modern tradition—and of boundless hope for man? What inquisition, what middle ages, are *we* to return to? *Our only* real past can only be the age of revolution, our great beginnings. Every dark doctrine of original sin to which *they* want to return is our prison house. [. . .]

## April 13, 1962

[. . .] Tea with Hannah and Heinrich—my forbidden pleasures![98]

96. Kazin would become increasingly doubtful of Wiesel's reliability. See Chapter 9, note 48.
97. Goucher College, private liberal arts college in Baltimore, Maryland.
98. Ann Birstein disliked Hannah Arendt intensely, largely because of Arendt's dismissive attitude toward her. At a National Institute ceremony (May 1954) where Arendt was to receive an award, she met Alfred and Ann at the door, invited him to sit with her in the front row, and told Ann to sit in the balcony. Subsequently Ann refused to meet Arendt and insisted on the same from Alfred.

## April 30, 1962

*Whistle Down the Wind*—Those children dancing round and round the hill after seeing "Jesus." Oh God, to be faithful to that. What joy. What joy. What blessing.

The growing consensus: History is only sin and error. History stinks. Only the Communists, it seems, now believe in history. As only the Catholics believe in "religion." The independents are left with the ashes. The "liberals" are left only with their liberalism.

Can't the free still have a belief? Is belief the issue only of dogma and slavery? This is the heart of the question.

Positive memory, not "nostalgia"—when we locate in a particular period, the values that are our particular concern.

This seems to be Beethoven day. Positive strokes. The world-shaking stroke. [. . .]

## May 18, 1962

Am struck in the book [*Starting Out in the Thirties*] by how much of a "Communist" in the religious sense I still am—I want a philosophy that will reach into *everything*. The religious value of "socialism" and the sacramental value of the poor is indeed the background of the struggle for individual authenticity described in the book. This is why this must be carried over *to* England, to the great day of Labor victory. The struggle *is*—not to give an absolute value to "history" itself, not to confuse the transcendent value that properly belongs only to transcendent factors, to *history*, or to any particular item in history. The real background of the struggle is the *urge* that made all those Cowleys and [Granville] Hickses and Obed Brookses and [Robert Gorham] Davises interesting in the *Thirties*.[99] So the period was dramatic and clear-cut in a way that only religious ages are, moments when masses expect a great renewal of life, when life really seems about to take a new direction.

Today history no longer makes sense. My fight is to show that it does, that the *continuities* of history are real. The fight *in* the book is to show that certain values (of which Socialism was the expression) are real. I no longer believe

99. Malcolm Cowley (1898–1989), literary critic, journalist, and literary editor of the *New Republic* in the 1930s; Granville Hicks (1901–1982), literary critic, journalist, editor of the Communist *New Masses* in the 1930s. In one of the harshest portraits in *On Native Ground*, Kazin calls Hicks "painfully limited" and "a little Calvin of the left" (421). Obed Brooks was the 1930s pen name of Robert Gorham Davis (1908–1998), critic and journalist, member of Communist Party in the 1930s. Davis, who taught at Smith College and Columbia University, took his pen name from an ancestor who founded Brooks Academy in Harwich, Massachusetts.

in Socialism, but I certainly believe in these values. History should never be identified with any one *creed*.

Reading the *New Statesmen*—poems by Robert Graves, who always invokes the muse but never gets her. Have yet to be moved by a poem. Frank Kermode—the university machine for critical insights. Everything is connected into critical aperçus.[100]

## May 25, 1962

[. . .] A little more self-discipline with people—a little more formality. It is not necessary to talk about everyone with everyone—or to say exactly what one thinks of everything. How malicious I can be! My God how I've lost my innocence—my terribly nice opinion of myself.

## May 31, 1962

The more I think of the professionalization and specialization that has driven the "poet" into a corner—that has made the writer ever less of a poet [at] all—the more I realize the aptness of Emerson's myth of the first man as the complete man, the ur-Poet, of Blake's myth of the Adamic man. Each specialization is a lopping off of the power to face the universe directly—each specialization is a progress, away from ourselves. No wonder that the "common man" today is the man who is satisfied with this specialization, with *his* specialization—the man who doesn't know any better, the man who doesn't have a "primal vision" to go back to.

No wonder that the writer constantly has this sense of a harkening back, not merely to his "primal vision," to himself as all vision, but to the connection between himself and mystery, as opposed to the modern connection between the infinitely subdividable subject as material.

In short, and oddly enough, man confronting himself as the source of vision has a sense of himself as spirit. The farther man travels from this original source of knowledge, the more materialized his view becomes. When he turns back, it is himself he can no long recognize.

100. Robert Graves (1895–1985), English poet, translator, and novelist, best known for his study of creative inspiration, *The White Goddess* (1948), hence Kazin's reference to invoking the muse; Frank Kermode (1919–2010), prominent literary scholar and critic, taught at Cambridge, University College London, Columbia, and Harvard, best known for his study *The Sense of an Ending* (1967). Despite his dismissive entry, Kazin admired Kermode and would later become a friend.

## June 1, 1962

Mark Cunliffe[101] on New York Jewish intellectuals, apropos of Goodman—they have the subtlest understanding of everyone, but each feels that he himself is misunderstood. Brilliant, positively brilliant. We are tied together by ties of "intellect" alone, as last night at Saul's with Lionel Abel.[102] Each one chopping away. But each dreads and distrusts himself, and tries to reach others only by intellect. This is the situation behind so much in the book—

## June 8, 1962

The poor Jew always feels his rise in the world as a romance and wants to tell his story to *everybody*. Look! Share my joy!—What a rise! The rise of David Levinsky,[103] the rise of Alfred Kazin, etc. . . .

Michael over last night, looking very slim and handsome. But both my children are so powerful, strong, hungry, lusty, direct, sensible and normal. [. . .]

## June 12, 1962

The more I think over Kennedy's speech and the call for a "technical and sophisticated" approach to economic problems, the more I realize that the animus behind the *thirties* book is the "free," moral approach, the revolutionary-ideological approach, of the time when society had *yet* hardened—when these problems had not yet become technical—when the single individual could still feel himself be equal to his "prophetic" and above all *critical* intelligence. [. . .]

## June 17, 1962

Mailer is really out of control in that [*Esquire*] piece on Jackie K.[104] Fucking it up, as we say. The piece has to be such a performance that if he feels he's not knocking them dead in the aisles, he presses down harder.

Exquisite
O see and hear the latest news—O come, see, and hear, intellectuals—

101. Marcus Cunliffe (1922–1990), British educator and historian, professor of American studies at the University of Sussex.
102. Lionel Abel (1910–2001), prize-winning playwright, essayist, and critic.
103. Refers to Abraham Cahan's 1917 novel *The Rise of David Levinsky*.
104. "An Evening with Jackie Kennedy, or the Wild Witch of the East," *Esquire* (July, 1962).

America, the land of wounded egoism. America, the land of limitless cultural self-criticism. America, where intellectuals know they are making and having an effect by watching the audience carefully as they slap its face. It is this *measured* and deliberate "outrageousness" that is so awful about Mailer in this *Esquire* piece and about Mary McCarthyism in general. [. . .]

## June 19, 1962

The important thing to stress about Isaac (and Saul) is that they were *naked*, lovably human, without ideology.[105] They were trying to make a stand on existence alone. Saul in Fulton Street talking about Lawrence and "nothing between me and the sky." The Rosenfeld circle—Dave Bazelon—the Posters—the musician and the Tarcov girl—Calder Willingham—the wall of pictures in the kitchen—The key book of this period—Dostoevsky's *Notes from the Underground.* But the sense of "openness," the thought of Isaac sailing in about Emerson. Isaac and Roger Caillois in the *Commonweal* (June 25, 1943)—marriage.
Isaac—Vassiliki—Ester—Arthur.
*Marriage*—the sense of always trying for a "new road."
Arabel—John Porter: Manny Farber
Saul—Anita. Dick—Felice
Midge Farber and Doctor Farber
Isaac's Feigenbaum—bared, pared, essential men.[106]

105. Kazin is describing people in this and the following June 20 entry whom he intended to include in *Starting Out in the Thirties* but some of whom would appear only later in *New York Jew.*

106. David Bazelon (1909–1993), writer and social critic, taught political science and English at the State University of New York at Buffalo; William and Herbert Poster were natives of Brownsville but, unlike the Kazins, were relatively well off. William Poster's essay, " 'Twas a Dark Night in Brownsville," *Commentary* (May 1950): 458–467, describes the importance of belonging to a gang in Brownsville; Kazin never belonged. "The Tarcov girl" is Edith Tarcov, whose husband, Oscar, was a friend of Bellow and Rosenfeld. Calder Willingham (1922–1995) was a novelist and screenwriter. Roger Cailloise (1913–1978), French intellectual and member of the French Academy, wrote on literature, philosophy, and sociology, edited anti-Nazi periodicals during the war, and worked against the spread of Nazi propaganda in South America. Vassiliki Sarantakis Rosenfeld, Isaac Rosenfeld's wife, helped support the family as a secretary at the *New Republic.* "Arthur" is Arthur Mallet, an officer in the English navy, stationed in New York. Arabel J. Porter would become executive editor of the literary magazine *New World Writing* (1952–1959). Manny Farber (1917–2008) was a painter and film critic. Dick and Felice are Richard Hofstadter and his first wife, Felice Swados. Anita Bellow is Bellow's first wife. Marjorie (Midge) Farber, who was carrying on an affair with Saul Bellow, had recently separated from Dr. Leslie Farber, a psychoanalyst (whom Kazin would consult in the 1970s about his own collapsing marriage). Feigenbaum, described as one of the "bared, pared, essential men," is the protagonist in Rosenfeld's short story "The Hand That Fed Me."

—Yet with all this anarchism, openness and utopianism, it is important to remember the competitive literary personalities.

How *formal* Isaac's style seems now—evidence not so much of a vanished age as of his own uncertainty choosing the "middle" term.—But the formality comes from a lack of *urgency*. Isaac was essentially negligent and absent-minded about his work—he used it as a way of clarifying and communicating his "life problems," his search for salvation. He used his work to clarify and to advance his own experience, where Saul has always used his life, in the grand manner, to advance his *work*.—The typical Jewish concern with one's self as a "problem," as a battleground. Trilling emphasized the *career*—Isaac his "soul"—but in each case the concern was personal; *art* itself became secondary. Exactly the danger—the boredom—that I feel about myself these days—the whole concern with the self, the career, the problem. Isaac became his own problem.

Isaac's great myth was "*naturalness*"—he wanted to look natural even more than he wanted to *be* natural. His surroundings had to be suitably "natural" looking, the constant Jewish effort of will to be natural.

## June 20, 1962

Now take a Jew like [Harold] Laski. The letters to [Oliver Wendell] Holmes [Jr.] really make me sick. They are so eager. How he plays up to the Justice. How eager to be his "lad," his son! That voice, as I remember from the Teacher's Union meeting of long ago, went on by itself—the suppliant flow. In Part III, the contrast with Eliot, the parfait *Englishman*, the actor, perfectly at home in his surroundings.

Finally in England to think of death—the separation from Asya that was already a death, and now and all those deaths in the Piccadilly Theater. [. . .][107]

But all those Jewish deaths frightened the spectators of their death in the movie. The Jewish fate was too brutal, too visible; it represented too obvious a foreshortening, of the usual cycle of life and death. It was not indifference *to* the fate of the Jews that I saw that afternoon in the darkness of the theatre—it was fear and embarrassment. The Jewish fate made one's own condition seem suddenly too obvious—it made the whole humanist effort too obvious a delusion. The Jews *scared* the spectators, and inevitably, when such things can be done to so many people, there is the fleeting thought that the people must

107. See note 38.

have justified such "punishment." The idea that the Nazis wanted the world simply to be "Judenrein," that they wanted simply to get rid of the Jews as a piece of *dirt*—This is what we still can't take in.

## August 6, 1962

La plage des intellectuels. To Wellfleet Beach they came, they came; upon Wellfleet beach they sat—the academic intellectuals, the literary intellectuals. And among the rare Wilsons, there were Stuart Hughes and Harold W. Solomon, Lewis Coser and Arthur Berger, Henry Graff and Alex Inkeles and Bernard Malamud and Hassan Asbekan and Mischa Stille and Jason Epstein and John P. Marquand, Jr., and Daniel Aaron and Mary Grand and Dwight W. Webb and Lee Halprin. There were Joan Sinkler and Arthur Trottenberg and William Ward and Jacqueline Miller and James LeShay and Philip and Maggie Roth—not to forget Bill Goodman and Bede Hofstadter and James Newman . . . and Arthur Schlesinger, Jr., and Richard Goodwin.[108]

Upon the beach they sat, discoursing, and loud was the sound of battle, louder than the waves. . . .

108. "The rare Wilsons" were Elena and Edmund Wilson, who preferred to spend summers in his family home in Talcottville, New York, well away from "la plage." Henry Stuart Hughes was a professor of history at Harvard and prominent activist for nuclear disarmament. Harold W. Solomon (d. 1967) was a professor of criminal law at the University of Southern California, married to Barbara Probst Solomon (1928–), writer and friend of Kazin and Ann Birstein. Lewis Coser (1913–2003) was an American sociologist who with Irving Howe founded the magazine *Dissent*. Arthur Berger (1912–2003) was a composer who taught music and composition at Brandeis. Henry Graff (1921–), historian of the American presidency, taught history at Columbia. Alex Inkeles (1920–), an expert on communication, social and political psychology, would become a senior fellow at the Hoover Institute. The Russian-born Mikhail Kamenetsky (1919–1995), aka Ugo ("Misha") Stille, was a journalist reporting on developments in America for the *Corriere della Sera* of Milan. Misha's wife, Elizabeth Stille, an editor for Dodd Mead, arranged the first meeting between Kazin and his future wife Ann Birstein on October 13, 1950. John P. Marquand Jr. (1924–1995), son of the American fiction writer John P. Marquand (1893–1960), was the author of the novel *The Second Happiest Day*. Dwight W. Webb was editor for Noonday Press. Lee Halprin is a philanthropist and supporter of liberal/progressive causes. Arthur Trottenberg was associate dean of the Faculty of Arts and Sciences at Harvard (1950–1968). William Goodman was executive editor at Harcourt, Brace. Beatrice ("Bede") Hofstadter was the wife of Richard Hofstadter. James R. Newman (1906–1966), an American mathematician and lawyer, wrote about mathematics and the history of mathematics for the general public. He is credited with describing the concept and coining the term "googol," ten to the hundredth power. Richard Goodwin (1931–) was an adviser and speechwriter for Presidents Kennedy and Johnson.

## August 7, 1962

What happened to the good old term, "man-of-letters"? It meant that *letters* stood for more than a craft—it meant the dominion for which letters had the key, over which it had authority. Now they are trying to make the critic a specialist in *criticism*, and even in certain kinds of criticism. The absolute division between critic as judge and the novelist as *producer* of literature means that the first has no real cultural authority and the second no real culture. [. . .]

## August 14, 1962

At Karen and Abe Burrows[109] for a dinner last night. Lovely people—fascinated by Abe's quickness—like lights going on, one, two, three, all over the pinball machine, the marvelous bounding up and down of the quick *Jew*, the great signal system, and apparatus for rapid assimilation and enjoyment. [. . .]

## August 20, 1962

The Jewish intellectual's gift, to see the Christian-liberal-"classical" world from the outside: to be a stranger to this culture, yet at the same time to see all the others as strange to *himself*. Hannah's gift—even when [she] speaks in "classical" accents.

## August 22, 1962

The background of [the] book [*Starting Out in the Thirties*] is contemporary history, the myth of it is history; and reading the documents on the Warsaw ghetto collected in Philip Friedman's *Martyrs and Fighters*, I feel as if history were living in me, just as if I were at a seder recollecting the journey out of Egypt. . . . So history, is certainly not an "advance," is certainly cyclical. This is its comfort. The past is real, I am tied to it. The world is real, because memories of it exist, participation exists. Each person takes up the story again, and so it really *is* a story that is about us all, and which we tell together.

Line in the Passover Haggadah, read in Warsaw, 1943—"Pour Out Your Wrath."

## August 23, 1962

The light looks a little "cooler" these days—the shadows are longer—the season is on another notch. Reading in Friedman's collection of documents on

109. Abe Burrows (1910–1985), humorist, author, composer, director for stage and television.

the Warsaw ghetto, I keep thinking of *the* problem: Jewish submission, Jewish passivity and quietism. It's as if the phrase used in the ghetto for death at the hands of the Nazis—*Kiddush ha-shem*, sanctification of the name—expressed the distraction, the God-intoxication, that made everything else unworthy. Death at the hands of the beasts, who were so "worldly" anyway. A contempt for those who were preoccupied with so little. Unfortunately, the Jews cannot be let off this much. The anxiety that has been the background of *my* life, reflected my parents' insecurity and panic; and in the midst of the terrible war, I had a sense that "history" was turning back to that. The civic insecurity of the Jews in Eastern Europe should not be confused with other-worldly virtues only. It was often the most religious Jews, in Friedman's account, who had the best morals. Is it really true, as Pussy says, that the Jews see themselves (ultimately) as a kind of sacrifice in the divine process of creation? The redness in the fire? The desired condition—pride, resistance, dignity—how is this made impossible by sanctification of the divine name? To believe in the Jews as a necessary sacrifice is to express a nearly Oriental fatalism. In this view the human being is actually held in contempt by God, is nothing to Him, merely exits to demonstrate His greatness. There is no incarnation of human purpose. There is only the Divine purpose and Divine will. . . .

Yet it is impossible to explain the terrible Jewish passivity on religious grounds. On the contrary, it was the mentality of segregation, the numerus clausus, the Ghetto, the pogrom; the background is Orientalism, authoritarianism, political tyranny. . . .

Unfortunately, the Eastern Jews had lived so long an inferior race that they *fitted* themselves to their discomfort and anxiety as my mother fitted herself to her bent back, and came to think of *this* as the natural posture and of their ghetto world as *the* world. They had grown into their suffering and anxiety until they could no longer tell what was normal. Centuries of oppression had internalized *them* into the fixed posture of oppression. The question was fundamentally not religious but *social*. The Jews had made a virtue of their weakness—like Uncle Tom Negroes?

## October 20, 1962

[. . .] AMONG STRANGERS.—How prosperous we are in America now, how forward-looking, how fortunate! We Jews are the most fortunate Jews that have ever been; and what defects and disabilities in our condition there *may* be, is being taken care of by psychoanalysis of the individual and by social research into the community. The fortunate Jew; the academic Jew; the Jew as writer, intellectual, spark. . . . But I think of Russia, of the fortunate Jews there; and I think of how we have been forced in a way to limit our great birthright, our great gift to ourselves; and I advise you, brethren, not to be lulled, either by our own prosperity and good-fortune or by the seeming good fortune of America itself. [. . .]

## October 25, 1962

Goodbye to the "good" Ida [a favorite Aunt], goodbye to that friendly face. There was a huddle of overcoats in the clean and modern Garbek Funeral Chapel this morning, and the corpse looked a blond and jolly kewpie doll. They had even smeared lipstick on her face.

A huddle of overcoats in the room. A circle of overcoats of familiar Brooklyn, Jewish faces grown older with the years. I feel as if the immediate human setting of my childhood was this huddle of overcoats.

Back to NY in a taxi with Pearlie nervously chain-smoking. The streets are thick with trucks—the sky overcast—endless pounding of repair work. A day like this—such an ordinary, flat, New York day. And so the dear and good Ida is carried out with lipstick on her mouth. The young clowns in that huddle of overcoats with their furry hats and yarmulkes—the old cheesy faces, faces swollen, faces shrunken—the glare of old lady faces contracted between the glare of glasses and the heavy lipstick. This aging of the immigrant generation, all in their overcoats.

## November 25, 1962

Coming back from seeing Katey to Sunday School, a damp, ordinary, even happy Sunday, I saw a woman standing over a trash can on the corner of 79th. I suddenly saw Mama in her—an openly suffering, intensely open kind of Mama—a Mama who suffered without pretense that she wasn't all suffering. Suddenly the dead appear again on 79th Street and Broadway. How suddenly rises up from my unconscious, my back mind, people—all those people I thought I could do without, all those people I pushed into the background, saying come near, but don't touch—And now I see Mama over a rubbish can on Broadway, *alone*, really alone for once, holding onto the wire. Oh what a sufferer, but how she hid it, had to hide it. And now one of the dead, a tramp alone on Broadway, cast-out in truth. Standing over that wire can as if she could puke, but her eyes madly searching the street.

## November 27, 1962

This constant lecturing, elucidation, referring-to of books, taking the books off the shelves and putting them back again—what *is* it, what do I possibly do for other people, for my students? The satisfaction that the analysis of literature gives me is intense and mysterious: it is as if I were reducing things to an order, the order of criticism, in which values are constantly invoked, arranged, set in order, in which *understanding* extracted from the book becomes an activity of the highest interest. But what is it that I do for my listeners, my readers? What is it about "literature," the sphere of literature, that I bring out? Do I really, at the New School at least, with these "progressive" minded self-improvers, do anything except invoke the magical accomplishment and those mysterious and superior personalities, the authors?—I feel to myself that these lectures to self-improvers, are useless, that there is no real contact with them, that the stuff of my lectures is translated into their terms; they do not meet the book, not even half-way; they use it as a way of demonstrating their consumption of culture. . . . Real criticism, in the classroom, with people who go out to meet the book, to seek its terms, to understand what this unique creation is—real criticism must be more precise, must seek to say what this book *is*, not to indicate the presence in little tootsie's world of the superior personality. . . . To seek to meet the book on its terms, to define and even to assimilate the unique creation that it is, to indicate the kind of thinking that literature alone makes impossible [*sic*, meaning possible]—this is what the real dialogue of the classroom must be about.

## November 27, 1962

The Tuesday Honors Seminar at City.[110] After all the mountainous blocks uphill, all the shit-stained and broken sidewalks, I suddenly find myself with kids in that seminar who are city intellectuals in my style, for whom ideas are instruments of salvation and who bore their way into a book to take away the certainty of a point of view. And suddenly in the midst of this dragging conversation about Baldwin[111] and Negroes, the real liveliness begins when we discuss the *uncertainty* of all values today. For these kids, though dear little Josephine Gattuso[112] expresses her environment as "dissolution," this

110. Kazin was the Buell G. Gallagher Visiting Professor at City College in the fall of 1962.
111. James Baldwin (1924–1987), an American novelist and essayist who wrote about his efforts to come to terms with his identity as an African American and a homosexual.
112. Josephine Gattuso Hendin (1944–) is Tiro a Segno Professor of Italian American Studies at NYU.

uncertainty has probably been lifelong—whence the irony, the sharpness, the tough little stance, as well as the shivery softness. Looking at them, I think everything is a question of values, values are our only home in the universe. We are guaranteed nothing in the world but the possibility—to *know* what we are doing. How Hannah's phrase comes back to me. And if we cannot know to ourselves what we are doing, even when we have to specify this value entirely for ourselves, locate this value in ourselves, then the only basis of integrity is gone. . . .

Fine kids, wonderful kids—gracefully serious—Miss Gattuso, Miss Halpern, Mr. Koch—gracefully serious, as we were not. The style is easier, but the contents are real, and very precious to me. I love them. They make me feel less lonely, less queer to myself in this time—I understand them.

## December 10, 1962

I complain about having so many things to learn in relation to "society," but the real point of manners is objectivity—objective consideration, objective awareness of others. The real point is not to get lost in this labyrinth of my own soliloquy, this sentence that it is so hard for me to end. . . . The power of understanding, which is all I really ask for from my writing, must make me see things, as I see my whole life now, as a kind of romance—a liberation from the darkness of self-tormenting thought to the light of understanding.

This is why my autobiography must be seen on a large scale, as a history growth, an illumination, like my essays themselves. A cherishing of what I have learned.

## December 18, 1962

The last Honors seminar before vacation—on *From Here to Eternity* and on war. I came away extremely dissatisfied with myself. If I believe that literature is important as pleasure, important as a criticism of life, then I *must* believe that values can be taught through literature. That is my aim as a teacher, that is all the fun of teaching—to bring things home to my boys and girls, to bring the world home to them. There is a world of imaginative possibility, in every sense, that I can teach students to see. There are hints I can give them. Why then aren't I more patient? Why am I interested in conversation with the really bright ones rather than in *teaching*—in showing the possible intermediate step—to the others? Teaching can be so absorbing that I'm sometimes finished by a class. But it is important to start from the student's point of view, from the student's level, and not use the class as a bloody way of getting ideas for my next article. The Northwestern thing [talk] should be on the writer's perspective in our immediate social and cultural setting—the Pomona thing on *teaching*. And the problem of teaching, of the "mass reader," *is* of the student. If we start by disliking him for being at the bottom, then teaching is not of him at all.

Every day the lesson comes back—forget your bloody, imaginary uniqueness, your childhood drama, and just live, act, *think*. What a world teaching opens up, if only I can think about my students for a change! Life opens up so excitedly, once the grip on childhood is really loosened.

## December 21, 1962

[. . .] Saw Hannah yesterday and I got the Eichmann ms. Hannah is in the *New Yorker*—special University Professor at the U. of Chicago. I was struck by my own jealousness and how much she has blossomed out. No need to argue for her against Ann now: Yet her insight, as always, is prodigious. She dismisses the English historians for playing at "parlor games," and isn't that exactly what I've meant about the nimble-tongued critics writing to each other?

The point about the English is this idea of a *class*, an elite, the dominators. You are *in* the special group if you can prove it by writing *to* it.

## December 22, 1962

Finished Hannah's study of the Eichmann trial and walked out into the streets dark with winter twilight. I walked and walked, shivering to get the wintry pure air into my lungs—to get the stink of so much evil, so much death, death—by the intellectual will, out of my system. At 23rd and Sixth, looking south I saw a bloody colored cloud over the roof tops. "The banality of evil" the *banality* of it all, the fearful ordinariness and inconspicuousness and in a horrid sense the *insignificance* of so much killing—as of the fearful selfishness and "respectability" of so many Jews behind it.

Hannah in her imperious yecke[113] way *is* one of the *just*. I come back to this. This is the lightning in her to which I always respond. She has the fundamental sense of *value*. She still believes in the right. Oddly enough, she

113. "Yecke," a good-natured, mildly derogatory term for German Jews.

still believes *in* the Ten Commandments. Her moral outlook is her magnetic point. She holds out, *alone*, for basic values. And the evil to be contemplated *is* "banal." It is under our feet.

## March 29, 1963
### [Berkeley]

Finally got to the conclusion of Hannah's pieces on *Eichmann in Jerusalem*—which is a magnificent conclusion, and makes clear just how swamped by "politics," by the ever-growing ferocity of "politics," so many of our arguments now are.[114] The Jews found themselves up against the most powerful, militarized state in the *world*: the amount of force directed against them was just incalculable in terms of the past. And as I read this morning's account of the suppression of Yevtushenko,[115] I realize what the essential image must be for Reno—the writer up against the *state*—not just dealing with "community" and *society*, but now under total surveillance by the *state*. The odds are all against him. He *must* be a good boy. Y. now acknowledges the criticism to which he is being subjected for allowing "Precocious Autobiography" to be serialized in the Paris *L'Express* "was aimed not at the destruction of talent but at its development," and called the publication of the autobiography "a major mistake prompted by thoughtlessness."

McCormick[116] quoting Collingwood in the anthology of censorship—the poem as an act of "pure consciousness." But it is exactly this purity which is intolerable to the heads of state now, and which they, as false intellectuals, particularly mind as an assumption of superiority. They work on us as the raw material for their notions of improvement.

## April 4, 1963

[. . .] Such a beautiful memoir by Nabokov in the new *New Yorker*,[117] the real playfulness of mind about the past—those sensory images as the only

114. Kazin was Beckman Visiting Professor at Berkeley the spring semester of 1963.
115. Yevgeny Yevtushenko (1933–), popular Russian poet, essayist, novelist, and film director who succeeded in criticizing the Soviet Union while avoiding the severe punishment suffered by other writers.
116. John McCormick and Mairi MacInnes, *Versions of Censorship: An Anthology* (1962); R. C. Collingwood, British philosopher and historian.
117. "The Lyre," *New Yorker* (April 15, 1963): 44–139.

*embodiment* of the past. The sense particularly of the sameness of the present and the past (the thing I always leave out of my Thirties book)—"It is a funny thing when you imagine yourself returning into the past with the contraband of the present how weird it would be to encounter there in unexpected ways the prototypes of today's acquaintances, so young and fresh, who in a kind of lucid lunacy do not recognize you."

## April 8, 1963

Rabbi Geffen[118] at 93 or something, still writes out in his diary what he has learned. Alfred Kazin, at 107, still writes out in his diary what he has learned. He has learned that the world is very big, and that there are many people in it, and that God's ways are mysterious indeed. He has learned that people do not particularly love him, that there is no reason why his extreme sensitivity to the slightest unhappiness or pain should be of great concern to others, and that if you leave a woman and sleep with someone else, the woman you have left has no particular reason for cherishing you anymore. He has learned, oh goodness me how much he has learned of this, that he is not the center of the universe, that personal things do not really count as much as he thinks they do, and that that mother standing in the window overlooking Sutter Avenue, watching for her only, dearly beloved son, etc., etc., is not with us, has not been with us for many years. [. . .]

## April 15, 1963

[. . .] Newton [Arvin] dead three weeks ago. It is hard to get used to the contracted span of everything nowadays. Here is Newton so full of his sorrows and troubles gone off as if he had *had*, a rich free life! Awful as he was in his creepy, clammy lonesomeness, he *was* an artist in his line and the grace of his books will perhaps be ignored by those unable to recognize it.

Palo Alto looked full of dead spots around the "rich" *seemly* houses. Louis K[119] as charming as ever—really admirable manners, warming *manner*. Has the gift of inserting what he wants to say in between the set periods of his manner. Admirable—soothing—kind. L. has a real gift for the social occasion—he confers a great deal on any group by being in it.

118. Orthodox Rabbi Tobias Geffen of Atlanta (1870–1970), best known for declaring Coca-Cola kosher.
119. Louis Kronenberger (1904–1980), critic, scholar, novelist, and biographer.

## April 16, 1963

[. . .] The book of life[120]—Lawrence was right—we are *touched*, touched right down to the nerve-endings in our fingers. That's what we want—the chink of the metal, dull silver as Josie drops the fork and spoons in twos into the drawers after drying them, the dull plash of the rain, the face of Sylvia Plath,[121] submissive, polite, alone sitting in my office up at Smith, the dead girl, the young pro, the girl whose talent was so fully formed that when I met her, it was already *outside* her, like the cold skills of a Bobby Fischer or a Heifetz in performance. She had only to press on the keys of the instrument to produce the right music. She could probably get no *personal* pleasure from writing well—her person really was not involved.

All *good* critics are frustrated writers. They are frustrated about the skill they are able to suggest so well because they work *close* to it without being of it. They are parallel to it and hence can see it in *the* most marvelous detail without being of it. I understand now why Edmund works so hard at his *journals*. They are *his* living novel, *his* unending book of life.

## May 7, 1963

Jimmy Baldwin spoke to a fantastic audience this noon in the great gym of the U. Every bench was filled and every available inch below was filled with students sitting on the floor. Behind me a little boy with a home-made placard which he held up. Lots of women brought babies. Jimmy was very good—had just the right tone and on the whole handled himself very well.

But it was the audience more than anything else that impressed me about this occasion. If I ever saw the excitement of a *public* meeting, this was it. The flow of feeling in the audience was extraordinary—it was a perfect example of a crowd filling up the present and *waiting* to be fulfilled.

A moment in time—the present itching for the future. Walked out inside this tremendous crowd.

Jimmy—not a politician, not a Negro leader but a *writer*. The best thing he said—the revealing characteristic thing: "There is nothing we cannot think about."

120. Lawrence called the novel "the bright book of life," the title of Kazin's 1973 book on American fiction.

121. Sylvia Plath (1932–1963), American poet, one of Kazin's students at Smith, 1954–1955; Bobby Fischer (1942–2008), American chess player and world chess champion; Jascha Heifetz (1901–1987), regarded by many to be one of the greatest violinists of all time, though some considered his playing perfect but mechanical, hence Kazin's reference to "cold skills."

## May 22, 1963

[. . .] Newton [Arvin] was amazingly *expressive* for someone so unstable and turbulent. He was really *gifted*. I can see this now in his charm, in his musicality. The professional cat-walker's urbanity he got into his discussion of literary judgments—a kind of suggestive *politesse* urbanity at its highest.

## June 5, 1963

Picture of the Pope[122] being borne from his Vatican apartments to St. Peter's where he will lie in state. Now the mumbo-jumbo begins in earnest—just a feeble flicker of the man himself still around. For me, his example has been overwhelming. These four or so years have gradually worked a revolution in me and in so many other people—I have a sense of moral liberation because of him. Suddenly it becomes possible to say—yea or nay again, right or wrong, to discriminate between good and evil in *everything*. The important point about this kind of *personal* faith is that it abolishes the pathos of distance which morally we feel about so many events these days. Clancy Segal,[123] who came over to the university yesterday, sat in front of the Greek Theater talking about the "brick wall" which radicals feel about political and social upsets of the supposed march of history. But there is a dimension of personal and moral freedom that is present in confronting what is happening so long as we are not afraid to call things by their right names, so long as we can say yea or nay. . . . I am more and more convinced that this dimension of personal freedom—the freedom to choose—the freedom to call things by their right names—is decisive. Only this individual sense of good and evil can abolish the pathetic sense of being a disappointed spectator and onlooker, a reader of the historical fortunes. History is *now*—"this society is mine,"—every day is the decisive stage.

## June 17, 1963
### [New York]

[. . .] Michael finally appeared around 12:30—I forgave him instantly for being late. My cunning son with Carol's beautiful blue-black hair (symbol of an inbred sensual personality even when I slept with her). We went down

122. Pope John XXIII (born Angelo Giuseppe Roncalli 1881), who died June 3, 1963, was admired by Kazin and many others for his apparent willingness, suggested by his convening of the Second Vatican Council, to turn the Roman Catholic Church into a more open and liberal institution.

123. Clancy Segal, British novelist, journalist, and leftist.

together to the Grand Central baggage room and together in a taxi brought the trunks back. Ann off to Cyrilly.[124] Thank God for another half an hour off. Then to 55th and [illegible] Avenue, Channel 13 educational television. A whole hour on Santayana's *The Last Puritan* with Augie Heckscher, Morris Phillipson, and (most interesting) Prof. Danto of Columbia's Philosophy Department.[125] Program cheered me up considerably. God, how I can bathe in cultural perceptions, in sheer play of critical point and critical wit. In the dusty rundown drugstore where I was having some coffee I felt pretty tired of time and felt as if I had had it. Then I revived in the Studio, and thank God for the program. I feel more like myself today. Talked to my father, talked to Jack Ludwig; and now here we are, having gone through this day without dying, without too much destruction to others and myself. [. . .]

## July 15, 1963

Reading Sainte-Beuve for this new piece, I am more and more impressed by the *public* interest involved in what he writes and whom he writes for. A medium of public awareness, as it were, a custodian of values for the public. Has its interests in his charge—is a repository and custodian of public values.

Isn't this the real European quality as opposed to the American, which confuses private interest with "liberty," and thinks of itself defending a value when it is defending only an interest?—Proof that it cannot elucidate this interest *as* a value, but can only affirm it, repeatedly and insistently, as an emotion?

Hannah Arendt's value for this generation of Americans is obviously her concern with the public standard, with *politics* as opposed to subjectivity. . . . And in regard to the Jews, her special concern is that the Jews *not* regard themselves as special cases, as an importunate and eternally aggrieved minority always, which puts them into the position of consciously amending justice and truth in order to get *their* human rights in. . . . The more the Jews regard themselves as special cases, as eternal outsiders and victims merely, the more they keep themselves from achieving this moral centrality, their perspective on the whole human problem, which is their birthright, their privilege, and their real history.

124. Cyrilly Abels (1903–1975), managing editor at *Mademoiselle*, a friend of Ann's.
125. August Heckscher (1913–1997), N.Y.C. Parks Commissioner and writer; Morris Philipson (1926–), novelist, essayist, and head of the University of Chicago Press; Arthur Danto (1924–), professor of philosophy at Columbia and art critic for the *Nation*.

The key to so many literary and historical issues in America is this absorption of religious liberty into economic individualism, and then into psychological self-affirmation merely, of one's "identity," God help us—the one thing we should take for granted by virtue of our birth, the starting point merely in any real sense of life. Unless there is some basic disinterestedness, some avowal of the public and common existence of truth, unless we can stop thinking of ourselves as special cases unjustly condemned to suffering, every day becomes an impossible struggle to satisfy one's "personality" limitlessly. And finally, the struggle becomes so unbearable that one wants to shut up one's personality entirely, to die. [. . .]

## July 20, 1963

[. . .] In the early '40's I entered Bohemia, I lived in the Village. For the first time I saw people dreaming aloud all day and the greater part of the day—people asking themselves: *What* shall I think, how shall I look to this one or that or to myself? The great difference from the early tenement and the evening-college life I knew in the thirties was that *then* I felt myself determined by everything around me and by the political explosions on the front pages. Suddenly, in Bohemia, starting in the forties, an eerie, dreamy kind of self-determination set in. This conclusively shows that personally, at least, the period of poverty was over. Poverty is the great determiner and conditioner. Poor people are held to it. In Bohemia, which has the masquerade of poverty, people impersonate poverty as they impersonate the artist.

April of 1962 when *Contemporaries* came out, I lunched with Harold Rosenberg at the Blue Ribbon. Today, 20th of July 1963, I remember, in relation to his support of Castro, that Castro put executions on television, and that in at least one publicized case, execution was held up because the cameras hadn't yet been set up. . . . I seem to see Harold at home, looking at executions on television (Hitler had the strangulations of the July '44 generals and conspirators (by piano wire, on meat hooks) put on film, too; Goebbels vomited when he saw the film.) I also seem to see Harold at home looking at action painters. Harold is the critic-as-spectator. Running up and down the gallery tracks of New York in his armored car, Trotsky lives again from his intellectual H.Q. . . . The creative in his own field Harold can't bear—Cal Lowell, Hannah, Saul. The critic in his armored car is wiser than the creative fool.

Bohemia—the stage onto which critics come out and play roles, Roman senators denouncing each other, sentencing each other to death. What shall I do with my life, with my sex, my fantasies—? What shall I do with my life? How shall I live—this moment, this week? Relatively unconditioned, undetermined, set free, to live how and why?

Bohemia was, even more basically, this bitter rivalry. And the claim to complete emotional "honesty," of absolute-personal bravery, was one particular vanity. The life of *possibility* was all. An actual book could not improbably be viewed as a sell out, but by not *finishing* anything, one could move the "tendencies" of a book about.

Connie Smith used to say, "I have my journal." Si Krim used to say, you're so *innocent*. The Posters especially used to feel the glory of their failure. Here is where Isaac, the ghetto dreamer par excellence, was in his glory—by not writing. Manny Farber and his little wife [Janet Richards].[126] . . . There was a dream, not only in marriage and of marriage, but a utilization of marriage itself as a fantasy. Manny the painter, looking at physical illness as the wounds incurred by his brave personal fight. But all the time looking out at the uptown Madison world of the *NR* [*New Republic*] with envy and despair.

## July 23, 1963
### [Wellfleet]

Has been cloudy and overcast since Saturday. Last night at Abe Burrows for dinner at Provincetown with the O'Connors. Abe at the piano playing songs of 1917. Immediately tears gush to eyes of A.K. Nostalgia unlimited. I imagined Trudy Weitz's apartment in Brooklyn, around 1931. Candles in the apartment, small huddle of adolescent hope and intensity. The scene came to life instantly in my mind. And I thought—why do I hug the past in secret and in silence so long? Because in that candlelit dark room off the Saratoga Library, looking back upon it now, there is so much sentiment and promise. That dark, young huddle sits outside a door, waiting for it to open. The past always as a promise of great

126. The journalist Seymour Krim (1922–1989), Manny Farber, and William Poster and Connie Smith, were part of a group that gathered regularly at Isaac Rosenfeld's Greenwich Village flat in the early forties. Janet Richards, Manny Farber's wife at the time, has published a memoir of her experiences in this group, *Common Soldiers: A Self Portrait and Other Portraits* (San Francisco: Archer, 1979).

new worlds opening. . . . No wonder that I hug it so much now, and why I hate to finish my book, to bring it out into the open, where it will dissolve into the actual world of experience. I want to keep all these instances of promise, that threshold forever keen and clear forever. . . .[. . .]

There are emotions, recurrent dreams, nightmare anxieties, fears of death, fears of being nailed down in a coffin and thrown into a hole in the ground (as Chekhov said) but these are always the same, they do not diminish by thinking about and by analyzing them. This "private" sector, as Hannah says in her book on revolution, has no light and reflects none—so nothing can be done about it.

What brought me out of my old hole of loneliness and despond was Ann, from '50 on. This was "public" life, true life, lived not by the solitary will seeking to pierce through by intellectual effort alone, but by companionship and understanding, by love and dialogue.

> "God grant me the serenity to accept the things I cannot change;
> the courage to change the things I can;
> And the wisdom to know the difference."

(Prayer repeated at the end of each meeting of Alcoholics Anonymous) [. . .]

## July 25, 1963

The beggarly Jewish radicals of the 30s are now the ruling cultural pundits of American society—I who stood so long outside the door wondering if I would ever get through it, am now one of the standard bearers of American literary opinion—a *judge* of young men.

## July 26, 1963

Reading [Georg] Lukacs with steady admiration.[127] He has the great Marxist strength of seeing society as a struggle, as a sense of *contradiction* between social profession and social reality—even between social hope and social necessity. . . . I suppose the essence of the Marxist appeal is to this dramatic and aroused sense of contradiction on every hand. Between the surface of life

127. *Studies in European Realism* (New York: Crosset and Dunlap, 1964), Introduction by Alfred Kazin.

and the basic reality. This sense of contradiction *made* the intelligent bourgeois of the 19th century into a social observer and novelist. . . . In America especially, the gap between the ideal, even abstract, freedom of constitutional tradition and precept and the evident facts of class antagonism and privilege made the *novelist*. This was the 19th century novelist's creative occasion and opportunity. [. . .]

## August 6, 1963

On the writing of Jewish history. Why do we know so little of our own forbears? Why don't Ann and I know even the maiden names of our grandmothers? Why is it so surprising to see a book like *The Promised City*?[128] Because Jews have had so little perspective on their own history. Because Jewish history has been so internalized that the insidedness of it, not to say the compactness and remarkably unchanged character of it, has permitted so little perspective. To write the history of one's own "people" or country, one must be able to see it in some larger perspective. Jews, on the whole, have not had access to this perspective. Either because they have seen their history as sacred, or because they have been too close to it and defensive about it, the kind of objectivity, which in its initial interest, sets the writing of history in motion, has been a recent development for them.

On the other hand, the vogue of autobiography among Jews—of the man who has made his way from the ghetto to the "great world"—Solomon Maimon, *The Rise of David Levinsky*[129]—even such books tend to be too tender to the Jewish experience (more tender than the authors really wish to be). The sense of guilt, the longing to belong, to belong again, all this is at one pole from the example of extreme "alienation" of Juden-hass, that Marx could still affirm.

Even the man who can go into these Yiddish records, like Moses Rischin, is virtually too close to the experience to be able to be objective about it. And in point of fact, such writers are documentary chroniclers not historians. For them Jewish history is still too central and sacred a story.

128. Moses Rischin, *The Promised City: New York's Jews, 1870–1914* (Cambridge: Harvard University Press, 1962). Moses Rischin (1925–), Jewish American historian, author, lecturer, editor, and professor of history at San Francisco State University.

129. Though told in the first person, Abraham Cahan's *The Rise of David Levinsky* (1917) is a novel.

## August 8, 1963

Suddenly occurred to me yesterday—*why* do I think that others are more intelligent, more probing and searching about commonplace things than I? The pleasure of working-things-out in my own mind, of thinking effectively, is so much my real day to day life. Yet I am always impatient, and the things that other people do methodically, I skip over. Impatience as a way of getting past material difficulties to my "real" life. But also because my mind is so often beclouded with fancies, recollections, daydreams, hurts, that my mind isn't clear enough at times to focus on specific needs and problems. A vast stream of undischarged matter, the "frozen sea," within us, Kafka thought that only a book can break up. Not enough engaged, too far outside things: a kind of loneness, as Mailer says shrewdly of Bellow, whatever else he says in this disgusting *Esquire* (July). Struck by Mailer, the madman, who in this respect is nevertheless too sophisticated, too savvy, to be so far outside as Saul is . . . and as I am. This being outside and alone, however, makes one's mental life all too dreamy and self-sufficient. There is not enough to engage it, to focus it, to direct it beyond what it expects to go. The lone self is always engaged in . . . what? nothing but saving itself. It returns back and back to the primal defense against the original anxiety-making situation. . . . It is this effort at self-saving that preoccupies the self, keeps it busy. And *bored*. [. . .]

Where does it come from, this preoccupation with the saving of the self? Where does this frightful distraction come from? It is all self-defense, and nothing to do with history. I brought myself up to contend with adversaries I thought were smarter and stronger than myself. I ran up and down my mind all day and all night long, looking for safe positions, for defenses against "the enemy." This cruel-self consciousness that I feel pressed over my brain like a vise every night—this inability to plunge into the middle of the stream—to forget myself, ever—this distraction, these daydreams and idle reveries. [. . .]

Somewhere I was exposed to some danger that forced me to arm myself, to resist. And now the resistance has become such a habit that it fills my mind with its recollected gestures and occasions, and often leaves me nothing to think about but this stale personal history.

The Jews' fright? My mother's? That cold winter wind and the orange rinds and coffee grounds spilling over the jagged edge of the garbage can outside the backyard on Chester Street. Going back to it, over and over again—how finally I saved myself in '43 after falling so deeply in love with Lou, and how long before that I *saved* myself.

Yet as I lie here, thinking of all these self-savings, I see the women and children in the gully, the wet earth, the German soldier smoking a cigarette and looking down at them, and I see the woman in the crowd saying to him contemptuously—"Go on, get it over with, kill us." Such love that woman had—for life, for her child—such contempt for her *own* life. Greater love hath no one than this, to give up her life. That Jewish mother, with all the anxiety of having been a Jew so long in Central Europe, surrounded by dogs who called themselves men, nevertheless, at that sublime moment, wanted to get it over with, for her child's sake. A sublime sacrifice of everything she had to give. And from such a background of anxiety, of anxious self-defense, of furtiveness and fear, of such long internalization, to say that to the Nazi solder detachedly looking down at her as he smoked a cigarette!

## August 9, 1963

[. . .] Never had it so good. Especially for those whose youthful strivings coincided with the throes of society in the thirties, the war was the national recovery act itself. And since the war, our fear of totalitarianism and our contempt for its pretensions have coincided so neatly with our prosperity and our becoming the intellectual standard-bearers of this country! The glossy respectability of Trilling (imagine a Jew in his position getting in trouble à la Wilson with the income tax); the neurotic self-defense of R. Hofstadter. Conservatism à la mode. . . . So the contradictions and conflicts are buried. Everything becomes a description of culture rather than an analysis of the social arrangements by which we live. Fatalism becomes our intellectual "privilege."

The key: *we* [Jews] have become the intellectual standard-bearers and leaders of the American community. And in some way the external image, held *below*, of the critic-and-intellectual leader on top has become the leader's own image of himself. Diana Trilling coming back from a night at Columbia finds the scene in the living room such as a successful literary *career* entails.[130] Emphasis on career rather than on works. But all this smugness hides a great boredom and sense of unreality. The rise of Lionel Trilling means that all these anxieties, naturally related to society, have become applicable only to one's position in society.

Lukacs, *Meaning of Contemporary Realism*, 122—"A character is *typical* . . . when his innermost being is determined by objective forces at work in this

130. See note 25.

society . . . the determining factors of a particular historical phase are found in them in concentrated form. . . ." In this sense my innermost being certainly has been determined by objective forces at work in this society. From my parents' steerage ship to this moment in Wellfleet, my innermost being (which I have always tried so hard to isolate and determine as x) certainly has been determined by objective forces at work in this society. In Trilling's sense there has been a "career," the great plebeian ideal.

So here are the problems of "success" (from the point of view of "career"). And there is my wife, in agony every day and every night, because she feels that as a novelist she is a "failure." Trilling thinks that life itself has changed in our time, after him the deluge: that is how much he protects his success, how little he believes in it, how self-conscious a creation it is. I in *my* "successful" way torture myself with self-doubt in order not to lose too rapidly my old image of myself as struggle. [. . .]

## September 8, 1963

Edmund W[ilson] in his wonderful "old" house on Route 6 in Wellfleet. Everything in this house passed down or acquired by someone who could recognize immediately its historical application to himself. By contrast virtually everything *I* own I have bought for myself or have had to decide its *merits* in relation to an entirely new situation. The crucial factor in the life of the "new man" who is the Jewish writer in this country is this lack of tradition. Sometimes, like Oscar Handlin,[131] he will try to interpret all American history in terms of immigrants. But no one can tell *me* that Edmund Wilson feels like an immigrant's son. Bill Gibson[132] and his wife asked people at the Arthur Schlesinger Jr.'s house the other day—have you *always* felt like an American? And I said—I've *never* felt like an American. But that's because I've given up trying to feel like an American. The lack of tradition is the lack of familiarity in many basic associations—and I know that I am outside them, trying to figure out what to do and what to think in relation to many basic American traditions.

Yet meanwhile the "Americans" feel deprived of what they all had. They feel that it's no longer their country. No wonder that the Jewish writer

131. Oscar Handlin (1915–), American historian, professor at Harvard, best known for his Pulitzer Prize–winning account of American immigrant communities, *The Uprooted*.

132. William Gibson (1914–2008), playwright best known for *The Miracle Worker*, a play about Anne Sullivan, who taught blind and deaf Helen Keller how to communicate.

comes in to fill a felt vacancy, that more and more ([Jack] Ludwig—Heller[133]—Saul B., etc., etc.), he writes as the lyricist of the absurd with an intellectual energy in inverse proportion to his connection of sharing this country with the old elites.

Lack of tradition=super-consciousness of what should be easy and self-consciousness instead of "society." Your name, your face, your manners, all are felt, no matter how flickeringly, to be issues.

What about the Jewish writer's local or personal tradition? Is it anything more than clannishness and the nostalgic even Oedipal pull of the old neighborhood? Is there a historical sense that will keep us from ourselves feeling the "emptiness" that Wilson noticed in moving into the Jewish tradition even for the purposes of study? Outside of the *family*, is there in fact a Jewish tradition?

The question arises because it is so hard to be "Jewish-moral" in the face of all these unfriendly, unfeeling objects *outside*. A tough materialistic, *factual* society redeemed for the writer only by its vividness, its staggering multiplicity of objects, pleasures, voices, people outside such a sensitive homesick stranger. How can I get into things by standing outside hugging my separateness?

The Christian dream of unity. The *only* answer to the question of how we can get over what divides us—the only successor to first the Jewish and then the Marxist dream of unity.

Christ's prayer—"that they may all be one, as thou, Father, art in me, and I in thee, *that they also may be one in us*; that the world may believe that thou has sent me."[134]

133. Joseph Heller (1923–1999), American novelist, best known for *Catch-22*, his satirical novel about the military during World War II.

134. John 17:21.

(15)

2-28-42/ Every once in a while some token, a sentence in a book, a voice heard, will recall for me the fresh instant delight in the sense of being a student of the American landscape and culture that I felt first two years ago, only after I had begun serious work on the book. The sentence this morning, fresh as a spring wind, comes from Constance Rourke's book on Audubon, on the sudden realization that his ornithology was the token of a national sense of scale, that like Whitman and the others he was a great voice of the American nationality. Yet what it does for me is to recall the excitement under which I lived for weeks on weeks early in 1939, when I suddenly realized, and for the first time consciously, that I had a passionate and even professional (sic) interest in American culture and literature. I remember now how in those weeks of almost incommunicable delight and energy and faith in the future I used to walk up and down the halls of the Metropolitan American rooms, looking at the portraits of solemn Colonial & Revolutionary figures--or pictures by Eakins, always a hero for my spirit--or dull glazed transcriptions of a Sunday morning in deare olde Flatbush in 1836. Pictures that suddenly brought back to my mind the delight I had always taken as a child in pictures of Colonials, in American history texts; delights in biographies of the American, at all times and in all conditions (when I was a senior at college, one of my jobs as a worker for NYA was to read and comb the DAB for biographies and lists of American college graduates; I never got tired of reading the stories), ......I have never been able to express the pleasure I derive from the conscious study of "Americana." As a writer and student of writing I get fulfillment out of only a very few American writers, actually; when I think of writing, I think always of Blake and Tolstoy. Yet the very words--"poet of the American nationality"--or the mere lists of Americans--Cope, James, Ryder, Peirce, Dickinson, Franklin--as in Lewis Mumford's little books, or the foreword to a book like Beer's Mauve Decade--or notebooks out of the nineteenth century--or the letters of WM. James, the curious sensation of talking of Albert Ryder and Henry James, of Whitman and Dickinson and Emerson, etc., in the same breath, gives me an extraordinary satisfaction. Why I'm not too sure; yet when I think of a career like Constance Rourke's or Wm. James's or Audubon's or so many others in the American vein--makers and movers and thinkers--great takers of notes--observers in the profoundest sense--I feel happy. I love to think about America, to look at portraits, to remember the kind of adventurousness and purity, heroism and <u>salt</u>, that the best Americans have always had for me.

Or is it--most obvious supposition--that I am an outsider; and that only for the [redacted] first American-born son of so many thousands of mud-flat Jewish-Polish-Russian generations is this need great, this inquiry so urgent?

Yet the most extraordinary element in all this is something it is difficult, perhaps hazardous, to express; that is, the terrible and graphic <u>loneliness</u> of the great Americans. Thinking about them composes itself, sooner or later, into a gallery of extraordinary individuals; yet at bottom they have nothing in common but the almost shattering unassailability, the life-stricken I, in each. Each fought his way through life--and through his genius--as if no one had ever fought before. Each one, that is, began afresh--began on his own terms--began in a universe that remained, for all practical purposes, his own.

Figure 1. February 28, 1942

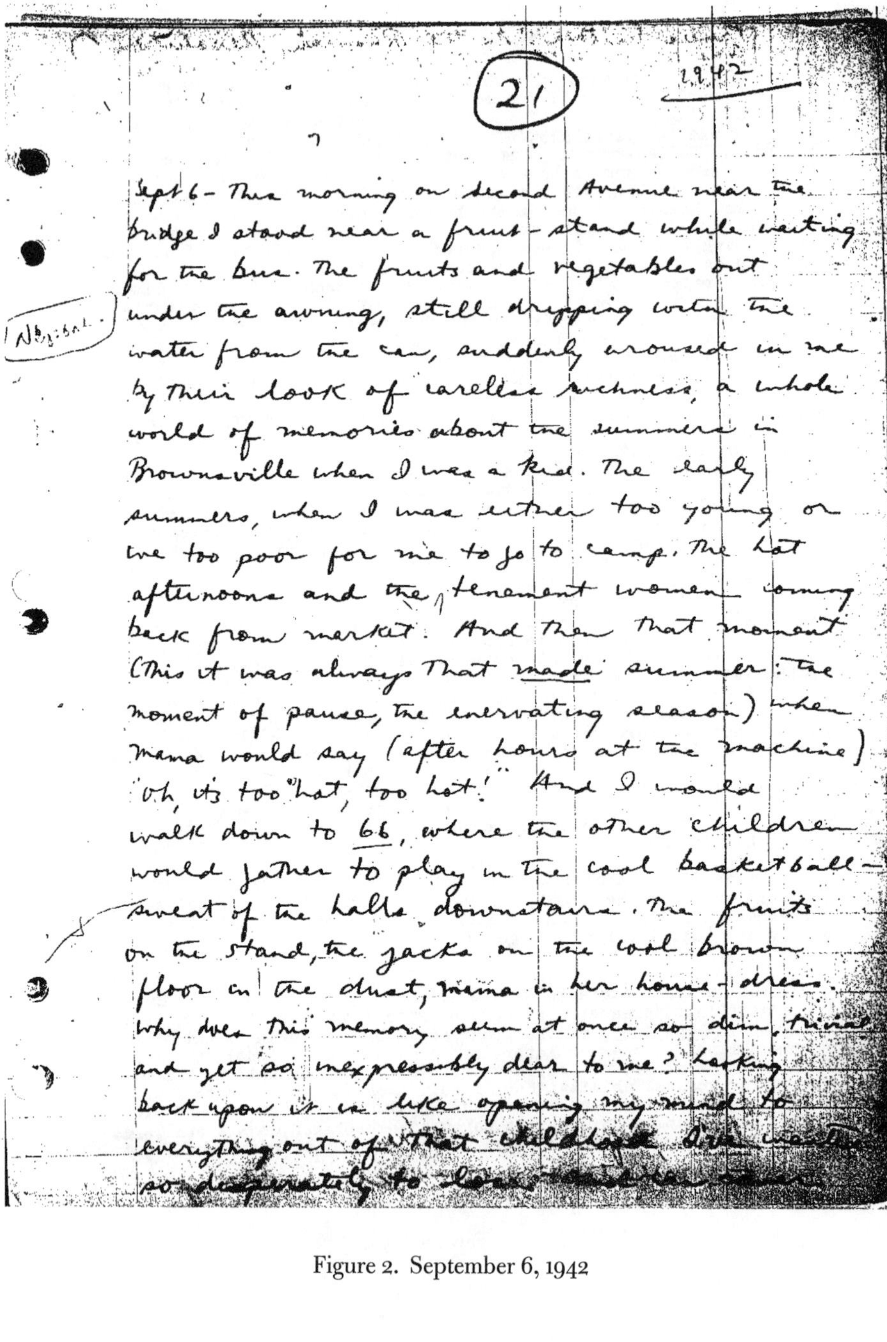

21

1942

Nostalgia

Sept 6 – This morning on Second Avenue near the
bridge I stood near a fruit-stand while waiting
for the bus. The fruits and vegetables out
under the awning, still dripping with the
water from the can, suddenly aroused in me
by their look of careless richness, a whole
world of memories about the summers in
Brownsville when I was a kid. The early
summers, when I was either too young or
we too poor for me to go to camp. The hot
afternoons and the tenement women coming
back from market. And then that moment
(this it was always that made summer: the
moment of pause, the enervating season) when
mama would say (after hours at the machine)
"Oh, it's too hot, too hot!" And I would
walk down to 66, where the other children
would gather to play in the cool basketball-
sweat of the halls downstairs. The fruits
on the stand, the jacks on the cool brown
floor in the dust, mama in her house-dress.
Why does this memory seem at once so dim, trivial
and yet so inexpressibly dear to me? Looking
back upon it is like opening my mind to
everything out of that childhood I've wanted
so desperately to [illegible]

Figure 2. September 6, 1942

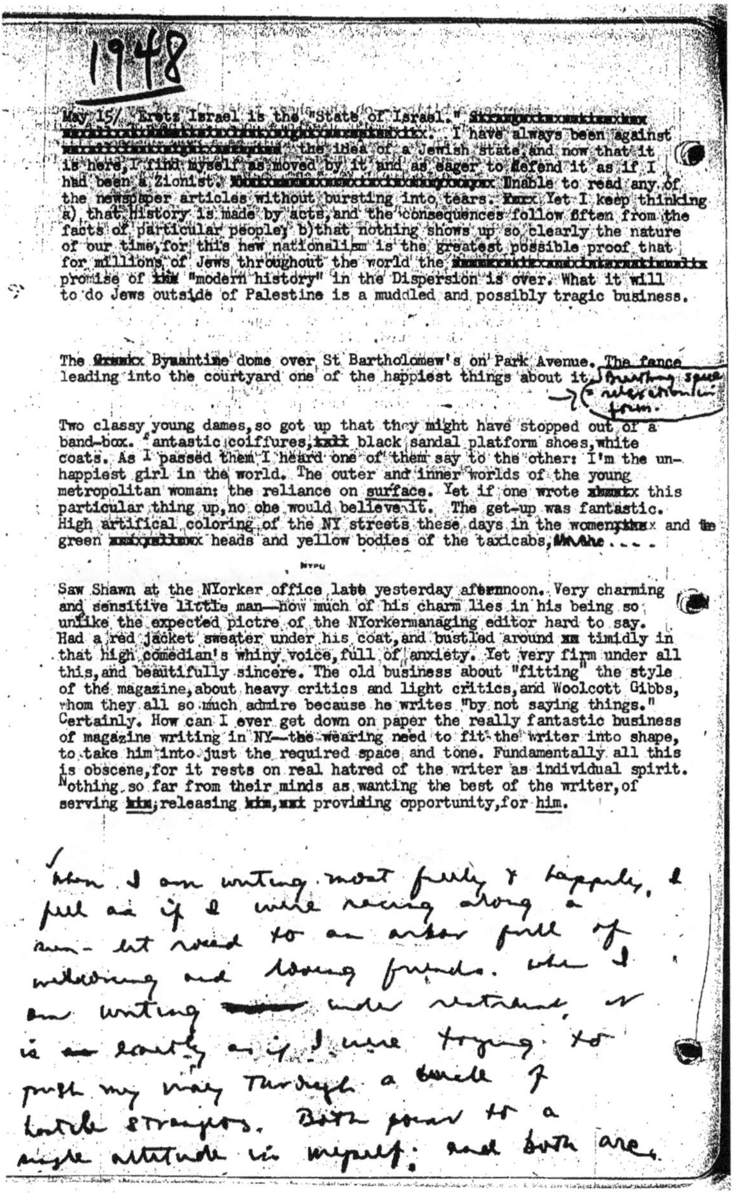

1948

May 15/ Eretz Israel is the "State of Israel." I have always been against the idea of a Jewish state, and now that it is here, I find myself as moved by it and as eager to defend it as if I had been a Zionist. Unable to read any of the newspaper articles without bursting into tears. Yet I keep thinking a) that History is made by acts, and the consequences follow often from the facts of particular people; b) that nothing shows up so clearly the nature of our time, for this new nationalism is the greatest possible proof that for millions of Jews throughout the world the promise of "modern history" in the Dispersion is over. What it will to do Jews outside of Palestine is a muddled and possibly tragic business.

The Byzantine dome over St Bartholomew's on Park Avenue. The fence leading into the courtyard one of the happiest things about it. Breathing space = necessary in form.

Two classy young dames, so got up that they might have stopped out of a band-box. Fantastic coiffures, black sandal platform shoes, white coats. As I passed them I heard one of them say to the other: I'm the unhappiest girl in the world. The outer and inner worlds of the young metropolitan woman: the reliance on surface. Yet if one wrote this particular thing up, no one would believe it. The get-up was fantastic. High artifical coloring of the NY streets these days in the women and the green heads and yellow bodies of the taxicabs, the . . . .

Saw Shawn at the NYorker office late yesterday afternoon. Very charming and sensitive little man—how much of his charm lies in his being so unlike the expected pictre of the NYorkermanaging editor hard to say. Had a red jacket sweater under his coat, and bustled around timidly in that high comedian's whiny voice, full of anxiety. Yet very firm under all this, and beautifully sincere. The old business about "fitting" the style of the magazine, about heavy critics and light critics, and Woolcott Gibbs, whom they all so much admire because he writes "by not saying things." Certainly. How can I ever get down on paper the really fantastic business of magazine writing in NY—the wearing need to fit the writer into shape, to take him into just the required space and tone. Fundamentally all this is obscene, for it rests on real hatred of the writer as individual spirit. Nothing so far from their minds as wanting the best of the writer, of serving, releasing, providing opportunity, for him.

When I am writing most freely & happily, I feel as if I were racing along a sun-lit road to an arbor full of welcoming and loving friends. When I am writing under restraint, it is exactly as if I were trying to push my way through a crowd of hostile strangers. Both point to a single attitude in myself; and both are.

Figure 3. May 15, 1948

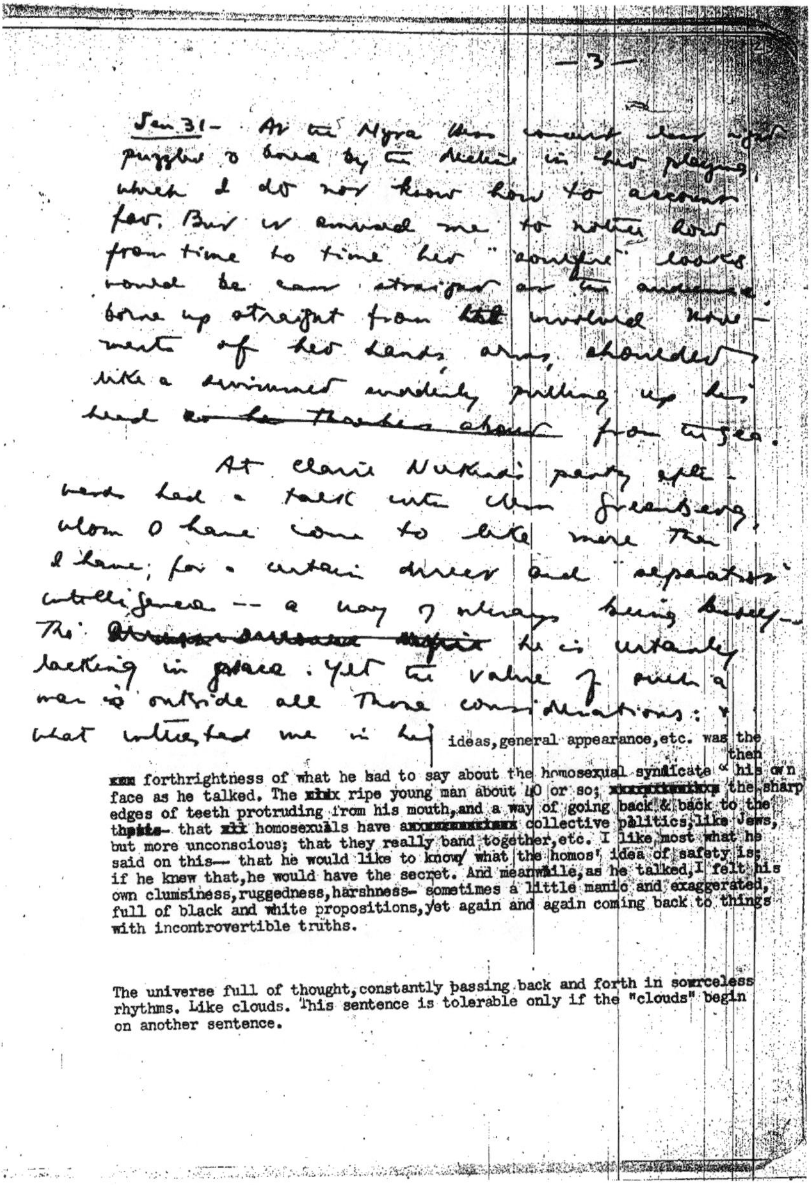

-3-

Jan 31 - At the Myra Hess concert [illegible] puzzled & bored by the realism in her playing, which I do not know how to account for. But it amused me to notice how from time to time her "soulful" looks would be cast straight at the audience borne up straight from ~~the~~ involved movements of her hands, arms, shoulders like a swimmer suddenly pulling up his head ~~[illegible]~~ from the sea.

At Claire Nicholas' party afterwards had a talk with Clem Greenberg, whom I have come to like more than I have; for a certain direct and "separatist" intelligence -- a way of always being busy -- The ~~[illegible]~~ he is certainly lacking in grace. Yet the value of such a man is outside all these considerations; & what interested me in his ideas, general appearance, etc. was the ~~xxx~~ forthrightness of what he had to say about the homosexual syndicate & then his own face as he talked. The ~~xixx~~ ripe young man about 40 or so; ~~xxxxxxxxxx~~ the sharp edges of teeth protruding from his mouth, and a way of going back & back to the thesis- that homosexuals have ~~axxxxxxxxxx~~ collective politics, like Jews, but more unconscious; that they really band together, etc. I like most what he said on this-- that he would like to know what the homos' idea of safety is; if he knew that, he would have the secret. And meanwhile, as he talked, I felt his own clumsiness, ruggedness, harshness- sometimes a little manic and exaggerated, full of black and white propositions, yet again and again coming back to things with incontrovertible truths.

The universe full of thought, constantly passing back and forth in sourceless rhythms. Like clouds. This sentence is tolerable only if the "clouds" begin on another sentence.

Figure 4. January 31, 1949

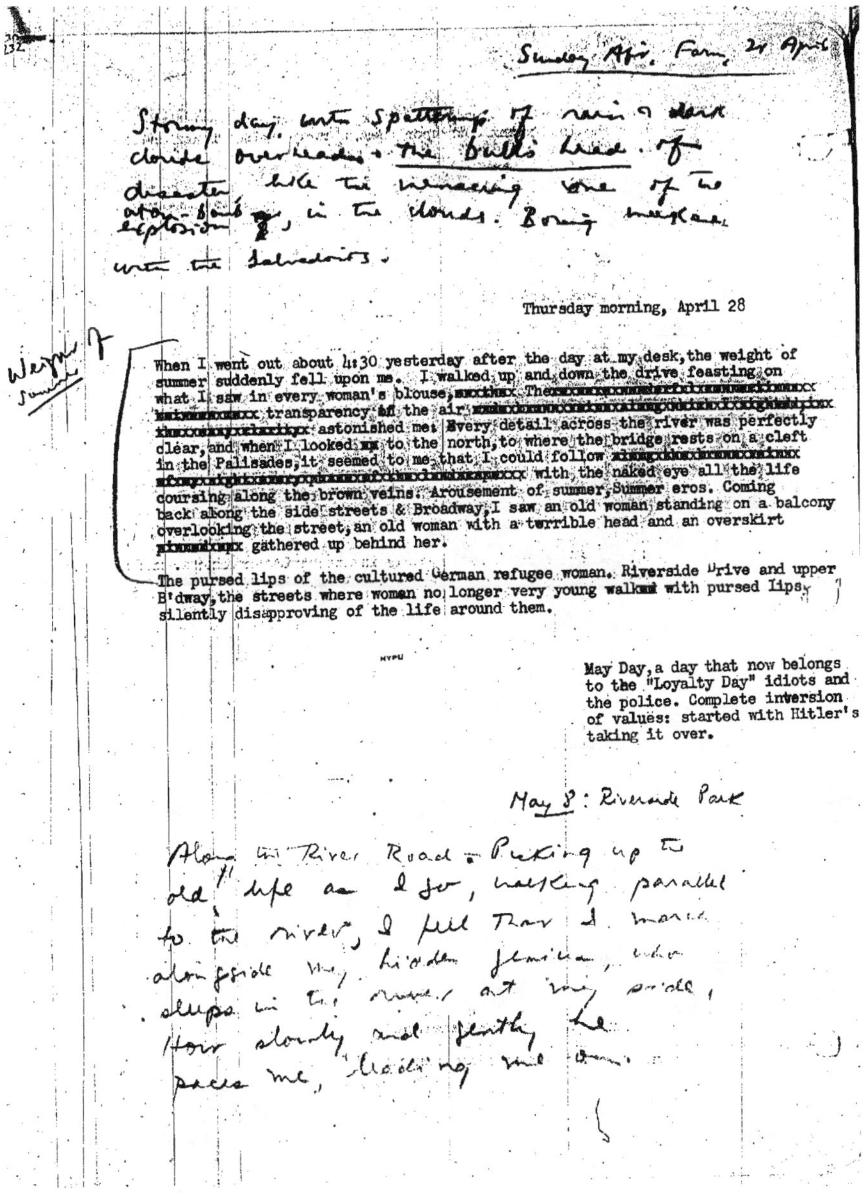

132

Sunday Aft. Farm, 21 April

Stormy day with spattering of rain & dark clouds overhead & the bull's head of disaster like the menacing cone of the atom-bomb explosion, in the clouds. Boring weekend with the Salvadoris.

Thursday morning, April 28

Weight of summer

When I went out about 4:30 yesterday after the day at my desk, the weight of summer suddenly fell upon me. I walked up and down the drive feasting on what I saw in every woman's blouse. The transparency of the air astonished me: Every detail across the river was perfectly clear, and when I looked to the north, to where the bridge rests on a cleft in the Palisades, it seemed to me that I could follow with the naked eye all the life coursing along the brown veins. Arousement of summer, Summer eros. Coming back along the side streets & Broadway, I saw an old woman standing on a balcony overlooking the street, an old woman with a terrible head and an overskirt gathered up behind her.

The pursed lips of the cultured German refugee woman. Riverside Drive and upper B'dway, the streets where woman no longer very young walk with pursed lips, silently disapproving of the life around them.

NYPU

May Day, a day that now belongs to the "Loyalty Day" idiots and the police. Complete inversion of values: started with Hitler's taking it over.

May 8: Riverside Park

Along the River Road: Picking up the old life as I go, walking parallel to the river, I felt that I march alongside my hidden feminine, who slips in the river at my side, How slowly and gently he paces me, holding me down.

Figure 5. April 21, 28, May 8, 1949

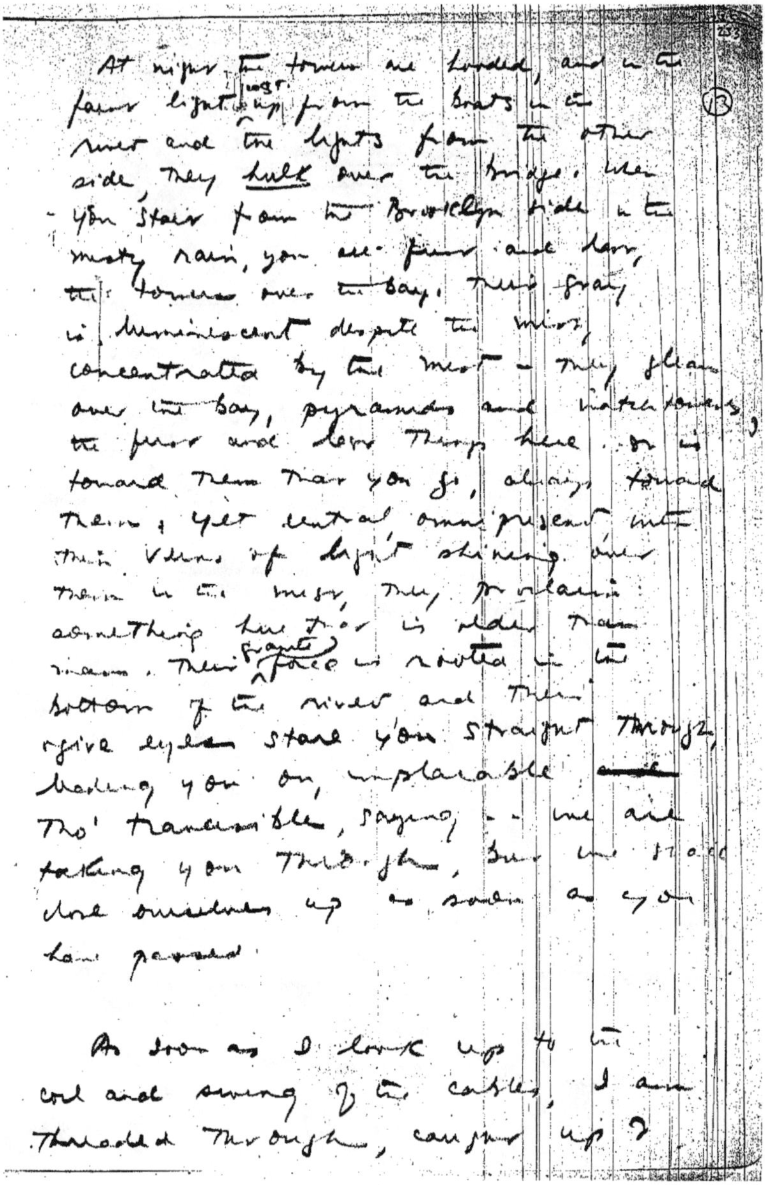

At night, the towers are lighted, and in the faint light ^mist up from the boats in the river and the lights from the other side, they hulk over the bridge. When you stare from the Brooklyn side in the misty rain, you see fierce and low, the towers over the bay. Their gray is reminiscent despite the mist, concentrated by the mist — they gleam over the bay, pyramids and watchtowers, the first and last things here. It is toward them that you go, always toward them, yet central omnipresent with their veins of light shining over them in the mist, they proclaim something that is older than man. Their ^giant face is rooted in the bottom of the river and their ogive eyes stare you straight through, bidding you on, implacable though traversible, saying — we are taking you through, but we close ourselves up as soon as you have passed.

As soon as I look up to the coil and swing of the cables, I am threaded through, caught up I

Figure 6. May 8, 1949

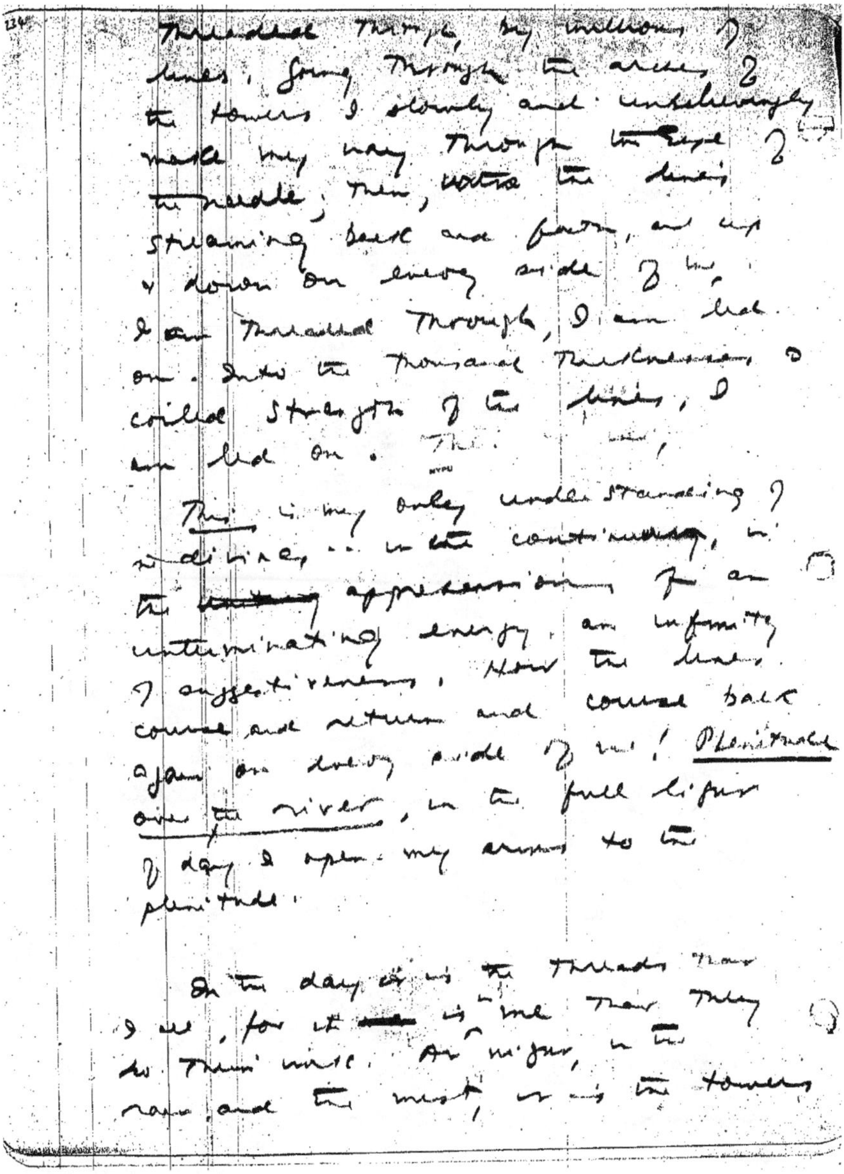
threaded through, by millions of
lines; going through the arches of
the towers I slowly and unbelievingly
make my way through the eye of
the needle; then, as the lines
streaming back and forth, and up
& down on every side of me,
I am threaded through, I am led
on. Into the thousand threadness of
coiled strength of the lines, I
am led on.

This is my only understanding of
the divine.. is the continuing, in
the apprehension of an
unterminating energy, an infinity
of suggestiveness. How the lines
course and return and course back
again on every side of me! Plenitude
over the river, in the full light
of day I open my arms to the
plenitude.

On the day it is the threads than
I see, for it is more than they
do their work. At night, in the
rain and the mist, it is the towers

Figure 7. May 8, 1949

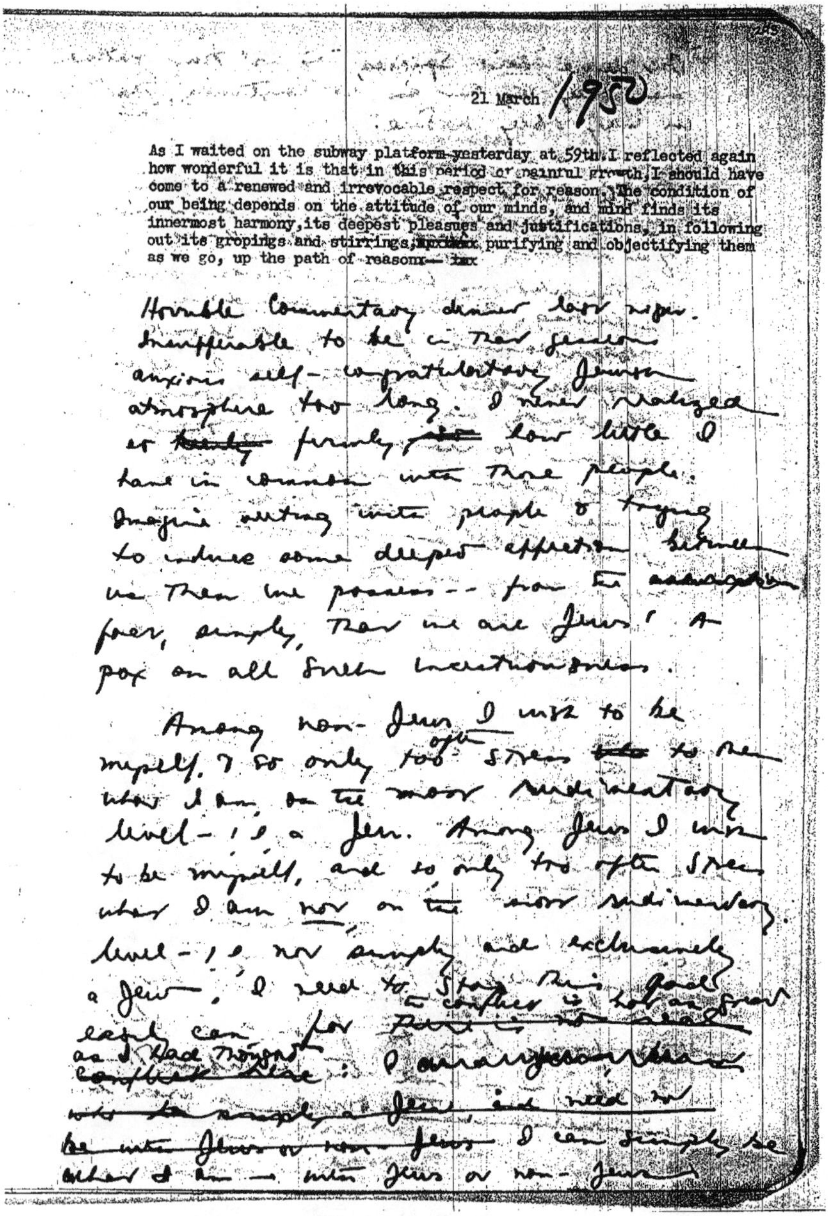
21 March 1950

As I waited on the subway platform yesterday at 59th I reflected again how wonderful it is that in this period of painful growth, I should have come to a renewed and irrevocable respect for reason. The condition of our being depends on the attitude of our minds, and mind finds its innermost harmony, its deepest pleasures and justifications, in following out its gropings and stirrings, ~~xxxxxx~~ purifying and objectifying them as we go, up the path of reason— ~~xxx~~

Horrible Commentary dinner last night. Insufferable to be in that jealous anxious self-congratulatory Jewish atmosphere too long. I never realized so ~~[illegible]~~ firmly ~~[illegible]~~ how little I have in common with those people. Imagine sitting with people & trying to induce some deeper affection between us than we possess — from the assumption, simply, that we are Jews! A pox on all such incestuousness.

Among non-Jews I wish to be myself, & so only too often stress ~~[illegible]~~ to the what I am, on the most rudimentary level — i.e. a Jew. Among Jews I wish to be myself, and so only too often stress what I am not on the most rudimentary level — i.e. not simply and exclusively a Jew. I need to stop this ~~[illegible]~~ conflict is not as great as I had thought ~~[illegible]~~ I can simply be what I am — with Jews or non-Jews

Figure 8. March 21, 1950

# 6
# The Sixties
## 1963–1969

IN EARLY 1963 KAZIN ACCEPTED A POSITION as Distinguished Professor in the English Department at the recently opened Stony Brook campus of the State University of New York. On September 27 he met his first class, initiating a weekly commute from Manhattan (spending two days and one night on campus) that would conclude in 1973 when he accepted a position at Hunter College and the Graduate Center of CUNY. After five years of freelancing and visiting professorships, he was relieved to have a permanent position. But he worried about the effects of his new security. Would he lose the edge that came with the daily struggle? Would the academic routine insulate him from the shocks and changes that made life interesting: "Middle-aged boredom. [. . .] Suburban ennui, flatness, nullity, insignificance, doom" (February 21, 1964). As it turned out, life in the sixties was hardly boring. If a steady job shielded him from financial uncertainty, it could not shield him from the ongoing difficulties in his marriage; nor could it protect him from the events that were rocking the nation—or from doubts and hesitations about how to respond to them.

There was much to respond to—the Selma marches, the Civil Rights Bill, the assassinations of Jack and Robert Kennedy and Martin Luther King, the escalating war in Vietnam, the upheaval on the campuses—and Kazin reacts to them all in his journals. But it is the war and what to do about it that provoke the most troubling questions. In a 1961 essay, "The President and Other Intellectuals," he had written that "when all is said and done action *is* the natural sphere of a mind, sane and hopeful, eager to revive the classic center of man's public activity" (*Contemporaries*, 458–459). But what kind of action? It was one thing to join peaceful marches for civil rights, to participate in read-ins against the war, to personally confront Vice President Humphrey in Washington on the Vietnam War, all of which Kazin did. But when peaceful protest failed, should intellectuals, liberals, thoughtful, right-thinking people join with students, including his son Michael, in acts of civil disobedience (barricading deans in their offices, taking over university libraries, disrupting classes)? Kazin deplored the confrontational methods of the students but took little satisfaction in his restraint. "Too much of what I see, too much of what I live, gets pissed away in all the attitudes of the spectator. Oh the intellectuals, the Jewish intellectuals, the commentators and scribes, the wisdom of non-doing" (November 22, 1967). He liked his teaching, for the most part; he enjoyed his distinguished professor role at Stony Brook; he was moving ahead on two new books and had plans for others; he led a lively and varied social and sexual life; he had reason to be content and much to be thankful for; "but all the while the thing on my mind is the insanity of the war, *the failure—moral failure—my failure—to do enough by way of resistance and response*" (March 4, 1968).

War and resistance, power and powerlessness, success and failure, are recurrent topics in the journals of the mid- and late sixties—contraries provoked by the Vietnam War but also suggested by Kazin's ongoing ruminations on the Jews, on Jewish history, and most recently and triumphantly, on the Six-Day War. "Every day since the Israeli victory early in June, I go to bed thinking: we are not as fit for killing as we were—we can be proud" (June 22, 1967). There were other reasons for Jewish pride. Having moved into the American middle class at a rate unmatched by any other immigrant group, American Jews were looking back in wonder on the distance they had come. Kazin had told a version of that story in *Walker* and would tell another in *Starting Out in the Thirties.* "Funny how long it's taken me to see what the book really is," he wrote in a November 6, 1964, entry: "a romance, a tale of the rise of Alfred Kazin, from misery, poverty, and literary chastity to power, intelligence, sexuality, reputation." He would tell it once again in *New York Jew:* "Write about Bellow and Trilling and Mrs. Trilling—about Jerome Wiesner and how many others who have 'made it.' *Success* has been our portion," he wrote in 1968. "The golden age of the Jews—the Age of our Success" (November 19, 1968). At a time of "insane big power mindedness," a time when "the whole theme of power [. . .] persistently engages me," Kazin took comfort in recounting the "rise" of the powerless to power and in reminding himself whenever he took up his journal of the source of his own power. "The word is my power, I have no other means of 'saving' myself" (March 4, 1968; June 27, 1973; June 17, 1969).

## September 29, 1963

[. . .] Started teaching at Stony Brook Thursday, 26 September, 1963. All very raw but pleasant. My immediate feeling is of how functional everything looks, bureaucratically assigned—a building that has nothing but corridors for students to walk in and teachers to listen to; offices that have nothing but desks and bookcases and files and pencils; even the chief administrative officer, Karl Drew Hartzell, looks to me with his sharp nose and his blank manner and his careful neatness as if he moved around nothing but blueprints and schedules. . . . The State of New York took a piece of ground, took the trees away, and on this barrenness has erected machine tools for learning called buildings and has hired machine tools for teaching called professors. The striking thing is the usefulness, usability, economy and dispatch. Everything wide open.

## October 13, 1963

[. . .] Writing in the Dark. Lying here at night I have many thoughts, and many odd figures clash in my mind. All night, indeed, inconsecutive figures pass and clash in my mind. But when I sit down in the morning to put a few sentences down, then I am no longer the host to these specters and dreams of the night, but someone who has to press words to an inevitable shape. Now it is not my dreams that take over, but my abilities alone; and for that brief period I am occupied with words.

Language is fundamental. They [words] are not "tools" but the primaries of which my picture is made. Without the right words, there is nothing. The dreams in my head are then not real, they are so vague that I don't know what they are. . . . I write in order to make these vaguely hulking shapes precise. I write to make them *mine*. I write to possess what would otherwise merely possess me.

## October 17, 1963

[. . .] The only way to have peace at S[tony] B[rook] is to let the kids talk, even to let the kids take over—not to instruct and guide and captivate all the time. Teaching *must* be really secondary—not a critic's notebook. Unless the *student* is in the center, it will be impossible here—I mustn't try to make *this* situation mine.

## October 19, 1963

Meeting held by *Dissent* at Hotel Woodstock on the Eichmann trial, and of course on Hannah Arendt's book. I hadn't planned on going, but when Stuart Hughes at the *American Scholar* dinner brought it up, I excitedly went with him. And then, like a fool, and under the influence of two quick martinis, I found myself actually walking publically to the platform and intervening in a way that makes me now feel like an utter fool. I was so irritated with Irving Howe's attack on Hannah that I triggered, absolutely gushed out like a cut artery. And at the moment I feel all the familiar, nauseous feelings of being profoundly dissatisfied with myself—of having let myself down, of behaving emotionally in front of a large audience. I keep asking myself—Was it wrong to speak up as I did? No, it wasn't; but I certainly didn't speak in the right place or to the right effect. I behaved emotionally and erratically. . . . I betrayed the whole tangled conflict about Hannah that has been going on in my mind so long, almost as a challenge to Ann rather than because I feel any of the old "commitment," as Ann called it, to Hannah. . . .

I feel that my *performance* was bad rather than it was wrong of me to speak. I feel ashamed at having been so obviously confused. I was defending Hannah *personally*.

There was certainly a lot of swank, even of contempt for Irving and [Lionel] Abel last night; and it is this egotistical show, I can see, this assertiveness on an absolutely unprecedented scale, that bothers me about my performance. There was I-can-talk-you-down about my bearing. I was trying to take over completely. Really big and aggressive.

## October 21, 1963

The era of indecision, of hesitant reaction, of indirect thinking. My era in this, but not mine alone. I keep looking for *the* position, for the philosophy that would round it all out and sum it all up. But even if "philosophy" in this major sense were my line—and it certainly isn't—I am not sure that it would be very meaningful just now. The rate of change in our time seems to me an absolute more positive than interpretations one can make of it. . . . I am convinced that my affection for Hannah has always been fundamentally a longing to be totally convinced—instructed—by her absolutes. After this awful *Dissent* meeting, which caused me so much shame afterwards when I thought of my intervention, I realize how much all this obsessiveness about Hannah has been about her as an "instructor," a *philosoph*. . . . The other day I was going to ask Bill Alfred about becoming a Christian.[1] When I read my piece (not 'alf bad either) about Eisenhower,[2] I know that my reactions are those of a radical critical "realist." The truth is that I never know what I believe in the abstract, and yet many of my fights with Ann and other[s] are about other people's positions, and it is often only after the fight that I can admit to myself how unsure I am of the position I have been defending.

The era of indecision is prevalent everywhere today. Maybe this is why linguistic studies have taken over in philosophy, and "analysis" in criticism. It as if *we* were being speeded up unbearably with the incalculable transformation in the external world. The observer cries out for a fixed point *because* he is not standing still. The outsider (a poor boy in the slums) can dream of Marxism as a *total* philosophy of salvation. The thinker involved in the middle of the presently continuous overthrow, and being bombarded with change as if they were particles, longs for "position" when in point of fact he can rarely stick even to ordinary rules of conduct.

1. See June 8–9, 1987, entry on Bill Alfred.
2. "The Sweet Music of Dwight D. Eisenhower," *New York Review of Books* (November 14, 1963): 1–3.

My autobiography has to be a narrative in which each piece of narrative justifies itself—it cannot have the character of an intellectual resolution; for even if I were to find one, it would be too obviously false to the facts, and in any event I don't think that it is in my nature to acquire one.

The philosophy of existence is the symbolic cont[emporary] philosophy—the philosophy of human reactions to phenomena, the philosophy of self-validation, as it were, the philosophy which fundamentally posits only the fact of existence in relation to the indeterminability of the all-sufficient cause. The Marxist is so full of the determinable cause that he sometimes makes the world itself seem indeterminable. The actuality of experience seems to yield to the official logic.

No wonder that people have killed and are killed for absolutes. They answer to some profound need for centrality and orthodoxy. Perhaps the doctrinaires kill because they are *not* as sure as they say they are or would like to be—So that in the act of annihilation one seems to realize what escapes one as a fiction?—opposite of the creative magnificence that is Shakespeare's negative capability according to Keats.

## November 22, 1963

Kennedy was shot around noon in Dallas this afternoon and died about an hour later. The fact is, when you have concluded all self-pitying thoughts about the inconsequence of the mighty when they are fallen, that the dead *do* have a very great power over us—that the last cry of the dying, though it is certainly not carried with any action, reverberates in our mind as a *continuing* effect. . . . Because we die, when all is said and done we live in consciousness on *this* side of life and not on the other, Kennedy's tragedy will have a larger effect on our lives than his administration. The final destructive blow taken against him and his silent subjection takes on continuing implications that his own actions did not. His somehow pitiful fate has become a major event in our lives.

Publically, his appearance was always *light*, ironic, witty in resource and charming. His fate is in its consequence incalculably heavy. He is a perfect example of the *prodigal* son—all that substance lost and wasted! We thought (because he tried to seem so) that America could be without the business of the Damocles Sword descending upon us—which is tragedy or fate (the tragedy being that we cannot resist its weight). In the end all the wealth, charm, easiness, youth, came to very little [very little in proportion to the ends expected of such advantages].[3] The tragedy is the Irish immigrant hope that enough money and charm and [illegible] would turn life into a "success," that the inevitable terms of life's bargain would somehow be changed.

## December 6, 1963

In the train going home. Well, I've done it again; and though I have a sick feeling of dismay and pain, there are moments when I'm not sorry. I seem to oscillate between solitude as the writer's dream of conquering his experience and falling in with all these ladies who are so attracted to me. I say to myself that it's not I who choose them as much as *they* chose me. They said the other week—you're dynamite for us. And what with the heady pleasure of the triumphant lecture and the drink, I found it hard to resist her. I found it hard to resist her. Could I have *not* touched her in the car last night when I came back to Sunwood? At the moment, honestly, I don't see how I could have. And though there [are] many sides to her character that I find opaque, I trust her not to play the fool. . . . At this moment, dismayed and remorseful as I feel, I can't help smiling at how the same pattern repeats itself. The writer's sensuality. I know that I couldn't have gotten out of that car without embracing her. [. . .]

After the *Commentary* symposium on the Negro, which I was too busy at Stony Brook to attend, there was the inevitable "big" crush party given by the Podhoretzes.[4] I went there and came back in a state of such moral fatigue and irritability with all those familiar faces that I must sit down here for a minute and put something of it down. David Danzig,[5] David Bazelon, Irving Kristol, Norman Mailer, etc., etc. The uncouthness of these people as a group, plus the uncomfort of standing for so long, and the sick stimulation of tepid scotch and water, makes for an atmosphere that is like a Jewish family feast in which the reproaches and hostilities and jealousies and grapplings become a thick, viscous medium in which you move.

My overwhelming feeling when I saw this group en-masse, en-pudding, as it were, all thickly cooked together in the room, was: My God, how tired I am of you all! And they looking at me with the same weariness and familiarity. . . . What

3. Kazin's brackets.
4. Norman and Midge Podhoretz. Podhoretz (1930–) was the editor in chief of *Commentary* from 1960 until 1995. Under Podhoretz the journal turned increasingly conservative in the late 1960s and 1970s, and Kazin ceased publishing pieces in it.
5. David Danzig, associate director of the American Jewish Committee, which published *Commentary*.

makes this group as a group so tiresome is its lack of manners, its lack of lightness, its lack of all those social graces that make a party. Louis Kronenberger notes the absolute lack of discrimination of topics, and I am struck by the disposability of everything. . . . The party is deductible, it is given by the corporation for the customers, and the "host" and "hostess" act as if the chief end of the party were to give themselves a kick. Struck by the oafishness of Norman Pod. drunkenly clowning in the entrance to the elevator. That lovely, blond girl (wife of the publisher of the *NY Review?*) looked really offended, and I couldn't blame her.

The faces stuck on the air as on hat-poles. Mrs. Roger Straus, toujours with the excessive makeup over her eyes and the ridiculously inappropriate "chic" hat and the choker . . . Mrs. Robert Gorham Davis, the ugly girl at the party who always looks tougher and more defiant than she needs to. . . .

Basically, the *Commentary* party is a collection of Jewish intellectuals who have made it. And all the prickly, sticky, aggressive, and hurtful tones and gestures that the lower-class Jew has in times past made me think that "life" is, are curiously emphasized by the thin and not very secure veneer of culture that attemptedly hides some of the more obviously unpleasant traits. I want! I want! I want—and now! A judgment of myself, a judgment. . . . Because it is so damnably hard to live with, in others as in oneself, this irritability above all things else . . . and impatience, and drive for quick, easy solutions of every problem. Every obstacle must be leaped now.

## December 10, 1963

Perry Miller died of a stroke yesterday in his study at Leverett House. The last time I saw him, outside the CBS building on 52nd street after an *Invitation to Learning* program, he looked flushed as usual, more distracted than usual, and vaguely embarrassed and unresponding when I argued with him about his unfavorable opinion of *Patriotic Gore*. Most times I saw him, he was flushed, wild, emotional, angry. And he was as jealous and competitive as anything could have been. Just to discuss anything with him on the air was to rub him the wrong way half the time. Yet I can't think of anybody in the "field" who was half as much a scholar, and who was simply so useful. He fascinated me because he was such a mixture of scholarly detail and choler. His temperament had nothing to do with his mind . . . or if it did, his temperament didn't enter into his books at all, except in a certain voraciousness of scholarly method . . . A career man in the best sense. How much he wanted to make a successful career of everything!—the "soldier" in the OSS, the scholar, the husband. . . . Those two tortured people at home, he and Betty, she with the piggy little eyes that [were] always red with weeping, he with that falsely robust "big laugh" and big voice. They looked together as if they had been pushing each other. She had got squeezed into a tiny little nut, and he had swelled into a kind of convention drunk. Perry could have been a character in a Sinclair Lewis novel. And yet he was the most scholarly and in some ways useful scholar of American literature whom we had.

## December 11, 1963

Bought the English edition of Hochhuth's *The Representative* [*The Deputy*] in the British Book Center on Monday, began it that afternoon and promptly began to have nausea and palpitations, especially when reference was made to the meat hooks with which the Kapos had to separate the bodies stiffened like "pillar of salt" by the gas.[6] I had to force myself to read on . . . and finally finished it yesterday. The irony is that when I got through I had the usual sense of being present at the newsreel of history, of being moved by *my* temporary participation in the horror and shock of the time, rather than by the play. Hochhuth is sophisticated; he is very eager to avoid obvious *bêtises*; some of the writing is even intellectually very neat, as when he has the satanic Doctor in Auschwitz say that all those horrors are an effort to make God speak. Yet the various settings . . . Rome . . . Auschwitz . . . a cellar . . . bring home in the old fashionedness of the "chronicle" technique of the costume play the presumption and folly of trying to make a play out of this. Obviously Hochhuth's play, which has the Christian spy in the S.S., Kurt Gerstein, as hero, is a declaration of the Protestant conscience against what the Vatican didn't do for the Jews. And this dramatization of contemporary history immediately sets up Catholic self-defense and Jewish bitterness on the same level. It is, like so much written in an attempt to be equal to the horror, artistically incoherent. . . . What are we supposed to think when we meet the "Doctor" (based on the infamous Mengele[7])—that this is the real Mengele, and therefore that the play is useful to us as a documentary portrait, or that this is an historical personage in his own right, though (as in Shakespeare) suggested by the original? In one way these questions arise precisely because Hochhuth is so tactful in his

6. Kazin's review of Rolf Hochhuth's play, *The Deputy*, "The Vicar of Christ," *New York Review of Books* (March 19, 1964): 1–3, contributed to the controversy surrounding the New York production.

7. Josef Mengele (1911–1979), known as "The Angel of Death," a physician at Birkenau-Auschwitz concentration camp.

manner, both as a German and as a playwright. If he were more "naive," less tactful, his play would have, if not more conviction, a little more force.

But to aim straight at the peaks of power, to attempt dramatization of both the Pope as a politician and of the entrance to the gas chambers in Auschwitz itself is to believe that one writer and one style (*his* one style) are enough to make "art" out of [what] Snow[8] rightly called the worst episode in human history.

Should it have been done? Hochhuth as a young German (he was born in 1931) is in a mood to take on everybody for the crime of Hitlerism. To a young German it is absolutely essential—and to a Protestant it is relatively convenient. But all the tact and discretion and critical sense in the world cannot hide the fact that this is an editorial in dramatic form. We cannot make art out of Auschwitz. We cannot turn the agony of our art into a newsreel and call it something else. Hochhuth is outside the events of our age not because he is German and born in 1931, but because we are *all* outside these events. Hochhuth says all the right things in his stage notes before Act 5, "Auschwitz or the Question asked of God." He knows that "it is common to the most momentous events and discoveries of our time that they make too great demands on the human imagination." Nevertheless, he has tried to put Pius XII in his cabinet and some unknown Italians and Germans, specimens of millions of victims, into the same play. . . . And when all is said and done about the excessive demand that Auschwitz makes on the human imagination, the politics of our time, which affords us so much illusionary "grasp" of the "total situation," and the journalism of our time, which makes it so easy [to] express and explain this "situation" in its entirety, combine to make Hochhuth's effort possible. . . . More and more it seems to me that we write these days as we suffer, in the same dimension. We suffer, that is, from the total alienation of our humanity—of our deepest tenderness and hopefulness as human beings—and the effect of this alienation from our own deepest, human feelings is to make us managers and the manageable, to make us hard, separate, instrumental, adroit. This is our suffering, that we no longer even know the deep part in which we unconsciously suffer. . . . But equally, this usability, which makes us so useful to everything and everyone but ourselves, makes us use Auschwitz *and* the Pope in his cabinet as events in the same play. We say "Horror!" about Auschwitz, but we don't doubt that we can put Auschwitz on the stage.

8. Charles Percy Snow (1905–1980), English physicist, novelist, government official, friend of Kazin's.

## December 15, 1963

Bitter cold for the first time this season. Went down to Hotel Adams on East 82nd Street to see the Meiklejohns.[9] They were just in from a matinee of "In White America," and in the evening were going to a party connected with "Hiroshima House" for the victims. And Meiklejohn told me that at the White House ceremony for winners of the Medal of Freedom, Douglas, Black, and Warren[10] went over to him with special feeling (because of his work in behalf of the First Amendment). It is for this that I love Alec. No one else I know just now is so much a symbol for me of the old libertarian American, the American with absolute good faith in liberty and liberalism and all good causes—the perfectly non-Marxist American, the American who has never felt any need of the apocalypse and is never depressed by its loss. . . . Alec Meiklejohn is for me the Socrates of the *American* enlightenment. He never seems depressed or ruffled, he is always unfailingly courteous, sympathetic, good-humored and aware, and for the same reason that he makes me (and so many others) feel in his company that they have to live up to this man, so he makes one feel that all the either-ors of the radical synthesis have been in advance of the facts. *Everything is possible*, is still possible, he seems to say with every modulation. My feeling about him is frankly one of hero-worship. I owe to him, from our few meetings in Berkeley last Spring, such renewed appreciation as I sometimes experience of American liberalism as a faith, of the teacher's job as a useful calling.

## December 20, 1963

I drove in from Stony Brook. Gusts of snow blew in the from the sides of the road and for the most part the driving was fast, monotonous, and vaguely ominous. The Long Island Expressway is always so crowded. Then when I got into the city, I decided to go up by way of Park [Avenue]. All those new office buildings of glass were lit up. The Avenue was sparkling with Christmas lights, and the effect was stunning in its brilliance—as if the heart of the city, the imperial avenue was literally made of light. . . . Christmas in New York with all the nostalgic old-American gestures toward the star and the tree, is really [the] celebration of the city's wealth. And this Friday evening before Xmas on Park Avenue, this wealth is experienced in *light*. Every window gleamed as a showpiece. . . . If a native is so astonished, a stranger would be blinded.

9. Alexander Meiklejohn (1872–1964), who had been dean of Brown University and president of Amherst College, was a philosopher and well known free speech advocate.
10. William O. Douglas (1898–1980) and Hugo Black (1886–1971), U.S. Supreme Court justices; Earl Warren (1891–1974), chief justice of the Court.

## December 25, 1963

[. . .] Yes, marriage hath many pains, and Ann is so cross and irritable half the time that I sometimes wonder if it is all worth it. Yes, it is. Nothing, but *nothing*, counts so much as living with a woman, and really living with her. I am a bad husband, I feel more and more that I am helpless before Ann's despondency and failures. Yet, what do all the affronts and pains in the world matter, what *do* they matter, by contrast with the sweetness and neatness that we have so often had in these last 13 years? When in my life have I ever had such intimacy with a woman at all? And it is a marriage that, with all the hysterical cries in our ears, is always recharging itself. God knows I don't love well, that I'm not patient at all, that I want just to write and have a woman to shore me up. . . . Yet when I really think at things as they are, at my family, at the privilege of my having a family at all, I wonder at my impatience and bad temper. . . . Nothing could [be] less significant than these brushes, these routines of family hysteria and personal anxiety. . . . I'm so much like my father, but so much more aware than my father, so much luckier.

One should never quarrel with women. The implicit meaning of the relationship is violated. It is better to give in, in form, than to violate the form. With women and in relationship to women, it is the form that counts, so that to fight with a woman is to concede an equality (in aggressiveness) that she does not want and that keeps a man from being a man with her. . . .

## January 18, 1964

Of the writers I have known personally and at all intimately, Hannah has surely been one of the few *originals*. Her originality consists in a peculiar moral steadfastness, a definite gift for seeing the moral implication of a position. Her originality plus a certain unconscious, personal Germanization in resistance to her American environment, gives her an imperiousness of outlook that is behind all these quarrels with her American friends. The breakdown of our friendship, I see now, really began at that spring 1954 meeting of the National Institute when she got her grant.[11] And obviously, it has been the competitiveness on my side as much as Ann's resentment, that explain the gradual falling away of our intimacy. There is no reason why one should try in personal relations to overlook the pains of such competitive jealousy and resentment. Hannah certainly blots out the other person, and you have to submit to her as final authority or break away.

11. See Chapter 5, note 98.

But her "originalness" rather than originality is one that I want neither to evade nor to sentimentalize. It is an originalness of personal outlook, a personal steadfastness of style, self-dependence in relation to herself and a crushing authoritativeness in relation to others. So the figure of "Erica Hauptmann" is at least becoming clear to me. The wars of rivalry, with Hannah at the center of the battlefield, have been really bloody.[12]

## January 27, 1964

[. . .] For me this endless autobiography has been, inwardly, an attempt at self-liberation, at private therapy, an attempt to lift all those hurts and frustrations from inward brooding into occasions of self-understanding and self-transcendence. It has been not so much the record of an education as an instrument of education. But in some way the emphasis on self has become a disease, my typewriter has stuck on the letter, "I"; and longing for transcendence, for objectivity, for sheer freedom from this self-reference, I find myself having, as Proust said, to write by moving an injured limb.

What happened in the '40's was just the beginning of the current sexual sophistication of the Jewish middle class. Everybody of my generation had his orgone box, his Lou, his great search for "fulfillment." There was, God knows, no break with convention, there was just a freeing of oneself from all those parental attachments and thou-shalt-nots. What has always been so wrong with my writing about Isaac, Lou, the village, the war, is my note of "you-have-changed-my-life," my priggishness, my air of innocence defiled. It is not Asya I have mourned all these years, it has been my own innocence. And so long as I write from the vantage point of that innocence instead of with the objectivity and honesty of a seasoned man who doesn't regret a single thing, who is grateful for all those wonderful girls and their gifts of love, I'll never be able to make anything useful of that episode and will continue to put my foot in the water and as quickly take it out. Which means that one is rooted in that early cycle of temptation and challenge and self-refusal, and one is forever sixteen, with the "future" always ahead of me.

The rhythm of an autobiography can never be as tight as that of a novel. For in a novel the action becomes, as it were, a single fact—in an autobiography

12. Hannah Arendt appears as Erica Hauptmann, a character in Ann's short story "When the Wind Blew" in *Summer Situations* (New York: Coward, McCann and Geohagan, 1972), 132–191.

silent reference is always being made to the shape of a man's life. . . . In an autobiography, as in history, there are "episodes" and "portraits" that "stand out"—there are moment[s] of artistic intensity, in short, when the speaker comes close to the pockets of his deepest concern. But basically every autobiography hangs on the value, or impersonation, given to the Me. The Me becomes the central myth, the corridor down which all the other characters walk, and what counts for the book is simply what single myth or interpretation the author of the recital is willing to give his Me, which one he will choose out of the many selves that he really experiences in his daily life.

Autobiography is a form by which the Me assumes, in historical guise, the control and significance that one would like to give one's life. The Me has become, in literary operation, useful. The Me has become a stock character for others. But this literary-autobiographical Me has to be as concentrated as any character in a novel. . . . He has to have authority, too, or the reader will not believe that the autobiographer has mastered his experience.

Autobiography deals with the delights of "personality" rather than character-in-action, in "portraits" rather than in *plot*. Which is why there are so few good autobiographies about oneself after a certain age, and why childhood and youth always provide the golden occasion.

## January 29, 1964

[. . .] Think of the Jews in the historical *drama* that has been wrought out of Jews and Christians. The Jews are on the stage, a "minority," being watched by a "majority," the non-Jewish audience. In Alexander Donat's memories of the last days of the Warsaw ghetto,[13] the Polish Catholics on their way from Church on Easter Sundays *watched* the helpless Jews flinging themselves out of the windows, and they applauded. The dramatic *role* which the medieval Jews played for Christians when they were being burned is like the role which Christ on His cross plays for those who surround him in the act of worship or who ruminatively look on.

The others look on. There is something fateful about the Jews, made for the center of the world's stage. They are always on stage or being thrown off stage. They are commented *on*. Even people who have never seen a Jew *know* about

13. *Jewish Resistance* (New York: Warsaw Ghetto Resistance Organization, 1964).

them as we know about famous criminals or celebrities or actors. The actor is expected to fulfill a certain role. There is a Jewish role for each Jew, which even Jews try to act out.

Does the actor act because there is an audience, does he act for the audience, would he not act if there were no audience? Because of the Jew's faith that God revealed himself in history, his sense of his own destiny is unfailingly dramatic. History becomes the drama in which he acts. He does not even complain that he is being watched by those silent ruminative people in the audience. The Jew cannot imagine a "Jewish" world. He always sees himself as a function of the majority, the "audience."

## January 30, 1964

How much of this helpless anger that rushes out of me at every detail of the Nazi murder of the Jews is tied up with my own feeling of guilt toward that Polish Jewish woman that was a Jew of maximum suffering and defenselessness, who always made me feel that I was not doing enough for her? I didn't do enough for her—her life was *so* miserable—I didn't do enough for our people when they were being slaughtered like cattle. I didn't *do* enough! This is my guilt and in some way my constant sense of fury and outrage at the Nazis is attuned to that old Jewish mother and her constant life of suffering. Yet if anything comes home to me as the solid, single growth of all these inner struggles to make sense of the Nazis, it is that the Nazis *were* defeated, that there is a stubborn power of resistance in man, a defense of his integral existence as a man. And for us Jews, who have so often sought to humanize the world so that human beings could live in it, a pessimistic identification of all being with evil is impossible. To be this pessimistic one must really hate life and distrust being, whereas, if you really adore life and are endlessly in wonder at it, the kind of mortification in regard to *all* things that my mother went in for becomes something to watch out and to fight—in behalf of life and joy. [. . .]

## February 8, 1964

The West Side is full of characters. In the Broadway bus you see old Hungarians with refugee caps, Negro pansy actors, professional Broadway types, mangled accents you cannot even identify, much less understand, and such a variety of the old that you feel the whole bloody neighborhood is nothing but an asylum. All the doddering refugees. [. . .] Broadway is a parody of old European cafe society.

Saul [Bellow] came in while the Bells were here. Friendly, laughing, transparent Saul: who like a precious jewel may let himself be handled, but who is impermeable. Over the years he's gotten friendlier, but he is just as self-contained as ever. There's a circle around him that you can't enter.

"We must deepen the channel in the brain." [. . .]

## February 16, 1964

There is a self, a Me, whom I race against. A Me whose identity is given only by Others—childhood influences, contemporary fashions, the setting of the family or the job, etc. This Me still gives itself marks, still counts progress by going from test to test. . . . And meanwhile I, the rational and contemplative and self-fortifying I, sees things that don't appear in the test. This I wants a breakthrough; this authentic self wants to be free of the self that can only race, succeed or fail.

Isn't this really why I want to write this book, to let the "real" self come through at last? The thinking, free self whose best insights are so often an astonishment?

My autobiography is not an *assignment*. It is a book in which I can uncover many delicious freedoms. Yet I keep chastising myself with this book, reproaching myself for my "cowardice," etc. when all the time there is only a story to tell. What happened. It happened.

The hero of an autobiography is this "real" self. The plot is this struggle between the "conventional" self, and the "social self," and the Me—the Me disengaged enough from circumstances to study them as harmful to "fulfillment" and "vision" and "integrity." The new self that we win back from old circumstances is the prior self that lost itself to circumstances.

When did it begin, this idea of the self as disengageable, wholly, from "society," as the first victim then the opponent of circumstances? When did it begin, this idea of the self as the hero necessarily alienated from society as his bad habit? Obviously when society began both to impinge and to fail as support: when it became a crowd rather than a community and a vast commercial inauthenticity. When nature became *our* nature.

Obviously this romantic version of the self is not enough for me. To feel oneself a prisoner to convention, a slave to social habits and expectations, is one thing.

But to feel that *oneself* is enough to admire and to trust, as opposed to the artificialities of society, is something else. And this is how far I have come from the *Walker* and its romantic doctrine, sufficient for a boy. For I don't believe that personality is enough to live a life by, I don't even believe that it is interesting for very long. The integrity of the self turned into the self-sufficiency and self-interest of the self. Personality became the absolute.

## February 21, 1964

When I was a boy, Deborah Gelb, the beloved, lived on the other side of that wooden fence on Rockaway Avenue. Every time I walked home from the subway and came to that fence (on the middle block, between the subway block and the home block), I used to feel all the sharpness of my love in my breast; and I would look across the fence, to the lights gathering in the evening on the windows of the Gelb house, as if the abyss between myself and the unseeing Deborah was remote enough for pain, too far to articulate my longing in.

Today on the train from Jamaica, Deborah recognized me and spoke to me. She's still very pretty, very cute looking—and is divorced, has three children (two sons of 19 and 20) and a little girl she was taking to her sister before she went off on a date. She was very eager to be friendly, she was amazingly eager . . . gave me her number at home, wanted to make a date. Obviously she was flattered and romantically excited by my few lines about her in the *Walker*; certainly she was not this much interested in me when I was puppy mad about her at nine or ten or whatever ridiculous age that was! Now she is divorced and interested in me. Her face is so pretty, a sort of really pretty version of Pearlie's—the same Slavic Jewish triangle. But although she was amazingly eager to see me, my over-all feeling was one of pity. She mistook my literary use of her in the book for a real interest.

Middle-aged boredom. Changes. Suburban ennui, flatness, nullity, insignificance, doom. From Brownsville to Long Island, the island that is my destiny, to which I always return. *Changes*. The real theme of the book, my real preoccupation, is entirely with that—Changes, metamorphosis, the change, or rather changes. The process of change, with that little boy staring at the fence still so vivid to my mind, but whom I cannot grasp, is a perfect paradigm of elusiveness of our body, our physical being, our life-marching-to-death. . . . The mind does not change; all that early longing is still baked into the inner man; and there are times, coming home from the university on Friday night when I just feel like whimpering, I feel so empty on that flat long island. But when I look at my double chin in the train window and take out my glasses to look at every word and count my energies and think of what happened to all that life behind the Gelbs' fence on Rockaway Avenue, I realize what it all comes back to, the only real theme: *Changes*, the whirling earth, the search for the unmoved mover, the unmovable, the principled constancy in all this whirligig. What is there to hold on, what, what? Not the "ideal" of a historic period identified with one's youth. Every day I say to myself—human nature *will* be satisfied.

History is the history of human nature—study human nature; study what the human *being* wants, how he moves, what he demands. History is the sum total of effect, the revolution set in motion by the demand of human nature. History is the history of the human abilities, demands, vulnerabilities.

## February [nd] 1964

Other People's Lives

To be a Jew is to be looked at by non-Jews in a certain way. Your experience is not their experience; and whether they look at you with sympathy or suspicion, they have to cross a certain barrier when they meet with you. But I, as a Jew, have in my turn so much of a barrier to cross when I try to imagine other people's conditions, that it seems to me that the real work of intelligence, of imaginative understanding, lies in this effort to identify, to understand, ultimately to participate in, other people's lives. "The human condition" is an abstraction; other people's lives, like our own, are made up of "conditions," which we cannot easily understand and do not wish to understand. So the real work of intelligence is to understand, to cross the barrier. And here the analysis of determinants is probably less useful than the gift of *presentation* through literature. The real achievement of literature has been, beyond anything else, to put us into other people's lives and to put theirs into ours.

But other people's lives, other people's troubles, especially other people's poverty is hard for us to take in. And probably a good deal of what we find so repellent in Communist countries is their poverty.

## March 14, 1964

[. . .] Analogy—my tendency as writer and critic to dwell on the "high-points" of a text, the emotional peaks, the "isolated beauties," instead of the *argument* of a book. My weakness as a literary scholar and as a writer is to opt for the creative moment rather than for the argument. But only the argument settles anything in a book; and analogous to argument in a book is the process-in-life which Carol, beyond anyone else I've ever known intimately, made me realize. The "argument" of Carol was beyond *my* behavior altogether. It was rooted and unchangeable. Things had to happen as they did. Emphasis on my efforts were as superficial to the drift as emphasizing passages from a book were to its argument. [. . .]

The idea was—that I would write *one* mighty confessional book, making up for the past and somehow changing it, resolving my life-problem. But I can see now that I am going to be working in autobiography as long as I live, that my book will be a narrative, not an *instrument* for "settling" my existence. . . . And perhaps the real story to be told (I caught a glimpse of it in the sketch of Isaac) is exactly this attempt to bring one's life to a resolution, this attempt to find a solution for everything, at every moment, and with everything I had. . . . It is this unrelenting and merciless search for a resolution that now lies behind me, that is something I can train my sights on.

## March 15, 1964

[. . .] Autobiography becomes art when it simulates history without submitting to it.

## March 16, 1964

To the poor Jews of the thirties, as to the desperate Negroes of today, "History" is all around to make a demand of. The door must open, a better world must come soon. There must be some immediate fruit of our effort. But the agitation of the Negroes, which has already provoked a sizable middle-class white opposition, is not accompanied by any ideological illusion of a brave new world, of white hearts made new and washed clean of their sin. Not only do they feel like a minority asking for rights of the majority—but they are looking for allies, who are not really there even when they seem to be. . . . Yet the real "ideological" or religious basis of the Negro protest movement *is* religious—a desire to have an entirely "moral" world, a world of peace-lovers, of attention to the sordid and neglected. It is not ideological in the millennial sense of communism, but it is religious in a more authentic, more harshly difficult way than millennianism. It does not have the mechanical expectancy of millennial movements, but it is moral in specific ways, not in vaguely general ones.

## March 30, 1964

*Monday*—Thoughts under the flu—the Jewish condition that Marx and Freud had in common: unmasking the secret motive of *them*, sex or class. Yes and rationally testifying to it as a condition that we share.

Memories of the Thirties—[Mark] Van Doren the sweet talker, turning everything into the sweet syllables of literature. *A sort of confidence man*—Everything turned into honeyed style, into intellectual "felicity."

## April 17, 1964

[. . .]

How you have suffered Alfred—That is the epic I've been unwilling to give up—"my youth," my great striving and fierce feeling, that daily atmosphere in Brownsville and later of daily conflict, fierce hoping. . . . And I've kept to this atmosphere in my book, trying in Part II to keep the whole boiling quality of the war years, the break with Asya, going away with Lou, etc., etc. Until one day I find myself in Stony Brook, chill and bored with being only the professor, the distinguished professor, bored with the objectivity I can muster as a critic, thinker and teacher; for such objectivity does not express itself in continuous feeling and brooding, but has limited aims and ends detached from myself.

*The Deputy* piece taught me that I can use materials of the '40s for truly objective, critical, thoughtful purposes. Every day in my teaching, every day in my living with Ann, I know what I can do as a thoughtful and objective man. And so I get lost, I feel lost—to give up all that striving, all that emotion!

The thirties book can yet be turned to real narrative, as the *Walker* was. But this outward-looking represents such a loss, this loss of the daily *Sturm-und-Drang*, that I feel empty and then get scared.

## May 5, 1964

[. . .] Louis Kronenberger's new book, *The Cart and the Horse*, is more about company manners. What interests me in Louis's writing is always its wit, not its expressiveness. He has the social gift, the gift of charming and witty conversation, *in* his writing, in a way that no other American I know has. He writes as if he were talking to someone ready to chime in immediately with his wit. It is really a *spoken* style (and often quotes, I am sure, many of his best sayings or those he has by the same gift provoked in others). In the mid-thirties, when I first met Louis, this social gift of his often made me suspicious. Now I welcome it as if it were that first martini of the afternoon. It *is* a bourgeois gift, and he well knows it, and why should he be ashamed of it? At least he does not fool himself with this gift, but keeps his eyes trained pretty steadily on the world. Objectivity is the only sanity for a writer, an objective conversation and *aperçu*, à la Louis, certainly a relief after the kind of incoherent self-absorption that Pearlie suffers from, or the kind of exhibitionistic shop-talk that Dan Bell rolls off in conversation *as if* to impress himself more than his listener. Dan's conversation is so automatic in performance; he rolls off what he has been thinking about, what he thinks he has lately discovered, as if it were a tape being played too fast. Nothing he says comes out of the encounter with the other; the other only sparks the performance.

What a neurotic set we all are—but in a particular East-European, poor Jewish style of personal aggrandizement. It is not so much our secret psychological "motivations" that make us this way as it is our manners. There is no tradition of self-restraint, of true politeness and inquiry. We feel *threatened* in the darkest kind of way, and we are always trying to rise straight up from every possible frustration. Our self is clamorous with indignant demands on everything and everyone. There is no ground on which we do not think we have a right to intrude our clamorous demand. And then, wearied with the inevitable frustration, we retire back into self-pity and misery. I look at Pearlie's face, white, miserable, strained; I think of my father, who at seventy-seven is as alone and self-absorbed and self-pitying as he was at seven; I think of the incessant tension between Ann and me, each of us demanding everything of the other and incapable of foregoing any of his demands on the other, and it seems to me that this absence of neutral ground, this driving yet fundamentally *despairing* demand on everything and everyone, is explained by something so simple as a lack of restraint, and forbearance in ourselves. We go at life like one of those monster children on television devouring cereal. We are manic with hunger. We feel deprived all the time. And somehow the boring and shallow sociologese of Dan Bell's conversation argues that so much inner deprivation closes up the perceptive faculties. What a cruel judgment on so much selfhood, that it should finally be incapable of *saying* very much.

Yet the writer brought up to middle-class urbanity and amenities, like Louis, knows nothing of the bitterness that we all start from. And every day I see on the streets of New York Negroes crocked, half-mad, ruined, of whose lives I know nothing. The given condition of early life is a fatality for almost everyone.

Gifted people can use this given early condition, but they can hardly escape it. For weeks now, ever since Northrop Frye[14] spoke at Stony Brook and then asserted to me afterwards that "reality is essentially a mental phenomenon," I have been talking back almost without knowing it. The givenness, the pull or gravity of these early conditions, is an overwhelming fact. The Marxists are wrong about freedom being the recognition of necessity, for if freedom is not a value in itself, we can never have it. But neither does freedom characterize us as we are. We are caught between the pull of "gravity" or determinism and the *necessity* of believing ourselves free. Frye's myth and rituals refer to the operations of the mind or imagination, not to the facts of experience. And for him literature is not a way of organizing experience or of rendering experience; it is simply a way of accounting to itself for itself.

## May 16, 1964

Saturday. That was a fascinating encounter, a week ago at our house, between Kronenberger and Ellison—fascinating to me because, with all his easy talkativeness and urbanity, Kronenberger is so "classical," objective, *firm*, by contrast with Ralph E., who like all my generation, is uneasily self-assertive, a bit sentimental in the clinches, wild and deep in his farthermost reachings as a writer, but in the last analysis, *subjective*, like all of us, in a way that the middle-class and Midwestern Kronenberger is not. Whenever I look into Wilson's jottings on the thirties, I am struck, similarly, by the scrupulous detail and *pointillisme* of everything, as opposed to the wild and always *personal* notes I tend to write on the period. [. . .]

## May 17, 1964

Sunday night. Came back from the Feiffers in Brooklyn to find that Dorothy Baker and Mercedes McCambridge were not coming over for dinner.[15] They had had a big fight about coming over and after several hysterical cancellations from "Mercy," I finally went over to get Dorothy—and found myself in that little room, in the house at 4 E. 64th with the most shrieking, screaming case of

14. Northrop Frye (1912–1991), Canadian literary scholar and theorist. His influential *Anatomy of Criticism* (1957), in which he argues that literature is constituted by "an order of words" corresponding to archetypal transhistorical patterns in the human imagination, left little room for the kind of historical/moral/political concerns that Kazin believed literature elucidated.

15. Jules Feiffer (1929–), cartoonist; Dorothy Baker (1907–1968), novelist; Mercedes McCambridge (1916–2004), actress on Broadway and in film.

hysteria I had ever seen. McCambridge threw herself in a chair, and her legs up; she pranced around the room as if she were stealing side glances at herself in a mirror. "Don't threaten me," she kept saying back to Dorothy, who sat small, pinched, in dark glasses—"Don't threaten me with the fact that you may die next week. We may all die next week!" McCambridge has just completed her run in *Who's Afraid of Virginia Woolf?* after 103 performances, and was obviously unable to let go of the violently dynamic part. But whatever the real or symbolic connection between the novelist (who has cancer) and the actress (who tried to commit suicide some time ago and who obviously has difficulties finding parts and who obviously feels she is a flop in all departments) the connection between professional anxiety, bad health, and the terror of death has become a blow that each aimed at the other as sickeningly as each aimed it at herself.

Ann says that so much fear of death makes one feel unworthy. To think so much of dying makes one feel contemptible and ignoble to oneself. When Ann said this, I thought of how much in Christian theological argument has depended on one's assurance of salvation—obviously as a guarantee of thinking better of oneself in the world. The contempt for oneself that McCambridge showed in her hysterical rage against Dorothy was also a fear of herself. To be unsure of everything is to lose status with oneself.

Anyway, I went over again after Dorothy had asked me to leave, and found her standing on the corner of 64 and 5th with her suitcase. Brought her back here for dinner and the night. [. . .]

## May 20, 1964

The twelve years of Hitler, 1933–1945, were the years of my apprenticeship, of my basic formation. During those twelve years, Hitler and Stalin were the prime builders of the new totalitarian system and the destroyers, at the same time, of the myth that politics could be the saving force and prime interest of my generation. The drama of those twelve years, ending in Hitler's defeat, was [the] painful last struggle for survival; and when it was over, one could only look back, "After the Apocalypse," as if the intensity and world scope of that struggle had left a permanent barrier between the two periods. After 1945, one picked oneself up, blinking in a little daze, to look at the world with entirely new eyes.

Those twelve years, of depression, of fascism, of Stalinism, of the Moscow Trials, and finally of Hitler's war and Hitler's terror, make up the setting of my book.

## May 29, 1964

[. . .] Ellison came down for lunch, the Department-about-to-hire-you lunch, and talked very soundly and very impressively about the translation of American experience into authentic works of the imagination on the part of lower-class men, Negroes, minorities, etc. This is something that never happens anywhere but in America, and it is this creative salt, not "ideology," that is the real substance of the book on the thirties—the *experience* of "lower-class" men is certainly different. . . . Then I look up at Susan Sunday,[16] and I realize how important it is to make the experience of my generation and of those days in the thirties come alive, how important it is to do justice to that experience, to show its relevance to artistic dignity in our toney middle-class world.

I have been hung up on the book only because of "personalities"; yet after all these delays, the book haunts me more than ever, and I am determined to do justice to it, to the truth of that experience, come what may.

Ralph *is* terribly impressive. With his beautiful light-Indian-Negro color, the Oklahoma accent, the scar just alongside of the right eye, and above all his sense of American experiences as something naturally flowing into and boiling up creatively in a literary mind of his kind of sensitivity, I find that I learn from him more of what I owe myself than I do from many writer-friends. This same evening, the Hofstadters just back from Europe were over for dinner, full of self-satisfaction and purring with tales of the Mercedes and the grand tour. Whenever I am with the Hofstadters, I feel in the air this self-consciously competitive ticking off of everything—academic accomplishment, literary accomplishment, motor-car acquisition.

## June 1, 1964

This disease of restlessness, which makes me increasingly difficult with the sentences that I read, with the people I know and even the people I love, which drives me constantly to something not here, something [that] appeals because it may *be* over there—what is this disease but the constant intrusion of self, this disease of constantly seeking my advantage in whatever I read and whomever I meet (exaggerated but true enough to be thought about seriously and critically)? So long as I don't lose myself in a subject or book; and I rarely do (my own

16. Susan Sontag (1933–2004), literary critic, theorist, and political activist from a later generation than Kazin's.

heartbeat, the rhythm of my longings and the fever of my ambition for *myself*, are in my ears as I read), then of course I am like a man turning things over impatiently and greedily. . . . It is a disease, a disease which I fight against, but which I have rarely understood so well as I do today; for with everything that can be said in extenuation and simple explanation of this disease, it *does* come down to this nervous self-protection and self-advance, and constantly leaves me, in relation to the subject, insufficiently curious, patient, devoted, and ever unappeased.

The writer as plebeian: the demanding, hungry self. Give us this day our life, our future, our needed "assurance." Give us this day everything—ecstatic sexual joy, food the minute we think of it, love without our taking pains for anybody but ourselves, mechanisms we do not have the patience to repair ourselves to be instantaneously, noiselessly and cheaply repaired. Give us, give us . . .! But to whom is this surly prayer addressed? Who is the magic agent of this unaccountable and quite unexpected benevolence?

Judishes hast, Jewish haste, Jewish egotism, Jewish self-centeredness . . . above all, greedy arbitrarily demanding minority thinking. We must make our lives right, we must get it quick, we must get it for ourselves, now. I despise Miss Sunday [Sontag] and Mr. [Lionel] Abel and so many of the Harold Rosenberg tactics in self-advancement and self-assertiveness and self-celebration, but look how I intrude myself on so much, and much that I can't get to the thing-in-itself that most of all I want to understand!

Leave myself out of the picture, for a while, for a "change," as we used to say, and most of this unrest and inner disturbance vanishes. A sacrifice is demanded of you, a gift to God himself: relax, put yourself out of the picture for the nonce, look squarely at the object as itself it really is.

The writer as plebeian has force, he has color, he translates "life" into terms of passion and power. But need it be *his* power that he seeks so much?

## June 5, 1964

[. . .] Began Serge's[17] *The Case of Comrade Tulayev*, and was immediately struck by the hurricane of feeling and bitterness in it—the intensity and evocative

17. Victor Serge (1890–1947) was a Russian revolutionary who worked for the Comintern as journalist, editor, and translator. He openly and bitterly criticized the Soviet regime.

sensibility that are the marks of the old Bolshevik or even true Socialist imagination. "Socialism" as an idea (I come back to my old preoccupation here) was the last great effort to communicate an effective idea of destiny. It gave meaning to the past, direction to the present, an association of triumph with the future. Since the breakdown of socialism as a religious or world-historical idea, there has been no other which has gripped the free and self-directing intellectuals of the world. And it is a fact that "nihilism," in the sense in which Silone spoke of it in his observations on the many casualties and suicides among writers in the forties, does represent the loss of this idea of destiny as something which man can not merely assure (the scientific-pragmatic illusion of the Enlightenment), but which man seizes on as a redemption of his true nature, obscured or lost in the circumstances of his daily life. To believe that your "right" destiny is not only assured but that all history points to it, that you can not merely create it but in a sense find your "true" nature by earnestly being faithful to your idea—is to create a model or paradigm of all reality, past, present and future—as opposed to the sense that your values are unsupported by anything but the biological accident of your own nature. [. . .]

## June 23, 1964

*Herzog* overwhelms me—Saul's greatest book and the book of this generation. He has learned from all his troubles and consciousness. *Equal* to the ambiguity of circumstances. The momentum of change so baffling and defeating of others in our generation, has in this book found its complement *and* consecration in the fully aroused conscientious[ness] of the intellectual hero.

The book seems to me of the most urgent importance and use. It is about *trouble*, *moral* trouble of the most excruciating kind, and shows how true consciousness can subtilize and deepen itself—*on* trouble. Herzog is a hero—in his confrontation of betrayal, and in the bewilderment and sickening loss he attains a consciousness equal to the maddening difficulty of circumstances and one which alone can minister to it.

Consciousness saves.

## August 16, 1964

Edmund Wilson at MacDowell Medal ceremony—the portly seventy man-of-letters (who belongs to letters). Big belly, white shirt, dark tie, dark suit, always formally dressed, always talking in formal sentences and on formal topics. Straight Roman nose, sensitive, but thin and controlled mouth. Red blotches of arteriosclerosis in his cheeks. So formal in his manner that any joke or crack on the part of another literally breaks him up—i.e., dissolves his formality. While on his side, behind the formality, the self-possessed but elephantine manner of the rubicund body, he plans mischief.

The big head, the big face, the man-of-letters always *at* letters, so to speak, assembling his information and digesting his reading and formulating his thoughts.

A big baby face, too: when he gets annoyed, when he pants out, he wants it all right—a flush comes over his face, he gets peevish. What he wants he wants, and what he doesn't, he rejects *immediately*. In touch with his own control tower at all times: amazing instinctive integrity, definiteness, flatness of reaction.

Above all, a man-of-*letters*, living on letters, for letters, thinking in letters. [. . .]

## August 30, 1964

The Wellfleet comedy, or social notes by the water. Professor Harry Levin's[18] Jewish nose is not a shame to him, as such noses sometimes are to Jews, but is really a periscope through which he carefully sniffs and sights what is going around him (meanwhile giving you now one ear and now another), surveying the opposition, sizing up his opportunities, awaiting his moment. After listening to Chavchavadze[19] singing "Stenka Razin" and other such ditties from ye old Russia of long ago, he said to me sotto voce, that C. had excellently parodied himself. . . . In the course of a few hours, Professor Levin's periscope having been folded up far below the water line, he managed to sink shafts into the late Perry Miller, the late F. O. Matthiessen, etc., etc. [. . .]

## September 9, 1964

[. . .]

Went over to Irving Howe's in the evening. Ariane [Howe's wife] has certainly made a difference to Howe, and he seems more likeable and more interesting to me than he's ever been before. We were all together there—Dick [Hofstadter], Howe, the [H. Stuart] Hughes . . . all my "history-minded"

18. Harry Levin (1912–1994) and Lionel Trilling were the first tenured Jewish professors of English Literature at Harvard and Columbia, respectively. Kazin disliked them both.
19. Paul Chavchavadze (1924–), the son of a Georgian prince, was a novelist and translator and a friend of Edmund Wilson and Elena Wilson.

friends, children of a common experience. I took away with me a copy of the new *Hudson Review* with the usual poisonous article by Marvin Mudrick,[20] a critic whose spitefulness and vehement nastiness have a way of reaching me as if he injected some poison directly into my veins. . . . Odd, here is a fellow whom I would guess to [be] an embittered, out-at-Santa-Barbara, English don. He writes with an intense bitterness and sense of his own higher standards as a critic that turns everything he scorns and dislikes into dirt. An angry, poisonous man, a "critic," who writes like a hunchback. Yet I have only to read him even on people I detest, like Diana Trilling, to feel that he is injecting poison right into me. . . . In my anxiety about my book on the '30s, I allow myself to side with someone who is purely and venomously an antagonist. I allow myself morally to be annihilated. . . . I plunge myself into the shadows exactly as I once did, seeing everything from the point of view of the hateful Mudrick, Merde-rick. . . . I yield to this viciousness as to a superior power. [. . .]

## September 10, 1964

There are styles in egotism as in everything else. Try it as the Leitmotif, of "Some Portraits":

H. R. [Harold Rosenberg]—the Maccabean. Never say die. Ruthless in-fighter. Never confesses to weakness, or to a mistake. When he betrayed his foolish French some years ago in an English magazine and was corrected, he turned on his critic and bit him hip and thigh. When a distinguished English art critic complained that H.R. palpably misread him and was an unfair polemicist, H.R. told him off: I don't let the author of a book tell me how to read him. . . . An intellectual rabbit-puncher in controversy and, as a critic, destructive of all other writers. Only painters count.

Yet he is an original, his egotism makes him original. He inspires confidence, pleasure, joy, because he is so positive. He is a street philosopher, an armed bohemian, a forward-looking man; carries you forward with him. [. . .]

## September 22, 1964

Party for Saul and *Herzog* at "21" of all places. Waiting downstairs for Ann, I amused myself by picking the customers for Saul's party from the regulars

20. Marvin Mudrick (1921–1986) taught at UC–Santa Barbara from 1949 to 1986 and wrote essays, many of them acerbic, primarily for the *Hudson Review*.

at 21. It was so easy! The girls, the old Chicago and Village girls, all looked as if they were wearing sweaty black tights under their party dresses. There was that unmistakable swarthiness of the girl intellectuals, with their olive complexions and fleshy noses; the Jewish men intellectuals looked ugly, stamped with the difference of their background and their trade. Thinking has stamped them, the ghetto has stamped them, they looked *pressed*.

All too familiar. The stale round of literary New York, the same people and the same cocktails and the same talk, repeated in the stale round of all our old friends from Chicago. A voice keeps on saying to me in the middle of the night, Look carefully, friend, look *deep*; there ain't any more than this. You've rounded the circle, there are no more spectacles than this.

So let them come in again, the old familiars, let us look at them again, with the fresh eyes of imagination—Arabel Porter and Katey Carver[21] and all the old loves, would-be loves, friends and near-friends, the hits and misses—even Vasiliki [Rosenfeld]. All so stale, isn't it? All so bloody familiar? But there isn't any more.

Saul, our plebeian princeling and imaginative king, standing there, gray, compact, friendly and aloof, receiving his old friends whom he had invited to 21. Funny to see Ruth Miller and Irving Kriesberg still lofty about Saul's "personal" kind of fiction. Saul alone of all the old gang has achieved first-class status. The sweaty girls who look as if they are all wearing tights under their party dresses, Harold R [Rosenberg] with his exhilarating command, Leslie Fiedler—Saul alone has made it, with the furious resistance of personal imagination to the staleness of the round. There's more yet for me, he cries in his heart, more, much more! Nothing is stale, he cries, if only you look at it hard enough, see in it aspects of human fate in general. Put your story on the universal stage of time, and the old Chicago friends will seem as interesting as kings in the old history books.

At the National Book Committee yesterday, Arthur Schlesinger was described (by Brendan Gill[22]) as "the most highly employable man of our time."

21. Catharine Carver (1921–1997), originally an editor at *Partisan Review*, did freelance editing for Saul Bellow and Leslie Fiedler.
22. Brendan Gill (1914–1997) wrote for the *New Yorker* for sixty years.

## September 27, 1964

The book will be all right, I now know, if I can only learn to do justice to all the other people in it—to see them, first, in terms of what they wanted and hoped from the period. I must get over seeing everything in the hard resistant terms of my selfhood. . . . The reason I am doing this book, for God's sake, is to turn the shallow outer phenomena into warm living phenomena in the consciousness of the author, and I must put these people back into life by giving them their right, by asking in every case what was *their* hope. The question to be asked first of every character in the book—How do *you* see it? Instead of this assault on Hook, why not a debate between Eastman and Hook?[23] The sterility of the final picture will be all the quieter and more convincing.

## October 7, 1964

[. . .] The real story of American literature, for me, the story it tells me and the story I would like to tell, is of time: the prophecies of the New World, the fantastic compression of time in the New World, the missing past and the unalterable dream of the future. What is Emerson talking about but future time, and what is James talking about, in his criticism of Hawthorne, but the lack of enough time to have made a deposit of tradition in the American's mind? Parkman's dream of the forest is a dream of time past, and Henry Adams's of the world future?

The book[24] could begin with Adams and his dream of scientific history as the free development within a relatively fixed sequence. It could deal with the Calvinist conviction of man's sinful past as the hold of the past, and then contrast this with the pervasive American dream of the free future.

## October 9, 1964

Jews like Judah Stampfer[25] and Elie Wiesel—Jews who are exciting to me simply because they still carry such a vibration from their religious training—Jews who when they meet you start off by talking about this vibration. Jews who are

23. Sidney Hook in *Out of Step* (New York: Harper and Row, 1987), 155, writes that despite Kazin's claims in *Starting Out in the Thirties*, he was not present at any of Hook's debates with Max Eastman.
24. Kazin would plan and work intermittently on *An American Procession* (1984) for two decades.
25. Judah Stampher (1924–1996), Israeli-born American poet, novelist, and scholar, taught for most of his career at Stony Brook.

electric in the old divine conscience. What is dangerous in the eyes of the world, yet what excitement they carry in their eyes and voice.

## October 12, 1964

*Critic and Creator.* Reading Frost all day for several days, and my principal sense is how much swifter, more complicated, honest, direct he is than I. Art is swift, powerful, condensed; criticism is long, so long in its unravelings of what was swiftly effected in its power. And Christians, in my experience, are so much more complicated than Jews, so much more at home in the world, so much less sentimental, so much cagier, so much more suspended in their disbelief. When a Jew says "tragic," he means his life: when a Christian of Frost's intelligence says it, he means the world, existence,—that which so few Jews can admit as problematical by its very essence, without solution, without hope, biased by its creator no doubt, but spinning along remote from his invisibility.

Frost was very smart indeed, very laconic, very direct, very honest, individual, independent, contrary. He had strong faith in his artistic powers, but very little faith in life, his life; the contrast of the pride of the artist with the vulnerability of the man, made him always interesting in strangely moving ways, you'd never know where he'd jump.

Independent, yet involved with people, triumphing over them and needing them in a way that made him as vivid as a beautiful young girl on the threshold of life. [. . .]

## October 23, 1964

Delusions of the critical intellectuals. That ideas rule literature, and they have ideas; that life is expanding all the time as ideas expand, and so they can be in charge; that they speak for modern literature, which is the voice of expanding and progressive consciousness.

Delusions of the intellectuals: that their self-pity is an indictment of the age. Nothing is so fine in *Herzog* as the way he nails this "Wasteland" psychology.

## November 6, 1964

[. . .] Funny how long it's taken me to see what the book really is: a romance, a tale of the rise of Alfred Kazin, from misery, poverty, and literary chastity to power, intelligence, sexuality, reputation, etc., etc. Why did I make all the time that even falling in love with Mary Lou was a fall? It was a rise—it's all been a rise. This has been a rising time in the most rising of all countries. We are all pushing as hard as possible to get more, more.

Susan Sontag, or the style-setter. The combination of chic and unseriousness in this article on camp is really funny.[26] Cultural amalgamation in this flip style that hides any real anxiety that is so pretentious, p. 525—"Loie Fuller, Gaudi, Cecil B. De Mille, Crivelli, de Gaulle, etc." I love that et cetera.

It's all elitism, self-conscious superiority based on a little foreign travel, homosexuality's daring, and that same enfant terrible quality that so many young women writers seem to need, feeling the most minor of minorities. . . . The fascination of Jewish intellectuals, Negroes and Puerto Ricans with homosexuality—a way of getting somewhere faster. Scandal, the counterfeit of fame.

Critic for the *NY Review of Books*—someone who argues brilliantly in behalf of the most arbitrary personal prejudices. The reasoning is superior, full of éclat, in the British fashion, i.e., designed to impress the opposition. But it is not honest, it is not large, it is not *true*, it is merely flashy—brilliant in its arguments.[27]

Yet—one has the sense in reading it that principles, or at least the articulation will bring principles into being is on the way. One has the English sense that standards exist. The English have this valuable *respect* for value even though they rationalize their judgments, i.e., disguise them as being more objective than they are.—They always pretend to be more reasonable than they are. [. . .]

## November 21, 1964

[. . .] The truth is I cannot bear to live without some of that inner glow in my heart, without the God I knew in my youth, without trust in my own reactions. I sometimes feel that the theory of fiction (on which Kermode writes, so brilliantly, in this *New York Review*),[28] and which is so crucial to the imagination of art in our time, calls for a stronger ability to endure the unreality of the world than I

26. Susan Sontag, "On Camp," *Partisan Review* (Fall 1964): 515–530.
27. The *New York Review of Books* published eighty-two articles by Kazin.
28. Kermode, "The Man in the Closet," *New York Review of Books* (December 3, 1964): 33–36.

possess. All these esthetic readings imply a central feeling of ambiguity that I can barely tolerate. I *have* to believe that the world is real *because* I observe it.

"The eternal mystery of the world is its comprehensibility"—said Einstein.

[. . .]

## December 17, 1964

Alec Meiklejohn died last night in Berkeley of pneumonia. The peculiar beauty of this old man is something I can hardly do justice to at this time—he made me, perhaps many others, want to *be* better, he made one look *up*, constantly. An extraordinary man, a beautiful, modest, unforgettable teacher-man.

## January 9, 1965

At Boston's New Year's Eve there were only professors and doctors at the Zetzels'[29] party, and I knew what the Genteel Tradition was—professors and doctors, doctors and professors. Like Harry Levin, the mask-like man. And now Eliot is dead, and I sit listening to his voice on records—what an actor, what a proboscis of a voice, penetrating, darkly and humorously and elfishly into so many corners of the genteel tradition. Sounds of words, colors of words, rhythms made into *characters*.

I saw him three times—in London at Faber and Fabers (and at Hamish Hamilton's party for Edmund); at Reynal's, after the war, when he walked about with Allen Tate, pleasantly soused; and in Rome, end of 47, when he read. . . .

He dominated us by the sheer perfection of his art, nothing else. Listening to Auden being roguish and impatient, and oh, so Christian, and boyish, to Dylan crapping off, Eliot by contrast comes through with stunning completeness.

That voice, that voice, darting into so many corners. . . .

## January 19, 1965

[. . .] The "rebels of good family" in the twenties created a literature out of their quarrel with their own class, their own society. Is it possible that the fondness for

29. Dr. Louis Zetzel of the Harvard Medical School was Edmund Wilson's physician in the 1960s.

"absurd" and "existentialist" novels on the part of so many Jewish "outsiders" today comes from the fact that they cannot quarrel with their own class, that their class is not important enough, or influential enough, to be quarreled with? Baltzell[30] is right when he says that the rebels-of-good-family in the 20's were far more rebellious and non-conformist than the outsider intellectuals are today. When you consider the enormous implications of the quarrel with their own, from Henry Adams to Wilson, you see the prime explanation for the lack of creative resonance and depth in the creative literature of so many "outsiders."

The outsider finds it so easy to say that the world is "crazy," about to blow up—it has too [much] tendency and too little *content*.

And yet this feeling of despair is all too genuine: it comes from living so much on the surface of things and by the will. This despair is in effect the solitude of an unremitting self-consciousness, of the lack of deep unconscious roots to our lives. When so much is up to *me*, my intelligence, my will, my capacity for survival, how can I help but despair at the unremitting effort it costs me to live—spiritually, at the same time, too exigent. [. . .]

## February 19, 1965

[. . .] Riots in Brooklyn, near-riot in the UN, stabbings in the subway, Republican cries to keep the war in Viet-Nam and Chinese cries to escalate it. We are all locked together in this subway car now, and people are flashing knives around us, and the little Keystone cops are not good at breaking up the melee and protecting us. The sense of danger is constant, and the sense of personal inextricability as we are all locked in on each other, bringing up images of the Jews locked into the gas chambers, crowds, always crowds these days making themselves immobile for slaughter. Mailer writes with this excessive American fluency, this supermarket plentifulness of personal sensation in which every personal sensation is cherished and enumerated and described with almost Elizabethan hyperbole.[31] Yet the atmosphere is staggeringly one of sexual nightmare, of aggression and basic lovelessness between people so pervasive

30. Professor of sociology at the University of Pennsylvania and author of *The Protestant Establishment: Aristocracy and Caste in America* (New York: Random House, 1964), among other works on caste and class in America, E. Digby Baltzell (1915–1996) is credited with coining the acronym WASP (white Anglo-Saxon Protestant).
31. *An American Dream* (New York: Dial, 1965).

that it is virtually unnoticed and unaccounted for. . . . Whenever I read Mailer, I have this sense of nightmare, in himself, communicated from him to me: and the energy of the writing, the sometimes frantic and at other times innocently showy fluency, is so clearly a kind of personal exhibition, in a world made up of other personal exhibitions, that the same over-cold ring and inflation of sexual experience (by putting it into terms of contest), found in the writing, makes the whole thing a kind of lonely narcissism. . . . There seems to be absolutely no attempt in this one even to create a hero dramatically separate from himself: the author suffers and writes in the same voice.

## March 15, 1965

Johnson before Congress asking for a special Civil Rights Bill to insure Negro voting. When the President speaks about these elementary concerns of justice, we are moved by the public articulation of our political hopes, our sense of our own political virtue, publically expressed. Yet what a brutally simple and demogogic style this is put in—and all this compelled on this politician by the incessant and widespread political protests following the terror exercised against the marchers in Selma! Thank God for the kids, for the churches, for the outsiders, for the conscience-bearers and the bearers of hope.

## March 24, 1964

Rain, rain, and rain from Selma to Montgomery. A huddle of Americans, white and black, marching in the rain, while ladies sitting in lawn chairs on the side yell "Nigger!" The US is trying on the idea of brotherhood, and it hurts like hell, and we will keep trying it. Selma is one of the great events in American history. It lights up our day. It is great, great, great. Religion as politics.

## March 30, 1965

Michael came over about 8:20, and we drove out to La Guardia to fly to Boston. Very Cold. There was a heavy snowstorm over Boston, and the plane landed at Providence. Much impatient waiting, then a bus to Boston airport. It was snowing and sleeting so hard that the driver (this on route I8) got out at intervals to wipe his windshield. But what with one thing and another—coach and taxi and subway—we got to University Hall in time for Michael's appointment with the Director of Admissions. The yard was thick with snow, and I hurried Michael along from Widener to the Chapel to the new Visual Arts building—so proud to show Michael to Harvard and Harvard to Michael. We had drinks with

Peter D at the Kaplans and dined with the O'Connors[32]—I felt so proud of my son, so astonished to see him grown up enough for an interview, "even,"—and when today, Tuesday, the 30th, I finally got him home to Englewood, I felt empty but very proud, terrible at seeing him off again, but *very* pleased indeed that we had both come this far.

## March 31, 1965

Dinner with Harold Bloom, Ludwig, and Levin in NY. Bloom, a really gifted, impressive and *nice* man—formidable to me, leaves me feeling like I know nothing and have read nothing of the English Romantics [about] whom I prate so much. I feel that it is time for me to settle down to some serious learning! By contrast with the Stony Brook brigade, Bloom looks *big*. Extraordinary how that round, vaguely baby, Jewish, unworldly face imposes itself, takes hold.

## April 2, 1965

Bloom. When he removes his glasses, you see an extraordinarily handsome face, straight nose, almost classical profile. When he puts his glasses on again and shuffles up his vest so that his shirt is all over the place and he stands there firing cannonades of lecture at you while he keeps scratching his hair, you lose sight of the very clear-minded and arrogantly possessed young scholar. Fascinatingly gifted and fascinatingly complex man; listening to him last night on Yeats and the Romantic Tradition, I realized that his interest is in literary history, and that he is a brilliant representative of an academician, which, as always, I am so out of that I can only suffer the exclusiveness, while I am on the academic spot, and not change it. . . . My feelings of chagrin and unworthiness during this period are just the old ability to see things from the point of view of any other than myself. I had a horrible four-in-the-morning crisis over this, but shook myself free of it eventually and got back to sleep. I don't look at literature as Bloom does, but I am certainly as much of a putter-downer as he is! This furious business of being one step ahead of the opposition and preparing a mine field for him to walk through! This furious drive to rise in the literary-critical profession by stealthily suggesting deficiencies, distortions, and debilities on the part of the

32. Peter Davison (1928–2004), editor at Atlantic-Little, Brown, and a poet. Benjamin Kaplan (1911–2010) was a professor at Harvard Law School and, from 1972 to 1981, a justice on Massachusetts Supreme Court. Edwin O'Connor (1918–1968) was a television critic for two Boston newspapers and a Pulitzer Prize-winning novelist. Davison, Kaplan and O'Connor were longtime friends of Kazin.

contra-position with whom you are discussing! The science of English literary history and what we think of this or that pattern in it. Bloom's thesis last night: there is a clear line between the Romantics, Yeats, Stevens, Lawrence.

## April 4, 1965

Bloom again, or romanticism as a lively subject in the English faculty. End of the New Criticism, which represented the School of Eliot-neo-classic and voulu religiosity. Bloom sees much in Shelley and in Blake's apocalyptic mode. What a change in the University since the school of Eliot! A good essay could be written on the Romantics and the *new* scholars.

"Writing In the Dark" will be on the relation of literature and *literary faith* to personal experience.[33] Literature as an aid, a solace, an instrument *in and out of the thick of life*. Literature as a factor in the humanist's, critic's, teacher's own life. Living by literature, living in literature, *living*-portraits of writers, estimates of people's literary capacity, literature as a *vademecum*, as a social tool, as a profession, as a drug, a gossip. The day to day life of the man who tries to get through life with the aid of only the subject he knows at all comprehensively, and precious little of it. [. . .]

## April 13, 1965

All these writers I am preparing to review just now—the French couple, Lasch and [Lewis] Coser[34]—remind me of the clear-cut position I can never seem to adopt: as a critic I enter too interestedly into the distinctive thought—and moral universe of each writer I study to be able to fault them for their position. . . . But equally I have become afraid of political "principle" too nakedly held; ever since the massacres of the war, I have been inwardly shaped by the terror of massive extermination; and, like the new anti-nuclear pacifists, I am afraid above all of aggressive political activity, of the *chances* of such wide-spread activity. In short, I am dominated by my fear of totalitarianism and fanatical extremism of

33. This would be the theme of *Writing Was Everything* (1995); "Writing in the Dark" did not become a book.

34. "The French couple" refers to Simone de Beauvoir (1908–1986), writer, philosopher, feminist, best known for her 1949 work, *The Second Sex*, and her lover, Jean-Paul Sartre (1905–1980), writer, philosopher, political activist, novelist, literary critic, and winner of the Nobel Prize for literature, which he refused. Christopher Lasch (1932–1994) was a professor at the University of Rochester, an American historian and social critic, best known for *The Culture of Narcissism* (1979).

any kind. . . . Yet meanwhile, whatever the intellectuals may support or oppose, the nation-states operate with the immoderation of unlimited technical change itself, and the badly frightened intellectual will not be allowed to abstain from choices that may help to bring on the same high-principled violence which he had hoped to escape.

## April 21, 1965

Finished the review of Lasch's fine book.[35] Ann in bed, petulant, miserable, cranky with me beyond words. Met my father at Borough Hall in Brooklyn and sat with him a while on the Esplanade. The old man looks feeble, for the first time at seventy-eight; angina now as well as the old coronary. We sat, we looked at each other, we tried to communicate, we were close after all. And going home, thinking of him, I thought of how little literature ever answers to this experience of being old and waiting to die, of so much blankness and loneliness. That line of Apollinaire's—I've never seen people for whom life is not too much. Life is too much for my father, who had been trying vainly all his life to be equal to this shell, his life.

In the subway going home I thought of how, when I was young, I thought that a great book, somewhere, would give the final word on experience forever. But up against experience like my father's, the poignancy as well of *watching* him, one man's truthful account is as useful as another's; there is no one way of establishing the uniqueness, the indescribable intimacy, of one person's experience. That intimacy, that inner truth, is the point, of course. What I've learned in my life more than any other is that there are few general rules, that the fatefulness of each person's life-situation is the central fact about him, that literature is meaningful only in so far as it turns to this inestimable, unweighable fact of a man's single experience. Death is not the same for all men, and obviously life is not either. What *I* have felt, what my father feels now, what Ann feels—these are incommensurable and expressive (not finally meaningful) only in a few words that catch the impact, the moment, the drift, nothing else. For months now, ever since finishing *Starting Out in the Thirties*, I ached and suffered over the intimacy of the narrative. Yet when I think of what else I might have done, I have to shrug my shoulders; I am glad of my book, it is a good book. But more than anything else I feel in touch with myself because of it, even though this self wavers.

35. *The New Radicalism in America, 1889–1963: The Intellectual as a Social Type* (1965), reviewed by Kazin in the *New York Review of Books* (March 20, 1965): 3–4.

Alarms, cries, shouts, screams: my anxious wife is on the rampage again tonight. I can't share what she feels, but I can be patient about it—I can wait it out, *not being her or bound to her*. I can, in short, be myself, wholly, and not tremble or suffer when the line is pulled. Eh? The only thing that will give me peace about Ann is to write about her, to be that detached.

## April 22, 1965

Dickinson. I *know* who she is and what she believes—what point she sees *from*—I know the speaker and the speaker's mind. This is my old friend, my old familiar, Emily—I read the poems with pleasure in *her* mind. This is what American writing so often comes down to for me—the familiar pleasure. So one must push the source of this pleasure to the critical limit, in study of the personal, intellectual, and religious sources of the pleasure—one must study this in depth, since to begin with "impersonality" is impossible to me.

## June 3, 1965

[. . .] Lunch with Bob Silvers, who is looking thin, ill, a little wormy. A wormy man, a courtier of literature, the editorial friend and help[er]. Love for intellectuals, would like to love them more directly—but he loves directly enough. He loves them in conversation. He loves them by *agreeing*. In the afternoon Katey and I went down to the Chelsea for a session of photographing with Inge Morath, Arthur Miller's wife. The poise, the self-characterization, the conscious charm, and international swish, of this woman. In her modest little two-piece black dress, her face in all its marvelous structuring stood out excitingly. Old playbills on the walls of Miller's plays, *Death of a Salesman!*—and the adroit, *modest*, playing it down presence of his Austrian wife.

It was June on 8th Street, and Katey and I walked over to the 8th Street bookshop and bought books. It was June, the golden month, and my golden girl, Katey, stood up in the bookshop and said, "Papa, go away and let me browse!"

Evening, dinner at the Howe's. The Podhoretzes, the Michael Harringtons,[36] and us. A good evening, exciting political talk. Felt at home with them all—felt easy. Ariane suffering.

36. Michael Harrington (1928–1989), political activist and founder of the Democratic Socialists for America. He is best known for *The Other America: Poverty in the United States* (1962), a book that influenced President Johnson's War on Poverty.

Kierkegaard—the last Journals. The sacrifice of Jesus Christ: an absolute. The one emblem of the Christian era: He sacrificed himself.

## June 7, 1965

[. . .] Henry Adams felt like a woman. Herman Melville and Walt Whitman felt like women, Hart Crane and how many others: all those sensitive, too-sensitive Americans and individualized consciences and sensibilities, under the impact of machines, machines, machines.

## June 15, 1965

[. . .] Went down to Podhoretz's offices and had drinks with him around the corner at Le Moal on Third. Good talk about the proposed introduction to the *Commentary* anthology.[37] Norman subtler by fifteen years than I, equally soft, rising to the bait with all his critical intelligence. Is on the drinking man's diet, and so ate paté off his knife. Home for low-keyed dinner and evening (so far) with Ann. [. . .]

## June 17, 1965

[. . .] O New York, New York, carousel and carnival of the too-rich, busy, full life, how can one ever do justice to your insane human fullness?

Baumann talks German in soft, warm voice—addressing herself to English, she lifts her voice several octaves and enunciates in a harshly clear, piping voice—feeds the data into this voice.

## June 18, 1965

Whole morning with Katey at the orthodontist, Natural History Museum, Brentanos, Soc. Library. On our way over to the [illegible] we met the Kristol ladies on the bus. Bea in her friendly "we-scholars" approach. Katey so beautiful in her blue raincoat. I had a letter in my pocket from Peter Davison announcing that Reader's Subscription would take care of at least 3000 copies of *Starting* (a joint offering of my book with Trilling's essays!), so I felt good. It had been

37. Kazin, "The Jew as Modern Writer," appeared first in *Commentary* (April, 1966): 37–41, which Norman Podhoretz edited.

raining in the morning, but by the time Katey and I had finished lunch, the sun was out, and I gleefully parked my raincoat and umbrella at The Excelsior. Happy day—father-daughter day. Katey kills me, absolutely kills me—the radiant face, the eager mind, the outstretched spirit. Her face smiles with the intelligence whose fullness she does not yet know.

We caught Fifth Avenue at the peak of the lunch hour crowd. A brilliant scene: I pompously told Katey that we were in the center of the world's most "important" city. I even said it was the biggest city, and Katey frowned, "London is bigger," she said.

Then a bad evening with Ann—one of the worst. We went down to dinner at the Blue Ribbon in a mood of tenseness: Ann wanted to talk about the McKay[38] offer, and I wanted to encourage her—but my mood was too good and hers was too bad, and after the first cold drops of concentrated martini, the fat was in the fire. She went off after I said I wasn't pushing her—a banality she took as a provocation. After more splutterings, she walked out on me, as she has from so many dinners. I walked up to Broadway, back to Sixth, and saw her come out of the restaurant—she had gone back. Bitter quarrel in the street, in front of the Algonquin—where I got so exasperated that I threw my umbrella down. On Fifth Avenue it ended with her standing across the street and silently mouthing her cries at me! Though I walked off, I followed her, concerned, worried, sick with guilt *and* anger with her at the same time. We walked surlily over to the new Weston for drinks, where we drank without talking to each other. Then we went over to Third Avenue for the silly Margaret Rutherford whodunit movie—on the way over, Ann bought a large giraffe doll, and we sat with it in the anteroom of the movie house, we put it in front of a seat from which it solemnly looked at the screen. To bed, two separate rooms, exhausted, tired, sick.

## June 27, 1965

[. . .] All these diaries are nothing but to keep in practice, to keep one's end up: the truth itself is always just out of reach, has to be struggled for, demands poise and exertion like a matador's: the knowing when the moment has come. The value of my journal to me is just that it is uncalculated and headlong and indiscriminate: that it is full of the stuff of life that one naturally feels superior to, the little crumbs that one disdainfully steps on. . . . The poor old whiskered

38. The David McKay publishing company.

lady in the bank just twenty minutes ago, who apologized for her life with each step, each step: and shuffling her way from the window, said to nobody, to the air, to God: "I've got to sit down before I walk again . . . I have to sit down before I walk again."

## July 26, 1965

Last night, rushing "home" to Yaddo after the violent, awful weekend with Ann at Peterboro and in Rochester, the phrase "ecstasy in consciousness" came into my mind. "Ecstasy in consciousness" for James, for so many writers of that "contemplative" kind. But now the business of living with someone, really living *with* someone takes you by the throat, chokes all the breath out of you, and then at the end leaves you grateful, oddly grateful, that this love exists. . . . Friday morning I sped to MacDowell and Ann, and arrived at her cottage studio feeling on top of the world. Yet all week I had been full of moral anxieties about the weekend, and sure enough I kept refusing her, refusing to fuck her passionately and directly with love. Why?—[. . .] because the sight of Ann in her MacDowell cottage, surrounded by so many, many flaxen haired, identical sophisticates, threw me off. We gave a little party for the "colonists" at her studio and then went back to the Peterboro motel. She was loving and exceedingly passionate, and though we started *sixante-neuf*, I didn't come in her mouth; and when she asked me to come directly in her cunt, I felt completely unwilling and muttered something about not wanting to be "tested." This set her off; and for hours she screamed at me in the horrible, little, Peterboro motel room. Next morning we went off to see Katey at Saipatuit—very cold on each other, but Katey so alive and marvelous looking that we couldn't help relaxing a bit. [. . .] But going out to dinner at that horrible Red Coach Inn on Route 44, the liquor stirring us up, I completely misunderstood something she reported having said about me to Reed Whittemore,[39] and the meal became a horrible, screaming fit. She went on and on obsessively and hysterically about Hannah and this and that, until I found myself choking on my food, pounding on the table, and rushed out of the restaurant.

We drove back to the motel on Route 44, and at three in the morning she awoke, cursing me, screaming "I hate you! I hate you!"—until the people [in the] next room began to beat on the wall. . . . I kept putting my hand over her mouth, I

39. Edward Reed Whittemore Jr. (1919–), American poet, biographer, critic, and editor, poet laureate consultant to the Library of Congress, professor at Carleton College.

was in such a horror of hearing her screams and curses again. . . . And yet, after all this she asked me to her bed. We fucked, and in the morning we made up for the whole weekend with the most delicious session we had had in ages!—We drove back to camp, had another lovely visit with Katey and her "bosom pal" Ann Johnson (of Berkeley), and then I drove her back to Peterboro. She was depressed, and I to my surprise was happy though exhausted by all the emotional turmoil of the weekend. . . . On the way back here from Peterboro, I drove wild and fast, and the phrase "ecstasy in consciousness" kept coming into my mind. . . . Somehow the weekend ended *happy*. My deepest sense with Ann, despite her oral violence, was again of her acuteness—and more than this, her demandingness for real physical love, which I realize to my utter surprise is possible with her. "I have a beautiful body," she kept saying, and "I mean to enjoy it."—One of the things that have always kept me back with her is my sense of having to work so hard at lovemaking with her, at her dormancy. Suddenly she has popped up as the demanding female, eager and anxious. And unless she feels absolutely loved, demanded, cherished, she retorts to the implicit insult in torrents of hysterical abuse. . . . And yet, my lifelong fear of being reduced by a woman, of being something less than the master and loving conqueror, has never been more out of place than with Ann, who wants me to love, to protect, to be in charge. And I feel so utterly one-of-two! What a pair we make, what an incredible *two*, what reciprocal fear and delights. As awful as I was first and she in retribution, so we were wholly in touch with each other after fucking in the morning. And the overwhelming importance of physical love to her now (I mean now openly) has been my feeling for so long—only I didn't associate it with Ann, with so much love.

## July 28, 1965
### [Yaddo]

[. . .] In the evening, to see the William Wyler film *The Collector*. Afterwards the Yaddo boys (and two girls, one of them being Zelda Popkin)[40] sat around in the Colonial and dissected the film, [Philip] Roth as usual giving the lead. . . . Roth is a sharp, logical analyst of character and motivation in whatever he sees and reads. I remember that in discussing *Herzog* he spotted all sorts of illogicalities; when he discussed *The Collector*, he took it apart, spotting every possible implausibility and moral confusion. He is always outside, vigilantly

40. Zelda Popkin (1898–1983), novelist and writer of mystery stories.

himself as the spectator and critic and judge. Everything is consciously sized up all day long. This extraordinary conscious intactness!

## October 4, 1965

The Pope's day in NY. It suddenly *was* a different day, and I felt, particularly in listening to his speech at the UN, that "the new way of doing things" that he was counseling in politics, as a measure to ward off wars, had become a blessed way of speaking. For a while the usual pettiness is suspended—for a while things lose their hard, horrid shapes—for a moment the useful hopes of peace and love begin to seem like possibilities. I found everything about the Pope's visit inspiring. I was particularly moved when I saw him walk into the great hall of the UN and representatives of 117 nations got up to greet him. The ceremony of all the world's nations—the ceremony of that symbolic linking—the ceremony that suddenly made an occasion of hope.

Oh Lord, Lord, Lord, for a moment in this usual desert the love of God somehow seems a possibility again, the sources of our life suddenly quickened by the old holiness, a feeling of sanctity brought back. Truly, "The truce of God." [. . .]

## October 26, 1965

Am beginning to thaw out after last week's separation from Ann. There was a moment in Sunwood, looking at the chandelier in my "secret" room there, when I really wondered whether it would not be best, all things considered, to get it over with, to hang myself then and there. But I knew that the chandelier wouldn't support my weight; and as usual, I had so many deadlines and classes to meet that I had to postpone my death. Suddenly, coming back Friday night, I found myself part of the family, my family, again. Kate is the seamstress of the family who sooner or later sews everything into a pattern on the thread of herself. Suddenly, in the midst of so much inner bitterness against Ann, I find myself rejoicing at the first proofs of her book, beaming on Katey in all things—and in all things find myself in a domestic daily West Side world so mixed-up in its humanity and absurdity, that the sheer drama of it holds me, and I postpone my death again. [. . .]

## October 26, 1965

Read in Podhoretz's selection of 20 years of *Commentary* and broke down in reading Sol Bloom's old piece on the Jewish dictator of Lodz and the children being taken out of the orphanages en route to the gas chambers, crying *Mir viln nisht shtarbn* [I don't want to die], 1943, the year of agony![41] I relive these days with such acuteness, as what don't I relive with such acuteness. But of course the ambiguities about Jewish cooperation with the Nazis are what make the material so hard to bear. . . . We Jews want to have the virtue of victims, and we do, but oh Lordie, the Polish Jewish leaders: (a) hoped that they could be "good" to their overlords, the Nazis; (b) they hoped they could "arrange" some compromise or appeal; (c) they didn't believe the Nazis could be this horrible; (d) they hoped to save their families or themselves; (e) this is the way they had always done things. [. . .]

## November 4, 1965

Thursday is teaching day, and teaching is damned hard work—for the literature mad professor, who still believes in salvation by the word, who is a fanatic of the word; the business of teaching is a business of selling the imagination of persuasion, of working the message of imagination into the heads of people who are passive by nature, uncertain by temperament, and by virtue of their age. "What do *I* know?" is the student's feeling, and he is right to ask. [. . .]

## November 15, 1965

One looks for one's father—one looks—one looks and then one realizes: I *am* my father.

The powerful people, made so by the war, and the powerless people, my saints, my Jews.

## November 20, 1965

Late Saturday evening visit with Cal [Robert] Lowell, my mad poet, my only genius. Cal excited by greatness, by comparing greatness. He is always making up verbal lists—the best historians, the best critics, the best stylists. Sometimes the lists are pure golden affinity-lists: George Herbert, Pascal, Thoreau, Hopkins[42]—because they all died by forty (?), because they were

41. Solomon F. Bloom, "Dictator of the Lodz Ghetto: The Strange History of Mordechai Chaim Rumkowski," *Commentary* (February 1949): 111–112.
42. George Herbert (1593–1633), English metaphysical poet and Anglican priest, one of Kazin's favorite poets; Gerard Manley Hopkins (1844–1889), English poet and Jesuit priest.

*religious* in the same genius way. Cal flitted easily from name to name and from subject to subject, but his sense of greatness, his sense of the great work, of the great moment in the great work, made me feel, again, as if I were breathing the unfamiliar, pure air at the mountain peak. He said, among other wonderful things, that Satan is Milton's hero because Satan has such a great *voice*, like Milton. [. . .]

## December 29, 1965

[. . .] I want to get deeper and deeper into the meaning of things, I want to get closer and closer to *reality*, to the deep meaning and felt relation of things.—I want to be *alive* in my mind, fully *penetrating*, not just "connecting" in the old moments' triumph over habitual loneliness—I want to be *better*, *clearer*, sharper, more proficient than ever! I want to be thoroughly *engaged* with the world. All these mildewed and bad vapors of soul come because I have exhausted the old epic of "self." *That* story is quite worn out for me, I want to be as precise and as disinterested as possible. A slogan for these really new days ahead—always the Other and the otherness of the world! I will *not* be satisfied with the mediocrity all around me! This conspiracy to blot out the higher intellectual and spiritual aspiration.

## February 8, 1966

Reading, reading, reading. The last few days have been full of endless reading. *Why* do I read so much? Why do I think I have to read everything? Why do I believe that print *always* has something to tell me? As a critic, I read and read certain texts, the beloved ones, so as to *possess* them. The rapture of the dancer, but before an audience. For the rest, reading so much shows an awful respect for "authority." They know. He knows. It's in print, that's how. . . .

But possession, of the critic's kind, the passionate effort at possession of the text, is another story. Read works of imagination, read to possess something more than information or "opinion."

The fascination, the terrible frictionless ease of a wholly cultural existence. A life suspended within life. Books don't talk back. Books can disturb, unnerve, but then you can always drop them. Literally, an indulgence of the self as [a] meditative, passive being.

## February 20, 1966

Sunday. A good week, a happy week, full of good thinking about Adams and great happiness between all three of us. Katey read a little of the *Walker* in an anthology that came and was suddenly, blissfully in love with her Papa— "I didn't know you wrote things like that! I thought you wrote only those silly critical essays!" Tonight I'm to read a bit of the *Walker* at the Town Hall "Read-In"; the book is so clogged with emotion, and clogged for me still, as I read it, that I cannot look at it without having a sense of the pastness of the past, the long-ago experience and the other man who wrote this book. . . . How quickly Katey is growing up, how quickly the cup of life fills up from the drops of time that seem so insignificant as they drop, drop, drop from the sun; how a few years mark *such* a difference in men, in societies, in careers. [. . .]

## February 20, 1966

Sunday Night. "Read-In for Peace" at Vietnam. . . . Lowell, Hellman, Kunitz,[43] Sontag, etc., etc. For most of the evening we sat in a great cavern below the stage, listening to the readers on the mike; as each one came down, he would look for approbation or something, I guess before sitting imperviously down to listen. I read a piece of summer, the trip on the El, from the *Walke*r—I read it well, with great pleasure; couldn't see the audience, the lights were so strong in my face; it was convenient, listening for the sound of my own voice. . . . Sontag bustling up and down, embracing Hellman, smiling with familiarity to Viveca Lindfors.[44] . . . She's made it—reminds me of the busiest little boy on the block. . . . A detective at one point jumped on the stage, asked the audience to sing "God Bless America" with him. . . . This was the only commotion: the rest was a sparkle of the good writers, the dullness of the poor poets, and watching, watching each other. . . . The literary market place.

## March 5, 1966

Saturday morning, the upper West Side. Through these streets pass some of the most unattractive people in the world. The smell of food in the streets, the cripples and junkies and drunks, the old Jews, the young Negroes, the grease smell over everything. This is my society; these are my streets. I walk thinking of this

43. Lillian Hellman (1905–1984), American playwright; Stanley Kunitz (1905–2006), American poet, taught at Yale and Columbia Universities.
44. Viveca Lindfors (1920–1995), Swedish stage and screen actress.

sycophantic review that young Alter[45] has written of Trilling, and yet I don't put this whole situation into *my* imagination of society, which is where it belongs. I keep pressing my brain with intellectual quarrels with *persons*; and my fantasies are to "correct" them, but if necessary to humiliate, to overpower them, to "crush" them by the *force* of my argument. . . . Literature, however, is a public act; the private quarrel and especially the private fantasy are by definition *irrelevant*. But the germ of so many public scribblings is actually these private grousings, these *ressentiments*. For the same reason that I hate so many poisonous critical statements as personal statements, I must *use* my inner resentments as possibilities for literary use. . . . Trilling, the pompously respectable professor, is a character in *my* imagination of society, not a person to argue with—the Jew's dream of literary England, of surpassing his servile state by culture. No one was ever so much the prisoner of culture as Trilling. No one was ever so much the victim of the genteel fantasy. The long conflict between us has always been over Trilling's conception of his *role* and of my scorn and my sense of being snubbed by him. I come back from Stony Brook with its poor prestige, its English department falling apart, to Alter's pious-moral subservience to Trilling, and inevitably I feel *sore*, insulted, and injured by the contrast. But meanwhile the real theme, *Jews as snobs*, *Jews as climbers* gets lost. But my long, sore conflict with Trilling is understandable only in the context of social role, the critic's aspiration to intellectual leadership.

## April 12, 1966

All my life I have lived between the strong pole and the weak pole. Weakness seemed my daily natural condition, even my destiny, until I became a writer in the '30s. Then, with the publication of *On Native Grounds* in 1942, authority was given to me, the authority of strength, the authority of my own capability—and now, my position. I didn't know what to do with it. I ran away from it. I didn't know how to be this new strong person. The more I think of what happened in '43, the more I realize how my own strength and new-found authority frightened me, and that after I had fallen in love with Lou and had begun to realize my long-starved sensuality, I became frightened at this, ran away into the old weakness again, tried to bury myself in guilt and shame. . . . My mother had said: Your destiny, mine, ours, is to be weak and sufferers, to deny our strength, to be losers. . . . No wonder that I have always referred back to *that* tradition in my mind . . . have been bound, internally, to that authority of weakness and pain, in order to get a little mother-loving, not to feel myself utterly alone in the world.

45. Robert Alter (1926–), professor of Hebrew and comparative literature at Berkeley, literary critic and reviewer for *Commentary* and other magazines.

Edel[46] said to me some years back: "You never used your authority as Trilling did." I never tried for position; I ran away from all the delights and strengths of being a critic, *my* kind of writer. . . . Always the consciousness of my internal weakness, always conscious of being surprised by my sane, active, responsible *public* role. . . . When, I wondered uneasily in public, would the "weak" self catch up with me, "the personal darkness," the old domestic tradition of pain? It caught up with me in '43—I allowed it to swim all over me. . . . And now, here, at the moment when that past has caught up with me in book form, I can see how I still use that weakness, that weakness, my mother's masochism and hypocritical self-denial, that Kazinian piety, to fight down every green and growing shoot in my heart. Marks of weakness, marks of woe. The struggle against the nea-sayers, against the enemy of supplicating weakness so that I would be let in, so that I would have a little warmth! [. . .]

## April 26, 1966

[. . .] To Washington with Irving Howe. At the Willard disappointed to find no Hersey, and the dispiriting cheeriness of Harold Taylor. . . . But we struggled on, our gallant and uninspiring group—Howe, Taylor, [Muriel] Rukeyeser, [Peter] Feibleman, Elmer Rice, Walter Teller.[47] . . . The press conference was good, we attacked (I especially) our great and immortal vice-president like anything, and sure enough, when we called on the great man as per appointment, he expressed indignation.[48] . . . Then he went into what-the-govt-is-doing spiel. . . . As Howe said, it was like listening to teacher . . . very boring. Astonishing to think how boring the 2nd chief can be. . . . He has arched eyebrows, wears a standard summer suit, a

46. Leon Edel (1907–1997), literary critic and biographer. Edel's biography of Henry James won a Pulitzer Prize and National Book Award in 1963.

47. John Hersey (1914–1993), Pulitzer Prize–winning novelist and journalist. In 1946 his *New Yorker* account of the bombing of Hiroshima became a journalistic sensation. He later published a novelistic account the last days of the Warsaw ghetto under Nazi occupation, *The Wall* (1950). Hersey taught at Yale, where he was a master of Pierson College. Harold Taylor (1914–1993) was an advocate of progressive education, president of Sarah Lawrence College (1945–1959), adjunct professor at the New School for Social Research and CUNY. Muriel Rukeyeser (1913–1980), American poet and political activist who regularly brought social concerns into her poetry. Peter Feibleman (1930–), American author and screenwriter. Elmer Rice (1892–1967), Pulitzer Prize–winning playwright. Walter Teller (1910–1993), American author and editor of nature books.

48. Kazin told Humphrey that he was "suffering from the Hemingway syndrome: you can never be tough enough, and you have to prove your masculinity." Carl Solberg, *Hubert Humphrey: A Biography* (New York: Norton, 1984), 293. Humphrey later wrote Kazin that he was saddened to be "selected for personal criticism on something which is a matter of governmental policy" (May 4, 1966), Kazin Estate, Berg Collection, New York Public Library.

solid color tie with a little HHH in the margin, and talks, and talks, and talks, and talks. . . . The most fascinating part of the day was the press conference: struck by the sharp, impersonal, cross-examination by the reporters[. . . .]

## May 20, 1966

[. . . ] I wonder if E[dmund]W[ilson] ever gets into his journals of the literary life anything as personal, harrowing, *mixed* as this. . . . I wonder if E.W., the literary surgeon of the culture-world, ever gets into his journals the incoherence that comes with the honest personal note with so much passion . . .

## May 22, 1966

EW [Wilson] thinks he is writing history whenever he sits down to his diary.

Young and old Milano—Dr. Andrew Milano with Papa Paolo arrived yesterday and [we] were extraordinarily taken with Dr. Andy. How sweet, good, kind, young, calm, right! And how *interesting* above all. . . . Paolo never changes, but does get sweeter. He doesn't believe anything unless it's in a book, and he worries over every new literary morsel for fear he may miss something.

Dinner Party at Uri Ra'anan's.[49] . . . The Soviet survey man from London, [Walter] Laqueur, [Zbigniew] Brzezinski (!!!!) the Soviet Expert from Columbia, by way of Poland; a very sweet old Jew who was deputy foreign minister in the Nagy cabinet; [Philip] Mosley from Columbia.[50] . . . The ladies, all looking like heavy sacks of wheat dumped in the corner, wore pastel shades that did not make their heaviness any more attractive. The men, all in white shirts, coats off, talked Kremlinology. Uri is now to be a professor at MIT. . . . He got mad at Ann's kidding him about his Israeli-status . . . but relaxed.

Then at Elly Frankfurter's,[51] 1130 Fifth—the art crowd, the glamorous young ladies in pajamas, the editors, the publicists. . . . The new style: Jason Epstein and

49. Uri Ra'anan, lecturer of government at Columbia University, former Israeli diplomat.

50. Philip Mosely was professor of international relations at Columbia University. Walter Lacquer (1921–), American historian of European history, professor of the history of ideas at Brandeis University (1968–1972) and University Professor at Georgetown University (1976–1988). Zbigniew Kazimierz Brzezinski (1928–), political scientist, professor at Columbia University, would become national security adviser to President Jimmy Carter from 1977 to 1981.

51. See Chapter 5, note 67.

his wife, who just look at you when you come into a room. How well we know you! What could you have to say to us? I told Jason I wanted to discuss my book for the Modern Library, and he said, non plus ultra, "I'm interested only in books for little Africans . . ." [. . . .] Elly Frankfurter, says A, has the "poule de luxe" quality. The girls at her party all looked like models grown a little old—very glamorous and very arch by contrast with "the sacks of wheat" in their pastel shades whom I had just seen at Uri Ra'anan's. . . . There was the incipiently angry Diana Tead Michaelis[52] (just divorced) looking very creamy, and au fond, sulky as the devil. There was the energetic Mrs. Don Allen, six foot-eight of woman, enough for a whole battalion to feast on. There was the inevitable Bowden Broadwater,[53] who comes on to people with his eyeglasses glinting in the light, his cigarette, his little smile, chatting his way to the front. In all the years I have seen Bowden Broadwater, I have never seen this little smile to deviate from its social falseness and its implied malice. . . . I had a long, long talk with Dr. Robert Lipton [*sic*][54] who is of course a professionally good listener, and listened and listened to my thoughts on power and death (in all of which he heartily concurred) with this fondling air of: "Oh, how true! Oh, how wise!" The more I see of psychoanalysts the more I see them as intellectuals: constructing everything around *theory*. As a human being, one finds oneself in the midst of a situation one wishes and tries to understand; as a doctor-intellectual, a curer of souls, one *knows*—or has to look positive.

## May 24, 1966

How these English snottinesses have the power to hurt us.[55] Why? Because they still represent to us—if not to themselves—so much cultural value, hierarchy, that even when they write from a Muggeridge[56] kind of irresponsibility, even then they are personal and underhand in a way no serious American writer would dare to be, we tend, against our better knowledge, to credit them with authority. . . . This was the comedy of Americans in London, Spring '45, and it is the comedy behind the career of a "notable" like Sir Isaiah [Berlin], the man who mixes only with other notables, who has turned the immigrants' many languages into the posture of the savant. [. . .]

52. Diana Tead Michaelis, television producer at WGBH.
53. Bowden Broadwater, married to Mary McCarthy, 1946–1961.
54. Robert Jay Lifton (1926–), psychiatrist and author of books on the psychological effects of war and violence.
55. *Starting Out in the Thirties* had received one of its few negative reviews from Robert Taubman in the *New Statesman* (May 20, 1966): 734–735.
56. Malcolm Muggeridge (1903–1990), English author, journalist, and television personality.

## May 25, 1966

Peace, peace, we cry, but there is no peace. Rusk[57] has given another speech, the same speech, grinding out the same "lessons of the thirties. . . ." In this damned war, one can only be for peace, act peace, live peace. . . . It will not do any good today, tomorrow, perhaps not for ages, but we must live peace, for the war-society otherwise dominates everything.

Was thinking the other day of the current literary scene, now so manifestly "literary society," that it is typified by Plimpton,[58] [Robert] Silvers, the [Jason] Epsteins. But at the annual Gab-Day of the National Institute and Academy,[59] one is more aware of the different circles—divided by generations—and of the underground sense of who's-made-it-and who hasn't. . . . There is the Jewish circle, the circle of the old painters, the academic circle, the lost generation circle, the circle of the homosexual musicians. . . .

The usual twaddle. [Allan] Nevins was chairman for the Academy and Kennan[60] for the Institute. As usual with so much repressed temperament, there was the little "scene." A young painter, very fairy, asked to receive an award for brilliant work in collage, began to throw little pieces of paper into the air. . . . Jacob Bronowski,[61] very Jewish-looking, very Cambridge in accent, orated some banalities about science and literature both having their roots in the imagination. Nevins got up to announce that the speaker had cast "such a spell" that he could hardly believe it was over. Very boring afternoon, relieved only by flashes of pomposity from Maitre Leon Edel, Maitre Lionel Trilling, Maitre Ralph Ellison[. . . .] Across the table, Ann sat next to Albee,[62] vicious eyes and dark glances, and his boy friend, a Pennington, whose name Ann got wrong as Peabody, but Albee told her it was all right, he could be called Peabody. . . . He was the homosexual version of the chorus girl—a blank, standard prettiness.

57. David Dean Rusk (1909–1994), U.S. secretary of state from 1961 to 1969.
58. George Plimpton (1927–2003), American journalist and editor, founder of the *Paris Review*.
59. Kazin was inducted into the National Institute of Arts and Letters in 1965; he would be inducted into the American Academy of Arts and Sciences in 1989.
60. George Kennan (1904–2005), American diplomat, political scientist, historian, known as "the father of containment," the policy the United States adopted toward the Soviet Union during the Cold War years.
61. Jacob Bronowski (1908–1974), English mathematician and biologist.
62. Edward Albee (1928–), American playwright, best known for *The Zoo Story* and *Who's Afraid of Virginia Woolf?*

Mrs. Julian Levi[63] kept flirting with me and showing a very large ring. Malcolm [Cowley] came over—looking very distinguished—and conspiratorially, friendly-like, asked me to join him in sponsoring Norman Mailer.

E. W[ilson].—"Bunny"—the diarist,[64] seeking to open up an intercourse with the world.

## June 7, 1966

[. . .] Allen Ginsberg, the guru of American undergraduates in the age of power. Was surprised to find myself so moved by the *Life* essay on him. So easy to laugh at Allen G.—that mixture of bed clothes, masturbation, Blake, Orlovsky's[65] girl-length hair. But the prophet will not be contained, especially if he starts from so much misery in Passaic. [. . .]

## June 8, 1966

*Papa, the superfluous man*, the man in everybody's way. The man who can't hear, who doesn't talk much. Papa whom mama talked down—Poor papa outliving everyone, always there, getting shyer and lonelier and more inward than ever—Poor papa whom *I* love and cherish all day long. [. . .]

## June 9, 1966

Walking along 14th Street on my way to Luchow's to meet the Daicheses[66] and Rab for lunch, it came over me: of course, the theme [of *New York Jew*] is "achievement" versus failure, power and its opposite, the heights of glory and the depths of humiliation. . . . Think from the very first of such obvious "failures" as: Isaac [Rosenfeld]; Weldon Kees; Robert Paul Smith;[67] [Bruce] Bliven; perhaps even Tom Sancton, the Southerner in New York, the power city. Think of the Negroes in the '43 Harlem riot, the Negroes abjectly learning their ABC's in the Great Lakes Naval Station, the Japanese prisoners in New Mexico. . . . And compare with this, such successes as Saul; Dollard at the

63. Mrs. Julian Levi, spouse of Julian Levi (1900–1982), painter and art instructor, director of the art workshop at the New School.
64. Bunny was a nickname for Edmund Wilson.
65. Peter Orlovsky (1933–2010), a poet and lover of the Beat poet Allen Ginsberg (1927–1997).
66. David Daiches (1912–2005), Scottish literary critic and historian.
67. The poet Weldon Kees (1914–1955) and the novelist, dramatist, and autobiographer Robert Paul Smith (1915–1977) were acquaintances of Kazin's during the war years.

Pentagon in Washington; the pseudo successes like [Willi] Schlamm,[68] who were really failures; the success of successes, the tycoon of the Power-Age, Luce . . . the exiles who felt like failures, refugees, the prisoners, the despised and soon to be murdered Jews . . . Erlich and Alter[69] compared with their proud jailers, Stalin, the brutal face, Hitler, the "success" of "successes," the maniac of success and power. . . . Natasha, Lou above all, . . . leading to the successes (Americans) and the victims (the English girl). . . . The world of naked power, of brutal, naked power, of *achievement* and the opposite. Robert Paul Smith said of his wife, "a failure." In his heart he said of himself "a nobody." He wrote from the worm's point of view, the ironic masquerade of all maniacs, subtle victims in American society.

Trilling, the would-be success, and his anxiety about it . . . Wilson during the war, "a failure . . ." The Posters in the Village, failures in the mud and darned glad of it, you bet—Connie Smith—[Seymour] Krim—all that bunch, the "failures" like Mannie Farber . . . The emphasis on naked achievement, and then, like Weldon, Smith, the others, the groveling in the mud . . . and Natasha.

Here is my theme, I thought, going into lunch, which was charming—but I was not sure why I was so expensively treating them all, except that the American always does, even in England. . . . Wonderful the way the English control their reactions, thus keeping the reactive forces intact—wonderful [the way] in which they choose not to hear when they do not wish to hear. And yet, Daiches's control, his personal dignity, his quietness, above all his surpassing competence, makes me think, always think of the identification with solid excellence, the quiet assurance of value, that makes such people as D.D. exciting to be with—not "personal" in the crudely aggressive way that so many Americans were during the war, that *theater* of their success . . . the release of all their pent-up energies.

But, of course, it is I above all who have sought success and who drove, drove, drove for advantage. Haunted by the false sorrowfulness of the mother always sitting on her own strength. Pitie pour les femmes.

68. See Chapter 3, note 80. John Dollard (1900–1980), a psychologist and consultant on soldier morale to the War Department during World War II, appears as Dr. Rosenkranz in *New York Jew* (76–77).

69. Henryk Erlich (1882–1942) and Victor Alter (1890–1943), Jewish anti-Fascists leaders and intellectuals, were murdered by the Russians who did not want to deal with Polish democratic leaders after the war.

The articulation in this notebook even of a sentence: release, satisfaction, self-satisfaction, hope. . . . And an objective reality exists. Your words in their synoptic connectedness support their existence.

## August 4, 1966
### [London]

Post-dinner visit to the Snows. Pamela in black beads, a little stouter than I remembered her, her accent more cutting than ever.[70] Snow a bald oldie, amazingly deferential and curtly shy in conversation. . . . The only rub of the evening was when we got on the Russians, more specifically Sholokhov with whom the Snows had stayed in Rostov-on-the-Don, and who, though admittedly "bloody" on the Sinyavsky-Daniel business,[71] is their friend. . . . Pamela's son by her first marriage, and Philip Snow were there—the latter a great young snot from Eton, a brilliant classical student apparently.

In the afternoon walked up Great Cumberland Place to Bryanston Square, then along Oxford Street and in Hyde Park. My old war haunts, almost unrecognizable now. . . . But the pacific quality of the people just the same, along with the heaviness of useless penny coins, the dampness, the vague uncomfortableness, the extraordinarily piercing quality of the voices—and the fact that when you have pierced the facade of this one or that one, the usual, undistinguished and uncertain human being appears.

## August 24, 1966

LONDON NOTES. English classes? Barons and villeins? More like different *tribes*, with different physical make-ups. Fine lunch with [Frank] Kermode at an Italian rest, in Jermyn Street. Was amused by the amused look I sometimes caught on his face. A nice fellow as well as an exceptionally brilliant one. . . . Went to National Portrait Gallery. Moved to tears by the marvelous John Linnell portrait of Blake—and by the galaxy of genius, room on room, besides. . . . Dinner at Marion Bieber's with mossy Prof. [George] Mosse and solid,

70. Pamela Hansford Johnson (1912–1981), novelist married to C. P. Snow.

71. Mikhail Sholokhov (1905–1985) is the Nobel-winning author of *And Quiet Flows the Don;* Andrei Sinyavsky (1925–1997), aka Abram Tertz, and Yuli Daniel (1925–1988), aka Nikolay Arzhak, were tried and sentenced to hard labor for satirizing the Communist regime.

bullet-shaped Leopold Labedz.[72] On and on through Europe with knife and fork.

## August 26, 1966

For the Jew making his way up from the ranks, the drama of society, the drama of *place*, is overpowering. That is why the Jew in England—[Harold] Laski, [Isaiah] Berlin, [Bernard] Berenson, just outside it—Steiner, Raphael,[73] so often figures as the collector, the expert analysis of place, influence and power. But to the Jew, so often suffering from social oppression, legal disability, prejudice punitive, there is also the great longing to make society a force for liberation, to find the Kingdom of Peace and Goodness and Righteousness here on earth—to find one's emancipation as a person through the emancipation of society—So, in any event, society affords a *drama*.

*History*, a belief in the existence of events prior to and superior to *the historian*.

## September 20, 1966

Full of the past? The Jewish Museum opened an exhibition on the "Lower East Side: Portal to America," and in the midst of blown-up pictures of East Side sweatshop workers, kids crowding the public libraries, a man in a Ludlow Street cellar desolately sitting by a table with a chalah, preparing for the Sabbath, there were hip cats in miniskirts, one young thing naked except for bikini pants under her transparent white sheath. Upstairs, the grimly exaggerated and old-fashioned song sheets and theatrical posters of the period—whose stars, [Boris] Thomashefsky, Bertha Kalish, Stella and Jacob Adler[74]—have that swollen look of old-fashioned theater people, who look as if they had been dining for years on applause, had filled their faces on the adulation of the public. . . . On the main floor, the photographs—by Lewis Hine, by Jacob Riis, the letters from Lillian Wald to the Warburgs asking for money to send some more urchins to the country, the faces of those stark years, 1897, 1910, 1912—an extraordinary visit

72. Marion Bieber (1922–2007) was an administrator and director of seminars for the Congress for Cultural Freedom; George Mosse (1918–1999) was a noted European historian at the University of Wisconsin; Leopold Labedz (1920–1993) was a Polish-born Kremlinologist.
73. George Steiner (1929–), American literary critic, philosopher, and translator, not one of Kazin's favorite people; Chaim Raphael (1908–1994), English scholar, novelist, and civil servant, friend of Kazin's.
74. Actors and actresses in the American Yiddish theater.

recounting a visit to the Hebrews in their squalor by William Dean Howells, *Impressions and Experiences*, 1906.[75]

The heavy clothes, the still-formal faces of the American Kaiserzeit, the last of the great, heavy bourgeois period: *the stillness of the faces compared with the storm beating around them* . . . the sudden immobility of the faces and bodies in the photograph compared with the excess of meditation with which we pronounce on them. Contrast of the living and the dead—of the over-active consciousness and the dead. "How they must have suffered!" "How extraordinary" we say, prowling around the luxurious halls of the museum, trying to have *the right thoughts* about them. The uneasy kindliness they inspire in us—they are now only a subject to our thoughts.

Yet *the shadow of fear* they inspire! The bedraggled, anxious, hemmed-in quality on which we so fondly gaze, now!

## September 22, 1966

First day of school, fourth year at Stony Brook. I think in advance that the routine is enervating, that I will be hopelessly mechanized and bored, but in point of fact, I am always excited—and the large graduate group, of which looks like 30! is the most exciting of all. Dealing with students: there is never a free exchange, they never tell you exactly what they think, they encourage on my part all sorts of dogmatisms, strutterings, authoritarianisms. . . . Yet, as is true of my kittenish girlish friend Mrs. Miriam Baker, students have this fresh and open quality, this willingness to learn, this readiness to be taught, to be themselves changed, that is the exciting thing about students. By definition, they are consciously in process: they feel themselves to be on the way to something else. . . . So the teacher talks, and the students (occasionally) feel themselves much impressed and illuminated. But since they are not on a par with *il gran professore*, and must hold their own counsel, the cordiality—ah, even the true *morality* of the relationship—is implicit. . . .

75. Lewis Wicks Hine (1874–1940), American sociologist and photographer who used photographs for social reform; Jacob August Riis (1849–1914), photographer and muckraking journalist, who used his camera to expose the poverty in New York City; Lillian Wald (1867–1940), nurse, social worker, public health official, author, and editor, pioneered community nursing programs. The Warburg family were a major banking family from Germany who contributed to philanthropic causes. William Dean Howells (1837–1920), an influential American "realist" writer, critic, and editor who encouraged and published the work of American minorities.

With Jack Ludwig to lunch, and then, while having my car looked over, by Janet the female mechanic, talked about my salary! Dick Poirier's[76] book, Sid Gelber, Dean Ross, etc. . . . Jack the unfailing bounce,—"what I told him, get the fuck out of here."

## September 24, 1966

[. . .] In my deepest happiness, I feel most Jewish! When I am closest to myself, I find most the reality of God as the totality of *truth*.

Wrote the above in the train. Then at Yaddo, great happiness—a feeling of sunlight, peace, ease, even "friends" among the Kronenbergers-Hicks-Cowley-Davises, and other assorted elderly parties. [. . .] Struck at the meeting by Eudora Welty's extraordinary feelingness and kindness. Granville Hicks's face congested—Louis [Kronenberger] bobbing up and down with the usual social ease—Malcolm [Cowley] looking astonishingly young and handsome, glossily, the benevolent man of letters—John Cheever's funny, private intensities leaking out of him (as they must out of me).[77] . . . Oh, all the "old" people in the arts, and what a show it was, when poor Robert Coates[78] could not speak and Malcolm could not hear!—But this morning, talking to Elizabeth,[79] was much touched by the message she relayed from some of the younger theologians—that whatever happens, *one must take it all into oneself, and so not be divided* . . . Truth.

## September 26, 1966

[. . .] MY JOURNAL, MY PRIVATE LIE detector—I notice in all excerpts from Wilson's famous journal that they are set pieces of literary-historical description, formal portraits, essays in miniature. How nice it would be to keep a journal like that, to leave a treasure like that. But so often I turn to this notebook as if it were my private lie detector, my confession, my way of ascertaining authenticity—and

76. Richard Poirier (1925–2009), literary critic and scholar, cofounded the Library of America; Sidney Gelber (1924–), Distinguished Service Professor and Leading Professor of Philosophy at Stony Brook; Stanley R. Ross (1921–1985), dean of the College of Arts and Sciences at Stony Brook.

77. Eudora Welty (1909–2001), novelist and short story writer, awarded the 1973 Pulitzer Prize for *The Optimist's Daughter;* John Cheever (1912–1982), novelist and short story writer, awarded the 1979 Pulitzer Prize for fiction and the National Book Critics Circle Award for *The Stories of John Cheever*.

78. Robert Coates (1897–1973), novelist and art critic.

79. Elizabeth Ames (1885–1977), executive director of Yaddo.

of recovering it—of making myself whole again. Talking to myself as I do here, I nevertheless find in the expression of private uncertainties a form of release, a clarity, from which I can start up again. . . .

## October 3, 1966

Lunch with Cal Lowell at Fleur de Lis. Cal very subdued, at the bottom of his cycle—terribly affectionate with me, full of intellectual fondness. He was talking about the old Yaddo business, and for a moment tried to indicate how strange his fanaticism of then seems to him now.[80] I found myself saying how far the river of history has carried us, how much it has changed. We pretend, all of us, at "consistency" of some sort. But politically it is virtually meaningless. Surely, it was this unseizability of the historical current that drove [Henry] Adams to fix "laws"—that drove him wild. The cruelty of change on a mind seeking *constants*.

## November 4, 1966

[. . .] Eliot's voice in "Gerontion," I found myself saying with surprise to my class yesterday—the great thing is to sound like a voice no one has heard before, but a voice that will remind everyone of his own voice, that will make one think of what the voice does for us (imprisoned spirits).

Dinner with the Steegmullers, the magic of Shirley the Hazzard.[81] When will we learn from a woman like this—with her incredible gentleness, the light that fills where she is, that love is a form of intelligence—a way of listening to the world, of taking it in, of rising above one's angry heart. . . . [. . .]

The Eternal Subject, the Holocaust. Gershom Scholem delivered an address to the World Jewish Congress in Brussels last summer, republished in the November *Commentary*.[82] The austerity of the man's reasoning, the deliberateness of his thought, the patriarchal gravity of his style, fill me with

80. In 1949, Lowell, on the verge of a nervous breakdown, tried to persuade the Yaddo board of supervisors that the executive director, Elizabeth Ames, had turned the place into a den of Communist subversives—a charge that Kazin and other Yaddo guests rebutted, saving Ames her position.

81. The writers Francis Steegmuller (1906–1994) and Shirley Hazzard (1931–) were close friends of the Kazins in the sixties and seventies.

82. "Jews and Germans," *Commentary* (November, 1966): 31–38. The Jewish philosopher and historian Gershom Scholem (1897–1982) initiated the first academic study of the Kabbalah.

boundless admiration and love. The Jewish father—in thought. The wise man. And now this patriarch speaks in the bitterest moral crisis of our lives, our history, perhaps of all history: (certainly as far as consciousness *is* history), making his way from thought to thought like a man walking from wet slippery boulder to boulder in a raging sea. [. . .]

## November 5, 1966

[. . .] Read Hannah on Brecht[83] in the *New Yorker*—an excellent series of reflections, done in admirably personal, tense, contemplative way. Marvelous use of the essay form to get away with so many judicial-moral reflections on the nature of the intellectuals, Germany, poets, and "forgiveness" of political sins. Hannah, another one of these intellectual matriarchs—the all seeing, all judging. But a marvelously gifted woman, and probably more gifted as a "critic" in the wide-open sense of *responding* to a particular deed, issue, thing, than anything else. The critic, like the "Jews" in that wonderful passage from Péguy[84] that old Scholem quoted, is always marginal to, is "elsewhere," *d'ailleurs*.

## November 13, 1966

[. . .] MICHAEL

The halls of Weld Hall were lined with broken glass from the Saturday night party. I woke the boy up, so eager to be a Harvard father. It was the usual struggle: why the heartburning? Michael looks as beautiful as those pale, long-haired, young Confederate soldiers in the photograph albums of the Civil War. We went to hear Allen Ginsburg read at Lowell Hall. Pretty bad stuff, very boring non-poems. Outside, [Peter] Orlovsky, the wife, was dusting off the family bus. . . . The radical students, benefit of Students for a Dem. Society [SDS], were dressed in Mexican serapes, cowboy boots, sweaters, ranchero hats, etc. A costume party: a *mating* party. The costume announces the type available—[85]

## November 28, 1966

[. . .] At Truman [Capote's] ball, the slithy, slender young ladies in blond cascades and white dresses and jeweled masks and fans—at Truman's ball, the

83. Bertolt Brecht (1898–1956), influential German playwright, theater director, and innovator.
84. Charles Péguy (1873–1914), French poet and essayist.
85. Michael Kazin was an SDS leader at Harvard.

most beautiful women I have ever seen.[86] Dancing with Jean Van Den Heuvel,[87] I felt all that slenderness in my hand, that cup of skin in my hand. . . . Truly, pleasure and the fate of pleasure? The bitterness rises in my throat—the sense of never coming near enough to beauty, of never having enough. Thank God for the candle that burned all that evening behind Lou's head when I fucked her! Thank God for Carol and Carla and Rose and Jean, for Celia and Elsie and Sylvia and Rosalind, for Alice and Vivienne—for the other Sylvia, for Lou, Lou, Lou! Quite a party, quite a party, but it's not yet over—

All the lithe, young matron ladies at the part, draw a single curve—

## November 30, 1966

James the articulator—the man who communicates every motion of his spirit in his prose. One feels about H. J. that whatever he had to say, he managed to say *all* of, to communicate all he had to say on any given subject. In a way, his completeness as an articulator is greater than his subject . . . he "chaws more than he bites off."[88] But he is the greatest renderer-up of his own treasure that one can imagine in a writer. The excitement he stimulates inevitably follows from his own voraciousness, his own need to be absolutely communicative and articulative of his own substance—

James's constantly pressing sense of consideration, his caressing social sense, as the energetic pulsations of his novels—a way of describing people as if one were welcoming them at a party—a way of constantly acknowledging little social facts. . . . A key in Capote turning everything into affectionate personal relationship—"society" becomes friendship, becomes affectionateness . . . and this we find in Whitman, too.

## January 7, 1967

Lunch with [Isaiah] Berlin on a Saturday afternoon at the Blue Ribbon. A very clever man, honest, kind, immensely well-informed—a real Jew-crossing-the-

86. Truman Capote's famous Black and White Mask Ball at the Plaza Hotel to celebrate the success of *In Cold Blood*. Capote (see Chapter 8, note 63) said that he invited the five hundred most famous people in the world. A CBS television crew filmed the arriving guests.
87. Jean [Stein] Vanden Heuvel, author and editor of the *Paris Review*.
88. Clover Adams, Henry Adams's wife, is alleged to have made this remark about James.

frontiers. An excellent *negative* critic: not much creative power there, but very quick to search out just how much there is in your thought. [. . .]

Berlin is a personage, a somebody, a personality. One is always aware of him as a figure of some dignity. Even his crooked, bothersome, "withered" (?) right arm somehow bolsters his dignity like an old man's cane. . . .

## January 18, 1967

The highbrow and the illiterate. The highbrow sitting in the bus stifling on his own thoughts, his too well made sentences, hugging his solitude, his *mental* existence. Up comes the man in the bus, assaulting him with a sentence like a bloody nose, an eczema in the eyes.

Carol, G___—the same surface of passion, the same enigmatically conventional depths.[89]

Peter Davison brought over Marietta Tree's daughter, Frances Fitzgerald.[90] The dear, little, artichoke heart, in a black dress. The perfect, little sexual jewel in the sleeveless black dress, the white, soft flesh on her arm, the big, big eyes.

## January 26, 1967

Oh God, the unending drama of everything, all day long the five-ring circus. I began the morning with such high hopes, writing at "Midtown and the Village." The phone rang: Felicia[91] (wanting to know if Jules F[eiffer]'s play would be suitable for the MacDowell benefit), called Bob Silvers about [Meyer] Zelig's book on Hiss-Chambers, and asked for Meyer Shapiro's review.[92] Worked, with growing uneasiness and sterility on that old *NR* stuff. Wilson's *Prelude* arrived in the mail. Went downtown to the Library to reclaim my typewriter from the

89. Here and in subsequent entries G___ refers to a former student with whom Kazin carried on an affair into the late 1970s.

90. Frances Fitzgerald (1940–), American journalist and author of the Pulitzer Prize–winning *Fire in the Lake: The Vietnamese and the Americans in Vietnam* (Boston: Little, Brown, 1972). Marietta Peabody Tree, socialite and Democratic activist.

91. Felicia Lamport (1916–1999), poet and satirist, was a friend of Ann Birstein's.

92. In *Friendship and Fratricide: An Analysis of Whittaker Chambers and Alger Hiss*, Meyer Zeligs, a psychoanalyst, argues that Chambers was a pathological liar and was lying about Hiss. In reviewing the book for the *New York Review of Books* (edited by Robert Silvers), Meyer Schapiro (1914–2006), professor of art history at Columbia and an old friend of Chambers, attacks Zeligs's book as unprofessional and biased.

Frederick Lewis Allen room, and discovered it had been stolen! It seemed to me funny at first, looking for it in that crowd of typewriters and not seeing it. Then to Osners, to pay for it. Home to find Kat Claman, Katies friend. Endless phone calls, girlish screams, locksmith, Kitty the new maid, Katie's camp; all day long, involved with Shapiro's review, with Edmund Wilson's boyhood, with bloody phone calls from editorial strangers, with plans for tomorrow's trip to Sag Harbor, etc., etc. Everything happening at once—we eat hamburgers to the sound of *Don Giovanni*, Beethoven mandolin sonatas . . . The simultaneity of all experience . . . The drama: and the only law in the midst of it is: Pay attention. Don't rush over anything. The more there is, the more to understand. Above all, precision to detail. Otherwise one is swamped.

## January 29, 1967

Sir Isaiah—fearful nimbleness, gamesmanship, of the Russian Jew—the superiority in maneuver of the *contestant.*

## March 5, 1967

Edmund's journal shows up the paucity of means that us critics and "moralists" have for writing our lives. It is hard for him to reach into the young EW, to get out of his own skin. He can only look one way, as it were—straight ahead. What are EW's tools? Fidelity to his own experience—the most intense faithfulness, great learning, great power of associativeness, and above all, dogged precision—to carry him over from one break in the usual flow of associations to another. Alas for the moralist! But one can be content with having so much, even if one does not have an inventive or resourceful imagination. . . . So we must see EW's discipline, his intense formality of style and attitude, as a *tool*, not an aesthetic matter. [. . .]

## March 8, 1967

[. . .] The happiest moment I ever had in my life, *writing*—the morning I described Bernie Davidson's mother in her last cancerous *look*—her hair strangely cut short, like a boy's—Forging those images, one out of another, all sealed in my memory, I had the joy of dealing with *things in themselves*, with what, for once, demanded no interpretation, no exchange into something else.[93] That absoluteness, that final definiteness, is what one seeks from writing—to

93. Bernie Davidson is "David," a chemistry student, a Marxist, and modern literature enthusiast in *A Walker in the City*.

find one's way to *that* final place in the mind. The happiness of the thing in and for itself that is the happiness of representation—and it makes a resting place in and for the mind. The creative act gives us that peace. [. . .]

## April 15, 1967

[. . .] Youth and age. Michael and Ann and Katey and me, my students. Saul and his hatred of the young. I was thinking, too, going up to Stony Brook Thursday morning, about the pompous, oily look of success worn these days by Professor Leon Edel, Professor Oscar Handlin, Professor Richard Hofstadter, Professor Saul Bellow; goodness, what successes we all have become, and how successful and happy and pompous some of us look!—Meanwhile my own youth suddenly seems aeons back, unbelievably old-fashioned, archaic, full of rotting tenements. . . . Everything is moving faster, faster, and the young are the biggest single sight on the face of time.

## May 5, 1967

The Lion in the path, the secret, central issue in everything we touch nowadays, the State, the High and Almighty State. We gave hostages to fortune, we children of poverty, when the State began its high almightiness in the thirties. By the forties it was in full gear as the war state, by the fifties as the welfare state. Now all bad dreams are of getting into trouble with this high almightiness. All success even in the intellectual field is somehow connected with the State. The scientist who abstains (Norbert Wiener) stands in such contrast to the scientist who gave his all and was crushed (Oppenheimer), while the vanity and success mongering of those second raters who have found their opportunity only by getting on the band wagon of the State;[94] and its propaganda stands in sharpest contrast to those who have had the *ability*—intellectually and morally to stand apart. [. . .]

## June 22, 1967

Drove with Papa to the cemetery. Almost eight years since that Saturday night in October when I saw Mama, already skeletal, heaving her last breaths. I was

94. Norbert Wiener (1894–1964), a professor of Mathematics at M.I.T., refused to participate in the Manhattan Project to develop the atomic bomb. After the war he refused to work on all military projects or accept funding from the government. The Berkeley physicist J. Robert Oppenheimer (1904–1967) directed the Manhattan Project and after the war served as the chief adviser to the Atomic Energy Commission until he was denied security clearance because of doubts about his political sympathies.

there. And now, in the Workman's Circle Plot, the graves so thick around hers. That day in 1959, the gashed earth for her grave stood out in the new cemetery fields. Yet it gives me some comfort to walk in that cemetery to see all those familiar, touchingly comic, made-up Jewish names. Every day since the Israeli victory early in June, I go to bed thinking: we are not as fit for killing as we were—we can be proud. Every time I think of what might have happened to the Jews of Israel if the Arabs had won, I find it easier to accept the audacity and toughness of the present Israeli position. By God, if you want to live, you want to *live*, and the difference between today, despite all the Russian-Yugoslav-Indian-Bulgarian yelping at the Israelis, and that day, June 5th, when the war began and Ann and I walked about in fear and trembling for the people, is enough for me. When I think of Mama dying under that picture of Herzl, of the touching faith of the Jews in the redemption, their only redemption, through Israel, I feel an inexpressible pride in our ability to live, to fight it through, to *live*. That is why Mama surrounded by all the Arbeiter Ring chaverim, "that their light may fall on me, and my light on theirs," fills me with a sort of joy, Khazak! Khazak![95] We have endured! Mama and her immigrant generation, with all that feebleness and misery, have somehow been redeemed, blessed, *recognized*, in this mighty persistence of the Jewish people. They won't kill us as easily as they once did. [. . .]

## June 24, 1967

What happened today? Happenings—What happens. Israel, Israel, Israel, my only happiness.[96] Read in tears that first book-length account of the Israel-Arab war. Was in ecstasy. I understand so much. Went over to Jane Shaplen's. Dr. Norton Luger, and internist.[97] Big, excited talk on the same topic. Israel, Israel. Israel. We agreed—the great rescue of Judaism will come from the Holy Place itself—The irony of "Jewish nationalism" is that *it* will produce a renascence of Jewish sacramentalism. Only among the Holy Places, our land.—I feel an immeasurable joy in the thought of this, our safety, our deepest love. It is Israel that will keep the flame of Jewish faith alive. What does anything else matter! The Jews will hold—They cannot *but* keep faith. Nothing else matters but that God lives, and that His people know Him—in their own land. [. . .]

95. Hebrew for "strong" or "be strong."
96. Kazin went to Israel for *Harper's;* his account of the visit was published as "In Israel: After the Triumph" (November 1967): 72–85.
97. Dr. Norton Luger was a physician at and founding father of the New York Hospital Queens.

## July 23, 1967

[. . .] Yerushalayim (To the Israelis and everyone else)

The *NY Times* appealed to the Israelis and everybody else for "imagination" on the question of Jerusalem, of which there is, the *Times* editorialist said sadly, so little in the world. But for the Israelis Jerusalem is *nothing* but a question of imagination—it is all imagination—it is their past—their raison d'etre. It is their Second Coming, Jerusalem Restored; everything else is discussable, not Jerusalem. Because Jerusalem is restored, they know that their God, the Lord of Hosts, lives as He always has—that miracles exist, that the historical destiny of the Jewish people is confirmed. They did not *expect* to be there in this way and to feel it this way, but now that they have, they *are* one with what they feel. The name, the place, the sacrifices of the place. Where human creative existence touches *immortality*—where the *unlimited* in time is made fully *manifest.*

The Chinese Jews of Kaifing-fu.

## July 25, 1967

Returned from Israel and am plunged right back into New York—and Sylvia. But what joy, what love!

## August 30, 1967

O these intellectuals (CCOB)—[98] Emotion disguised as *logic.* How easy to prove anything—temporally. O'Brien the diplomat, the intellectual smoothie—!

How susceptible I am to the girls. My heart full of Beverly this morning, of Rae in my half sleep, of Sylvia the dark enchantress, of Mrs. Paley in her bikini, of Marta in her kindness—of Giselda in her car—of Celia in my dreams—of Vivienne at the peak of fucking—of Mary Lou and Jean the poet and Rosalind and Rose and Carla. O delicious girls all—but for me every day there is a new susceptibility, a new hope, a new love. *Neue Liebe, Neues Leben.*[99] I am endlessly attracted, endlessly hopeful. [. . .]

My son the revolutionary. How tempestuous life is straight at home—how unbearably dramatic. [. . .]

98. Conor Cruise O'Brien (1917–2008), Irish politician, international statesman, and influential journalist.

99. "New Love, New Life," poem by Goethe, set to music by Beethoven.

## October 2, 1967

Carson[100] was pure sensibility, pure *nerve* along which all the suffering of the South and the Smith family passed. She was all *feeling*, an anvil on which life rained down blows. She was all *effect*, never will—subject—drive. Tremulous, elfin, self-pitying charm. Always great problems of *identity*. Internality of the American Dostoevskian sort without the slightest political sense of the world. The southern *isolato*—the Southern longing to give "love," to effect an instant embrace.—How well I remember coming down in the train with her from Yaddo during the war. She drank Sherry constantly from paper cups, and when the soldiers noticed her filling her cup from the bottle and got familiar and rambunctious, she expressed some pretty intense resistance to my pleas that she stop.

Love—loneliness—orphanage—the silent cry of the forties: the lure of the abnormal. The boy-girl Reeves Mc[Cullers]—David D[iamond]—Newton Arvin—Truman Capote. Do you remember how she pranced around in the garden at Yaddo imitating a lunatic in front of those visitors who wondered what the place was?

## October 10, 1967

Went down to Brownsville with David Durk, an old Amherst student, now a detective. Durk was actually more interesting. Brownsville looks as if it had been hit by a foreign enemy. Saw an amazing number of burned out, gutted buildings. A Mr. Windt, a postman at the corner of Sutter and Rockaway, told me that the Puerto Ricans along Sutter Avenue next to our old house were trying to get "assimilated"; they had little stores, were making an effort. The Negroes, not. They mostly live on welfare; and often enough, it seems, they rob from the poverty program, use it as a racket, while organizing political protests against it. The dreariness of the old house, the old streets, on a foggy, rainy, October Tuesday. I was amused to see how the postman, Windt, and the druggist at Eastern Parkway and St. John's Place, who have been there for 40 yrs, and the old Jews talking Yiddish and slopping their lunch at the Brownsville Community Center on Stone Avenue—to say nothing of the old Stone Avenue Talmud Torah, still intact, and Belmont Avenue in all its pushcarts, still intact—how all these remnants of my youth moved and *satisfied* me. Everywhere, it seems

100. Carson McCullers (1917–1967), novelist and short story writer, best known for *The Heart Is a Lonely Hunter*, *The Member of the Wedding*, and *The Ballad of the Sad Cafe*.

I go looking for signs and survivals of my youth, which is why I am always moved by Jews, and why I hope that writing *my* narratives of the war will bring me back to that vanished period, and why I found myself in Brownsville at all today, thinking of writing an article on what has happened, on Negroes and Jews. [. . .]

## October 15, 1967

After the holidays, after the big purgation. I went through Yom Kippur with a total sense of dislocation, fasted, went to the beginnings and the end of the service at Rabbi Birstein's old schul, and as usual in synagogue or even on a big Jewish holiday, found myself totally *outside*, watching and listening with the smallest portion of my mind. I can never look at the prayer book without being stupefied by its sameness, its repetitiousness. The congregation moves me by its folk character—i.e., if you are not a Jew and not brought to these ceremonies, gestures, smells, faces, it must seem utterly meaningless. The prayer book seems to me a constant plea to this Oriental potentate, a stupefying litany of submission. Yet, put this old schul, these white-faced old men and fat women on a string of Jewish history, and why, the whole thing becomes (as part of a succession) unbelievably stirring and fascinatingly enigmatic. . . . The problem, as always, is how to be a "Jew" without "Judaism"—how to live in the history (as one's only way of keeping it) without simply becoming a *worshipper*: by which I mean someone bent to *this* cult.

## November 14, 1967

[. . .] Called Michael, to discover that he has been officially admonished by Hahvud. The letter from one of the senior tutors concerned a sentence, something like, "If our society is to have a future, Harvard must"—do what? cultivate respect for the views Harvard men do not agree with? Michael does not agree. Napalm manufactured by the Dow Chemical Co. is to him an evil that justifies interfering with Dow's representatives on the Dow [*sic*, Harvard] campus. But meanwhile, napalm gets manufactured just as much as ever—and lands on N. Vietnam peasants with the usual regularity. But I do like Michael's sense of outrage. . . . Everywhere today the American who has any imagination and conscience tries to relate himself to this superpower we have become, and fails. In the old days I am reading about in Ellen Moer's "biography" of *Sister Carrie* and *An American Tragedy*, the American related his agrarianism, his provincialism, his innocence. Now he relates his overwhelming sense of death and destruction.

This is the typical existentialism radicalism of our day, involving the middle-class individual's sense of his own survival, full of anxiety, inner struggle, with material idols he loves and cannot bear to sacrifice; but essentially, dealing with "life" as a whole, not specific political ideas and solutions.

## November 19, 1967

Here it is Sunday morning, gray and leaden, and suddenly Cal Lowell is on the phone talking about St. Paul and St. Louis and Cato the younger, moving in and out of history with what a perspective! Marvelous unprovincialism of the gifted man. Cal's new poems, especially the one about Caracas—"city without a center"—and about Leone the tough presidente, and the blood as hard as rock—show what a little radical experience can do for a poet! Great to have him reading these poems on the phone just now. What a privilege.[101]

The wintry look. Everybody in Zabars is dressed like an artist. The last word in *individuality*. The middle-class Jew as professional bohemian.—Make it new all the time, baby. The Fiedler disease—the role-players—winter role, summer role, morning role, play role. *The great society* full of actors playing many parts.

But no one is so "creative" as the newly prosperous, professional Jew, who feels out of it—business.

## November 22, 1967

The theme that lies at the heart of everything I am trying to say, to seize, to understand—the theme that was at the heart of the "Vicar of Christ" essay,[102] that has haunted me for ever since '43—that is surely the basis of whatever is good in the Adams, James, Emerson to Dreiser book—i. e., the American-Puritan literary experience: the difference between the actors and the bystanders, between the stage and the *pit*, between the protagonists and the moralists, between the revolutionaries and the commentators, between Christ and the Christians, between the young and the old, between the alive and the merely watchful, between the glowing act of love and all the ruefulness and interpretation thereof—

101. Robert Lowell's "Caracas," published in *Notebook 1967–68* (New York: Farrar, Straus and Giroux, 1969).
102. See note 6.

That life consists in acts and actions, in performances and deeds, and that too much of what I see, too much of what I live, gets pissed away in all the attitudes of the spectator. Oh the intellectuals, the Jewish intellectuals, the commentators and scribes, the wisdom of non-doing! Oh the Trilling syndrome, the James syndrome, always the beast that never sprang from the jungle!—at a time when everything teems with existence with struggle towards a revindication of our human nature—"action," not merely in the work of art, but as a positive attitude towards life, to be one of the actors, not the spectator; fills one with the hope that life's thirst will yet be satisfied. William and Henry: the therapist who became an actor in his own mind—fiction as symbolic action. Action as a *necessary* fiction. [. . .]

## November 27, 1967

[. . .] Society—politics—force—power: the ruler, the medium and the ruler. I read with the greatest admiration Noam Chomsky's meditation on resistance in the current *NY Review of Books*.[103] His moral understanding of the abuse of power in Vietnam *and* his scruples about activism, both do him honor. But fundamentally, the violence of US power in Vietnam calls out of him, as out of us, a strategic and complex resistance, which comes down to: how can we make the monster rest? How can we stop it even temporarily, not how can we overcome it? The Soviet examples prove beyond all else that state power never relinquishes itself—least of all if and when it is founded on revolutionary action. It never modifies itself seriously. It is *we* who moralize, who subtilize, who sacrifice, who abnegate—the great state power never does—

All I ever asked is a bit of real estate for myself, *my* place in the sun—all the struggles in the world are for "land," property—one's own piece of God's earth.[104] [. . .]

## December 9, 1967

[. . .] Everyday, everyday now, the Big State, the Crusher; Russia putting some young writers on trial for sedition, subversion; America the All-Righteous, Hubert Humphrey defending the Vietnam War to his old Dem. pals in Minn.

103. Noam Chomsky, "On Resistance," *New York Review of Books* (December 7, 1967): 4–12. Noam Chomsky (1928–), American linguist, professor emeritus at M.I.T., political activist, author of more than one hundred books.

104. Alfred and Ann hoped to buy property on Cape Cod or possibly in the Hamptons. In 1981 he purchased a house in Roxbury, Connecticut, which he referred to as Kazin Acres.

by cleverly asking—what is *your* alternative? First the Crusher moves in, kills, destroys, establishes itself all over the place; then refutes the critic, the poor individual, by asking—and *your* foreign policy? Put up or shut up! First they turn us into their victims, then they win their cheap victory by mocking us for not being able, instantly, as individuals, to undo the *evil* they have done.

The religion of words. Emerson lived before the age of semantics and the science of linguistics and the passion for anxiety as critical *doubt*—For him words were *absolutes*, straight from his heart to the listener.

## January 7, 1968

[. . .] Dr. Spock, Rev. Coffin of Yale, Mitchel Goodman, Marcus Raskin[105] have been indicted by the government, in Boston, for counseling resistance to the draft And where am I in all this? It's true that I don't believe in civil disobedience, but the Vietnam war is so sickening that anything is justified against it.

## January 23, 1968

On this lonely, crucial Brooklyn Heights day, I ended up in a Longchamps opposite City Hall talking to Sylvia. I was moved by her sharp wit about many things, about her directness, but above all by the way in which she practically fastened me to the table with her insistence on the central issue that I have *not* sufficiently asked for satisfaction, for the joy of my senses—and that I have substituted for it a search for approval. Looking at her extraordinary lips, which I so gladly tell her are like the "lips of a cunt" (and into which I would as gladly slip my prick as I have into her cunt), I think—how easy life would be if I had her all the time—if the rooted and easy love-making I long for beyond anything else were there, for me with her! But I know that in my heart of hearts this is impossible—that this—she—is not what I want to bring my life down to just yet.—When I came home from the long purgation of a day, it was inevitable,

105. Dr. Benjamin Spock (1903–1998), an American pediatrician, whose book *Baby and Child Care* (1946) was a best-seller for years, was a highly visible activist against the Vietnam War. William Sloan Coffin Jr. (1924–2006), chaplain of Yale University, was a leader in the civil rights movements of the 1960s and a prominent activist against the Vietnam War. Marcus Raskin (1934–) was the codirector of the Institute for Policy Studies. Mitchell Goodman (1923–1997) was a writer and activist who organized the antidraft protest that led to the indictment and trial of Spock, Coffin, himself, and Michael Ferber, a Harvard student. Raskin was acquitted, the other four convicted. The conviction was subsequently overturned.

after so much emotion, that Ann and I would fuck. *Inevitable too, that after I had come alone and then sucked her into coming that she would weep by herself* as she had been by herself when I was in her. *So bemused by her suffering*—always looking at this picture of her life. So we go on—today is "calm," if sad—so many days, more and more days, have not been calm at all. But I sit here in a faint glow of recovery, and much of this intactness just now I owe to Sylvia. A remarkable girl, a love maker.

## January 27, 1968

Pamela Jacobs, that earnest but literal student in my American lit. course, has blossomed out into *one of these kids for whom Emerson-Thoreau-Melville-Whitman become a revelation, a transfiguring* of the universe. This kind of revelatory power, that the Romantics can exercise over the mind of a student is very moving to watch—the routine paper and exams smell with excitement, *Great!*

## January 30, 1968

*Literature and Revolution.* The accession to a hitherto undreamed of consciousness that certain writer-aristocrats accomplish in 19th century Russia, was accomplished for the working-class (comparatively speaking) by the Russian Revolution.

## February 3, 1968

What will not be forgiven me by the reader of these diaries is my obstinate unhappiness. And quite right. This is what I do not forgive myself. Lord, what a disease, what sentimentality, what rhetoric! What excuse for not living!—Above all, what self-centeredness!—Because I have been one of those who have hugged unhappiness to keep from living. And *this* is a sin.

## February 19, 1968

Mailer's *The Steps of the Pentagon* [*Armies of the Night*] is an extraordinary thing—it finally cracks open the hard nut of American "power," and shows how much more there has been in it, for the non-fiction novel, for personal observations and agonizing involvement, for incessant dramatization, than we had realized. It brings sensibility up to a par with the guilty, frantic, but endlessly involved and fascinating world-activity of U.S. just now.

At Elly Frankfurter's party a week ago Friday, Mailer in his lapelled vest, jutting ex-pug belly, and inhuman actor's look of "taking it all in," annoyed me so much that I said some very rough things to him. I said he looked like a pig, and he did. A pig of American prosperity.[106] But I realize now that Norman's inhumanness is that *he* is always nothing, a blank on which his mind is writing some new part for him to play and that the method of incessant confrontation which makes up the scenario of *The Steps of the Pentagon* is his extraordinary way of locating and dramatizing.

I especially like Mailer's use of "frankness" as his way of dramatizing the present *and* his sense of the endless implication of being (temporarily) a *casualty*.

## February 23, 1968

This unbelievable availability of women. I have the spark for many of them—Miss Baker runs in and out of my office crying "I love you!" And I know that I spark Mrs. Beverly Lawn and possibly Mrs. G. Lord, just as certainly as I do Mrs. R. Miller, Mrs. J. Gordon, Mrs. W. Wilson and others. The women are "emancipated," bursting with possible love—and every one of these detests her husband, feels she has inwardly *suffered* from him. Each of these, so far as I know, has this beef. But to the spark, me, their "greatest" charm is that they are "available"—to the point where all this lovely female wealth blends into a composite figure and while far from falling in love, I feel that I am always at the peep show, always outside, exchanging glances even when one goes beyond all this. Available, external, untouched in what I am even if you fuck em over and over. The place where the frustrations make love—love as occasion.

## March 4, 1968

Kenneth Clark, the Negro psychologist, is reported saying to a professional meeting that dry rot has set in, the terminal stage to American democracy as we know it, because of the continued oppression of Negroes, the Negro-white war in U.S. in effect. . . . The more closely you confront the U.S. inability to settle the Vietnam war, the more you face the total and massive inanity of the bourgeois life in the U.S. today, the more you realize that it is exactly this unsettled and by normal standards, unsettleable social crisis we are suffering from. The air

106. In Peter Manso's *Mailer: His Life and Times* (New York: Simon and Schuster, 1985), 465, Kazin recalls that Mailer responded by challenging him to a fight (which Kazin laughed off), then later expressed surprise that Kazin had given the book a positive review in the *New York Times Book Review*.

is poisoned with hatred, greed, exploitation, the insane big power mindedness of the ruling group in the U.S. Even the efforts of big business to "alleviate" disorder show how inanely limited and shortsighted are the conceptions in the highest places of what is wrong with the U.S. "You live badly, my friends. Is it necessary to live so badly as this?"

## March 4, 1968

Villanova University, Pennsylvania. Heart of the Main Line, beautiful homes of stone, charming people, with that special softness of the young Catholics. (They are *very* motherly in looking out after you and are *not* afraid of strong drink.) Exquisite manners. The revolution inside the Catholic fold is wonderful if unsettling to behold. Everybody is a liberal here—Father Burt, who teaches theology, begins with Nietzsche and the 19th century Death of God! Mr. Kelley, the young head of the Honors program has an effete-nose-in-the-air look, but is actually very nice and soft. I've never had an easier, more comfortable academic-lecture period. But all the while the thing on my mind is the insanity of the war, *the failure—moral failure—my failure—to do enough by way of resistance and response. We are being engulfed by the disorder that is the inevitable price of so much injustice.*

## April 5, 1968

[. . .] Dr. Martin Luther King was slain in Memphis yesterday, and today is like no other day. The truth is—it will take an American revolution "between the races" to change the relationship between white and Negro. *Nothing is more important, and* if this happens, all other relationships will be transformed. The Negro—the complete *outsider*—is the key to the American *revolution*. [. . .]

## April 12, 1968

Good Friday Eve of *Pesach*

Went down to West 2nd Street to see Pop in his new apartment. *I always have to cross a river to make a very long journey indeed to see my pa.* Nice surroundings—nice apartment. We walked along the boardwalk in the direction of Brighton. The Half-Moon Hotel is now an old-age home. The Boardwalk is full of old, old Jews sunning themselves. Going back, I had such a spasm of loneliness that I could hardly sit up straight in my subway seat. Called Dick Hofstadter from a subway phone, and after a long walk with Ann up to Claremont Avenue, went up to Dicks's. A long, meandering, pleasant talk punctuated by whiskey sours. Dick can look so scared, just talking, he looks *angry*. His tight lips, his ugly upper look. Has the *angry* look of a sick man.[107] But his intelligence is an extraordinary *grace*—and makes up for anything. Amazingly adroit and *elegant* mind.

## April 28, 1968

Red Sunday at Columbia, with red flags flying from one window and the SDS militants (who occupy four buildings, the Negro souls occupy a fifth) sitting on the ledges outside the windows raising their fists in movie Communist salutes. Columbia's gates are barricaded, cops all over the place, students milling around. Something bad may yet come of this. Meanwhile the Old Left (D. Bell, I. Howe, A. Kazin) are as sure as anything can be that all this is bad, the New Left is having a field day of gleeful dishonesty, and it is not impossible that the police will yet come into clear the buildings of students; the Negroes, at least are supposed to be armed.[108]

Yesterday, the peak of the anti-war rallies. 87 thousand people marched in protest against Vietnam; and the Sheep Meadow when Ann and I got to it, looked like a vast campground with the different banners in place designating the different troops of the Left. The polarization of life in the last few years—polarization in the classic European US political style—has suddenly given New York an atmosphere of unbearable political excitement. There are vibrations of some tremendous unrest. And the immediate consequence is that the old-fashioned bookish solitude is as difficult for middle-aged scholars as it for young students.

The American Left: the middle-aged passives (rational and passive, don't change for the sake of change), the young Maoists (down with the whole power structure, liberate Columbia's buildings), the Nihilist fuck-you Negroes. The young Middle-class SDS are unguilty about everything except the Negroes.

## April 29, 1968

*Politics, the great Entertainment.* The kids outside the Columbia gate, busily milling about so impressed with themselves for being *There!* The

107. Hofstadter died of leukemia in 1970.
108. On April 30, police cleared the Columbia buildings of student protesters in a raid in which 150 students were injured and 700 arrested.

"honest" are the passive. The *actors* (not the dishonest) are the histrionic *movers*. Bell-Trilling vs. SDS = *moralists and actors.*

Ann screamed me down the stairs again this morning—and my first thought all day was naturally: *what* did I do wrong? *Why* did I do it wrong? But I didn't do anything wrong! It wouldn't have been any different any way I did it! That is the final meaning of so much effort. It wouldn't have made any difference!

## May [nd] 1968

[. . .] To office—to Columbia, empty, milling about of students still stunned by police raid on campus Monday night.[109] [. . .] The crowd at Columbia is the dull, uncontested circumference within which I sit in the reverie of all this university disorder and my own personal disorder. But what happiness to feel the *simultaneous* vibrations of so many events, thoughts, dreams in my mind. What happiness to record the rhythmic impression of this immense vibration that is the concert of so many things. Veritably, veritably, this is the age of our *riches*, the stream of life is irresistible just now.

## May 23, 1968

I loved and am loved! I love and am entangled on every side! It is not like the old days, when the withdrawal was so easy on every side—Carol the evasive one—the Secret One—Superego.

I am a critic-teacher-authority to so many, but to myself, a raging *id*, a volcano of passions. The book I am trying to write must be my passion now—a passion of *thinking*, a passion of intellectual *rightness* and authenticity.

## May 25, 1968

[. . .] Revolution is crucial. So is fucking. So down with mental events! Up with narration (time is the greatest possible happening). Down with looks and smiles and up with happening—*process*-development and the God (that greatest of all mental events) who gets recreated every day—whom *we* create—the spirit of time, God: The crown of Time. [. . .]

109. Kazin had rented a small office on the Columbia campus where he could work.

## June 8, 1968
### [Yaddo]

Hot June day, sitting in a Saratoga bar watching the endless profusion of C.B.S. on Bobby's [Kennedy] funeral. The train, as I write, 3:45 P.M., is almost 2 hours late to Washington, for the crowds at each station are so great. At Elizabeth, N.J., people rushed out to the tracks, and two people were killed. Incredibly moving reprise of Lincoln's funeral train procession to see the train with the black wreath over the locomotive, the flag-draped casket in the last car, the many, many cars, slowly making its way from city to city. The hot, sun-baked crowds on the platform at Trenton, and all over the country, people joining themselves to this as they watch! Yet utter the word democratic, the word en-masse. [. . .]

## June 29, 1968

Finished Roth's *Portnoy's Complaint*—savage, endlessly inventive satire of the Jewish son against his parents. Very funny, dirty, impressively clever, but not easy to be fond of. Alas, children are like their parents, and the fierce revengefullness of the son is like the fierce proprietariness of the parent. Tel arbre, tel fruit—All genitals, mother hatred and mother fucking. The way out: the son is a "case." We are all "cases."

## August 31, 1968

The SDS spirit started up in the young kids. When: three or four years ago? Now, after Humphrey-Daley '68, the American leftist kids have achieved what they wanted (with the bitter reaction and help of Daley), and American "liberalism" is more and more a rhetorical plea on the part of middle-aged people—*not* a common ideal just now. Humphrey is the living embodiment of American "liberalism" just now—but his plea for "consensus" will fall on even more deaf ears than has Johnson's. The U.S. is now openly and noisily the country of extremes, of unending opposition, of dynamic irrationality. [. . .]

## September 3, 1968

[. . .] So let me think about something else for a moment. Literary history, history as reflected in book reviews, the topicality of book reviews, the excitement, the momentary issue that a book creates. Later on the book is forgotten but not the issues themselves. The novelist is right to feel that he can get buried in literary "history"—that the trend becomes overwhelming.

Looking back, one sees that while the individual book is forgotten, books group themselves into issues, into polemics—more polemic now than there used to be—

## September 9, 1968

Talking to Edmund W. is like talking through a megaphone. There is a great silence between words, then a great shouting. The deliberateness and formality are overpowering. He smiles a lot to himself in answer to points he sees no need to answer. On the low couch (he sits on the high sofa up against the wall) the ladies, auxiliary to A.K. in this instance (on a chair), the ladies keep falling over, there is no place for them. When EW pours from his evening pint of scotch, his eyes glint, he looks as he must have looked in bed with a girl. But otherwise, now, it is granddaddy Wilson, with his granddaddy little glasses and his white round face and his shrunken manner. He said "I keep thinking of old age as an abnormal state that will pass, but it doesn't."

Michael with us Sunday and Monday. A lot of arguments. Everybody in the family seems exasperated with me; and I feel crawly and self-conscious to the point of madness, unused and unhappy, idle and impotent and angry and stupid.

## October 20, 1968

Hannah's introduction to Walter Benjamin in this week's *New Yorker* of all places, is really the epilogue to the inner sufferings of that whole group of brilliantly gifted German Jews—Benjamin, Kraus,[110] Kafka, the murderous angel, by extension Hannah herself, who made a wholly inner world out of the outer world, spiritualized their despised Mosaic religion into the fiery but ethereal discriminations of their culture, and were at such loggerheads with themselves about their attempt to meet Germany without *altogether* losing their Jewishness, that in effect they not only predicted disaster all the time but positively welcomed it. As the only end. . . . The extreme spiritualization of everything (with excursions like Hannah's into "politics" as pragmatism) is what I see most in these writers. The cult of contemplativeness and inaction. The extreme bourgeois delicacy. Definitions, definitions. . . . One finally meets so much

110. Walter Benjamin (1892–1940) was a German philosopher, literary critic, essayist, and translator. He is credited with coining the term "modernism" and has exerted considerable influence on recent critical theory. Karl Kraus (1874–1936) was an Austrian writer, satirist, poet, and playwright.

internal profundity with despair. These people identified mortality with their own effort because all they wanted was to make the definition come out right for themselves, not to make it work for others. They were transcendentalists without a movement, utterly solitary and pleased to remain so.

As for Bell,[111] [Arnold] Beichman, Kristol, Trilling, etc., I shall henceforth *ignore* them. No more anger at these stuffed shirts. *Ignore* them.

Trilling. I thought that my own feelings were bad enough, but it turns out that his animus against me is even worse. And what has it been about all these years? T. cannot stand my temperament—he cannot stand the ghetto Jew in me—he cannot stand my vitality. L.T., the would-be gentleman—the little gentleman.

## October 26, 1968

[. . .] Mailer on the conventions at Miami and Chicago is sometimes too rhetorical—trying to get it all into a sentence, to absorb it all into his consciousness. But this is why the "reporting" is so stupendous—absolutely brilliant: Mailer doesn't feel that he has to *know* anything, but he does have to think it out for himself, to confront it in every stabbing pulsation of his consciousness. He really takes it all on, for himself, to himself, *in* himself, and that is why it makes such a powerful impression. It is all confronted as writing, not "researched" except in the forests and jungle vines of his brain.

## November 1, 1968

Ralph Ellison broke up the *American Scholar* dinner again this evening. A forthcoming article on drugs, students, etc. had not been shown Ralph, and beginning on this he went on, remorselessly, stammering a little and talking very pompously, to deny that he was an Uncle Tom, to talk about himself in the thirties, forties, fifties, sixties. Later that evening, when I had gone to bed, he called me—for the first time in many a moon—but I knew it was he, didn't take the call, and listened with fascination to Ann fielding his remarks—"I'm of a great sincerity about this."—During the monologue, I played with coins, but whenever I looked up, I noticed Barzun staring ahead with great aplomb. I had seen him earlier at Steele Commager's and it occurred to me that Barzun, with his inhumanly clear and perfect sentences, his perfect address, his imperturbability,

111. Daniel Bell (1919–), sociologist and Harvard professor emeritus, is married to Pearl Kazin Bell, Kazin's sister.

must be another one of these foreigners (pace Dr. Amy Baumann) who has transformed himself, in order to be an English speaker at all. He manufactures sentences, he emits thoughts, with a proficiency that I find deadly. I keep trying to imagine him in his underpants, but it is impossible.

Hannah at this dinner finally awoke all my long-dormant dislike of so much patronage. She was trying to put me down on the thirties book, and actually had the nerve to tell me, because she had just come on the book, that it must have been just recently published![112] She also loftily explained to me that the "Imag[ination] of Society" book[113] would undoubtedly be my best. . . . I always associate the Century (where the dinner was held) with unpleasantness now.

Hannah, Pearlie, Dick too in a way—so many estrangements. Losses. That *I* have chosen to have?

## November 19, 1968

The winners and the losers. Jews and non-Jews: write an essay on what we successes owe the others. Write about Bellow and Trilling and Mrs. Trilling—about Jerome Wiesner and how many others who have "made it." *Success* has been our portion—which may be why Philip Roth and Bruce Friedman can write only about sexual anxiety. The golden age of the Jews—the Age of our Success. The *End* of The Story *was* "Making It."[114] Write about "the rewards of a successful literary career," about *Making It*, about [Norman] Podhoretz and Shanker and Hofstadter and [Irving] Kristol. Like the German Jews. The sweet smell of success. Like Chametsky and Roth. *The Jewish success*. Alfred again, Bede Hofstadter, Robert Brustein, Jules Feiffer, Byron Dobell, Harry Levin, Irving Ribner, Edward Saveth, Bernard Malamud, Mailer, Barbara Solomon, Marcus Klein, Robert Silvers, Jason Epstein, Leon Uris, Daniel Bell, Harold Rosenberg, Irving Howe, Albert Shanker, Robert Coles, Mike Nichols, Elaine May, Abe Burrows, Leonard Lyons, Leonard Bernstein, Jules Feiffer, Peter Gay, Nathan Glazer, Thomas Lasch, Saul Bellow and Saul T[ouster], Ray Horowitz, Charles Frankel, Mark Rudd, Michael Kazin, Steven Kamin, Herbert Weisinger, Sidney Gelbart, Isaac B[ashevis Singer]

112. Kazin may have been correct that Arendt was putting him down by professing to have recently learned about *Starting Out in the Thirties;* she had read at least parts of it following its publication in 1965, referring to it in an October 20, 1965, letter to Mary McCarthy, *Between Friends* (1995), 191.
113. One of the titles Kazin considered for *An American Procession*.
114. Kazin is referring to Norman Podhoretz's *Making It* (New York: Random House, 1967).

and Herman Kahn—Hans Morgenthau, Hannah Arendt—Herbert Marcuse and Herbert Mitgang—Karl Shapiro—Meyer Shapiro—Oscar Handlin—Leon Edel—Carl Kaysen—Beny [Benjamin] Kaplan—George Steiner—[115]

115. Jerome Wiesner (1915–1994), professor at M.I.T., science adviser to Presidents Eisenhower, Kennedy, and Johnson. Philip Roth (1933–), acclaimed American novelist, friend of Kazin's; Bruce Jay Friedman (1930–), American novelist, play and screenwriter; Albert Shanker (1928–1997), president of the United Federation of Teachers from 1964 to 1984 as well as president of the American Federation of Teachers from 1974 to 1997; Jules Chametzky, professor at University of Massachusetts at Amherst, founder of the *Massachusetts Review*, author of *The Fiction of Abraham Cahan* and *Our Decentralized Literature: Cultural Mediations in Selected Jewish and Southern Writers;* Robert Brustein (1927–), American theater critic, playwright, director, and producer; Byron Dobell, editor at *Time, Esquire, New York*, and *American Heritage;* Irving Ribner, Shakespearean scholar, professor at SUNY-Stony Brook; Edward Saveth (1915–), writer on immigration; Barbara Probst Solomon was U.S. cultural correspondent for Spain's primary newspaper *El País* of Madrid; Marcus Klein, literary scholar and critic, author of *After Alienation: American Novels in Mid-Century*; Leon Uris (1924–2003), American historical novelist, author of *Exodus;* Robert Coles (1929–), American author, child psychiatrist, professor at Harvard University, author of more than eighty books and hundreds of articles, winner of the Pulitzer Prize for general nonfiction and a MacArthur Award; Mike Nichols (1931–), writer and director who produced and acted comedy routines with the actress Elaine May (1932–); Leonard Lyons (1906–1976), American newspaper columnist; Leonard Bernstein (1918–1990), American conductor and composer, wrote music for *West Side Story;* Peter Gay (1923–), Berlin-born American historian, author of more than twenty-five books, professor of history at Yale University; Saul Touster, professor of American studies and legal studies at Brandeis University; Raymond Horowitz, prominent art collector and founder of the Mr. and Mrs. Raymond J. Horowitz Foundation for the Arts; Charles Frankel (1917–1979), American philosopher who wrote about value theory and the philosophy of history, assistant secretary of state in charge of education and culture from 1965 to 1967, a post he resigned to protest the Vietnam War; Mark Rudd (1947–), political organizer, a leader of Columbia's SDS movement in 1968, later a cofounder of the Weather Underground, a radical violence-prone organization established to protest the Vietnam War; Herbert Weisinger (1913–1999), dean of the Graduate School, SUNY-Stony Brook; Herman Kahn (1922–1983), military strategist at the RAND Corporation, who analyzed strategies and consequences of nuclear war; Hans Morgenthau (1904–1980), prominent figure in the study of international politics and law, known for his classic work *Politics Among Nations*, an eloquent opponent of the Vietnam War; Herbert Marcuse (1898–1979), German philosopher, sociologist, and political theorist associated with the Frankfort School of Critical Theory, one of the fathers of the New Left, author of *Eros and Civilization* and *One-Dimensional Man;* Herbert Mitgang (1920–), reviewer and editorial writer for the *New York Times;* Karl Shapiro (1913–2000), American poet, the fifth poet laureate consultant to the Library of Congress in 1946; Arnold Cooper, a professor of psychiatry at the Weill Cornell Medical School and the Payne Whitney Psychiatric Clinic; Aaron Asher (1929–2008), prominent editor of leading writers, husband of Linda Asher, who was a translator and editor at the *New Yorker;* Arnold Newman (1918–2006), American photographer, noted for his portraits of artists and politicians as well as for his abstract still lifes; Joseph Machlis (1906–1998), professor of music at Queens College CUNY, author of *Introduction to Contemporary Music;* Victor Goldin, associate director of the department of psychiatry at Beth-Israel Medical Center.

Ann Birstein—Carol Bookman—Arnold Newman—Arnold Cooper—Aaron Asher—Linda Asher—Joseph Machlis—Victor Goldin—L. Silberstein—Susan Sontag.

## December 3, 1968

[. . .] This beautiful *diary:* my speech . . . speech at the root. The existentialist thinkers en ce regard: speech as the resolution of the chaos of the life-death cross.

## December 6, 1968

A woman like that [G___], having to make up her own mind about everything, having to think and *order* everything out in secret, a woman like that, a natural revolutionary under her always-correct expression. You are the revolution I sought, I told her, which is not altogether true! But she is a revolutionary for herself, as women have to be, and so helps those in contact with her—those who reach her—to be a little revolutionized too. The firm shining lips, the extraordinary sweet smelling crop of hair at the cleft, sensuously gifted (like our old Lou) but incredibly intact, attentive, clever, a *planner*.

## December 8, 1968

[. . .] I shall write of Roth in terms of the family (Jewish obsession with their own) and of show biz, which in Jewish history succeeded socialism—the Jewish writer as outrager, provocateur, "shameless" fellow, his way of saying "I am *not* a goyim!"—Roth and the Jewish cult of purity. Desecration of the *food*. Wallowing in it.[116]

## December 10, 1968

[. . .] Emerson the highest product of American capitalism, who is of course against the "material" side of capitalism. The pure individualist product of so deeply engrained an individualism—who wants, on the basis of individual man, to be spiritual. Emerson always appeals to this private legend or fantasy of the past. The present is not quite real, or defined, to him. The future is pure abstraction—

116. Kazin reviewed Philip Roth's *Portnoy's Complaint*, "Up Against the Wall, Mama!" in the *New York Review of Books* (February 27, 1969): 3.

Capitalist psychology—man can find everything he needs in himself, without any help. He is his own best strength. The "soul" meaning the man himself is all—

## December 14, 1968

Roth and A. K. Eat, eat my child, eat! So one recovers in bed, either with another or oneself, this immense "gratification," with the penis used as a fork or spoon to shovel the gratification. Somewhere in earliest childhood one sucked and was sucked; all parts of that primal female body were available to us, and ever after one waits for that bliss to return again. Glutton. Be committed to me alone, she says, love me for myself alone. But how can one explain to her that it is Woman one loves, the feminine principle as the necessity to gratification, and that in a time of unlimited consumer satisfaction in so many things, when people are indeed hipped on getting, enjoying, moving, feeling with the swirl, when the difference between the sexes are always breaking down, when the one-body principle seems to be acting as flatly as the one earth-space, the one space-time-continuum of simultaneous information and entertainment in which we live—how can one explain that the male is committed to his *enjoyment*, to his freedom and movement—in a word, to his infant nostalgia? Complete possession is the norm, as the baby was nothing but its possessing enjoyment. Now the man is a pluralistic universe; many different forces and traditions contend in him; and above all, he *knows* that he is in a world of many others, many other pluralisms possibly even more complex than himself; and so longings for these ancient streams of connection and pure gratification are intermixed with shocks and guilts and, above all, *uncertainties*. There is no firm *language* for the adult male embarked on a career of voluptuous enjoyment. He lies to no woman more than he lies to himself—lies in the sense that he improvises positions and postures (morally speaking) for him to live by in this hand-to-mouth existence. Interesting contrast between the fullness of the temporary gratification that he can get and the leaps, falls, and fissures in his internal moral existence. He is egged on and on; however, he obstinately pursues this destiny of gratification because the idea of being loved "entirely" (even in the moment on the bed) of being loved for "himself alone," suddenly does heal the breaks and fill over the blanks of the normally beset existence, when and where he realizes every day that he is *not* King and Adored Object.

The little Jewish boy does grow up to think of himself as all-cherishable, and it has taken the contemporary sexual revolution to persuade him that his obsession with fucking is by no means strange or unfulfillable. . . . But the closeness of this dream also explains the irritability, the pride negativism, of so many other responses to existence. The negative *politics* of everyday, as it were. Hence Roth: who is the distilled end product of the American Jew not as "hero" or martyr or revolutionary, but the *son*, the son as consumer. Eat, eat, I need to eat!

## December 20, 1968

[. . .] Roth looks like Pinter—These sharp-nosed young Jews of the post-war generation. The sharp nose *is* very important—They are *sharp*.

## December 21, 1968

There was this stupid, showy dinner party at the Arthur Gelbs'; and Arthur M. Schlesinger, Junior (very Junior) was there, and I thought, what a prodigy, what a young, young man Arthur always is, what a pout he always has, and how provocative (like a child) he always is. Arthur the prodigy, the young man, even at 51 he is alternately the most charming and the most insufferable of brats. Arthur the liar—with his sense of some authority to lie to!

Northrop Frye writes in a language that is all his own, "criticism," a language so special to him and so exaltedly abstract and intellectually, donnishly witty, that I ask myself how we ever could have said five words together at that time at Sunwood. The abstractness of it all is what is so interesting. The trouble is that people's separate languages are really people's separate minds, the convolutions in the brain are the parts of the speech, and each looks helplessly at the "parts" of the other. The convolutions are hidden—but horribly penetrating. We are made by these minutest subdivisions, these infinitely small, cellular differentiations—and we are the last to explain these highly personal differentia. [. . .]

## December 25, 1968

Poor BOYS GROWN RICH, or The Beatles—*The Yellow Submarine*, it moves, oh it moves through a sea of dreams. In the end "all you need is love," but meanwhile, o love, o love, what riches in these visions, these cartoons of our dreams, what power of movement and fantasy, what visions of *riches*, in these poor boys from old barren seed Liverpool. I sat at the film this afternoon in a perfect ecstasy of recognition, and thought—of course! Poor boys always understand each other. When I was young, oh when I was young, I thought my mother and father were all the world, that's how poor *I* was. And I tried to change my mother and father—I had nothing else but them, and being somewhat dissatisfied and even desperate (shall I say) I tried to change them, what else? But now that I am grown rich—oh now that I am grown rich, there is no need to change anybody! Ours but to pick and choose from the great garden of our richness!—Still, brothers I know in poverty, brothers in the mean and broken streets of Liverpool, 1945, I rejoice in the yellow submarine that floats oh floats through these streets *and* seas of dreams.

The songs work like acrostics, backward is the same as forward, and the acrostic is a design: all you need is love, luv, love, (glove). Love is all you need.

## December 27, 1968

MLA convention at the Americana. A bunch of over-age SDS's broke up the American literature meetings repeatedly with utterly phony, trumped-up charges of police terror. How these guys like the atmosphere of confrontation. I'll not soon forget the line of young instructors forming before the stage while old, gray, bald Henry Nash Smith[117] made his weak remarks. *Pour la reste*, I listened to Dick Poirier reading the bad, new critical prose over the question of Chicago and thought, what a phony.

This was a wholly provoked incident, based on a few posters in a hotel lobby, and leading to deliriously self-righteous rant on the part of Lauter and his wife Florence Howe and the others. I watched all this with the greatest contempt. My soul cannot live on this pseudo-revolutionary fare. [. . .]

## January 5, 1969

FATHERS AND SONS. On this fine Saturday, enter Michael, in two shades of corduroy, brown boots, moustache. We had lunch at Nocital, a Mexican joint on West 46th, and as usual, when the four of us get together, we make the place jump with the violence of our arguments. Michael, who later on was all suave honey with Daniel Bell when the Bells came over after lunch, jumps at me like a bull, and I jump at him with quieter but even more intense feeling, then Ann joins in, and Katey, and the four of us are hollering and quoting and what-not like drunken peasants at an Irish wake. The amount of violence that is

117. Henry Nash Smith (1906–1986), professor at Berkeley, noted Mark Twain scholar, best known for his book *Virgin Land: The American West as Symbol and Myth* (1950), one of the first books of the "myth and symbol school" that shaped American studies at midcentury.

set up between Ann and me is always *something*, but when Michael introduces his conversation-by-political-slogan, my reaction to him is one of vehement disapproval. . . . And yet, I ask myself, what is it that makes these political dogmas the occasion of so much heat? Because they are the symbols, if not the occasions, of such idealism and truth as we have. People still come to blows over the Roman Catholic and Presbyterian versions of the truth in Northern Ireland. With us, we want to remain idealists and faithful souls of one kind or another, and politics is the way we reproach or approve each other. Michael seems to think that I have betrayed the leftist directions of my youth, I on my part think that the socialist thing, one way or another, betrayed *my* idealism. It's no good my trying to say to him, I care only for art and literature! Of course I don't. The real question behind all the heat: where do you find truth? Truth as all-operative from one set of principles, one perspective? Michael's SDS line irritates me as much because it is always colliding with the truth as because it is so abstract and sometimes down-right false. Yet compare Michael talking about Cuba with so much love because workers in a factory worked all night and all day to supply food to the North Vietnamese with margarine-faced Prof. Dr. Rostow, who in his interview with the *New York Times* today (January 5) says with the ridiculous lordliness of the high diplomatic world: "Cuba is a nuisance, dangerous still, but manageable." [. . .]

## January 23, 1969

[. . .] Hannah's calls to politics, to the public space, to communication, to directness—all are a good example of criticism in action, criticism that must lead to action, that is a form of action. But it all takes place in a world made up of ideals as distinctions within and from the actual world—it is the refugee's ideal republic, it is the German democrat's eternal dream.

Hannah my teacher, Hannah, the eternal educator. Reading over these essays, *Men in Dark Times*, is like a resume of all the insights, and many of the quotations, that Hannah the teacher propounded over the years from 1946 when I first met her. How hard it was—is—to explain to Ann that it was Hannah's ideal classicism that won me to her—that it was her "knowledge." I noticed years ago that otherwise we were always silent between quotations, looking for topics—which I generally initiated to get the ball rolling, of course. Some of this awkwardness was no doubt the difference in our cultural-national styles. But fundamentally, it arose because Hannah was the teacher of so many of us relatively uninformed young intellectuals; and she taught and taught, until we walked out on the teacher—who wanted, German style, only to keep teaching and to keep the taught in her sight.

What peace—if one saw oneself *only* as a servant of truth. Objectivity with the *fiat* of death.

Writing is fucking—a form of ecstasy—but it lasts longer—the *other* is not this usable, wastable, exhaustible. [. . .]

## March 5, 1969

Looking back on "my generation," my greatest sense of what happened is of being overwhelmed by events, of being tossed up and down in this ever turbulent sea of "politics," history, war. Here and there, as with Jim Agee, there is a wistful upward shoot of "spirituality," an attempt to link up with the super-individualists of the 20s. And from this point of view Isaac's furious "sexual," search, like my growing "Jewishness," is an attempt to save something from the spiritual numbing, the constant threat to life, the anxiety, the money-making, the empty, bourgeois responsibilities. The truth is that loyalty to the unconscious values of the self is almost the only privilege one is sometimes left with in this day and age. Everywhere else I am conscious of a cheapening, of a routine, of a devaluation, of a baseness, that drive me farther and farther away from myself, that makes this long "journey" away from one's heart, one's deepest conviction. What I demand, above and beyond everything else at this moment, is integrity to *myself*—[. . .] some connection with *value*. "I cannot live this way! I cannot live this way!"[118] [. . .]

## March 7, 1969

The visiting Englishman, Prof. Plumb,[119] at Hofstadter's dinner. Good form—above all, stout fella. Never lets his side down. Is formidable as a debater, as an arguer. Compared with the softness and vacillation of Americans, the Englishman, especially the visiting one, is always solider on his feet and especially, more rational, in his conversation—Never lets the side down. Is always thinking in behalf of English power. "England is a much juster society than America."

118. Kazin may have been loosely quoting Leo Tolstoy, who upon learning of men being hanged for trespass, reportedly said: "It's impossible to live this way, for me at any rate, and I shall not do it"; quoted in Henri Troyat, *Tolstoy*, trans. Nancy Amphoux (New York: Doubleday, 1967), 612.

119. John Harold Plumb (1911–2001), Cambridge historian.

## March 25, 1969

My unconscious: the clotted Jewish past, the whole (mysterious) history of the collective Jewish self—

## March 26, 1969

Nabokov. Utterly exceptional man, exceptional even in his original aristo situation. So exceptional that he has to *ward off* other writers, exceptional to the point where his sense of reality is so multiplex and confusing that he has learned the art of dissociating himself from "the dream of reason" and has the ability not to mediate between them but to present them as alternate versions of reality, as tricks in his bag of tricks. . . . Exceptional in his dream of attachment, exceptional in his linguistic-scientific *naming* ability (Linnaeus). . . . The furious competence of the aristocratic-intellectual-Petersburg Russian, rivaling the Western world. . . .

The unity of time to the artist-observer. Time as a great circle whose circumference is *everywhere.*

Vladimir the innocent. Pure and Good. And *loving.* The outer shell of Nabokov, the egotism dissolves, and one is aware of dealing with the gifted and exceptional *child.* The isolato. Great piety in his memoir—utterly decent man. (The test of the Russian barini not to mean *harm*). Vladimir's instincts are utterly *pacific.* The country of literature—the country of *his* imagination.

V. the rhetorician tries out sentences to see where he will land. Loves experiments in *perception*, loves to establish and disestablish mental laws. Driven by a need to *create* reality. Has basic thesis—the fear of silence, *of not knowing—to keep in touch.* Obsessive immortality.

Words are *too* important to V. They have magically *denotative* powers. The peculiar importance of scientific, descriptive terminology to the Russian intellectual. Russia and *personal* gamesmanship—The acute Russian sense of *rivalry. Thinking* everything out in exile, silence and cunning.

## April 26, 1969

1740 hours. Protestant and Jew in American Literature. From the green, golden, towpath. RWE believes that nature is something for men to think with. It is comprehensibility (and in his case expressiveness) incarnate. It is the beginning of "natural" thinking—thinking according to nature, by the light of nature, according to the (great) book of nature. Everything is open—everything possible. There is nothing inherently different from men (witness Plato's eternal realm), only the first cause (which too lurks in nature—at the end of the labyrinth so to speak).

What has always bothered *me* in all this is the applicability and practicality of everything. There is sublimity of course, but no mystery. Whereas nothing is so obvious about the Jewish *condition* (to say nothing about the Jew's God) as its mystery. Why the Jews at all? Why do they persist? Why, without a supporting religious mystique, be a Jew at all? Why the long persistence of the Jews, the deep-felt rationality of their suffering? Mystery, not comprehensibility, like the varieties of Providence. The Jew's God is *hidden* and the Jew's fate is always mysterious. By contrast, Emerson is open, radiant, a poet of unlimited perception as possibility. Nature is not divisible. *Nature is really the mind of men disclosing itself in evidences of design all around him.*

## June 5, 1969

Frankie Fitzgerald invited us to a big evening bash, at her mother's, Mrs. Marietta Tree. Mrs. Tree is beautiful and glamorous and sharp as a knife. The evening turned out to be political. Galbraith[120] mockingly introduced Norman Mailer; and Mailer, advancing his latest social theory, New York City to be a separate state, argued in his usual boxer's style, arms defiantly across his chest or hands viriley making a point. He argued to win, not to persuade; the literati who made up most of the evening laughed a lot at him. But I was, as always, impressed by Mailer's devotion to the job in hand, his passion for mastery. His thinking is always along the line of a social *model.*

The fabulous looking New York party girls. Each as her own model. The air of being intellectually detached and sexually available. . . . Intellectuals as spectators yet also "glamorous." Bessie Cuevas, Linda Asher, Alexandra Allen, Mrs. Halberstam.[121]

120. John Kenneth Galbraith (1908–2006), Canadian-American economist and public intellectual who taught at Harvard and served in four Democratic administrations. His best known book is *The Affluent Society* (1958).

121. Bessie Cuevas, descendent of John D. Rockefeller, social activist; Mrs. Halberstam, spouse of David Halberstam (1934–2007), Pulitzer Prize–winning author.

## June 17, 1969

[. . .] This [journal] is my true autobiography. . . . I am racked by so many old pains, yet continually try to lift myself by thought, by ideas, by words that are warm when I put them together—because to prove such a relationship is a flush of joy. . . . But so often the words of others, words in general, outside the demonstration of a connection, are like closed books behind doors. . . . The word is my power, I have no other means of "saving" myself. But for thought to hammer at the closed door! Creativity is the demonstration of secret connections . . . between words. The immediate connection is all. Beyond, the writer seeks in vain to remake his life . . . to *make* life . . . to attain his dreams on earth.

## June 26, 1969

"Guilt" is felt as flouting an authority whom one believes in—whose values are in some sense your own, have even taught you what values are. But during World War II the widely diffused sense of guilt also became a way of trying to find values, in the absence of meaningful authority. The American war novelists who write like clowns (Vonnegut,[122] Heller, etc.) are, even when they have been participants, literally onlookers as Vonnegut [and] the Germans' prisoners remained "out of it" during the destruction of Dresden. The guilt of so many non-participating, non-suffering Jews like myself is really an attempt to give the Holocaust "meaning"—our suffering *is* a way of re-establishing authority. More and more I realize how much the literature of the second World War, on the U.S. side especially, is literary, an affair of onlookers. . . . The American wants to be part of it, to create his morality by becoming part of the universal suffering. But he can't. . . . And one reason for feeling like an onlooker in the midst of it is his lack of a common past with the others; so that the profound sense of isolation that the Jews had in Nazi Europe, the sense of their own strangeness and superfluousness in the midst of the European community, suggests the strange "cynicism" of the American soldier—who doesn't in this case have to be a Negro—who feels that he is physically but not morally one of a team. . . . His memories are singular, his moral universe in war is too often limited to himself. . . .

The Hitler war—the age of the primal sin, killing on such a total scale that man saw himself, everywhere, in an image he could never forget—

122. Kurt Vonnegut Jr. (1922–2007), American novelist noted for his black humor, perhaps best known for his science fiction work *Slaughterhouse-Five* (1969).

The actors and the onlookers—suddenly the onlookers saw themselves on the stage.

## August 24, 1969

[. . .] I know that for me the writing of this non-fiction novel [*New York Jew*] can only be created by relationships, by the amount of feeling on my own part. . . . Otherwise, it becomes "reminiscences" of writers merely. . . .

Impossible to write such a book unless you are strong in the legs: i.e., take full responsibility for your experience . . . say I because that is what there is to say: that has been the focal member. . . .

The book is not the story of initiation—but of the story (total) of a generation . . . of a period in history seen from the point of view of a middle-aged man who has come . . . TO THINK OF DEATH. . . . The initiation is not the essence, it is the total life-view. . . . It is about winners and losers, life and death.

This book will be written, is being written, not from the point of view of a young man, an initiate, but from that of a mature man looking back. . . . It will not be the lonely story of a young man's shivery initiation, but that of a whole group in and through time. . . .

## November 25, 1969

Political nuts all over the place—or the wars of religion. Aunt Nechama and Uncle Boris[123]—the political messianism of the oppressed. *Tout se dispose en forme de politique* [everything takes a political form] because these are statements of aspiration or fantasy not requiring anything but *self* articulation. Radical politics—anti-radical politics—*where*, so to speak, do the realities behind these statements take place? Ideas—ideologies—wars of religion.

*I am the lion in the path.* I am the lion in Michael's path (according to my Jungian friend Jeff Satinover)[124]—I certainly seem to be the lion in PK's [Pearl Kazin's]

123. A cousin of Kazin's mother, Nechama Heller, and her husband Berl, both fiery radicals, were frequent visitors at the Kazin household in Brownsville.

124. Jeffrey Satinover (1947–), American psychiatrist and psychoanalyst who teaches at the C. G. Jung Institute in Zurich.

path—And God knows I am that in ABK's [Ann Birstein Kazin's] path. Lion! Be a lion!

## December 20–22, 1969

My father sits up in bed, trying to speak.[125] He sits up, smiling a little, saying "corn" "corn." Son? Son? so much for an outworn, 82 year old body, for the man looking up at me with the hatred of the dying (not my father, no, not my father—the old man sipping his liquid food through a straw). A bald-headed Yankee, in the other bed, says about the food served up to him—I won't eat this shit. Who ever heard of apple-sauce for dessert? Merciless bodies, decaying bodies—I never loved Charles Kazin, my father, so much as now—I know I identify with him, alas, alas! with the paralyzed old man! No, I love him, I love him—and in despair over his helplessness. . . .

## December 30, 1969

Edwin Fischer's 1938 recording of the Bach Piano Concerto No. 5 in F. Minor. The slow movement is played with such subtle falls from note to note that you hold your breath at the beginning of each phrase to see whether it will surprise you again by rising when it should be falling. Little curves of mental space that are as meticulously various as algebraic relationships. Pure line—pure development all within a space so limited that it gives the highest possible value to the relationship between one note and another. [. . .]

In the slush and torridly crowded subway to 158 E. 58th, Dr. Nathan Stockhammer, now Katey's shrink. Clever bearded fellow in his early forties or so, took us gently over the coals, called the right turns just as we were coming to them, and we made them. He saw the bitterness, the violence, the stupidity. So there was a flare-up in the taxi, too, and the rest of the evening was the usual. Muck. Just muck.

125. Kazin's father had suffered a stroke that left him partially paralyzed and aphasic. He died on September 23, 1970.

# 7
# New York Jew
## 1970–1977

"THE DEATH GOD SUDDENLY WALKS INTO the distracted, sodden New York Party!" Kazin wrote in an October 17, 1975, journal entry. "And suddenly life becomes a *book*." On December 27, 1969, his close friend Josephine Herbst had died in a New York hospital, her "hot dying hands, just like the hands of BB [Berel Birstein, Ann's father] and GK [Alfred's mother] ten years ago this year." On September 23, 1970, Alfred's father died in a Brooklyn nursing home. A month later, he learned of the death of Richard Hofstadter and Ben Seligman, two friends from the thirties and forties, followed in two weeks by the death of Heinrich Blücher, Hannah Arendt's husband and Kazin's confidant. "In these few weeks I have lost Papa, Dick, Ben, Heinrich, I think to myself: where have they gone?" (November 4, 1970). More losses would follow—his teacher and friend Mark Van Doren and Edmund Wilson in 1972—"our great tree has fallen"—and Hannah Arendt in 1975. The deaths were deeply troubling—"my overwhelming thought is that the serious people are gone, have gone, are going one by one"—not least because they reminded him of time passed and passing and of his own age. "Looking out at the dusk dripping down into New York, I seemed to see the dark taking over everywhere, taking *me* over. So little time left. The impossible thought of becoming sixty!" (June 12, 1972; December 5, 1975; December 10, 1974).

A writer who had typically looked to his youth for inspiration, Kazin spent much of the seventies worrying about change and decline, about the arc of his career, about the ominous trends in his marriage—and about the uncertain fate of the city he loved and that seemed under new threats daily. He worked on three major projects in the seventies—*Bright Book of Life,* a critical study of contemporary fiction, published in 1973, *An American Procession,* which he would not finish until 1983, and *New York Jew* (1978), his last autobiography, chronicling his life from the war years into the seventies. Though it contains accounts of visits and teaching assignments in Europe, Russia, Israel, and New England, *New York Jew* is primarily about Kazin's life in New York City. Like the two earlier autobiographies, it conveys the wonder and sense of expectation that New York could always elicit from this Brownsville native, except that by the seventies, the "unreal" city in the distance had become very real and its problems everywhere evident. "*The Walker* [. . .] was a fable of youth, sweetness, and search," he wrote in a May 22, 1974, entry. "The *New York Jew* is about a world of real conflict—a world of *people* only and wholly. And it is a book about shipwreck—in a city and a country riven with the deepest kind of conflict."

In 1976 Kazin saw the shipwreck up close. He had resigned from Stony Brook in 1973 to take a position at Hunter College and the Graduate Center of CUNY. In the intervening years he had watched the city lurch from crisis to crisis: the crime rate mounting—"*100 muggings a day*" (September 23, 1972)—its finances in disarray, the south Bronx burning, the middle class rushing to the suburbs, the tabloids screaming—"The Last Days of New York!" "New York is just a failure." On May 28, 1976, during final exams, City University failed to meet its payroll and closed its doors. It would reopen weeks later, many programs cut and faculty let go. Kazin had seen it coming. Journal entries speak of strikes, blackouts, garbage piling up on the streets, "a world coming apart. . . . The great big, dissolving center—New York can't be governed" (May 22, 1974). But even as he registered the strikes, the murders, the screaming headlines, he continued to be entertained—and appalled—by his "New York characters" (on the street, in the subway, at a party or the Century Club), to discover and rediscover forgotten neighborhoods, and to rejoice in the energy and variety of a city whose present and past are inseparable from his own. "The city is unbelievable. Such commotion, such pressure, such violence, such quiescent rage. Yet the outsider-insider feels connected to it—by his mind, his past, his past now being a book?" (May 22, 1975).

## March 11, 1970

From the Diaries of a New Yorker: The fat necked chauffeur of the Club Car took us from Nightingale by way of Williamsburg Bridge to Menorah [home for his father]. Williamsburg-Ridgewood, the Old El on Brooklyn Broadway: nothing but tattered signs of hardware stores, Venetian blinds, plumbing, trucks. Max Wiseman, the director of Menorah, is a writer—did things for the *PR* the other day—so it looks good for Pop—though the lunch was horrible—funny with poor old Gedaliah trying to get something out of his teeth while Wiseman and [I] talked literature. Back by way of East Side, Delancey St. . . . Dazed with relief and happiness; I went into Nedicks for a hot dog. Jamaican Negro was talking to NY Negress about how beautiful his island is and how walking keeps him young. Put my food before me, gave me a sidelong glance just as I was fishing in my overcoat pocket to pay him, and said something about Jews and money. I was in no mood for nonsense and told him off. He said something about everybody being a Jew when it comes to money. Jesus was a Jew, I said sentimentally, but this got overlooked in his point about money. . . . Pursued my hot dog into the Hebrew National on Times Sq, when the counterman at the dairy counter (yet) said fifteen, made it sound like thirteen. Not easy to communicate with your fellow New Yorkers. To drinks at the Algonquin with Hilton Kramer[1]—Josie's literary

1. Hilton Kramer (1928–), art critic and cultural commentator; Leslie Katz, critic and editor.

executor—and Leslie Katz. Katz thinks that the young are barbarians—Kramer's hair is very long in the back, he talks with elaborate fatigue, and I left them in a hot argument whether Katz should publish a little "keepsake" volume of Josie's letters. To home, the usual bang-bang. Ann off to see the Grove Press film festival. . . . Endless war—no let-up. . . .

## March 21, 1970
### Deya [Majorca]

Suddenly another world—orange trees, country roads, the Mediterranean off in the distance, the unmoving faces of old Spaniards, *the Franca Roja, the sense of time enough.* Wandering up and down the town, led by the mission poet John Hall, we ran into Robert Graves outside of one of his houses beating a carpet in preparation for the visit of his god-daughter, who is a member of the Norwegian ballet. Graves showing us around the house showed his usual passion for knowing everything about every little thing and putting you to the test about it. [. . .]

## March 31, 1970
### [Palma, Majorca]

Ran into Leonard Boudin of all people at this hotel. What interests me about him most is not his championship as a lawyer of "unpopular" left causes but the surly, half-blind, typically, *physically* malformed old City College men with the gift for pure abstraction (in his case *chess*). How many of these zealous Quasimodos have I seen with malformed eyes and stomachs and the look of a medieval Arab discovering *Aristotle*. Jean Boudin, his wife (sister of I. F. Stone's wife), very tiny lady, clucking madly about how terrible the U.S. is in an effort to sympathize with her absent daughter, Kathie, who was last seen running naked out of the bomb-destroyed house on West 11th Street.[2] Oh God this total Jewish impatience with the world—these irritable generalizations of total alienation in behalf of *politics*.

2. Leonard B. Boudin (1912–1989), prominent civil liberties attorney and activist who represented Daniel Ellsberg and Dr. Benjamin Spock, both of whom advocated resistance to the Vietnam War. His daughter, Kathy Boudin (1943–), was a member of the Weather Underground, convicted and imprisoned from 1981 to 2003 for participating in a robbery of a Brinks truck in which a guard was killed. Isidore Feinstein Stone (1907–1989), investigative journalist who self-published *I. F. Stone's Weekly*.

## April 8, 1970

Back in New York after that lovely escape to Spain. I realize more than ever now, reading Orwell's *Homage to Catalonia,* what an unreal, quiet, subdued, utterly obedient country it has become. Orwell writing about the battles around Huesca, writing about battle, is so completely engagé in every fiber of his being, is so much at war against INJUSTICE AND EVIL, that by contrast, every line in Hemingway about Spain—about war—is that of the spectator. Orwell[3] is truly the Christ of our generation—that passed through the fire of total commitment before the horror of the total war. . . . What is most striking about *Catalonia* is the absence of "literature," the drivingly insistent honesty, the total, integral militancy of politics, and the act of writing the truth. . . . I am struck by the immediacy of his visions (confessed as such), the way certain scenes linger in his mind, by his effort to be utterly truthful about the engagement of himself in and to war—This is truly war *at the bottom*, not from the literary gentlemen's point of view—and I notice with particular admiration both the detail of his privations, annoyances, frights—and his disciplined detachment from exaggerating the importance of *his* sufferings.

In his own way Orwell had a lot of "military" experience as a policeman, soldier in Spain, volunteer in the General Popular Militia in Spain. . . . And he is disciplined as a result. The discipline is in his writing and in his refusal to make too much of his *literary* personality—though he shrewdly uses it in the sense of depending, as writer, entirely on his honesty, his factuality. . . . The writer as hero is *not* one of his myths. The self blends into the text as—ideally—he blends into the war. . . .

3. George Orwell, pseudonym of Eric Arthur Blair (1903–1950), English author, novelist, and commentator, fought on the side of the elected Republican government in Spain against the Nationalists led by General Francisco Franco and other generals and supported by Italian Fascists and Nazi Germany. Shot in the neck and disillusioned with the tactics of the Communists who had betrayed the Republicans, Orwell returned to England, where many on the left did not want to hear about Communist treachery. In *Homage to Catalonia*, Orwell acknowledged that while the war was a political "disaster," it had left him "with not less but more belief in the decency of human beings." Ernest Hemingway (1899–1961), also a supporter of the Republic, participated in the Spanish Civil War as a reporter for the North American Newspaper Alliance. In Madrid as the city was being bombed, he wrote a play, *The Fifth Column*, about the war. In 1940 he published *For Whom the Bell Tolls*, a best-selling novel also about the war. Hemingway was less interested in the contradictions of the war than in the displaying the heroism of certain participants.

Orwell is all "politics," meaning not only ideology (not his strongest point) but, literally, togetherness. . . . A point about him, as about Zygelboym,[4] *the readiness to think himself a sacrifice*. . . . Very important point about this generation of ours. . . . By contrast, the radicalism of the "kids" together has an inescapable quality of play-acting . . . and of deliberate provocation—trying it on for size. . . .

## April 26, 1970

[. . .] Clever, all too clever—all these novelists trying to *solve* the problem of the "contemporary" by cleverness. So Bellow: he has to have the last word in *Sammler*. Snubbing his own characters—giving them marks for virtue. Their lives do not come up to his understanding.[5]

## May 7, 1970

Monthly dinner of the Century Club. Never trust anybody over 77! Hundreds of gray hairs in black evening coats, self-consciously listening to old Dean Acheson[6] defaming the youth as carriers of violence, defending Rhodesia and South Africa—Acheson being charming, lordly, the state secretary still, architect of our foreign policy, etc. Oh Lord, save us from these successes.

## May 19, 1970

Had dinner with Michael at the Tsen-Tsin restaurant 125th Street, under the high girders of the El. He was coughing, he was pale, he was unshaven, and I was trying with all my might and main to show a) that I "sympathize" with his goals, b) that I am concerned about his leaving school again and drifting about, as he has done increasingly. . . . But it was no use. He goes his way, he goes, he goes, and I watch him with my heart sore. . . . He is and will be a sacrifice . . . a human missile, taking no thought for himself. . . . I could insult and outrage him by calling him a rentier, a parasite, etc. . . . But it is stupid and untrue. He is a sacrifice. He want to *be* a piece of the action.

4. See Chapter 2, note 24.
5. Kazin published a highly critical review of *Mr. Sammler's Planet*, "Though He Slay Me," in the *New York Review of Books* (December 3, 1970): 3–4, provoking Bellow to break off relations.
6. Dean Acheson (1893–1971), U.S. secretary of state in the Truman administration, helped design the Marshall Plan and plan the creation of NATO.

## May 21, 1970

[. . .] Mrs. Roy Tarlow, formerly Mrs. Olaf Helmer, formerly Mrs. Hans Meyerhoff, formerly Mary Louise Petersen—is as beautiful as ever, looks like the white haired mother of the girl I was once so infatuated with. I'm glad I went, by god and after all—because I had forgotten how gentle, how compliant she is, how courteous a listener. . . . She exists, always has, as the coefficient, the willing and able partner. . . . She listens, she devotes herself to you. By god and by gum I'm glad I had this brief visit. . . . I came out *liking* her again—impressed with her lovingness and her sympathy—sun warmth . . . I go around sniffing for sympathy like a stupid dog. . . . I mustn't dwell on this—or I will take my life, I'm so unhappy. . . .

## May 24, 1970

The power of the Jews has always been disproportionate to their numbers—now it is disproportionate to the military power being leveled and that can be leveled against the military power of Israel. In the U.S. everything done since the war has expressed the blind, natural excess of American wealth and power—the power intoxicates, it overwhelms, it bribes. . . . It leads to domination, to "imperialism." It is the great, brutal fact of life . . . and Americans who in themselves feel afraid lean on this power, identify with it. . . . Hence the flag business, the construction worker patriots no longer defend the war.[7] . . . Nobody does . . . they [are] defending the "flag," the icon of this national power on which everything rests. . . . The intellectuals are driven mad by this power if they try to do anything except just enjoy it, to be part of the system. The minute they step out of line, they are threatened. . . . In other words, the flag worshippers say, Do not get out of line, Do not make a fuss—or you will lose all the possible benefits of being part of the system. The collaboration . . . the bribery. . . .

"The war is coming to an end" . . . hence the bitterness. . . .

Picasso—Creativity is a sense of destruction—

## June 3, 1970

Papa Louis Ginsberg and his son, Allen Ginsberg, read their poems side by side at the Pen club. Papa has Yiddish overtones in his speech, writes sentimental,

7. Kazin would deliver a speech on May 28, 1970, to eight hundred members of publishing houses on the misuse of the flag by proponents of the Vietnam War at Dag Hammarskjöld Plaza, a version of which, "Our Flag," was published in the *New York Review of Books* (July 2, 1970): 3.

wistful couplets, and has about as much force (granted his age) as any other pious, goody, goody Jewish immigrant. Allen the "fag" looks like Samson, breathes in deep when he comes to a long period of interlocked epithets for Moloch, and expresses so much force, bass voice, rhythmic intensity, horror of and saturation in the poem as a piece of the living violence it is struck off from that the contrast of father and son is the contrast between immigrant weakness and native strength, between "poetaster" and poet. . . . Allen looks and sounds more like Samson . . . and HIS violence is equally striking. Only a very powerful country could have promised so much of itself in the shape of a counter-culture—

In Jews emotions often take the form of "ideology."

What is narrative? Narrative is a throwing forward—an acting out—an impersonation of objectivity—a masquerade leading to our hoped-for objectivity.

## July 3, 1970

Sharon Hotel, Herzlia [Israel] Friday morning.[8] Arrived late last night from Frankfurt after a long day in the airport waiting to get to the El Al counter, then to have our baggage examined for Arab bombs. The whole long day under the Holocaust consciousness of Dr. Fackenheim—days and days now of obsessive Jewish self-consciousness—i.e., of our existence as Jews, of our particular experience as Jews. Dr. Bauer of the Hebrew University went back alone to Belsen after we had made our pilgrimage in the rain on Wednesday, July 1. This whole experience, I've decided, has been to screen us individually as Jews, to put the "Jewish" experience at the center of our consciousness, to make us see Jew and think Jew all the time. And if, unlike the victory season right after the '67 War, when I was here last, I feel the Jewish obsession this time without a lifting of the heart, it is because I associate so much pain, lunacy, and outrage with so many Jews I have recently suffered—not merely Ann, but the madly ambitious [George] Steiner, who has plots like in Shakespeare and is *so full of his life*, every moment at the moment, that I can hear the pistons madly clacking in his brain.

8. Kazin, Elie Wiesel, and Rabbi Emile Fackenheim were among a group of prominent Jews who traveled to the site of the Belsen concentration camp and then to Israel on a trip organized and funded by Josef Rosensaft, a Belsen survivor and wealthy art collector.

Jews, Jews, Jews—without faith, without the old religious feeling of being central to and teacher to the universe, it becomes *the* psychological experience par excellence, the burden of the greatest enigma. The Yiddish-accented Polish Jews come straight out of the shtetl, the religious speak from Mt. Sinai. But for the others psychology becomes the Thing—psychology, the study of effects, for the pressure of the historical burden on the individual Jew is, as a cause, dissipated into individual *reactions*.

Somewhere I had come to believe that *Jew* and my *family* were identical. Nothing in the years since has been such a surprise to me as the fact there are so many different *kinds* of individuals and that there are the abysses between them.

So I must clear my mind of these old childhood identifications before I can see the "Jewish problem" for itself. Can a Jew ever see it for itself? Does it even exist outside of these intense primordial family relations? Has the "Jewish experience" ever meant anything to me outside these relations-identifications? I've looked to "The Jews" for the prolongation of my family. *Chaverin! Brethren all!*

*Belsen*, July 1st—the cemetery park in the rain. Such a *small* place. Within ¼ of a mile were packed in 58,000 people. There were 13,000 unburied corpses. Sparse and totally inadequate documentation of the Nazi period in the hall.

## July 16, 1970

After the long talk with Michael last night, the good talk for once, I was—I am—so full of the dammed-up feeling of so many years that I can hardly breathe calmly. All this lifetime feeling, all this long passion of the heart, all this longing—all this anger—all this bitterness, all this love, all this seeking—I feel as if I were the site of many storms. Everything keeps thundering through me. . . . Michael was here, my son was here, everything is still possible, I keep saying to myself, everything can be done so long as there is intactness, dignity, peace of mind, love for the Other instead of the old selfish bitterness—

These floods of feeling . . . at Menorah, watching Pop weeping in the bed and hearing Lefanecha[9] being derisively repeated around him. The swollen bodies

9. Lefanecha ("Before Thy Face"), the first word in a Hebrew prayer often said by children in the morning. In *New York Jew*, Kazin writes that his aphasic father repeated the phrase mechanically and nonsensically in his speech to the amused irritation of the other patients.

and hanging faces—hanging at an angle, drooping like the hanged. . . . The subway book indeed! The line of pure concentrated feeling. And what is the language for this. . . . The feeling of being *exceeded*, faces that top the sensorium—of oneself turning wholly into a possible register of what is too much for one. The note of strenuous suffering.

## September 23, 1970

In the late afternoon—Charles Kazin, my father, my father.

## September 26, 1970

He must have died between half past five and six in the afternoon. I had been talking about his possible cancer to the head physician, Dr. Jacob Handelsman. By six he was dead. Then, between Wednesday (we were on our way to the cocktail party in honor of Steegmuller's *Cocteau*) and this morning, Saturday, September 26th, the family descended, the telephone rang endlessly, there were the Bells and the Bells and the Bells, and still more Bells, as is seemed, though there are really only three of them . . . and the idiotically artificial, false service. They already had his coffin in by the time we got to the open pit next to Mama's grave, and there I was, shoveling in earth, stupidly reading in transliteration the Burial Kaddish—and seeing the Rabbi (Berzon, $50 for the morning) yawningly reading his newspaper . . . and looking at my children, my wife, my aunt, my uncle, my cousins. . . . Oh mystic ties of family! I have never been closer to Mike and Katey. . . . Yet the preposterous comedy of family connections where people are not connected. . . .

My old man will no longer prowl the boardwalk, my old man, the most solitary man in creation, unable ever to communicate his loneliness, my dear old Brooklyn walker and prowler, forever looking, dragging his bad leg. This last year was always one of such incommunicable pain. . . . The loneliest man in the world had aphasia and couldn't communicate . . . except to say LeFanecha . . . Before You . . . Before You.

The man we knew so familiarly as Charles Kazin suddenly appears ferociously, ominously changed as a *coffin*—staggers and frightens us as an object at the bottom of a deep hole, an *object* on which *we* who knew him, now throw *sand*.

## November 4, 1970

Heinrich Blücher died on Saturday, October 31—In these few weeks I have lost Papa, Dick [Hofstadter], Ben,[10] Heinrich, I think to myself: where have they gone? The "essence" of it all is silent, like God. Yet standing at the pit of silence, the direction which we seek somehow, though it has not "found" us, points us toward where we must go. Hannah was wearing an old-fashioned black dress, black stockings, and looked like death. Heinrich was 71 yrs old, they have lived together 30 years, and Hannah said of losing him—an *unimaginable* catastrophe. She was making philosophical distinctions even in replying to my question: was it at all expected. Yes, in the long term it was expected, but in the short term, an unimaginable catastrophe. [. . .]

## November 22, 1970

[. . .] Home again, days of the usual anguish with Ann, insult, violence, reconciliation. . . . Of course she is right when she calls me a mama's boy. . . . There is an infantile sense of desertion in me still, an aching loneliness, a longing for attachment, for the reassurance of being loved, that is infantile to the point of insanity. . . . The question is: why, at my age, knowing how temporary and shallow and even unmeant (on both sides) these assurances can be, do I long so for it, like a poultice, an aspirin, an amulet. Why after so much knowledge of how this mechanism works, do I still long for "love" beyond anything else—give up my soul for this sometimes . . . why is it so hard always to face the truth, the privacy, the lonely room. It's as if I had never got tired of testing, as if the problem had all possible solutions in the fascination of trying it over and over again.

My friend Dick was an early, emotional, nostalgic friend. The historian Richard Hofstadter, was something so entirely different—over and over, since his death I have been trying to accustom myself to the duality (or the single professional Richard Hofstadter behind the impression of duality). . . . [W]e, all of us, even daughter, "Kate," have an intellectual dogmatism, assurance, beyond our deserts. I sometimes listen to myself in class, with listeners, laying down the law . . . and think of the contrast with the whimpering child. . . .

## November 27, 1970

At Hannah's. Coffee with the widow. The German Jewish austerity and intellectualism are moving as ever—the photograph of Plato's bust, the functional

10. Benjamin Seligman, labor economist, Kazin's friend from the 1930s.

apartment meant for very plain living and the highest thinking, the quotations from David Grene[11]—"he who lacks Greek is not quite a human being." But the best thing about being with Hannah is that she is herself so ambitious, vain, bright, that it is not so much first things as the highest places one becomes aware of. After all these years, conversation with her is still as stiff as a diplomatic conference . . . and probably one reason why it is so stiff is that human and friendly as she is, she does in a sense hold court, invite an exchange of gossip, reminiscences while keeping her citadel, her PHILOSOPHICAL MIND, inviolate from your unphilosophical mind. She is by gum and by golly a Leader, an Oracle—when she talks about her successes, her following at Chicago etc., it is with modest laughter. But she does believe herself to be the Chosen One; she does have this attraction for many people because of her profound sense of herself as a central figure in the central subject, Philosophy—and it is a relief, frankly, after so much sodden acceptance of the second rate to feel the ambitiousness and self-confidence of a figure like this.

## December 15, 1970

Wednesday morning—lovely day inside. . . . sent off "Gedahlia" to the *New Yorker* yesterday and realized more than ever how much all this autobiographical stuff is based on the mythology of the working class, the deprived, the exploited, etc. Must put this into all the education part, both in the Army trip and in the English section. Trying to be a teacher to the anonymous, the unknowns.

I have been writing this notebook for more than 30 years now, and I "realize" more than ever how much it is made up of . . . "realizations" instead of happenings. Every day a little illumination, every day a little more mental stretch and deepening. . . . But there must be happening suspended of meaning . . . not impatiently brought to the climax (and dismissal) of meaning . . . solid blocks of narrative for the sake of . . . the sense of happening. Wittgenstein: don't think, look!

Plenty has replaced scarcity everywhere, not least in bed. . . . Affection rules rather than passion, the romantic idea of the exclusive one. Monogamy becomes a function of scarcity rather than of emotion . . . emotion of Availability.

11. David Grene (1913–2002), professor of classics at the University of Chicago and cofounder of the Committee on Social Thought, an interdisciplinary Ph.D. program in modern and classical thought. He is best known for his translations of ancient Greek literature.

## December 22, 1970

The Century Club is a habit, and people who are habits go to the Century Club to prolong their habit. . . . Sat with Dick Rovere[12] at drinks (he's as nervous . . . nervous with me . . . nervous as he was in 1939), glad to hear that his son, Mark, is back from Vietnam. Arthur Schlesinger going up the stairs looked small and fat. . . . The bust of G. Washington at the head of the stairs . . . the mellow, old landscapes . . . the old men have this look of being weathered in the service of coming here to eat lunch. The whole thing so preposterously an act of old-fashioned gentility, servility, the behavior of gentlemen, that past the outside door you have to catch your breath. C'est tout a fait un autre chose [It's an utterly different world]. . . .

## December 30, 1970

[. . .] I went down to Washington [for the Conference to save the Soviet Jews] thinking that I would wall myself into the hotel room, finish with myself forever down there. I came back, thanks to my two old Jews Heschel and Singer[13] (but especially Singer) in a state of exaltation. . . . In his dry, ungiving, utterly skeptical way, Singer reminded me *not* to make any claims for myself, to give over. . . . His father, a rabbi for fifty years, never received a word of praise in his life. . . . To praise God is enough. . . . Suddenly I understood better the awful monotony with which Jews praise God. . . . It is the eternity principle, the deepest one a person can grasp. It is so funny going back late into the 6:30 plane from Washington and seeing the empty seat between them, waiting for me. Heschel with his funny, phony, little beard nevertheless looked everybody's dear old man. . . . Singer, the plucked chicken, all white skin, in his black suit and nondescript tie. . . . Nothing for us Jews to do but give homage . . . to say the word that is *not* for us. . . .

Give me your blessing!=*You* are a blessing!

12. Richard Rovere (1915–1979), reporter and journalist, wrote the "Letter from Washington" for the *New Yorker* from 1948 to 1979. He and Kazin became friends in the late 1930s when Rovere was writing for the Communist *New Masses*, from which he resigned following the Hitler-Stalin pact of 1939.
13. Abraham Joshua Heschel (1907–1972), Warsaw-born American rabbi, prominent Jewish theologian, and philosopher. Isaac Bashevis Singer (1902–1991), Polish-born American novelist and short story writer who wrote in Yiddish, was awarded the Nobel Prize in literature in 1978.

## February 21, 1971

Gass[14] is not a *natural* novelist but a man thinking. His admiration for Gertrude Stein, his fellow-thinker—the other analyst of literature.

O'Hara the old machine, the old pro. Cheever the performer (*New Yorker* as the great editorial mother) . . . Salinger the cute child . . . Updike the professional young man.

The essence of biographical criticism (Nigel Dennis on Pinter as actor) is the sense of a *mind*, the properties of a mind, what strength and or weakness this mind possesses. . . . The mind has character more than a person has. . . . This is the essence of Johnson's *Lives*. In the mind qualities are virtues or defects—sins. . . . Not Sainte-Beuve, tel arbre tel fruit, but as the mind . . . the mind's tendency, the mind's natural *virtue*. What used to be meant by "soul"—i.e., what the mind most deeply *represents*. . . . True, the work of art is an action, and actions count especially, but there is a logic between character (the mind's character) and action. [. . .]

## June 3, 1971

Old men—When I walked into the "Gallery" of the Century for the festivities before tonight's dinner, I saw dozens of indistinguishably white haired men in black suits, all milling around so that they became even more pieces of each other. So muted, respectable, repressed looking. "Would you want to find yourself dining some night with Bella Abzug?"[15]

Old men. J. Edgar Hoover's[16] bloated, swollen, red face, sitting next to Nixon at the government conference on the killing of policemen. The insane vanity of the man. Administrators, by accident administrators, have a power so great (as not to oppose hand guns) that the caprice of it all is as bad as the policy.

14. William Gass (1924–), prize-winning American novelist, short story writer, and essayist, taught philosophy at Washington University.
15. Bella Abzug (1920–1998), social activist, feminist, and the first Jewish woman to be elected to the U.S. House of Representatives.
16. John Edgar Hoover (1895–1972) was the first and longest-serving (1935–1972) director of the Federal Bureau of Investigation, which he helped found. The tenure of subsequent directors was limited to ten years.

## June 13, 1971

Sunday, 13 June 71, at the Deep Hollow Ranch in Montauk. Edmund's Talcottville Diary is in the *New Yorker* this week. All discipline rather than natural interest—an effort to open up an intercourse with the world. When I think that "Gedahlia" and "The Girl from the Village"[17] were rejected by the *New Yorker* and that these dried-up fragments of E.W.'s old soul are published because they are by E.W., I have to laugh. But then I have to laugh anyway; for a moment comes when not just being a literary intellectual is a private fact (E.W.'s classic situation) but the open, suffering, deeply clamorous personal record that *I* write as opposed to E.W.'s simulations of objectivity. From behind his caged voice, E.W. describes the degradations inflicted upon the old stone house in Talcottville in exactly the same "disciplined" tone of voice in which he describes his daughter Helen flying through the windshield in a terrible motor accident. But he never once says "my daughter" anymore than he ever called Elena "my wife." On the other hand, what persistence, what obdurate elegance in putting together all these pieces as elements in the old American's attempt to measure change *from* the locus classicus of the stone house.

A giveaway to Edmund's attempt to politicize his income tax troubles. It was *after* he was called in by the IRS that he started looking up examples of America's preparations for biological and chemical warfare. [. . .]

## June 17, 1971
### [Los Angeles]

Didion and Dunne, the pair.[18] Of course he came along to lunch, though I had invited *her*. We ate at Scandia on the Strip, and then drove back through the Malibu Canyon. In September 70 the Malibu hills were on fire, and the surfers in the ocean kept surfing. The hills and the ocean. At dinner, Didion in a long skirt and full of body language. She often cradles herself in her own arms, in the well-known woman's self-protection against the cold. Her face runs the gamut from poor old Sookie to the temptress with long, blonde-red locks. She can look at you and past you without the slightest hint of a concession. The *unspoken* is a most important part of her presence in the world. The unspoken ripple with

17. Both appear in *New York Jew*.
18. Kazin interviewed Didion for a *Harper's* article, "Joan Didion: Portrait of a Professional," (December 1971): 112–122. A writer best known for essays that merge personal observation with cultural analysis, Joan Didion (1934–) was married to John Gregory Dunne (1932–2003), a novelist, screenwriter, and writer of nonfiction prose.

bald John Dunne was often there. She once almost took a knife to someone—probably Noel Parmentel,[19] always the relation in the NY story.

Brian Moore[20] and his wife to dinner. Brian's accessibility and charm made an interesting contrast to Didion's many silences.

## January 26, 1972

My own private planetarium at night here in this corner bedroom. Lights coming on in New Jersey, cars moving in pulsing arcs made by the headlights, light-brimmed planes floating in a sea of air. Stars and satellites and planes and cars on the New Jersey shore. Highways newly cut out of the Palisades rock. Meanwhile the city towers rim you round with their concentrated glimmer. The mass chain electrified [. . .]

Black man as victim=anti-hero. Eloquence of the Negro sermons in *Moby Dick* and *The Sound and the Fury*. *The White Negro*. The Jewish anti-hero as surrogate hero. *Above all, the fluency of narrative, the power of the narrator—The subversive anti-establishment pose as in Mailer's White Negro. From Ellison to LeRoi Jones:*[21] *the inflamer.*

Ellison the Christian and spellbinding celebrity. The comedy of his recent conservativism. The comedy of Howe-Ellison, of Podhoretz-Ellison, of Ellison the lecturer. *God's trombone*[22] *is the phrase for old Preacher Hickman*→ a contrast with the political playing-the-game Blacks—from Negro to Black. In the American arena. → But Ellison is a real *storyteller* and not a moody private poet divided from his *activist* political role. *Black nationalism: a way of disturbance. Unsettling the white middle class instead* of trying to join them by way of Malraux-Melville-myth-(Lord Raglan). [. . .]

## February 10, 1972

Ingrown, anxiety laden bookworm, who in the spirit of E. Wilson and other such bookworms, has kept this notebook since college in order to open up

19. Noel Parmentel (1927–), witty, acerbic journalist, early mentor and close friend of Joan Didion. "I never saw ambition like that," he once said of her. "It was ferocious, flabbergasting."
20. Brian Moore (1921–1999), acclaimed Northern Irish novelist.
21. LeRoi Jones (1934–), later Amiri Baraka, controversial African-American dramatist, fiction writer, and essayist.
22. "God's trombone" refers to the black preacher Hickman in Ralph Ellison's long-awaited and posthumously published novel *Juneteenth*.

an intercourse with the world. But there are so many lines of life outside the too straight diagrams which this diary contains. . . . The trouble, the trouble, is that one tries to avoid "trouble," conflict, the endless conflict of everything with everyone and with oneself. So that holding on to the straight lines, the intellectual pattern, one misses the heart of the matter, the unexpectedness, the things beyond your formation—which lie in the fascination of all opposition, conflict, disagreement, estrangement, quarrels.

## February 19, 1972

According to Claes Oldenburg, Baudelaire[23] once remarked of talent that it "is nothing more nor less than childhood rediscovered at will—a childhood now equipped for self-expression, with manhood's capacities and a power of analysis which enables it to order the mass of raw material which it has involuntarily accumulated." Claes—"Everything I do is completely original. I made it up when I was a little kid."

## April 26, 1972

Met Isaac Bashevis Singer in the Braniff waiting room at Laguardia. It turned out that he too was going to Texas Christian U. in Fort Worth—though he thought it might be the University of Texas. We had a *most* interesting talk *en route*. He knocked everybody in "fiction" from Kafka to Wiesel, but as usual fascinated me by his interest in the occult, his faith in the cabbala, his vegetarianism (which began when his parakeet fell into the bath and drowned), his essential indifference to his surroundings (he was prepared to stay *four* nights at the Sheraton in Fort Worth in order to go on to St. Paul by way of New York itself), his total in-turning to himself.

He makes an impression on all around him even when they are not exactly sure who or what he is. His bags (which he insisted on carrying at all times) were crammed with mss. in large manila envelopes. He writes on loose pages torn out of school exercise books and said among other wonderful things, that the Jews hypnotize the outsiders and then get hated when they themselves desert "their" cause (i.e., first Christianity and then Marxism). He brightened up (without the help of any strong meat or drink whatsoever) at dinner, became positively

23. Claes Oldenburg (1929–), Swedish sculptor, known for his large replicas of such everyday objects as a clothespin, a hamburger, an apple core. Charles Baudelaire (1821–1867), innovative French poet, essayist, translator of Edgar Allan Poe.

pixieish at times. The essential solitude of the man, a kind of genial indifference to the world while happily tasting its money, prizes, etc. (his *only* recreation is travel) was very noticeable. *It no longer matters where he is;* he does not believe in anything outside his creative mind and fancies. When I referred to the scene in *My Father's Court* where his father, the rabbi, simply closed the window on a woman who could be heard being raped, who was screaming, he said with a boyish smile of self-recognition, "That's me!" Does not care to read very much. Says his incessant writing for the *Forward* is his "laboratory." [. . .]

## May 21, 1972

[. . .] Evelyn Hofer[24] does make me see things through her eyes, and I think that I shall put her into the book, among my artists. . . . We had a pleasant lunch in the Sunday sweetness of Fleur de Lis, and then I pulled and hauled her to see Elie W. on Channel 4 at 4. God, what a disappointment, what histrionic identification of himself as a conscious *symbol* of the Holocaust. Not to mention the really unnecessary propaganda for Israel. . . . Elie: "I am most at home in Jerusalem when I am not in it." His face, his gestures, his speech, all so self-consciously Elie the Auschwitz Victim that the incoherency of his religious views, the rhetoric about the Messiah, somehow jarred more than ever.

## June 12, 1972

Edmund [Wilson] died in Talcottville in his sleep (Thank God for that). Our great tree has fallen. He was all history-minded and is now a piece of history. I can never think of him without becoming historical-minded. History as one's own submission to Time. Time personally regarded. Edmund's bitterness at what time had wrought to *his* private earth ship of time. The decline of the American republic and all that. Literature as the tradition—and then the favorite subject of literary critics. The collapse of tradition. Always "the sense of an ending."

Edmund was a modern. A modern is a member of a privileged caste, part of a tradition, who revolts against it. The revolt is personal. *We* contemporaries live in revolutionary time—when the issue is the enforced equality of the whole human race. And mass society. And the revolt against this by the counter-revolutionary spirit that tries to drive certain races out of the human race. [. . .]

24. Evelyn Hofer (1922–2009), German-born photographer who worked primarily in New York and Mexico, friend of Kazin's.

I dreamed that I was in Chicago with Isaac Bashevis Singer but somehow lost him and ended up riding through some pretty grimy Chicago streets with Jackie Kennedy. She was very talkative and friendly. She pointed down her body and said about the late president, "He liked to screw." Finally some blond Yale type (also friendly) appeared at her side, and we amiably rode through some pretty terrible examples of urban renewal. [. . .]

## September 23, 1972

Violence unceasing. The key is always self-justification. The justification of the *physical*. There is nothing we may overlook. There is no higher principle.

In the subway—"All blacks are enemies of Christ."

NY—*100 muggings a day*

## October 13, 1972

[. . .] Katey in, party for Kotlowitz at Barbaralee Diamonstein's.[25] The usual. Barbaralee is enormously attractive, but so supple and swivelly that after hugging you with enough affection to send two other people to fucking in public, she immediately sweeps on to another guest. For Barbaralee there is always another guest, and another. . . . [. . .]

## October 20, 1972

[. . .] My 14th Street barber had a red tip of a nose when I took my haircut today, and I asked him if he had a cold. Says he has never had a cold in his life, but that he does drink a whole bottle of his father-in-law's homemade white wine every night for dinner. He does not eat all day, but when he returns to his wife in Howard Beach, Queens, she sets out seven different dishes for him every night . . . and "I never spend less than three hours on my dinner."

## November 9, 1972

After the McGovern debacle. The truth is, god damn it, that I *am* impressed by McGovern's defeat—impressed by the futility and arrogance of minority

25. Barbaralee Diamonstein, television writer and producer; Alex Kotlowitz, American journalist, best known for *There Are No Children Here: The Story of Two Boys Growing Up in the Other America.*

righteousness. The intellectual left, the young left, cannot win—they can only force domination over others.

The majority may not always be right, but *the broad mass of the people* know their own interests.

## December 25, 1972

My mother was illiterate—but passed on the customs of the Jews like a blind priestess.

## January 25, 1973

Case of Charles F. Lee ended finally, with a guilty on one charge and a split jury on the other two. [. . .] Elia Kazan took notes all the time, obviously saw us as a play he was in, played the part of the man of reason, the honest direct fellow.[26] Always wore work pants, desert boots, always struck a conscious attitude of friendly, direct, populist good sense. . . . Each time we had vowed not to deliberate any more with Larry Jones, it would be old Kazan who would make his pitch for let us reason together. [. . .]

## May 7, 1973

How the State of Israel reminds me of myself, and how myself reminds me of the State of Israel. Excessively forewarned, forearmed (if not excessively), always on the alert . . . every moment between ecstasy at being delivered and the apprehension of annihilation. [. . .]

## June 19, 1973

In Paris I thought the people absurdly "correct," walking with almost a military air of self-importance. . . . I disliked their firm air of purpose. . . . But my God, in New York, in this rainy, soggy June, half the people I see seem to me distended, mad, sloppy, and eccentric, and self-indulged to the point of physical incoherence. . . . At the corner of Times Square I heard a sickly looking man cry out, I DON'T HAVE TO APOLOGIZE TO ANYONE? HEAR? NOT TO ANYONE?

26. Kazin and the director Elia Kazan (1909–2003) served on a jury that convicted a police officer for bribery.

## June 27, 1973

Met Nelson Aldrich at the Century for a discussion of possible *Harper's* articles. Aldrich was wearing a carelessly elegant three-piece off-white suit. With his hair parted young-style down either side of his head, his lounging style, he looked enough the great grandson of Sen. Nelson Aldrich, the first cousin once removed of Gov. Nelson Aldrich Rockefeller.[27] A lot of bandying around, soon the relationship became definitely teacher and pupil. . . . Aldrich wants me to write an article on paranoia in American life. He thinks paranoids have a great sense of plot. . . . I was thinking: ci-devant American aristos have a great sense of plot. . . . Interesting that my lunacy takes the form of "guilt," because I want to overcome the "strong" around me . . . and Aldrich's takes the form of paranoia . . . or how did we become what we are? . . . Interesting that *I* have no sense of plot, only of character and of solitary effort. . . . Whereas the whole theme of power that persistently engages me is, well, only *partly* the idea of power as nefarious.

Paranoia in the Pynchon[28] sense: sooner or later implies that the powers that are supposed to be don't themselves know what they are doing. And the "innocent" fall in with the (bumbling) plot.

## July 16, 1973

[. . .] Ann: I joined the Pulitzer Prize committee to keep her from winning the Prize.

## July 27, 1973

New York Will Kill Me (Title)

Summer . . . five murders in one afternoon . . . Blacks with hair parted at intervals down the scalp ... This mysterious pressure ... of other people ... of the everlasting strangers we live with. . . . The pressure seems to be in the air. [. . .]

27. Nelson Aldrich was senior editor at *Harper's* and former Paris editor of the *Paris Review*. Nelson Wilmarth Aldrich (1841–1915), was a United States senator and leader of the Republican Party. Nelson Aldrich Rockefeller (1908–1979) was governor of New York and later vice president of the United States.
28. Thomas Pynchon (1937–), American novelist noted for his complex plotting which at times suggests a paranoiac's fantasy. Kazin was on the Pulitzer Prize committee in 1974 that voted unanimously to give Pynchon the award for *Gravity's Rainbow*, a choice vetoed by the Pulitzer board, which described the book as "unreadable," "turgid," "overwritten," and "obscene."

NEW YORK JEW. We are pushed along, we have been long determined . . . yet there continually arises before us the theme of "destiny," the arc-design of our freedom on earth. Destiny before us, destiny pushing us from behind . . . the two selves we live with all the time . . . of man as "God," all *mind* (which is the only possible definition of God and the reason we are tantalized by our resemblance, in so far as we are conscious of mind) . . . and the historic human self, incorporated in this most historic entity, the body. . . .

Jews are peculiarly determined . . . having [been] so much shaped by history and since they so much live *to* their ancient history. . . . But meanwhile "history" as freedom, mind, . . . i.e., God, rises up before us . . . saying in effect you will know who you are if you will find out just where you are on History's (supposed) timetable.

Call this the crunch. The crunch between the keenest, sharpest idea of transcendence . . . and the most intensely determined kind of character structure. . . .

*New York Jew* We are the perennial instructors—because every real novelty is a thing of mind and believing in nothing so much as God, i.e., perfect mind, perfect freedom. The terrain of the mind seems endless. *We* have found our way into the subtlest folds and refolds of the world as the terrain of mental freedom.

Isaac Bashevis—"We have hypnotized them." The spell of this compulsive mind—This *identification with God as destiny*, perfect freedom—*my life, my life.*

## October 2, 1973

Auden in the midst of us. As a New Yorker, Auden was so terribly accessible, a homosexual drugstore cowboy. . . . I remember his sitting with a young man in a house on Montague Terrace that I visited while house-hunting after the war . . . saw him at a party with Dwight Macdonald, lamenting that the "lower orders" had made it impossible for the better people to get taxis . . . and then there was Auden at our party, asked for by Erich Heller. On the whole, my immediate impression of him was always as a party fellow . . . on the make . . . Chester Kallmann's[29] famous boyfriend (and how disgracefully he stooped

29. Chester Simon Kallmann (1921–1975), poet and lover of W. H. Auden (1907–1973), with whom he collaborated in writing librettos.

to review Chester Kallmann) . . . Auden in the midst of us . . . always around . . . so friendly, so ironic, staring with smiling eyes for a pickup or a note . . .?

## October 4, 1973

Philip Roth, the male shrew.

## December 24, 1973

[Philip] Rahv died yesterday at his home in Cambridge, age 64. No one ever tried so hard to look strong, to feel strong, with the faith of the old-fashioned "revolutionary intellectual." That was *his* super-ego . . . but on this side of the Messiah Philip certainly had his silences and breakdowns and confusions—which I guess at. The revolutionary front held in public. [. . .]

## December 27, 1973

Thirty years . . . the end of the war . . . and now we are seeing the end of the war boom. . . . The thirty years were the "golden age" of American Jewry . . . the golden age to the depression generation . . . it seemed to mark with the unlimited sense of power created by the war a wholly new period in every sense. . . . Because America was superpower . . . and we could not really believe that wicked, atheistic Russia was more than a moral challenge to us . . . it was that all right.

I see the book coming out of this second war psychology in every sense—The history of the boom . . . of wars and profitable wars.

## December 30, 1973

New York's towers look this bright morning as if they *do* scrape at the sky. My upthrusting NY, my lofty New York, my heaven-shaking city. *I know how to do it* = I know the storyteller in myself—all the way ahead or *You Must Change Your Life*. [. . .]

Murray the Kempton.[30] It's odd, he said to me on the phone when he was fizzled one afternoon, that I can persuade people I don't love that I do care for them—but I can't persuade the people I do care for that I do, that I do. . . . He is

30. Murray Kempton (1917–1997), journalist and former Communist, friend of Kazin's. In a 1997 tribute, "Missing Murray Kempton," *New York Times Book Review* (November 30, 1997): 35, Kazin claimed that Kempton "was the most acute and cultivated columnist since Mencken."

a man who uses words well, sometimes brilliantly, but he always claims that he meant something else . . . when I take him up on something he has written that I don't understand.

In point of fact he is your betwixt and between fellow, who knows what he *feels* but essentially, not what he *thinks*. And one responds to people in terms of what we know them to think, not what they "feel:" in front of us—the writer, the persuader, the advocate . . . the word user, the slick word artist . . . all this patina, all this brilliant irony . . . to cover up the gap in the man (and he doesn't know that this gap exists) between what he thinks and . . . what he thinks. . . . Because in his heart, he is not clear to himself. . . .

We understand ourselves only and just when we become one with what we think. . . . Otherwise, we are at war with ourselves . . . And words become our arms. [. . .]

Kempton, the psychic wrestler. His rhetoric easier than mine: the Southern politeness, the air. . . .

## February 23, 1974

Saturday afternoon . . . Lunch with Amos Elon at the Century. As usual, Israelis inspire me—I saw so much talking to him! God in us . . . (the mind as God) . . . and the tension between American "ideals" and American realities. . . . At the next table, Barzun and Colin Davis (?)[31]

Anyway, I saw a lot this afternoon. Thank you, Israel. Thank you, God.

## April 28, 1974

[. . .] Hot, open Sunday. NY is all warmth and crowds today. Millions, positively millions! of kids, each with one Indian feather stuck in his hair, walking in an endless crowd down CPW [Central Park West]. Suddenly, looking at the marvelous show of photographs of Manhattan at the New York Historical Society, you feel close to the city. Positively neighborly again. Kertész,[32] the

31. Colin Davis (1927–), English orchestra conductor.
32. Andre Kertész (1894–1985), Hungarian photographer and photojournalist; Andreas Feininger (1906–1999), German-born photographer, best known for his stark black-and-white photographs of Manhattan.

European, Hofer, the European, Andreas Feininger, the European. In the midst of all that mass, that stupefying incongruity that makes a pattern, your heart catches at the snow on a rooftop, the endless chimney pots that go up and down the roofs of old Manhattan houses. The Europeans are now as spellbound by the futurama of NY as the young Americans are. . . . Sam Falk, the *NY Times* photographer, another *quartier* painter. Fulton Fish market: the old sheds and storefronts with their slanted low roofs look positively Dutch.

## April 29, 1974

[. . .] Then to Hunter, where I found this in my letter box:

"Dear Mr. Kazin: I am the woman cab driver with the BA from the New School who drove you from 14th Street to West End Avenue last winter. During the ride you most kindly offered to help me in my work. Enclosed are two stories I have written. I think they are different, one from the other. I would truly appreciate your reading them. Very truly yours, Barbara Schaffer." [. . .]

## May 2, 1974

Just below the stairs, going down to the 14th Street subway, in the shadows, a dusty professionally old Black whimpers for alms in a tiny, tiny, little voice, a thread of a voice, that sounds like something from the Spanish. Coming up a moment ago on my way from the Yaddo board lunch, I saw a weathered black gent talking to her, in that slow drawling, all too patient, ironic voice. A voice below the business cycle in which Americans usually live. *A voice that had the sound of old legends in it.*

The life behind the NY rock.

## May 20, 1974

A Day Like This. Start with the presentness, the city sense. "The girls in their summer dresses"[33] gaily walking down Broadway to the subway, so fresh, so fresh, o maidlach! Knees flashing. The middle-aged men poring over the figures in the *Wall Street Journal*. . . . The old man, with all his winter clothes on him, lying up against the storefront, endlessly scratching at his hair, scratching it away. . . . The black with the remarkable cheekbones and the immense reserve. . . .

33. "The Girls in Their Summer Dresses" is the title of a short story by the writer Irwin Shaw (1913–1984) featuring girls walking the New York streets in the summer.

The city as this immense collage and montage. . . . The present so dazzling. . . . The man with the broken nose: "Put your money where your mouth is!" [. . .]

Walter Benjamin: describes the unconnectedness of all things in the big city, objects ricocheting off us.

## May 22, 1974

The *Walker* was a boy looking for his identity. It was a fable of youth, sweetness, and search. The *New York Jew* is about a world of real conflict—a world of *people* only and wholly.

And it is a book about shipwreck—in a city and a country riven with the deepest kind of conflict.

*A world of women.* [. . .]

The news on the TV, the news in the morning. The judgment seat . . . literature as an institution. . . . The students as your new mass audience. Teaching literature. Holding on to certain fixed concerns in a world coming apart. . . . Literature is conservative, but all the middle-class writers make like radicals . . . trying to transform the world.

A world coming apart. . . . The great big dissolving center—New York can't be governed. . . . Meanwhile, the uprush of women . . . the sense of battle in the air: down with patriarchy. . . . Adrienne Rich on Beethoven.[34] . . . One has this notion of oneself as a fixed identity, but action speaks louder than criticism.

[. . .] At the National Institute shindig, the annual lunch: Trilling with his hooded, sunken eyes, his poignant, but proud expression, the cigarette always in hand like a Paris boulevardier's cane. . . . That air of weary experience, of vanity and immense caution: a bit like Luther Adler,[35] you know, old chap? Styron: bloated, petulant face. Warren,[36] spouting away, and never a word do I understand. . . .

34. Adrienne Rich (1929–), American poet, essayist, and feminist. In her poem "The Ninth Symphony at Last as Sexual Message" Rich argues that Beethoven was "A man in terror of impotence/of infertility," an observation that enraged Kazin.

35. Luther Adler (1903–1984), son of Russian Jewish actors Sara (1858–1953) and Jacob Adler (1855–1926). Luther was primarily a stage actor who appeared in *Awake and Sing!*, *Gold Eagle Guy*, and other plays produced by the Group Theatre in the 1930s.

36. William Styron (1925–2006), American novelist best known for *Lie Down in Darkness* (1951), *Confessions of Nat Turner* (1967), and *Sophie's Choice* (1979). Robert Penn Warren (1905–1989), novelist, poet, and literary critic, the only writer to receive a Pulitzer Prize in both poetry and fiction. Kazin was not enthusiastic about his fiction or poetry.

## June 3, 1974

[. . .] The Jewish intellectual (our greatest son, Marx) versus *tout simple*, the *Jew* (Kafka) who contains all these times in himself. [. . .]

The Christian idea of the future—based on the individual. The Jewish idea: the *past*, the *group*. [. . .]

*A Jew is someone who is always remaking his life*. Renovation *endless*. [. . .]

*Emerson made me a Jew*. What a Jew owes *Christianity* for his Judaism.

## September 7, 1974

The unbelievable power of women—over me! Everything I do and think has sooner or later to cross the road that is Ann . . . The big woman now. . . . And somewhere, "Remembrance is redemption" (the Baal Shem Tov),[37] there is the longing to reproduce some early bliss, to be at home with myself, thanks to SOME WOMAN . . . and when the first cracks appear, when disturbance, negativism is in the air, by golly if I don't get very mad . . . in both senses of the word.

Prisoner of sex! Prisoner of women!!! The sacred fount! But it occurs to me that the men I was most attracted to, the deep friends, like Dick, were exactly the same. I look around me and ask myself if there is any man I like who doesn't have this same "prisoner" quality. . . . Except that some of them, like Dick, seem to have managed it better than I, being less greedy, and being able to stick to one woman at a time, instead of stupidly trying to be so many things to several women at once, comme moi. [. . .]

## October 1, 1974

Hunter is a *city*.[38] Mass scene. Everybody pops up, sooner or later. So the teaching business=passing on your experience=becomes more real than ever.

37. "Forgetfulness prolongs the exile; in remembrance lies the secret of redemption," a statement attributed to the Baal Shem Tov (1698–1760), a mystical rabbi generally considered to be the founder of Hassidic Judaism.

38. Kazin became a professor at Hunter College and the Graduate Center of CUNY in the fall of 1973.

## October 15, 1974

Lost in a whirlpool of memory. All his dreams, conversation, momentary impressions en route are pieces of this jig-saw puzzle he still dreams of putting together: every fragment exists as the obligato to still another fragment!

## November 15, 1974

Ann. I sit down to write about this terrible day, when she was so near to suicide (and I believe it) and find that I cannot write about it. Not easily. To see her destroyed, so supine, so helpless. The threat is very real, very great.[39]

David Bell's Bar-Mitzvah [in Cambridge]. There was a portable Ark in Phillips Brooks's house, which suddenly reminded me of the portable Ark in front of the Wall in Jerusalem after the 1967 war. Rabbi Ben Zion Gold, from Poland and a camp, was perfect in his tact.[40] The party was very nice. I always dream of some great purpose to accomplish when I get to Cambridge-Boston. But then I see the neat houses along Francis Avenue, the dream-like Harvard I never went to (young men in the gleaming, circa 1895, Santayana and such taking the horse car into Boston), and I get tired. . . . Early this morning, in Pearlie's kitchen, I looked at the early risers walking behind the fences on their way to the Sunday papers, and I didn't envy them one bit. Rode over to see Elizabeth Bishop, who now lives on Lewis Wharf. City debris with rubbery, comic-strip faces and little Happy Hooligan hats were fishing in the harbor. Then the plane to New York, and who should be on it but [John Kenneth] Galbraith and [Wassily] Leontief. G. pressed me to take a taxi with them as far as the Carlyle, and as he made points about my review and similar cultural matters, I felt his big body, big bones, all prehensile, all reaching out to make a point. Very active brain, talked brilliantly as his big body squeezed me against Wassily. Loves to take over, to shine in confrontation.

39. Ann was admitted to the Payne Whitney psychiatric clinic on November 18 for observation.

40. David Avrom Bell (1961–), son of Pearl Kazin Bell and Daniel Bell, is an American historian of France at Princeton University. He was previously dean of the faculty at Johns Hopkins University. Rabbi Ben-Zion Gold was director of Hillel at Harvard University. He is the author of *The Life of Jews in Poland before the Holocaust: A Memoir*.

## November 29, 1974

Thinking of Barzun, "more style than substance," style as substance, the visitor to these shores—it is this note of the "superior" style that I must get into the description of the European visitors during the war—Brecht, Chagall.[41]. . .

## December 5, 1974

[*New York*] *Jew* is like the *Walker*, is the *Walker*—the story is nothing (so far) but the shock of novelty . . . the new experience . . . experience itself to the man let out of the ghetto restriction. . . . In a way the Henry James letters testify to this same sense of "nascency," of a new man seeking to be born, yes, but essentially being stamped into a new form by the impact of these experiences, by the impact of the "world . . ." ne rien plus. . . . And the document of this nascency is always the report from the senses. The inner impact.

Barzun, Trilling, the endless prating of "*culture*." They mean not works of art but a vaguely synoptic tradition in space and time—*the cultural continuum of the upper classes (the non-desperate classes)*. And this (inert) tradition as an object of *criticism*.

## December 10, 1974

Sitting in Press's[42] office, looking out at the dusk dripping down into New York, I seemed to see the dark taking over everywhere, taking *me* over. So little time left. The impossible thought of becoming sixty! Then, like the spare lights in the rigging of the boats alongside the piers in Brooklyn Heights, lights began to wink in occasional office windows on the horizon. Especially in 500 Fifth Avenue, the office building whose legend 500, in the biggest possible letters, holds my eyes every time I sit in Press's dental chair. The lights began to come on, the lights began to come on! And I thought, Dios mio, how I want to live, to live to every possible moment the hidden God reserved for me—to live, to live, to breathe, to think, to see . . . to have it all, *yet*. God grant it. God keep it.

41. Marc Chagall (1887–1985), Russian-French artist, was one of the great modernist painters of the twentieth century as well as one of the most versatile, working with stained glass, tapestries, ceramics, stage sets, and canvas. He is best known for painting evocative and exuberant images out of Jewish folklore.

42. Dr. Press has replaced Leuba as Kazin's dentist.

Und in den Nächten fällt die schwerer Erde[43]
aus allen Sternen in die Einsamkeit.
Wir alle fallen. Diese Hand da fällt
Und sieh die andre an: es ist in allen.
Und doch is einer, welcher dieses Fallen
unendlich sanft in seinen Händen hält.

Yukio Mishima[44]—"I want to make a poem of my life."

## January 18, 1975

[. . .] *Our great men*—Jewish heroes—always for Delmore [Schwartz] heroes of thought. Joyce Ha-Melech, Joyce our king. The people are rooted in the past, but the heroes are always pushing out the boundaries of the *supposedly* known world. Reading Lévi-Strauss[45] in the plane roaring its way to Rio *through lightning, 35,000 feet over the Amazon and the jungle, I am dazzled and overcome by the unexpected fullness and independence of thought*. The Jews are an old habit-worn people, but every gifted "king" is an undefinable new event. [. . .]

## March 7, 1975

Blacks smoking in the subway. Blacks pushing you in the subway. Blacks eating hot dogs over you in the subway. Blacks around you here and near and everywhere. And then a Black in the subway sees you reading Whitman and nods at you in salute of generous, generous, expansive, all-loving Whitman.

## March 13, 1975

To be a Jew is to be determined from birth. To be a Jew is to believe that there is some transcendence. Within this determined condition or beyond it? At the

43. A song by Rainer Maria Rilke (1875–1926): And in the nights the heavy Earth/Falls into solitude from star to star./We all are falling. This my body bends./And look at the others: Fall remains their calling./And yet there's One, who holds all this falling/Forever tender in His open hands.
44. Yukio Mishima was the pen name of Kimitake Hiraoka (1925–1970), a Japanese poet and playwright.
45. Claude Lévi-Strauss (1908–2009), French anthropologist and a dominant figure in the structuralist school of thought. He argued that the "savage" mind is essentially the same as the "civilized mind" and that the underlying structures in human thinking are universal.

moment, thinking of the fatigue of the Barondess party[46] yesterday, of the money pressures on me, of the tattered angry whimpery state of my soul, I nevertheless cry out against all determinism of my condition, and with a free heart opt for joy, for difference, for independence, for fantasy, for love impossible, for love made possible, for all possible craziness, so long as it is joy and there is joy. Not to be numbered among the tired urban reflexes! Not to be included in the ranks of the normal kvetches!! To be free of my determined condition! An everlasting yea and yea again!!!!

## May 1, 1975

New York characters. Saul Steinberg,[47] met with at Lexington and 72nd. An involved jockey cap buttoned up to a hood on top—several mufflers inside a splendid tweed jacket. The whole costume as impressively zany as Steinberg's drawings. Any meeting with S.S. is a study in impressiveness. He takes you in, studies you, speaks in a slow, reflective tone which seems to swallow you up! Takes your measure, is taking your picture, no doubt. And he is letting you see him. . . . Very slow, studied, still the visitor to these shores. Looking at these things, comes out with humorous pronouncements: Brendan Gill kamakazied with his book. Thinks himself Mr. *New Yorker*. "I divorced Rome some time ago."—taking in the whole slop and "media" language of our time *for his own*. Painting his picture with all the local brushes.

Vagrants, beggars, madmen, screamers. . . . In the course of one (cloudy, rainy) morning, I saw Jesus Christ, dark as they come, furiously walking down 14th Street, pushing people out of his way. . . . Women screaming in front of post boxes. . . . Man in overalls and sneakers and beard (toujours la barbe) begging. What a procession of what Himmelfarb[48] would call just a "subculture" of poverty. But what a subculture!!

Embassy officer in Vietnam before leaving burned 2 barrels of money—2 to 4 *millions* of dollars.

46. Dr. Jeremiah Barondess, Kazin's physician and a personal friend, was the president of the American College of Physicians. He was the husband of Susan Kaufman (1926–1977), author of *Diary of a Mad Housewife* and a friend of Ann Birstein's.
47. Saul Steinberg (1914–1999), legendary cartoonist for the *New Yorker*.
48. Gertrude Himmelfarb (1922–), historian of Victorian England, wife of Irving Kristol.

## May 7, 1975

Two elements in my "story"—what is given and what I made of it. Where I found myself and what I did to . . . master it, to understand it, to evade it—and now—to express it.

There is the dialectic of your autobiographer: a man playing tricks retrospectively with his life. But as Eliot noted about the writing of his kind of personal-emotional poetry, you must accept the original experience. . . . [. . .]

## May 15, 1975

Adams wrote from the high places about the low places. . . . The drama of the *Education* comes from the complexity of power relations—from the seemingly unstoppable velocity of the power instruments man has created. I write from the low places, about the low places; I start with the sense of freedom, openness . . . but then the complications of my own nature, the complications inherent in all political relationships, the unstoppable century . . . the flooding forces. All this creates the tension and drama in my own book: emerging from the ghetto, my hero discovers that the outside world is a million times more complicated than he had dreamed of. . . .

He dreams of the ghetto again because he would like to return to the comparatively simple relationships he had earliest—relationships he outgrew in fact, relationships he believed he could master—relationships so introverted . . . that left him alone.

Into a world so full of false bottoms—of intricate intimidations. . . . But a world full of manifold *surfaces*—and the many relationships between surfaces—

Brownsville is the road which every other road in my life has had to cross. And the "world" is the crossing, the cross, that Brownsville has encountered.

The Man Who Has Risen—A Man Who Has Risen. [. . .]

## May 22, 1975

The city is unbelievable. Such commotion, such pressure, such violence, such quiescent rage. Yet the outsider-insider feels connected to it—by his mind, his past, his past now being a book?

After the floating, moist ferry ride yesterday, a black and a Puerto Rican fighting each other madly on the Times Square platform when one tried to get out of the train and the other *in* at the same time.

At the Volvo garage, 50th and 11th Avenue—you can hear the boats and whistles on the river. It is these *thoroughfares*, these *apexes* of movement and power that make you feel that you are back to the dream again—*coming to the city over water.*

The Indian lady in the supermarket at 7th and 15th. That distinct air of pride, proud bearing, along with the most complete air of strangeness in the sing-song English and the olive skin. . . . I remember the Indian doctors in East London . . . that air of authority coming at you from some great hollow— [. . .]

## July 23, 1975

What a blessing—God means that our lives are not entirely in our hands, that our life does not entirely belong to us—that there are connections all the time, under our noses, behind us, to which we can make reference—on which we can call.

Bellow amazes me all over again with Humboldt [*Humboldt's Gift*]. Another in the long line of gallery portraits—This centering in book after book on the individual comes from Saul's sense of himself deriving from the free powers of the universe (the Jewish "God") and from the ability to use the whole social machinery as subject. Emerson spoke of Nature and the me—everything outside me being the Not-Me. . . . Saul regards the American society as one form that the universe happens to adopt in this hemisphere—and it is the Not-Me. . . . On the other hand, Other People are stages along the development of the Me. . . . The style rests so much on the abilities of Jewish humor to cram the antipodes into every sentence. . . . Always the marriage of heaven and hell . . . or rather, of our God and their world. . . .

Sundown. The meaning of it has been the allness. . . . The eating up of oneself when this deserted child thing begins . . . the son of lonely parents—the lonely, the lonely . . . and nothing was any good until Asya came into my life. And the book, and the chance to make bridges. All the time in my head. . . .

Saul is wonderful. . . . He has decided to become immortal. In the midst of this life—and many marriages—"Charles Citrine"[49] has discovered that the outside world is all in us—*we* are nature, by a perfect correspondence. . . . That mock Englishman, Tom Sterling, said that nature *lasts*, nothing has gone wrong with it. Saul sees himself as Nature.

The effect of such a book, such a man on us. . . . How he turns me on. . . . What is it *but thinking the world differently?* This is the only test of a real book, it influences us by turning our usual mental life inside out. . . . All the time Saul was thinking, thinking of making life different by an act of superb imaginative projection. . . . We become supernatural, in this book too, by turning ourselves inside out. . . .

How marvelous. How grateful I am. Here I have been mooching along, more than half wishing for easeful death, waiting for the fire to blot me out completely . . . to turn me into dumb gravel on the road, and Saul is insisting that he must continue! continue!

So it is all a matter of philosophy, or active religion. . . . You must see it all differently—rethink everything . . . pull the rug out from under *their* feet.

You begin by finding new names, show up the old name words as *inactive* . . . too long inert—You begin by making every word new by the intense honesty with which you use it. . . . *Their* words are no good. . . . Ours have become dull, sick habits. . . .

Start again. . . . How do you know but ev'ry Bird that cuts the airy way, Is an immense world of delight, clos'd by your senses five?[50]

For so many centuries of revealed religion people at least tried to think out every part of the creation. . . . Then naturalism, or seeing only what is natural to us, we left most of the creation unaccounted for and unaccountable—and so left closed to ourselves what is seemingly "unnatural" in us.

Absorbing so many other people, so many other minds, I became passive . . . too fond indeed of this passive stance; so it turned into masochism, an intellectual

49. Narrator in *Humboldt's Gift* (New York: Viking, 1975).
50. "How do you know . . ." from William Blake's *The Marriage of Heaven and Hell.*

masochism, by god and by goody . . . a way of masticating on everything from others, and macerating myself in the process.

## October 4, 1975

Trilling gave them a point of view, an attitude, a handy phrase . . . a leading idea. I gave them a lot of history, from every point of view? What my book needs most urgently is a basic philosophy to leave them with at the end. . . .

## October 10, 1975

The air is poisoned, the scene is excessive, the people are comatose, the headlines are threatening, the sirens on the police cars sound like maddened whales. Drunken blacks are lying between the garbage cans, silly Jews with white Victorian sideburns wearing form-fitting sports jackets are jauntily making like swingers. Everything is high, excessive, noisy . . . the young men with beards look pathetic as patriarchs. The women are most frightfully confused . . . and on the whole seem to me much less intelligent and stable than I had anticipated. [. . .]

## October 17, 1975

THE ORDER OF RELEASE

All this emotion. All this Me and Me and Me again. A withered, frightened man on West 72nd Street wearing a black hood and carrying a tiny poodle next to his belly. He is made of this bent and bending fear.

The only way out is all the way out. The cacophony of Me and Me is just too much.

The Order of Release—1970—Papa, Dick, Heinrich—Not only the shortness of the time, but the *surprise*. The death God suddenly walks into the distracted, sodden New York Party! And suddenly life becomes a *book*. The day may be long, but the years are short. . . . Time becomes a series of punctuation marks . . . arranges itself in memory . . . becomes a story.

The only release is to get it all down. To be faithful to the inwardness of one's real existence in the mind. The contractedness of time and the contraction of language. [. . .]

## November 7, 1975

Numbers, numbers . . . Trilling died Wednesday night (the 5th) and has the longest obituary since Gen. MacArthur.[51] A still, solemn, soundless triumph for Lionel, who wanted public position more than anything else, and has it. I wonder if he was ever very happy. I wonder if he ever wanted happiness more than he wanted the position he got as a critic of "international prestige." I wonder if being happy in Claremont Avenue ever meant as much to him as being at Oxford. . . . He was so constricted, so *public.*

An old-fashioned fame: the last "man of letters." A tight man . . . somehow this painful, mournful morning I think of him, as I do of Ramy,[52] always making a point with the cigarette in his hand like a classroom pointer. The old-fashioned Russian intellectual with the cigarette smoking in his hand. You see him sitting down, concentrating, talking.

*The Jew totally mesmerized by a culture that no longer existed.* . . . The cultural lag here is stupefying. . . .

"*We are so conscious of each other.*"

## November 19, 1975

Allen Mandelbaum[53] officiating at meeting of English grad students. Scruffy beard, hideous striped shirt and even more hideous striped shirt [*sic*, meaning tie]—all with a kind of instinct for the excess that will be in perfect bad taste. But smokes constantly through a long, bobbing cigarette holder and talks with nervous, high-falutin', super-imagistic academic prose that is like Groucho[54] making for a professor. The key words are all abstract: great blobs of images. . . . Looks like a poor shtetl Jew trying to get out of the rain, in borrowed clothes, but talks like . . . a James character *deranged.* Talks in code, a poet's language plastered onto the bureaucratic necessity.

51. General Douglas MacArthur (1880–1964) officially accepted Japan's surrender on September 2, 1945, and oversaw the occupation of Japan from 1945 to 1951. He was fired by President Harry Truman for insubordination during the Korean War.
52. Ramy Alexander, mutual friend of Kazin and Paolo Milano; see April 2, 1988, entry.
53. Allen Mandelbaum (1926–), Dante scholar and translator, chairman of CUNY Ph.D. program.
54. Julius Henry "Groucho" Marx (1890–1977), American comedian and movie actor, starred in thirteen films with his siblings as the Marx Brothers, later the witty host of the television game show *You Bet Your Life.*

The Order of Release: the poisoned air—from the excess materialism—above all from the mountain of obligations—

## December 5, 1975
### [dated December 4, 1975]

*And I only am escaped alone to tell thee:* Job.[55]

Hannah died Thursday night, Dec. 4, 1975, while entertaining friends. My first thought was that I had been struck from behind. How my overwhelming thought is that the serious people are gone, have gone, are going one by one.

The Academy and *personal* powerlessness. All about writing by non-writers. But when the intellectuals became "advisors," then the Academy shifted from null verbality to special pleading.

Hannah at the *Commentary* dinner, 1946—Hannah in Morningside Drive, still taking in boarders. Hannah, the conservative, clear thinker=penetrating you, yea, with those maxims from classical politics. How she influenced us.

Hannah and memory at Manomet. The Beethoven Cello Sonata in A. The books that had been stored in Paris—the photograph of the sculptured Plato on her desk.

Hannah in Germany, 1952. Hannah and time-tables. She liked to read time-tables. Hannah putting on her eye makeup. Her sexual appeal directed to literary influence on young credulously adoring and grateful American writers.

## December 8, 1975

Coming back from Hannah's funeral. Unbelievable . . . not least, the feeling that she enlisted. To see Jovanovich and McCarthy in tears as they delivered their tributes! Hannah, the magnet. . . . What moved me most, oddly enough, was Hans Jonas's memory of Hannah and himself in Rudolf Bultmann's seminar in the *New Testament* at Marburg.[56] "We were only the two Jews in that seminar."

55. "I only am escaped alone to tell thee": *Job* 1:14–15; also the epigraph to the Epilogue of *Moby-Dick.*

56. William Jovanovich (1920–2001), chairman of Harcourt, Brace, Jovanovich; Hans Jonas (1903–1993), German-born philosopher, Alvin Johnson Professor of Philosophy at the New School for Social Research in New York City from 1955 to 1976; Rudolf Karl Bultmann (1884–1976), German theologian who taught the New Testament at the University of Marburg.

Hannah standing out even among the brilliant students of 1924—her eyes, fascinating . . . her toughness and her own vulnerability.

Women play such public roles . . . and are, as who just said it, "saboteurs" within.

New York and Hannah. The boarder, the police locks, the German expressionist pictures, the Chinese restaurants on the corner—above all, looking at America through *her* eyes. She exercised that kind of authority. The key point *was* Jonas's—She was like no one else.

## February 6, 1976

Irene Worth in Tennessee Williams's *Sweet Bird of Youth*.[57] You cannot keep your eyes off her—certainly I could not: the woman, "all woman," as they say, the woman up to her neck in the sheer labor *and* passion of survival. The body enthralls you, the face . . . she is like some screamingly human index, fever chart, of what it takes the whole day through to keep alive. . . . Only women have quite this closeness to what counts, the sense of our life in us, rising and ebbing. [. . .]

## February 20, 1976

Early morning sorrows. If it were not for the teaching and those other of my children! and my hope that my inside narrative will yet come to something!! I am saved every day by the teaching, by "school," by the renewal it seems to bring. . . . [. . .]

## February 28, 1976

[. . .] The Media Men (type of John Leonard):[58] they thrive on the surface irony and above all the absurdity of things. The visible scene is in such disrepair, and such contradiction to what is supposed to be, that anything you see and even look at furnishes an example of derision.

Whereas I still believe in the centrality of truth. The Media Men could not say that the center does not hold. . . . The key is that there is no center. . . . And

57. Irene Worth (1916–2002), stage and screen actress, a favorite of Kazin's; Tennessee Williams, playwright, best known for *A Streetcar Named Desire* (1946) and *Cat on a Hot Tin Roof* (1955), both of which received Pulitzer Prizes.

58. John Leonard (1939–2008), literary, film, and cultural critic.

along with this ec-centricity, the prevailing sense of a lot of dust on the surface, lies the *bitterness*. [. . .]

*Slaves in Egypt*

Dick—Trilling—Schwartz—etc. All of *us* victims of the "old" morality. Looking back from the relative laxness of the 70s, we look to me now as victims of conventionality.

*Because* we believed, like Broadway's *Tevye*[59] (that demonstratively U.S. Jew) in *tradition*. We were under the spell of a *continuity* that broke up under our eyes, and the dupes.

Winners and losers. The news media men *dramaturgy*

The murders—murders—murders.

They are as much flotsam and jetsam
As the material they report.
Flies settling temporarily on
The dust and as quickly.

## March 14, 1976

[. . .] Papa was always looking for the exit. And with good reason—that raging life-force in Mama to which he (and I) submitted so completely because it seemed to be *protective*. [. . .]

The "Woman's Movement," insofar as it is a minority movement, resembles all other minority movements; pushy, seeking all possible support in the "movement." The Jewish movement is exactly the same sociological and political phenomenon except for the intuition of a transcendental truth that was worked into its still mysterious sense of closeness.

Oddly enough, what is *different* and in a sense redemptive about the Jews as still another pressure movement is exactly the *closeness*, the *talking to God*. Their sense of being agents of some higher purpose. *The movement!*

*No wonder Papa was always looking for the exit!*

59. Tevye, a central figure in a number of the stories of Scholem Aleichem (see Chapter 9, note 84), appears in the musical and film versions of *A Fiddler on the Roof*.

## April 18, 1976

[. . .] Bill Sheed,[60] Vidal, etc., feel surrounded by Jews, pushed by Jews, burdened by Jews. Jews are their *present*. Jews are a Saturday night party in E. Hampton with talk about the Holocaust between the delectable epicure courses.

For me, crippled, malicious, outsiding Sheed, the Jews are the *past*. This past is what I am trying to reach. I want to get back to my God, to Law, to His will. I am so tired of my own! But here is Sheed (quoting Vonnegut) on the relative intelligence of (mostly Jewish) writers. Mailer, the great earth's astronaut at the top of the list. Roth would come out dumber than you suspect.

Jews are "smart." Some Jews are smarter than others. We are crowding *you*. John (Jack) Fowles[61] says that he starts talking Southern with a vengeance after an evening of Jews. They do insist so on their own ethnic etc. identity. We are crowding *you*, Mr. Fowles and Mr. Sheed and especially Mr. Vidal. Jews—Jewish intellectuals, Jewish writers, *everywhere*. Even the fairy across the road is named Sinai Mordecai Waxman! How these Jews push even their Biblical place names in our faces. Are we *never* to be free of their relentless, cultural opportunism, their incalculable intensities, their freakish irritable solidarity, their constant invocation of Israel.

Even at Yale, by God, the exegete par excellence, flowering Bloom, brings up the Cabala (a "cabal" says Christopher Ricks)[62] in order to "revise" conventional opinion about Wallace Stevens.

Jews, stop pushing us together by *your* very existence! Stop with the past already! Stop with your infernal repetition. [. . .]

## May 25, 1976

From the moment I began to keep my notebook, on marrying Natasha, I felt blessed with a new way of seeing. I would stop excitedly in the winter street to

60. Wilfrid Sheed (1930–), American novelist, biographer, essayist, satirist; Gore Vidal, American novelist, playwright, essayist, and political activist.
61. John Fowles (1926–2005), English novelist and essayist, author of *The Collector* and *The French Lieutenant's Woman*.
62. Sir Christopher Bruce Ricks (1933–), British literary scholar and critic who taught at Yale University and is currently professor at Boston University.

enter the description of the short circuit a sled's runners made through a path of muddy ice. I *saw* things now I had never seen before: the deep doors on Remsen Street—the piled-up colors of the cars waiting to be loaded onto the freighters to Latin America at the foot of Columbia Heights. . . .

Above all, I felt in the Big City on the brink of simultaneity—and that getting things together might change me. I was so parent-oriented, so tradition bound, so rooted in my own tracks, that the new life after marriage with Natasha felt like a world apart.

## May 28, 1976

Lord, Lord, the pain *is* my pain and nobody else's—

Tim[63] and friends were libertarian in style. . . . They opposed the American State in the name of freedom, peace, non-violence, etc. . . . But all the time they were secretly supporting a totalitarian state . . . which, like Cuba and China, they saw only in terms of personal wish fulfillment.

The 60s were the *shattering* time. The old "faith" was destroyed=disaffection became the tool of irony, not elitism.

My Promised City—How easily they try to write off New York: "New York, oh yes, Yes, I seem to have heard of it"—the Governor's executive assistant during this long day of turmoil that ended at midnight with the City University being closed.

The Promised City was not Jerusalem, whose walls make too much of a Son et Lumiere show on the front page of *Hadassah* Magazine—not Moscow certainly—not Rome for its luxe et volupte in the hot, summer afternoon—it was the city I grew up in—the harbor—the Heights—the ferries—the endless connections to Europe and America at once. It was the great world city—The Promised City was above all the solidarity with the other people on the sidewalk that I felt this morning crossing over to the 72nd street subway.

It was the echo I felt yesterday, Black Friday indeed at the City University, talking on the phone to Allan Mandelbaum about the repercussion of great political events in America when we were young in Europe. [. . .]

63. "Tim" is the pseudonym of Michael in *New York Jew*.

The end of Promised City could be the mad "holiday" scene at 14th and Sixth. A car with black and Puerto Rican young, dressed in baseball caps with orange visors, ran into a Cadillac. The Cadillac owner obviously went off to find a cop; the baseball players, sitting on each other and laughing in the back of the car, are all over the street, all over the Cadillac, waving back outraged drivers trying to get past or around. Complete snarl, everything in a state of perfect Memorial Day heat, bad temper, hurry. . . . [. . .]

The crowd swallowing you up—New York is dying. I am on my last mile, etc.—but the overabundance of people, orange baseball caps, broken sidewalks, potholes in the gutter—all swallow you up like the most severely unimpressable process of nature.

## June 3, 1976

The Party and the Fire.[64] From Betty Friedan's windows, 1 Lincoln Plaza, one looks down on the great square of Lincoln Center with memories of Venice as the "drawing room of Europe." Only the river, from that most elegant and expensive height, seemed to balance the beauty of the square and the lights. In the midst of a rumble with Dr. Lipton [*sic*, Lifton][65] about the survivors of the Holocaust and "neurotic survival guilt," one saw this great fire, raging, truly raging, on several Weehawken piers over in Jersey. The trivialities of the literary cocktail party suddenly become a kind of collective excitement in the face of that blazing insistency over in Jersey. And when Mrs. K and I came home, that fire in our windows, we fell into a fine, rapacious lovemaking.

You see New York from a distance—the island. You see it from the heights always looking down. . . . It is always this picture of itself, the approach to the city—except when you are right in the middle, below, toiling your way through the choked streets of debris.

## July 7, 1976
### [Ames, Iowa]

Dinner with Abigail and James Van Allen. James discovered the radiation belt around the earth that is now named for him, and he is endlessly fascinated

64. Betty Friedan (1921–2006), writer, activist, and feminist. She cofounded the National Organization of Women and is best known for *The Feminine Mystique* (1963). Her party is the final setting in *New York Jew*.

65. See Chapter 6, note 54.

by the constitution of Jupiter—the most "fantastic planet of them all." With his thick Dutch nose, his perfect look of surprise when anything out of the way is said to him, his commonplace clothes, his commonplace jokes, you would think him just the nicest run of the mill Hawkeye. . . . But his head is really among the stars, and the "niceness" is that perfect non-personalism, his complete absorption in the object of study, that is in such contrast with Birdseed [Ann] last night, putting herself, her old jokes, eternal PS 17 into everything.

When Van Allen describes anything, it is exact, it moves, it has distinct *frame*.

## July 8, 1976

Thoughts on nearing the end: of the first draft [of *New York Jew*]—

1—It has all been happier, fuller, *riskier* than I had allowed myself to say. Primarily, it has been a leap into experience, a need to open doors, to get out, to mingle, to see, to get in as much as possible. A positive greed for experience—for all possible satisfaction—to satisfy all possible curiosity—to be in there, to be in the saddle—to get hold of the situation—to be right in there.

2—I am a cultural "conservative" because "culture" is conservative. I think of myself as a "radical" because the "system" is rickety—because it is run by knaves and fools—because there is no reason to believe that "culture" is being sustained, or can in any way provide security or safety.

Neglect is the greatest and easiest temptation of all. Bypass the drunken black at the corner. "We have a hundred million in Brazil, most of whom we don't need."

The spectator in the audience does not know what the writhing figure on the stage is suffering—what he is suffering—what he is going through. A Jew has had experiences that other people simply don't understand or wish to understand. [. . .]

## August 15, 1976

[. . .] Bellow came on with his eyes *confronting* you. The sense of some overall, private confidence was enormous. But his private radar never stopped studying you—and warding off anyone who might obstruct his assured progress—

## August 21, 1976

Writing *On Native Grounds* felt to me—to us—to be a political act. The country was on the move—*we* were on the move. *We were learning America.* FDR was part of this larger movement of break up and reform—A movement, things moving literature in direct relation to the energies of society.

## August 27, 1976

Akron—Hilton Hotel and Schmotel. Thinking obsessively about Bellow as "success," as the man who of us all somehow did it right. It's really a quality of intelligence, of matter-of-fact—[Harold] Rosenberg has something of this successful pirate too—*the invader and marauder of an entirely new country.* The ability to smell out opportunities—above all, *the ability not to let oneself down, not to lose necessary morale.*

It's all been a triumph of self—*a triumph of the favorite son*, the son who, gifted with so much love, became a conqueror.

Success story—"winners and losers"—above all the triumph of the self in a culture wholly commercial, competitive, and acquisitive. [. . .]

So much "triumph of the self," so much psychological man means that the last chapter [in *New York Jew*] must be about *Him*, *It*, and not just *You*. . . . It must be about God's world, *duration*, as opposed to man's world, all this transiency, all this running against time closing down on you— [. . .]

## September 13, 1976

Reading Waugh's *Men at Arms* with the greatest possible delight. Only Waugh caught the real truth about English "class relations." It's not a struggle between different classes but between different *species*. The grimace of perfect dislike and derision they throw each other!

## November 2, 1976

Carter elected. And at least for the moment, I couldn't be happier.

## November 9, 1976

Meeting of the Distinguished Professors at the Grad Center to do something about the financial avalanche that may move down on us beginning

1977–8.[66] I did know most of their names, but looking around me I saw, principally, INTELLECTUAL VANITY, vanity of such a narcissistic, posing, self-declaring, pompous, gesturing kind that the smirking and posing finally reminded me of the ridiculously heavy, meerschaum pipe and purple, black cigars that one bearded gent alternately stuffed his mouth with.

The academic class: the "professionally trained"—how much I know, how clever I am, especially in skepticism about everybody but myself. . . . The "critical" attitude.

## November 28, 1976

[. . .] The thing about Hannah more than anything else: she believed in lasting relationships. The Hitler nightmare was a break with lasting relationships, with lasting values. Now we put this "classicist," this believer in permanent values, up against Bellow, who resented being told anything about Faulkner by a Kraut, against [Paul] Goodman, who shocked her by leaving a mound of peanut shells all around him, by Mary McCarthy, who after trying to insult her at Rahv's house became her frenzied acolyte, by Cal Lowell and Randall Jarrell. And me. [. . .]

## December 7, 1976

The writer is always a volcano. In Kipling the feeling is so strong, so recessive, that it cannot find a home on earth and takes refuge in supernaturalism, in "ghosts," above all in this genteel British end of the century cult of evil—of a beast in the jungle.

What and who is this beast waiting to come out at us? This visitation—this vastation or devastation, as the Jameses used to say, of *their* evil spirit? It is the volcano pouring out its fire and ashes—literature can express the fiery volcano (and forget not that a fire was practically Blake's favorite symbol and certainly his favorite idea of *force*) *but literature does not restrain* it. The myth of the writer as Prometheus, the fiery rebel, remains a personal obsession. And as with Dreiser—Malcolm Lowry—a character may prefigure the ordeal the writer will live through! The writer has his volcano in his hands. . . . It seeks G.

66. Kazin was on a committee elected by the faculty that recommended the university begin charging tuition, limit admission (open to all New York City high school graduates) to the top 20 percent of graduates, and close a number of the community colleges.

*Our bookkeeping culture.* Was Kerouac a homosexual or not? How many times can you come? *Your sexual habits and preferences, etc.* is your identity. *You have no other soul you can really call your own.*

Shaw: In Stockholm all people speak the same language.

## January 17, 1977

Out of the provost, of all people—Bellow is always looking for something to fit his sense of the wild, daemonic energy at the center of our life—of our universe. I take this up and realize that "our God" is always a God of fire and thunder—an angry, wild man God—so far from the sweet, beneficent God of "Love" that it is clear that the Christians invented something in the shape of beneficence that is entirely *new.*

## January 28, 1977

Norman, Oklahoma—the mind turns down through the plains battering the bare shingles of the world. *I could not be more alone*—key to Chapter 7.[67] *I Confess* . . . the cold war and the McCarthyite terror turned everyone into himself, made this an age of psychology, self-scrutiny, confession, and extracted confession. The self became the locus of what was really a political age. But politics as the opposition of interests could not be allowed—The self lied about its fatal importance to itself under the mark of *guilt.*

The self could not sustain itself alone—the age of the totally "free" individual belonged to the era of capital accumulation—and this rapacious accumulative self remained the model when the actuality was the frightened, burdened, inwardly fugitive *citizen.*

Psychological man, Romantic, opposing man versus the *citizen.* Arendt knew politics, as we all did, only through literature and its maxims. The onslaught was met with precious quotations, didactic examples.

Trilling and Arendt as the teachers of the deradicalized intelligentsia.

*I confess—I confess* to what? I confess *to whom?* To authority—to government—to *power.*

67. Refers to chapter 7 of *New York Jew*, "The Times Being What They Are," depicting the response of former radicals to the anti-Communist hysteria of the McCarthy era.

But those who lived in the literature and by literature knew power only as a threat from *them.*

It was at this point that the Holocaust began to sink in. The century was a century of ever-increasing power, and inquisition was the symbol of this power.

The Hollywood ten-twenty-forty, etc. could not admit that McCarthyism—"*loyalty*" derived from totalitarian fashions of the age set by Russia. They claimed exemption from the system they practiced on each other—on Albert Maltz.[68]

The self turned and turned in its gyre.[69] "Great art is not personal like that," said Celine. But politics had become "personal" like that. The fault, dear Brutus, lies in ourselves.[70]

Because the aggrandizement of the self as consumer went parallel to the aggrandizement of *power*. And sharing in this power we become victims of it.

I confess—I confess—I am the victim of my childhood, my circumstances. I am not guilty because I am the present looking at my past and am therefore not responsible. I am only my own historian.

What I want is to be relieved of my suffering not to make an accounting of the power, the system of interests.

So began the drinking, the "relaxing," the treatment of solitude as a prisoner in his cell to be *jollied*. The reality of the prisoner in his cell is to think his way out, but solitude was viewed as an ailment or delusion. And loneliness was *real*, because the social contract was the topmost most visible reality.

Deradicalization was urgent but not very factual. [Irving] Kristol—there is no real poverty. The state takes care. But the *self* appeared everywhere: every self claimed to count.

68. Albert Maltz (1908–1985), novelist and screenwriter, blacklisted in the 1950s.

69. See Yeats's apocalyptic poem "The Second Coming," which begins "Turning and turning in the widening gyre/The falcon cannot hear the falconer;/Things fall apart; the centre cannot hold."

70. See Shakespeare's *Julius Caesar*, a speech by Cassius: "The fault, dear Brutus, is not in our stars/But in ourselves, that we are underlings" (I, ii, 140–141).

The "self" we agreed on was the guilty self, the self in imaginary flight from and revolt against the power-state. But the flight was interpreted as *flight from self, as a psychological tribulation only*. Guilt was located only in the single party, this mysteriously flexible and useful pronoun, *I. Eye. I confess. Eitel. I tell.*

Hannah—"I never in Europe saw people suffer like this." The turning, gyrating self under the daemonic eye of power. Especially for Jews, who had just lately been condemned to death *en bloc*.

Eliot on *Sacre du Printemps* and a clue to the "*obscurities of* the soul."[71] *I confess* means that I wish to eliminate *all* obscurities of the soul.

## February 4, 1977

A slave to the *New York Times*. . . . A slave to the whole spectrum of liberal opinion, of necessary world news. . . . A slave to this side and that side of "the world." News from afar, and news, opinion, news. *I have to listen*. This is the world!

## February 18, 1977

Naipaul[72] is a man of three continents, so that in his writing he seems to swim between them and to be the spectator of each. The novelist's detachment, his disinterestedness takes in Naipaul the form of situations and above all of persons in unexpected places (like the autobiographical ship's memory at the end of *In a Free State*), but the tone is always the same: a certain intellectual depression, a consciousness of being caught that as so often happens in pain produces a terrific sharpness, a depressed lucidity, a picking out and level emphasizing of situation and color.

The Key point is that despite his masterly handling of so many situations, you are aware of a particular Naipaul tone of rootlessness, compassion, a certain

71. T. S. Eliot wrote that Stravinsky's *Sacre du Printemps* "evoked the screams of the motor horn, the rattle of machinery . . . and other barbaric cries of modern life"; quoted in Monroe Spears, *Dionysius and the City: Modernism in Twentieth-Century Poetry* (New York: Oxford University Press, 1970). Eliot likened James Frazer in *The Golden Bough: A Study in Magic and Religion* (1890) to Freud for "shedding light on the obscurities of the soul."

72. V. S. Naipaul (1932–), Trinidadian writer of Indian ancestry who won the Nobel Prize in literature in 2001, probably best known for *A House for Mr. Biswas* (1961).

sorrowfulness and an intellectual pointedness about Others. . . . It does remind me of the way so many Indians behave . . . "abroad."

He does not raise his voice. He dramatizes everything and dramatizes endlessly without being "dramatic." He somehow slips into the shadows. Perhaps it is this that explains his lack of world fame, in the style of Nabokov or Graham Greene. . . .

Not to forget that he is a Natural novelist, a thinker for whom the novel is a form of "social inquiry." . . . The fortunate artist, locating himself in so many different situations—

Lack of world fame, of course, due to his being regarded as a creature of so many different situations, from the East Indians, who were brought in after the emancipation of the slaves—

Key is the novelist as thinker—everything understood without explanation, but the *characters* offer explanation.
Stendhal: "I must be clear or the whole world around me breaks up."

## February 27, 1977

Why and how did I sacrifice my dignity like this? Why and how did I allow myself to *become* this bawling, brawling contestant—? *Where* and how did I slip back like this?

## March 5, 1977

Meeting to welcome Vladimir Bukovsky[73] at Stuyvesant, packed, turned into a near-riot when to this bitterly anti-Communist audience both Mike Harrington and Russell's old evil genius Ralph Schoenman began "Comrades and Friends" appeals for "socialism." Socialism indeed. As Bukovsky got up to speak, a small, slight figure, a Trotskyite or something in the aisles bawled out. "You're being used!" To which Bukovsky could only [say] that he was doing the "using." Schoenman with his hayseed beard that looks like the cutting edge of a crude, medieval ax stared—glared?—steadily at the audience before and

73. Vladimir Bukovsky (1942–), Soviet dissident, spent twelve years in Soviet prisons; Ralph Schoenman (1935–), leftist and activist, former personal secretary for Bertrand Russell.

after he spoke. The ego of the man and his infantile belief in his infantile talk about "revolutionary socialism" were monumental. Bukovsky quietly and acidly represented the school of experience. "In Russia what counts is not the left camp or the right camp but the concentration camp." Pavel Litvinov[74] with his charming, open, healthy, somehow beaming baby face (looked to me very much like grandpa) began by saying "I am not a socialist."

So the meeting, overloaded, overheated with television cameras as well as with stocky, violent-feeling Russians shouting to Schoenman "Bolsheveek!! Out! Boo!" left me with the depression and exhaustion proper to meetings of Russians about Russia. Every single Russian around me radiated the unbelievable emotionality of carrying in his mind and heart the consequences of the Revolution. The landslide of political madness and fanaticism came down on them, and they are still mentally under the rubble even when they seemed to be walking about in the open air.

## June 9, 1977

Finished the book [*New York Jew*] this afternoon and I can say thank you *Lord*, from now on I am more likely to write about *you* than about me. I am liberated from autobiography—I have *done* all the confrontation with myself that I can take. Now I go on to a *bigger world.*[75] [. . .]

## June 12, 1977

Literature conservative. The nineteenth century as the enduring center of literature—not only into the 20th century *but well into* this century, precisely because we are so corporate, organized, and so a *single VOICE* seems more distinguished than ever.

*The Great Voice* and the elocutionary style in all these Victorian moral commanders—Emerson, Marx, Carlyle, etc.—*the voice* speaks for its moral authority (these great voices are all ex-theological) and it still has a congregation—still expects to be listened to.

74. Pavel Litvinov (1940–), Russian physicist, imprisoned for five years for participating in the Red Square demonstrations against the 1968 Soviet invasion of Czechoslovakia.

75. Kazin would continue to publish autobiographical pieces, including his "journal book," *A Lifetime Burning in Every Moment* (1996).

How did *they* see themselves? On the whole as virtuous and above all expanding personalities. The historians Adams and Tocqueville[76] had (naturally) an ironic and dispassionate perspective. But Emerson probably thought himself wholly virtuous (only the *writer* in him made him feel ironic about himself and see the irony in human ambition). Thoreau's self-approval is monotonous to the point of being unbearable. Of course it was all for his writing—his own life.

Hawthorne and Melville at least knew themselves to be troubled men.

The century ends in this prevailing sense of secular apocalypse. But the apocalypse was indicated in the revolutionary violence that followed *man taking his history into his own hands*. William James's bathtub was overflowing.

*Our* distorted perspective based on the obvious contrast of the good old century with 1914. What is hardest for *us* to grasp is the evident conscious secularizing of religion, its universality, its hope, its promise of redemption, the ministerial oratory.

## July 3, 1977

[. . .] For these intellectuals, from *PR* to the *NY Review*, the mystical absolute is "Modernism," i.e., overthrow and overturn in the "artistic sphere" as in the political. . . . Yet the great modernists themselves were seeking to preserve and re-create tradition, perhaps even their tradition, to make art out of their nostalgia in the face of "modernization."

The audience—the consumers—the critics of modernism created an Absolute; the modernists themselves, qua creators, were interested in the Great Return. The consumers—readers—audience, constitute a consistent and homogeneous *mass*.

## August 4, 1977

[. . .] Bach in the morning—these many notes, these neurons and synapses of notes, these endless circuits of notes, sound to my brain as the elements of my brain. My happy, waking consciousness is made up of these notes.

76. Alex de Tocqueville (1805–1859), French political thinker and historian, best known for his brilliant analysis of American society and politics, *Democracy in America* (1856).

AMERICA—the vision I had reading *American Humor*[77] on the subway platform—the seeming illimitability leading out from every *sentence* in Emerson—The openness, the spiritual confidence, all these signals to the then immigrant brain still exist, within the context of the century of *theories*, of *natural history*, the discovery of *production* as the secret of *advance* and *enlightenment*, above all of the proud *self*, the single soul.

Marx arguing *for* his vision—Nietzsche the great debater always arguing against the "moral tradition." [. . .]

## August ?, 1977
### [dated August 2, 1977; out of page order]

He and she.[78] He looks down at her crumpled, bloody, bone-splintered body—she who was always so immaculate in her white pants suit, and platinum hair, and thinks of Hardy's dead peasants saying in the poem "Friends Beyond," *death gave us all that we possess.*

The shock of her dying after so much mental strife and bourgeois *angst. The ax that breaks the frozen sea within us.*[79] (He is full of literary quotations to the end, the habit of quotation for which she most scorned him.) She escapes him in death—because it is all so terrible as in some way, to be mysterious. To obey an impulse so! The willfulness of this shocks him as her "drive" shocked him in life. *He never understood her.* She never understood herself. Literature is representation, *not* "understanding."

77. Constance Rourke, *American Humor: A Study of the National Character* (New York: Harcourt, Brace, 1931).
78. Sue Kaufman (see note 46) committed suicide by jumping to her death. Kazin hoped to write a story about the incident but never did.
79. Franz Kafka: "A book should be an axe to break the frozen sea inside us"; letter to Oskar Pollak, January 27, 1904.

# 8
# Love and Politics
1977–1984

IN A MAY 13, 1978, ENTRY KAZIN MARVELED at the changes that had recently occurred in his life. "I feel like Ulysses transported in his sleep. Something mysterious happened this year; something decisive beyond words, clearing up my life, putting familiar things in unfamiliar places and making the unfamiliar more and more *intimate.*" He was right about the changes, and right that they would be decisive for his future. While completing *New York Jew,* Kazin had applied for and received a fellowship at the Center for Advance Studies in Behavioral Sciences at Stanford University for the 1977–1978 school year, to be followed by a William White Professorship at Notre Dame. He would return to New York (and CUNY) in the summer of 1979—but without Ann. Following a series of loud arguments that brought police to the Kazins' Stanford apartment, Alfred had moved into a motel. In the winter of 1978, the marriage collapsed, a casualty of years of domestic strife and countless infidelities. There was a more immediate cause. In the spring of 1977 Kazin had met Judith Dunford. The daughter of immigrant Jews, Ignatz and Edvig Schwartz, who had settled in the Bronx, Judith, age forty-four, had heard Alfred lecture when she was an undergraduate at Mount Holyoke and remembers being "overwhelmed," "swept away." The meeting had led to more meetings—Judith was separating from her husband at the time—and in a matter of weeks to a love affair that promised the kind of happiness and companionship no longer found in their marriages.

The survivor of three failed marriages, Kazin was wary of repeating the past. But by the spring of 1983 he had decided to marry. "I dragged my feet so long—dragged it right into this kitchen on a rainy holiday morning—suddenly wishing that I had met her [Judith] 60 years ago" (May 30, 1983). There were other changes—some of them happy (Michael's marriage to Dr. Beth Horowitz, the purchase of a house in Roxbury, Connecticut), some much less so (a heart attack in 1982, "a day and an hour that will live in infamy" (February 16), and breaks with longtime friends, including Francis Steegmuller and his wife Shirley Hazzard). *New York Jew* and the response provoked by its satiric portraits had damaged relations with others. And though he had gained some new friends (Philip Roth, Saul Steinberg, Isaac Bashevis Singer), Kazin felt increasingly estranged from a growing number of former acquaintances and "more and more out of it" (October 4, 1981).

Following the completion of *New York Jew* in 1977, Kazin had returned to his book on nineteenth-century American writers, now called *An American Procession.* He devoted most of his time at Stanford and at Notre Dame to this project, tracking his progress and projecting plans in his daily journal entries. Published in 1984, it received mixed reviews, some praising it (justly) for its distinctively personal engagement with writers Kazin had spent a lifetime reading and teaching, others noting that it lacked the dramatic structure and critical verve one hoped for from the author of *On Native Grounds.* Kazin had plans for two other books—*Our New York* (1989), an extended autobiographical essay to be published with photographs by fellow Brownsville native David Finn; and "Absent Friends," a look back at friends, family, and acquaintances (and a few enemies) who continued to occupy his thoughts and dreams "in the infamous watches of the night" (October 16, 1982). Though the latter project never materialized, it gave Kazin the opportunity to reflect further on people who had played an important role in his life—"Each year their shadows lengthen, they become bigger somehow, bulkier, more intrusive . . . even more critical: They may not answer me, but they certainly provoke me to interrogation" (March 27, 1979).

Another development altered Kazin's life and mood in this period—politics. A radical from socialist Brownsville, he had always had political interests; but except for the antiwar protests in the sixties, he had largely avoided direct political confrontation. "I do not consider myself one of those 'armed intellectuals,' " he wrote to a student on April 29, 1980. "It is not my mind, not my style, not in the least." The 1980 election changed this as Kazin watched the "Reagan Revolution" move the country sharply to the right. That Reagan's agenda was being championed by former liberals and radicals, many of them friends, now neoconservative "arrivistes," deepened Kazin's animus and guilty conscience. "The great liberal Kazin," he wrote in a February 5, 1982, entry, "is just an observer, a *bloody book reviewer*. [. . .] All these moneyed gangsters and friends of other moneyed gangsters! . . . and it all passes before my eyes with a cluck, cluck." Kazin did more than cluck. He attacked the country's domestic and foreign policy in articles and speeches, directing his angriest polemic at those neoconservatives who had once championed the poor and the weak and now sided with the rich and powerful. In March 1983 a piece he published in the *New York Review of Books* attacking a recent gathering of neoconservatives of the Plaza Hotel elicited more fan mail than any other article he had written. On October 20, 1983, he delivered a speech attacking Reagan's policies, "The Strange Death of Liberal America," at the Great Hall of the Cooper Union (where Lincoln had delivered his famous speech describing his views on slavery in the free states). He had few illusions about his influence, but he was determined to do what he could. "The toughness, inflexibility, absolute rottenness of these ex-comrades," he wrote the day before Reagan's reelection. "You have to fight them *hard,* but they are in power and after tomorrow's Election Day, God help us all! they will be nastier to deal with than ever" (November 5, 1984).

## August 15, 1977

[. . .] The Gathering Of The Forces—the gathering of hope . . . force, power, strength. All my books are about the unleashing of hope—they are all about a new life, "presciency" as the new girl said, *newness,* the springs of courage.[1]

## August 16, 1977

Start with the acceleration of history in the last of *this* century. The pace of *massedness,* collectivism, violence, never lets up. Man has mounted science and is now run away with. *Things are in the saddle* and ride mankind.[2] The power is an extension of men but is not *in* men. It is the Pandora's box of limitless "power" of things and over things.

So you look back at early America as the 19th century place of the "fixed things."

[Henry] Adams is driven wild with intellectual ecstasy by the seeming limitlessness and replication of the law of acceleration. At the same time he cherishes the fixed *point,* the point of rest, the observation post! So you get the "historical" sense fully satisfied. At the same time there is the continual sense of the absurd and illimitable chaos! Breakup indescribable! The flood come again! Adams sees human history as *cosmology.*

## October 4, 1977
### [Palo Alto, California]

The Center is not only a meeting place of "social scientists"; it *is* a piece of social science. Life has become so socialized, such a "society" of specialists, that what fascinates me about the place, even as it scares me, is society watchful, everyone watching everyone else, everyone playing it cool. . . . I think of all these eruptions—Delmore erupting, Ann erupting, Alfred erupting—the whole immigrant-writer flaming sense of indignation, especially my madwoman's feeling that her fate is always in someone else's hands. . . . And contrast this with what one can only call the silent treatment. I know what you think you know about me and the social contract between us is to say nothing.

1. This and the following entry look ahead to Kazin's next book, *An American Procession.*
2. "Things are in the saddle/And ride mankind" is from Ralph Waldo Emerson's "Ode, Inscribed to William H. Channing."

So what a laugh to come out of 68 Pearce Mitchell[3] with Ann constantly erupting and screaming, hysteria and bitterness unbounded, and to be enveloped in the soft modulated good mornings of the Center. All day long we pass each other on the way to the coffee urn and the toilet. All day long we pass each other. If I could only pass by my madwoman, and she me!! [. . .]

## December 18, 1977
### [New York]

St. Vincents—the Kingdom of Heaven is within you—the great gospel of the 19th century.[4] Romantic self-liberation. Within Romantic self-liberation. Within *you.* But the most obvious sight around me this hospital week in NY has been the *crowd*, and the chief aim of the crowd is to duplicate one another, to hide in one another. [. . .] The body is slow, slow as time—the mind alone is important, impetuous, "successful," free. This week—this week of my body's imprisonment! I am so fettered—but no use to talk about any of it. My mind will be free—my K, my immortal K, will yet soar.

## January 12, 1978
### [Palo Alto]

1300 Oak Creek Drive, Apt. 306. Moved in and feel like the unexpected survivor the moment after the battle is over. The field is littered with corpses, and I feel spent—but I am here.[5]

## January 28, 1978

Night Thoughts, Night Spasms—I always demanded of women, demanded, demanded. And of course became angry and abusive when the tender, loving care was not forthcoming. So why do I get uneasy when chez Schwartzie [Judith Dunford, née Schwartz] everything is offered? Because I think it will soon be withdrawn?

Etc., Etc., with the psychology. But isn't it also true that my mind is not like hers and hers and hers and that the sense of being exceptional, of being my own mind and like no one else's has led to this devouring self-examination? From time to time I think of what it must be to love *solidly,* to regard the other

3. An apartment complex in Palo Alto.
4. Visiting New York, Kazin slipped on the ice and broke his left shoulder, necessitating two operations.
5. Alfred and Ann have permanently separated.

as simply unimpeachable, whom I can entirely respect (say like Lucy D. or even Dick H.)—someone *I* look up to but do feel spiritually at home with. I seemed to have settled so easily for my wives and sweethearts—have settled on *them* with too many compromises hanging between me and them—have in my quest of "satisfaction" and "love" become conscious (God forgive me) of their *use value.*

I suppose a man so suspicious of women shouldn't complain if they turn on him. And yet before this almighty and terrible tribunal of my heart I plead not altogether guilty—that I *have* loved. Oh, well, Tribunal, let your servant depart in peace. If I have offended, I have certainly paid and paid for my offenses. [. . .]

## February 7, 1978

Home now, after this long terrible day at the Center, my heart full of dread about Ann's coming. And of course she ended it, as I could have predicted, kicking my door and shouting "Drop dead." But my wife, my nut, is not what interests me at this moment—that subject is certainly exhausted, or should soon be. What I want to know is: I feel so enmeshed in some pitiless law that says, Kazin, you are what you are and you are suffering what you are suffering for the same reason that B. follows A. You are caught in the sinews of inexorable law! There are necessary consequences. And my freedom? My sense of my self as a free being? All I can do, I guess, is to affirm it, to believe it, to act on it, to prove it as a necessary paradox in the face of "unalterable law."

Unalterable? I can do nothing? I have started by writing this. To write is to form a thought out of nothing. There was no thought before I started to write this. I am Man Thinking. I am thinking this page; I am thinking my life.

## March 14, 1978

Under the big California sky all these little specialists at the Center. Knowledge is power; specialization is more power; pride is the final power of the little specialists. At lunch, the unforgettable sight of Dick Epstein crooning away about insurance lawyers and his recent consultation in New York while duck-grave Ruth Bader Ginsburg[6] (who could be the daughter in a shtetl picture of an old Jewish family), sits delicately eating her salad and expressing, what, displeasure? outrage? boredom? One will never know anything from this duck face. . . . [. . .]

6. Ruth Bader Ginsburg (1933–), who taught at Rutgers and Columbia Law Schools, later became an associate justice of the U.S. Supreme Court.

## May 3, 1978

[. . .] What a day, what a New York day . . . from the Cavett Show (little Dick Cavett,[7] with the smile branded on him as if from birth) to the Woodwinds blowing so beautifully at the Century. . . . Schwartzie so gallant all the while, amid the gray heads at the Century, gray, gray white public old age! The wives, she says, look as if they all sat on the board of the Met. Museum. [. . .] The Cavett audience asked questions after the show. One black (when I had said Brownsville) "did you wear one of those big hats?" Like the chassidim? Yes, to every unit meeting of the Young People's Socialists League.

## May 13, 1978

[. . .] When I see where I am now, when I think of where I have been, when I awake each morning to the California sunshine and this just barely familiar room, I feel like Ulysses transported in his sleep. Something mysterious happened this year; something decisive beyond words, clearing up my life, putting familiar things in unfamiliar places and making the unfamiliar more and more *intimate.*

## June 26, 1978

I feel humiliated, devastated, etc. by this onslaught against me in today's *Book Review,*[8] but the truth is that there is not a single line about Trilling that I would take out of my book or apologize for. I *knew* that the Columbia acolytes would organize this demonstration against me, but I did *not* suspect that so many "old friends" would join in. Anyway, if I feel *exposed* and very much alone at the moment, that is *all* I do feel. And will have to keep cool—and silent!—and just bear up.

## June 28, 1978

A long haul to Berkeley to speak at the Writer's Conference. Isaac Singer and his Alma, Isaac looking a little bent at 73, naturally, but as exceptional, unexpected, and above all as funny as ever. I had forgotten that he always comes on *plain* and plain as can be. . . . Everything he says and recalls is already a story in its *detail.*

7. Richard "Dick" Cavett (1936–) was the host of a television talk show that typically had more intellectual content than those of his competitors.

8. A letter in the *New York Times Book Review* (June 25, 1978): 54, signed by nineteen people, including such "old friends" as Frank Kermode, Howard Mumford Jones, and Arthur Schlesinger Jr., complained that Kazin's portrait of Trilling in *New York Jew* was a "grotesque misrepresentation of the truth."

Husband and wife wrangle over details of a car, a hotel, that Isaac remembers one way and Alma another; and it is the plainness that gets me; no fine feathers, no "grace . . ." and no pretense either. I am here, and this what I remember, and this is what I want to say. Or to put it another way, outside of his imaginative world, he is as "ordinary" as anybody can be. Which is the way a writer should be.—But how can it be after so many years here, that he is so *much* outside English?

My audience at the writers conference did not like me very much. I mean did not "understand" me very much. Words like "contempt" for parents and "violation" of the actual people were tossed around. Thinking about what I said to Gardner Lindzey[9] at lunch—how utterly singular each person is to another, secretly to himself, how hard for these great, alien, overbearing galleons floating around each other—ever to meet.

## July 14, 1978

Harold Rosenberg died—more and more, alas, his kind of slashing critical intellect will seem unnecessary, as that kind of criticism (of everything) disappears. [. . .]

## August 6, 1978

A quiet moment to sit down with myself in 14th Street and mediate on the state of my soul, which is not good. Someone dropped an egg outside the main entrance to my palatial habitation, and the sight of the yellow yolk coagulated somehow to my goings and comings (amazing how a bit of garbage will endure in New York) is enough—as in 1950, when I saw nothing but shit on the Upper West Side—to make the requisite background to all my uneasiness. . . . Anyway, it is somehow typical of the old man's return and the old man's weariness with everything I see here that trudging back on 11th Street past St. Vincents, I saw a dark haired lady who improbably turned out to be Edna Phillips with the ridiculously dyed hair. O Edna! O Delmore! O West 11th Street and *Partisan Review!* O Philip and Natalie Rahv!—I feel as if a glacial age has passed—and over me. "The past was not real unless you had lived it yourself." Okay, I have certainly lived it.

And now to the *American Procession* and the contextual definition of freedom—which means an idea of freedom, oddly enough like the man chained

9. Gardner Lindzey (1920–2008), a psychologist and president of the American Psychological Association, was director of the Center for Advanced Study in the Behavioral Sciences, in which Kazin was a senior fellow.

to the wall who says to the other man chained to the wall—"Now my idea is this. . . ."

The motif is I dwell in *possibility, a fairer house than prose*. . . . If freedom *is* an idea, it needs some concurrence. . . . I was thinking, driving, driving from California to Indiana that RWE's famous belief in correspondences (shades of Baudelaire) is a perfect example of what one can call romantic *sovereignty*—the world is really in my head, because the world that is such a neat double of my head—"Nature is meant to serve," the poet is nature's priest, etc.—simply lends itself to the nature of human intelligence,—so that one sees in the distance the shape and tone, the lovable familiarity, of what is nearest, one's own thoughts. . . .

RWE believes that "life consists in what a man is thinking of all day." Rubbish. But life does take its shape and tone, its volume, from our minds. . . . Everything is recast in personal consciousness, as personal consciousness—and though we hardly glimpse the truth, remains somehow an item, a property, *of* our personal consciousness.

So? So this explains the haunting sense of familiarity—the delusion of immortality that we connect with the persistence of our mental apparatus, our "subconscious"—(there is nothing else to tell us who and where we are. . . .) But the *what* we are is harder to get; this explains the haunting sense of something yet "beyond,"—it is just beyond our personal involvement, our Gott betrunkenes state. The beyond becomes shadow=outline—*the image of outer space* absolute=of our floating, almost entirely submerged at times, in this sea of thought. . . . [. . .]

## September 9, 1978
### [Notre Dame]

The Big Game, The Big Crowd. As I write, Sunday morning after, the great field across the way is dusty-empty. . . . Yesterday the crowds, the cars, were all so great—not to mention the funny hats, the beer cans, the hospitality centers at the open back door of the station wagons, that for a few hours it did feel like a festival. Some festival. When I went into the great stadium with Frese,[10] Dolores,

10. Dolores Frese (1936–), professor of English at Notre Dame. In May of 1978, after being denied tenure, Frese filed a class-action law suit on behalf of herself and sixty-six of her female colleagues against the university, alleging gender bias. She won the suit, which was extensively covered by the national media, securing her tenure and opening doors for women in academia and elsewhere.

Matthew Frese, the sight of the utterly jammed stadium did feel exactly like a "dream"—the image of a stadium crowded to the rafters was so complete, an image resting on my eye—an American too sealed off to be credible. . . . [. . .]

## September 27, 1978

At Notre Dame I not only live next to the cemetery, but life here is so quiet and oh! so private! that I sometimes feel I am living in it. [. . .]

*These are very plain people and I lead* a plain life. "*Fish Tues. Sat. 2:45.* All you can eat." [. . .]

## October 2, 1978

Reading Bellow's new story in *The New Yorker,*[11] with Katie asleep upstairs. In the story—a confrontation of *now,* the winter of 1933, of the single person in a world of *unassimilable objects,* I seem to see myself in Bellow's story. The shock of Katie's exploding on the street the other night after I had stupidly given voice to my bitterness against Ann. She threw the books down on the pavement and screamed at me—and Ann—for mucking up her life so long, the two of us.

The solitary, solitary world of Bellow's fiction—and ours. The world is *all outside* and there is no *relief* (the story is in part a satire on Christian religiosity). *But there is consummation.* A man ever alone in the Chicago winter during the Depression finds it mysteriously in himself to penetrate objects by describing them with excruciating precision. You never bind these objects to yourself—but you do handle them, so *distrustfully* that the illusion of possession is established.

What a school of experience. What a rain of blows. And the single I, still looking for Mr. Green, is surrounded to the point of ecstasy by recognizing so many power sources around him.[12] The "pathos of distance," the ecstasy of it—the distance the yawning gap creates so many "finds" for the enquiring mind rising to so many tasks of consciousness.

So—keep your distance, [illegible] boy! No plea for love, forgiveness or mitigation will shorten the distance.

11. "A Silver Dish," *New Yorker* (September 25, 1978).
12. Kazin is referring to Bellow's 1951 story "Looking for Mr. Greene."

Bellow more interesting in such a story than in his novels which get too much drawn out with self-concern. The scenario laid out in a story—*slamming the issues at you*—is the crux. [. . .]

Why Bellow excites: the press of consciousness is a model—we want to be alive with this vitality.

## October 5, 1978

[. . .] He longs for stability, domesticity—he dearly loves Schwartzie, yes indeed—and puts himself to sleep dreaming three in a bed. Is moved to tears, O yes indeed, by every particle of Jewish History . . . but would not be capable of following the Law for a minute, even if he could read it! Every morning gets up to walk in a clear direction, forwarts!, and by the end of the day, around news time, when he and the world need a little sustaining drink, finds in some mysterious fashion that he had gone backward.

I have just drawn the outline of the Jew as Hero . . . A Portrait of the Jew as Perennially Young Man. . . . The world is his, has always been his, has never really been encumbered. He has a sense of the infinite, yes indeed, of the farthest possible gift of extra-world and extra-time . . . yet he worries over every least triviality. . . . [. . .]

## October 10, 1978

The secret of my book, the compelling energy behind my book [*An American Procession*] will be my love for these writers and for their *native* experience. I have been released by Schwartzie as if from a dark cloud to celebrate the material that has haunted me so long—and that *haunts* me, surrounds me, pervades me, because *I believe in it.*

## October 13, 1978

With HJ, we *stretch* our imaginations. James's greatness—The flowing, expanding wave of consciousness that is his real *medium* gets *us* to expand our own consciousness. *This* is the American advantage—as a young man he saw that the American spiritual tradition had "spiritual lightness and vigor"—and just as he compared his "gaping" self in *A Small Boy and Others* to "the visiting mind," so his real strength is like Whitman's "Spider." It is an American trait—the famous *bootstrap* myth—must be connected to the expanding individual consciousness. [. . .]

## October 27, 1978

Alas, Alas, I must give up Astoria [G___],[13] the whole, long day, wonderful as the physical ecstasy that it always starts from, there can be no satisfactory future life for me there. Ungrateful heart! Ungrateful lover indeed! [. . .]

## November 16, 1978

[. . .] New York: is there a character anywhere like Gordon the Lish,[14] with his natty sports appearance, sophisticated hair (gray that suggests goyishe blend), his poker playing with you over the smallest, slightest conversational matter? The editor and ghost writer who lives by telling one writer stories about another; and in my case, told me (as Weinstein[15] did) what stories other writers make up about *me.* Judith, who was present at the Century with The Lish and me, says that the Lish is addressing not me but my "persona." The "persona" of the well-known literary critic? The persona who sits on *New York Jew* and my other fables of my life? Anyway, telling me the outrageous scene painted about me by Ozick[16] (in my own house I called her a Jewess, took my rain coat and stormed out) I ask myself if Madame O (the only cunt like thing about her is her opening initial) knows she is telling lies or just tells lies automatically, making up stories as she goes along?

You have to hand it to O—what use indeed is "reality?" Especially if you look like the last copy of a 1936 tabloid left out in the rain? Of course writers—so long as they are writing—must never be pitied. On no account whatever! Re-reading William James's *Pragmatism* in the plane yesterday, I was struck again by his total assertiveness, unmistakable effort at *mastership* (lays down a line of thought as belief that he means you to adopt, and no other). . . . Truly, 'tis not the "persona," as people fondly say about the assumed character of a writer but *the line he puts down with every line* that is his real person, and I don't mean "persona." [. . .]

13. See Chapter 6, note 89.
14. Gordon Lish (1934–), editor at Alfred A. Knopf, formerly fiction editor for *Esquire.*
15. Weinstein may be Allen Weinstein (1937–), professor at Smith College, author of books on Soviet espionage in America, including *Perjury: The Hiss-Chambers Case* (1978), a sometime friend of Kazin's.
16. Cynthia Ozick (1928–), writer, novelist, essayist.

## December 14, 1978

Today is Sunday, now is mid-afternoon; I came in Thursday, have been living with Schwartzie in her new apartment, and God help me (and her) I do feel married as I never did, I think, with Ann. . . . Idiotic and mad etc., etc. as it may all seem, I have made up my mind to accept this happiness, not to qualify and fight it—I feel a great calm with Schwartzie, mixed with an incredible excitement. . . . Noting this at random in the 14th St. studio, I am impressed not only by her great intelligence and wide-awake critical scrutiny of mind, but by the blessed fact that our conversations, about anything and everything, hold me to the mark, will not let standards drop, will not sacrifice "reactions," from the intellectual gut of our being so to speak. . . .

Sufficient unto this day is the happiness thereof? I feel that if I can keep my head screwed the right way for once, and trust my heart, that something very blessed and beautiful is in store for both of us. . . .

Anyway, I seem to see the packed up windows of Park West, 100th and Columbus, in a more tender light. . . . What a set of personalities NY presents as soon as I get down to the street. . . . So many of the upper West Siders especially look as if they were about to have an audition. . . . For what part that the city doth present? [. . .]

## January 18, 1979

The function of literature, the raison d'être of literature, is to make a *difference* in our lives; whether by pleasure or transformation. And perhaps they are not so different.

## February 2, 1979

Before Dawn. In N[otre] D[ame] it is always before dawn. . . . My dreams are improving. Martha Kaplan called me in some perturbation to announce that Elie Wiesel had taken out a court injunction to prohibit me from writing about the Holocaust. [. . .]

## February 21, 1979

[. . .] The Lives Of Our American Poets: In all his photographs Melville presents a stony gaze, eyes abstracted, not a hint of compliance with the photographer as the world's messenger. . . . You cannot call his appearance "distracted" in the pleasant sense you would attribute to a book worm; it is stony, the face made of the same materials the man writes about. He does take on the color of the world, damn him!

## March 27, 1979

ABSENT FRIENDS The dead vanish to themselves as if they were of no further importance. Yet each year their shadows lengthen, they become bigger somehow, bulkier, more intrusive . . . even more critical: They may not answer me, but they certainly provoke me to interrogation.

The dead writers as absent friends . . . still yammering in your ears, by night even more than by day . . . dropping their smooth, silky poison into the porches of your ears as you lay sleeping.[17] . . . And how these writers, these presences, these menaces, these taking-overs, how they crowd you in one season of your life and disappear in another.

I have to imagine them walking, breathing, crowding, loving, talking to me. Just as I dreamed of Beethoven startled out of his wits by a recording of the Hammerklavier, so I have to describe Blake (and a few others) talking back to the constant reader, the lovelorn reader, the nudnick reader. . . . This is the third who walks beside you[18] as you saunter through the sub metropolitan glades of Highland Park with Bessie from Belmont Avenue.

## April 3, 1979

[. . .] The Fool could have learned more from completely loving one woman than he has ever learned skipping from book to book, life to life.

## April 30, 1979

[. . .] How did this Brooklyn *actor* [Whitman], this street smart journalist, rover, narcissist gain the confidence to sing of "myself." I am large I contain multitudes, *the myth of democracy as limitless personality.*[19]

17. Allusion to the ghost of Hamlet's father describing how he was poisoned by Claudius while asleep: "With juice of cursed hebenon in a vial,/And in the porches of my ears did pour/The leprous distilment" (I, i).
18. "Who is the third who walks always beside you?" from T. S. Eliot's *The Waste Land*, line 359.
19. "I am large; I contain multitudes": section 51 of Whitman's *Song of Myself*.

W's ability to combine, to alternate the feminine and the "male" roles—"loving comrade"—the universe his only one complete lover and that is the poet. Fundamentally, the myth of the *peaceable kingdom,* of American quietism, does depend on a "passively" self-righteous role. . . . Man is a vessel who gets filled with God. In every case this feminine role is a cultural ideal transferred from religious sanctity. . . . The American non-guiltiness (as opposed to primal goodness unexperienced in life) sees the feminine, sees "peace," as a positive ideal. Though it originates as a contrary to the American world of unlimited free enterprise . . . W's favorite metaphor of elusiveness, of flying, of You will hardly know who I am or what I mean,/But I shall be good health to you nevertheless, /And filter and fibre your blood.[20] [. . .]

## May 1, 1979

This loathesome Smerdyakov,[21] who calls me at night, begins with some special insolence, "Hi there, Al," and then proceeds to make some mock-cultural remarks. . . . The trouble with this nightmare type is that even when I take the phone off the hook and try to get back to sleep, the strange suspicion comes up that he is not *real,* that he is an invention I direct against myself. . . . So much peculiar meanness . . . nemesis . . . seems the product of my own fears. . . .

Melville at his big desk, in his dark room: he thought and thought, and finally, as he thought, came to the end of thought.

Thinks in riddles. . . . How he loves to hobble himself in *Clarel*—to give a flash and to be gone.

## May 8, 1979

Lunch with Bellow at the National Arts Club in Chicago.[22] Saul, quiet, very cordial, elegant and precise in his speech and manner. Struck by the difference that the years do *not* make. Sad in a reserved kind of way. Puts things unmistakably without emphasis. The waiters all bowing to him. O Mr. Bellow!

20. "You will hardly know who I am [. . .] blood": from the penultimate stanza of Whitman's *Song of Myself.*
21. A liar and sadist in *The Brothers Karamazov.*
22. Kazin's and Bellow's first meeting after a rupture in their relationship following Kazin's critical review of *Mr. Sammler's Planet* in the *New York Review of Books.* Bellow received the Nobel Prize for literature in 1976.

I asked him what Stockholm was like. He quoted Gregory[23]—"I know St. Peters is the largest thing of its kind but I want to get out of it." I do understand his difficulty in enlarging himself all the way. And I guess the whole quarter of a million or whatever it is, went to *her* lawyers. [. . .]

## June 20, 1979

[. . .] The truth is that I cannot bear to look at *New York Jew*—it all seems to me such a series of reactions to (a series of "provoking" people, Ann being last in the series and somehow the sum of them all). . . . I look at the book now and wail to myself, where am *I*, where is *my* mind, my strong and immortal self? Like the "Jewish tragedy," the war in which this book was born—reaction *to*, flight from, complaint against, instead of some sweet strong solitary affirmation—or as old Walt says, "assurances."

## July 2, 1979

Coming in from the airport, the riot begins: the driver in fury at a slowpoke in front of him, explains that such an asshole driver comes out only on Sundays. "Professionally speaking, one shouldn't drive on Sunday. Who drives on Sunday? Beggars, nuns, old ladies. . . ."

THE NEW YORKER . . . "THE EFFICIENT WAY TO REACH THE TOP"

## July 22, 1979

My only politics seems to be defense of the victim, amnesty, and down with the excesses of the state. . . . But "powerless"? as this may be and even a sacramentalized powerlessness, the ideologies of the right and left remind me of their pseudo-scientific monocausality. The first thing a principle does nowadays, if it is really a principle, is to kill somebody. . . . There must be sacrifices to the "truth," i.e., the formula. Although ideology always includes utopia, the utopia is the end term of a wholly tyrannical way of thinking. . . . [. . .]

*The "New York Book."*[24] New York as the old pleasure ground and culture ground—NY as communists—New York as happiness in the meeting of all

23. Bellow may be referring to Pope Gregory I (c. 540–604), who in 590, while still a monk, was kidnapped and carried off to the (old) basilica of St. Peter and consecrated pope against his will. It is also possible that Bellow is referring to his son Gregory's response to St. Peter's Basilica.
24. *Our New York* (1989).

these *new people*—NY as endless variety—as the good old summertime at Coney Island and Steeplechase and Aurora Park—NY as *initiation*—NY as the *nation in review.*

## July 28, 1979

Wake up, wake up! So tired this a.m. from all these nameless dreams, from counting the score of so many cares. Feel as if I had been trampled by a hundred-volume novel. Spent hours reading Podhoretz's *Breaking the Ranks.*[25] Oh God these little ideological cretins. A whole book to tell you what Diana thought of Jason's thoughts of Lionel's thoughts of William Barrett's thoughts . . . And calls it "politics" when there is nothing, but nothing in it about American *life.* The brutal simplifier! The brutal, little mind of Norman Podhoretz! [. . .]

## August 4, 1979

[. . .] Bach Day on WFMT in Chicago and I am so ravished by the most complete brain in musical history that I hate to turn it off. ANGELIC FORCE . . . to be defined as complete harmony of mind, soul, talent. . . . Where the most perfect artistic intelligence comes out as goodness, gaiety absolute confidence. . . . God prayed for one human mind like Bach to do justice to creation, and Bach prayed that God would just be there.

## August 16 or 17, 1979

Left Notre Dame August 15—arrived New York Aug 16 . . . A long hard pull and now, except for my dear Schwartzie, [what] am I doing in this over-charged, over-populated, over-geschmutzed city. . . . I dare not even write what I feel and fear about our heroine [Ann Birstein], whose sickness, as usual, dominates and occupies everybody. What an uproar she does create. But I do have to put down here, since I am the historian of New York???!!! that one John Halpern put fireworks on top of the tower of Mr. Roebling's bridge,[26] and not only had no Idea that this might cause extreme hurt to someone or other, but described it a) as a piece of sculpture b) as his protest against the government's economic

25. Norman Podhoretz, *Breaking Ranks: A Political Memoir* (New York: Harper and Row, 1979).
26. A twenty-six-year-old artist, John Halpern, was tried and acquitted of planting a bomb, which Halpern called an "environmental sculpture," on top of a tower of the Brooklyn Bridge. The "bomb" proved to be only fireworks that, it was determined, would not have harmed anyone or the bridge.

policy. . . . Here, ladies and gents, we have a perfect illustration of unlimited "consciousness raising."

While speeding my weary way through the mountains of Pennsylvania, I caught a most bewitching evangelist. The performance was remarkable, because the galloping fool mesmerized himself into such rhythmic repetitions that I had the strangest insight into the secret vascular disorder that poetry can be—and because he lingered with such oratorical self-love on his words that when he got to the end of the word "God" he curled it up at the edges, so that it became "Godda."

What Godda wants for you, he pronounced, is for you to understand that he has your life, your destiny, your FATE, entirely in his hands. . . . The message of submission and of God-as-magic-dispensation of EVERYTHING was really remarkable.

## August 20, 1979

What bothers me in New York: not "Christopher Street is our turf," on a Gay leaflet . . . not even the terrible end-of-summer crowds . . . not even the rudeness and off-handedness, except as it relates to my old, aspiring and rejectable self. . . . It is the shuffling old man in the supermarket whom even other old men turn away. . . . It is the reminder of rejection, of being nobody. . . . So it is the blacks playing saxophones in the torrid, Calcutta subway—the drawn, taught, unspeaking faces—everyone on guard. . . . I, yes, "know it all too well"—i.e., I remind myself of my old self at every turn, waiting for the door to open. [. . .]

## August 25, 1979

[. . .] I trotted over to the services at Campbell's Funeral Parlor for Jim Farrell. . . . There was a cross in this theater where I have seen off so many people—Harold Solomon, Harvey Breit, Mark Rothko,[27] Sue Kaufman . . . the theater with the easily arrangeable stage scenery. . . . This time over Jim Farrell!!—a cross . . . Kurt Vonnegut turned out to be a very peppery admirer of Jim's as a social realist—and the critic of the cross . . . "Nice try," he said with

27. Harvey Breit (d. 1968), American poet, playwright, and editor for the *New York Times Book Review*. Mark Rothko (1903–1970), painter known primarily for his abstract forms, who committed suicide in 1968.

old-fashioned bitterness . . . and then, of course, "When he arrives at the pearly gates I am sure he will as always handle himself well."—I am thinking [of] Jim and his works for the *Times,*[28] and realize one thing to stress is his hold on the "common reader."

Farrell was always at his best writing about "hard times," writing out of hard times. . . . When the terrible grip of old fashioned American capitalism releases its hold on him he has only a very soupy language for the emotions. [. . .]

His prime "political" insight was the common man as consumer, the fool of the commercial, the illusions created . . . *An American Tragedy* . . . but he never saw himself as a "leader" of opinion or sided with the "leaders"—which is why he would remain a radical.

The consumer psychology, nevertheless, leads to American pathos—the little man squeezed to death, no language for his desires but the one They provide. [. . .]

## September 27, 1979

Tour with David Finn, ending in Brownsville and then Brooklyn Heights. When you get a little removed, just a *little* removed, the ant-heap and the ant-struggle somehow don't seem so inflictive on the old memory. I didn't recognize Chester Street at all—the old shul looks as if it had been left to burn down. My old block on Sutter Avenue has been completely eviscerated, nothing but rubble, brick. . . . Pitkin Avenue looks like those hastily rebuilt lines of sheds in post-war Cologne. . . . And everywhere, black, black, black . . . black all over everything and black all the time . . .

I felt *nothing* all the way. . . . It is present New York, the inextricable mix, that gets me. Finn Minn Tinn the quiet p. r. man with the cigar and the Jaguar. . . . What interested me was the studious non-reaction of the driver, Howard, a nice North Carolina black, slightly hard of hearing. . . . Eastern Parkway and Kingston, the Lubavitcher chassidim . . . spread over a lot of houses. . . . Two young questioned us about David's picture taking. One of them had that virginal pink face and pink nose (framed in ear locks) that I always associate with the yeshivah bocher blinking his eyes as he rises out of the Talmud.

28. "James T. Farrell, 1904–1979," *New York Times Book Review* (September 16, 1979): 9, 30.

"It is because so much happens. Too much happens." I am pressed on every side by New York and by all the opportunities, commissions, temptations, etc. Pressed. . . . Last night to the YMHA to hear a cellist Frederick Zlotkin ruin the Bach sonatas. . . . The performer was a dud, but the audience was great—so many attentive, "cultured," young people, so much attention!! The culture rite of New York. . . . And all those dark, breathy streets to make my way past . . . loaded with my load of books-books-books.

## October 7, 1979

Didion aroused by Mailer's death book. Didion is excited by terminal feelings, and fills up the front page of today's *Book Review* by extending her usual end-of-everything traumas to the whole West. But these elegies are usually put into the snappiest possible prose, and that is the key to contemporary "smartness." End of the Road, but snap, snap, snap to the measure. [. . .]

## December 13, 1979

[. . .] [Yaddo lunch] Malamud, as always, so stiff that he unconsciously struts. Something humorous in a novelist with this much flexibility of imagination being proper looking to the point of being peremptory . . . A fundamental alienation there. His stiffness would amuse me if it weren't so pompous. . . . Cheever with beautiful hair, marvelous NE accent, all social wit and wisdom, comes running into the lunch with such effect. . . . Robert Gorham Davis seems to be losing his teeth, jaw wags. . . . The immovable Gordon Ray.[29] The "development" man from the firm of Alexander and Alexander, Mr. Oakes. . . . I was deeply impressed by the rich, wise, knowing, and very plainspoken Alexander Aldrich,[30] whom they call Sam, and gave the development boys what-for.

I do admire the Wasp way of telling someone off in a perfectly low measured voice. All facts, sir! You are a fraud, sir!

## January 6, 1980

[. . .] My besetting anxiety and confusion: that the creative mind can and perhaps [does] act for itself alone. That there is no "order," no equivalence, no balancing out in this world of disparate minds. . . . In the subway, my heart pent up with the

29. Gordon Ray, president of the Guggenheim Foundation.
30. Alexander Aldrich, attorney with the firm of Helm, Shapiro, Ayers, Anito and Aldrich, city attorney for Sarasota Springs.

ugliness, the craziness, the despair, I think that if I lash out I will make my protest help recreate the balance of the world. . . . No, we think alone as we die alone. . . . We think for the sake of thinking as we die for the sake of life carrying on. . . . There is no final summing up. There is no "justice." That was my childhood dream, that things would work out. . . . Think of it, my best thoughts may go unheard! [. . .]

## January 24, 1980

An evening with the immortals of the Academy Institute on far off West 155th street. Lillian Hellman tottered up to read her tribute to Janet Flanner but could not continue because of her recent eye operation. . . . In a heated discussion whether the Institute should move from its regal but somehow inaccessible building, Ralph Ellison gave me and everybody else fits by reciting his life in his most beautiful tenor voice, lingering auspiciously on every closing syllable and made it clear that words come first, sense comes after. . . . At the end of my little tribute to Jim Farrell, bright, up-with-it Shirley Hazzard wanted englishy to know what other writers take for granted in Chekhov's saying that what other writers take for granted the writer from the lower classes pays for with his youth. Honey, it's money! But I desisted. Oh the bright, alert worldliness of Miss Hazzzzzzard. . . .

What a tedious embarrassing evening . . . what bores these immortals are . . . no one in sight under 58, and most amusing to me, Madam President, Barbara Tuchman,[31] rasped like the most officious yenta, interrupting, chiding, underlining. . . .

The contrast between the ride up, those tired, huddled masses breathing to be free, the crowd yanked out at 137th Street, then rushed back in again to the train to continue its way to heavenly 158th Street . . . the contrast between the withered academicians and the worried mass in the subway cattle car. . . .

As Francis [Hazzard] Steegmuller finished reading the Hellman paper for her, she lay with her head back, her eyes covered in thickness of glasses. . . . I shall never forget the bitterness in that face. To be 75, to be in danger of losing your eyes, and to feel that all your youth is with you as a writer's often is. . . .

And trouble deaf heaven with my. . . .[32]

31. Barbara Tuchman (1912–1989), American historian, best known for *The Guns of August*, which won the Pulitzer Prize for general nonfiction in 1963.
32. The complete line from Shakespeare's Sonnet 29 reads: "And trouble deaf heaven with my bootless cries."

## January 31, 1980

Moved out of 14th Street last night and am sitting here by the window, by the desk, by the phone, by my book . . . Alles in Ordnung [everything is fine] . . . so why sitting on the can, going through the daily motions, do I suddenly weep? The sculptor who moved me, John Sanders, said to the noise of his truck pounding in our ears, "New York is a hard town." He loves the hard town. Sculptors in stone, in metal. . . . Why do I weep? Because it is hard for me to give up *anything*. The sheer physical necessity, to say nothing of the moral necessity, to make a choice: I try to overlook. . . . But it will not be overlooked. Thou must renounce!

## June 24, 1980

The writer is not the legislator, not the creator-demiurgo of value (this is what drove Nietzsche crazy). He is the restorer, in part, in very small part. And his restoration (Sartre is a prime, glorious example in our time) may see the future in one direction, while he is helping to create it in another by creating a public of *minds*.

Deconstructionism deconstructs the I as an organized entity, projects onto language structure what really belongs to individual mind.

Superego "The division of the psyche that develops by the incorporation of the perceived moral standards of the community, is mainly unconscious, and includes the conscience."[33]

Writers are *actives*, never passives. The momentum of language put into action is to *change* things.

## August 14, 1980

I am daily tormented by these political monsters—a monster is someone who wants to inflict an extreme ideological fixation on someone else. But my politics consists in thought, not practice; which means that I shiveringly oppose fanatics but do nothing myself. I stay out. I do not even know whether I shall vote, though I do feel a great need to vote against that would-be monster R. Reagan.

33. Kazin is quoting the *American Heritage Dictionary*.

Saul Steinberg, who is all "European" still, said that he hated Roumania, long a colony of Turkey, because the Roumanians thought of themselves as a crooked colony and having to do crooked things.

S. noted a little complacently, that Harold Rosenberg didn't know whether to take him as a "greenhorn" or as a new arrival from—Paris.

## August 24, 1980
### [dated May 24]

The Big Event[34] . . . drove out in handsome, August sunshine to the "estate" of the Horowitzes—well nigh 150 people, endless refreshments, blue napkins, rock band (which ended up with Havah Negileh and Dayenu)—relatives, ex-wives, sister, daughter. . . . Oh my, what a day for my son and Beth Carrie to get married on, and what a spectrum of feelings I went through between 1:40 when I arrived and some 7 or 8 hours later when I at last retired from the fray. . . . Mario[35] took over briefly as father of the bridegroom when the cake was being cut; marvelous to see what a cocky, brash, little fellow Carol has been devoted to all this time. . . . Ann made a lot of emotional, imploring faces. . . . Kate was stocky, over-blond, "strong"—I was amused to see her irritation when to Mario, of all people, I discoursed on the lack of acquaintance with literachoor among the peepul. . . .

Anyway, Michael and Beth looked just lubberly, and I was desperately glad to get back to Judith. God bless my children and God bless the Constitution of the U.S. and Down with Ronald Reagan and so what else is new? I am back to Henry James in THE BOOK. Pray for me now and in the hour of our consummation.

What a milestone Mike's marriage signifies for me—I feel as if I have been lurched ahead to a point on life's horizon where I did not expect to get but which is so far ahead that I am excited even by the contraction of time it represents.

THE WEDDING . . . Michael's mother and father looking at each other in ill-concealed distaste . . . Michael's mother very genial and matronly all through the event, a ready, cordial, expectant smile unfailing on her lips. Rich uncles

34. Wedding of Michael Kazin and Beth Horowitz.
35. Mario Salvadori (1907–1997), Michael's stepfather, professor of civil engineering and architecture at Columbia University.

of the bride, great-uncles I should say, coming up to me (whom they didn't know from Adam and Eve) boasting of how long a journey they had made to arrive here. Grand uncles introducing themselves, somehow, not so much by name and affiliation as by the air of hard won prosperity that is the real laurel wreath hanging over a Jewish wedding. . . . Mutters from Joe Birstein about the source of the bridal papa's wealth that had made this lavishness possible etc., etc.—What I noticed most rising to my gorge in this recital is my ridiculous ressentiment. . . . If ever a man had reason to be grateful these days c'est moi. . . . And so (it now being 5 PM and time to get back to my Dreiser studies) I do, and at last sign off with malice toward none . . . And may it be so. . . .

## September 10, 1980

Harold Clurman died.[36] Gabby dear Harold, who would start talking a block away as soon as he saw you, and with that adenoidal, gasping rush, rush voice (not unlike Mailer's) would wrap you round and round in talk. Everything had to be explained, *settled* right now. . . .

## November 2, 1980

I am haunted by Sir Isaiah [Berlin], The Court Jew who always knew *everybody* at the top and who still makes me quiver with resentment when I think of the snubbing I received from his unseeing back at the Santa Caterina Amalfi [Hotel] in 1947. But all this childish resentment apart, I have to confess my fascination with the intelligence of the man as well as his social resourcefulness. From the moment he was named Isaiah, a certain magic fell upon him! Every honor and great chance fell his way including such a late date marriage with a daughter or granddaughter of a Russian Jewish baron. Sir Isaiah O.M.—the conversationalist—the social star—but also the friend of liberty, the noble Russian Jew sprung from an ethical tradition that he *has* carried on.

I am tired of feeling small—of harking back so much to my own ghetto beginnings—tired of the litany of struggle—tired of so much envy and resentment. I write all this to discharge my self-sickening bile. *Basta!*

The *Fascination* Of Sir Isaiah. At last I come to the point. The name, the background, the intelligence, the social resourcefulness and, yes, what Elena

36. Harold Clurman (1901–1980), founder and director of the Group Theatre in the thirties, husband of Stella Adler, friend of Kazin.

Wilson used to praise as the "niceness," the thoroughgoing Jewish idealism—all this has made him a compelling figure to Englishmen, Jews, Russians, and the like. . . . And, as he smilingly confirmed the story about Churchill and "I. Berlin," he enjoys his own legend.

97th Street—birds wheeling and pivoting, low, between the buildings.

## November 6, 1980

[. . .] The shock of RR's election has been absorbed by me. . . . I recognize that business is business, money rules the roost, and am sort of looking forward to Ronnie's presidency: it puts things into ascertainable order. . . . No question that Carter's fumbling style was depressing us all. . . .

"The New Deal is over at last." In 1980. . . .

Something must be noted about Podhoretz's contempt for merely "domestic" issues. . . . I quote from an interview in the *Book Digest.* Like Kristol, NP is also down on the "intellectuals" as a class—claims in the *Digest* (December 80) that "there developed a new ambition. It was actually to be recognized as a group best able to govern, a new ruling elite.

"I think we have a whole new intellectual culture developing of which I consider myself a part. . . . We tend to be part of what I call the 'New Nationalism,' an aggressively positive attitude toward this country, its culture and its role in the world."

"What does Reagan think? He's been very cordial to me . . ."

## February 18, 1981

One advantage of getting "old." So many people do not share my past that I am unexpectedly free to invent it—even to seem to occupy it. And the cultural lag *parmi les jeunes* [*among the young*] not only gives me "authority," but for a brief moment allows me to deceive them, confuse them, as well as to just plain puzzle them.

## February 19, 1981

Pursued all night by the furies of do this do that . . . I dream of "not caring." Lord! Lord! Oasis dear in the midst of Reaganland, Podhoretzland,

Brezhnevland![37] Teach me not to care, teach me to sit still! Teach me to float off at my ease—to "play it!" whether cool or not. . . . Having tried so long and so hard to reach the goal, and having gone so far beyond the piss pool off the men's room in the Rockaway Avenue station, I now find myself doing all this, doing it and doing it—and to what avail? So I dream of that perfect trip to the fjords, to the house with the lake, to the Bach unaccompanied flute sonatas, to being *in* her all day and night, to that day in Rome amidst the plane trees, stopping for a cool dry wine on my way back from the Vatican museum . . . and above all, Lord! Lord! to having enough time. . . . I have never felt so excitedly, so blissfully alive until now, when the numbers begin to press on me.

And the dearest dream of all, to have it all back again—to have it *all*, not to sacrifice! Lord! Lord! indeed . . . The open mouth pressed against the window pane. [. . .]

## March 7, 1981

Ugly Duckling. I talked to her a lot—just talked. . . . She became the survivor. "Shana"[38] was picked up in a raid and murdered in a ditch. The Ugly Duckling always had a lot to say about handsome, attractive ladies *close to her* like Shana, Sophie, Paula, etc. But in the end she was the "Survivor" and through her son, still is there . . . still dominates. . . . He talks to her a lot . . . the old fellow in his 60s, or even his 70s! Still measures other women by her . . . by her famous moral superiority. . . . [. . .]

We could end on fifteen-year-old Sadie Tolmach in the summer of 1931 . . . whom I saw just that summer, madly caressing her breasts on the hilltop overlooking the reservoir in Highland Park. . . . I haven't seen her for 50 years; and I can't forgive myself, the 16-year-old virgin and nincompoop, for not having enough imagination to sleep with her. . . . I can't forget her scorn . . . her elusiveness, how she skipped out of life! What Sadie comes to in the end is so much thinking of her . . . of that 15-year-old, of old Brooklyn—what might have been! First Encounter Beach. [. . .]

Gita, who railed against the police during evictions and helped put the furniture back.

*I was formed in perfect sympathy for her* . . . and alas, for suffering women, not for proud and happy women—

37. Leonid Ilyich Brezhnev (1906–1982), general secretary of the Communist Party of the Soviet Union and the political leader of the country, from 1964 to 1982.
38. Shana, Gita Fagelman's attractive sister, was murdered by the Nazis.

Her body, like my feet, tokens of a bygone primitive era—*fossils.*

Hannah the intellectual, the visionary intellectual, the God seeker, who wrote of politics as The Great Fall,[39] longed for the "public world"—expressing the most private vision.

## March 27, 1981

Friday morning. Leslie Farber,[40] dead of a heart attack at Roosevelt Hospital. A sudden death? A great shock to me. What a dear wise if sad man he was in the last years—and what a change from the peppery hard-drinking rather mettlesome fellow I remember in some restaurant in the Village during the war years. He was all occupied with dear Marjorie in those years—a scrappy unhappy couple they were.[41] Then she went into a Big Decline.

Leslie—a sharp fellow but also seeking a logos—even by way of Martin Buber! He makes me think of Rioch and "you don't know what goes on upstairs"—the lonely analyst, the self-contained painter in Provincetown, the daughter of medical missionaries in India. . . .

## April 16, 1981

Fifty years ago this Spring! Walking down that wide sidewalk from Columbus to Amsterdam on 97th Street, I suddenly felt in the puff of warm air that has at last had the decency to appear in this neighborhood that I was walking those heavy, sunlit, wide, clean streets, Bushwick Ave, Evergreen Ave, the happy graduation spring of 1931. 1931 is an obviously improbable date to remember just now, but I remember every detail of Julian Aronson's[42] kindness to me, playing the Kreisler recording of the Brahms concerto, beginning to write. All that . . . And Highland Park. All that . . . What I have most fixed in my mind just now, however, is the clean, empty, *available* sidewalk. [. . .]

39. Kazin is referring not to a book but to "the fall" or "the break" in the Western traditions, a recurrent concern in Arendt's writing.
40. Kazin's psychoanalyst in the early 1970s.
41. James Atlas in *Bellow* (New York: Random House, 2000), 86–87, writes that Marjorie Farber was having an affair at the time with Saul Bellow.
42. High school history teacher who encouraged Kazin in his writing.

## May 14, 1981

Alan Wald, assistant professor at Ann Arbor,[43] a sort of historian of the Left—wrote a book on Jim Farrell as a "revolutionary socialist." Is interviewing old timers for a book on the Anti-Stalinist Left . . . A long pleasant argument with him at the Grad Center. Felt every time I was talking about the past that I was talking into the *air*, he was so solemn and militantly left. The inevitable arguments turned him a bit churlish. [. . .] But what struck me more than [anything] else: [I] felt when I was talking about the 30s and such prehistoric periods as if I were a novelist writing a novel, making it all up . . . His own mind so abstract that the notion of these old Commies and anti-Commies as being led by intellectual *pride* really astonished him.

## May 19, 1981

Absent Friends indeed . . . People I brushed against and never took into my soul, much as it would have been difficult with an almost Hahvud man crying "Heel, Clovis!" but (and what the devil was his name?) Varian Fry[44] of course, hurray for Varian Fry, whose wife was Eileen, daughter of that heavy English couple in Provincetown. Varian Fry, succeeded me on the *NR* literary desk, and who, unbeknownst to me until the Washington conference on exiles from Nazism last year, turned out to have been the Scarlet Pimpernel of his time, rescuing Jews and lefties from occupied France because *his manner was so perfect, his accent so good*. . . . I never saw the man for that manner, that accent!

## June 16, 1981

Tuesday a.m.—THEY MADE IT . . . GRANDEUR AND MISERY OF THE JEWS, 1981!!

Visit to Bashevis the Singer for photographs by David Finn and daughter.[45] A big dusty apartment (no curtains overlooking Broadway) . . . Singer in a ridiculous thin-lapelled suit and dark tie looking as if he were on line to see his Creator. His "chaos" room, which Alma calls the "garbage" room, is lined with endless certificates, diplomas, testimony to his various honors . . . even

43. Alan Wald, author of seven books on the American left in the twentieth century, is currently H. Chandler Davis Collegiate Professor of English Literature at the University of Michigan.
44. Varian Fry (1907–1967) rescued Jews from Nazi Europe. In a December 1942 issue of the *New Republic*, he published "The Massacre of Jews in Europe," documenting the slaughter of Europe's Jews.
45. For *Our New York*.

framed certificates from some Jewish lawyers' group and election to the National Institute and the American Academy of Arts and Sciences . . .

I found him cagey, depressed, full of tiny little jokes and unexpected jealousies (Solzhenitsyn[46] has hundreds of acres in Vermont, is a millionaire; but, of course, the Jews do not want unlimited acreage, just a bankbook—so they can go off lightly when the trouble comes.)

The Jews, the Jews, the Jews—the repetition of it sometimes drives me mad—from Begin even to our latest martyr Timerman.[47] . . . Why is it harder for a Jew to forget that he is a Jew than it is even for a black? Because of all that history, no doubt, the tug of the past . . .

In any event, the present period of Jewish "success" will some day be remembered as one of the greatest irony . . . The Jews caught in a trap, the Jews murdered, and bango! Out of ashes all this inescapable lament and exploitation of the Holocaust . . . Israel as the Jews' "safeguard"; the Holocaust as our new Bible, more than a Book of Lamentations . . .

Add Liebling[48]—"Sheenies who are meanies." (the *New Yorker*'s hatred of the "intellectual.")

## August 18, 1981

Became owner of Roxbury House. Great closing ceremonies at offices of Woodbury Bank's lawyer James Ryan. In these small towns everybody knows everybody else, so everybody knew where to find Mr. Ryan, though nobody had an exact address. A great outpouring of checks. Those vultures Howard

46. Aleksandr Isayevich Solzhenitsyn (1918–2008), Russian novelist, dramatist, and historian, best known for *The Gulag Archipelago* and *One Day in the Life of Ivan Denisovich*, winner of Nobel Prize in Literature in 1970. He was exiled from Russia in 1974 and returned in 1994.

47. Menachem Begin (1913–1992), the sixth prime minister of Israel, signed a peace treaty with Egyptian President Anwar Sadat in 1979 for which they shared the Nobel Peace Prize. Jacobo Timerman (1923–1999), an Argentinean Jew, who described his imprisonment and torture by the Argentine government in *Prisoner Without a Name, Cell Without a Number*, reviewed by Kazin in *New Republic* (June 1981): 32–34.

48. A. J. Liebling (1904–1963), who wrote for the *New Yorker* and disliked the company of the Upper West Side intellectuals, refused to attend a party at the Kazins' because "sheenies who are meanies will be there." The quotation is from Raymond Sokolov's *Wayward Reporter: The Life of A. J. Liebling* (New York: Harper and Row, 1980), 310.

and Probst,[49] may they perish, stripped the house bare. Somehow, thanks to Judith, the shock was not as bad as I had expected when I heard the news first from David Gordon. But there will be so much time, money, energy, and above all self-control expected from this unruly and incompetent house owner that I feel quite stunned.

Roxbury and environs are beautiful. The grass is growing wild around my house, but for the first time in my life I own a house. I pray for calmness, proportion, sense.

## October 8, 1981

On the way to this big bash thrown by John Russell[50] at "Glorious Food," a fancy caterer who also provides little dinner parties for THOSE IN THE KNOW, Judy and I were, of course and always, too early. [. . .] The dinner party was full of celebs. . . . I like John Russell and I like Rosamund Russell,[51] but I hadn't anticipated their being quite so "In"—Jackie herself, Irene Worth, Frankie Fitzgerald, actors, actresses, the head of the Morgan, etc. I was talking, drinking, talking, eating, and even though Judy hung back I could see that she too was fascinated by the show.

Of course came too early. We always do.

John Russell has this great gift of enlisting you in his stammer, drawing you in to his stammer. Unlike the repellant grimaces of say a struggling stammerer like Ted Hoagland,[52] John's necessary face movements expresses the most wonderful, affectionate, enclosing pantomime. All wonderful, wonderful, wonderful! he seems to be saying. Wonderful of you to come, wonderful to see you! And he is a *good* man. . . . But another such party and I will die.

Jackie looked so much like Jackie that I thought for a moment it was an actress playing Jackie. The face has become as professional as an actress's.

49. Maureen Howard and Mark Probst, previous owners of the house.
50. John Russell (1919–2008), art critic for the *New York Times*.
51. Rosamond [Bernier] Russell, much-admired lecturer on the arts and fashion who gave frequent talks at the Metropolitan Museum of Art.
52. Edward Hoagland (1932–), writer known for his nature and travel writing, was a student of Kazin's at Harvard in 1953.

## October 25, 1981

The House is wonderful, a great release (as well as a great expense) . . . 24 degrees when we woke this morning. . . . Thinking of the House reminds me of their Houses: Emerson's clerical gown he wore for lectures—how little Dickinson refers to the inside of her house, though many of the famous "symbols" are undoubtedly about rooms and passageways in her house—Whitman's rootlessness and slovenliness about any particular habitation he happened to find himself in—Melville's attempt at some kind of "dignity" and status in E. 26th St. (not to forget Eleanor Metcalf's description of his iron bed in one room and Elizabeth's white covered bed in another).[ . . .]

Like Van Wyck's grand corner central house in Bridgewater—like Hawthorne in the Old Manse—like Poe forever seeking a house—like Dreiser on the upper West Side writing *Sister Carrie* or like Eliot seeking our Old Home—like Pound the eternal Bohemian in Rapallo. [. . .]

TALKING OF HOUSES! Thoreau's hut, or is it the road that was his real home and the shift to the overstuffed mansion of Mark Twain in Hartford—William Dean Howells on Beacon Street (not to forget the mansions on Beacon Hill of Parkman, Prescott, Lowell).[53] Craigie House in Cambridge.

Henry Adams across from the White House—James in hotel rooms all over Europe—then Eliot in London lodgings. . . .[54]

## December 21, 1981

Katie in and looking marvelous, fresh, clean in soul . . . hair old-fashionedly long, barrette fastening the still reddish blonde locks. . . . As she says, Iowa has been a fantastically lucky thing for her.[55] . . . Sitting in the Swiss something

53. Francis Parkman (1823–1893), American historian, author of *The Oregon Trail: Sketches of Prairie and Rocky-Mountain Life* and *France and England in North America;* William Hickling Prescott (1796–1859), American historian of nineteenth-century America; James Russell Lowell (1819–1891), American poet and critic, professor of languages at Harvard, editor of the *Atlantic Monthly*.
54. In a November 15, 1981 entry, Kazin thinks of another comparison: "Everything very o.k. though the house (living room by the stove) can be taken for a broken down Southern mansion in [William Faulkner's] *Absalom! Absalom!*"
55. Cathrael ("Katie") Kazin had earned a Ph.D. in English at Cornell University and was at the time an assistant professor of English at the University of Iowa. She would give up that position to earn a law degree at the University of Pennsylvania.

restaurant on East 40th, facing the library (Kate virtually the only female in this hard packed herd of young businessmen—terrible rush, terrible food, but both of us happy to be together), I talked of the strange fated place, that Iowa has been in my family's life, remembered Sophie cooped up for years in far off Clarinda,[56] the letters Pearlie and I used to write with dreary dutifulness to the Superintendant of the Asylum . . . and somehow the connection between long dead Sophie and Kate? K says that waking up one morning and putting on the radio, what should she hear but a tape (which I do not remember having made) of [my] reading the Sophie story from *Starting Out in the Thirties*. . . . [. . .]

## January 21, 1982

Judith is my happiness. Judith is the warm bed, the ready word, the endless interest. The world is not only snowy and cold, day after day this horrid winter; the world is evil, and will not get less so. But Judith is the middle of the world, the word within the world. Last night, in an absolute fever of merriment as we were going down on the Columbus Avenue bus to the concert at Alice Tully, I suddenly had a flash: sometime in the late 30s, on a quiet, near-empty bus with Asya, myself enjoying the total quiet, the unexpectedness of that bus, Lexington Avenue or some such. In the middle of the New York mess, I thought *then,* here *we* are! And so it was last night in the bus.

Incredible luck. Let me for once be clever enough to sustain it. [. . .]

## February 5, 1982

Friday morning. Chill, chill, especially from slit mouth Ronnie our terrorist president. The great liberal Kazin, who wants no one to be harmed and is perpetually astonished by every show of meanness, greed, violence, and general duplicity, is just an observer, a *bloody book reviewer,* when it comes to reading the noospaper. All these moneyed gangsters and friends of other moneyed gangsters! . . . and it all passes before my eyes with a cluck, cluck.

This looking, this mere looking-on, is becoming a disease. After a day's work of reading and commenting on other people's works and lives, I look on as the little puppy dogs do their commercials and acts on tee vee. I look on as slit mouth Ronnie utters more and more of his totally lying crap—I look on (this is

56. See Chapter 1, note 56.

pornography spreading from the cunt to the capital) at the strap off the shoulder, come hither glance on the cover of *Playboy*. . . .

## February 16, 1982

NY hospital—arrived midnight February 10, a day and an hour that will live in infamy.[57]

Today, Tuesday morning 16, February 82, first time the old head is even clear enough to put down date and whereabouts. Suffered minor heart damage. Bloody intensive care unit—monitoring—endless record-keeping. Helots staring at EKG screens and keeping records. Science fiction—needs helots and a lot of technical equipment. Above all, *an army of obedience.*

They are trained, as slit-mouth Ronnie would say, knee jerk "liberals." Only—they are not "liberals" at all. [. . .]

## April 21, 1982

There was nothing A. MacLeish turned to that he did not turn into still another success.[58] And when you survive the hollowness of his poetry, of his speeches, of his successive ideas as conservative—New Dealer—anti-Fascist, etc., etc.—you realize that what he had was "eloquence," the ability to speak to large groups of people from some vaguely distinctive upper class place of his own. He had enormous charm, Archie did, great presence, ease; but above all he knew how to address the public in everything that could be made a matter of public concern. In a positive sense he was the poet as politician, the poet in the public place. And this was an advantage, natural to his liberal era and his advantageous upbringing, that a great many more talented poets today have no notion of at all. . . . At *Fortune,* at Harvard, at the Library of Congress, he was somehow in the center, not skulking in the closet.

## April 27, 1982

Much concerned with Hannah ever since the *NY Review* asked me to review the Young-Bruehl biography.[59] Thinking over our whole strange and truncated friendship over the years, the volatility as well as the nobility, the conceit and the vulnerability, the Prussian egotismus and the soulfulness, the real love of God,

57. Kazin suffered a heart attack after arriving at the hospital.
58. The poet Archibald MacLeish died April 20, 1982.
59. "Woman in Dark Times," *New York Review of Books* (June 24, 1982): 3–4, 6.

I realize that her fond quotation from Augustine, "Love means that I want you to be," is more than ever my firmest and most grateful connection with her. It is this concern with being and her fright in the Nazi experience of not-being, of all our not being, that I remember best. . . . And of course her *fame* as a teacher and exponent of political wisdom in the American context. How grateful we all were to her, how much her crisis thinking seemed to us something altogether new and deep in our lives—McCarthy's addiction to her, like the addiction of so many, really based on *our* political anxiety. . . . Which Arendt shared with an intensity beyond us, but which she complemented with her extension of anxiety into thought relatively scarce in the pragmatic day to day, ad hoc American contest.

Her judgments became pretty ad hoc too, but she could always put them into a wider and deeper context.

The friendships based on political anxiety—on the sense of fright. . . . The usual academic spectatoritis was outside of this—she never achieved a "new science of politics," anymore than anybody else did, but she did offer us who were frightened a new vista—couched in the language that took its inspiration from the extensiveness of German idealism. [. . .]

## May 28, 1982

[. . .] AMS[chlesinger] Jr. greeted me as he appeared on the 15th floor. Expressed "concern" about my illness. Arthur always blunts my exasperation with him by being a perfect gent.

## June 17, 1982

[. . .] F. Steegmuller would have grimaced. S. Hazzard would not have noticed. But my obsession with the Steegmullers, night and day, is really becoming sick. How I hate to lose old friends, if only because they are connected with the Ann period! And how I hate recognizing F's snubs and little faggy airs of distaste. . . . Heart burnings undeniable, but over what?? Reminds me of the put down I experienced chez David—Ruth Glass in Lunnon during the war. Really, I am absurd in my fear and horror of "breaks," yet of course I have made more breaks with the gentry than they have made with me. 67 years old and I haven't changed a bit, except externally! Deep resentment and even bitterness—yet I have to sit down to write this in order to clear my mind even a little of all the . . . *burning*. Truly, *I* have done the breaking, and I must accept that unexpected view of my own assertiveness and even harshness. . . .

## June 29, 1982

[. . . ] Old Saki B[60] for dinner last night and good talk from him about the behaviorists at Stanford Center "taking over the world." I knew exactly what he was getting at—the current realists always give you *evidence* based on selections from the outside world. And you are supposed to react to the stimulus. *There is nothing else in the picture.*

Saki is wonderfully naive about himself, however; seems amazed that in getting psychoanalyzed (for the first time, age 46) he is being relieved of the usual child self-centeredness. Says he is truly monogamous and romantic, and doesn't want to flit about. Asks my advice religiously! Yet he is also sly on occasion and related a story about ABK at Stanford, when they had invited me to take the Cole chair, getting into a flurry with a gent at a dinner party, insisted that she was not Mrs. Kazin but Ann Birstein, and when the gent was properly ironic, told him to fuck himself. Ann is always a lot of trouble, isn't she, even in apocrypha?

I finally got Saki out of the house by offering a walk. We walked up Broadway to about 108th, and then he walked me back. Like old times? Hah—the streets positively *smelled* of menace. [. . .]

## August 23, 1982

[. . .] Dinner at Arthur Miller's—the adorable, beautiful Barbara Ungeheuer[61] in a red dress—quite lost my heart to her again. . . . Inge Morath[62] talks in a kind of yell—the conversation of Jews at the prosperous dinner table with ex-Germans! Friedl Ungeheuer, an economics writer for *Time,* quick, efficient English, light charm, very knowing about everything, talking about being a boy during the war. Frau Ungeheuer, of noble Catholic lineage, carefully explaining that a relative died in Dachau and that her father kept a low profile during the war as a farmer in the Black Forest.

Arthur M. with his 400 acres! Lost on his own property recently. Benignly overseeing the evening feasts. I like Arthur, have always liked him, for being so plain and doggedly honest—for being so business-like, which helps to explain

60. Sacvan Bercovitch (1933–), professor of American literature at Harvard.
61. Barbara Ungeheuer, wife of Friedel Ungeheuer, economic correspondent for *Time.*
62. Inge Morath (1923–2003), photographer and wife of playwright Arthur Miller (1915–2005).

why I like plays about business—and corruption. But who would guess from his stolid demeanor that he sees life as a stage performance??

## October 16, 1982

So what does this anxious sleeper brood over in the infamous watches of the night? Why he is not more famous, not a "celebrity" like Other People. He nudges other people in these broodings, complains, tries to make things right, desists for a moment and then starts over.

ABSENT FRIENDS! The dead (Hofstadter, Schorer, Leslie Farber). The renegades to the extreme right (Allan Weinstein, Lucy D., Norman Podhoretz, etc. Types he has never liked, like Leslie Fiedler, Capote, Vidal). Old wives and sweethearts/Asya . . . Haughty betrayers—Steegmuller . . . Bureaucrats: Barzun, Kappy Kaplan. Bureaucrats—Jason [Epstein], Anne Freedgood . . . police officials (Arnold Beichman). Celebrities—never in his orbit—Updike, Schlesinger. People he has mocked and betrayed: Leon Edel, the sculptress. Actors playing the Holocaust circuit: Wiesel. Actress playing lit—Sontag—Rae Brooks/bitterness personified: John Brooks.[63]

The Double Women: The Doll (Sue Kaufman) and the Sleepless Night (Elizabeth Hardwick). Peter Davison—but the serene death, Jane Davison, so tremulous when I knew her—so brave sitting before the rock in which she now lies. Mighty Hannah.[64] [. . .]

People like Barzun and Trilling, no democrats as cf. with a really democratic and eager soul like Edmund W. [. . .]

63. Lucy S. Dawidowicz (1915–1990), historian, best known for her account of the Holocaust, *The War against the Jews, 1933–1945* (1975). Truman Capote (1924–1984), novelist and short story writer, best known for his "nonfiction novel" *In Cold Blood* (1966), was a friend more of Ann Birstein's than of Kazin's. Harold ("Kappy") Kaplan, journalist and chief press officer of the United States in Paris during the postwar years. Kazin visited with him on his trips to Paris. Anne Freedgood, editor at Random House. Rae Brooks, book reviewer for *Harper's*.

64. Elizabeth Hardwick (1916–2007), American literary critic, essayist, novelist, and short story writer and cofounder of the *New York Review of Books*, was married to the poet Robert Lowell. She and Kazin remained friends for most of the time they knew each other. Jane Davison was a student of Kazin's at Smith College and later married Peter Davison, Kazin's friend and editor at Little, Brown.

## January 9, 1983

Plaza Hotel meeting of these righteous neo-conservatives offers another chance to play "Swift."[65] In a society so tumultuous with corruption of every kind, when money is the constant on everyone's lips, when the most frightful sacrifices are exacted of the marginal people for the sake of national "defense" (more Orwell newspeak), it is truly wonderful to think of a political avant-garde leagued with the government and propagandizing for "democratic capitalism." And talking of the "Free World" as if the phrase ennobled people instead of directing them to what is flagrantly not-free in the current world, in America itself. [. . .]

## January 18, 1983

For the Plaza piece: it more and more appears that these ideological conservatives are examples of the Marxist belief that ideology is just the window dressing for power. Power in America, economic, social, financial, corporate—money as the bloodstream without which we do not do for a moment—money the one constant on everybody's mind—and yet these jabberwockies see themselves as influencing people? No, they are simply in a warfare with other intellectuals. The whole thing is a sideshow to the reality of American power. Intellectuals just cross with other intellectuals on the usual plane: if you don't agree with my key to salvation, you must burn, for you are threatening me with extinction.[. . .]

## January 21, 1983

[. . .] The Plaza piece will have a smashing end: Andropov[66] in the Kremlin is shaking in his boots because of the power of anti-Communism displayed by Midge [Decter] and friends at the Plaza. But actually, the real point of the conference will be that "we are two nations." Tom Brokaw on Channel 4 visibly shudders (let us say grows becomingly sad) as the screen shows an outstretched man on the sidewalk at Madison Avenue in 12 degrees January cold. But just as the Midges worry about AMS. Jr. saying benevolent things about Russia, so the whole point of the conference will be the middleclassness, the sheltered

65. "Saving My Soul at the Plaza," *New York Review of Books* (March 31, 1983): 38–42.
66. Yuri Vladimirovich Andropov (1914–1984), general secretary of the Communist Party of the Soviet Union from 1982 to 1984.

bourgeois insularity—exactly the same thing that promotes feminism and other middle class professional passions.

Thomas Powers[67]—the current period is one of preparation for war.

## February 18, 1983

Since my publisher Bob Gottlieb[68] is as fixated on 19th century literature as I am and is for all his *voulu* flamboyance as conservative in culture matters as I am, he understands, sympathizes with, and admires *An American Procession* (as I do). But Bob's magnificent office overlooking New York is chock-full of Pop Art *chatzkes* and his desk faces a large Coca Cola advertisement which shows pure American models, blond and fresh faced young American boys and girls reaching for the Coke. And Bob himself, with his husky "sexy" voice and actor's manner, still looks like Woody Allen even though he would like to have the authority of Balanchine or old A.A. Knopf himself. What is significant is how much the publishing business depends on a literary sensibility like his—full of piety and good taste—and how much it is and flourishes as a business. The Knopf office to a visitor may resemble Yaddo or the MacDowell colony. Young secretaries in corduroy slacks, knick-knacks and photographs and funny pictures and graffiti all over the place. Even the café au lait mail boy pushing his wagon looks as if he were contemplating a scene in a novel. Yet the business gets done—*relentlessly*, as in all successfully smart American business—while everyone feels like an "artist."

## February 19, 1983

Arrived at the Roxbury house to find that the pipes had burst, the kitchen floor awash, the toilets out. While Judith and the boys labored, I managed to have the tremors. It was such a "shock." And I was more or less shocked and ill for much of the weekend. Such a delicate organization, this Kazin! Everything must be just so, and on time, or otherwise we play Proust!

67. Thomas Powers (1940–), author and intelligence expert, won a Pulitzer Prize for national reporting in 1971 for his articles on the Weathermen, a violent offshoot of the Students for a Democratic Society.

68. Robert Gottlieb (1931–), writer and editor for Simon and Schuster, Alfred A. Knopf, and the *New Yorker*. He is also an expert on ballet. Woody Allen (1935–), actor, writer, comedian, and film director.

To play Proust in an 1870 farmhouse in SW Connecticut is not the most manageable of roles. The point of this note is that I was really ill, slept on and off most of the weekend.

## February 26, 1983

Shabbos morning. It is a mark of my essential loneliness and "cast-out state" (call me Ishmael, Herman!) that no one knows so much of the physical conditions of the NY streets as I do—no one gazes so attentively at the dreck, the fissures . . . Because these have been my green fields all my life—and because I seem to have lived in these streets more than anywhere else. A thousand years ago, when I was still living with Carol. I remember being struck by the long, even line of the tops of the houses—the straight line of them.

## March 9, 1983

The forward movement and the back. There are days, too, many days, when I feel engulfed in routine and a helpless lurch toward death. [. . .] At such moments "looking backward" seems the only relief. I am a nostalgia specialist and at the flash of an eye can put myself back into memory.

But actually it is the forward movement that saves me, and only that. For life does come down to thought, and it is the regular duty, the need to write x and to review y, that keeps me going. Literally. This morning, the letter to Michael about Soviet dissidents, the lecture to prepare for Missouri on March 18th, the Hawthorne seminar tomorrow, etc., etc., all keep me thinking—and what else is there, or rather, what good is anything else compared with this? This moment of thought in this one great book of my life?

## March 20, 1983

Reading in the *Times Magazine* about Aaron Lustiger, now Jean-Marie, Cardinal and Archbishop of Paris,[69] I was moved, even wept, as I always do at some magic and seemingly miraculous conjuncture of the Jews and the Christianity they have spawned. Don't ask me why this sort of thing always moves me so much—particularly that I have returned from my all-with-the-Jews period, 1943–1982, the forty years that I lived entirely with the Holocaust and which ended for me

69. Cardinal Jean-Marie Lustiger (1926–2007), whose parents were Jewish. His mother died in Auschwitz.

with Begin, Sharon, Shamir,[70] and the war in Lebanon. The idea of embracing "the son of God" is as strange to me as ever, and "Yeshua," that myth of my boyhood, has been utterly savorless and meaningless to me for a long time now. But the synagogue, alas, means equally nothing—and the idea of someone like "Cardinal" Lustiger, so much of my own *mispoche*, moves me precisely because *he* has active faith—and I wander about in culture—about-religion as much as ever. [. . .]

## April 5, 1983

To write about Cal[71] is to enter into the Great Disturbance—not only of the man but of his generation and of the country in the unexpected ascent of the postwar years that drove everyone crazy. Poetry, however, is supposed to be the enemy or at least the solvent of disturbance; it may mirror the uneasy and death driven heart but does not imitate it. . . . Poetry is all contraction where life is all diffusion! But Cal diffused, spread out to the point where his poetry was running after his life—and his life was in streamers . . . diffused in "lacy jags." Poetry in America could never be anything but "personal," for the only tradition it had was American energy rather than the classical art of harmony.

The real poles Cal worked with and between: the "elegance" of condensation and contraction—the centrifugal impulses of the American character and psyche, a teeny-weeny side of American poetry. The most accomplished, [Elizabeth] Bishop—the cutesiness of Moore[72]—the household econom[ic] feminization of

70. Yitzhak Shamir (1915–), prime minister of Israel from 1983 to 1984 and from 1986 to 1992; Ariel Sharon (1928–), prime minister of Israel, 2001–2006. Israel attracted considerable criticism for its June 1982 incursion into Lebanon when Menachem Begin was the Israeli prime minister and Ariel Sharon was defense minister. The incursion, which cost more than twenty thousand lives, achieved the end sought by Israel, forcing the removal of the Palestinian Liberation Organization from Lebanon. Sharon, however, was forced to resign as defense minister for allowing the Christian Phalangist militia to enter the Sabra and Shatila refugee camps, where they killed hundreds of Palestinian and Lebanese civilians.

71. Kazin reviewed Ian Hamilton's *Robert Lowell: A Biography*, "The Case-History of Cal," in the *Times Literary Supplement* (May 6, 1983): 447–448.

72. Marianne Moore (1887–1972), modernist poet, whose *Collected Poems* (1951) won the Pulitzer Prize and National Book Award for poetry. Richard Palmer Blackmur (1904–1965), critic and poet and director of the Christian Gauss seminar at Princeton University. In *On Native Grounds*, Kazin wrote that Blackmur's criticism "displayed so devouring an intensity of mind, so voracious a passion for the critical process itself, that it became monstrous—an obsession with skill, a perfection of skill, that made criticism larger than life . . . and never touched it" (440).

so much American poetry, soon swept up in Blackmurish pseudo-profundity by academic critics who write like failed poets. [. . .]

The Lowell attic—the world of things—heirlooms—all that stuff, all those ancestors and relatives, associations and quotations, almost too many people to write *to.*

## April 16, 1983

[. . .] Sunday afternoon ride to Brooklyn Museum to see the exhibition on The Great East River Bridge. [. . .] The terrible trip back across Canal Street to Manhattan Bridge, remembering how many times the mass scene made me feel lost even before I was actually lost . . . the BMT trains across Manhattan Bridge grinding grinding—and then I realized Brooklyn Bridge as the *found* place, the inexpressible lofty and secure place in the midst of New York's confusion and vertigo, the babble of tongues. . . . I was lost from home, I lost myself, until I found the bridge—all the rest was nothing compared with the *find,* the place, once found, to which one could return again and again.

Always there, mysterious, spidery, incredibly *there.* [. . .]

## May 30, 1983

Lord, Lord, what happiness, excitement, sharing, interest, curiosity unlimited in being married to Judith.[73] I dragged my feet so long—dragged it right into this kitchen on a rainy holiday morning—suddenly wishing that I had met her 60 years ago! [. . .]

## July 4, 1983

Dinner last night at Cornwall Bridge with Philip Roth and the beautiful, soft, adorable Claire Bloom.[74] Philip surrounded by his possessions: the vast lawn, the enormous house, cartoons of himself in his study (except for a framed photograph of Franz Kafka). . . . We began the evening in a dome on the lawn framed in an enormous mosquito net . . . and enjoyable as it was looking at Claire Bloom and listening to Philip's shrewdness, watching his pointy nose and pointy instrumentalist personality, what I enjoyed most was the sight of so much Acquisition. . . . Apparently Philip, like Updike, was the beneficiary of

73. Alfred and Judith married on May 21, 1983.
74. Claire Bloom (1931–), English stage and film actress, married to Philip Roth.

an enormous sum from the Franklin Library for their putting out his works in library edition with his signature on thousands and thousands of sheets.

Then the long, long drive from Cornwall Bridge at night through the winding CT countryside, the silent, white houses, the tall, white reproachful Puritan steeples, all ghostly, but still authoritative in the moonlight. . . .

## July 15, 1983

I see that Woody Allen[75] is back, psychology and all, but back. The Chameleon man. I was afraid that the Jews had ceased to be "satirists" and *outsiders*, that the Marx Brothers had been completely eclipsed by the Podhoretz Brothers. . . .

Of course the Jew as "analysand" is still better than the Jew as ideologist of current American power. Power works in different ways on us Jews! Some it totally turbulates and destroys . . . Some it turns entirely inward (Kafka) . . . Some it hires as cheap lawyers.[. . .]

## October 30, 1983

[. . .] Relaxed, almost slumberous evening beginning *Little Dorrit.* What I never get over in Dickens is a) the temperament, the authority, the driving, sardonic over-all view of everything, the most synoptic talent imaginable, b) the stealthiness of people moving through clotted, decayed Victorian London and the secret life they lead. Moving out of the shadows. This is the Dickens idea of his talent as well as of the hiddenness of so many lives at the time and the conspiratorial nature of all emotion that is in any way protest. "Making it" not allowed to everybody. Dickens is the great example in the momentum of his style itself of the necessary minute victory over suppression organized by the Victorian church and the system of exploitation. . . . Into the shadows they sent, they thought they sent, Charles Dickens. Out of the shadows he leaps like Satan, to dominate the world that held him cheap—but above all to lend this world some *magic.* The magic is in the presto chango of his mind. The magic is all in the magician. How I would have liked to watch him write! It must have been one of the most exciting transformation acts in history.

75. Kazin is referring to Woody Allen's film *Zelig*, a fictional documentary of a chameleon-like character who assumes whatever new identities and looks suit him.

## November 14, 1983

Big, early crowd Lincoln Center to see Joe Murphy inaugurated as 4th chancellor of the City U. [. . .] Moving ceremony, whites and blacks, repeated references to the disadvantaged, the city as the center and locus of everything, the need for public education. I was misty eyed for a while but got over it. My people, my university, my city, my lower class, my black and white! Joe Murphy speechifying looked as if he were wearing his soft velvety academic cap as a baseball cap. But the public man praised Socrates as a democrat and knocked Plato as an elitist. [. . .]

## December 9, 1983

[. . .] Meeting the quality passing through the Century—Kingman Brewster,[76] who by god looked as noble as Kingman Brewster should have looked. Robert Lekachman[77] in a corner of the hall, waiting for someone. He left the club because the ladies are not admitted as members. Of all the many injustices and ordeals that every day rack me in the U.S. this is not one of them. [. . .]

## January 2, 1984

Frozen, cold, and days and days of preparing to "review" the *Oxford Companion to A. Lit.*[78] My eccentric need or *wish* to know everything about a man's career. Career, after career, which on a sequestered morning like this in the winter country does get to look like so many gravestones. The fascination of dates—nationally and scientifically considered. Above all, the continuity of letters, the eccentricity or tragedy or shining celestialness of certain careers—and of course! *the secrets, the tidbits, the drama, that the gravestones don't have room to list.*

## January 7, 1984

[. . .] ORWELL: OR THE BAFFLED SOCIALIST—the will of the party made possible by the supineness of the mass, of the working class.[79] In *1984* the total

76. Kingman Brewster (1919–1988), educator, diplomat, president of Yale University.
77. Robert Lekachman (1920–1989), economist, former colleague of Kazin's at Stony Brook.
78. "A Cornucopia for Browsers," *New York Times Book Review* (January 29, 1984): 3, 33.
79. Kazin would give a talk, " 'Not One of Us,' " at a Library of Congress symposium, May 1, 1984, on Orwell's *1984*. It was later published in the *New York Review of Books* (June 14, 1984): 13–14, 16, 18.

impotence and slavery of the people is an effect of totalitarianism. But I believe that Orwell thought of this supineness as a cause. The English working class did not believe in equality; it lived on protest, as the intellectual class among Socialists (O. himself) lived on *protest.*

"Socialism" in its original meaning: what Marx constantly referred to as civil society would turn from conflict into (for the first time) harmonious and cooperative social relationships. Leninism turned the existing myth—the wretched are the power of the earth (Saint-Just)[80]—into a fable of dominance by the "wretched," the proles—(we have been naught, we shall be all) that somehow magically, by eliminating the exploiters, makes all men equal. . . . He gave the game away by positing the inability of the workers to speak for themselves. The Party!

All this is the myth of the avant-garde, the elite, what Pound called the "antennae of the race." "Intelligence" rule . . . The inside track belongs to the best brains, etc. So why should they not profit from the hegemony granted them by nature?

Lenin disproved Marx—as Marx had already disproved himself—not the material rules but the "meaning of the material." Politics is more decisive than economics, because politics makes decisions.

Meanwhile, the noble myth of the cooperative society, the just society, the international union of the workers (who had no fatherland of their own) is totally obliterated by the necessity of endless conflict, perpetual struggle, permanent revolution. . . . The myth of revolution as the dynamic of history shows that the very idea of conflict was more important to "socialism" than the old ethical idea of cooperation.

## January 8, 1984

A night at the opera (Friday) with the rich. Arthur Carter[81] had us in his box at the Met, along with the builder Arthur Fisher, an orthopedic surgeon Dr. Leon something. The assembled wives flittered—Mrs. Fisher in earrings that Jude

80. Louis Antoine Léon de Saint-Just (1767–1794), French revolutionary who served on the Committee of Public Safety contributing to the "Reign of Terror." He was executed at the age of twenty-six.
81. Arthur L. Carter, investment banker who owned the *Nation* magazine and had recently started the *New York Observer*, for which Kazin wrote occasional pieces.

is sure cost not less than 80 thou. So there we sat at *La Bohème,* ridiculously (as always) over dressed by Franco Zeffirelli, whose sets, while brilliant, dwarfed poor Mimi, made nonsense of Rodolfo and Marcello, and in the second act produced such a sumptuous Paris street scene that more Parisians surrounded Momus's café than can normally be found outside the Place de la Concorde. [. . .]

Anyway, there were we among the rich, watching the poor, poor bohemian artists starving freezing and dying in a Paris garret. Too bad the dopes couldn't like us Jews have made it to America. Amazing how the only richies I ever meet are Jews. [. . .]

The Fishers had one of those super, large Cadillacs waiting at the door to take the rest of the company to supper. . . . We were driven home by Carter's chauffeur Paul in his Mercedes. The performance was not so much undistinguished as drowned in finery, Zeffirelli's as well as Arthur Carter's. What an insistent little prick! What dynamism! Rich, rich, rich, rich is all he ever is and all he ever talks about. Rich, rich, rich, rich! The little blonde wife, a marriage therapist or something like that, looks scared.

## January 17, 1984

[. . .] Watching that statuesque (truly) Kim Novak [in *Vertigo*], I thought of how in Russia dumpy, bearded, endlessly acquisitive and competitive Paddy Chayevsky[82] regaled me with accounts of how she had pleasured him. Poor Paddy, now some more than a year dead—vanished; Kim Novak with all that sleek blondness and opulent sexiness. . . . What one remembers, like a dietetic, wetly savoring in his mind the taste of chocolate, is the image of rodent-like huffing and puffing Chayevsky recounting the joys of Kim Novak sucking him! My first thought when he recounted the scene was of how unattractive she must have thought him. But no—he was somehow a power (for the moment) in Hollywood, and there is something about the entertainment business that breeds that jocularity.

## January 19, 1984

Dinner at Wassily Leontief's, Washington Square . . . Prexy Brademas[83] of NYU, his *very* handsome, physician wife, who used to be a model, was married to the

82. Paddy Chayefsky (1923–1981), American playwright and screenwriter, was in a cultural delegation, including Arthur Schlesinger Jr. and Kazin, that visited the Soviet Union in 1959.

83. John Brademas (1927–), member of the U.S. House of Representatives for twenty years, where he cosponsored 1965 legislation creating the National Endowment for the Arts and the National Endowment for the Humanities. He was president of NYU from 1981 to 1992. Robert Osborn (1904–1994), writer and satirical cartoonist.

multi millionaire Briggs, the auto body man, had 4 chillens, left him because of "repeated infidelities." An artist and his pliant wife, Robert Osborn, very handsome Waspish fellow in his 70s, I suppose, who is definitely condescending. Helen Frankenthaler,[84] whose drawl reminded me of all the drawling remarks, at once vulnerable and ironic that Helen F. seems to drag with her from dinner table to dinner table.

After 45 years in Cambridge, the now famous Leontieffs are now in Washington Square. Wassily seems to me utterly unchanged from 1947, when the "Mozart of economics" first charmed me at the Salzburg Seminar. He is perpetually the Slavic foreigner, the brilliant mathematical economist, who unbelievably still says, in the midst of some story about meeting with upper echelon Soviet personalities, "of course I speak Russian." I never forget anything he says, especially since he tends to repeat the same personal reminiscences, like the unforgettable aunt who was in a Soviet camp from before the war until Stalin's death in 1953 released her—and who only then discovered, in far out Siberia, that there had been a World War! [. . .]

## February 1, 1984

Last night, good love with Jude after party for Yehoshua[85] at Doubleday's fourth floor apartment above the store at 53rd and Fifth . . . Mrs. Howe at the party—good looking Israeli but not very interesting—noted that the apartment had no bedroom. That she could see . . . Yehoshua charming, very much alive; Mr. Irving Howe a bigger Klutz that ever. No manners, no grace, just a head like a pot belly.

On my way to the party stopped off at Scribner's bookstore and looked into a book about his Joosh and Quaker ancestors by my favorite NY Victorian, James Thomas Flexner.[86] . . . Amazed to read that he is now 75 years old. My favorite clubman, the Centurion par excellence, always looks so comfortable. Important in my epic of wandering the NY streets (and sometimes finding a home) to note the "aristos"—the upper class, like Francis Steegmuller (all that taste, all those beautiful pictures, Capri almost all the year—on Jewish money from the dead Beatrice, no doubt) . . . and oh, oh, oh that impeccable taste. I shall never

84. Helen Frankenthaler (1928–), abstract expressionist painter.
85. A. B. Yehoshua (1936–), Israeli writer, friend of Kazin's.
86. James Thomas Flexner (1908–2003), prolific author, best known for his Pulitzer Prize–winning biography of George Washington, a regular at the Century Association.

forget the frown, the horror, with which he pointed to the dust on the frame of Beatrice's picture. The picture, thanks first to Steegmuller, then to his dopey nephew and the dope's broken-down Mercedes on Water Street, that brought me Judith and this new life![87]

Israelis at the Doubleday party for Yehoshua, smiling to themselves—Mrs. Howe tells me the Hebrew word for someone who has left Israel is someone who has gone *down*; someone entering the Zionist paradise is defined as *going-up*. They watch the American Jews, but the American Jews do not watch them. I do—but can't say that it is very worthwhile. They have become another people.

## February 12, 1984

[. . .] Lunch Friday with Harold Brodkey[88] at the Empire Szechuwan . . . He came on like one of those weird characters in Dostoevsky who imposed themselves on you by their . . . strangeness . . . who act as if they want to commit hari-kari in your kitchen . . . Frightening, yellow sun glasses ("French Hunter glasses" he complacently explained), scruffy four days beard, sweatshirt . . . Miserable, malicious, defensive, openly at the end of his tether . . . bright in a desperate last-moment sort of way, but so anxious about himself and his unfinished novel that he extracted pity even as you wanted to kill him for letting his misery wash all over you. [. . .]

## March 19, 1984

Big luncheon party yesterday, John Russell-Rosamond Bernier . . . in their rented country house somewhere around Redding Ridge . . . Everything, as always, "in the best of taste," though some of the guests were distinctly not. I enjoyed meeting Werner Hofmann, a Viennese now head of the Hamburg Museum and present holder of the Meyer Schapiro chair in Art History at Columbia . . . The son of the novelist Jean Guéhenno,[89] a consular official . . . his rather sour wife, a French-American lawyer. . . . Anyway, the drinks flowed, the lunch mounted up, and everybody was on the best of behavior. . . . Russell at these lavish lunches and dinners he gives (and I have never seen him at anything else) looks like an

87. Judith Dunford met Kazin when, through a series of coincidences, she returned a picture to Kazin painted by Bea Stein, Steegmuller's late wife.
88. Harold Brodkey (1930–1996), novelist and short story writer.
89. Werner Hofmann, director of the Museum of the Twentieth Century in Vienna from 1962 to 1969 and of the Hamburg Museum from 1969 to 1990. Jean-Marie Guéhenno (1949–), U.N. undersecretary general for peacekeeping operations.

ambassador out of Henry James, or a military attaché in his own country's uniform—he is so *external* looking to the scene he makes possible . . . the bathroom hung with his honorary diplomas, citations, etc. All this concentrated gentilesse makes me want to send the dishes flying, of course, but not before I have eaten!

These are gentlefolk, and I am no gentleman, nor do I wish to become one. A gentleman, however, has this advantage over a savage like me in that he never makes a mistake in public. . . . I probably commit more gaucheries in public, in speech and manner, than I ever do thinking at my work. . . . The gentleman is admirable, John Russell I admire enormously for his surface and his scholarship. He is a perfect example of the critic-as-teacher. . . .

But what shall we say of that stammer, that nervous repetition of words? Shyness l'anglais, Lord Warburton[90] to the life. . . . But isn't the stammer a way of translating his native thought into the language of American society.

## April 2, 1984

[. . .] Body-Mind . . . I finally made some sense of the Orwell, after two tries, and taking a shower, was amused to see the mighty, strong prick on me as a result of my . . . writing thoughtfully and well.

## May 2, 1984

Washington, the Library of Congress [. . .] final say-so on *1984*? [. . .] The Orwell conference itself not much—Denis Donoghue[91] looking very tall and handsome, very crisp in his not altogether secure "British" accent. . . . Every once in a while I was astonished to hear a narrow Irish "t." [. . .] The academics I seem to see more of than anyone else—so easy to talk to and to talk with—they recite, I recite—never an intellectual surprise except from someone like Denis Donoghue, so much smarter than the rest . . . A "foreigner" among these yokels, of the *mind.*

## May 20, 1984

[. . .]Arthur Schlesinger, the perfect courtier. Intelligence of the most flexible. Manner (public) absolutely flawless. Never at a loss. No matter what you ask

90. English Lord in Henry James's *Portrait of a Lady.*
91. Denis Donoghue (1928–), eminent literary critic and scholar from Northern Ireland.

AMS Jr., or what demand you make of him (in a social way), he responds instanter with a fib—if he needs one. [. . .]

## May 21, 1984

Yeats the "heroic," the powerful, the only positive great poet. Out of insignificant, powerless Ireland—unable to free itself of either British Empire or Roman Church. What a lesson for the *powerless* poets of the most powerful nation on earth.

But Yeats found myth, the sediment of history and *history's* imagination, in the interstices of Ireland and its seemingly rudimentary, historically powerless, religiously potent, state. The poet bulked large in this small and (historically) "ineffective" country. Not because it was ineffective but because it enabled him to invent a past.

We have only individual *past,* the psychoanalytic past! No great poet in common—except as *migrants hither* and wanting (in money) the redemption of our poverty.

Ireland—"bogland"—Seamus Heaney[92]

Why I miss the trolley cars. Because unlike everything and everybody else in the U. S. they did not swerve from their ancient path. And because as a boy (thousands of years ago) I went to Coney Island in a trolley car, and saw grass growing between the tracks and because it was an open trolley, with the conductor on the side hopping from row to row to collect his fares (his left arm holding the rail as he hopped) and because it seemed to me then (as does not happen now on the bus) that the other passengers were all my family, all Brooklyn. And because as we neared the sea, and could see its blue glare on the surface, everyone (at least in the back row) burst out singing.

## May 29, 1984

When it comes to music, I am a poor violinist and have only the most rudimentary technical knowledge. But am I an echo! Half the night my mind kept buzzing back phrases from the slow movement of the *Death and the Maiden* Quartet. Could not get that "tread," that beautiful heartbreaking and ominous tread out of my mind. Could not walk away from it. Again and again I find myself *possessed* by certain passages. . . . Yet if I took out my fiddle to play any of them, I would

92. Seamus Heaney (1939–), Irish poet, was awarded the Nobel Prize for literature in 1995.

be distracted and thinking not of the notes but of the words that might possibly describe them. [. . .]

## June 7, 1984

The Journal Book must obviously turn on the enormous changes—the lifetime of changes—that I embody and that the great City of Noo Yuk embodies. . . . I cannot walk anywhere now without thinking of how transitory things can be. And this too shall pass. And passes, passes, passes, as quickly as time passes. . . . But I alone am left to tell thee.

O fury fused.[93] [. . .]

## June 10, 1984

Roxbury—White among the piercingly red rhododendrons! How comes it Father Mendel?[94]

Talking over coffee this morning to Judissima about Mel Lasky and that generation of City College anti-Communists: Lasky, Bell, Kristol, Lipset,[95] etc. . . . A generation of tireless sociologists of the Kremlin—all of them born around the time of the Russian Revolution and all of them born anti-Communists!

Bellow is the leading *mind* in his novels, The Voice, but there is no *character* in his novels that begins to resemble a man so entirely self-centered, pathologically touchy, yet so intelligent . . . A character driven to portray low life (dept. of humor) but no one less careless of life in the gangster fashion . . . The favorite of the mother becomes a conqueror . . . but in this case a conqueror always at war with his . . . troops. . . .

Inquisitive beyond anyone else, but as afraid to look into himself, as to touch a hot stove. The more I go on with this, the more I seem to be sketching THE JEW . . . domineering (in terms of curiosity, true pupils of their Lord) but always at war

93. "O harp and altar, of the fury fused": from Hart Crane's *To the Brooklyn Bridge*.
94. Gregor Mendel (1822–1884), priest who first discovered some of the elementary laws of genetics by experimenting with generations of pea plants.
95. Melvin Lasky (1920–2004), journalist of the anticommunist left, editor of *Der Monat*, a German Language monthly, supported by the C.I.A. and the Marshall Plan during the Cold War. Seymour Martin Lipset (1922–2006), sociologist of politics who taught at Stanford and Harvard. He was later a senior fellow at the Hoover Institute.

with the rest of the human race . . . Because most people are intelligent enough to resent their being excluded from the Jewish priesthood of the intelligence . . . the acolytes of *their* Lord, His favorites.

What was it Melville said in the Journal of the Holy Land? Doomed or luckless are the favorites of Heaven. . . .[96] [. . .]

## July 17, 1984

Lunch yesterday at the Players Club with Bob Giroux.[97] His practiced voice—trained by the Jesuits at St. Regis?—but a very natural bonhomie as well. Surprised by the *literary* quality of his book on Shakespeare's sonnets. . . . He has been working on this "Book of Q" since his student days at Columbia. . . . Told me that he and Berryman were rivals for this famous Columbia fellowship to Cambridge, that he was actually ahead of Berryman,[98] but that Mark Van Doren neglected to tell him that there was money to the fellowship as well as Cambridge, so that he turned it down because, of course, he needed a job. . . . There was perhaps no need to assure him that if he had gone on to be an "English" prof. he would not have done so well as he has. . . . The book publisher! The protector! Talked a lot about Jean Stafford[99] (which was a main reason for my traipsing down to Grammercy Park on this fearfully hot day). . . . Jean always described herself as broke, but left the big Hamptons property (left her by Liebling), worth several hundred thousands, to her cleaning woman! Stroke, aphasia in her last years, an unpublishable manuscript, crypto novel, out of which Bob extracted a story the *New Yorker* gladly published. . . . I told him about her idiotic acceptance of Oliver Jensen[100] when we were all at Yaddo—"he sent me a dozen long stemmed American Beauty roses!" Liebling, who once refused to visit me with Jean because, according to the biography by Raymond Sokolov, I was one of the "sheenies who are meanies," turns out by all evidence

96. Kazin is referring to the following passage: "No country will more quickly dissipate romantic expectations than Palestine—particularly Jerusalem. To some the disappointment is heart sickening. Is the desolation of the land the result of the fatal embrace of the Deity? Hapless are the favorites of heaven." Herman Melville, *Journal of a Visit to Europe and the Levant, October 11, 1856–May 6, 1857*, ed. Howard C. Horsford (Princeton University Press, 1955), 141.
97. Giroux wrote *The Book Known as Q: A Consideration of Shakespeare's Sonnets* (New York: Athenaeum, 1982).
98. John Berryman (1914–1972), poet, winner of 1964 Pulitzer Prize for *77 Dream Songs*.
99. Jean Stafford (1915–1979), novelist and short story writer, former wife of the poet Robert Lowell, winner of 1970 Pulitzer for *Collected Stories of Jean Stafford*.
100. Oliver Jensen (1914–2005), founder and editor of *American Heritage* magazine.

to have been one of the world's supreme snots. . . . What a Eustace Tilley[101] character in truth, though he ate himself to death, the pig! I shall never forget the slobber with which he ate those chickens at our house! [. . .]

## August 15, 1984

[. . .] [At Alfred A. Knopf's memorial at Campbell's funeral home.] A very aged and crowded company . . . John Hersey, who at 70 is as lean and earnest and looks as terribly "good" as he did in his youth, read the famous names AAK had published . . . Pat Knopf, putting aside all revanche in that turmoiled family, read a very affectionate tribute to papa. . . . Without fuss, said his father's second wife had given AAK the love and tenderness he had never known before. Then some Juilliard grads play the Hayden Quartet Opus 76 #5, as AAK had requested, the son: "thank you for coming"; and as I had expected, the largest old-age literary social gathering of its kind ended with the flight of notables for the limousines lined up on Madison Avenue as for a Mafia funeral. [. . .]

## August 22, 1984

[. . .] Drive up to Amherst and Henry Steele Commager—405 S. Pleasant Street . . . Henry, in white shirt and tie and jacket, in his porch study. Studies upstairs . . . typewriters . . . endless cartons of papers and of course the shelves and shelves of books. Back in the 50s, when I lived in that paradise, Henry still ordered books from English booksellers by the carload. . . .

Looked very well for 82 . . . Young wife, Mary, perhaps half his age, who does errands and is professionally chipper. Upturned nose, merry laughter. Henry complains that he cannot finish any of his many projects. It was my impression that he moved to Amherst in '56 in order to get on with his work. Writes frequently for the *LA Times* Op Ed page . . . As always strong in constitutional argument and fact. Leave it to Commager to know how much the U. S. pays Castro each year for our naval base ($5000) and that after cashing one check, Castro scornfully refused to cash the following ones.

Very impersonal, charming, talked about Steele[102] as if he were no more agonizing a topic than the weather! Steele used to laugh at his father's wanting him to do

101. The supercilious cartoon figure with the monocle who appears on the anniversary covers of the *New Yorker*. See note 48.
102. Commager's son, Henry Steele Commager Jr., a classics professor at Columbia, died earlier in the year of cancer.

a history of classical scholarship in America. And Henry actually, with a smile, wondered why Steele should have specialized in Latin when Greek lit was so much greater and when S had had the privilege at Harvard of Werner Jaeger![103]

I tried to hint that Steele had something in common with Horace, but this did not get much attention. Henry the old fashioned bookman and scholar in *excelsis*, books, books, books! Steele was very different, quite a cynical wit in his way.

Amherst more crowded and "modern" than ever. A heterogeneous young population . . . Bus shelters, smart shops. Had a look at my old house, 155 Woodside Avenue, now occupied by the Mass. Institute of Humanities, was closed by the time I got there after 5. What a beautiful house that is—in the turmoil of life with the Witch, I never took it in, I guess, that this was a prime thing. I remembered the copper beech and the wonderfully extended porch. Peeking in one of the windows, I was amazed by the elegance of the stairs and the grave shadowed beauty of room after room. What a fool, that Witch! And what a fool me! [. . .]

There is no "personality" outside the way we think and what we think about—all the time. Commager is a charming "old-fashioned" man, the very picture of the true scholar in his college house, surrounded by books, books, books. . . . But he is alive mostly to "history," and the way he thinks is the constitutionalist way—he thinks by precedent and by the historic arguments these give him. [. . .]

## September 8–9, 1984

Big Visit from Michael. Strapping, big, energetic, clever, still fixated on the idea of "socialism," but smilingly admits that the "*Nation* is to the left of me." Why I go through a million cycles of guilt, pleasure, acknowledgment of reality and accompanying refusal to accept reality about a married man of 36, I do not know—*except that I will not let the past alone*. That is the besetting ailment and sin—I want to keep remaking the past until it becomes a different affair of father and son—a father who lived with his son, saw him grow up, had some effect on his upbringing and thus saved him from that rigid, unimaginative mother who actually kept Michael from any religious upbringing—on the ground that on religious questions "one cannot be sure."

103. Werner Jaeger (1888–1961), noted German classicist who moved to the United States in 1936. He taught classics at the University of Chicago and Harvard University.

Obviously, too, I want Michael to be, "intellectually," more like me. Which is very funny indeed, since I would go crazy facing anyone who thinks and talks and acts with the eccentric assertiveness and/or articulation that is my life. . . .

All these fusses and feathers—the important point is that Michael in his sheer existence, in the way he moves and eats and talks, is a constant astonishment to me. The "Other!" Though I sometimes cannot tell whether we are father and son or vaguely fraternal, the important fact to a solitary like myself, who has hugged his peculiarness and solitariness and Kazinness so long, is that Michael Kazin exists for this hypocrite lecteur.[104] . . . [. . .]

## September 10, 1984

[. . .]Afternoon tea with Eric Bentley[105] on Riverside Drive. Eric thin, milder, and silenter than I had ever known him, suffering from anemia. Hope it's not AIDS. Eleven rooms, one of his twin sons occasionally lives with him. Eric used to be quite edgy, smart, arrogant in an offside English way, and oh my, such a radical—from the days he set Black Mt. College on its ear!

A lot of Columbia gossip. Says that Oscar James Campbell,[106] a vociferous anti-Semite in the old Columbia style, didn't know that Trilling was Jewish! And that Mrs. Trilling was recently much offended by anti-Semitic remarks made at a dinner she gave Barzun and his young Texan wife. . . . I told Eric about Barzun's long-kept secret: that his mother is Jewish. He noted Barzun's spectacular ability, as during the '68 strike, to keep himself apart. Eric now regrets resigning his big Columbia chair as a result of the strike . . . is teaching at Maryland. [. . .]

## September 12, 1984

Watching the young Korean girl at the "vegetable" store this morning, watching her compulsive orderliness at the counter and her eager energy, I thought of how the tenement Jews of my youth used to work. The Orientals of NY are metropolitan Jews of the 80s. . . . They even have the dual language system! One for themselves, one for the Goyishe customers.

104. See Eliot, *The Waste Land*: "You! hypocrite lecteur!—mon semblable,—mon frère!" which itself is a quotation from the last two lines of Baudelaire's introductory poem to his collection of poems *Les Fleurs du mal*. In English: "Hypocritic reader—my double—my brother."
105. Eric Bentley (1916–), noted critic, editor, actor, playwright, translator.
106. Oscar James Campbell (1879–1970) taught English literature at Columbia, 1936–1950.

Mama toiling early in the morning—Papa toiling—Alfred toiling—piling it up, item by item, adding it up, making things come out neat and right!

## September 14, 1984

[. . .] At dusk, sitting in the *Newsday* office in Manhattan, Murray Kempton[107] talks and talks on the phone—in effect writing his life, his long broken and deteriorated life, in that bright Wasp Baltimore accent—but at once oracular and profane (still the radical) delighting me even as he breaks my heart. What a fluent life! What memories suddenly remembered from the phone! As he was on a landing barge approaching some bay in New Guinea, there was no evidence of the Nips, so he took out Conrad's *Victory* and found himself reading a description of the "most beautiful bay in the world"—the very bay he was in—[. . .]

## September 23, 1984
### [dated August 23]

"Unsere Ist Eine Optische Zeit."[Ours is a time for seeing.] Funny as it was to see that above the ruins of Cologne in 1952, the *triumph* of the visible is the most obvious fact about New York when you walk about, as I have in all these glorious days of late September weather. . . . Not just the amazing new buildings (and in New York the native is continually just as "amazed" as the supposed provincial, whoever that can be in these days of national hookup and incessant air travel from pole to pole), but the way the silhouettes merge at certain hours of the light, and the way the "skyscrapers" toss and turn as they seem to fight each other—before they subside into the general amazement (not always to be looked at too long) of New York, the technical marvel. [. . .]

## November 1, 1984

Keeping this journal, this incessant daily record—I, too, am reporting to "an invisible court." But the point of trying to put my day in order (after I had lived and left it in the usual disorder) is that I do try to change myself, to put my soul in order. (What a thought in this ravaged and ravaging time.) Amazing, isn't it, to want, still, to follow out some invisible moral design? [. . .]

107. In a 1997 tribute, "Missing Murray Kempton," Kazin claimed that Kempton "was the most acute and cultivated columnist since Mencken," *New York Times Book Review* (November 30, 1997): 35.

## November 5, 1984

That new rightist maniac Lynn[108] managed to throw me, but good, with the most vicious attack on all my works in yesterday's *Book Review.* I can see that in my haste to answer his original nastiness in reviewing Virginia Carr's[109] book on Dos Passos, I didn't make clear my own objections—anybody's but Lynn's!—to Dos's later career. Anyway, for a man so eager for "golden opinions" of himself, I can neither keep out of fighting these born again rightists nor take calmly the consequences! [. . .]

The toughness, inflexibility, absolute rottenness of these ex-comrades. . . . You have to fight them *hard,* but they are in power and after tomorrow's Election Day, God help us all! they will be nastier to deal with than ever. [. . .]

To walk down Broadway on a sunny, warmish, Fall day is to feel oneself another Dickens, Balzac, Dostoevsky. . . . There is nothing in humanity you cannot see, and especially now. [. . .]

## November 20, 1984

[. . .] In the Eastern shuttle coming back from my lunch at Brandeis and visit with Evelyn Handler[110] and the Dean (Anne Carter), Elie Wiesel, who languidly invited me to sit with him. . . . Elie's nose is somehow more protuberant, his cheeks more sunken, that publicly suffering face more discreet than used to be. . . . Teaches the Humanities at Boston U. every Monday, just every Monday—death of Socrates, death of Moses, death of Jesus. . . . As Judith comments, he's always full of death. . . . But what an angle, what a nose for the dramatic! Anyway, I steered away from all grievances and we had a good talk about . . . general topics. As the plane doors were about to close, some unimaginably Hasidic characters in full regalia came in, and I asked Elie if his characters always followed him. [. . .]

## December ?? 1984
### [dated December 12, 1984 but out of sequence]

[. . .] Tired but happy, marched off to the NY Yacht Club for *American Heritage* Xmas party. . . . I had always admired the sculptured, convex trimmings on the

108. Kenneth Lynn, "A Raw Nerve Touched," Letters to the Editor, *New York Times Book Review* (November 4, 1984).
109. Virginia Spencer Carr (1929–) wrote biographies of Carson McCullers, John Dos Passos, and Paul Bowles.
110. Evelyn Handler was president of Brandeis University (1980–1983), the first woman to hold that position. Anne Carter was dean of the faculties at Brandeis.

outside of the building at W. 44th Street. But the "Model" room where the party was held left me dazzled. If you want to know what the richy rich, the old Shamrock racing Newport 20 story yachts like to do with their money, here are the models . . . in a room whose very size (and the easy talk it makes possible: voices straight up to the top, no effort required to make yourself heard) gives you a sense of the movers and shakers behind New York life. As it was.

43rd–44th Street—what a level duplex of importance. . . . At the party, an unrecognizable Chester Kerr, but still the editorial jerk I knew years ago. Party prattle about a relative who wanted [a] cathedral for a marriage party of 7 people, and the rector wore golf shoes.

Barbara Klaw, daughter of Irita and Carl Van Doren[111]—how I loved Irita, that dazzling, busy hair . . . that air of the '20s flapper . . . and her ready smile . . . her confidence . . . her association with Wendell Willkie, who died surrounded by books. . . . Reagan will die surrounded by box office figures. These *washed* out editorial intermediaries—so discrete, so polite and wan—Cf. Klaw with her parents. [. . .]

Irita and Carl had such style—Carl's very haircut was flamboyant—those literary characters of the twenties—they *looked* and *sounded* decisive. And they were sexually so much a pair—a pair broken up—that you could not look at one without thinking of the other.

Of course they were no great shakes as minds—but how they looked! The *style* of the 20's—they could not write a line (Carl) without sounding off a bit of dash—[. . .]

## December 28, 1984

New York Landscapes in the Snow of Yesterday—These great heaps of stone and steel and aluminum rearing over you as you delicately make your way through the melted snow at the corners. [. . .] New York Landscapes . . . one key to it all is that it *is* an "all." The obvious incongruity of the buildings, the deadly alliance of rich and poor, the choked up streets, above all the constant pressure of noise and "too much music," all—amazingly—does constitute a whole.

A city like this, imperial, heedless, full of margins at the edges and money splendor at the "heart," is an amazingly coherent contraption with suggestions

111. See Chapter 5, note 7.

of organic integration to it. . . . As Amuricans say with gritted teeth, it woiks. . . . What works? The city works. . . . It falls apart in bad weather, and there is an aggressive roughness running through it that shows what counts (though what counts is not what remains) . . . Money, money, power, and a kind of second generation immigrant assertiveness. . . . But it does work even as it stupefies and beats you down. . . . Because you have to live here, you worship at this shrine. . . . The powerhouse feeds you. [. . .]

# 9
# Last Years
1985–1998

ON JUNE 5, 1985, ALFRED KAZIN TURNED seventy, the mandatory retirement age at City University. He had begun regular teaching late in life, and he worried about his limited pension. Living in New York was expensive; he had a mortgage on his Connecticut house; and he paid Ann $17,000 dollars a month alimony. Anticipating financial difficulties, he began seeking additional sources of income—teaching courses at NYU and Drew University, conducting occasional seminars at the Graduate Center, applying for grants. He would sign up for semester stints at George Mason, Cornell, Barnard, and Brown; and he would continue to write reviews and essays while working on books. In the thirteen years between his seventieth birthday and his death on June 5, 1998, Kazin published five books and more than fifty essays and reviews, taught dozens of courses, and lectured in Spain, Amsterdam, Copenhagen, Berlin, and Salzburg. Financial concerns were one reason for the extraordinary effort; equally important, he feared the consequences of slowing down. "It is the forward movement that saves me, and only that. [. . .] It is the regular duty, the need to write x and to review y, that keeps me going. Literally" (March 9, 1983).

But going forward was often very hard. Kazin had had a heart attack in 1982 followed by bypass surgery, and he experienced recurrent chest pains. He suffered from chronic shoulder and back trouble as well as a bleeding ulcer for which he was occasionally hospitalized. In July 1991 he learned he had prostate cancer. "Who, me? A nice old fellow like me what never done nothing to nobody, etc.?" He urged himself, "So now we must work harder than ever. That old joke about the coming of a terrible world flood that would wipe everything away, and the Rabbi said, 'We have just a few weeks in which to learn to live under water' " (May 29, 1991). The work led to the publication of three books: *Writing Was Everything* (1995), *A Lifetime Burning in Every Moment* (1996), and *God and the American Writer* (1997). Of the three, *Lifetime*, his "journal book," caused him the most difficulty. He had hoped to publish a book of his journals since the late 1940s; now in his eighties, he doubted he could work his way through the six-decade "pile up of words" held in the Berg Collection. In the end he settled for a compromise—a series of retrospective meditations on events and people in his life prompted by past entries, many of them substantially rewritten. More a memoir than a diary, they represent a last look back on his life reconsidered after his fateful meeting with Judith Dunford in the late seventies.

In the final two years of his life, Kazin wrote less frequently in his journal, and many of the entries are lengthy passages quoted from the *New York Times*. The majority of these are about Jews, Jewishness, and Israel. Kazin, who had long been fascinated by the paradoxical extremes in Jewish history—the "high and low, the first man and the last"—hoped in the time remaining to him to bring his ideas together in a book, *Jews: The Marriage of Heaven and Hell* (February 4, 1988). But the project never reached the planning stage, and it is unclear how serious Kazin's intentions were. He wondered whether his now almost obsessive preoccupation with the subject of Jews was a kind of homesickness, "some longing, still, to be back home with the people surrounding me in my childhood" (August 20, 1997). Gathering material on Jews and reflecting on the triumphs and failures in the Jewish past may also have served as an alternative to the services (and community) of the synagogue. For Kazin, unobservant to the end, his Jewish interests remained largely a private matter: sympathy, even identification, with Jewish victims; reverence for rebels, artists, thinkers—"from the blessed Spinoza to Einstein, it has been the great Jewish intellectuals and thinkers who have been the true rabbis (teachers) of the world" (May 15, 1997). He acknowledged that his heterodoxy could leave him feeling spiritually lonely—"Can one really worship the Jewish God privately?" he asked himself more than once—but he felt he had little choice (April 13, 1988). "I just am what I am," he told a reporter from the *Jerusalem Report* who pressed him on his faith. "I have my own feelings." As with so much else in his life, Kazin could be a Jew only on his own terms.

## February 5, 1985

Out to Drew on the snowiest night of the year to begin my Humanities course with a lecture. Endless plodding along 80. [. . .] Lots of sweet Methodist types in my enormous audience . . . this will at least be a change from the frenzied position takers. [. . .]

Nature! Great nature! I still don't have a proper fix on the nature-landscape book, am drowning in my notes and transcripts.[1] . . . The fact is that "nature" is too big and despite everything we pretend, too lawless—lawless to us—to be anything but subjective. . . . But landscape is an attempt to make a home for ourselves out of this immensity, which we drink up in so many subjective, narcissistic, utterly arbitrary ways. . . . Landscape is to get a "fix"—above all, it is the attempt to turn our homelessness into an image that will give us a sense of location. [. . .]

## March 29, 1985

[. . .] Thinking about Chagall in NY during the war, when he once met up with Isaac Rosenfeld and me on Yom Kippur, 57th Street. I feel a comradely twinge

1. *A Writer's America: Landscape in Literature.*

toward a fellow Jew when I remember his speaking Yiddish to us and admitting that though he could not get himself to work on the High High Holy Day, he was sauntering on to Pierre Matisse's[2] gallery for a look (no doubt at his own work). Chagall and Vitebsk did summon up that feeling about Jewishness being a kind of sealed treasure, so deep within oneself. . . . And what is it? In my case, the sense of all those others who have gone the long, long road. Solidarity . . . especially with those who so silently died at the hands of one power mad group or another.

## April 2, 1985

Gentlemanly dinner at the Century for Dan Aaron, who at 73, God bless us, looks a fresh faced fifty, and was as usual charming, nice to everyone. . . . The dinner was "hosted" so to speak by Kenneth Wilson,[3] who is another charmer—and there were Allan Williams the publisher, [Richard] Poirier (whose gravelly, far off voice I did not recognize), Byron Hollinshead of *American Heritage*.

As usual Arthur M. Schlesinger, Jr. stole the show. At least for me. His knowledge of American "society," his very quick mind, and above all his experience at such dinners makes him fascinating. Despite the troubles we have had, I have to confess that Arthur (and I am not forgetting what a fibber he can be when it comes to his authority figures) is the nearest thing to a Howells with Adams-like intelligence and political emotion that we have. I am always amazed by his familiarity with current fiction as well as with the various notables whom his brother-in-law relationship to Anthony West[4] (among other people) has put him in touch with. Arthur has been everywhere and knows everybody, and I have to say with some ruefulness: has the sharpness that comes from social experience. . . . My mulish solitariness these days certainly has its limits! [. . .]

## April 20, 1985

O what a farce is like; what a farce it is[5] . . . my old friend Elie Wiesel (who has incorporated the Holocaust into himself) is on the front page of the *Times*

2. Son of the French painter Henri Matisse (1869–1954), Pierre Matisse (1900–1989) directed the Pierre Matisse Gallery on East 57th Street from 1931 to 1989.
3. Kenneth Wilson (1936–), theoretical physicist who taught at Cornell. Byron Hollinshead was an editor at *American Heritage*, later editor in chief at Oxford University Press.
4. Anthony West (1914–1987), British writer, son of the novelists Rebecca West (1892–1983) and H. G. Wells (1866–1946). Rebecca West and Schlesinger were friends.
5. President Reagan's controversial visit to the Bitburg cemetery in Germany where a number of Waffen SS soldiers were buried.

haranguing the Goyim (Secretary of State Shultz stolidly staring ahead) on what the Germans did to us. . . . And on the tube Elie is talking, wheedling rather, to our great Prexy (also staring stolidly ahead but with his usual determined look of attention to something he hasn't the smallest interest in or knowledge of or whom to ask for some real help), telling him that power must submit to our suffering. . . . And all the while, praising our great President, even sorrowfully forgiving him. . . .

As Judith says, the only proper thing for a really indignant and outraged Jew would have been to send a telegram refusing attendance at such a ceremony. A Congressional Gold Medal to Elie—the whole thing is beginning to stink to high heaven as the most shameless personal aggrandizement in the name of dead Jews. [. . .]

Wiesel looking at himself instructing the Pres of the US on the front page of the *Times* may be puffed up with Hungarian vanity—but it all makes me sick, disheartened. Because nothing has changed—the Jews are the margin of history, always on the bias, and when they are heartbreakingly in the right, they appear to be intrusive, wrong, outside everything "normal." [. . .]

## May 6, 1985

[. . .] People who have been through some extreme experience—say, my favorite Wiesel—can exaggerate, invent, lament, mythologize to their heart's content (and that is their object, not "truth"), because they have been hallucinated by the experience. . . . Birstein used to say that Elie lied, tout simple. . . . And of course he does. And he certainly dramatizes in public to the point where whatever was private and somehow terrifying for all sorts of reasons (the death of his father) has become just . . . public words.[6]

How would it be if Wiesel pictured in a story—a story based on the lack of memory he shares with the big Jewish and sympathetic public that knows nothing, really, of the camps—he can say anything—and because he has this gift of dramatizing in public and bringing in the Jewish tradition, Rabbis, lamentations infinis—he so imposes himself on this public that he becomes in private (intermittently) the Suffering Servant, "Our Teacher Of The Holocaust," as the *Times* columnist Shandberg[7] put it, that has become his life?

6. See note 48.
7. Sydney Shandberg (1934–), *New York Times* reporter, noted for his coverage of the war in Cambodia.

The point of all this: the Nazis did create a world so awful that they treated it as a storyteller his fiction, while their victims were so marred and distorted (many of them) that they cannot bear to remember "exactly." [. . .]

## May 11, 1985

Peter Manso's *Mailer*, a biography as told by loads of NY literati, relatives, ex-wives, u.s.w. . . . This is the cocktail party I never went to, would have disapproved of if I had gone to—but nevertheless is a running account not merely of Mailer's life, his affair with America, BUT the collective autobiography of all the speakers—[8]

Has left me feeling more and more the loner, moralist, aloof spectator. Oh my gosh, what Diana Trilling thought of Lillian Hellman's getting Norman to cancel the blurb he had written about Diana's book of pieces! What is interesting is of course and mainly the attraction of Mailer for all these people, the way they (especially the non-novelists and literary critics and even unsuccessful novelists like Chandler Brossard)[9] were pulled to Mailer by his success, his "fearlessness," his (especially) ability to be a "radical" while proving in every Zeit that its Geist was his Geist and that he was the most American, the most ruthlessly characteristic American of all!

Because Mailer was in it all, the big expansive over-prosperous Americano postwar period of brag, bluster, and overweening confidence—and the rest of us were not. . . .

Mailer the ur type of a certain period—without the extraordinary lift to American ego, no Mailer . . . as this period will sink into history, also no Mailer. The chorus interpreted this period through him, but he *incorporated* it, he did not represent it. It is the incorporation that makes the public personality, Wiesel and the Holocaust, Mailer and domestic expansiveness. Everything to become public and "legendary" for its own time requires a *story*. In Mailer the period in all its temptations became the story. [. . .]

8. Peter Manso, *Mailer: His Life and Times* (New York: Simon and Schuster, 1985). Kazin is in fact a guest at the "cocktail party," describing his impressions of and encounters with Mailer. U. s. w.: Und so weiter, "and so on."
9. Chandler Brossard (1922–1993), novelist and writer for the *New Yorker*.

## May 26, 1985

[. . .] Thinking All The Time is what this damned [journal] book is all about. It is all stream of consciousness, stream of *thought*. . . . And rolling with the punch that life gives you . . . constantly shipwrecked on the rocks in your little boat but just as that damned river keeps rolling along, so does thought, thought, thought in this hungry brain. . . . It is this *incessancy* I have to get into the book . . . the very fragments and sputtering and interruptedness that are so hard to read are the real connecting stones, the primary elements, of the book.

## May 29, 1985

Dinner last night with Bellow at the Gerald Freunds.[10] In this latest epiphany Bellow comes with son Adam and girl friend as well as wife. . . . In the more than forty years I have known him, Bellow has always appeared and reappeared at intervals like some wandering star. . . . This time, almost seventy, he appears with white on white shirt and bow tie, thin as ever, congested in his usual cold conceit, with that same trick of opening his eyes wide at intervals to show what his famous and much practiced conversational power is taking in. Sitting back (Adam's hand on his knee) the little pasha evokes in me, as usual, admiration for his adroitness and his gift of the apposite quotation as well as absolute loathing of the self approval in which he sits encased like a cat in a milk bath. He did not even try last night to offer much conversation, and I, determined not to taunt the little "conservative," went on talking just to avoid a case of the blahs . . . sitting encased in his conceit as in frozen grease.

But, as I say, the "star" reappears at wide intervals. The last time I saw him, must be the lunch in Chicago, he was still on stage, but courtly, since he had been reading my account of him as a young man in *NYJew*. . . . Before that it was Bellow at the Century, Bellow on the Viking boat ride, Bellow at the Rosenbergs lifting a salami out of his suitcase. And going steadily backwards, Bellow in Wellfleet, Bellow in Queens, Bellow standing on the toilet in his little flat on Riverside Drive to look at the river. . . . Forty three years since we met at the *New Republic*. And he still has that trick of widening his eyes, practicing "observation," sitting congealed like frozen matzoh ball soup in his conceit.

10. Gerald Freund (1930–1997), first director of the MacArthur Foundation Prize Fellows Program. He was formerly dean of the humanities at Hunter College. James Atlas reports that the birthday party turned into a political quarrel which abruptly concluded when Bellow left without saying good-bye: *Bellow: A Biography* (New York: Random House, 2000), 517–518.

. . . To cap the occasion, Peregrine Freund, immer die ingenue, brought out a birthday pie with two candles, one for Bellow (June 10th) and one for Kazin (June 5). Peregrine doesn't know from nothing which made her hostessing the party perfect in its irony. . . .

But I was struck by her saying about Gerry that nothing fazes him. . . . He does have a remarkable *surface*, Gerry does, just as he has that perfectly "German" or neutrally Jewish face! The foundation man in a world of surfaces . . . always polite, impeccable—I suddenly realized that there was more to him than I had expected from all the polite gestures we've exchanged over the years—

## June 1, 1985

Roxbury—God how I hate these princelings baked in their own conceit. The Big Ego always throws me into a rage—no doubt of envy as well as principled antagonism to dictators, despots, spiritual bullies and the like.

Bellow finding a good word to say for Franco! Because he "saved Jews."

That bad evening with Bellow at Gerry Freund's comes to me days later as primum examplum of *ours* as a lost generation—poor boys, "intellectuals," to their fingertips, brought up to be adversaries of power types and the "established order"—who now turn out to be voices of "privilege," *messengers*, auxiliaries, "conservatives"—but I don't suppose that SB's disgust with Chicago is anything but "personal," an affront rather than a prime index of our civilization.

AN EVENING WITH THE LOST GENERATION . . . Karl Shapiro, Alfred Kazin, Saul Bellow, Bernard Malamud, etc. . . . Now in their 70s, still smoking, hale and hearty sex lives. . . . Of course, some of us wear white on white shirts like Jewish dentists or brokers or nuclear engineers . . . and some of us have had as many wives as Henry VIII, as many mistresses as Dracula or Jack Kennedy. Resolutely thin, carrying on as usual, determined not to sink like our fathers, but o my! how our social opinions reflect our top lofty incomes, and what excuses we do find (we who once had no trouble execrating everyone in power) for those in power.

Who would have dreamed it? that life should have offered us so much—in shovelfuls. We are such [as] dreams are made on, and our little life is rounded with . . . prizes.[11] . . . Our President belongs to our club—the man taken everywhere as an illiterate dope is the most cunning turncoat of us all.

11. See Prospero's act IV, scene 1 speech in Shakespeare's last play *The Tempest*, taken by many as the playwright's statement of intended retirement: "We are such stuff/As dreams are made on; and our little life/Is rounded with a sleep."

## June 4, 1985

Amos Oz[12] at the Century—the officious black at the desk looked startled when Israeli style Oz appeared sans necktie. Very moving talk about Jews in general, Israelis. . . . He is short, handsome in a sort of Russian Jewish Kibbutznick style, very nice. . . . What interested me most in the talk: he covered his head (as if in mourning) when I spoke of "desanctifying the Holocaust, Elie Wiesel," he was very funny recounting stories of would-be intellectual Ben Gurion (then defense minister as well as p.m.) summoning Private 18 year old Oz to his office at 4:30 in the morning for a 7:30 in the morning debate about an article Oz had written in the Labor paper *Davar* satirizing BG's pretensions to an intellectual (and quoted Sir Isaiah on BG's illusion that Weizmann and Jacobtinsky were intellectuals).[13] [. . .]

## June 29, 1985

Grand birthday dinner thrown at Uzi's? Third Avenue fancee Italian restaurant for Papa, Kate, Beth, Judith. . . . My dear son looked magnificent in beard, was generous and tactful in every regard; and while I found myself not able to talk to Cathrael very easily, I was pleased to see her chopping away with relish and love to Dr. Beth. . . .

Michael is the son and *brother* I've always longed for. I used to feel like an elder brother in the long agonizing days when he was growing up with hostility to me. . . . Now that we are intellectually of the same age, so to speak I feel like a spiritual brother. . . .

Singer popping up in a story called, "Miracles."

"I've long been convinced that there is a hidden Messiah in every Jew. The Jew himself is one big miracle. The hatred of the Jew is the hatred of miracles, since the Jew contradicts the laws of nature."

12. Amos Oz (1939–), Israeli novelist and journalist (a favorite of Kazin's), as well as a professor of literature at Ben-Gurion University.
13. David Ben-Gurion (1886–1973), first prime minister of Israel; Chaim Weizmann (1874–1952), first president of the State of Israel; Ze'ev Jabotinsky (1880–1940), Zionist leader, author, and soldier as well as an early leader of the Zionist underground organization Irgun.

## July 1, 1985

[. . .] Spain still on my mind. Rereading Josie's *The Starched Blue Sky of Spain*,[14] which is of course well written but so emotionally packed that it makes my feelings sink. . . . Josie could be all emotion, as I've noticed women under the influence of ideology can be. The ideology bears them downward.

But reading Josie on our Holy War 1936–38 and thinking of Bellow having a good word to say for Franco when we had that dinner at Freunds, I realized that Ovid had nothing on me when it came to Metamorphoses—the only possible title for the Journal Book, and change, change, change is what it is all about. With endless yearnings for the Unmoved Mover, for something beyond what old Billy Blake called this "universe of death."

Not only from shift to shift, wife to wife, life to life! But the concealments within the beloved—take Josie! Reading her evasive comments in the Spain essay on the murder of José Robles,[15] I think of all her other concealments. And of mine, and why I like thrillers so much—the concealed spy, the turncoat, the secret adulterer, the love of telling lies . . . Anna J.—and her fascination with homosexuality all the while she was sweetly lying next to me. And dreaming of something, someone, whatever it was, the Other—if only whales that talked, dolphins that could do arithmetic.

We are such stuff as lies are made of, and our little life is rounded with a book.

However, in another part of the forest that is Broadway—I was respectfully saluted and just as respectfully saluted back—the bearded, oldish Jew with bicycle and pail, sponges, etc., who goes up and down Broadway washing winders. I had first seen him at the Fleischfuhrers, Harry Oppenheimer, who

14. "The Starched Blue Sky of Spain," in *The Noble Savage* 1 (1960), republished in *The Starched Blue Sky of Spain and Other Memoirs* (New York: HarperCollins, 1991). See Chapter 3, note 71. A writer on the activist left during the 1930s, Josephine Herbst wrote proletarian fiction and columns that recorded conditions in Depression America and described events in Spain during the Spanish Civil War. She was a friend of the writers Ernest Hemingway and John Dos Passos (1896–1970).
15. According to her biographer, Elinor Langer, Herbst was less than "straight" in her account of what she had heard had happened to Robles (a friend of John Dos Passos's who had been murdered by the Communists); but Langer warns that like so many "inner complexities" of the Spanish war, there may have been "no straight." *Josephine Herbst* (Boston: Little, Brown, 1983): 219–225.

to my pleasure, sneaked him a bill with a gesture of solidarity. . . . Today, seeing him unlock his chain around his bicycle, I realize that in this sinful, lying, treacherous noisy, totally corrupt, and undependable world, I was seeing one of the just. . . . Don't laff! I know this! [. . .]

## July 7, 1985

[. . .] A journal is a history of moments, of passages. It is a continuous chronicle only if the author is a continuing type . . . an obsessive type. It is a history of rallies, of recoveries, of reestablishing oneself in life after the usual shocks, blows, outrages, and attempts at murder. One may well ask what a few words of self-encouragement written at daybreak, when the world seems to be reestablishing oneself, has to do with so many . . . outbreaks, horrors, rapines, etc., etc. But what else except the act of memoria is there available to us—the act of definition[. . . .]

## August 13, 1985

[. . .] What struck me most [reading the *Nation*] (in the comfortable air-cooled surroundings of the Society Library) was the violence of the ideological comment. It was interesting to learn from that Stalinist monster Cockburn that young John Podhoretz is a senior editor of the Moonie paper in Washington. Not so interesting to read that Podhoretz Sr. is "a mass murderer whenever he sits down to write or stands up to speak."[16]

Podhoretz admittedly is a killer. Cockburn is a killer. I begin to feel like a killer when I read these killers. Berlin 1933. Petrograd 1917. . . . Why *this* much savagery? It is because ideology becomes the more fervid and uncontrollable the more fixed it gets in time. . . . Because it becomes identified with one's own righteousness . . . Because each ideology has a unitary explanation of the world and its sinfulness . . . Because intellectuals have nothing in this world but their "notions," and protect their property as if it were life itself.

16. Alexander Cockburn (1941–), Irish-born American journalist of the left, wrote columns for the *Nation* and the *Los Angeles Times*. "The Moonie paper" is the *Washington Times*, founded in 1982 by the Unification Church of the Rev. Sun Myung Moon (1920–) to offer a conservative alternative to the *Washington Post*. The neoconservative John Podhoretz (1961–) is the son of neoconservative Norman Podhoretz. Norman Podhoretz and Cockburn typically went for the jugular in their columns, "mass murderer" presaging the kind of "attack journalism" now common on talk radio and cable news. It reminded Kazin of the "bomb-throwing," "Stalinoid" language and name-calling practiced by the 1930s partisans of his youth.

And me? I am just against extremism in every form. I am not a super idealist like Chomsky . . . or a self-important genius who knows what is good for every government in the world. But all this is no longer "politics" in the old American sense of the word. . . . It is ideology . . . and ideology is the theory that *nothing* is the lesser evil . . . that political ideas are necessarily at war with other political ideas . . . that only *our* ideas shall survive. [. . .]

## October 4, 1985

Since the above, some eight days ago, I have written over 30 pages first draft of the Pound lecture for Alabama, "Teacher" for Louis Rubin's[17] Algonquin Press book, the Yaddo memoir for the group of memoirs they are putting out there, and this morning hope to get on with the last chapter of the book. . . . Slightly breathless, for this week has included two classes at NYU, the usual seminar at City Graduate Center. I am so pent up that I find it hard to sleep except on those now all too frequent nights when I take Halcion, and often strain to catch my breath as I walk. The steps going up the exits at the 96th St. subway are hard. Yet I pound away, all this steady work and my exuberance having lunch with a younger fellow like Wm. Patrick Kelly III[18] from Queens and drinks after the Melville seminar yesterday with Derek Miller and Carol Saltus—sometimes makes me uneasy. . . . how long can this last?

## June 20, 1986

The journal book is not a book of anecdotes; it is not a record of my times. It is about my lifelong compulsion to keep such a book. It is about the consciousness that cannot rest except in such a book. Everything will follow as a book—is already there—once the compulsion is faced. No use in pretending that I am more "humorous," equitable, and easy going than I am. I am unappeased and unappeasable. [. . .]

I shiver when I read day after day of my journal and come across the same anger, the same unappeasability, the same heart, the same, the same unrest and anxiety.

17. Louis Rubin (1923–), American literary critic, scholar, editor, cofounder of the *Southern Literary Journal* and Algonquin Books, established Southern Literary Studies at the Louisiana State University Press.

18. William P. Kelly, literary scholar and critic, became president of the Graduate Center of the City University of New York. Carol Saltus and Derek Miller were students of Kazin's at the Graduate Center of CUNY.

But that is the barest infliction of my consciousness. Which now must be taken straight.

Yes, a suffering, a hungry lifetime, a hungry soul, often a bitter soul. But that is why I have already written it out in shorthand, day after day. "A Lifetime Burning In Every Moment."

## August 16, 1986

I can never lose the feeling that there is some great party going on to which I have not been invited—I have this at least in common with Freud—the sense that I am not easily likeable, that I come on as someone vaguely aloof or unapproachable. No doubt there is still a lot of self-conscious proletarian youth in me. But I live so much alone to myself (like Wilson, whose "friendships" and attachments were always literary matters, often enough just intellectual scholarly exchanges) that I suppose it is foolish to complain of others when again and again I feel it more *natural* to be alone. Still, there is a gnawing loneliness, a sense of living apart. . . .

And the worst of it is how I resent the social gift in others, I laugh, seeing Rose Styron[19] at the slightest gathering looking as if she had been greeting people merrily, professionally, all her life. But there is a gift there, a long bred talent for sociability, that I certainly lack. And it makes me bitter, bitter. When I am not working.

## August 18, 1986

Last night. Judith and I had eaten at the Chinese restaurant on 97th Street, had bought a container of milk at the Hispanic grocery next door, and were walking up Amsterdam Avenue to our corner at 100th admiring the Episcopalian Church on the corner. Suddenly I felt someone right behind me, and before I could quite realize what had happened, a young black boy in a blue tee shirt, with something like "Lights" (some club name?) on it, insidiously removed my wallet from my left side pocket and sped off.

I chased him a little calling "Stop Thief!" exactly as in the movies or whatever, and one fellow at the corner actually took up the chase for a little while. A goofy

19. Rose Styron, poet, journalist, civil rights activist, spouse of the writer William Styron.

fellow standing there could have caught the "perpetrator" as they say in Police jargon, but he didn't, and kept on apologizing to me in a very belligerent way, explaining that everything is fucked up, that he had decapitated a lot of people in Vietnam. But ridiculously, he was solicitous at the same time though angry at me for seeming to accuse him of failure.

Police station. 24th Precinct. We rode around in a squad car to all the known "drug corners" where young hoods are supposed to hang out. Strutting, very assertive, Hispanic cop, who had to be told over and over and still over again just where I had been robbed. Police station—enormous American flag behind the lieutenant's desk. . . . Howling from the detention cells in the rear. Intelligent, helpful Patrolman Morales, who took down my statement. I was afraid that the blank checks in my wallet, etc.

We had just wearily (and a bit traumatically) gotten into bed when lo and behold, another good samaritan, who had found the abandoned wallet in front of his house, called us up, delivered same. Turned out to be a black Buddhist, full of conscious rectitude . . . Dancer, actor, etc. from Philadelphia. Tall, quite stage-type . . . We drank a glass of wine in honor of his helpfulness. And so to bed.

## August 19, 1986

To my utter bafflement, Podhoretz's latest, *The Bloody Crossroads*, has been sitting on my office desk all these months with an inscription "Alfred, Why *Can't* We Be Friends?" Unless this is a joke perpetuated by someone else, I can only say in response that this "bloody" volume, indeed, written with a rusty hatchet, is most interesting for what it leaves out, the U.S.A. itself. There is nothing, nothing by someone styling himself "anti-Communist" on every page about the life lived in the cities, on Midwestern farms, by the corrupties [*sic*] eager beavers on Wall Street, by the drug-maddened class everywhere [. . . .]

## October 8, 1986

The career of Norman Mailer—from the "outlaw" to the slightly punchy, fat, little fellow in the dinner jacket.

I have been going over the 1981 journal before sending it on to Dick Cook.[20] Astounding, how evocative my writing is, naturally, rather than analytic—which it

20. See the Introduction of this volume for my meeting with Kazin.

is when I have to be, to bear down on the subject. And what is evocativeness? It is the release of a hidden spring, the articulation of a voice you have been carrying around all this time without knowing that you have. Evocation is . . . "religious"—it is a summoning forth of a scene, a place, a destination, a principle, that is central but . . . (again) hidden. . . . Yeah, it *is* the past breaking out in your heart—if by the past you mean that which lies beneath the surface of the conventional social world. . . . It is the release *unexpected;* it is a call from the most truly soul-part of you. It is the part of you which more than anything else believes in *Unity:* which is what religion is all about. [. . .]

"My Mother's Windows." There was this shining Polish girl Anne Mattus who occupied the next violin chair in the F. K. Lane High School Orchestra. And how she shone. . . . We used to walk home with our violin cases. And one day Mama, washing the windows on the Sutter Ave side, saw us—saw the shining, gleaming Poilesha. She had something of a fit, immediately demanded knowledge of my relationship with the said Anne Mattus . . . etc., etc. I did not tell her that we used to pet in the Highland Park Cemetery perched on a convenient slab or mound. . . . But I remembered this reading Naipaul's very accomplished, but very, very distant, stranger-like account of his early days in the English countryside. Because "My Mother's Windows" is the key to this—the despotic Jewish mama surveying everything, her windows her eyes.

## October 25, 1986

[. . .] This brooding, painful episode with Martin Peretz's singing with the *New Criterion* and all the other contemporary inquisitors in the matter of my once sacred "Spain." I called my piece "The Wound That Will Not Heal," and it hasn't . . . it never will.[21] Spain is deep in my heart, truly a sacred memory, for all the bitterness I feel equally about Stalin-Russia's tortures and appropriations there. . . . What I am feeling most, I guess, in the context of Peretz's arrivisme, is the forgetfulness of people like that.

21. Kazin, "The Wound That Will Not Heal," *New Republic* (August 5, 1986): 39–42. Ronald Radosh in " 'But today the struggle': Spain and the Intellectuals," *New Criterion* (October, 1986): 5–15, attacked Kazin and other intellectuals for perpetuating the notion that the Spanish Civil War was "the one pure cause of the 1930s," long after it was clear that Stalin had intervened in the conflict for his own "cynical" purposes, had engaged in atrocities as brutal as Franco's, and had betrayed the democratic ideals of the Republic. Martin Peretz, publisher of the *New Republic*, seconded Radosh's case against Kazin and others for supporting the "illusion" of the sacred Loyalist cause—"Changing Minds," *New Republic* (November 3, 1986): 42.

This letter to myself, which is what the journal really is. Like all writing, it is an attempt to uncover such depths and secrets, such forgotten passageways as me soul contains. . . . But isn't there a mistrustfulness of others in spreading so much, *confiding* so much, to my own voice?

## November 2, 1986

How I rush to this notebook in the morning, can't wait to have this communion with such thoughts as I have! [. . .]

Funny to think of Newman,[22] a Jew from Cleveland, as an American hero—but he is, partly I think because he *is* Jewish, there is a wealth of experience in that face that corresponds to the glamour/poignance of so many European actors and actresses. Let's face it buddy—even a Jew with such handsome regular features has kept an air of gravity plus cunning . . . he's been around not just in the tough sense and so has a reserve, a kind of worrisome wisdom (worrisome not least to himself). . . . [. . .]

## November 13, 1986

[. . .] Extree Extree—Jewish Nobel Laureates honored by "Jewish Academy Of Arts And Sciences"—Elie Wiesel, that amateur Jesus of Nazareth, pictures smiling ecstatically (in tuxedo) next to Bashevis Singer. Bashevis earned his prize by writing; Elie got his prize by pulling one face of anguish after another until people couldn't stand it anymore and decided that he was the Jesus of the Holocaust. But look! Brethren! the old Jesus was hanged on the cross and then became God. Elie's credentials are the hell of Auschwitz and Buchenwald . . . so he gets the Nobel Prize for "peace." [. . .]

## November 29, 1986

[. . .] Roxbury is lovely but the intellectual company is, how shall I put it, all money. "There's nobody here except people with money."

## December 26, 1986

O My, the Show People of Roxbury. Big bash at the Styrons—Lennie Bernstein in an orange shirt, some sort of exotic "prayer" shawl draped over his expressive

22. Paul Newman (1925–2008), actor, film director, racecar driver, and humanitarian.

shoulders, smoking away, talking to eager young girls. Mike Nichols, the serpent in the garden as Judith calls him—Claggart to the life, said not enough money was coming in just now, wanted to get un-used to the money. Arthur Miller a bit tight addressing me as usual on the subject of his latest openings. Benevolent, even comradely in a Jewish-1915 way, but would never think of saying a word, *asking* a word, about anyone else's work. I did not see her, but apparently Caroline Kennedy (Schlossberg) was there. The Pete Gurneys, daughter a graduate of the Yale English school, now a financial officer at the ad agency whose long name still ends in Benton and Bowles. That little rat, Jerzy R. Kosinski, thought Conrad was a good subject to bring up with him, but it didn't interest him very much.[23] All the while, host Bill Styron looking a bit subdued as usual these days; we talked about Randall Jarrell's possible suicide, Bill's own depression. And I talked to him about William James's own breakdown and his resuscitation through faith.

What in hell am I doing with all these theater types?

## January 7, 1987

As I was hunched over my typewriter at the Graduate Center, enter Irving Howe looking flabby and sad, complaining that he is out of things generally. . . . Of course the only reason he knocked at my door was to repeat his invitation to write for the NY number (whatever that is) of *Dissent*. . . . Irving needs me occasionally oddly enough even for chronological solace in the face of the army of "theorists," academic Marxists and so weiter [and so on]. But as long as I have known him, he has retained an attitude of mistrust, rivalry, positive aversion at times, that makes even the most "sympathetic" talk, *comme hier [like yesterday]*, debilitating in the end. I may yet come up with something for his bloody mag, but sincere conversation between two people who agree more than they disagree, there will not be. [. . .][24]

23. Mike Nichols's manner and appearance apparently reminded Judith Dunford of Claggart, the scheming villain of Melville's *Billy Budd;* Caroline Bouvier Kennedy (1957), a lawyer and author is the only surviving child of President John F. Kennedy (1917–1963) and Jacqueline Bouvier Kennedy (1929–1994). A. R. "Pete" Gurney (1930–), American playwright. Jerzy Kosinski (1933–1991), Polish-born American novelist, best known for the controversial novel *The Painted Bird*. Kazin thought him a literary confidence man.
24. Kazin did contribute a piece, "They Made It," to *Dissent* (Fall 1987): 612–617. It was his only contribution to what he called "the dullest magazine in the world." Kazin to Dennis Wrong, October 25, 1970 (Kazin Estate, Berg, New York Public Library).

## March [nd] 1987

[. . .] Malamud[25] the passive, the quietly unrebellious "sufferer" saw in his Oregon exile what an everlastingly fantasy-world lay in his own experience. It was not the "new life" but the "old life" that became his successful alchemy, turning Morris Bober's grocer and the "Poilesh" into gold.

He even invented a Malamud language, a magical-immigranto Brooklyn language—which would catch the mingled skepticism and experience-laden quality of his characters.

His compassion, so natural, so automatic and self reflective—at the end of *The Tenants*, his "Jewish" faithfulness, indistinguishable from that of any other mutely respectful Brooklyn Jew. The "Take Pity" story as the ultimate in Jewish spiritual pride.

Remembering "Bernie" and the changeover to "Bern"—Cowleys' snottiness to "Bernie" at the Yaddo meeting. . . . Malamud walking the West Side streets after his first attack and breathing with satisfaction that he had done his appointed round as he came upon me waiting for a bus at Broadway and 86th.

Sly "Bern" breathing "Are you available?" to a lady across from the dinner table . . . Bern at the Plaza Oak Room giving me lunch (and a dollar to the head waiter) but growling about what Hannah Arendt had said about me as "historian" rather than "critic."

*Anyway, the powerlessness that we all grew up with* and the strategies with which he had to overcome them as storyteller . . . To say nothing of afflicted brother "Eugene."[26]

The raw facts of life in depression, lower-class Brooklyn. Before the Jews turned academic and turned literature into a theory, before the Jews turned middle class and found their religion in the Holocaust and the State of Israel. The bitter dialogues. [. . .]

25. Bernard Malamud died on March 25, 1987.
26. Eugene Malamud suffered from schizophrenia and lived much of his life in an institution.

## March 30, 1987

I work in fragments, am only an "essayist," diarist, paragraph writer. I work with separate pieces of stone, piece on piece on piece! But I will get the building built. [. . .]

## April 5, 1987

Emory U motel, Atlanta. Death turns so many people interesting—some it even makes "celebrities." The Compulsion to Keep a Journal. The strangeness of being alive—so often I am unreal to myself and so is the "world." At the same time my overwhelming sense of my own experience—the holiness of my experience—engulfed in my experience, constantly amazed by myself as my own recording angel, the need to get it down, to frame it, to record the passage from yesterday to today. And the overwhelming blaze of simultaneity—as well as the old ghetto days amazement at being in *this* world.

## April 11, 1987

[. . .] My compulsion to keep this journal: the mad excess of experience, to say nothing of the past, all those "missing persons," who loom larger as time goes on, to say nothing of the simultaneity of everything in this "mad rush of life,"—plus my inability and unnecessity to invent anything in this daily riot of life—the brain screeches get something of this down! Schreibt und Geschreibt! [Write and record!] As great old Simon Dubnow[27] said to his fellow Jews as he was taken away by the Nazis. . . .

Plus (amid many other signs of madness in the head) my refusal to give up anything I know, anything that has ever occurred to me. . . . Who else, praising this German film of Rosa Luxemberg, would nevertheless protest that they had "forgotten" she was a Jew, and Leo Jogiches,[28] and how many others! "You must know everything."[29] "You must not forget anything." Kazin the nag, the obsessive—and yet, like Tolstoy (!) I keep this journal above all to prove that I *exist*. That means the same as: this lifelong, gnawing, consistent, yet generally

27. Simon Dubnow (1860–1941), Jewish historian, author of *World History of the Jewish People* (1925–1929), shot by the Nazis in Riga, Latvia.
28. Leo Jogiches (1867–1919), founding member of the Spartacus League, lover of fellow Marxist Rosa Luxemburg (1871–1919), murdered while investigating her murder by German government troops.
29. "You Must Know Everything," Isaac Babel short story.

unconscious sense of solitude. Who is to say where this loneness, inwardness, splinteredness that has been a tidal effect of being—where it comes from? But what I do know before all else is that everything around me (except my Judith) reinforces it—that no matter how much I enjoy things I do not *respect* them, do not feel part of them—and that there are very few people whom I respect enough to "love" even when it seems wrong not to feel love toward [them].

## April 14, 1987

[. . .] Party for Andrei Voznesensky[30] yesterday at Arthur Schlesinger's. The usual mob of beautiful people—which included a wistful looking Jackie Onassis somewhat timidly making her way through the crowd . . . Jason Epstein, face swollen with too many lunches and dinners, with that usual look of snotty superiority from Jason as both "intellectual" and Random House big shot. . . . What was funny: as we were gathering up our "wraps" from the Schlesinger bedroom, Arthur hurried in to swallow some aspirins, muttering about the excess of people, party. . . . We talked a little, as you can with very intelligent Arthur, about Sidney Hook, the Spanish Civil War, the medieval opinions high at the U of Chicago. . . . Arthur is always intelligent, and best of all in this society, courteous. . . . To function that well as a public character is a solid attribute.

## May 2, 1987

The pilgrimage of The Outsider—Kazin, of course, but also Judith and principally Malamud.

Thinking of my excessively bookish, timorous, totally "idealistic" and visionary youth, with its lack of observation and realistic common sense (the loveless marriage of my parents, the rivalry that was to become vicious as well as pathetic in the case of PK [Pearl] as well as so many others—I realize that the key to Malamud was his belief in magic (writing being the principal magic) . . . stemming from outsidedness. And the fact that all his situations, not just the baseball one in *The Natural* but the "Jewish" ones beginning with "The Magic Barrel," the theme of the marriage broker and the "arranged" marriage so characteristic of Russian Jewish "arrangements," were all archetypal rather than actual. But the archetypal *was* our actuality—this is the significance of

30. Andrei Voznesensky (1933–2010), Russian poet, essayist, and author of the successful rock opera *Juno and Avos*.

the Jewish writer's dealing with "history"—the long Jewish past so embedded in us. [. . .]

I remember most of all his walking about the city "dreaming," dreaming aloud—it reminded me of the importance of such walking about, of its solitariness as well as its search for knowledge. . . .

## June 7, 1987

The Compulsion to Keep a Journal. Out of a sense of vacuum, called loneliness or exclusion or feeling the "marginal" man. The same as "Missing Persons," the longing for the Other, the Other being God as well as various persons. To be *there*, in a certain measure out of *here*. To get over this lifelong feeling that there is some terrific party going on to which I have not been invited.

But of course one's solitariness, one's damned studious solitariness, is the other side of the coin. To be there, yes! But also to be able to come home to myself. A certain distrustfulness of people. Perhaps above all a certain distrustfulness of myself. So that wonderful as Judith's love is, I am always faintly surprised. Looking for the joke, as it were. Not loneliness but a loneness, a feeling of having grown up at the end of the world. Of securing myself in solitude, this everlasting studiousness, "You must know everything." And all the while knowing that there is oh! much, much to be learned, even of the past, from my contemporaries.

So: the journal as a record [of] one's solitariness. Talking to myself! But also a longing to pass over to the other side, to "only connect!"

Coming back from the Village this Sunday afternoon, early evening, I realized that the above is true enough but really not to the point. The journal is above all a form—a form of reflectiveness, for stray reflectiveness, aperçu, etc. It is a dreamy form, sometimes so dreamy that it seems to write itself. Because one is writing to oneself, and in a very real sense *for* oneself. Informal, fragmentary, introspective as all hell, no particular connection between one entry and another. Pieces of the day, pieces of time. Above all, it is a monologue. A form of self-instruction, self-admonition and purification. It is (alas) a way of communing with oneself, of trusting nothing and nobody so much as one's very own self. So it *is* a form of loneliness. But the entries pile up and up, and perhaps more than most writings, somehow add up to a life itself. In its very lack of formal art. In its confessional and prayerful need.

## June 8, 1987

Also true: notes are "fantasies" (Proust). . . . There is something disengaged about them, fragments indeed, just as the "diarist" is at the farthest remove from being "engage"—there is something about the reflectiveness, the inherent casualness, of journal notes that makes for the strictest irony. One is not embattled. . . . Anger surfaces in a journal like mine, or should I say despair, but the heat never lasts very long . . . goes against the grain. These are *personal* notes, and too much emotion of the resentful or aggressive kind somehow dies down. Like making faces at oneself in the mirror.

## June 8–9, 1987

Harvard, for the PBK exercises. I was "PBK orator";[31] and very interesting and satisfying it all was, getting up in Sanders Theater before that responsive group. The evening before, Prof. Elliot Forbes (Emerson's great grandson) officiated a very small and *very* stiff dinner. The poet Amy Clampitt, a nerve-torn poetess, indeed, as shy and any moment on edge as Emily D. must have been—Mrs. McKinsey, the always smiling, already ready Radcliffe PBK President. The great grandson, a professor of music, the great Emerson nose as prominent as on his cousin Amelia Forbes, whom I met at that 70th birthday dinner thrown by an anonymous benefactor in 1975 . . . very donnish, old Cambridge, whimsical. . . . I was walked around the Yard before the exercises by Bill Alfred, who was wearing a bent fedora in the June heat and of course the unreasonably warm kind of suit that as I remember Bill picks up in thrift shops. [. . .][32]

Bill Alfred is one the *quaintest*, most remarkable characters I have ever known—with his rumpled old clothes, his sweet, sad, whispery voice, the Irish bachelor from Brooklyn (half Welsh, hence the Alfred), he walks and talks, the Lowell Professor of Humanities at Harvard, as if nothing except academia has ever worked out for him—certainly not relationship with a woman, and above all not his chief desire, to succeed as a playwright.

I remember thinking [Alfred's play] *Hogan's Goat* was going to be about an old Irish pol—it turned out to be a severe play about infidelity and some such

31. See Chapter 4, note 24.
32. Elliot Forbes (1917–2006), American conductor and musicologist, known for his Beethoven scholarship; Amy Clampitt (1920–1994), American poet, winner of a MacArthur Fellowship; Amelia Forbes Emerson edited diaries and papers of Ralph Waldo Emerson; Elizabeth McKinsey was director of the Bunting Institute at Radcliffe College; William Alfred (1922–1999) was Abbott Lawrence Lowell Professor of the Humanities at Harvard University.

sinfulness in a good Catholic family. (When I asked Bill in the yard yesterday if he missed the Latin mass, he answered, proudly, that on the occasion of his heart attack some years back the priest came to him to say mass and said it in *Latin*.)

I always think of him as something of a bachelor-Irish "saint"; I certainly find irresistible both his sweetness and the link to old Brooklyn. . . . But what a strange human being, when all is said and done, what a throwback, and how odd that he should have succeeded preeminently at Harvard as a scholar (of Anglo-Saxon!) while giving the impression of being down at heels, out of pocket, everywhere else. Where in thunderation did he get that bent, weathered, just barely salvageable fedora to wear in the June heat??

## August 4, 1987

O that famous compulsion to keep a journal! It came from some ridiculous belief that the actual, daily account of things would enable me to deal with them—to make sense of the experience that always seemed to be in *pursuit* of me. And then—in my harried sense of life I had no "time" for invention, no need to "play around" with forces, incidents, developments that always seemed to me dangers to allay, threats to get over.

Perhaps it is only now that I can see how much I was "inventing" the character so assiduous and even storm-tossed in making these notes. Inventing, too, the curious illusion or hypothesis that there was an exact transcription between experience and my journal report thereof. The whole business, not just the daily transaction between the event and the journal, was in invention. I was inventing myself as a character, in my own way inventing a form. Above all inventing "reality" as something always outside of me that I was pursuing—when it was not pursuing me!

What I did not admit about the daily note-taking, my daily report to myself and/or the mysterious tribunal to whom I was reporting and confessing, was that the undertaking, in *my* own use of it, was an invention, a way of life. I was filling up my solitude and, by being so obsessed with the immediate, the exact transcription of a vast complex of many-layered reality, recognizing every day that "I don't know what I think until I see what I've said."

The variety of subjects—the "world" in all its contradictoriness—public and private—

## October 19, 1987

The cultural vertigo of New York, the endless spectacle and merry-go-round. Last night, St. John the Divine,[33] dedicated its "Poets Corner" (shades of Westminster Abbey!) to Emerson and Mark Twain, and I read from *Huckleberry Finn* and "Twain's" ferocious War Prayer of 1904–5. The plumy voice of Canon Morton—Dick Wilbur[34] reading Emerson poems, Bill Jay Smith from *Life on the Mississippi*, dear old Poirier from Emerson's Journals and Essays in a peculiarly aggressive gritty voice. Anyway, all this happened as part of "Vespers"—and what a show the elegant Episcopalians do put up—the procession of the choir in lovely, red hymnal vestments, each of us holding a lighted candle, enormous echoes rebounding through the virtually empty cathedral; I was much edified by the spotlights playing from corners down on the vast, vast emptiness . . . a big cultural event, and there was Rose Styron with her amazingly vivid blonde-gray hair, turtleneck, Rose the most versatile socialite I know. Even flew to New York from Roxbury in Arthur Carter's helicopter!

Remembered in the midst of all this theatrical holiness, the great vaults, the amazing awesomeness, meant to overpower the poor medieval peasant with the subtle busyness of the Gothic style, that the last time I was at "Vespers" was Spring 1945 in Yorkminster . . . the handful of thin, tight, hungry-looking people who attended in those pews parallel to each other before the altar.

## October 29, 1987

[. . .] Reading Truman Capote's *Answered Prayers*[35] (pointless title in this case, but so cutely Capote)—at first I couldn't believe the near-pornographic boasting and strutting of the "Jones" narrator-protagonist, but realized that

33. The Cathedral of St. John the Divine, located at 1047 Amsterdam Avenue in Manhattan, is the largest cathedral and Anglican church and the fourth-largest Christian church in the world. Sometimes called "St. John the Unfinished," the cathedral was begun in 1892, and construction continues.
34. Richard Wilbur (1921–), poet and translator, was appointed the sixth poet laureate consultant to the Library of Congress in 1987 and twice received the Pulitzer Prize for Poetry. William Jay Smith (1918–), poet, was appointed the nineteenth poet laureate consultant to the Library of Congress from 1968 to 1970.
35. *Answered Prayers: The Unfinished Novel* (New York: Random House, 1987).

the book is full of story-telling talent, that he certainly carries this smelly stuff right along. But, N.B.! the sexual boasting and the name dropping are all of a piece! Das heisst: only the "big name" queers are the real notables, standing out from the crowd, living just as they like (Tennessee, Natalie Barney, even Ned Rorem, though he is not really important, not enuf, and so is put down). . . . Homosexual sex is the ultimate distinction, if combined with enough fame and mazuma. It permits the infinite variety of shocking, even "unnatural" poses, fixtures, adventures. And above all it is for the sake of sex and spectacle alone. No sentimental nonsense about it.

What drew Truman, I guess draws us, is the literally lurid, the shock violence associated with so much money and sexual "freedom." From the beginning "T" knew how to grab attention, how to turn his (to himself acknowledged) freakishness into the greatest publicity. . . . Then he became the pet monkey, court jester, of New York big, big money "society," amusing the Paleys and the like, a gossip conduit par excellence—yet all the while sharpening his knives on them, as he did on everything and everyone. . . . Why all this malice? To show off his "knowingness" about people, of course, to be in the know beyond everyone else. But also, since no such "society reporter" is ever without some moral reproach at the very doings he is enjoying, a certain horror at the ultimate separateness, shallowness, luridness. . . . Note how the only warmth, very covert, appears when people are suddenly incapacitated or moribund. . . .

Capote was the most gifted and, in his own way, the deepest of the "smart" (Ritz Hotel, beautiful people) NY writers. . . . What is most signal about him and his frightful, but truly graphic, distinct, palpableness in *Answered Prayers* is that he regarded himself as a freak and went up against a world he fundamentally regarded as overblown, contemptible, narcissistic . . . but a world that accepted him only as . . . (his word) *entertainer*.

In this world Mailer is the parvenu as fantasist . . . it is his dream world, one he thinks he can master through the swagger of his style. . . . For Mailer sex was the first great "fantasy"; but of course he betrayed the Jew in him by turning it into world revolution, ideology, mastership through "idea"; Capote, who, as he repeatedly said, had had sex with everything and everyone, even "fire hydrants," needed no such fantasies based on sex . . . he had the weary habitue's scorn of romanticism . . . though of course dying for "love."

The "society" writers—Capote, Mailer, Vidal, old New York's Auchincloss—then the pitiful Jewish patients and East Hampton crowd—Judith Rossner and the like . . . Or the old *New Yorker* gang, from A. J. Liebling, Jean Stafford, and the like—[36]

## October 30, 1987

[. . .] Last night's dinner at Cafe de Paris (49th and 2nd) with Philip Roth and Claire Bloom. The dinner was superb, the restaurant charmingly unpretentious and somehow *right*, and having made my way to the place in the face of the densest, screamingest, impatient evening traffic I have encountered in ages (like an army moving straight at any schmuck in the way)—a boiling, screaming river of traffic threatening to flood the very pavements—I found that once the subject of Arthur Miller and *Timebends*[37] had come up, Philip wouldn't let go, insisted on wiping the floor with Arthur north south west and east—bad writer, no thinker, even his marriage a disaster . . . on and on.

Philip always thinks in straight lines, fancies himself a specialist in common sense, but when he goes bang, bang, bang like this (and I have been through the performance before) I realize why I see him only for sort of formal dinners perhaps three x a year and despite the edge he fosters, am always glad to see him depart in all his prosperity and self-satisfaction. The cleverness, the sharpness, the continual *edge* somehow turn even an evening, to say nothing of his fiction, into *performance*. There are no purely meditative, unexpected moments, no reflection outside professional ones. The competition is really keen!

That pointy nose of his. . . .

## November 18, 1987

[. . .] My journal book must replicate the "associationism," the catch-as-catch-can, and the impressionability that are of my pattern. . . . The moment to moment life, the impulse and waywardness . . . but above all the characteristic of wonder, the sense of awe, the struggle against limits, the insatiability and of course the "moodiness."—This up and down so deep to my inner weather. [. . .]

36. Louis Stanton Auchincloss (1917–2010), American lawyer, novelist, historian, writes about the private lives of the American Brahmin class following in the tradition of novelists Henry James and Edith Wharton. Judith Rossner (1935–2005), novelist, best known for *Looking for Mr. Goodbar* (1975).

37. Arthur Miller, *Timebends: A Life* (New York: Grove, 1987).

## December 2, 1987

Jimmy Baldwin dead in Paris. New York's very angry man. So talented, so expressive, but above all so vehement in behalf of the suffering blacks and not to forget expressively angry and suffering Jimmy Black. More than any other black writer Jimmy B was an emotional powerhouse, always facing you down with his anger. When he wasn't camping. I remember him a little from Paris in the '50s, when he was pals with Ann and was flighty funny. "A Negro Looks At Henry James," the great article for his new Joosh magazine called *Commentary*. Then in the '60s, when he was invited to the White House, and sat near the radiator in 110 Riverside Drive [AK's apartment], getting hotter than the elevator, getting too hot for Richard Poirier, who began to quibble with him over his anger, anger, which was so set-up, so professional, so charming! I suspect that Jimmy will be remembered not so much for his essays, powerful as they were, but for his kind of angry dominance of his material, for standing out so, in every sense. As he said, "What more do I need: I'm already black and homosexual." Trying to figure out, still, whether those stories way back about his being hetero and being a lover of Midge Decter (??!!!) had any truth to them. . . . Whenever in these last years I saw [him] on the street, he seemed to occupy it with a conscious conspicuousness, even when he sort of swayed and camped his way down the street. [. . .]

## January 12, 1988

[. . .] Why do I hate Sidney Hook so? Why have I always regarded him as a deadly enemy to *my* spirit? It is because he personifies everything I resented and even *feared* in the intellectual arrogance of the left, in the circumscriptions of imagination, in the logic-chopping, and above all in the polemical aggressiveness of the street fighter. Since these habits of mind have accompanied him all the way to Ronald Reagan, the Hoover Institution, etc. [. . .]

## February 4, 1988

[. . .] [Leo] Szilard 1898–1964—working with Fermi at Chicago, he developed the first self-sustained nuclear reactor based on uranium fission. One of the first to realize that nuclear chain reactions could be used in bombs, and instrumental in urging the U.S. to create the first atomic bomb, he latter opposed nuclear warfare.

That night in Wellfleet, Schlesinger mewed that Leo Szilard was "crazy." And certainly my brief encounter with him showed him as a beggar in the courts of power, a poor suppliant Jew where before that he had been one of the "makers and finders" of the new age. . . . Brings back my favorite notion of the Jew in history, high and low, the first man and the last, the nearest to God (as he thinks) and the pariah, the "prophet and the bounder" (Proust), the most creative and the most abject, the most "in" and the most "out."

God's first born and yet the most proscribed . . . nearest to what even the future anti-Semite John Jay Chapman[38] called "the heart of the world" and yet the most despised. [. . .]

## February 11, 1988

[. . .] My recurring image of the Jews—the High and the Low—the Jew as scientific wizard, even as leader of a government enterprise (Oppenheimer) and then the pariah. Over and again, and not just because the Jews lacked political power. Something inherent in their marginal, their parvenu, their over-intellectualized and moralized situation. Because there is always that distant monitor, that God who bewitched them forever by actually speaking to them—after they had first invented him. And where did they find Him in the first place? Telos everlasting some fixed ultimate end. . . . Life must be lived *this* way and emphatically not any other way.

The rise and fall of the Jewish wizards.[39] . . . The pretentious, somehow self-distorting figure of Oppenheimer. Thinking of the one time I saw him, in that very "British" terribly refined bookshop years and years ago not far from the Harcourt office—Oppenheimer was right behind me, drawlingly asking for a *German* translation of a Dostoevsky novel. . . .

The eternal dichotomy, power and the powerless, and never the twain shall meet. But the meaning of the "modern" world is the acceleration and concentration of power in forms never before imagined, much less realized. The "modern" world, one of *knowledge* and more and more one of heedless routine *application*. The concentration of this power in a few physicists' heads, became something more than "the mind of the race."

38. John Jay Chapman (1862–1933), essayist, an acute critic of Ralph Waldo Emerson, and, according to Edmund Wilson in *The Triple Thinkers*, "probably the best letter writer that we have ever had in this country."

39. Kazin was reading *Nuclear Fear: A History of Images* by Spencer R. Weart (Cambridge: Harvard University Press, 1998) for a review, "Awaiting the Crack of Doom," *New York Times Book Review* (May 1, 1986): 1, 40–41.

## February 21, 1988

Thinking of Irving Howe and his mulishness. "Comrade Morpheus"?

All these "New York Intellectuals" ever had was their dream of revolution—the trouble was that they had no utopian feelings of any kind, could not imagine what this "new" society would be, were incapable of this, saw themselves as intellectuals, agents of change, heavy thinkers. But all the while their "revolution" agenda was not even their own, and really had very little pertinence to American life, except in the 1930s—where there was a lot of discontent if no uprising. It was the uprising they were fascinated by, Trotsky as the armed bohemians' leader, the big speechifier and word man—not the new society. And now that the "uprising" dream is long, long behind them (feudal Russia took care of that), they have nothing to say, to show. And, as in the "age of revolution," they still represent a collective mood, an immigrant heritage, rather than individual power. [. . .]

## March 20, 1988

[. . .] Through Tompkins Street to the River. What an effect of long-lived-in, old New York, East Side New York, Tompkins Park give[s]. Like being in the slum parts of Dublin . . . the less picturesque parts of Florence. Old, very old! The almost indecipherable memorial to the General Slocum (1904).[40] . . . Walked along the river . . . looking across to the gritty factories, foundries, warehouses of my dear old, old Brooklyn (as in the 19th century pictures, a church steeple rising above the industrial muck). A cut leading down to the river, Gowanus Creek. . . . At the widest part of the island, you get this amazing view, so much prettier than the new skyline at the Battery, of midtown. The profusion, the mass of New York, weight on weight, but unlike the chocolate-covered brownstone city of the 19th century what I see is the springiness of all those different buildings thrusting themselves sometimes antically against the sky. The "electric vitality" of New York, as always, the effect of this mix, this grand mix.

Person and place. New York and I, I and New York are so bound up together that I cannot look at a picture of the *Forward* building in Sander's Grove Press book

40. The P.S. *General Slocum*, a paddle steamer, named after the Civil War officer and New York congressman Henry Warner Slocum, caught fire and burned in New York's East River, taking 1,021 people to their deaths, New York's greatest loss of life from a disaster until the September 11, 2001, terrorist attack.

on the Lower East Side without bursting into tears—so much does it bring my father back.[41] Talk about having too much "New York material!" that material is my life; and now that I am about to write still another New York chronicle, and this in the "last act," I realize that my hesitation, as usual, is because every street is part of *my* story and my story is set in street after street of New York.

## March 22, 1988

[. . .] Israel was bruited to be the "normal" state for the Jews, the place where the Jews would, at last, lead a "normal" existence. I have always suspected that there would be endless conflicts between Israel and the Moslem world, and my *deepest* suspicion is that the third world war might very well start there. [. . .] This is not the time to ask why the Jews are always (almost always) out of step, in some extreme position. . . . Maybe the messengers of God, because they bring the Holy Message? All irony and bitterness aside, the question remains: where and how is this tribe, our tribe, to become "normal"? What does "normality" mean for a people always "ahead" of the rest, and just as routinely "below," everyone else, condemned to total "extermination"? There will never be peace with Israel. What began as an experiment in resettlement on "democratic Socialist" principles, or Tolstoyan, what-have-you, is now a power struggle to the death (as in the Bible), but now with the whole Moslem world, and intrinsically with the whole Third World. . . .

Answer of the true believers: none of that matters . . . just obey the Torah, and live it. . . . And if we must die for the sanctification of the name. . . .

My distant cousin Seth Schein, a classicist who has joined the Graduate faculty, dropped in the other day. In the course of the conversation he let it be known that his grandfather, old Orlikoff, had some reputation as a "Hebrew scholar," Talmudist, etc. I remember the old geezer as a haughty, impatient seller of kitchen ranges, with a face (just like his son David's) as deeply indented as the landscape of Switzerland. It now comes over me, only now, that what I saw in old Orlikoff was, of course, contempt for my poor, unlettered parents, still stuck in poor, old Brownsville. How much of my (unconscious) life has been not competing with my father, Freudian style, but making up for him. Admittedly, I am an "Oedipal" case, considering my lifelong fantasies of making it with married women, with displacing the husband, even humiliating him in front of me as I make love to his wife. It was

41. *The Lower East Side: A Guide to Its Jewish Past in 99 New Photographs*, Ronald Sanders text, photographs by Edward V. Gillon Jr. (New York: Dover, 1980).

surely the mother, however, who was more the center of some energy for me to conquer than it was the father. And I claim to be the only one—"I alone am left to tell thee"—who cared for my father, who remembers him. I cannot forget, as I write this, the scene at the funeral parlor where those rats Dan and Pearlie sat (it seemed to me so light-heartedly) at one side of the coffin. How cooly, indeed, they took my father's death. As they did his life. Anyway, I put this down, on the brink of writing my text for *Our New York*, remembering how much there was to redeem. Alfred the redeemer. The avenging angel. It is still up to me, as it always was.

## March 26, 1988

My affection for Angus Fletcher,[42] whom I playfully call (to myself) not only "Angus" but "Angst." It is that patiently suffering face as well as his elegance, Britishly good manners, etc. Angus, always deteriorating or on the brink of devastation, yet the good teacher, bearing up, doing his duty by his students, etc. I could never admit my "attachment" to him, it would only embarrass him as a homosexual. And I must admit that what I find so endearing in him is this combination of some obvious distinction *plus* the fight he puts up to survive. Strange but undeniable: he has great charm for me.

## April 2, 1988

[. . .] Paolo Milano died in his sleep in Rome early this morning. Andy [Milano's son] called me. He would have been 84 in July. God how I miss him—what a big space he occupied in my life, in my "development." One of those European teachers, the émigrés who taught me—like Hannah. But Paolo was sweet, full of deportment, terribly bookish, essentially a follower. . . . I remember dear Ramy Alexander (né Alexander Goldstein in the great port city of Odessa) saying "Paolo doesn't believe anything unless he reads it—in a book." Faithful, European-faithful Paolo, the good disciple, the faithful teacher and friend. . . . Putting down these first impressions now of my loss, I think of Paolo as a prime friend in those intoxicatingly unsettled years right after the war—the European intellectual, the bright new spirit in the Village that somehow gave presence to the "last intellectuals"—Broyard,[43] Lionel Abel, Harold Rosenberg, Milton Klonsky. . . . [. . .]

42. Angus Fletcher (1930–), Distinguished Professor of Comparative Literature at CUNY.
43. Anatole Broyard (1920–1990), critic and editor at the *New York Times*, whose posthumously published memoir of Greenwich Village in the postwar years, *Kafka Was the Rage* (1993), Kazin admired. Milton Klonsky, New York poet and essayist, one of the group who gathered at Isaac Rosenfeld's apartment in the 1940s.

## April 12, 1988

I'm so busy, so frantic half of the time, defending my ancient interests on the battleground of criticism, that I simply underrate and obfuscate the intense amount of speculative thinking that goes on in "theory." The way to appreciate this, I see now, is to remember the hoary, pious elders in the academy of my youth—how utterly primitive they seem to me now by comparison with the really impressive mental activity that goes on now. What held me back was, as always, my intellectual piety—my desire to see the creative process honored rather than the furiously abstract intellectual. And I shall never believe that a whole university of critical thinkers is equal to a single page of *Crime and Punishment.* Nevertheless, I have been too much a stick in the mud about all this—not willing to be more curious about the subject.

The key point: the university as a domain and even *center* of intellect. Irresistible. I am never so alert and happy anywhere else.

## April 13, 1988

[. . .] There are public Jews and private Jews. But can one really worship the Jewish God privately? Once there were *hidden* Jews, but even they prayed *together* in the attics and cellars and the sewers of occupied Warsaw.

To admit that one is a Jew is already to commit oneself not only to God but to community—whether or not you believe that (like extreme Islamic sects) you belong to the "People of God." There is no "private Jew." That is just genteel affectation—a social mannerism—a way of living in a society you do not trust. . . .

## April 20, 1988

There are days, even mornings, which mark a decisive turn. Like Jackson being defeated in the NY primary, like the total Black-Jewish division in NY that Jackson—and that ape Koch—has helped to bring about. Like the brutality of the Thatcher government in dismantling what is left of the welfare state. . . . Like the increasing brutality of the Israelis, the whole take-it-or-leave-it policy on deportations and the rest.

A point in history after which things will be *definitely* different. Oddly enough, the latest news under the ax of history reminds me of the sensations I used to have at this season in Pineapple Street after the war—early spring, a softer light in the sky, fleecier clouds, a sense of having arrived at a point of no return.

Fascinating, of course, to think that all these things not only have sharper consequences, but that their sharpness also consists in their being cut off from their antecedents. Militant, daredevil, fuck-you-all Israel is, on the books, the child of the Holocaust, as Jackson is the descendent of slavery. But as power entities, the embattled state and the embattled Black politician move independently in their consequences, no matter how many appeals they make to the past. That is the lesson of every day now: that the past, the different pasts, are all dead. As the Roman Church is not the consequence of the "sacrifice" of Jesus, not even the continuation (as it is) of the Roman Empire, but a powerful entity in itself. . . .

What am I getting at in all this? That history becomes a book, a fable, a set of symbols . . . that there really is no continuity between the "sacrificed" (whether in the Holocaust or under slavery) and those who, in their name, are very busy sacrificing others. Sentimental idealism (my pervasive fault) or as Mike Abrams[44] says, my "humanistic radicalism," this is the arm-chair attitude toward history. The actors and agents are independent entities, new forces in the current drama of power relations. The past was "sacrifice?" The present is all power, and the people being sacrificed have no access to the language codes and dominating symbols of the people who have the power and whose only interest is in getting more and more of it. The "probation report" on the criminal is of no relevance. The present deed is everything. The appeal to the past is only a way of eluding the ax of *present* history.

## June 19, 1988

[. . .] G___,[45] now rather broader than she used to be, face looks a bit swollen. Has been carrying on with other men, as for so long she did with me, with a frankness to herself, a "level" common sense, that belong to a great military strategist. No sentimental "guilt" or psychoanalytic nonsense, close as she is to the great commercant of these things. Her steady determination in matters of the heart, like her wonderful avidity in bed, make all things possible. Never

44. Meyer "Mike" Howard Abrams (1912–), prominent and extremely influential American literary critic, an expert on Romanticism, best known for *The Mirror and the Lamp: Romantic Theory and the Critical Tradition* (1953).

45. See Chapter 6, note 89.

look back! And de l'audace, l'audace surtout! How much I owe her for that steadiness, that level common sense, that totally Mediterranean, sub Napolitana, matter of fact. When she talked about the very serious operation her husband had undergone earlier this year or something, there was oh just the hint of an ironic little smile. She would not be devastated by his death. On the other hand, she is *fundamentally* loyal, I suppose because of family.

What struck me most was the little physical changes in her. No longer the fetching school girl in the blue coat, with briefcase, who used to walk up 14th Street waiting for me to come down the stairs and catch up with her. A great romance, a very great romance. Needless to say, she wore a dress that allowed me to see her beautiful breasts swimming in and out of sight as she moved.

## July 23, 1988

[. . .] The city my teacher, guide, landscape and landmark, my native ground in truth. My strongest images of this influence: born into a community, with the most intense tradition of both locality and tradition. The community was the world. But as I grew, I became aware of New York as a whole series of communities, and this became [my] first sense of the "other." . . . Street to street, those equally sized city blocks as the very ground of my life. Doing the street over and over, the same street leading to other streets. . . .

And then the city itself, far-flung, mysteriously full, containing so many discoveries. . . . Life never ceased to discoveries—But I musn't forget the amazing resources within my tenement existence. Willie Bernstein (whom I hated and who hated me) nevertheless confiding to me at twelve that he had discovered a great poet, his name Ezra Pound. . . . The Glenmore, Saratoga and Stone Avenue libraries.

No question that I threw myself on the city—256 A Sutter Avenue was the nest to return to, but "the city" in truth now, all of it, became the world. [. . .]

All things come related in the City. And this interweaving finally makes for that continuous sense of apprehension which, along with the delight of and in discovery, is the alertness that stamps the true city man. Anticipation.

I was formed by anxieties that had nothing to do with me. My parents' characters, the sorrowful, bitter picture carried here of Russian Jewry. The arduousness of working class life.

But along with that, as in the classical Jewish community pictures in the New Testament, was (in the form of socialism) the burning passion for emancipation, for deliverance. The idealism and devotion were as intense as the sense of limitation, and of course grew out of it.

"Making It" was definitely not a substitute for that sense of "historic" purpose. . . . And comradeship. . . .

Circle on circle ever-widening, beginning at the margins of the city and widening to include the whole city.

## November 24, 1988

THANKSGIVING DAY Rejoice! THE CRY FOR JUSTICE

After the long day, or almost two days of commemoration of Primo Levi[46] at NYU, I found myself sitting across the table at Beatrice's Restaurant from a rather vain Italian-born medievalist, whose name I had difficulty in catching. He had the usual smug opinions about everything—another "reality instructor." Praising Thatcher and the end of socialism in Europe, he countered my objections to her injustices against the North, the trade unions, the workers in general, by noting with the usual self satisfaction of the type, "there *is* no justice."

No. There is no justice, no final justice in human affairs; the struggle for existence makes for too much competition. *But the cry for justice* is eternal because it comes from the condemned, the pariahs, the proscribed, the forgotten, the homeless, the dissidents, the outlawed.

Thinking of this for my little speech [for] the *Tikkun* dinner, December 19. Thinking how my own background and the old association between socialism and the *idea* of justice—of mama and the eviction,[47] of the 60,000 unemployed in Union Square with the police training machine guns on them, and, of course, the Holocaust, of the Jews cooped up in the freight cars taking them to their death in Poland, how they were not allowed the slightest dignity for their toilet needs, how when they got to a station and were let off for a spell, how they

46. Primo Michele Levi (1919–1987), Jewish-Italian chemist and writer, best known for his account of the year he spent in the Auschwitz concentration camp, *If This Is a Man* (1958).
47. In "The Cry for Justice," *Tikkun* (May–June, 1989): 77–80, Kazin recalls his mother defying the police and carrying furniture back into an apartment from which a family had been evicted.

squatted over the railroad tracks, of the derision and scorn of the Germans, who, of course, saw in their pitiful state fresh evidence of their being sub-human, a sub-species, and thus deserving of everything put on them.

The cry for justice is so heard on every side today that only an ideologist can say that one party is completely right and the other completely wrong. But it is plain just now that the cry for justice that comes up very powerfully from Arabs in the occupied territories—and for which over 250 people, many of them young people, have been killed by Israeli army and police—that their cry for justice is certainly louder than that of Defense Minister Rabin talking about the early struggle of Labor Zionists.

America! How the Jews have been transformed—politically, religiously. . . . Remembering just now the scene in John Hersey's *The Wall*, where the Jews holding classes in the sewers of Warsaw say that they pity the rich Jews of Hollywood, who cannot know such a depth and sharpness of experience, one thinks of the formerly condemned in America, like Wiesel, and how many others, pursuing their celebrity . . . their successful public careers. All this in such contrast to Primo Levi's account—and his likening Begin to Arafat.[48]

The condemned in New York—the homeless in Madison Square Garden—what an amazing civilization. At the same moment the American Jewish Committee publishing one of the most reactionary magazines in America [*Commentary*], and one which only recently practically justified some of the Nazi murderers among us because of their intense anti-Communism.

[*New York*] *Times*, Thanksgiving Day. Jewish leaders, notables meeting with John Sununu,[49] Bush's appointed chief of staff, and how well satisfied with his attitude to Israel. *The assurances he gave them*, all under the leadership of Jacob Stein, a national co-chairman of the Bush For President Committee and past chairman of the Conference of Presidents of Major Jewish Organizations. (Weissman to Truman, I am the president of 100 thousand presidents.) [. . .]

48. Cf. Kazin's essay comparing Wiesel's reliability as a witness unfavorably with Levi's, "My Debt to Elie Wiesel and Primo Levi," in *Testimony: Contemporary Writers Make the Holocaust Personal*, ed. David Rosenberg (New York: Random House, 1989), 115–128. In response, Wiesel accused Kazin of "lending credence to those who deny the Holocaust," *All Rivers Run to the Sea: Memoirs* (New York: Random House, 1995), 336.
49. John Henry Sununu (1939–), governor of New Hampshire (1983–1989) and chief of staff under President George H. W. Bush.

"Among the organizations represented at the meeting were Hadassah, The American Jewish Congress, the National Council of Young Israel, the Synagogue Council of America, the Rabbinical Assembly and the Union of American Hebrew Congregations."

All of which reminds me of the scene at the Allenby Bridge in 1967, the broken bridge, the Arab women carrying up and down the elevated and depressed sides of the bridge all their worldly goods, even refrigerators. . . . And of the Israeli soldier standing watch over them, rifle at the ready, who observing my face, said "Don't forget the troubles *we've* had!"

I am not likely to forget them. Or to cease observing how American society in all its wealth and distraction and wastefulness creates so many conditions in which we forget the cry for justice. Thinking of Elie Wiesel and how the American Jewish middle class fastened on him as a symbol of the Holocaust and as a surrogate for their own religious vacancy.

## December 25, 1988

The "lonely" country made lonely by its lack of attachment to anything but material advancement.

*The Compulsion To Keep A Journal*, out of personal tribulation and self-pity to the proud and aroused critic (of many things, not least his own life), who puts these things down in private because it is not always possible to speak one's mind in "public." And in private, too, because there is where the heart lives, there is your treasure, your inmost life, your constant life . . . the life that you do not share with anyone—not with the people you love most—the life, the mental life, the ongoing life, that you cannot tell from yourself. Your very "soul." [. . .]

## December 29, 1988

[. . .] Why in hell do I ever think of writing, for all its tribulations, as anything but joy? To look forward to the morning's work, to do your morning's work, and then to feel that you have paid back something of your debt to the Creation. . . . And with this, to look at things more sharply, attentively, and above all more *lovingly*, with the senses and coordinates aroused by the act of writing (this act of supreme attention), and still in place, still vibrating. . . . Thank you, Lord, for giving me my work, such a chance as so few people ever get.

## January 31, 1989

[. . .] Afternoon, wandered over to the Violet café at NYU to have tea with Doctorow.[50] Charming, mild, I was very taken with him. Of course our conversation, in which I was trying to get him to say something about the moral significance of all that murdering and criminality in *Billy Bathgate* became a classic example of the dialogue between "creator" and "critic"=he emphasizing how much the book came from a single metaphor, was all within the language which moves it, constructs it—and I talking, almost against my will, from the "outside." But it was a lovely meeting, diminished something of the loneliness and insignificance (professionally speaking) I feel these days. [. . .]

## February 5, 1989

As Jesus identifies himself in the life-force by his father-intoxication, My father, Our Father, Abba, so Harold Bloom identifies himself in the literature-force (his key word is "strong") by ranking Freud with the great writers—or father, by making Freud the *grammar* essential and inherent to the great writers. Which makes Freud Bloom's son. The son really, in Bloom, makes himself heir to and replica of the father. The agon of the Oedipal myth, the son fighting the father so as to replace him, provides Bloom with his driving myth—there are primary figures whom the son, critic, comes to resemble by dwelling on the strength he has to conquer.

## February 11, 1989

[. . .] I suppose if I had continued in the line of *On Native Grounds* I would have radical democracy as my message. The book remains after forty-seven years, important to a lot of people for the "mythology" that went into it unbeknownst to the author[. . . .] What happened instead of continuity on that line was, of course, the disillusionment with radicalism as a *program*—I certainly remained faithful to the ethos, and in myself incorporated it, I see now, as the democratic *agony:* i.e., hope of liberty, equality, fraternity, and the hope not only constantly deferred but open to shocks and horrors when you consider the pool of life in which you have to swim in New York.

I see now, however, that the "autobiographical" books, my personal history, do convey the aspiration and torment of democracy—the setting New York City,

50. E. L. Doctorow (1931–), American novelist, short story writer, and essayist, probably best known for *Ragtime* (1975), a historical fiction set around 1900.

"where seven million people live in peace and enjoy the benefits of democracy": (Wasn't that the old WNYC invocation?)[51] [. . .]

## February 23, 1989

Dinner party at Louis and Adele Auchincloss, Louis so bright and cheery, always primed for cordial interchange and Adele with the mysteriously bad teeth for a Vanderbilt, with that extraordinary sweetness and presentability of the very, very rich. Thinking of the first millionaires I met back in "socialist days," a Miss Crane of Crane plumbing, who walked and looked and smiled so benevolently, as if she were an air plant or lived on perfumed cushions.

Interesting woman who is actually teaching in Julia Richman,[52] a Mrs. Martha Suthpen . . . the hard-bitten Will Gaddis[53] and his girl friend Muriel. I actually got Gaddis to talk about his life, and began to understand why he looks and sounds as if he doesn't *want* to talk. Divorced parents, sent to boarding school when he was 5, himself a problem at Harvard, when he broke the sacred rule of not getting his name into the papers, and was "sent down" = allowed back only if he would live in the yard, in freshman dorm, so he refused.

The Auchincloss house 1111 Park Avenue at 90th Street looking exactly like the designated and inherited interior of an Auchincloss novel. All his books in library bindings, his own study with first editions of Edith Wharton—the dining room with its ancestral portraits.

The dinner party—going through the proper motions. Every gesture counts. Watching yourself perform. Manners as a ritual, confirming the cast's sense of its own status. No one plays the crazy. Arthur Miller was supposed to be present but couldn't make it. I kept thinking of what Arthur's hoarse directness and blue work shirt would have done to the evening's performance. [. . .]

## March 26, Easter 1989

"Only in New York"—on W. 96th Street, just outside the church, a decent looking fellow with a package, who suddenly stopped in front of a tree (and a poor looking tree it is) and on a sudden impulse, ***kicked it.*** [. . .]

51. Kazin is correct; it was a pre–World War II theme of announcers on radio station WNYC.
52. A comprehensive high school on the Upper East Side.
53. William Gaddis (1922–1998), novelist, best known for *The Recognitions* (1955). The reasons for his dismissal from Harvard are uncertain; he may have been involved in a drunken brawl.

## April 21, 1989

Lunch yesterday with Anatole Broyard at Orso's on W. 46—his favorite. Odd how, despite all my wariness with Anatole, I fall in with his "clever" style, become friskier and more profane and reckless. Yes, yes—one "falls in." Yet for the first time in my experience Anatole, whom I privately think of as a riverboat gambler just in from N'Awlins, was positively wistful at times, didn't shoot down every writer whose name happened to come up. [. . .]

## May 31, 1989

[. . .] Israel settlers, more and more taking over, occupiers and *racists*. You hear me, you bloody patriots, racists! From this morning's *Times*, 20 settlers "detained" (you may be sure it won't be for long) for killing a 14 year old Palestinian girl. Rampaged through the village Kifl Harith, setting fire to a house and crops and firing submachine guns in a reprisal for a clash with stone-throwers in which a rabbi was injured.

One settler who said he took part in the attack told the Israeli radio: "In our opinion we are a part of this entire country, and *every Arab village is also our place*. It is only the army's orders that keep us out of villages."

The march of Zionist progress. Atavism. Settlers stoned on their way to pray at nearby "tombs of Biblical heroes."

## July 27, 1989

[. . .] to Knopf's, where I encountered my editor Gordon Lish in the throes of post-operative pain and incessant pissing [. . .] A lot of the usual trying to find the Grand Pasha about my journals, but I didn't wait to find out the latest about not seeing him. I called Lynn Nesbit and guess what, "I am driving him to the country tomorrow," so there. The fact is that the journals scare even me when I look them over—so much longing, so much resentment, so many names to worry about even if they don't sue me for libel: Hah Hah [. . .][54]

54. The "Grand Pasha" probably is Kazin's old friend Jason Epstein, who was editorial director of Random House, which owned Knopf, where Lish was senior editor. Lynn Nesbit is a prominent literary agent. *A Lifetime Burning in Every Moment*, a memoir based in part on Kazin's journals was published by HarperCollins in 1996.

## August 12, 1989

[. . .] Reading Eric Foner's *Reconstruction* for my big Lincoln piece.[55] Admirable, endlessly informative about the period and the country at large during the *Wawh*. But only those in the know, like yours truly, know the irony—so much of this inherited from his Stalinist fanatics Father and Uncle, the Foners![56] Of whom Hofstadter used to say in amazement, "They read only first-hand sources!" If Patriotism is the last refuge of the scoundrel, the Black cause is the last refuge of a defunct Stalinist. But what Papa and Uncle couldn't accomplish in a general book of history, the "young" Eric has. And he is De Witt Clinton professor of history at Columbia, Dick's old chair! *Ça vous amuse, la vie?* Yes, Father, occasionally life is an absolute riot. And if I had time to tell you more . . . !

Now that my "book of life," this journal, is being read by one or another editorial persons, I find myself being more conscious here that I write what may actually be read by others! But I foresee that it will be published only after me demise, and in very attenuated and by then unintelligible form. And I had hoped, just once, to get some real dough in my own lifetime!

## September 12, 1989

Amused to be asked to write for the 75th anniversary of the *New Republic* an article in which I am invited to be frank in my evaluation of the paper.[57] Being just a year younger than the paper and having grown up with it since I first began writing there fifty-five years ago, I am tempted. Tempted by what? By the *inner* history, the endless ups and downs, hysterical loyalties and revolting betrayals of the "progressive" tradition, elitist gentlemanly and always well supported by wealthy patrons (now the editor himself). The *NR* has always been a liberal, "progressive" island in the vast sea of American complacency, but what strikes me most at this moment, getting some preliminary thoughts down, is that it

55. "A Forever Amazing Writer," a review of Lincoln's *Speeches and Writings, New York Times Book Review* (December 10, 1989): 3, 39.

56. Eric Foner (1943–), American historian and professor at Columbia University. His father, Jack Foner (1910–1999), taught history at Baruch College until he was dismissed in 1941 along with sixty other New York teachers for alleged communist influences on their teaching. In 1979 the New York State Board of Higher Education apologized to Foner and the other teachers for a gross violation of their academic freedom. Jack's brother Philip (1910–1994) was a labor historian and activist. Richard Hofstadter was the chairman of Eric Foner's Ph.D. dissertation committee at Columbia.

57. "*The New Republic*: A Personal View" (November 6, 1989): 78–83.

has always agreed with the historical moment—isolationist in the '20s, virtually fellow traveling in the '30s, madly pro-war and "progressive" about the New Deal when the New Deal had been jettisoned by its father—and in the age of Peretz,[58] disillusioned pet-liberal without throwing the baby entirely out of the bath, staunchly and often aggressively pro Israel at all costs, but glued into the various fashions and follies of that company town WA.

Still, a "minority" paper, not a mass organ, and with the kind of literary drama-movie coverage (especially the occasional art piece) that bespeaks a "high" level of culture and is addressed to the professional, smart, chic audience that loves to read criticism as intelligence.

Peretz's leadership has been too strident, too irritated with the "Marxist" and "Woodstock" elements among the young whom he is aware of as a Harvard teacher in his spare jours. All the earmarks of the parvenu, but is true of the professionalized Jewish middle class, the people "who have risen" more quickly and dramatically than any other in American life. On the same charity board with Frank Sinatra! Knowing all the big wigs in Israel and where-not. The post-liberal bitterness. [. . .]

## October 21, 1989

[. . .] Read my Mississippi paper—Faulkner and religion—to the usual Grad Center gathering. I waded through so many puddles on my way to the *Times* to deliver my Lincoln review, then to the P.O. and the Grad Center for my reading, that I was wet from shoes and socks to terrible "raincoat," which is definitely not impermeable. So having changed to a pair of socks that I bought on the way, I read my paper without my sodden shoes! The only audience I can imagine so friendly to me by tradition and instinct—Kazin now the old fart—that they seemed delighted rather than shocked. [. . .]

## October 24, 1989

Lenin supposed to have said when he was finally ensconced in the Kremlin—"My head is swimming!" *My* head swims every day at the changes in the Evil Empire—Today, news of the Hungarian Republic—the Russians admitting that their bloody

58. Martin Peretz (1938–), then the editor.

war in Afghanistan was illegal and immoral—three hundred thousand marching in Leipzig for a separation of the East German State and the C.P. . . . One of the many reasons why I would hate to die in the next thrilling ominous decade swerving relentlessly into the 21st century—I would have to miss all the thrilling developments and the Big Quake that may erupt politically in old Stalin land.

O Alexander Cockburn and other such assorted shits who have so long defended Russian totalitarianism in the name of "socialism"!

## October 26, 1989
### [dated November 26, 1989]

The only thing to say about Mary McCarthy's passing is that it somehow marks (more than the death of Trilling, Rahv, etc., etc.) the passing of a turbulent critical style related to past utopian dreams and immeasurable bitterness therefrom. After Mary, everyone else will seem bland. The last link (one of them) with an American idea of "*socialism*." But Mary and I, we had [the] 19th century childhood necessary to so much 20th century assertion. Like the Romantic generation that went nuts for the French Revolution, and then was driven nuts by the Revolution itself, so we in respect to the Russian Revolution. American Socialism—meaningless term—*radicalism* no longer quite exists because of its lack of any *international* idea. [. . .]

## December 1, 1989

Inducted into the American Academy of Arts and Sciences, along with [Elizabeth] Hardwick, [William] Gaddis, [James] Merrill, [Helen] Frankenthaler. The solemnity of it all in that vast, empty assembly room, especially laughable when the big discussion came up whether or not to abolish the damned thing. [Ralph] Ellison piped up, no, he believed in hierarchy. The delicious Maggie Mill,[59] brighter and straighter than ever in a marvelous blue dress with a multi-colored ribbon for a sort of belt, is leaving. At lunch I was bombarded by a guy next to me in open collar, protruding undershirt, no tie, who turned out to be Julian Schnabel.[60] He went on

59. Maggie Mill, executive director of the Academy.

60. Julian Schnabel (1951–), American artist and filmmaker. Harrison Salisbury (1908–1993), reporter and correspondent for the *New York Times* in Moscow who received the Pulitzer Prize for international reporting in 1955. Milton Babbitt (1916–), American composer, noted for his electronic music. John Johansen (1916–), prominent American architect who taught at the Yale School of Architecture. His wife, Ati Gropius Johansen—the daughter of Walter Gropius (1883–1969), the founder and director of the Bauhaus School of Design in Germany, and Johansen's teacher at Harvard—is a graphics designer specializing in children's book illustrations.

and on to me and Edna O'Brien next to me about how he still loved his wife though they are no longer living together. Paul West, Mary McCarthy's husband, looked at me with silent, profound reproachfulness. He should only know what I had to say on the subject of that infernal busybody and town scold. Arthur M. Schlesinger's tribute to her made me realize, not for the first time, what very different universes he and I live in. What fulsomeness! What love! Leon Edel's tribute to Cowley amazingly left out his real contribution—the portable Faulkner and Hemingway. And so it all went, on and on and on, though I cannot forbear to note that Jl. Schnabel asked me several times what I thought of his painting (no reply on my part), that Harrison Salisbury looked very old and worn, that E. Hardwick (as expected) knows everybody fondly, and that the whole long afternoon, full of wine and gossip and academical self-importance. [George] Kennan, noble, solemn, aggrieved; the composer Milton Babbitt writhing like a cornered boxer; Karl Shapiro very wistful and out of it; John Johansen (architect) turned out to be the husband of my old Black Mountain student and charmer, Atti Gropius. [. . .]

Ken Galbraith, looking slightly bent though still foresty in his old age. Rather benign. I've always liked the compassion that gets into his writing on social subjects, something unknown to that social whirlwind, AMS Jr.

As Groucho said, I wouldn't belong to any club that had me as a member. And I don't feel like one of those ponderous academicians. I have Cowley's seat, who succeeded Van Wyck Brooks. I am the fourth (Seat 43) after Edwin Howland Blashfield,[61] Brooks, Cowley! Each of whom seem to have lasted in his "seat" a very long time. For my part, I am more and more aghast at the speed with which everything is moving, liberating, revolutionizing, oppressing, shooting—each event made even faster by the speed with which it travels to the TV screen, the distraction with which we all look at it,—*the speed with which I am traveling out of life*. So fast that it takes me longer and longer to fall asleep, everything getting to be such a pressure cooker in my head.

## January 17, 1990

[. . .] Whom do I write for? For anybody who will read me. Whom do I write to, directly to? Nobody but myself. I hear every word as I write, it bombards my privatest, most intimate sense of existence—in immediate sensations. The need

61. Edwin Howland Blashfield (1848–1936), American painter noted for his portraits and murals, wrote and lectured on art.

to write to myself—because there is nobody I can talk as I do to myself. All very odd. [. . .]

## January 20, 1990

I once reminded Philip Roth that the Jews were born in the desert, not in Newark. I don't think this made any impression on [him at] all. After reading his latest, *Deception*, very clever, very Roth, and very forgettable, I feel that Roth lives mentally in a tunnel, packed in all sides by two subjects—Roth as novelist, Roth vis-à-vis women. His intensity gets more and more subterranean . . . the image to which he often recurs, himself the artist in a small room working all day, reminds me of the small, even locked, room into which he puts *me* as I read.

His acute awareness of "the affair," the bed and board relationship. Less interested in sex, though he likes to have even his women characters say "fuck" the way he does. Maybe that's why. His intense, afflicted, sometimes screaming sense of his own Jewishness comes down, ritually, to a kind of shell game. Things are never what they seem, he likes to work on the reader, even to show him up.

I think of him as a yenta, a shrew. What I hadn't expected in our insignificant relationship is how easily aggrieved he gets.

Jewish intensity—to get so over-involved in the smallest details of living. In Roth the kitchen has been replaced by the bedroom.

Of course this intensity turned out to be irrelevant to the most frightful details of living. Like getting killed just for being a Jew.

## February 2, 1990

[. . .] Mailer awarded the Emerson-Thoreau Medal by the American Academy. I was on the committee but did not want *him*, the swaggerer. I wanted Vann Woodward.[62] Anyway, Norman made a speech. It is all about THE WRITER THROUGH THE AGES AS NORMAN MAILER. Actually, his lectern style (this is an old paper of his, read many times "over the heads" of his academic audiences) is interesting because his swagger is so social-minded, so full of the charm of presenting himself as merely human, full of doubts and failures etc., etc. like

62. The historian C. Vann Woodward (1908–1999).

everyone else—more than anyone else. It is that aggressive charm which begins by confessing how bad he is, then uses it to mount to his real point—uniqueness of the novelist.

But he does say something very relevant to me. Of a first book, written way back then. Times so different from our own. How comfortable (for the last time) it was writing a novel, *The Naked and The Dead.*

"One was the sum of one's own history as it was cradled in the larger history of one's time. One was a product."[63]

Mailer has this way of turning his compunctions into charms. "The prescription, therefore, is simple: one must not put out a job with any serious taint of the meretricious. At least the prescription ought to be simple—but then, how few of us ever do work of which we are not in fact a bit ashamed? It comes down to a matter of degree."

No novelist of his "standing" has lent himself so thoroughly to the meretriciousness of American fashions—of sex as ideology—of the most contemptible palaver to show his connection with the mob—End of An American Dream. Regards from Marilyn.[64]

## March 24, 1990

[. . .] There was a nice lunch in WA yesterday with Rick Hertzberg and Leon Wieseltier.[65] Leon the prankster and punster looking (as he says) like George Washington in a circumambulating mop of white hair (and him not 40 yet). Weird. But the talk was fast and good and full of gossip, and I was so moved by being with friends again, I felt that the past had stood up. . . . [. . .]

## April 30, 1990

Rainy, cold day in Roxbury. Judith and I met on this day in 1977, thank the Lord. The most unexpected bliss of my life.

63. Norman Mailer "The Hazards and Sources of Writing," *Bulletin of the American Academy of Arts and Sciences* (February, 1990): 26–36.
64. Norman Mailer, *An American Dream* (New York: Dial, 1965); *Marilyn: A Biography* (New York: Grosset and Dunlap, 1973).
65. Hendrik Hertzberg and Leon Wieseltier (1952–), editor and literary editor of the *New Republic*. Kazin was a friend of Hertzberg's parents, Sidney and Hazel Hertzberg. See June 20, 1959, entry.

My function, my whole delight as a critic is in reading minds, distinguishing the quality of minds. If the Journal Book is to have any authenticity, it must swell [*sic*] in those regions where the real problem of my life [is] what to do with a mind like mine, strange enough to myself, inaccessible and even facilely marked down by minds so utterly different from mine! This is the situation I so easily suffer from as "solitude," aloneness. . . . Yet the exercise of that mind is what I love most in writing. . . .

[. . .] The first premises of my life in an immigrant community was that everything was up to me. The man who has risen. The fight back. People could be argued into this or that. Pressure could always be applied. The way out was the way up—and through.

Yet all the while, what a secret, good fortune was mine, in the interior life, in the life of the mind, in this graphic certainty of words, words, words alone being the tracery of the mind. [. . .]

## May 28, 1990

[. . .] Turning back to Karamazov and The Grand Inquisitor, I feel as if I were reading back to the most crucial and *intimate* texts of my old education. 1915 is much, much closer to Dostoevsky's century (and Tolstoy's and Melville's) than it is to 1990. Like most intellectual Jews I am a 19th century man, still occupied with the prophesies of the 20th century rather than with the actualities I have lived through, continually stumble through, and in my ignorance of science, apocalyptic nationalism and the kinds of mind capable of performing the Holocaust, Katyn Forest, etc. I feel like one [of] those Faulkner characters who prays that life may stand still for a moment, for only a moment, that the reel may go backwards.

## June 5, 1990

The fall of Rome was nothing compared with the "fall" in the heart of Alfred Kazin when he was first unfaithful to a wife (1943). He regrets nothing, especially not the extension of his experience (what a way of putting it) that came with his fall. But to this day (and today I am seventy-five years of age) he cannot think without a gasp of pain of all that it cost him then to be unfaithful to Asya. And what it costs him still.

## August 3, 1990

[. . .] Peter Davison[66] called me the other day, still hot for my Journals, and finally came out with "don't think me untoward," but might it not be okay,

66. See Chapter 6, note 32.

finally, to have my precious life blood after my death? I may yet be lucky enough to complete *The Almighty Has His Own Purposes!*[67] And just as I got too hopelessly depressed trying to get something of the endless Journals, it may be just as well to leave it all for Judith—and Davison?

There is something really arresting about the idea of J reading me—so much of which is without the details of loving other women in the old by and bye. . . . I've always been so afraid of putting down anything about the "small hotel" and love in the afternoon with MacDougall Street—or to use a name J figured out, "Astoria!" But now that I seem to be teetering on the edge of admitting, awaiting, only a posthumous existence for these notes. . . .

The only use of a Journal is in the details. Everything else useless to me and my eventual reader. The lovely ease and freedom of the Journal form, so inviting to sink into, should make this kind of precision all the more possible. But I am not a novelist, so the detail is there for the pleasure of being precise, of staying alert, of taking in the mischances, the accidents, the utter intoxication and unending strangeness of being this self, yet never really content to believe that one knows fully what a "self" is. . . . *The connections alone make it all worthwhile.*

## August 7, 1990

Finally got through the [Denis] Donoghue review,[68] thanks to J's last minute suggestions and cleaned myself up for the big lunch at Algonquin with Vartan Gregorian.[69] It turned out that the Algonquin wasn't serving, the Century was closed, Sardi's was under repair. "Greg" with briefcase and umbrella, never silent for a moment, ran me up to Ragah's on 48th Street, big Indian place, don't you know, all the while pouring out a steady stream of jokes, observations large, small, and sometimes acute. He was greeted along the way by fan after fan—one even hailed him from inside a taxi! I told him all Times Square lacked was a big sign VARTAN IS BACK! . . . He was greeted most enthusiastically by the soft footed waiters at the restaurant, and he told me with his usual cheery smile that he was a favorite of theirs because he had not crossed a picket line years back when they were on strike. . . .

67. Published as *God and the American Writer* in 1997.
68. "Habits of Home," *New Republic* (September 24, 1990): 44–46, review of Denis Donoghue's memoir, *Warrenpoint* (New York: 1990). See May 2, 1984, entry.
69. Vartan Gregorian (1934–), president of Brown University, former president of the New York Public Library.

What an amazingly bright, cheery, smiling, glib, but occasionally wise, little man. With his chin beard, his infinite knowingness about so many different things he did remind me of a Levantine trader or shopkeeper, so wise in the ways of this commercial world, so wise about himself and family, but at the same time poised above this busy, busy world.

He not only entertained me, he really instructed. Talking about his presidency of Brown, which he said was difficult but which he seems to be handling with the greatest ease and confidence, he said—repeated—that he has no contract with the university, refused to have one. "This leaves me free. This is my security. I could leave at an instant if I felt like it."

Now how many people do I know whose insouciance in the all crucial matter of a job leaves them so free and joyous? [. . .]

## August 9, 1990

More [John] Cheever journals in the *NYorker*, August 13 issue. If ever there was a document for my precious book on the 20th century American writer's abundance in despair, this is it! He is so friable at least in these selections—God knows what Susan C.[70] or Gottlieb or whoever left out, the usual high and mighty editorial standards of civic prudence settling on [illegible] so quick to break down and have doubts about his work. But the beautiful sensitivity of C's stories depends on his morbid sensitivity. They are entirely stories of crisis, I mean of the continuing kind, the kind that does not end with the resolution of a story but goes round and round the world after the story is completed. . . .

But it is the self doubting that is so fascinating, neurotic weakness that is amazingly representative, for though many, many writers might not need to throw themselves on the ground and howl like Cheever, we do have the American—drawing entirely on himself. There is a terrible strength in this (as I can testify) as well as a frightening weakness. So religion, and especially in this case the Church (Episcopal, very high?) becomes the only grace, the only transcendental country, the only release and repair. Existence in itself is day to day an absolute trial, for truly C is on trial (again I know whereof he speaks). . . .

70. Susan Cheever (1943–), writer and novelist, daughter of the novelist John Cheever, worked with Robert Gottlieb, editor in chief at Alfred A. Knopf to produce *The Journals of John Cheever* (1991).

So sexual anxiety and the need to hit the bottle, just to provide a little morale! That's what his religion (and that of a lot of other people) come to, the only real hope in this excruciating *personal* world. All reminds me of the Kafka story about the terrible machine. "The Penal Colony."

## October 14, 1990

The Jews will last longer than Israel will. I've always had a sense of foreboding about the place as well as great pride—if no particular sense of belonging. The "belonging" refers to the time when they were naturally there (by conquest of course) but that was so long ago that it seems from much of the Bible that they were always there. And didn't Abraham my true father (my eternal father) cross over into it from Mesopotamia?

Sooner or later, I feel, the beleaguered, aggressive, totally defiant Israelis will find "the rest of the world" too much for them. As always, it will be—it already is—Jews vis-à-vis the "rest of the world." [. . .]

## November 7, 1990

Erich Heller dead in a retirement home in Evanston. I feel above and beyond my fascination with his exceptional personal culture and slightly too overpowering personality . . . that he was one of the last links with European Jewry before and after the war. I remember how his face lighted up, how his Anglo-American speech no longer seemed necessary, when he was at Hannah's talking his native language and in full company with what he was most used to. . . . How bitterly disappointed he was not to be taken by Harvard after that brilliant lecture I heard him give, "The Hazard of Modern Poetry," with MacLeish introducing him with unusual praise. He was essentially very conservative, like Hannah—like Kafka!

## December 6, 1990

[. . .] Lucy Dawidowicz died and got buried right away without the papers carrying any notice of the service. Joe Weisman told me some weeks ago that she had prepared her own funeral service. Maybe she also presented her fellow fanatics on the right with a list of politically correct people to be admitted to the service. She had become a pain, a bore, truly a fanatic, but her death does indeed diminish me—as do the deaths of recent [persons]—Erich Heller, Leonard Bernstein. The old Jewish guard is retiring from the fray, leaving the world to the deconstructionists, the punk, funk rock bands—and the four Administration figures—Bush,[71] Baker, Scowcroft, Cheney, who are alone running the Gulf Crisis and alone will send so many American kids to death against the latest tyrant.

Lucy and her "ilk"—no wonder that the Israelis have achieved their ghastly isolation. Jews, Jews, Jews! the greatest successes in history from an intellectual and religious viewpoint, but despite the richies in America, the greatest failure. Shamir, you bullet headed bastard, you too are a failure, like the virtuous peace party in Israel. . . .

## January [nd] 1991

[. . .] Last night, the streets were wet, and seemed to reflect the thousand and one brightnesses streaming from the still lighted shop windows and street lamps. There was a friendly fog in the middle. The whole thing suddenly gave me that strangely familiar feeling of having returned to the last years of the nineteenth century—a feeling borrowed from my lifelong fascination with Victorian London, but mostly from the Saturday nights of my boyhood, when my father regularly took me down to the lower East Side for the meetings of the Minsk branch of the Workmen's Circle.

Broadway was so *condensed*, is what I mean, like a stage set, and while furiously lit up, was also deep in shadows.

I have never lost this association between shadowy dark streets and suddenly finding myself in another century. When I first came to Rome and stayed on in winter, I would walk in the amazing shadows covering the narrow alley-like streets between shut-in palaces and churches as if in a trance of memory. I had been here before! And if I came out into Trastevere on a busy night, the arc lights over the stands selling everything under the sun plunged me back into the Brownsville open market area on Belmont Avenue alongside of which I grew up.

Joe Liebling used to say of the streets painted by Maurice Utrillo[72] that they made you want to weep. For me the old Jewish streets of the lower East Side, where I have never lived, talk to me of Charlie and Gussie Kazin before I knew them. I am

71. President George H. W. Bush (1924–); Brent Scowcroft (1925–), national security adviser under Bush and Gerald Ford; Richard "Dick" Cheney (1941–), secretary of defense under the senior Bush and later vice president under George W. Bush.
72. Maurice Utrillo (1883–1955), French painter of cityscapes, particularly of Montmartre.

still looking for them on this dark Saturday night. They were married on a Saturday night, which is about as much as I will ever know of their wedding. [. . .]

## March 7, 1991

Thursday. Morning. The Jew as wiseguy and petty egotist. After all the doctors yesterday, I hailed a cab at York and 68th St. A sign facing the passenger: SURPRISE! THIS IS AN ENGLISH LANGUAGE DRIVER. HE KNOWS WHERE YOU ARE GOING BETTER THAN YOU DO. Reminds me of Ann's driver, who ended up "Whaddya want from your mother god bless her?" The driver in his cab, sort of feels like a king over the Third World Competition. [. . .]

## April 22, 1991

"Pogrom in Pennsylvania," ran the banner headline in the *Jewish Daily Forward* when a black was lynched in PA—sometime early in the century. What I can never get over, remembering Brownsville in full, was the sublime, the ever-credulous, the unbelievably *universalizing* idealism of those poor Jews—so long as they were Socialists. The moral resonance of that early Jewish-Socialist-Bundist belief in a "better future" is something prehistoric, now that "socialism" in the hands of despots, sadists, opportunists, and (shades of I. Kristol) total *Realpolitiker* turned out to be the seed, the formula even (the National Socialist Workers' Party!!!) of the most terrible people in this hopeless century. *Hopeless because always at the mercy of events.* And even when total domination of the Gulag and Auschwitz did not rule the roost, at the mercy of technology, which made life easier or more productive in many small particulars, but more and more made man dependent—a slave of another kind.

Every morning noon and day the News! makes me remember the guy in England who wanted to throw out the Government Issue radio—"I've heard nothing but bad news from that machine ever since it was given to me."

## April 30, 1991

[. . .] THE JEWISH PRESENCE in modern American culture (meaning lately) comes from the end of the "radical" period. I remember Bert Wolfe,[73] ye old

73. Bertram Wolfe (1896–1977), a friend and neighbor of Kazin's when he was living in Brooklyn Heights in the late 1930s, was a founding member of the Communist Party U.S.A., later expelled from the Party by Stalin. Kazin uses Wolfe as a foil in his caustic portrait of Mary McCarthy in *Starting Out in the Thirties*.

pristine Communist, saying of my interest in Jewish affairs, that it was "neurotic." Of course this was a period, as Mrs. Wolfe recalled, when Communists meeting in international conclave laughed that the reason there was no rep from Africa was that "we couldn't find a Jew willing to put on a nose ring."

The old radicals—Hook, Schapiro, etc.—were still aloof from purely "Jewish" concerns. Too nationalistic, as the Budapest (meaning Sasha Schneider)[74] said in 1960 concerned about his going to Israel—even showing too much sympathy.

## May 19, 1991

One should die as William Blake did, joyously singing hymns on one's deathbed. One must almost believe that all the cards are not in yet, that there is indeed a second chance. That is the morning feeling, as the night is always something else. Morning begins with Björling[75] singing, all the way from the heart. I know why I am so obsessed with this life's notebook—Each day is a new start. Each day, still, has everything to show me and to teach me. I write in order to learn, and life is nothing but a learning process. Something always unfolds, like the seed long hidden beneath the snow. [. . .]

## May 29, 1991

[. . .] Very very hot. Last night, extraordinarily brilliant new moon. Just as it was rising, among the "inessential houses," a yellow, gold disk, I heard from Dr. David Wolf that my prostate is badly enlarged and that the blood samples show the possibility of cancer. Who, me? A nice old fellow like me what never done nothing to nobody, etc.? So now we must work harder than ever. That old joke about the coming of a terrible world flood that would wipe everything away, and the Rabbi said, "We have just a few weeks in which to learn to live under water." [. . .]

## June 7, 1991

[. . .] What has always kept me in life and exhilarated me has been the confidence in my own judgment, my strange gift for feeling out the quality of talent and

74. Alexander "Sascha" Schneider (1870–1927), violinist and conductor, member of the Budapest String Quartet.
75. Johan "Jussi" Björling (1911–1960), Swedish tenor, one of the leading operatic singers of the twentieth century.

mind within the text I am reading. A hidden touch of objectivity, as welcome as a spring of the freshest coolest water in the desert! As a good critic I am first astonished by gifts that I do not possess, then excited by the chance to make contact with them through my analysis.

And then there is the strange mixture in very gifted writers, like Bill Styron, of tremendous imaginative vitality and life-force mixed in with great doltishness. Mailer, essentially a fantasist, in whom the novelist's cunning intelligence, very considerable, is so mixed up with subjectivity that expresses itself pseudo-intellectually in myths about sex and conspiracy. And so it goes. There are no great general myths, nothing that gives out the sense of life's origins and destiny—of hope. . . . There is just this grinding personal ambition. Of which Mailer is the most feverish athlete. [. . .]

THE COMPULSION TO KEEP A JOURNAL—is very mysterious. Although it is as easy and natural for me to keep my notebook going all these many years—like falling into bed—the obvious ease of writing to oneself alone and for oneself alone (no editor to be immediately over you) the fact remains that these minutiae, these notes, observations, prayers, quotations, etc. *are* written for someone who is not altogether ME. There is a deeper part of myself than the ordinary wide-awake and social one that I strangely satisfy by the freedom I feel in writing this. Some older part of me, anarchistic and spiritually outlaw—that does not have to answer to anyone. Yet demands that I foster it, engage it all the time.

Here I am entirely private, all myself, as I cannot be talking directly to another, where the very nature of dialogue has rules we cannot flout in talking to another. But this monologue? It is really an interrogation of sorts, seeking an answer. Why it is a form of prayer.

It is the privacy—detail that will see me through.

## June 11, 1991

In *my* youth, our hearts were touched with fire. Something in our poor old tenement Jewish life, uplifted by the ideals and energy of the Jewish labor movement and the messianism of our fathers' primitive Bund Socialism, gave me images of value I have never lost. Is this why I keep returning to the "Jews" as the moral center, the value place, in a world in which there seems to be little to affirm except through the memory of such long-cherished idealism and world-outlook?

Not the Jews as such, though I do feel for the idea of the "people," but the Jews as a memory tradition religion of value . . . despite everything they as ordinary human beings can do to counteract the . . . "Promise."

## June 14, 1991

Jews who do not believe in the Messiah—meaning that they have never heard of it—are like everyone else and as a tribe not particularly interesting. What makes me interesting to myself, what makes my old youthful background among immigrant Jews in a tenement interesting is the secularization of the Messiah. There was a promise indicated to all trivial doings and habits—something great awaited us—and it was not just that primitive evangelical Socialism arising from within the Russian-Jewish working class mix, it was the rapture of some immanent expectancy, the radiance of believing on every hand and for whatever reason, that something great and good was coming.

Though he tarry, yet will I await him with perfect faith. [. . .]

## August 9, 1991

Friday morning. Radiation station—in the midst of death we are in life.[76] To my amazement there was this early morning crowd at the radiation station waiting to get their dose before, no doubt, leaping off to swimming pools and picnic tables in the fair countree. A cop with the regulation American flag in his sleeve. A pious Jew with yarmulke. Busy executive types coldly perusing the business pages of the *Times*. To my grief, a number of young women. Tis all as had been said about our inimitable Bush time—life and death so ridiculously mixed up together. And as I prepared to make my way in and wondered if it was superstition or belief that would lead me to kiss the mezuzah on the wall, sure enuf the secretary said to me softly but unmistakably, "When do you expect to pay your bill?"

What a scene this would make in a play—the crowd glumly sitting together, each one with his and her calculation of how much time we have left. Sure enuf, one pompous gent probably not much younger than I was orally reviewing for a young lady across from him the sacred numbers of how long his parents and grandparents had lived. All late eighties and early nineties; so when he had

76. "In the midst of life we are in death: of whom may we seek for succour, but of thee, O Lord, who for our sins art justly displeased?" from the *Anglican Book of Common Prayer*.

finished this little piece of autobiography, he sat back with a smirk, fondling the delicious soft leather of his super briefcase, which had an extra pocket. For some reason this bloke was not carrying a watch, and every interval had to ask his fellow comrades in cancer for the time. I came home after necessary errands—Judith furious with me for not letting her know I would be delayed—so intensely worried. A lesson for me, but what with another blowup on Route 7 between us because I was in the left lane when the book says I should be in the right, I arrived at little gray home in the West so emotionally drained that for hours I lay on my old bed in the office as if my legs were resisting my effort to get up. Truly, this summer is a season in hell. Yet there are absurdities as well as persisting anxieties. . . .

## September 9, 1991

What I need to say most in Roxbury Sunday: that I always thought of literature as the prime form of education, and that the content of the great books seemed to me as a matter of course the direct content of life. . . . It was not so much the great books, or the supposed masterpieces, but what went on between writer and reader as a form of transmission that somehow had in it the possibility of human regeneration, of action toward some resolution of the eternal problems of life. To read was, comic as it may seem, to engage in a virtuous action, to be in touch with minds so much more experienced and better trained and gifted than yourself. AFTER ALL, READING PLATO WAS LISTENING TO SOCRATES, even being interrogated by him. . . . Reading the *Iliad* was to undergo all the horrors of hand to hand combat in war, and to read the *Odyssey* was like skirting just above sea level in the Mediterranean, while to read *Anna Karenina* was to fall in love with the most radiant if undependable of women. . . . And so it went . . . the Milton epigraph above the entrance to 315 [of the New York Public Library] . . . A GOOD BOOK IS THE LIFE BLOOD OF A MASTER SPIRIT, and somehow you entered that.

## October 9, 1991

The reason I keep this journal, my other self, is that distrusting the world as I do while endeavoring to keep up my love of it—the creation I mean—is that there are things I say to myself that I cannot say to anyone else. If any of this is to be published, let them overhear me. I will not address them directly.

Far from whining over my loneliness—and in a sense I have never known anything else, except in the beginning with Asya and in the past recent years with darling Judith—I cherish it, I love it, I need it, I live on it. My private world I bear like "a chalice through a crowd of foes."[77] [. . .]

## November 6, 1991

[. . .] The idealism on which I grew up was the product of a very small, Europe-oriented, Biblical tradition. Suddenly it turned out, in the breakup of colonialism, that the world was indeed a very large, complex and confusing place full of many differing races, traditions, religions, cultures, to say nothing of an infinite number of holocausts not much regarded in history. This is what drives Jews crazy, that gets people like Bellow to sneer "where is the Proust of the Papuans?" etc.

What drives Jews like me crazy is the sheer arithmetic of multi-culturalism, the fact that we are no longer center stage. If we are "the heart of the world," as that non-lover of the Jews John Jay Chapman admitted, it is because too many other races and peoples regard themselves, suddenly emerging in the light of history (something written by the West alone). Everybody wants to be recognized—to which we reply, if the challenge is met at all—that we no longer have a common world, just many, too many, societies and clans, and that anyway, we have so long been "culture" that we cannot, just because it seems inevitable politically in the over-crowded Disunited Nations, esteem you as we esteem ourselves. Egalitarianism, especially in the culture sphere, sooner or later omits all questions of merit.

Unfortunately, the sheer accumulation and aggregation of "peoples" on peoples, now means that "culture" is secondary, if that, in the world's mind. You cannot play the desert father shutting the door on the pagans, or the divine solipsist in his cork-lined chamber. "Culture" itself has become anthropology, education appropriated by the media and the endless clichés of a wholly commercial society in which only an occasional church demurs from the ethos of competition and profit.

## May 30, 1992

I never expected to be this old—old. I never thought it would come to this business of counting the time, pressing the time, negotiating as it were with time itself, bargaining with the implacable god, so that I would live to finish

77. From James Joyce's "Araby" in *The Dubliners*.

this book made up of my journals, a book that is itself not just a record of time lived through and through, but one that attempts in the act of writing to open up a new perspective on time, to see it in a new light so that the old enmity will not persist to the very gates of death. With my prostate cancer, my arthritis, my damaged hearing, my this and my that, the doctors, the hospitals, the many colored pills, and assorted medical orderlies and accountants always on my tail, I am made to feel so passive an object that only writing restores my sense of manhood, of being actively myself in the old style.

Yet it is not any present weakness or disorientation that troubles me—I am not a writer dying like Dick [Hofstadter] or Anatole [Broyard], Dick with the mss. of his projected American history under his hospital bed at Mt. Sinai, Anatole shrewdly writing about his dying, aiming at the first possible publishing season after his death even as he went through the agony of not being able to pee and swallowing hundreds of pills in a single week. What worries me is my diminished interest in the purely personal as a subject for writing—and here I am, having to carve into myself, go over so many experiences of which I can say, with Alice B. Toklas,[78] "I forget, but I do not forgive." Or to put it another way, I don't feel macho and commanding enough to prey on my past at the moment. I cannot confess even to Judith, regretful as I feel about my lack of sexual ardor, how relieved I am to have done with sex. I feel in fact as Sophocles is supposed to have said in his eighties, grateful that the tigers of lust are not tearing any longer at my vitals.

So what is going on about the journal book? the fact that I keep on refusing to use the journals themselves. Of course, the pile up of words there seems impossible to break though. But the real problem, with myself of course, is that I do not feel myself to be a problem that needs redemption. Not even about dying. I wrote the other personal books in order to redeem my experience, and make a new person of myself. I suppose as they say nowadays that I invented a self to write about. But God's own truth deep in my belly is that on the brink of 77 I am just the person I want to be, am perfectly satisfied with my mind and my soul, if not with the natural decay of my body. In some way I have been trying, through the obsession with *A Lifetime Burning in Every Moment*, to bring back the spirit of biting crisis I have so often lived through—especially in regard to the

78. Alice B. Toklas (1877–1967), partner of the writer Gertrude Stein. Stein's best-selling book *The Autobiography of Alice B. Toklas* is really the autobiography of Gertrude Stein.

"personal" side of my writing. No wonder I keep inching say [*sic*, away] from that theme to write just about "Jews!"

So this page ends very differently from the way it began. The truth is that I am not worried about death—I just want to have as productive a life as possible. I am worried about Judith's having to pay back advances I have not earned before my death, and of course I do want to go out with a bang, a really personal book of thought as central experience. I want to discover what I have to say about my obsession with religions—and I want to write about other people. Etc., etc. wherever the journals will take me. The opening figures in my mind as a satisfactory type.

## July 16, 1992

The Democrats at Madison Square Garden this week. The politicians except for dear Mario[79] are as boring as can be. But I feel right at home with most of the delegates I see on the floor. And most of all, I recognize in the Democrats' noisiness, rowdiness, passion, and turbulence everything I love about America—the visceral populism. So to speak, the angry sense of all our striving over the years, the militant and emotional temper. I haven't the faintest idea who "Bill Clinton" is, but the South is in many ways the region most open to change, and it may be that this baby, if given half a chance after the Bushites throw all the shit at him, may yet be able to exercise some fresh intelligence in the White House.

Cuomo speaking of "An American Family." Only immigrants' sons speak this way.

## September 3, 1992

[. . .] I grew up thinking that "Jews" was another name for anyone dispossessed, persecuted, constantly vilified and easy to "exterminate."

## January 10, 1993
### [dated January 10, 1992]

Every night, reading Rousseau's *Confessions* in delight. The studied innocence combined with the projection of absolute egotism, not to forget the gifted writer's sense of the necessary detail. He swims through a sea of women, everywhere

79. Mario Cuomo (1932–), governor of New York, 1983–1994.

women tenderly taking him up. Infinitely adoptable by women, yet an adventurer by birth and character with a gift for extracting general principles. There is something in the combination of so many unsuspected traits in Rousseau that makes up his literary personality. I have never encountered before a writer so full of "ideas," so bent on bearing his heart. The copiousness of the narrative is refreshing—no tight-lipped modernism here. I am also impressed by the adventuresomeness open to him in the pre-revolutionary rigid class structure of the time. The lackey who was allowed extraordinary freedoms at the table—and will soon have them in bed.

## January 13, 1993
### [dated January 13, 1992]

A low point in the year—everything in the murder-torn world is like the weather. Judith in tears thinking about all the political horrors and everyone else seems to be able to do nothing about. But ah! the clean, white fellow from Nebraska sitting every day on a rag, corner of 95th and Broadway. We cannot get him to agree to a hospital. He is just dying on the corner of 95th and Broadway, of AIDS probably, meanwhile tonelessly looking at us and everything else without anger or mistrust. The good Jewish liberals—"what can we do for you?" He would like a hot chocolate. And he could use a Tylenol. Meanwhile smoking a cigarette, just sitting there on the corner of 95th and Broadway. [. . .]

## October 31, 1993

[. . .] The best experience of all this "family weekend" was having lunch Friday with L[eon] W[ieseltier] in the fancy restaurant next to his office on 19th St. "The last of the true believers"[80] as Ann calls me in her malicious novel, happy beyond words talking about transcendence with L, another religious nut, but Leon certainly cooler about it all in a philosophical way than me. I was so buoyed up about it all that to my surprise after all the trouble I have had with my left foot, I walked for miles in WA in the glorious Indian Summer weather, thinking again how eventful WA always is for me[. . . .]

## August 1, 1994

My lost city. Every day I see why I wrote OUR NEW YORK. The Pageant Bookshop at 109 E. 9th has closed an era in which Fourth Avenue proclaimed itself the

80. Ann Birstein, *The Last of the True Believers* (New York: Norton, 1988).

"Book Row Of America." Nothing said in the story about Dauber and Pine on lower Fifth Avenue. When Nat Pine came to my old apartment at 110 Riverside Drive, he would not only accept my review books for sale but, if my old edition of Dostoevsky came into view, give me his appraisement of the translation. I remember Dauber's son when I was eager to acquire the 11th edition of the Encyclopedia Britannica, saying—"For that price you're getting, you can schlep it yourself!" The distinctive musty smell, the dim lights and owlish and taciturn proprietors of the old 4th Ave bookshops, with names like Biblo & Tannen, Schulte's, Aberdeen and Green books. Who was it in that old bookshop who when called to the phone would announce in a loud voice "On the wire!" [. . .]

## August 9, 1994

[. . .] The whole fun of keeping a journal is talking to oneself, and if one is as extreme a loner at heart as I am, talking to oneself and is easier, more affable and honest than talking to the usual faces at a party. [. . .]

## October 21, 1994

Great talk at lunch with Yaron Ezrahi,[81] all by ourselves this Saturday in the big reading room of the Century. Fascinating in his independence as well as his bubbly intelligence. Said he got more "secular" when for 48 hrs after Baruch Goldstein murdered the Hebron Arabs at prayer, not one Jewish cleric had anything to say about it.[82] Moving story about former Sec of State Shultz, who as prof at U of Chicago had a favorite student, an Israeli. At the 6 Day war the student flew immediately back to Israel and died in action. Yaron says Shultz is close to tears when he recounts this.

These loose limbed forever voyaging Israeli intellectuals! But Yaron is a swinger in the deepest, most honorable sense. He really thinks for himself. His journal book, which he says he owes to my telling him about mine, is to be published by Farrar Straus.

81. Yaron Ezrahi (1940–), professor of political science at the Hebrew University in Jerusalem, friend of Kazin's from the Center for Advanced Study in the Behavioral Sciences at Stanford. In his celebrated quasi-autobiography *Rubber Bullets: Power and Consciousness in Modern Israel* (New York: Farrar, Straus and Giroux, 1997), 298, Ezrahi credits Kazin for indicating how autobiography can provide insight into authoritarian politics.

82. On February 25, 1994, the Brooklyn-born Israeli physician Baruch Goldstein (b. 1956) murdered 29 Muslims and wounded 150 others while they were at prayer in the Cave of the Patriarchs in the West Bank city of Hebron. Goldstein was finally killed by surviving worshipers.

## March 4, 1996

ED [Dickinson], she fights out as a lone woman the drama of being "saved" and "not saved" that is the heart of the old orthodoxy.

Meyer Schapiro dead at 91. Grand full page obituary by John Russell about our boy, who arrived in NY at 3 away from the "odious" anti-Semitism of Lithuania. Soon after the war I took his glorious class in modern painters at the New School, full of painters and writers. The attentiveness Schapiro inspired as he beautifully stood there thinking out loud, weaving his mind around the painting being shown on the screen. Those gloriously expectant days, right after the war. Anatole Broyard caught the atmosphere of the time in his memoir, *Kafka Was The Rage*. Standing on the roof of the New School with a girl, the madly learned Schapiro addressed me on the subject of *Belgian surrealists!* That night Irving Howe and I talked about Solzhenitsyn. "Somewhere downtown."

Jews, my Jews, something more to feel with you, brothers! 19 killed in Jerusalem bus by suicide bomber from Hamas. [. . .]

## October 30, 1996

Talking to myself in this notebook is like walking through a crowd holding your decapitated head in your hands without a soul being the wiser.

## March 7, 1997

I live in fear and suspense—fear of being found out, of being proved guilty of transgressing the authority first lodged in me by Gussie Kazin (who was herself all fear as well as a great manager), and the suspense of wondering when and how I will meet my death. Meanwhile, I have everything in life to fulfill me—and so rarely feel "fulfilled." So fulfillment is nonsense. The only fulfillment is when you merge with the universe—in death. The very idea of fulfillment is trivial, sentimental, and a travesty of religious expectation of losing yourself in God.

Am full of conflict preparing to write *Jews—of seeming disloyal, of being too critical. Hell!* the only thing is to put the conflict in.

What joy and relief this lonely Sunday to be able to set down things here as they are—to capture the tides storming back and forth in my soul; I must never be too tired to write in this book—*it is the one place where I can deal with the unexpected* that every day is made of. It is easy to think that every day is the same old routine—that tomorrow and tomorrow stuff that a murderer like Macbeth is drowning in guilt and therefore doesn't see the wood for the trees. But life is ever new, and the day is its constellation right in my head.

## March 28, 1997

I weep over so many experiences of Jews taken together, but quickly shake off my tears when I think of the individual Jew (not least myself). That is because I was brought up as still another instance of the historic Jewish family, tribe, collective. Gershom Scholem accused Arendt of not loving the Jews as a people, and she replied that one could not love a whole people, just God. Goes to show you how different she was. The emotions, the incessant stress and yearning for deliverance imprinted in me from earliest infancy in Brownsville surrounded by Jews, Jews, Jews, are a world apart from my efforts as an adult thinking mind to understand what is primordial, superstitious, savage, credulously obedient in the rituals of Jews operating as a religious community and not praying without a quorum. So much of intellect in psychic retrospect of all this is founded on memory as a tradition of Jews telling themselves their own story of piety. [. . .]

## April 28, 1997

[. . .] The more I think of "Jews: The Marriage Of Heaven And Hell," the more I see their religious separatism and self-satisfaction in this separatism as the primal cause of anti-Semitism. The Jews positively gloried in being "different," and such was the force of the spell Yahweh had laid on them, they could not help feeling "superior" even in the bleakest ghetto.

The spell was of their collective destiny in this world (hence the ease with which this led to *Protocols of Zion*[83] and such conspiracies to rule the world). And as the sacredness of Christianity became thinner in the 19th century, racial (and therefore political anti-Semitism) grew out of the theological anti-Semitism natural to a church founded by Jews that most Jews had no *religious* reason to join. No doubt Marx had good reasons to think of the Jewish question. But socially and politically Jews were always in the wrong, whether they were "monopolists" or contemptibly "sub-human," as a leading Nazi general in Russia called them to justify their "extermination."

83. *The Protocols of the Learned Elders of Zion* was a widely distributed anti-Semitic text purporting to describe a plan for worldwide Jewish domination. It was in fact a plagiarism from various satirical texts unrelated to the Jews.

The strength fervor and spell of Jewish unity [was] not created only by their afflictions through history. The strength of Christianity lay in Paul's persuasion in the resurrection of Jesus and the conviction [of] individual salvation. Nothing is so lonely as the sense of one's own mortality. The Jews (Sholem Aleichem)[84] believed they were together in death—"so that my life may be on them and theirs on me." The Christian was assured by his *theology* that he [was] "saved." The Jews felt themselves already "safe"—in death as in life, they could not imagine being without each other.

## May 15, 1997

Jewish orthodoxy has nothing to say about anything—except obeying the Law and thus continuing in the way of your parents. (Gershom Scholem the great exception, but he was not an observant Jew. He minutely studied orthodoxy without practicing it.) From the blessed Spinoza to Einstein, it has been the great Jewish intellectuals and thinkers who have been the true rabbis (teachers) of the world. And the liberal Jews trying to hold on to the fringes of the prayer shawls (Kafka!) are just as shallow when they harp on "Jewish identity." What a depressing routine all this has become. [. . .]

## July 20, 1997

The unending chain of information about Jews, then and now, every then seeming a now, while every now immediately brings up its inevitable parallel in a then. I want to write about the triumph and agony of the Jew, the marriage of heaven and hell indeed, for so many Jews who have absorbed the many, many endless catastrophes of the past even as they feel themselves to be the smartest, the most influential in thought, righteous, etc., etc. But like Penelope's unweaving every night of what she had to weave in the day, I feel I am drowning in sheer information—so any shards of which call for me to put them into my book though, as is customary with the Jews, everything now already happened then and can be sickeningly familiar. Yet I cannot leave off recording, recording everything freshly published. Jews world over are always in the news, are (as in the Gospels) center stage even when or because they are the enemy, the pariahs, the outsiders, the irreverent. [. . .]

84. Sholem Aleichem was the pen name of Salomon Naumovich Rabinovich (1859–1916), a Yiddish author and playwright. The musical *Fiddler on the Roof* was based on his stories about Tevye the Milkman.

## February 23, 1998

Abe Ribicoff[85] dead at 87 in the Hebrew Home For The Aged in Riverdale. His son Peter (?)—was a student of mine my first year at Amherst. Sullen when I stupidly asked to learn more about the Governor. Greatest vote getter in CT history. Pushed JFK for the Presidency from the time they met as freshmen Congressmen 1948. [. . .] How wonderful he was on the podium in 1968 with the police fighting the antiwar crowd outside the convention hall, protesting the "Gestapo" tactics of the cops while Mayor Richard Daley and gang shouted "Get Down! Get down!" Then cupped their mouths and shouted an obscenity at Senator Ribicoff that few television viewers had difficulty lip reading. "How hard it is," Ribicoff scolded back, "to accept the truth when we know the problems facing our nation." [. . .]

## March 18, 1998

Ever since I received the news of my cancer (in the bone yet) I have been more conscious than ever of having constantly to deal with this formidable stranger—stranger to me than ever—my BODY. Dear me, what a lot of trouble he hands me every time I struggle up from a chair, get into and out of bed. Etc., etc. A lot of trouble, pain, inconvenience and sheer helplessness. And all the time my mind is singing, my soul, spirit, call it what flying around of its own accord. What a division, my friends, what a dual self I walk around in—these days. No wonder one starts embracing supernatural agencies and whimpering "Get me outta here!"[86]

85. Abraham Alexander Ribicoff (1910–1998), member of the U.S. House of Representatives (1949–1953), governor of Connecticut (1955–1961), and U.S. senator (1963–1981). He was secretary of health, education, and welfare under John F. Kennedy.

86. This is the next to the last page of the extant journals in the Kazin Estate. The final entry on the page is on the "Religious Right."

# INDEX